# If St. Peter Has Hounds

*A day with every mounted British pack*

Tony Harvey

Foreword

*by Captain Ronnie Wallace M.F.H.*

All Profits To The Hunt Servants Benefit Society

Published 1998 by
Paul Rackham Ltd, Manor Farm, Bridgham, Norwich NR16 2RX

Typeset by CSC Design & Reprographic, Southolt Road, Worlingworth, Woodbridge, Suffolk IP13 7HW Tel: 01728 628549

Printed by Planagraphic Ltd, Farthing Road, Ipswich, Suffolk.



ISBN 0 9534425 0 0

This book is dedicated to my four grandchildren
Daisy Vaudrey
Christopher & Margaret Wells-Furby
and
Wilfred Jenkins

# If St. Peter Has Hounds

## *A day with every mounted British pack*

*So back to my toast to this greatest of sports,*
*Here's to hunters and hounds – and spare Reynard a thought.*
*May we follow the horn till it's our turn to die,*
***And if St. Peter has hounds he will hear us all cry***
*Tally-ho, tally-ho, tally-ho,*
*Hark forrad, good hounds, tally-ho.*

**Suffolk Foxhounds** *L to R, Dick Colson, Mrs Anglea Miles Hon. Sec., Paul Rackham M.F.H., sponsor of this book.*
Photograph taken by Jim Meads

# Contents

## FOREWORD

*by Captain Ronnie Wallace M.F.H.*

To have hunted with 286 packs in this country, which comprises all the mounted packs whether Foxhounds, Harriers or Stag Hounds, and to have attended hunting occasions with various packs of Beagles as well gives some idea of Tony Harvey's dedication to the chase.

This book is an intriguing description of the logistics involved in such an undertaking and the way in which horses and accommodation were arranged.

In addition Tony hunted the Easton Harriers, from all accounts with conspicuous success; this comprises two Masterships of over twenty seasons.

These achievements are all the more notable by a person who was not brought up to hunt. In fact those who come fresh to the sport, and obviously harbour a feeling for it in their genes, are often the keenest of them all. Our author was brought up to work with heavy horses on a big arable farm, but his father must have been a discerning person too; he suggested without warning that Tony borrow a horse which was available, learn to ride it proficiently and then join in with the Easton for a day's hunting. He became a rough rider and horse breaker, whipped-in to the hounds, learnt lessons from that and advanced to huntsman in his own right.

He is a purist in his concept and particularly enjoys the establishments which practice the hunting of the hounds without too much interference. Those Masters and followers who appreciate "the hooroosh" of hounds, manoeuvred by quick staff work may not always concur, but his comments on his experiences sometimes with praise and sometimes not, make interesting reading.

I commend this tome, and that is what it is, for the perusal of devotees.

# Author's Preface

My wanderlust started in 1971 when I had that idea that, as I was a Master of Harriers, it would be fun to hunt with every pack of harriers in the country, these being mainly in the West Country, the north and East Anglia. Little did I know what it would lead to for when I had stabling arranged hundreds of miles from home it made sense to hunt with as many of the local packs of foxhounds as possible while I was there. This eventually led to the idea to try and hunt with one hundred different packs and when this was achieved, the visiting bug was so great that I just had to carry on and try to hunt with them all. There was one stage when I was tempted to give up the idea when I still had about twenty-five more packs to visit and these were all over the country. The fact that I did complete the record was due to my good friends Anne and Tony St Quinton who very firmly told me that if I gave up then I would regret it for the rest of my life and made me go on. 1 shall never forget that night in their home when I read through all my hunting diaries and they had Baily's Hunting Directory open and wrote beside each hunt's entry the date I had been with them, and then made a list of those left.

The whole thing would not have been possible without the help and support of so many people. Firstly, to Sheila my wife who not only kept the ship sailing at home during my long absences but also dealt with the piles of filthy breeches, etc., on my returns. To my late brother Robert who kept an eye on my pig farming business. To Kenny Warne, my head stockman, in whom 1 had a hundred per cent trust. To my Master's Secretary, the late Rupert Montagu, who attended to any problem that arose in the Easton Harriers and also helped greatly and very enthusiastically in the planning of the trips. To Jim Wickham, my Kennel Huntsman, in whose hands I could leave my beloved harriers with every confidence, and to Hilda Wickham and all the girl grooms who have accompanied me and turned out the horses so well, often from very indifferent stabling. To all my hosts who have allowed me to stay with them and have made me so welcome, but especially to Tizza and Colin Plumbe who not only put up my horses, my groom and myself in fine style on so many occasions, but also conveniently moved from Yorkshire to Worcestershire and finally to Scotland, thus giving me bases in all those areas. To the farmers and landowners without whose cooperation and generosity the noble sport of hunting would not exist. To all hunt servants to whom we all owe a great debt of gratitude for their dedication and willingness to work long hours. To all Masters for allowing me to follow their hounds, and especially to those who invited me to ride up with them or, even better, with their huntsmen. To quote Surtees, 'I was there to please myself and not to astonish others", and my pleasure was in watching hounds, listening to them and observing the country and how it was run. At this point I would like to stress that the opinions I express in this book are of necessity only drawn from one day's hunting and should not be taken as an accurate description of that pack. Lastly, but certainly not least, my sincere thanks to a great friend, Paul Rackham, who for many years was a neighbouring Master when he had the Suffolk Foxhounds and insisted upon and achieved the very highest standards with them. He not only generously offered to sponsor this book, but also suggested that the profits should go to the Hunts Servants' Benefit Society.

Tony Harvey, 1998

# HARE-HUNTING MAP

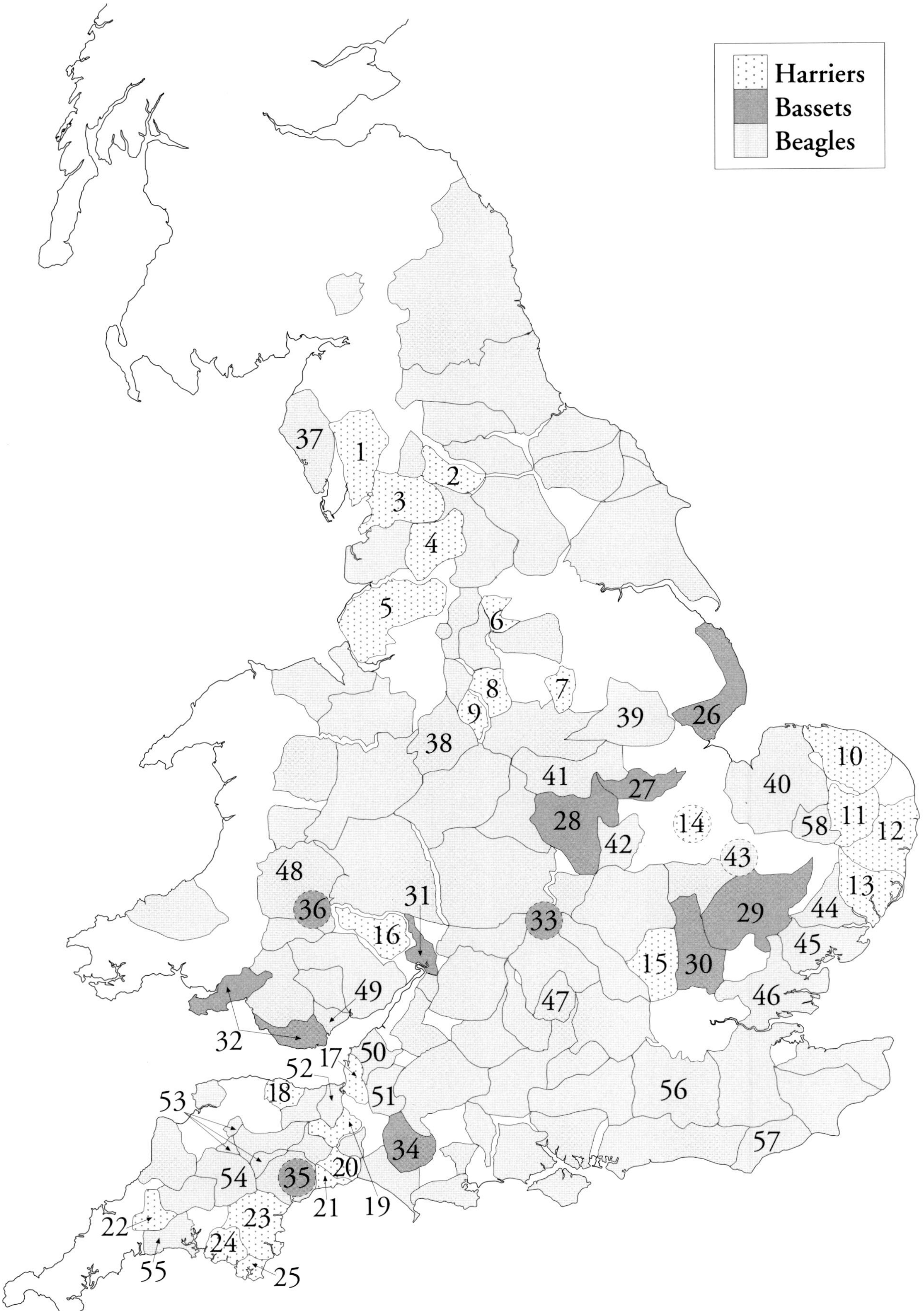

# KEY TO HARE-HUNTING MAP

## *ALPHABETICAL ORDER*

### *HARRIERS:*

| | | |
|---|---|---|
| 15 | Aldenham | 30/1/74 |
| 21 | AxeVale | 21/3/73 |
| 22 | Bolventor | 17/3/73 |
| 14 | Cambridgeshire | 31/1/66 |
| 20 | Cotley | 25/3/78 |
| 23 | Dart Vale and Haldon | 15/3/73 |
| 11 | Dunston | 26/10/68 |
| 13 | Easton | 5/11/53 |
| 8 | HighPeak | 10/11/82 |
| 5 | Holcombe | 31/1/71 |
| 18 | Minehead | 31/1/71 |
| 24 | Modbury | 16/3/73 |
| 10 | North Norfolk | 19/2/74 |
| 4 | Pendle Forest & Craven | 26/1/71 |
| 6 | Rockwood | 22/2/75 |
| 16 | Ross | 17/10/80 |
| 7 | Rufford Forest | 18/2/75 |
| 25 | South Pool | 24/3/73 |
| 9 | Staffordshire Moorland | 15/11/90 |
| 19 | Taunton Vale | 20/3/78 |
| 3 | Vale of Lune | 27/1/71 |
| 12 | Waveney | 29/1/66 |
| 2 | Wensleydale | 19/2/75 |
| 17 | Weston & Banwell | 16/1/80 |
| 1 | Windermere | 29/1/67 |
| | Sennowe Park | 22/1/74 *(private)* |

### *BASSETS:*

| | | |
|---|---|---|
| 27 | Albany | 16/1/82 |
| 35 | Crealy *(country loaned)* | 21/11/81 |
| 29 | De Burgh & N. Essex Harehounds | 20/3/76 |
| 26 | East Lincolnshire Harehounds | 2/1/82 |
| 33 | Four Shires Basset Hounds *(by invitation)* | 28/12/9 |
| 34 | Huckworthy | 2/2/91 |
| 36 | Hydfer | 16/10/82 *(approx)* |
| 31 | Leadon Vale | 18/1/92 |
| 32 | South Wales *(now Vale of Glamorgan and Gower)* | 11/1/92 |
| 30 | West Lodge Harehounds | 16/12/89 |
| 33 | West Oxfordshire *(now included within the Four Shires)* | 17/10/81 |
| 28 | Westerby | 19/10/92 |
| | Bradley Vale | 3/4/87 *(now the Ryeford Chase Griffon Vendeen, hunt by invitation)* |

### *BEAGLES:*

| | | |
|---|---|---|
| 52 | Beacon | 28/2/81 |
| 37 | Black Combe & District | 14/3/70 |
| 51 | Chilmark | 22/3/80 |
| 50 | Clifton Foot | 21/3/81 |
| 45 | Colchester Garrison | 24/3/76 |
| 48 | Glyn Celyn | 15/9/87 |
| 46 | Mid-Essex | 7/2/79 |
| 43 | Newmarket *(by invitation)* | 16/12/89 |
| 40 | Norfolk | 22/2/79 |
| 54 | North Dartmoor | 9/11/88 |
| 38 | North Staffordshire Moorland | 2/12/8 |
| 41 | Oakley Foot | 17/11/90 |
| 39 | Per Ardua | 8/11/78 |
| 57 | Pevensey Marsh | 9/2/83 |
| 42 | Pipewell | 17/11/90 |
| 47 | Radley College | 8/2/83 |
| 55 | Redhill | 26/3/81 |
| 44 | Sproughton Foot | (1968) |
| 56 | Surrey & North Sussex | 2/3/82 |
| 53 | Taw Vale | 15/3/83 |
| 49 | Wentloog | 15/9/87 |
| 58 | Wimbish | 29/1/77 |
| | Bell-Irving | 30/8/75 *(private)* |

## *NUMBER ORDER*

### *HARRIERS:*

| | | |
|---|---|---|
| 1 | Windermere | 29/1/67 |
| 2 | Wensleydale | 19/2/75 |
| 3 | Vale of Lune | 27/1/71 |
| 4 | Pendle Forest & Craven | 26/1/71 |
| 5 | Holcombe | 31/1/71 |
| 6 | Rockwood | 22/2/75 |
| 7 | Rufford Forest | 18/2/75 |
| 8 | High Peak | 10/11/82 |
| 9 | Staffordshire Moorland | 15/11/90 |
| 10 | North Norfolk | 19/2/74 |
| 11 | Dunston | 26/10/68 |
| 12 | Waveney | 29/1/66 |
| 13 | Easton | 5/11/53 |
| 14 | Cambridgeshire | 31/1/66 |
| 15 | Aldenham | 30/1/74 |
| 16 | Ross | 17/10/80 |
| 17 | Weston & Banwell | 16/1/80 |
| 18 | Minehead | 31/1/71 |
| 19 | Taunton Vale | 20/3/78 |
| 20 | Cotley | 25/3/78 |
| 21 | Axe Vale | 21/3/73 |
| 22 | Bolventor | 17/3/73 |
| 23 | Dart Vale and Haldon | 15/3/73 |
| 24 | Modbury | 16/3/73 |
| 25 | South Pool | 24/3/73 |
| | Sennowe Park | 22/1/74 *(private)* |

### *BASSETS:*

| | | |
|---|---|---|
| 26 | East Lincolnshire Harehounds | 2/1/82 |
| 27 | Albany | 16/1/82 |
| 28 | Westerby | 19/10/92 |
| 29 | De Burgh & N. Essex Harehounds | 20/3/76 |
| 30 | West Lodge Harehounds | 16/12/89 |
| 31 | Leadon Vale | 18/1/92 |
| 32 | South Wales *(now Vale of Glamorgan and Gower)* | 11/1/92 |
| 33 | West Oxfordshire *(now the Four Shires)* | 17/10/81 |
| 33 | Four Shires Basset Hounds *(by invitation)* | 28/12/91 |
| 34 | Huckworthy | 2/2/91 |
| 35 | Crealy (country loaned) | 21/11/81 |
| 36 | Hydfer | 16/10/82 *(approx)* |
| | Bradley Vale | 3/4/87 *(now the Ryeford Chase Griffon Vendeen, hunt by invitation)* |

### *BEAGLES:*

| | | |
|---|---|---|
| 37 | Black Combe & District | 14/3/70 |
| 38 | North Staffordshire Moorland | 2/12/89 |
| 39 | Per Ardua | 8/11/78 |
| 40 | Norfolk | 22/2/79 |
| 41 | Oakley Foot | 17/11/90 |
| 42 | Pipewell | 17/11/90 |
| 43 | Newmarket *(by invitation)* | 16/12/89 |
| 44 | Sproughton Foot | (1968) |
| 45 | Colchester Garrison | 24/3/76 |
| 46 | Mid-Essex | 7/2/79 |
| 47 | Radley College | 8/2/83 |
| 48 | Glyn Celyn | 15/9/87 |
| 49 | Wentloog | 15/9/87 |
| 50 | Clifton Foot | 21/3/81 |
| 51 | Chilmark | 22/3/80 |
| 52 | Beacon | 28/2/81 |
| 53 | Taw Vale | 15/3/83 |
| 54 | North Dartmoor | 9/11/88 |
| 55 | Redhill | 26/3/81 |
| 56 | Surrey & North Sussex | 2/3/82 |
| 57 | Pevensey Marsh | 9/2/83 |
| 58 | Wimbish | 29/1/77 |
| | Bell-Irving | 30/8/75 *(private)* |

# Acknowledgements

***Paul Rackham***

Last Autumn on an auction meadow in Norfolk I came across my old friend Paul Rackham. As we walked round together looking at the carriages that were for sale, he asked me about my book. When I told him it was shelved for want of a financial sponsor he immediately said "Send me a copy". Paul's backing was a great boost to my morale and I set about finishing off all the last minute details. I thank Paul for his motivation and encouragement, for giving up his valuable time for meetings and for offering the use of his offices and staff at Bridgham Manor.

***Bridget Wells-Furby***

Bridget, my eldest daughter, has been a tower of strength and encouragement to me in writing this book. She advised me and spent endless hours typing out the manuscript as I read it out to her (my writing being almost indecipherable), then corrected the worst of the grammatical errors.

***Geoffrey Sale***

Geoffrey has been a great support to me and has proved invaluable as a proof-reader and for the painstaking way that he researched the spelling of place-names, especially the Welsh ones.

In his role of editorial advisor he liaised with my sponsor and offered sound advice on all aspects. I am deeply indebted to Geoffrey for finding Mary Goffe and persuading her to illustrate this book and for driving her to our many meetings.

***Mary Goffe***

Mary's contribution to this book is tremendous. Since she was introduced to me by Geoffrey Sale, she has put all her enthusiasm and skill into producing the drawings. It must have been very difficult to take notes while I described various situations and then go home and interpret them so successfully. Her patience and ready smile have made her a pleasure to work with.

***Honorary Secretaries***

Thanks are due to all the Hunt Secretaries and members who responded to my request for photographs, many of whom obviously went to a great deal of trouble to find the most appropriate one available.

***CSC Design and Reprographic***

Special thanks are due to Linda Foulston for her design skills and the personal interest and extra effort that she has put into this publication.

# Chapter 1

## Suffolk Beginnings and The Fell Packs

I was born, as was my father, at Braiseworth Hall, in the small parish of Tannington, near Framlingham in Suffolk. Braiseworth Hall, which is a moated farmhouse, gets its name from Peter de Braiseworth who was one of William the Conqueror's knights and this was his portion of the spoils. The house was not imposing and grand as the name might suggest but is best described as a large rambling L-shaped farmhouse. We made our own electricity and the drinking water came from a well beneath the kitchen floor and was pumped up by an old cast-iron pump which stood beside a large stone sink. The kitchen was entered by a stable-door (i.e. the top half opened without the bottom half), and led into a dairy where huge hams were laid out in scrubbed wooden mangers. They were covered with salt and resembled snow-covered rocks.

From the kitchen door it was only a hundred yards or so to a long line of farm buildings of which the principal one was the carthorse stable and that was where all my interest was centred for longer than I can remember. Fourteen Suffolk Punch geldings stood along one long manger at "bait-times" and at night were either on the meadow in the summer or in a large covered yard in the winter. The horses were a very important part of the farm. They did all the carting of the farmyard manure which was a lot of work as there were hundreds of bullocks and pigs on the home farm and the six other farms which belonged to my father. They also carted all the harvest – in sheaves when I was young and later the strawbales after combines and balers appeared – but the major part of their year, and the hardest work, was the carting of the sugarbeet which usually took from late September to late January or early February. We children were an integral part of the carthorse scene as we "drove away". This meant taking the empty waggon into the field and the loaded one back to the stackyard. I was one of six children and the four elder ones, who were born quite close to each other, all drove away along with the sons of the farm men. If we were not there, a man would have had to have done the job so each one of us children released a man for pitching and loading. At harvest time it would be quite normal for ten children to be driving away, all spread out at different stages between the stackyard and the field which was sometimes a long way off. We did this job from a very tender age and I, being keen, was doing it full time at six years old. When we were so small it was considered too dangerous to climb up the wheel and walk along the shaft to get onto the horse's back so the men at either end would lift us off one horse and onto the next. As I grew older I became more and more wrapped up in the carthorses and wanted nothing else but to be with them, but when Ferguson tractors, which were small and light and suitable to replace the horses, appeared, the horses were sold. The last ten horses and every piece of horse equipment were all sold by auction on the farm. My world had come to an end and I can still remember the empty sick feeling in my stomach which lasted for some months. I worked on the farm with the tractors but could never put my whole self into it as I had done with the horses.

**Monty** – *The author's first hunter*

Photograph donated by Susan Scott

One day when I was about sixteen my father came into lunch and said that he had been with Major Clay, our vet, who had mentioned to him that there was a cob to lend out. He went on to explain how Mary Mann, who lived in Dennington (the next-door parish) was pregnant and wanted to find a home for her cob until she could ride again and would I like it. I was very excited and set off on my bicycle after work with careful directions from my father as to how to find Clay Hill where Mary lived. This was quite an adventure as I had never been so far from home in this direction before on my own as, with the exception of a visit to the dentists in Ipswich once every holiday, I hardly ever left the farm. I arrived at Elm Farm and was shown Monty who I had no hesitation in saying I would have. The lack of hesitation was because I was desperate to have a horse again and not from any of Monty's outstanding qualities (of which there were many) because at this time I knew nothing about any other horse than the Suffolk Punch.

# MAP 1

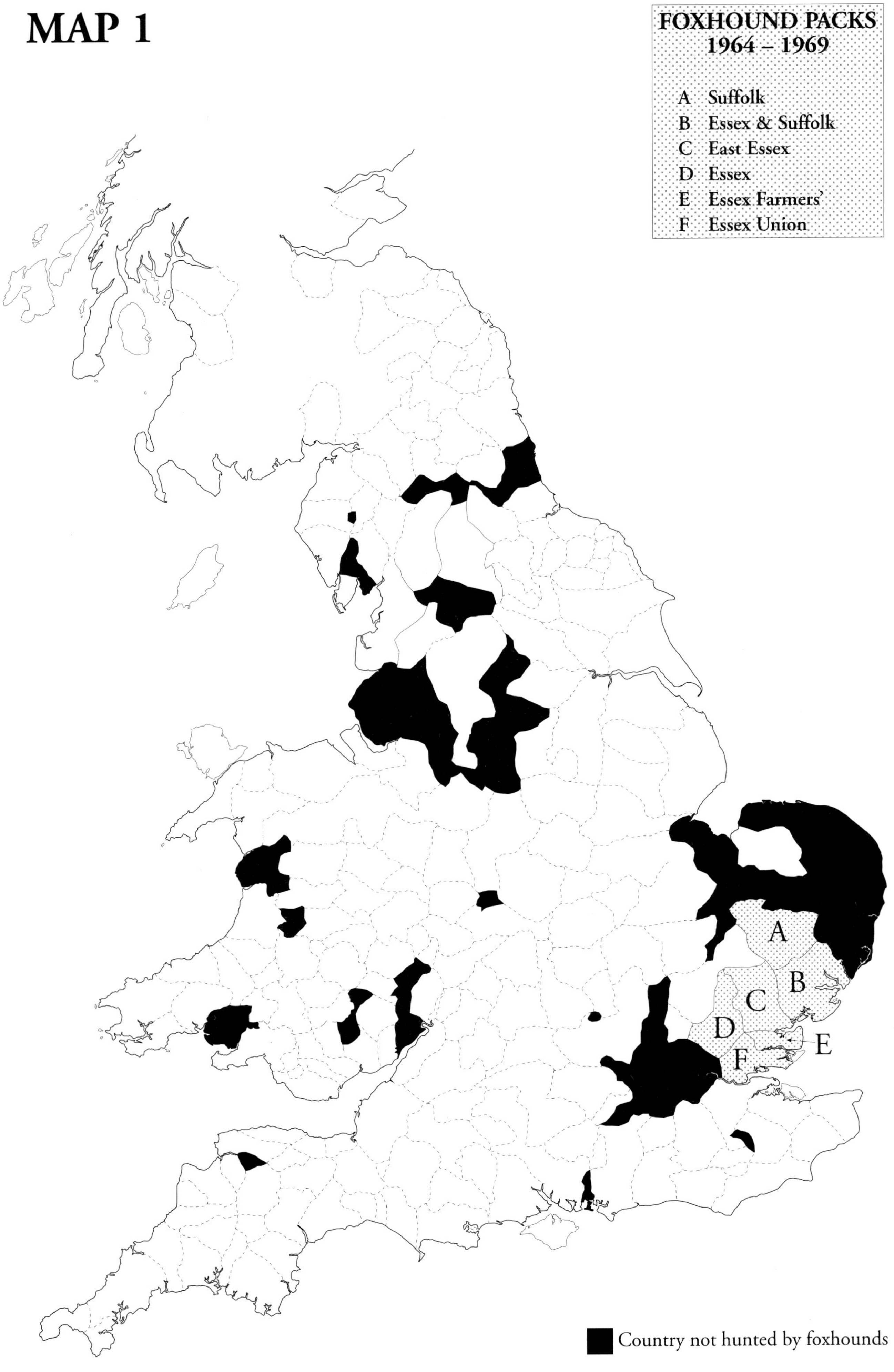
FOXHOUND PACKS
1964 – 1969
A Suffolk
B Essex & Suffolk
C East Essex
D Essex
E Essex Farmers'
F Essex Union
A
B
C
D
E
F
Country not hunted by foxhounds

To my utter dismay, Mary firmly suggested that I ought to ride him to see if I liked him. If I could have wriggled out of this I would have done, but Mary was quite firm and I did not want to risk losing my chance to have him. I climbed onto a saddle for the first time in my life and walked round the meadow. Then Mary told me to trot and then the acute embarrassment began as, of course, with never having been in a saddle before, I could not rise to the trot and just lumped about as if I were bareback which was what I had been accustomed to. To my great relief Mary said I could have him and with his saddle and bridle still on I led him trotting home beside my bicycle.

At the farm there were some large loose-boxes for the one or two carthorses which would have been bullied when they were all together in the large covered yard so I put Monty into one of them. All the horsemen were pleased to see a horse back on the farm even if it was not a "proper" horse, in other words a Suffolk Punch. I was off on Monty whenever I could, either before seven in the morning or after tea, and when my father saw my feeble attempts at trotting he said "Boy you must have some lessons." I felt this was most *infra dig.* as I was considered to be a good horseman with the carthorses but I accepted the inevitable and cycled down to Framlingham for lessons with Miss Gallienne with whom I struck up a friendship which has lasted to this day. I soon picked up the rising to the trot but apart from that I am afraid I must have been a very disappointing pupil as I was not interested in going into such finer points as "leg-aids" and so forth. After a few lessons I stopped going because it was harvest-time and never recommenced my lessons. This I was later to regret as I have so often wished that I had been taught to ride properly and understand how to place a horse properly at a jump, instead of just riding at it anyhow as was my style, or rather lack of it.

When my father could see that I was really enjoying Monty, he said that I ought to have some breeches and not always ride in my farm overalls and boots. The very next Tuesday, which was market day, he took me to Ipswich with him and, when he had finished his business in the market, he took me to Edwards in the Buttermarket where I was measured for breeches. They were tailor-made for me and cost eight pounds ten shillings. This seemed a terrible extravagance to me as this was considerably more than a farmworker's basic weekly wage at that time. After harvest was over and we started on the sugarbeet the work day ended at four-thirty and there was time to ride in the evenings. I was able to use my new breeches although mostly I still rode in my overalls as it took too long to come into the house to change.

One morning in November at the breakfast table, during a lull in the conversation, my father grunted,

"Boy, the hounds meet at Worlingworth Swan. You ought to go."

When my father made this type of remark it was a mixture of an order and a suggestion with rather more emphasis on the order. I was both excited and scared at the same time as I wanted to go but was frightened of what I would be expected to do when I got there. My father had never hunted, nor had any of my family, but he had always spoken of seeing our local pack, the Easton Harriers, on the farm and had never complained about the hunt although, of course, in the carthorse days, they were an undoubted nuisance as the carthorses would be unsettled all the while hounds were within earshot and the younger ones would have to be held for hours at a time which was a waste of manpower.

When the great morning arrived I was so nervous I would have given anything for a good excuse not to have gone. What to wear was the greatest problem but I had been taken off to Ipswich again to buy a riding cap and I eventually set off for the meet dressed in my brown wide-cut breeches, with a pair of socks pulled up to the knees which had been my father's when he wore plus-fours. My heavy, ankle-high, farm boots were washed and polished for the first time in their existence and, with my ordinary sports jacket, collar and tie, and my new riding cap, I was kitted out as best we could. When I got to the meet at about ten-forty-five, I was too shy and embarrassed to go right up to the pub so I partly hid in the gateway of Grange Farm, two hundred yards from the pub, and waited. The **Easton Harriers** traditionally moved off at the Master's pleasure, as opposed to moving off on time, and after what seemed an eternity as I sat there with a whole horde of butterflies in my stomach, they eventually moved off at twelve o'clock. I still remained hidden, rather like a cap-dodger. The first draw was a long, narrow field opposite Grange Farm and I think I might well have gone home at that moment as my nerves were very much on edge had it not been for the fact that there were two of the wives of our farmworkers standing nearby who would have told everyone that I had chickened out. I followed well behind the rest of the field down the field and near the bottom a hare got up and they were away. The cry of the hounds thrilled me and made me quiver all over but the excitement of it all did not overcome my fear when I came to the first ditch. I jumped off Monty and pulled the reins over his head, jumped over myself and he followed.

In this undignified way I negotiated the first five or six ditches as we followed a circular hunt on Bulls Hall land, until hounds finally crossed onto Chandos Farm which belonged to my father. I hung back but Captain Bernard, the Master and huntsman, had noticed this lad lurking in the background and made enquiries as to who he was. As the Captain had killed

**Easton Harriers:** ***The author 'chickening out' at the first ditch!***

his hare on my father's land, he wanted to present me with the pad so he shouted for me to come up. As I did not want to lose face by getting off I hung on to the mane with both hands and somehow managed to keep on Monty's back. I rode across to him but, of course, did not know how to receive the pad so I jumped off and took off my hat. He gave it to me and at the same time told me how pleased he was to see me out hunting, and that he hoped I would come again. When I got home I told my mother and father about the day and about the pad, but naturally neither of them knew anything about taxidermy or that I ought to have it mounted on a shield, so I nailed that pad over the door of Monty's box where it stayed for many many years. I have often wished that it had been properly mounted as it marked the beginning of a new life for me.

Owing to pressure of work I did not hunt again that season until March when the work had eased. The Easton were meeting at the Kelsale Rising Sun so I set off to hack the ten miles or so but became lost soon after leaving Dennington (from where I had fetched Monty). As I got into Badingham I saw a man ploughing headlands with a pair of horses, who I later knew as Butcher Baldry, and I asked the way. With various other enquiries I eventually arrived at the meet, to see Captain Bernard sitting with his hounds on the edge of the main road, the A12. I do not remember much of the day except my great excitement and the thickness of the hedges and the wetness of the fields, most of which were still unploughed and so wet that we had to pull up our horses and walk across some of them. Hacking home, I saw a very angry farmer trying to catch an old Suffolk mare off a meadow who had been excited by the hounds and was not acting her age.

During the following summer Mary Mann asked for Monty back. My father said he would buy me a hunter and duly took me to Cambridge Horse Sale. I was so excited that I can remember trembling all over as if I had some terrible fever. There were lines of horses and ponies standing in the ancient stalls at the market and father rather liked the look of a four-year-old chestnut mare. She had one of those fancy descriptions in the catalogue which did everything but amount to a warranty. They are usually meant to trap the unwary and it succeeded in this case. Her name was Flame and father bought her for sixty guineas, then telephoned home for the farm foreman, Frank Bloomfield, to bring a lorry and fetch her. I waited with the horse until Frank arrrived. My state of excitement was such that I persuaded Frank to stop twice so that I could check her during the sixty mile journey home. We took her to the vicarage which my father had just bought and had told me I could use the stables and the two little paddocks. In hindsight, I realise that she had probably only been backed a few times. When I put the saddle on her in the stable she froze and then started to buck on the spot. When she calmed down a little, I led her out and lunged her in the paddock. She put her head between her knees and bucked and bucked for circle after circle. Needless to say, I did not get on her, and discussed my problem with the old horsemen on the farm. They were more or less unanimous in their advice.

"Yow want to git on har in the middle of a ploughed fild, bor," they said. " She'll a-had enow by the time she git to the rood."

I did as advised and lunged her round on the ploughed field getting ever nearer the centre of the field and as she stood with her legs slightly spread-eagled with exhaustion, I put my foot in the stirrup and swung on. She made a few desperate attempts to buck me off and would undoubtedly have succeeded even in this plough if she had not been so exhausted. I walked her around on the plough and trotted a little, and eventually came out on the road and rode back to the stable. This process was repeated daily on a sliding scale until I could get on her at the stable. I then carried out some rudimentary schooling using some aids unique to me, and taught her to jump ditches on a lunge line. I hunted her quite often next season after I had developed the technique of not actually asking my father for a day off. Instead, I just went and accepted the mostly quite mild telling-off at teatime. I must add that this was not exactly a day off in the modern sense because there would be probably a lorry with ten thousand bricks to unload in the dark, or a load of minerals to carry into the mill after tea, several times a week.

During the next summer, I had a serious disagreement with my father and in these circumstances mostly one or the other gives way, but here there were two stubborn souls together. The upshot of this was the age-old one in which the young man tells his wise father that he can manage perfectly well on his own without any help from his sire and departs. My father immediately emphasised the "no help" part by selling Flame. I did not exactly depart as I continued to live at Braiseworth Hall but had no part in the farm and maintained a frosty relationship with my father. Once the heat of the row had died down I realised that I had to decide what I was to do to earn a living. Not unnaturally I turned to the only thing I thought I was any good at, namely horses. News came to me that Mr and Mrs Pulham of Home Farm, Kettleburgh (of whom Mrs Pulham was years later to be my Point-to-Point Secretary), needed someone to break a horse for them. Someone else had already tried to break it and had failed. I tried my best at the Vicarage stables at Tannington but could not overcome the harm my predecessor had done. The farm horsemen told me that if anyone could break it, it would be Jack Steel of Bulls Hall in the adjacent parish of Bedfield as he was the best horseman in the area. I went to see him and he said he would not mind helping if I did not involve him in the row with my father. His remedy was to set the horse to work harrowing on Bulls Hall so I found myself once more at work on the land crab-harrowing on one of the fields I had crossed on my first day's hunting. The horse was eventually broken and, to prove the point, Jack rode it back to Home Farm.

This introduction to Jack Steel provided me with a chance to earn a living and we set up a form of partnership breaking and dealing in horses. This was at the time when it was just becoming fashionable for everyone who could afford it to have a pony for their children. Trade was good and I spent two very happy, carefree years dealing in everything from Shetland ponies to Suffolk Punches. One day I bought a chestnut hunter mare called Blaze from Buxhall for forty-five pounds, rode her home and advertised her. The man in charge of the Blythburgh Hospital bought her for seventy-five pounds on condition that I hunted her once, and after this day's hunting I liked her so much I wished I could have kept her. When I delivered her, I made him promise that I would get first refusal if they ever wanted to sell her. I eventually bought her back (for fifty-five pounds) as my first hunter after I married and she stayed with me until she died, giving me many seasons hunting with long and hard days. During my two years of dealing I carried on hunting as a part of my business, either riding an improver, or showing off one with a view to selling.

Life changed when, in 1957, my father bought Kings Farm in Tannington which stood at the bottom of a long lane and had no electricity or water laid on. He had thawed out a little during the intervening two years and said that I could use the buildings rent-free if I wished. I had by now met the girl I was going to marry and this made me take a more serious view of the future. I left my carefree dealing days and started to work hard for a living. I started pig-keeping at Kings Farm which was especially difficult as, with no water laid on, all the water had to be carted out of a pond with pails. I sold my car to raise extra capital for this venture and bought Ben, a strong cob, and a float to look after the pigs. The system was to buy the meal from my father's mill at Braiseworth Hall and take it down to Kings Farm in the float; after feeding, the float was used to muck out the pigs and then I would drive home again. I built up the business until I had four hundred pigs and, in addition, six hundred laying hens which I kept upstairs and downstairs in the house, a lovely beamed, thatched farmhouse. Sheila, my intended, gave me her full support in this venture and would often come to wash eggs for me on Thursday afternoons, her half-day off from her job in the local Post Office. I would either bicycle to see her or drive Ben in the float, but she did not moan about having no car to go out in, despite the fact that her sisters and friends' boyfriends had motorcyles or cars. From Kings Farm I earned enough to buy Glebe Farm at Badingham the spring before our marriage in October 1959.

Glebe Farm was an extremely modest little farm with thirty acres and it was my intention to keep pigs in an intensive style. I used my very limited capital to build new piggeries and the modernisation of the house had to wait until more capital was raised from the investment in the piggeries. Sheila bore this with patience for most of the time but we were both highly embarrassed when Captain Bernard, Master of the Easton, called in one afternoon after hunting and asked to use the lavatory. We did not have one, in the modern sense, only an Elsan pail in an old pantry, and it was into this small room that the revered mentor was shown. Four years later, when I took on the Mastership of the Easton, we still did not have a flush lavatory and I often used to laugh and wonder if I was the only Master of a mounted pack who did not have one.

During the 1959-60 season I was invited to sit on the Committee of the Easton Harriers, along with my friend and neighbour John Capon, and we both accepted. This seemed very daunting at the time as there was such a gap between our age and the ages of the rest of the Committee members, and we sat there amongst such wise sages that our presence seemed of little consequence. A whole generation seemed to be missing. Years later I realised that this was owing to the War, when many farmers stopped hunting and never made the effort to start again at a time when horses were on the way out and were considered very old-fashioned, while shooting was being much better organised and far less trouble.

I had not had a hunter, or hunted at all, for the two seasons I had my pigs at Kings Farm but then I was given the chance to buy back Blaze. I started to whip in to Captain Bernard without really realising that I was doing so as the hounds were very out of hand and wild and the Master needed all the help he could get. For example, when moving along a road, I would get ahead and stand guard at every open gateway or gap in the same way as if sheep or cattle were being driven along the road. This was, as far as I was concerned, normal behaviour for a pack of hounds as I knew no other, so I accepted it and happily did my bit to keep them going. Captain Bernard's kennel huntsman, Ernie Nunn, was over seventy and had suffered a bad fall on the way to a meet. Both these facts contributed to him being rather less enthusiastic than in his younger days and he was quite happy to let me try to whip in. He would offer advice, quite firmly but not always in a very diplomatic way. For example, in my earliest days I rode without a hunting whip and, hacking home one evening, he called me up beside him and growled, "If you can't afford a whip, I'll give you one." End of conversation.

I "whipped-in", in a very amateur way, for two seasons, which involved some long days, sometimes being away from home for up to eleven hours as I had no transport and would hack the eight miles to the kennels and then go on with hounds to the meet which could be up to ten miles, then back to the kennels by dark, and the final eight miles home in the darkness. I can still remember clearly covering the final stretch on the road above Glebe Farm, and seeing Sheila silhouetted in the open kitchen door, anxiously listening for Blaze's hooves ringing on the road.

Captain Bernard and Ernie Nunn resigned as Master and kennel huntsman respectively on 30 April 1961. There were no applications for the vacant Mastership although it was advertised in the *Horse and Hound* and the local press, so the Committee decided that it would try to run the hunt. A professional huntsman, Nick Brooks, was appointed with myself and Mrs Kingston-Smith as amateur whippers-in. It was the popular belief that the introduction of a professional huntsman would steady the hounds and put an end to their wildness. Both of us amateurs and the professional put in as much time as we possibly could during the summer and were fairly confident about the impending season as we were able to walk out with hounds in a fairly relaxed manner, even if we were ever vigilant for signs of them running off. However, our confidence was misplaced as, once the harvest was cut and the fields open, all the old instability returned and they were itching to break away. As soon as we started mounted hound-exercise the real trouble began. They chose their spot opposite some barbed wire and just disappeared. The Easton country at that time was overrun with hares and they hunted their own private hares all day and well into the evening, some being picked up as late as nine-thirty at night many miles away. It was after this incident, and the flood of complaints from farmers, that the Committee decided to put down the whole pack with the exception of six bitches (who would not hunt again but would be bred to preserve the old bloodlines) and the unentered young hounds. I was not involved in the obtaining of draft hounds but foxhounds and some harriers and even a couple of otterhounds soon arrived and we had a scratch pack to start the new season of 1961-62. We did have the inevitable few rogue hounds given to us which was not at all helpful. I have likened it to kicking a man when he was down, but from it I learned a lesson and never once drafted a hound with a serious fault to another pack. What a change it was to whip in to a steady pack and it was not long before our scratch pack was running beautifully together and we had some grand fun, most of the foxhounds being delighted to be allowed to hunt hare.

In the next season (1962-63) the Committee appointed a professional whipper-in, Pledge, who would also groom the hunt horses. I continued to whip in with him as often as I could get out but was relieved not to have to go on a regular basis. Then, in December 1962, on a sudden impulse I offered to become Master during a Committee meeting. When I returned home I had to break the news to Sheila. Her only reaction was to say that she supposed she would never be able to eat fish and chips out of the paper again. However, she was much more understanding than my father who firmly told me that I was an idiot and "didn't I know that Masters of hounds should have their living come by post?" In other words he was saying that Masters should not have to work for a living. By the time the Mastership details had been agreed it was too late to change any staff arrangements so Brooks and Pledge stayed for my first season. To mark my first season as Master (1963-64), Captain Bernard gave me my first leather-bound Hunting Journal and out of the great respect I had for him, I have rarely had a day's hunting anywhere since that I have not recorded in this and subsequent diaries.

**Norwich Staghounds.** *Henry Bothway, Joint Master and huntsman, leaving Pulham Market, Norfolk.*

Photograph kindly loaned by Mr Robert Bothway

It was during my first season as Master, in the spring of 1964, that I was introduced to French hunting and heard the word "venerie" for the first time. A Frenchman, George Lamiot, was starting a new pack to hunt the fox in Normandy and had been in correspondence with John Graham, a member of the Easton and a past Master of the Waveney Harriers. As a result I went to France in my pickup truck to take a draft of three and a half couple of harriers which were horse-shy after being ridden over or jumped on. They were of no use to me but in the French forests they could hunt well away from horses. This introduction was to alter my view and deepen my understanding of hunting and with the benefit of hindsight I can easily say that I learned more venerie from a few evenings at George's fireside than I did in seasons of hunting my own hounds. During this and subsequent visits to France between 1964 and 1975 I hunted with fifteen different packs of hounds, staghounds, beagles, harriers and boarhounds.

Prior to this, I had had several days with the Norwich Staghounds which were a pack of "carted" deerhounds which means that two deer were brought to the meet in a special trailer. One of them would be released and given fifteen or so minutes start before the hounds would be laid on the line. There was little or no venerie attached to this form of hunting as the scent of the stag is strong and lasts for a long time. In places where they hunt the wild stag, on the other hand, there is considerable venerie involved as there are many other deer and hounds can easily change lines when hunting. However, there was no chance of changing stags in Suffolk and it was a case of sit down well into your saddle and ride. There was no time to spare and no thought of finding an easier place to jump. Anyone who faltered, or who stopped to help someone in trouble, would be lucky if they ever saw hounds again. Hunts of between twenty and twenty-five miles were quite common and the deer was often "taken" over twenty miles from the meet. "Taking" the deer involved catching it so it could be returned to its trailer for the homeward journey. "Taking" was quite a problem as it would come to bay either backed up against a thick hedge or, more probably, in the middle of a large pond.

The **Norwich Staghounds** had traditionally met in the Easton country four times a season, at Eye, Laxfield, Debenham and Saxtead, and each year for four years or so I had joined them at Saxtead. This was before I kept a hunting diary so I have no exact dates but one day stands out in my memory. In comparison, it probably is still the most extravagant thing I have ever done and done at a time when I had only a thirty-acre farm and a most enormous overdraft, frequently being summoned to Ipswich to appear before my bank manager. Some of the Easton members were going to share a hired lorry and asked if I wanted to join them. I agreed and my share of the lorry was two pounds ten shillings. I decided to hire a horse and went to Barbara Buller at Grundisburgh. She offered me Poobah who was a real, quality, seven-eighths bred Point-to-Pointer and way better than anything I owned. The hiring charge was five pounds and to have spent seven pounds ten shillings on a day's sport was terrible. As I have said before, it was well over a farmworker's weekly wage. However, much as it struck my conscience, and in a sense it still does, I have never regretted it. What a day we had. The deer was turned off on Herbert Breese's farm at Saxtead and ran via Kettleburgh nearly to Wickham Market, turning left and running to Great Glemham and, after a run of about twenty-four miles, was taken at Woodlands Farm, Peasenhall, at about four-thirty, just as it was getting dusk. Every obstacle had to be taken without regard and my new mount sailed on over everything without a hitch. At the end, I leapt off and eagerly helped to take the deer which was in a small pond, and became soaked in water and mud in the process. It was during the taking of this deer that I met Stanley Tompkins who was fanatically keen on staghunting. Stanley told me what to do and when as we were taking it and we quickly became friends. We were later to enjoy many days together.

Another early experience of hunting with other packs came on a Wednesday in December 1964 when I was confined to my bed feeling very sorry for myself with a bad cold. Sheila went shopping to find some delicacy to cheer me up but just after she left, Alan Bridgeford, a high-ranking member of the Easton who lived at Little Chopins, Coddenham, telephoned to say that the **Essex & Suffolk Foxhounds** were meeting there that day and would I like to come (Wed 3 Dec 1964). I immediately telephoned the kennels to ask for a horse to be ready as I kept my personal horses there with the hunt horses. I dressed in double quick time and was just going out of the door when Sheila came in with the tempting goodies and did not seem at all pleased with my rapid improvement. She vowed it would be the last time she made a fuss of me when I was ill and, thirty years later, I know she meant it as she never has!

The Master, John Jiggins, was hunting hounds and made me very welcome. I was amazed at how grossly fat the hounds were and the Master, seeing me looking at them, explained to me that some people had commented on that point but that was how *he* liked them to be! The first fox would not go away and after dodging in and out of Oak Wood for an hour or so was lost, but the second fox at two-thirty gave us a run to Henley and back. John Jiggins invited me into the Sorrel Horse at Barham where the landlord, Tom Jefferies, was famous for keeping a wonderful cellar of fine wines. I do not remember sampling any of the fine wines but the last entry in my diary for this day reads "Came home in high spirits" which just goes to prove what a wonderful tonic a day's hunting is, even when the sport is not very good.

*"There's a doctor in boots, with a breakfast that suits,*
*Of home-brewed ale and good beef.*
*To his patients in bed, "I have come," he said,*
*"To console you in hope of relief".*
*To the poor his advice gives away,*
*To the rich he prescribes and takes pay,*
*But to each one he said, "You will shortly be dead,*
*"If you don't go a-hunting today."*

In the course of the day I had been kicked on the shin by another horse and when I came limping into the house, expecting sympathy from my wife, the only response was that it was no more than I deserved.

The following Monday (8 Dec 1964) I had another day away, although this had been planned some time in advance and was not an impromptu jolly as my day with the Essex and Suffolk had been. I had decided that I wanted to see the **Cambridgeshire Harriers** because I, along with all the harrier world, had heard so much about them and I set off with four friends – my neighbours Chris and Sara Bigden, Christine Dickinson and Terence Saffell. Christine was later to marry a French Master of hounds, Jean Bocquillon of the Picardie Valois, and forge a lasting link between the Easton and the Picardie Valois, and Terence was to become the Honorary Secretary of the Harriers.

**Essex and Suffolk Foxhounds.** *Meet at Denny Wood, New Forest, by invitation, 2 March 1982. Joint Masters George and Mary Paul.*
Photograph kindly loaned by Mr George Paul

It seemed a very long way to the meet at the Flint crossroads at Heydon and we had to pass through several towns which are now bypassed, but we arrived in good time and were welcomed by the Master, Mrs Betty Gingell. Our host for the day was also very welcoming and before we moved off he insisted that we all returned to his house after hunting for tea. He pointed out his house on some higher ground behind the pub. We moved off and hounds were drawing when our host stopped back on the road and spoke to a lady in a car. As he was cantering up a smooth grass track to catch us up his horse's foot broke through a rabbit hole and he had a bad fall. A message came up to Mrs Gingell who was waiting with her hounds that the fall was serious and everyone stood still. After the doctor arrived it was confirmed that he had broken his neck and was dead. To this day I have always believed that he had stopped back to warn his wife that he had invited five extra for tea. How terrible to be killed on your own farm within sight of your house and on a smooth grass track. How true is the saying that a fall on the flat is always the worst.

The journey out was full of fun and excited anticipation but the return was of solemn faces and quiet words and the shock of it seemed much worse for the fact that it was not exactly a hunting accident as he was not jumping or doing anything dangerous.

**Cambridgeshire Hariers** *Mrs Hugh Gingell with her Harriers at the Flint Crossroads*

A couple of months later the Norfolk and Suffolk Foxhounds met at Glebe Farm by my invitation. This came about after a long row which started when Mr Henry Bothway, Master of the Norwich Staghounds, decided to start a pack of foxhounds in place of the staghounds when they were disbanded. They were to be known as the Norfolk and Suffolk Foxhounds and a great row broke out over their country as they registered all the countries previously hunted over by the old Norwich Staghounds. This was made up of the old Dunston Harriers, the Waveney Harriers and the Easton. The Dunston hierarchy were so intermingled with the officials of the Norfolk and Suffolk that they made no objection but the Easton and the Waveney, under their Master Lord Somerleyton, objected most strongly. As foxhounds usually take precedence over harriers this would have meant that the harriers would have had to ask the foxhounds' permission for every meet of their season. Clearly this would have been an intolerable situation for us as we had always been independent of foxhounds since there never have been any foxhound packs in our country and both the Waveney and the Easton fought tooth-and-nail. This was all very difficult for me, a young and inexperienced Master in his first season, but I was greatly helped and supported by Captain Bernard and after many months of battle the Masters of Foxhounds' Association held a tribunal in London. Lord Halifax presided over the meeting and both sides gave their evidence rather as if in court. I would have preferred for Captain Bernard to give the Easton evidence but he said that, as Master, I must do so. He stood beside me as I gave our evidence but it was all very nerve-wracking. My main point was that the Easton farmers' would not accept two mounted packs. This I could state very firmly as the old Norwich Staghounds had a terrible reputation for riding roughshod across country, leaving a trail of damage behind them. Lord Somerleyton's objections were, I believe, on similar lines. The decision made foxhunting history as for the first time ever the MFHA supported our cause and the **Norfolk and Suffolk Foxhounds'** country excluded the Easton and Waveney countries.

This had been a hard and bitter struggle but to show that there were no hard feelings Sheila and I and some friends went to their Hunt Ball. Whilst there I went across to Henry Bothway's table and asked him if he would like to bring his hounds to a lawn meet at Glebe Farm. He agreed and the occasion took place on 3 Feb 1965. As hosts, we had a good stock of whisky and gin ready for the meet but were caught out as they all asked for either cherry brandy or port. The first draw was Bruisyard Big Wood which proved blank and this set a precedent for the whole day. Every wood between Badingham and Saxmundham was drawn but all proved blank. It was dark as we hacked back to the meet but, as a small consolation, the Bothways, Henry and his wife, stayed on the evening for dinner. I had a few more days with them later but they usually could not find foxes so, after a while of trying to hunt fox one day a week and drag one day, they soon disbanded.

It was a year after our trip to the Cambridgeshire when I again hunted with another harrier pack but this time the trip made our journey to the Cambridgeshire, which I had thought so long and exciting at the time, seem like nothing. It was brought about by the necessity for some forward thinking as Master of the Easton. The Easton country had been mostly arable with some meadows around each farm and fields of between three and ten acres. They were surrounded by very high and wide hedges which made riding to hounds an urgent business otherwise they were soon out of sight. But the times were changing. The big hedges were mostly gone by 1966 and the foremost farmers were bulldozing ditches in to make larger fields. Ironically, the pioneer and clear leader in this exercise was my own father who, with lots of determination, a small bulldozer, and gangs of men draining by hand, soon had large fields, and his "two-hundred-acre" was famous throughout the county. The traditional Easton country which had been perfect for hare-hunting was disappearing rapidly, aided and abetted by larger and larger Government grants as farmers were urged to produce more home-grown food. The word "conservation" might not have existed as no-one had ever thought of the need to use it.

All this made me realise that there must be a great change in the style of hunting in this part of the country. There would be no more riding to hounds in the sense of following their line. Large, well-drained fields were mostly sown with winter wheat and the future of hunting must be to keep the horses on the edges of fields and watch hounds from a distance. This in turn, of course, meant that hounds must hunt themselves and not look to the huntsman to cast them or to be with them when they were drawing. Although the country was disappearing rapidly it was not far advanced in most areas so it was quite easy for me to realise how reluctant hounds were to be completely away from me. I gave this problem much thought and discussed the future with as many knowledgeable people as I could find.

John and Elizabeth Graham, who were both very keen on hunting, lived at Brundish Manor, quite close to Glebe Farm. Elizabeth was a very good cook and she and John often gave very good dinner parties. Inevitably the conversation was mostly of hounds and at one of these parties I was airing my current problem when John, who was much more cosmopolitan than me, came up with a suggestion. There was a pack of harriers that hunted in the mountains of the Lake District, he explained to me, and they must, of necessity, be totally independent. Well into the port stage of the dinner it was decided that we should go to the Lake District and see for ourselves these mountain harriers which were, of course, the Windermere.

I telephoned the Master of the Windermere, John Bulman, and explained that I was looking for a stallion hound that would breed independence into my hounds. He suggested that we might like to combine our visit with their Hunt Ball and, knowing how much Sheila and I enjoyed dances and parties, I accepted. Just before he rang off he said,

"And don't bring any of your fancy southern clothes".

Sheila was bitterly disappointed about this point and just could not understand how they could have a Hunt Ball without dressing up!

John Graham, Sheila and I set off for this journey in January 1966, a very exciting one as, although I had been to France, I had never been further north than Thetford. We stopped for lunch in a pub and from the juke box Nancy Sinatra was blasting out "These Boots Were Made For Walking" which seemed appropriate as we were going to hunt on foot. I can still feel my excitement at our first sight of the "mountains" (as we called them) of the Yorkshire Dales as we travelled along the A66 from Scotch Corner until we got into the Lake District proper and were quite awestruck by the fells. We found our way to the kennels at Dungeon Ghyll in Great Langdale and, after looking at the hounds, we had tea with John Bulman's parents at the Dungeon Ghyll Hotel. We had Cumberland rum butter left over from Christmas on delicious home-made scones which left a lasting memory in my taste buds. We were not impressed with the hounds in kennel, being all types and sizes with a few beagles mixed in. There was very little of the real original Windermere blood left except one or two who had the blood of Windermere Chorister in them, but they did not have good conformation and had sterns so curly and gay that they started to turn a second circle, rather like a pig's. The idea of introducing Windermere blood into the Easton did not seem such a good one when I had seen them so nothing came of my original plan, but meanwhile the fun continued.

We were hurried off back to the Britannia Inn at Elterwater to book in and John told us to be ready by six o'clock to follow him to the Ball. He arrived with his wife and we followed his van in our car, terrified for our lives as he drove so fast. There was a light covering of snow on the ground and the hills seemed so steep and the walls threatening serious trouble to any one who skidded. After what seemed a very long journey we arrived at the Plough Inn at Selside which was full to overflowing with genuine country folk. The atmosphere was tremendous and after a while order was called and I heard my first ever hunting song. There was another song and then the Master ordered everyone out and over the road into the village hall which was full of trestle tables with plates of ham and pickles and so forth, already in position. In front of the plates of ham were cake stands loaded with various cakes. What a wonderful old-fashioned spread!

After the meal was ended, John Bulman made a short speech thanking all catering ladies for their efforts and then ordered everyone out back to the pub where singing started in earnest. I shall never forget that singing, especially the man standing on a beer crate to sing "The Place Where The Old Horse Died". The Master then ordered everyone back across the road and within a few minutes the hall, now cleared of tables, was full of people – a ratio of six males to one female. Soon dancing began in earnest and Sheila had a wonderful time, dancing every dance. The atmosphere was electric with unforgettable characters by the dozen. Shepherds' sticks stood in corners and every now and again a collie dog peeped in through the door and someone would growl "get back". It was all over far too quickly and people drifted away except for the inevitable few in which, as the Master's guests, we were included. The privileged few were gathered in the kitchen at the back of the hall for more drinking. Beer bottles were quickly produced, the tops removed and were handed round. Sheila must have looked a trifle taken aback as I heard John Bulman say,

"Nay, lads, nay. You cannot expect Mrs Harvey to drink out of a bottle."

After only a slight pause, a cracked cup with no handle was produced for Sheila to drink from.

This little party lasted another hour or so with me noticing that every now and again a bottle was put behind the curtain. Years later I discovered they were for the policeman outside. What an unforgettable night, and one that was to alter my life for ever as I became firmly hooked on singing from then on.

Next day we hunted on foot with the **Windermere Harriers** from the Britannia Inn at Elterwater. Sadly, this was one of the very few occasions on which I made no entry in my diary, but I can remember clearly seeing hounds hunt up into the cloud, then hearing them hunting along inside it, until they dropped down out of the cloud again further along the valley. I can also remember a great party in the bar of the Britannia in the evening with John Bulman standing near the fire playing his accordion and singing songs. During this evening I met many people, including Colin Plumbe who was to be a lifelong friend. Colin was amateur whipper-in to the Windermere along with Peter Noble and both were great singers. Next morning the landlady was very understanding and gave us lightly scrambled egg before we set off home feeling very jaded but very, very happy. Back in Suffolk I waxed on about how wonderful I thought the Lakeland hunting and singing were, and was surprised to find that the old generation of the Easton members knew lots of the songs as they had been sung up to the War when the tradition had died out.

A year later I decided to make another trip. I had no trouble in getting companions and Terence Saffell, Ernie Calver, Geoffrey Ingram-Smith and I decided to make a little holiday of it. After an excellent day's hunting from Wilby Swan on Thursday 26 January (1967) we left Suffolk for the Haycock Hotel at Wansford-in-England, near Peterborough, arriving too late for dinner. Going into Peterborough we soon found a Chinese restaurant open and studied the menu. Geoffrey Ingram-Smith went very pale and said he definitely did not want lychees as he thought he had been scraping them off the bottom of his boat. We all rocked with laughter. Moving on next morning we lunched at the Morritt Arms at Greta Bridge and arrived in good time to have tea with Mr & Mrs Bulman senior at the Dungeon Ghyll Hotel. We looked at hounds in kennel and then went back for dinner at the Britannia. There was to be another singsong in the bar that night and at the end of dinner I said I was going to have a glass of milk to help keep me sober as these lads were really hard drinkers. The other three decided that if I (whose drinking ability was well-respected) thought I needed milk then they ought to as well. It all worked too well and the four of us sat completely sober all night and did not get going in quite the same way as our fellow hunters. My friends told me in no uncertain terms that they did not think much of my plan! However, they were all very hearty at breakfast the next morning which might well not have been the case.

The Coniston Foxhounds met at the Britannia at nine o'clock and, after seeing them away up the fell, we went with John Bulman and his **Windermere Harriers** to Gate Ghyll near the Ullswater Foxhounds kennels (Saturday 28 January 1967). It was very amusing to watch John drawing the fellside as, in the midst of the party the previous night, Ernie and Geoffrey had vowed to keep with him all day, saying that they could not see what all the fuss was about, and that if he only walked, of course they could keep up with him! Terence and I watched the pair put up a really good show but as anyone knows who has hunted in the fells the local people have a style of walking up the steep fellside which looks easy and unhurried but is impossible for flat-country people to follow and keep up with.

This day's hare-hunting I could easily claim to be the best I have ever actually *seen.* I stood with Terence at the fell wall (that is the highest wall which follows the contour of the fell) from where we saw the find and could see the hare most of the time during the run. The fells provided a grandstand view as we stood halfway up on one side and could see the whole hunt laid out before us on the opposite side, very often having both hare and hounds in sight at the same time. Particularly, we could see her doubles, and her twists in and out of holes in the wall, and then look back to watch the hounds work it all out. We would then look around the fellside again and find her still going, keep her in sight for a while, and then again watch hounds work out her wiles. While watching her on this day I saw clearly for the only time in my life a five point double. I was really quivering with excitement as hounds slowly hunted up to this amazing double and spent about fifteen to twenty minutes working it out then went on to kill her in some sedges. It is difficult to describe how perfect this all was. The hare was never pushed hard and the only time hounds saw her was at the kill as John had laid them on her line without them seeing her. This delightful hunt had lasted just over the hour.

Another very similar hunt followed and the hare went to ground in some rocks and was left. The third hunt was again just as good, if not better, and she was killed in the rough grass at the edge of a little brook.

I was walking with John as he drew for the fourth hare and as she sprang up, he said,

"I think I know her, Tony. Would you like to see a hare go to ground?"

I said of course I would and he said, "If it is her, she will go into that gryke in the rocks," and pointed out a slit-like opening in a rock face well up above us.

I climbed up to it, and took up a position within sight but well away from it and then watched and listened to the hunt below. Eventually the hounds and followers disappeared round to the left of my hill and I was very tempted to follow them. However, I stayed still and was rewarded for my patience as Puss came along unhurriedly and sat on a tussock about five yards from the gryke. She sat with an ear cocked back and listened to hounds hunting her line slowly up to her, and the leading hound was actually in sight before she hopped across and disappeared into the gryke. Hounds hunted right up to it and one harrier actually marked at it. So ended the perfect day with houndwork of the best – hounds never pressing their hare, seldom helped and working out all the doubles for themselves. I have so often thought of this day and how perfect it would have been to teach someone about hunting as there was everything harehunting stands for right across the valley laid out before us in full and easy sight.

We walked back to the White Horse and, as it was after "Time", stood in the backyard with a glass of beer and a ham roll, the adrenalin still rushing round my veins. We went to see the Ullswater hounds as they were nearby, and found that they were just home from a week's hunting in one of the valleys and had hunted every day that week. They had killed fifty-two foxes that season and three that day. As we entered the kennel, all the hounds were asleep on a raised bed along the far wall. They were bedded on dry bracken, and not a hound raised its head except for one who gave a faint "whoof". This I could hardly believe as most packs would have bayed frantically at four strangers. John Bulman asked about a particular hound he knew as a puppy. The huntsman went to the bench and, putting his hand behind the hound's head, drew it off. It stood as if drugged and gently swayed like a drunken man. I do not suppose I will ever again see a pack of hounds so tired. I wondered how some of the Stud Book foxhounds in the grand packs would fare hunting five days in a row and was sure that they would not be fit enough to kill three foxes in the open on the last day. They had justly earned their rest and we left them to sleep in peace.

Back at the Britannia, we thoroughly enjoyed our dinner before returning to the bar where yet another evening of singing, stories of hunting and accordion playing went on until the small hours. This time we did not use the precaution of a glass of milk and entered into the fun and singing with the greatest enthusiasm. It was two-thirty before we finally staggered up the stairs, having had an exhausting day. On our way home the next day we stopped for lunch at the Old Bell, Barnby Moor, which was next to the kennels of the Grove and Rufford, but shortly after rejoining the A1 we ran out of petrol and had to push the car to the next garage. We finally arrived home at eight o'clock.

**Dunston Harriers.** *Children's Meet at Bergh Apton Manor, 29 October 1996. Acting Master, Mr Robert Bothway, leading hounds, with kennel Huntsman Wayne Reeder, behind.*



During the season 1967-68 I resigned the Mastership of the Easton. I was completely heartbroken as I loved my hounds dearly, but as a result I wrote to the last Chairman of the recently-disbanded **Dunston Harriers**, a pack whose country had lain to the north of the Easton's, stating that I was prepared to re-form the Dunston if he thought the country would welcome such a move. My offer set the ball rolling towards its re-establishment, but in the end Robert Bothway, the son of Henry, was appointed Master of the newly re-formed pack. I was disappointed but nevertheless stated that I would give them some good hounds. Naturally I would not have missed the Opening Meet of the new pack and presented myself at the Poplars at Fundenhall, home of Robert Bothway (Sat 26 Oct 1968). I was eager to see how my draft of hounds would fare amongst all the others which made up the new pack. I took my best horse, Stonebow, who had been turned out to perfection by my good girl grooms, and was pleased to be so well-mounted as the beginning of a new pack had excited the imagination of the hunting world and there were ninety-six horses and over two hundred people on foot. This size of field was not ideal for a harrier pack and the hunting was not first-class, although there was some good music in covert for half-an-hour when a fox was found and was rattled around with hounds clear of horses for the first time in the day. At four o'clock tea was served in the Master's home and, as if that was not enough, his father, Henry, insisted that I called at his home on the way back for drinks. The day ended with yet another first class dinner party with John and Elizabeth Graham at Brundish Manor. This party was very memorable because my fellow guests included my venerie idol, George Lamiot, and I was introduced to Bunny Longman whom I discovered to be a Norfolk veneur, and to John and Hazel Parker who were later to be instrumental in encouraging me to go to Exmoor to hunt with the Devon and Somerset. This enjoyable day was, in a sense, to cause me to waste the best opportunity of my life to do several hunting tours. I had two first class girl grooms and four good horses all in their prime and, for the first time in years, was free of the tie of hunting my own hounds. My financial position had improved considerably since the days when I had taken on the Mastership in 1963. I was now keeping four times as many pigs as I had left Glebe Farm and was now living at Tannington Hall which I rented from my father (who had bought the farm in 1967). Even so, keeping two grooms would have been extravagant if they had not also worked on the farm, particularly straw-carting at harvest-time. I was never again to be in as good a situation for hunting around the country but I settled into a pattern of hunting Tuesdays and Saturdays with the Dunston and Thursdays with the Easton. I thoroughly enjoyed the venerie of harrier hunting and loved every minute of it although in hindsight I wish I had travelled more widely.

The time was not entirely wasted, however, as I managed to hunt with eight more packs during the season 1968-69. The first of these, according to my diary, was the **Sproughton Foot Beagles** although I am sure that I had actually hunted with them before this time and not written up the days. They were our local pack of beagles and their country lay within those of the Essex and Suffolk and the Easton. The beagles came to meet at our local pub, the Tannington Three Horseshoes and Sheila and I invited them to come to the Hall afterwards for tea. This is another time when I bitterly regret not putting more detail in my diary. They did not draw on my father's farm as the big open fields were not conducive to good hare-hunting, but we hunted in an area on Lord Stradbroke's estate which still had its original fields and hedges. This was ideal for beagling and I remember introducing my brother-in-law from London, Tony McCowan, to beagling.

**Sproughton Foot Beagles.** *At Castlings Hall, Groton, 11 Dec 1968. L to R, Miss Paul, Master and Huntsman, Bob Durham, Mark Clayton. "The day Charlie left the bitches behind".*
Photograph kindly loaned by Mrs Margaret Nockold

I had been explaining about doubles and other problems of scenting hounds when I heard a change in the note of hounds' cry. They were behind a high hedge at the time but I said to my brother-in-law, "They've changed to rabbit."

"Now," he said, "This is ridiculous. I have found everything you have told me very interesting but I cannot believe that you can know what animal they are hunting when you cannot see them."

Just as he said that we heard the sound of whips cracking and cries of "Ware rabbit". He did not forget that for years, and often brought it up in conversation.

The tea afterwards was to set a pattern for many years to come and, the pub closing soon after, the beagles have met regularly at Tannington Hall on the first Saturday in October since then.

Rather more adventurously than simply hunting with my local pack of beagles, I decided it would be fun to try to hunt with every foxhound pack in the counties of Suffolk and Essex of which there were five at that time. The invitation to hunt with the first of them came in a round about way through the Hennessy family who were good friends and great supporters of the Easton. They had several times invited their friend Bill Bulman to hunt with the Easton and I can remember how taken aback he was at his first Easton meet. He took a look around the crowded pub packed full of laughing happy people drinking as fast as the landlord and landlady could serve them and when he eventually was allowed outside to get his horse he looked at his hostess, Julie Hennessy, and said,

"Whew, they drink every drink as if it were their last."

Bill returned our hospitality by inviting Julie and me to hunt with his local pack, the **Essex Foxhounds**. I provided a horse for Julie and we set off together in the lorry for the meet at their kennels at Harlow on 29 January (1969). We called to pick up Julie's twin sister Yvonne from Aldham on the way as Bill was to provide a horse for her. This is one of the many times when I regret my early slackness in not writing more in my diary. However, I do remember that the hounds looked very fit and hunted well together as a pack. They found almost immediately, flew for two and a half miles or so and then marked to ground where it was left, but we spent the rest of the day hacking from one blank covert to the next. I had arranged for Crawford Stopher, who worked for me, to bring my pickup truck and take the lorry home. This was because Bill had invited us to stay for tea and because I had accepted a dinner invitation at the Saffells for that evening and would be stopping there on the way home. Once the horses were gone, Bill, who was later to become Master of the Essex, took us to his home for "tea", and this was a tea to beat all teas. After a gin-and-tonic we changed out of our hunting clothes to sit down to a steak-and-kidney pie. Pudding was followed by an elaborate cheeseboard, and we ended up with vintage port. At about six o'clock we left with all three of us in the front of my pickup. I am not sure if it was that I was genuinely lost or if it was lack of concentration due to being in such close proximity to the lovely twins, but I do remember going in and out of Essex three times on the way home. The blank coverts did not seem to matter so much as we laughed our way home, dropping off Yvonne at Aldham, then Julie at Martlesham, finally arriving at the Saffells where my wife and friends were waiting for me. After a quick sherry I sat down to dinner to which I managed to do justice in spite of having had "tea" at four-thirty.

**Essex.** *Opening Meet at Matching Green, during the Mastership of Paul Carden (1966–72). TheMaster Paul Carden, and Huntsman Tom Watchorn.*

Photograph kindly loaned by Miss A Parrish

Four weeks later I made a second trip to hunt with another Essex pack (Tuesday 25 February), this time the **East Essex Foxhounds** who were meeting at Huntsmans Lodge, at Foxearth near Sudbury (actually in Suffolk). Again I took a friend with me, this time Nona Shand, and we both thoroughly enjoyed the hospitality at the meet which was just as well for again we were not to have much sport. The first hunt is best described as a short, sharp one, and then hounds drew for hours before finding a second fox which was quickly lost. This was a day of blue haze which is one of the surest signs of a very poor scent. We finally arrived home at six-thirty.

This bad scenting day was not enough to put me off visiting and the very next Saturday (1 March) I set off again to hunt with the **Suffolk Foxhounds**, this time taking my friend and neighbour Ernie Calver with me for his first day's foxhunting. He took his own horse, Rupert, and I took my best one, Stonebow. Hounds met at Lawshall, near Cockfield, and there was a large field assembled outside the Swan. My friend was very disgruntled about this

**The Suffolk Hunt**

Photograph kindly loaned by Mrs Angela Miles

sort of meet and could see no sense at all in sitting on his horse *outside* the pub! Hounds found almost at once and went away at a great pace. I was thrilled to hear the lovely voice and horn blowing of Tom Batterbee, the huntsman, who was quite outstanding and the best I had ever heard. During this run hounds changed to deer and we all enjoyed a great gallop before they could be stopped. The second fox gave us a grand hunt of forty-five to fifty minutes with hounds putting themselves right at every check. Towards the end of this run I jumped some rails under an oak tree. Stonebow rose higher than I had expected and I hit my head and gave my neck a severe crick from which it has never fully recovered.

**Waveney Harriers** *Mrs James Wells Jt Master*
Photograph kindly loaned by Mrs James Wells

The next visit came about because John and Hazel Parker, whom I had met at John Graham's dinner party on the evening of the Dunston Harriers' Opening Meet, invited me to have a day with them. Their local pack, the **Waveney Harriers**, was adjacent to the Easton and were meeting at the White Horse, St James, on the Wednesday (5 March) following my day with the Suffolk. "The Saints" country is famous with both motorists and hunting folk because of its being a few square miles of a maze of narrow, twisting, roads, with tiny fields, high hedges, and masses of tiny commons, all looking exactly alike and all named after saints. Motorists dread never getting out of it, and some refuse ever to enter the maze, even in daylight. In contrast, "the Saints" were loved by hunting people for the very same reasons, mostly the small fields and big, rough hedges, and anyone who could keep with hounds in "the Saints" was counted as a real "goer". Sue Gooderham was my companion for this day and we managed somehow to find our way to the meet. There was bright sunshine after a white frost which is usually a sign of poor scent but, to my surprise, hounds were able to hunt quite well, and slowly and carefully worked out some difficult checks. At the meet I had noticed that most of the hounds seemed to be old ones which would account for them being able to hunt in these conditions, and the painstaking way in which they sorted out the checks. The country was mostly grass or stubble ("the Saints" being too wet to plough until the spring) and we had great fun, killing a brace of hares in classic style.

After a day with the Essex and Suffolk from The Lion's Den at Great Holland (which finished in the centre of Clacton with the mounted field surrounded by supermarkets) on the following Monday, I arrived home at six o'clock, made an immediate turn-round and left for Essex with my horses Paddy and Embassy, and my groom Josephine Bugg (10 March). Due, perhaps partially, to the great fun we had had with the Essex Foxhounds, Yvonne Sharp had invited me to stay at Aldham Hall with two horses in order to go with two more Essex packs. Josie soon had the horses settled down and I spent an enjoyable evening with my good friends. The dinner was first-class and the whole evening such fun and I certainly needed no rocking when I finally went to bed. This was the first night I had spent away from home with horses in order to have a day's hunting, and had I known what a long road I had started myself on I would never have slept a wink. The experience served to whet my appetite for travelling with horses and set a precedent for many jollies to come. The following morning Yvonne, who was going to ride my other horse, and I set off in good time for the meet of the **Essex Union Foxhounds** at the Whitmore Arms at Orsett (Tues 11 Mar 1969). When I pulled into the car park the landlord rushed out, shouting abuse and demanding how I dared to park in his yard without permission. I was completely flabbergasted but had

**Essex Union.** *Meet at Orsett, 1969.*
Photograph kindly loaned by Mr Philip Mitchell

some sympathy with him after he calmed down and explained that the hunting folk usually took up all his carpark, without giving him any custom, and went away leaving a mess for him to clear up. He agreed to let me unbox there and in return Yvonne and I went in and had a few drinks.

Yvonne knew some of the people in the field and introduced me to them, and especially to Major Mitchell, the Secretary, before we moved off to draw around the edge of the town. Hounds found quickly and we were soon cantering up a street towards some traffic lights where we had to stop as they were red, kicking on again when they changed to green. People looked in astonishment from the pavement and when we reached a "washeteria" the Field Master made a sharp left turn up an alleyway and eventually led us onto a rubbish tip where hounds were marking their fox most beautifully. As I drove back to Yvonne's, I was full of admiration for the Master, Mrs Marion Wilberforce, who kept hounds going in such conditions but thought it was definitely not my type of hunting. In 1984 the Essex Union merged with the Essex Farmers'. The whole day was an eye-opener for me. Firstly, I had never not been made welcome by a landlord at a meet, secondly I had never drawn so close to the edge of a town and been hunting up to traffic lights, and lastly, I had never heard of a "washeteria" before.

On the Wednesday morning my hostess said that she did not think she could manage to hunt a second day running so I went on my own to the meet of the **Essex Farmers' Foxhounds** at the White Horse at Dengie (Wed 12 Mar 1969). I had not really allowed enough time to get to the meet and, as always happens when you are late, I took the wrong road. Eventually I came up behind a horse box trailer with a horse in it and thought I could follow that. It was a terrible mistake because after a few miles it turned into a farmyard. I carried on a little further and then the road ran out and I came to a lonely signpost with an arm carved as a human hand which said "Public Footpath to Ostend". It was only then that I knew that I was really lost because, although I am not brilliant at geography, I knew I ought not to have been anywhere near Ostend.

When I eventually found the meet it was necessary to park some way off and, as I walked up to the pub, I could hear singing coming from the bar and bitterly regretted being so late. For me, it was like a home-from-home, with the atmosphere in the pub so much like the Easton, and the Master, Alan Ratcliff, and the huntsman, George Peverley, gave me a really genuine welcome which always makes such a difference to a day's enjoyment when away from home. Conditions were very, very wet after a night of torrential rain and the field was consequently rather restricted in where it could go. Hounds hunted very well all day and I was most impressed with the style in which George hunted them and especially his beautiful horn-blowing. He was champion many years in the professional class of the horn-blowing competition at the Horse and Hound Ball. Little did I realise that I would meet him again years later in south Wales when the hotel which was my base for a two-week hunting jolly turned out to be his "local".

I drove back home that evening having thoroughly enjoyed my first, although short, hunting jolly, and already looking forward to my next trip. Next day I hunted with the Dunston (Thurs 13 Mar) and was very late back but a party of us set off at six-thirty for another trip to the Lakes to finish the season. Once more we arrived at the Haycock Hotel at Wansford-in-England too late for dinner and went into Peterborough for a Chinese meal, which was only memorable for the fact that Ernie Calver offered the Chinese waiter some of his snuff and choked the poor fellow so badly he could not carry on serving. We left the Haycock the following morning and drove comfortably to the Skelwith Bridge Hotel which was quite near the Brittania where we had stayed previously but which was fully booked by the contingent from the Pipewell Beagles. We arrived at five-thirty and just had time to change before going to the Windermere Harriers Hunt Ball and dinner. This was not to be a village hall type Ball but a grand affair where we were told we could wear our "fancy Southern clothes". Held at the Belsfield Hotel in Windermere, we commenced the evening with a formal dinner with set speeches. A visiting master shocked everyone by his speech replying for the visitors. He said that he really could not praise the hounds as they were such a motley lot all different sizes and types with a few beige beagles and the only decent dog in the pack had no stern at all – then he went on with a shocked and silent audience. I think he had intended it to be an amusing speech but had seriously misjudged the loyalty of the Windermere members to their Master and hounds.

With the formalities over, the dance started, or rather, more accurately, the bar filled to overflowing and some couples started dancing. It was a wonderful sight to behold. There were hunt evening coats from various packs, both green and red, dotted around everywhere and mixing with men in suits, some dark, some brown tweed, and sports jackets of every type. On the dance floor could be seen equally varied fashions twisting or shuffling around the floor, with patent dancing pumps alongside strong brogues and a fair sprinkling of heavy walking boots. The atmosphere was incredible with the ballroom in full swing, and singsongs coming from the bars, little Albert Benson in full voice in one bar and in the other an even smaller

Ted Potts singing "One Step Forward and Two Steps Back" with most realistic footwork to match.

I blew in the hunting horn competition but came nowhere and a local Master blew hard and long but fainted from lack of oxygen. The Ball ended at one-thirty and we all piled into the bus to go back to the Britannia where the landlord, who had been at the ball with us, did not take much persuading to open up the bar. We sang heartily until four in the morning. It was not surprising that we were in such good spirits as the landlord was rather tight and could not be bothered with the optics, pouring straight from the bottle. As he was not at all steady on his feet, if we held out our glasses on the forward sway, at least two doubles guggled out into the glass. He was also not counting very well, and all rounds, regardless of size, were two pounds which was well in our favour.

**Blackcombe & District.** *Meet at the Pennington Arms Hotel, Ravenglass, in 1960s. Mr Tyson Cowman (Master) on right, and Mr Alan Edwards (Huntsman) on left.*

Photograph kindly loaned by Mrs M E Gregg

The morning after the Ball we had agreed to go to the joint meet of the **Blackcombe & District Beagles** and the Windermere at Ravenglass (15 March 1969). This joint meet of the Windermere and the Blackcombe is in the beagles country, and was a regular event to end the season for both packs. The country was very kind to us jaded folks, and scent was not good so keeping up with hounds was not at all difficult. The beagles and the harriers ran well together, but at each check would more or less divide and cast round in their respective lots, rallying to the cry of whoever sorted out the line first.

We went back to the meet at four o'clock where about 120 people went upstairs for a "Tatie Pot" (Lancashire Hot Pot) tea and a good singsong. There was an appointed MC who called upon each singer in turn. I sang for the first time in public (barring Easton Harriers), and I sang "The Ballad of the Easton Harriers" written by myself to the tune of "It's a Fine Hunting Day" and later on I sang "The Place Where the Old Horse Died". We left at six-thirty and the singing was still going strong. My most lasting memory was of a giant of a gamekeeper singing "The Miles and the Road to Dundee". After a good venison dinner at Skelwith Bridge, we went round to the Britannia and started off singing again with the landlord shutting the bar at three-thirty on Sunday morning and pushing us all out. We arrived home in Suffolk at nine o'clock the next evening, very tired and deliriously happy.

# MAP 2

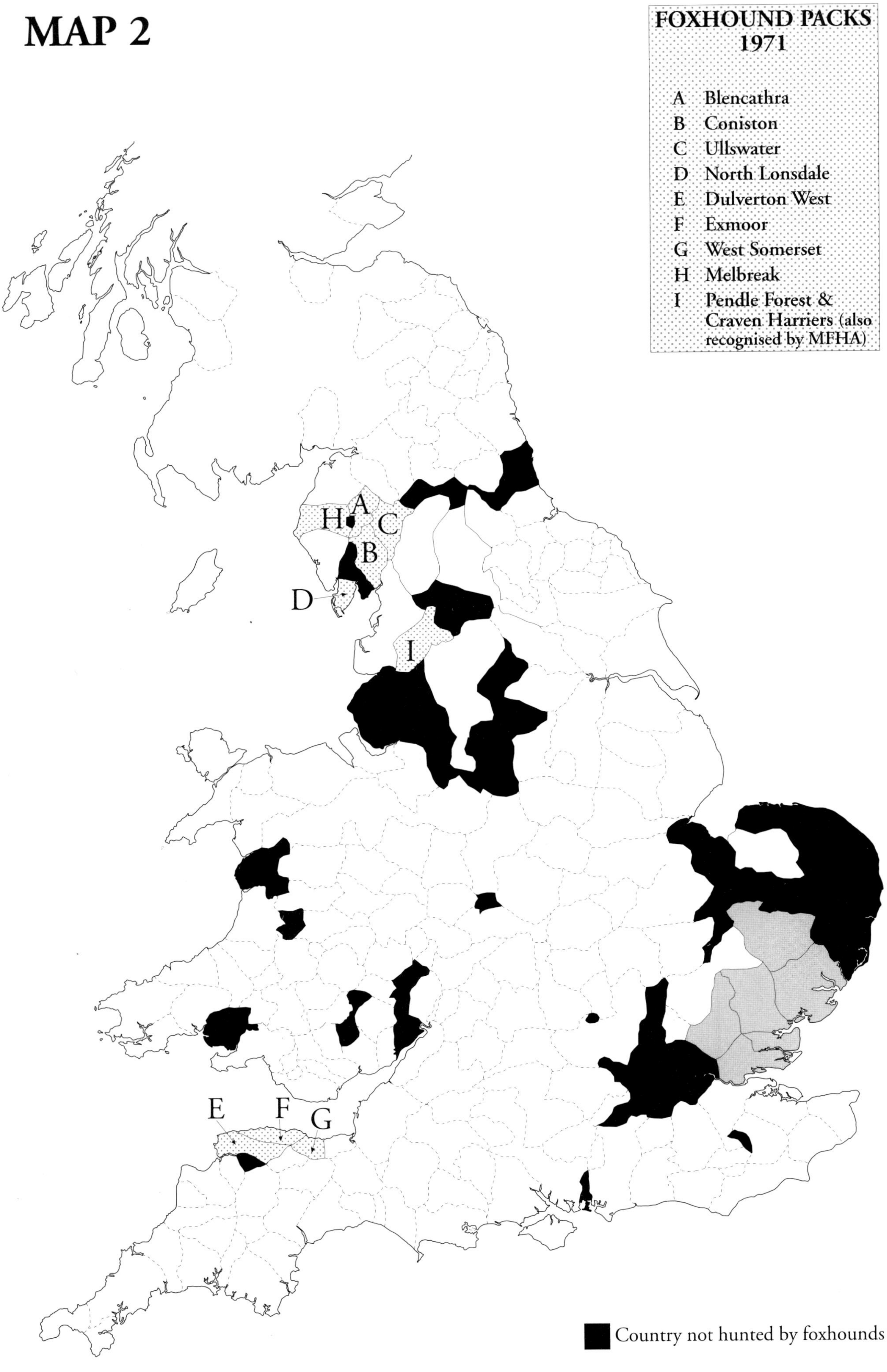
FOXHOUND PACKS
1971
A Blencathra
B Coniston
C Ullswater
D North Lonsdale
E Dulverton West
F Exmoor
G West Somerset
H Melbreak
I Pendle Forest & Craven Harriers (also recognised by MFHA)
A
B
C
D
E
F
G
H
I
Country not hunted by foxhounds

# Chapter 2

## The First Jollies – Hornby and the West Country

During the 1970–71 season I agreed to take on the Mastership of the Easton Harriers again, at the request of Captain Bernard. He and I were both on the Committee of the Masters of Harriers and Beagles Association and we were having drinks before lunch after one of the Committee meetings when, with a bevy of famous Masters around him, he asked me, or to be precise, beseeched me, to take on the Mastership again. In such august company the proposal seemed like an honour and in a moment of weakness I agreed. This was not officially confirmed by the Hunt Committee until the 19 February 1971 but I had given my word in front of so many Masters that it was as good as a contract. The immediate effect was rather like a man whose doctor has told him that he has only six months to live and he realises all the things he has not yet done in his life and how much he would have liked to have done them. The effect on me was to realise how much I wanted to travel and enjoy hunting jollies and how I had just thrown away that chance by agreeing to the Mastership. It was during these thoughts that a challenge presented itself to me – what fun it would be to try to hunt with every pack of harriers in the country, twenty-nine of them at that time. I had already hunted with five (the Easton, Dunston, Waveney, Cambridgeshire and Windermere) and a study of the hunting map showed me that most of the others lay either in the Lancashire/Yorkshire area or down in the West Country with some odd ones like the North Norfolk within reach of home, the Eryri in Wales, and the Ross in Herefordshire . I fondly imagined that three or four trips from home would achieve this ambition. Oh, how simple life is to the naive. Little did I know that it would take twenty years for me to achieve it.

Stanley Tompkins, whom I had met whilst helping him to take the stag with the Norwich Staghounds years earlier, farmed in the Dunston country not far from their kennels, and I had become firm friends with him and Kathleen his wife. Naturally I talked about my idea and Stanley said that he would love to come with me on every trip that he possibly could. He and I studied the map and decided that we would go "up north" first. Arranging stabling and so forth at this distance was not easy but luckily I had the enthusiastic help of Helen Briscoe. I had met her and her husband Bernard when hunting with the Windermere and when I broached the idea to her she thought it very exciting and set about finding somewhere which could accommodate both us and our horses, at a reasonable price, for a week. She telephoned to say that the Castle Hotel in Hornby was prepared to clean out its old stables which would give us six stalls and to ask whether we thought our horses would be able to manage in stalls if they were used to loose boxes? If so, could we manage to bring all the necessary hay, food, and so forth, even the straw? I said I thought we could manage. Stanley decided that we ought to go in his lorry as mine, although slightly larger, was much more dilapidated and very slow. He told me very firmly that his Bedford had an overdrive and could go at over fifty-five miles per hour. It was quite a problem to fit a whole week's feed and bedding, plus two horses each (Nina and Jim for Stanley, and Stonebow and Paddy for me), into one lorry but somehow we managed. Stanley brought his horses over to Tannington the night before so we were able to load the lorry before settling down to our evening's fun.

We left at six o'clock on the Sunday morning (24 January 1971) with Rita, my wife's young sister aged sixteen, to groom for us, and we arrived at the Castle Hotel at four o'clock. Rita was very anxious about the horses as it was the first time she had been in charge of any horses other than mine and was especially worried about the stalls and that the horses would have to stand tied up all night. She set about arranging a system of string to lengthen the halters so that they would be able to lie down. During the evening Bernard and Helen came to see that we had settled in all right and the landlady asked Rita if she could help restore confidence in horses in her children who had been badly frightened by their own pony. This request proved difficult as they were very excited about the horses being at their parents' pub and were constantly running in and out of the stables which meant, of course, that with stalls they were right behind the horses' legs. To make matters worse, they nearly always had an Alsatian dog with them which brushed against the legs of one of the horses and was badly kicked. Rita told us later that the thing she disliked most was the responsibility of washing our breeches and the thing she liked best was being able to walk into the hotel after seeing us off and be waited on at table for breakfast.

After all our trouble in arranging to transport and accommodate our horses, the first day of our jolly we hunted on foot as there were no mounted packs going. We decided to have a day with the **North Lonsdale Foxhounds**, a foot pack which was meeting at Appletree Holme, Blawith (Mon 25 Jan 1971), and this gave the horses time to settle down after the long journey. As the meet was so far away, we left before breakfast. We got lost in Kendal, ending up in a breaker's yard and then stopped for breakfast at a cafe but they were so slow serving us that we were late arriving at the meet. Luck was with us and we saw hounds crossing the road in front of us in full cry and we followed with the other car followers until they killed. We later saw this huge fox as it was placed in a Land Rover. I left the road and walked with the huntsman, George Ridley, but we could only draw blank so at three o'clock I telephoned the Master of the Vale of Lune Harriers, Mr Temple, to ask permission to visit his kennels. I thought the hounds looked rather rough but enjoyed seeing the kennel huntsman, Jim Hawkins, again. Having a coffee with Jim we recalled his days with the Cambridgeshire Harriers, and the fact that he had applied to be my kennel huntsman. I explained how I had telephoned the Master, Mrs Gingell, for references, to be told that he had changed his mind and was not going to leave the Cambridgeshire. This was the reason I had not followed up his letter. He was furious about this as he said how much he would have preferred the Easton to the Vale of Lune. This surprised me as their country was all grass.

**North Lonsdale.** *Meet at the Red Lion, Lowick, 1970–71 (not far from Appletree Holme). Huntsman George Ridley and, second from right, Alec Swann, Hunt Secretary.*

Photograph kindly donated by Alan Bolt

That evening we invited Bernard and Helen Briscoe to dine with us at the Castle Hotel and were later joined by Jim who chatted to Rita and told her which routes to take when exercising to see the loveliest views. The following day we went with the **Pendle Forest and Craven Harriers** from the Tempest Arms, Elsleck, which was near Skipton (Tues 26 Jan 1971). At the meet we were warmly greeted by one of the Masters, Mrs MacAlpine, who introduced us to Mr Reg Hindley, the Senior Master, and others, including George Steel the professional huntsman whom I had met at Peterborough Hound Shows. The hounds were a very smart, level pack, clustered around George and staring up adoringly at him. The mounted field impressed us greatly as nearly all were on top class hunters, beautifully turned out, the whole sight resembling a smart Leicestershire meet, although on a smaller scale.

We first drew an area of moorland and rough meadow which showed little scent, then crossed a main road into a piece of country most easily described as classical – good firm going, with top class permanent pasture, fenced with thorn hedges and post-and-rails. I had never seen the like, except on hunting prints, and looked with trepidation at the rails. For someone

**Pendle Forest & Craven.** *MJRBannister M.H. (on grey in the middle), Bob Napper, Huntsman (right) and Harry Hindle, amateur whip (left)*

only used to Suffolk ditches and a few odd gates, the sight of real fences was a terrifying sight. I took comfort from the knowledge that Stonebow had done many seasons in Leicestershire with his previous owner, the legendary Geo Henson (Master for many years of the Blankney) and he told me himself that whenever he went into Leicestershire he would always take Stonebow as his first choice. Hounds found at once and hunted for almost an hour before killing, Stanley and I both receiving a pad. I had left it all to Stonebow, just clutching tightly to the breast plate as we came into each successive flight of rails. Hounds soon found again and in all they ran almost continually for three hours over this classic country. I soon learned not to go up the hills as George Steel explained to me, saying, "Think of them, sir, as the handle of a pail. It is easier to go round the rim of the pail than over the top of the handle, but it is the same distance."

Also I realised for the first time that serious damage could be done to grassland. The skid marks of horses coming downhill are as much to be avoided as damage to winter wheat in the Easton country where we had fondly but mistakenly imagined grass-country packs could do no damage. Another first for me was actually riding a horse up a real hill. I had never done this before and it was quite an experience. Since then I have ridden up much higher hills and mountains and realise that these were mere pimples as hills go, but I was very impressed at the time.

When we had boxed up, George Steel insisted that we go with him to kennels to see the other hounds and have tea with him. It was a proper hunting tea, with boiled eggs and toast, and lots of cups of tea with a drop of whisky in each. George was in top form and was continually teasing his lovely young wife about being an artist and spending too much time drawing and painting, and asking whether she realised she was supposed to be keeping house for him. It was a perfect end to such a wonderful day's hunting, to have tea with such a loving couple. That evening Bernard and Helen had invited us to dine with them at their favourite restaurant, Crooklands. Owing to the tea-party, we were rather late getting back to the hotel which consequently made us late getting to Crooklands, with the end result that we found ourselves locked out on our return to the hotel. Luckily Rita's bedroom opened on to a fire escape and she let us in through a French window after having a shock seeing two figures outside her room.

However, we were up in good time the next morning for our day with the **Vale of Lune Harriers** which we had seen in kennel two days before (Wed 27 Jan 1971). This was Helen's local pack but sadly she had to work and could not come out with us, although Bernard was going to follow on foot and took us to the meet at Biggins. Mr Johnson, the Senior Master, greeted us all and introduced us to his Joint-Master, Sandy Temple (whom I had asked to visit the kennels), and Ben Johnson, the Honorary Secretary, to whom we immediately paid our caps. As we were going to our lorry to unbox, we passed a man leading his horse out of his lorry. Without introducing himself at all, he growled at us, "I hope you've paid your cap". I replied that I had done so, and always made a point of finding out who the Secretary was and to pay at once, to which I received a solemn glare in return.

Hounds soon found and, after two fields, there was an awful row as hounds went right through a lambing flock. No-one had contacted the farmer although he was only 250 yards from the meet. We later found out that this was typical of the way things were run and that the Vale of Lune were sadly mismanaged. This was my first taste of stone walls. Paddy did not know what to think of them at all, but I was lucky in that the first few were quite low and I was able to get him over. He still stopped at the high ones although I was able to get him over in the end, with

**Vale of Lune Harriers:** ***"A heart as brave as a lion!"***

the exception of one where I was truly left and the hounds and field were out of sight. Luckily, Bernard came along, took a few stones from the top and replaced them after I was over. After that he jumped anything reasonable and appeared to enjoy himself, going on at the walls willingly. The huntsman, Jim Hawkins, was performing over unbelievably high walls and was riding a 14.2hh pony which was somewhat of a local celebrity. None of the field even tried to follow him and I still have a clear vision of him jumping those walls. When he was coming towards us all we could see was his head and his horse's ears, both of which disappeared as he got to the wall just before he sailed over as light as a bird. It turned out that the growler from the meet was also Field Master. He did not go on at all well, and for the first half of the day we were well out of touch with hounds most of the time. Later Mr Ben Johnson told us to go on with Jim and hounds. This put us on show as the field were then watching us attempt to follow Jim. One alarming jump I shall never forget was a sheep wire fence with barbed wire on the top which ran along the crest of a bank, but with Jim and Stanley gone I had no choice but to go also. I felt sorry for Jim Hawkins – hounds were rather out of control and he only had an old gentleman of over seventy to help him. To end the day we had a sharp run across country with hounds "going on to cry" (i.e. running to where they could hear hounds hunting) in the distance, which turned out to be the Lunesdale Foxhounds. I helped the old man whip-in as Jim did his best to sort out his harriers from the foxhounds and get back to the meet. The overall impression of the day was of a heavenly country badly mismanaged. It needed good farmer relations and a whipper-in. To those of us who struggle to keep going in winter wheat it seemed such a wicked waste to spoil such lovely grass country for the want of a little knowledge and effort in running the country properly.

After dinner at the Castle Hotel we went to meet Mr Newton Bacon, Master of the Holcombe Harriers, and his charming wife Kate, who were later to become our very good friends. I had telephoned to ask permission to hunt with the Holcombe and he had immediately insisted that we went to have a drink with him and get to know him before the day. So genuine was the welcome we received that by the time we left, we felt as though we had known them for years. Once again, it was necessary to creep in through Rita's bedroom.

We were slightly late getting to the nine-thirty meet of the **Coniston Foxhounds** at the Low Woods Hotel, near Windermere, the next day (Thurs 28 Jan 1971), and hounds had moved off and were already running in a wood above the hotel. We car-followed for an hour or so and then by luck we saw the hunted fox come out onto the main Windermere-Ambleside road and run off and on it for a mile or so. When the hounds arrived Anthony Chapman, the huntsman, cast the hounds forward until they hit it off up the hillside. We could not bear to simply car-follow any longer and we set off up the hill behind Anthony and hounds. Hopelessly outclassed, of course, by Anthony, we were soon left behind, but came across them marking at an earth. I watched with great interest as this was my first sight of terrier men at work. He was soon dug out and, after giving Stanley and me a pad each, hounds had their reward. We dined at the Fenwick Arms and gave a special thank-you party to Rita for looking after our horses so well in the difficult circumstances. Helen joined us for this dinner and I know that she would not mind me telling this story as she was such a good sport. Helen was a tall, strongly-built girl with a lovely face and figure and always looked fit and healthy. It came as no surprise to me when she asked for a pint of beer for an aperitif. However, I was surprised when she kept level-pegging with us as we were drinking gin-and-tonics and she had consumed about four pints by the time we went in to dinner. She ordered a substantial starter with a T-bone steak to follow and when we were seated at the table, I asked her what colour wine she would prefer.

**Melbreak Hounds** *on Low Bank, Buttermere, with Huntsman Richard Bland (Pritch), from the Buttermere meet, c. 1980.*

Photograph kindly loaned by Jock Small

"Oh, I shall have a pint," she said, and this one slid down easily with her starter.

When the T-bone arrived it was the largest I have ever seen and although the plate was oval-shaped it protruded over each end by an inch or two. I asked if she would have some red wine but was told that she would rather have another pint. How I wish I had a photograph of that healthy, happy girl sitting in front of that T-bone steak, with ample vegetables piled on top and a full pint in her hand. We were barely able to conceal our amazement as it all disappeared so easily and gracefully that it might have been an omelette and a glass of milk.

**Holcombe Harriers.** *At Balcarress near Haigh, the Master, Mr Newton Bacon, on the left with his longstanding Huntsman Alec Sneddon.*

Photograph kindly loaned by Mrs Kate Bacon

It was lucky for us that the **Melbreak Foxhounds** were hunting on the Friday as it meant that we could have a full week's hunting, even though the horses could have a rest (Fri 29 Jan 1971). The meet was at Stockhow Hall, Ennerdale, at nine-thirty. We were slightly late finding the meet but heard hounds running so joined in at once when they crossed the road and followed along the valley until they marked in a badger sett. This sett was so large that one hound was completely inside and appeared to be lost for a while but later reappeared. Hounds had split earlier and the huntsman, Harry Hardisty, took hounds on to where he could hear the others running. These again marked to ground. Stanley and I had quite a hard climb up the rocky fellside to where they were marking and there we met Joe, a splendid local character. Hounds were marking in a rocky place and Harry Hardisty shouted down to a man in a Land Rover to bring up a crowbar. We watched him climb up to us with the heavy crowbar about six feet long across his shoulder. He did not stop for breath even once and when he got up to us his cigarette was in his lips with a long length of ash on the end completely undisturbed. Stanley and I just could not believe that that climb could have been made to appear to be so easy!

The huntsman had taken hounds up above us and they stood looking down and bayed frantically when the crowbar was used to move some rocks. The fox soon bolted, almost over Stanley's feet, who holloaed it away with great gusto, and our new-found friend Joe said, "Eh, lovely bolt, lovely bolt." Hounds went away downhill with a great cry and ran unaided for almost an hour before entering some Forestry where there was no scent. On Joe's advice we stopped and went to the pub with him and had a very amusing time before making our way to Helen Bristow's for a cup of tea. We ate a very hearty pheasant dinner at the hotel and Bernard and I took Rita and Cathy (the waitress at the hotel) to the North Lonsdale Hunt Ball in a local village hall. This was one of the delightful Balls held in the fells and is basically a dance in a local village hall supported by local hunting folk. This was so crowded that it was difficult to dance and, feeling rather lazy after eating so much pheasant, I only managed one dance with Cathy, but the girls were in great demand and danced almost every dance. Before going home we were told that the Lunesdale Foxhounds were having a singsong the next night and we promised to go.

The next day we set off to the last meet of our tour, the **Holcombe Harriers** at the Last Drop Inn, West Bromley (Sat 30 Jan 1971). We had three horses in the back and four of us in the front, Stanley, Bernard, Helen, and myself, all squeezed into the cab. We arrived feeling rather like sardines and were warmly greeted by Newton and Kate Bacon. We thought that Helen's horse was the smartest turned out at the meet. There was a long hack to the first draw, but then hounds found at once and ran up a slag heap, another new experience! They went on over moorland with stone walls, one of which the Master's horse refused and he invited me to go on. I thoroughly enjoyed a splendid burst across the moor, riding comfortably just behind his lovely hounds which were going with a glorious cry until they lost the line in some very dense Forestry. This run across the moors had been my first experience of bogs, and I was in serious trouble several times, just managing to get out. Stanley and Helen were not so lucky as both their horses went down but managed to struggle out with help from other people. There were also deep holes from subsidence due to the coal pits below the surface. These were hidden by long grass which added extra excitement to the run. I was full of admiration for the way Alex Sneddon, the huntsman, hunted his hounds, and recorded in my diary that night that he had them in perfect control.

He drew again and got a fox away, and we had a very fast hunt with a five mile point to beyond Bolton. Stanley and I pushed on ahead of the field (at the invitation of the Master) and with that glorious cry ever louder in our ears we were horrified to see them dropping down a steep bank onto a railway line on the edge of Bolton. We swung left and Stanley rode down a long flight of stone steps to the railway line, with me

***The Holcombe Harriers: "Where there's a will, there's a way!"***

following. We then galloped through streets, stopping at two sets of lights, and I wished with all my heart that we had kept with the huntsman, and was dreading losing hounds. After a few more lucky guesses and street crossings, we were once again pushing on over lovely stone walls until we were reunited with Alex. The three of us came up to hounds marking at an impossible place. Alex was dismayed to find that he had only five and a half couple up at the earth and decided to retrace his steps. His route included jumping a fair stone wall, just one pace short of a river so there was little room to land before fording it, and then jumping another wall from a narrow bank on the other side – all very exciting but unnerving for a ditch-jumping Suffolk hunter. On the way back we picked up hounds and members of the field until they were all on.

Arriving back at the meet at six o'clock we were fortified with a hot-pot and when we eventually left at about seven o'clock we received some very strange looks from the general public who were arriving for dinner all decked out in their best Saturday-night finery, to find us stumping out in filthy, muddy clothes. We arrived back at Hornby at eight o'clock, had a quick bath and dinner, then went on to the Lunesdale Foxhounds' singsong in the local village hall. We took Rita with us and she was the centre of attention. In our capacity as chaperons we had to keep a close eye on her. I sang "The Warson Hunt Song" and "The Jolly Old Country Squire", and was presented with a silver cup, an impromptu creation in silver paper. This was a wonderful and most suitable end to our hunting tour and we returned home to Suffolk on the following day, fully satisfied with our first experience. We had been away for a week and had hunted with six different packs of hounds, three harriers and three foxhounds', which seemed a great achievement.

Our spring trip to the Lakes was by now almost a tradition in the Easton as we had been every year but one since our first in 1966. The 1971 party consisted of Nona and Jimmy Shand, Kathleen and Stanley Tompkins, and Mary and Ernie Calver, as well as Sheila and me. We stopped for a delicious lunch with Pam and David Reynolds (Masters of the Pipewell Beagles) at Chester House, Birchester, near Wellington, arriving at the Langdale Hotel at eight o'clock. After dinner we went to the Travellers' Rest at Grasmere where the Ullswater Hunt Supper had been held. We were hoping to get into the singsong afterwards but the landlord was very protective of the foxhounds' tradition and would not let any strangers near the room that the Ullswater members were in. He almost threw us out of the pub but luckily John Bulman, Master of the Windermere Harriers, came out to the Gents, and saw us, and invited us in. Ernie Calver and I both sang.

Next morning we lost ourselves getting to the nine-thirty meet of the **Ullswater Foxhounds** at Kentmere by taking the road to the wrong Staveley, so we were late, arriving in the area to find hounds split and people hollering everywhere (Thurs 11 Mar 1971). With such pandemonium going on, I could not resist a major sin when I saw a very tired fox cross a wall. I encouraged a few hounds onto this line, and they took it into some farm buildings. When I thought I had lost it, Stanley saw it away at the back of the buildings. Hounds drove on to kill it in the river below and this is the only fox I have ever personally hunted and killed. I did not know that Stanley could run so fast. Whether he was out of control going downhill, or not, I am not sure but he was almost up with hounds when they killed. There was a good singsong in the Britannia that night, all of us from the Easton and a good gang of Pipewell Beaglers but only one Lakelander, Peter Noble. I am sure that the visitors the previous year had so outnumbered the locals that they had spoiled the special Lake District singing atmosphere which was why Peter Noble was the only one at the Brittania this year.

I did not put the name of the meet in my diary but the **Blencathra Foxhounds** provided our next day's sport (Fri 12 Mar 1971). Hounds soon found and ran along the fellside for a mile or so, with us following in a car and had both fox and hounds in view all the way along. The fox came down into the valley and ran the valley bottom very fast for four miles. I have never seen hounds drive on at such a pace but eventually they came to a check on the road. The huntsman, on foot, obviously could not possibly have been there and, indeed, would not have been even if he were on a thoroughbred horse, so there was no-one there to cast them over the road. When the huntsman did arrive no-one told him where they had checked so he started to draw again up the fell. They found at once and went over the top and although we tried our best we saw nothing more of them.

That evening we again went to the Windermere Harriers Dinner and Ball at the Belsfield Hotel in Windermere, where Colin Plumbe, now married to Tizza, had kindly arranged for us to sit with them. There were fifteen entries in the horn-blowing competition and after three heats I won the final against Bernard Briscoe. I was presented with a hunting horn made from a cow's horn which had earlier been stolen but was recovered and still hangs in my study. Having attended the Ball, we duly went to the traditional joint meet of the Blackcombe Beagles and the Windermere Harriers at the Pennington Arms in Ravenglass (Sat 13 Mar 1971).

This was now the third year in succession that I had attended this meet on the seashore, although the previous year our party (which consisted of Sheila and me, Ernie and Mary Calver, Sue Clough, and George and Sue Gooderham) had been lucky to make it. There had been a thin covering of snow that morning and much discussion of whether we could get over Wrynose and Hard Knott passes. As I had never heard of either of them I took no part in the conversation. If I had known of them I would never have tried but we all went in a convoy with the Pipewell contingent in the lead. Half way up the steep and twisting road of the pass the wheels started to spin and with a big drop off to one side of the road I was greatly relieved when Ernie Calver jumped out and put a rock behind the wheel. We turned back and went the long way round, arriving at the meet at the Pennington Arms slightly late.

On this occasion the weather was exactly the opposite and, as we drove over the dreaded passes in baking hot sunshine, Jimmy Shand entertained us with tales of racing over the same road in the RAC rally. It was far too hot for hunting purposes. Hares were difficult to find but we did have two little hunts and hounds caught their second hare. It was about one-thirty when the two Masters decided that enough was enough in this heat and blew for home. We had driven in the car up the hill to where they had drawn, but Nona Shand and I decided to walk back and we dropped down off the hill and walked along the beach back to the hotel. I think that this must be the only time I have ever walked on a beach on the way back from a meet. We sat down in the big upstairs room at two o'clock for our "tatie pot" and the singing was soon in progress. Christopher Curtis from the BFSS was there and thoroughly enjoyed the singing. I sang "A Jolly Old Country Squire" and Mary and Ernie also sang. We had to force ourselves to leave at four-thirty as the singing was still in full swing. We would not have left so early but we had arranged for a mini-bus to take us all to the Plough Inn, Selside, for a Windermere singsong. This was a great mistake as the landlord had been greedy and had advertised the singsong in the local paper. It was so crowded as to ruin it, and most of us went for a walk. We did have a pleasant hour and a half of singing after eleven o'clock, the highlight of which was Albert Benson singing a song about himself and his cockfighting adventures in Ireland, "The Cocks They Crew, The Feathers They Flew". He was a tiny little man with the most enormous hands, and he had a habit of striking the top of a table with the flat of his hand to emphasise parts of his song. I can still see the half-empty glasses jumping about on the table as he struck it.

Next morning we started for home, calling at the Rockwood Harriers kennels to meet the Masters, John Loy and Bob McCready, to look over their doghounds, and to select a stallion hound. I decided on Pickwick for whom in later years I was to become very grateful because all his progeny improved the voices of the Easton kennel. On 17 March 1971 at a General Meeting of the Easton Harriers I was officially installed as Master and the next morning I drove back to Yorkshire to fetch Pickwick from the Rockwood kennels and back again in time to attend the dinner to mark the end of the Easton season.

Our jolly to Lancashire in January had been quite a topic of conversation and talk about it had spread as far as our neighbours, the Waveney Harriers. The Chairman, Desmond Long and his wife Isla, and John and Hazel Parker, had the previous season been down to Exmoor for the spring staghunting and, as they were going again, they invited me to join them. They kindly included me in their reservations at the Crown Hotel, Exford, one of the traditional venues for the folk who flock to Exmoor at the end of every season, and booked my horses into some spare stables nearby. Rita again agreed to groom for me and the old Ford Thames lorry managed the journey in ten hours. As there was no sense in wasting the time of the long journey, I had a tape running with songs that I wanted to learn. Poor Rita! How sick she must have been of hearing "The Female Drummer" which is a long song and needed to be played over fifteen to twenty times before I could learn it. After unloading the horses we found Rita's lodging next to the stables and I saw her settled before going to the Crown where my friends were already relaxing as their man had brought down their lorry and they had travelled comfortably by car. Looking back, it sounds very mean not to have had Rita in the hotel with us but it was twelve pounds a day at the Crown compared with two pounds ten shillings "all in" at her digs. To be honest, her digs would have been much more suited to my pocket as it was not just the price of the hotel, but keeping up with my friends who were respectively Chairman of the Norwich Union and a turkey magnate who was knocking on the door of Bernard Matthews. My grandmother used to say that "pride feeleth no pinch" and however big a hole the bill knocked in my pocket I have never regretted it. Those five-course dinners in the evenings with excellent food and wine, and the wonderful hunting atmosphere were well worth the occasional twinge of a guilty conscience. What made the experience particularly special was my friends knowing so many of the other people staying there and introducing me to them, so that I felt like one of a great big party.

While we were enjoying a cup of tea the conversation inevitably turned to which pack we would hunt with the following day. To me the next day, which was a Friday, would not have held much hope but one of the party got up to read the list of meets which had been cut out of the local newspaper and pinned to a beam. I was totally amazed to find that there was a

**Devon and Somerset Staghounds.** *Meet at Brendon Two Gates, 1970. The Masters Mr R H Nancekivell (far right) and S J Westcott (far left), the Huntsman W Perry (next left) and the Rawle brothers, Fred, Dick, David, Tom and Bob (from the left).*
Photograph kindly loaned by Mrs S Bazeley

choice of three or four packs each day of the week, all within easy reach of Exford. The decision for the first day's hunting was the **Dulverton West Foxhounds** who were at Brightworthy, near Withypool (Friday 26 March 1971). I decided to take Stonebow and sat in the high winds, admiring the well turned out hunt staff but was somewhat taken aback to see that the famous Mrs Smythe was on a little cob and every now and again during the day she would often swing her leg over to the near side so that so that she appeared to ride side-saddle. This I later found out was to ease a painful condition in her hips. Looking back, I had made a big mistake in taking Stonebow, my bold-jumping hunter, and leaving behind Embassy, a neat, nimble, cobby type of hunter who would have been much more suited to the steep and rough ground of Exmoor.

Hounds drew hillsides and rocks thoroughly but did not find until twelve-thirty. I was thrilled to view a fox away down a sheep-track. There was some beautiful hound work in the valley below as hounds persevered to hold the line in the strong wind. Hounds swung round the hill and over the ground we had previously drawn, past an open earth that was pointed out to me (which was all very thrilling and interesting for an inexperienced foxhunter), round in another circle, then to ground in the earth he had previously passed. After watching the digging for a half-hour or so, my friends said they were cold and were going home so I went with them. Greeted by the landlord of the Crown, we quickly fell into what was to become the normal routine – sitting down to tea and scones before bathing and preparing for dinner.

The next morning, while we were having breakfast, Rita came into the dining-room looking very worried and told me that Stonebow was very stiff. As soon as I could I went to the stables and was surprised to see just how bad he was, but thankful that it was only stiffness. I took my hunting whip and chased him up and down the road which soon loosened him up. We then set off for the meet of the **Devon and Somerset Staghounds** at Mounsey Hill Gate (Sat 27 Mar 1971). I was completely overawed by the whole spectacle of the meet even though I had expected to see a large and impressive mounted field. In comparison with an Easton Harriers meet this seemed to cover a tremendous area, with over one hundred horses standing in small groups scattered over the moor, and others still hacking in across the moor from various directions. I said good morning to the Master, the legendary Mr Nancekivell, and then looked for the Secretary. I had been warned with considerable emphasis about the bogs and the advisability of following a local person, so as I paid my cap I asked the Secretary who would be the best man to follow. Without a moment's hesitation he said,

"Dick Lloyd, if you can keep with him."

Although I had been staghunting in France, the tufting had been done in dense forests and I had been unable to actually observe it, so I watched with great interest as the tufters, about three and a half couple, drew Hollam. After being stopped three or four times on unsuitable deer they eventually got a young stag away and the main pack was laid on at Comers Gate. All this was absolutely fascinating to a Suffolk hare-hunter, knowing precious little of other forms of hunting, and I was amazed how unhurried was the process of laying on the main pack. Once the main pack were settled on the line, they fairly flew and I stuck to the tail of Dick Lloyd's horse as he crossed Exmoor with apparent ease at a pace which terrified me, going down a precipice at a canter that I would not have even considered walking a horse down a few days earlier. My little grey gelding, Paddy, was rather outclassed but was coping as well as could be expected with the pace, and was fit enough to keep going. After a while a long and very welcome check occurred, especially for Paddy who was somewhat blown. After information received, hounds were lifted four miles to Emmettis Grange where he was fresh found and away to Ricksy Ball, and he was taken soon afterwards. I had stuck to Dick Lloyd nearly all the way, but had lost faith once and stopped at a place where he appeared to just gallop into a bog which was a mile or so across. I watched as he just kept galloping on, his horse at knee depth in this black slime which seemed to have a hard bottom. I decided he knew what he was doing and galloped in after him but this loss of faith nearly cost me the hunt as I was left behind. As I kicked on into that black bog I do not think I have ever put such trust in another human being before or since. He, of course, knew the moor like the back of his hand and I ought not to have worried. The day ended with a good party at Jo and Peter Prior-Wandesford's who were friends of the Longs and the Parkers, and I was luckily included.

The next morning it was the same story of stiffness with Paddy, only much worse. I have never seen a horse so stiff except one with azoturia. He actually had to sway his whole body to get his legs over the step of the stable and it was quite a time before he could even walk properly, let alone begin to trot. After an hour or so, I decided he was all right to leave. I would have judged him to be very fit as he had been carrying me hunting hounds in the Suffolk plough for a full season but the steepness of the hills used different muscles and the length and speed of the run had been much more than either of us was accustomed to.

The following day we went with the **Exmoor Foxhounds** from Bradley Moor Gate (Mon 29 Mar 1971). It was very cold and windy so I was glad that hounds found at once. We had a fast five-mile point where hounds turned and hunted back again. As hounds were turning back I saw Jo and Peter Prior-Wandisford crossing the river where hounds had done, so I left the main body of the field, thinking that I had found another informed local pilot. I was wrong, and missed the hunt back. I eventually caught up again to find them at a check which they could not resolve. They soon found again but this fox was headed and went to ground where it was left. A third fox was found quite quickly and ran into a very boggy place where Isla Long's horse got into serious trouble. It managed to struggle out and gallop off without her, but got wedged between a stone wall and a wire fence. I went back to the meet with Isla as Stonebow had cut himself badly on a rock. Having come home early we had more time to enjoy the cream tea in the Crown and, over the scones and jam, we studied the list of meets for the next day and decided on the **West Somerset Foxhounds** who were at Brompton Ralph (Tues 30 Mar 1971).

**Minehead Harriers** *Jt. Masters Lt. Col. Jim Collins and Mr S G Westcott*

Photo kindly loaned by Lt. Col. Jim Collins

I arrived late for the eleven o'clock meet as, despite our study, we had thought it was at eleven-thirty. However, the Parkers were much later than me so that made me feel better. Hounds drew off the moor, down a most beautiful valley and, after an hour or so, found and we saw some lovely slow houndwork, as they worked the line out of a quarry. I stood on the edge of this huge quarry and watched them put a fox away but I am not sure if it was the same fox they had hunted so slowly into and around the quarry. We then enjoyed a very fast hunt for five miles with a three-mile point, almost all through overgrown lanes like green tunnels. I had never galloped so far without seeing where I was going, as I just dare not raise my head, simply following the horse in front. How pleased I was that I had Paddy, my smallest horse. Hounds marked to ground in high rocks and I climbed up on foot with the huntsman. This was a large earth, and the entrance was so big that four and a half couple of hounds came out of it as he blew them away. The Master, Jack Stevens, made me very welcome. He said he had been Field Master for seventeen seasons in Oxfordshire, before coming to Somerset and I have a lovely memory of him leading us over a very trappy post and rails at the bottom of a steep place. At the end of the day there were only four others besides us and, as we hacked back, a fox was viewed running along parallel with us on the opposite side of the valley. Hounds were laid on and we had an exciting twenty-minutes worth of sport, losing the line in some heavy sheep foil. So ended a most enjoyable day.

However, bad news from home was to break up our party. Fowl pest had struck the Parkers's turkey flock and they had to return to Suffolk to cope with this potential disaster. They consequently missed our next day's sport with the **Minehead Harriers** at Stile Down (Wed 31 Mar 1971) but Rita was able to have a day on her favourite, Stonebow, as the Parkers had kindly given me the use of their horses in their absence. My first impression of the hunt was the appearance of the huntsman who, I presumed, had obviously reverted to his cubhunting clothes, as his coat was patched and shabby and he was wearing rubber boots. I was most surprised to be joined by Joe Parravani from the Waveney Harriers, as I did not know that he was down in Somerset, although he had told me that he went down at times. Hounds drew for an hour and marked a vixen to ground in Honey Combe and left her. As we drew again, I met a most gorgeous girl exercising a Point-to-Pointer, and afterwards Rita mentioned at every possible opportunity that I could not take my eyes off her.

On the Dunkeries hounds found again on Robin Howe, and ran on to Bincombe and North Hawkwell, through West Harewell, to Stile, when, on advice from "Sinbad" (but who he was I cannot remember), we went up through some very, very steep woodland, and as soon as we were up at the top, Desmond Long heard the huntsman down at the bottom so we were faced with a very dangerous and frightening ride down again, slipping for most of the way. Rita was even more scared than I was so I had to pretend to be brave. Once down, there was "Sinbad" again, who pointed out to us the way the huntsman had gone, having had a very good joke at the expense of the visitors. We could only follow footprints of the huntsman's horse but came up with him just as he killed his fox. The field included an extraordinary visiting American, who had had only a few riding lessons for the sole purpose of hunting in England. Hounds did not seem very steady on sheep or cur-dogs, but a lasting memory is of a lovely view of a large herd of deer on the Dunkeries.

**Quantock Staghounds.** *Meet at Triscombe Stone, spring 1971. Huntsman Alfie Giles.*
Photograph kindly donated by Mrs R Thrower

This put me in the right frame of mind for my last day's sport with the **Quantock Staghounds** from Crowcombe Park Gate (Thurs 1 Apr 1971). I rode Colleen, Hazel Parker's horse. The tufters were working from eleven to three-twenty in very steep, scrubby country and I noticed that they worked mute and wondered if this was often the case with tufters. Deer were everywhere, and the difficulty was getting the right one away on its own. I followed the Secretary, Mr Bird, and after getting up a very steep place saw the whipper-in's daughter let out the main pack without permission. She duly received a rocket from the Master, Mr Thrower. Hounds hunted with light cry and little drive for an hour or so, when the hunted deer joined three others and ran to the sea where it was left. The huntsman was handicapped by being mounted on what appeared to be a nappy horse and the sheer number of deer. The tufters put in a great deal of difficult work but were assisted by a wonderful character in his eighties. He had a wool scarf round his neck and no teeth, but rode at a flat-out gallop in amongst the deer to help separate the desired one. His black coat was that lovely shade of green which happens to very old black clothes; I've only seen it before on the surplices of very old clergymen but my daughter assures me that she has seen it also on the gowns of very old academics. It was an eye-opener for me to see how comparatively little notice the deer took of hounds as they would stand and watch hounds go by at only a few hundred yards distance. Lastly, it amazed me to find that these hounds hunt stag two days a week in a country that I was told was only twelve miles by seven.

We drove back to Suffolk the next day. This had been another week-long trip and I had hunted with another six packs. Only one of them, however, had been harriers (the Minehead), so I had not made much progress in fulfilling my ambition and now, with the prospect of taking on the Mastership of the Easton again, it did not seem that I would have very many more good opportunites to go away.

# MAP 3

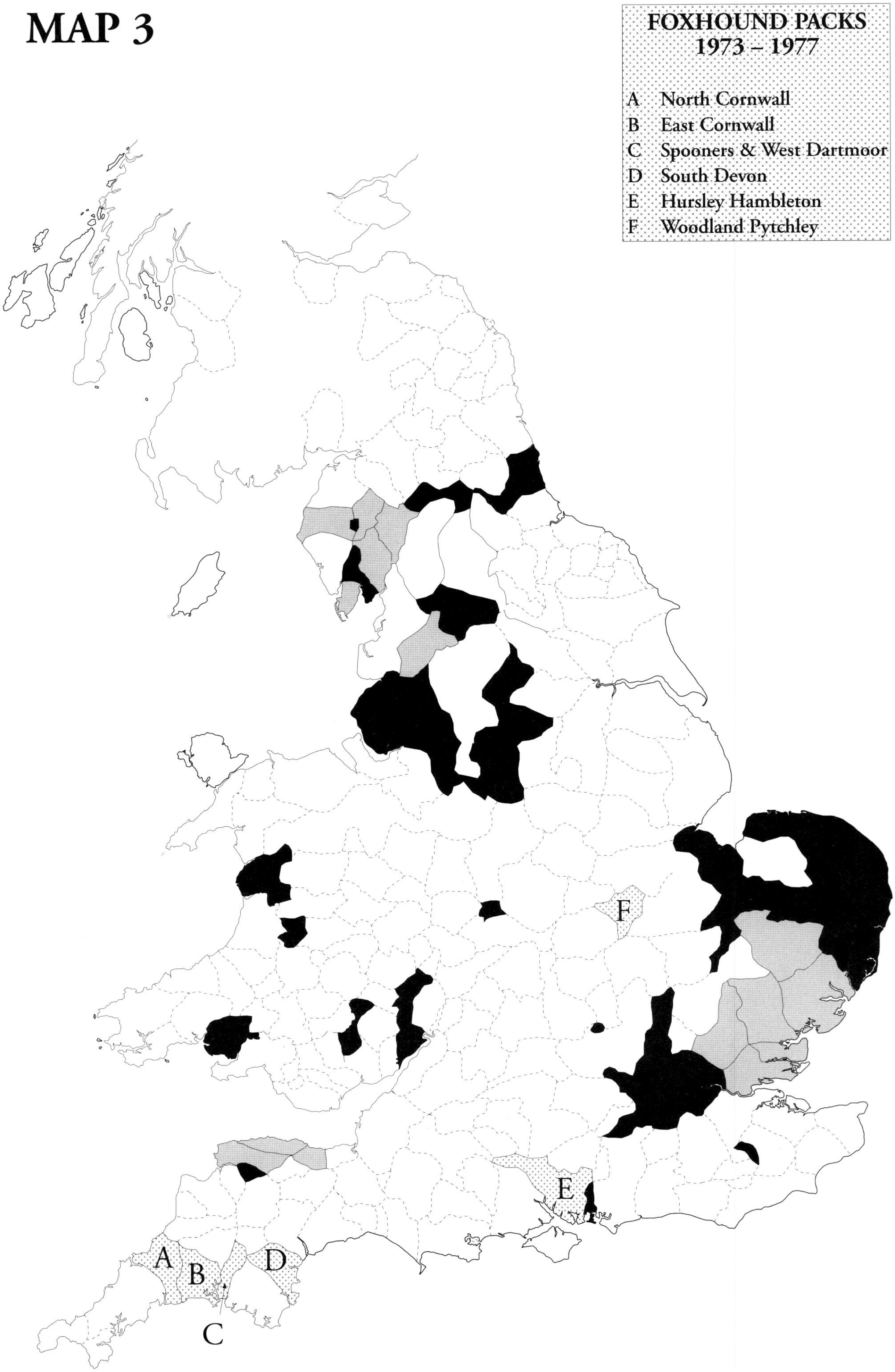
FOXHOUND PACKS
1973 – 1977
A North Cornwall
B East Cornwall
C Spooners & West Dartmoor
D South Devon
E Hursley Hambleton
F Woodland Pytchley
F
E
A
B
D
C

# Chapter 3

## The West Country Again

Having met Kate and Newton Bacon while staying at Hornby, our friendship was furthered when Newton asked me to judge the puppy show of his Holcombe Harriers in 1972. Newton suggested that I come up to Mount Pleasant, Gressingham (near Lancaster), to stay with them for the weekend. The plan was to have a day with his local otterhounds on the Saturday and to go to the puppy show on the Sunday. I decided to break the long journey to Lancashire on the Friday by calling in to see David and Pam Reynolds (of the Pipewell Beagles) at Chester House for coffee, and then on to the Castle Hotel at Hornby for tea so that I could renew my acquaintance with my hosts of the previous year. They told me that after our visit they had advertised hunting holidays in the Horse and Hound but had had no takers. After arriving at Mount Pleasant I settled down with Newton in his private bar and we primed ourselves ready for a first-class dinner to follow. When dinner was over Newton, while chuckling quietly to himself, suggested to Kate that they might take me to meet "Mr Squiggley-Figgley" (in reality, Mr Francis Shrigley-Feigl).

After making the necessary arrangements we went off in Newton's car so that I could meet this man who ranks amongst the most eccentric people I have ever met. On the way, Newton explained to me that he was a Czech immigrant and that his father, when he left their village for the 1914-18 War, gave his son instructions to keep the whole village supplied with game and venison, and this he did until the war ended. Francis Shrigley-Feigl lived at the end of a long drive in the village of Wray in a castle-like house called Cragg Hall which had been used for the rearing of turkeys until he had bought it. We crossed a courtyard with knee-high weeds growing between the flagstones to see his pet badger who had been shut out of the house (where he normally lived) as he was inclined to bite ladies' legs if they were wearing skirts, the sight of bare flesh proving too tempting. When we entered the house we were greeted by a total of eight dogs and the first thing I noticed was the cold, damp feeling, like a house which has been empty for years.

**Kendal and District Otterhounds.** *Hounds drawing keenly watched by Mrs Kate Bacon on the far bank. Mr and Mrs Bacon were regular followers of these hounds.*

Photograph kindly loaned by Mrs Kate Bacon

The house was so crammed full of priceless furniture that one had to walk through what seemed like passages between the pieces, not unlike a saleroom. A widower, he lived there all alone and the dust on this furniture was so thick that it was impossible to see what sort of wood the pieces were made from. He led us to a huge sitting-room where there was a tiny little fire burning, a few sticks and a tiny log, and for all the impression it made in a room of this size, it might as well have been a candle. Francis was tall, lean and very softly-spoken, and quite fascinating to talk to as he was the sort of person who could talk intelligently about anything. The evening went far too quickly. On the way home, the Bacons told me that not even the water was laid on in the house, or rather, that he had had the meter disconnected so he did not have to pay the bill. He carted water from a pond at the bottom of the long drive, and in summer, when the pond dried up, from the Bacon's house. When he hunted, on a fat little cob called Minny which somehow squeezed itself into a tiny trailer, he used to wrap himself up in foam rubber. One day he had a bad fall and was carried unconscious to hospital where the doctor looked at him, amazed, and then asked a nurse why a mummy was out hunting. When Francis awoke, he was for some time convinced that he was in heaven. After his death there was a lorryload of silver and pieces of his furniture which made over £25,000, and one piece over £50,000. His entire estate was valued at well over a million pounds.

The **Kendal and District Otterhounds** were meeting at Mitton Bridge to hunt the Ribble and the Hodder rivers (8 July 1972) and, although Newton and

Kate hunted with other otterhound packs, these were their local pack and their favourite. This was my first experience of otterhunting and I was interested to learn about the sport. The hounds were mostly otterhounds with a few old foxhounds thrown in to add some drive, I was told. Apparently pure otterhounds are inclined to dwell on the line, enjoying every particle of scent before moving on, so the foxhounds provide the drive to actually catch anything. They drew downstream a little way and marked in some roots. I shall never forget the glorious sound of those lovely otterhound voices marking. They then drew upstream and as I walked along the river bank I met Mrs MacAlpine and Mr Pickles, Joint Masters of the Pendle Forest and Craven. Although we did not find, there was some drag and the music and the whole atmosphere was lovely, as we walked along watching the huntsman with his pole in the water below us.

We stopped for lunch in the next pub upstream which had wall-to-wall carpets in every room and which was more suited for the other customers who looked like tennis-players in their white plimsolls, than us otterhunters in very muddy boots, but no-one seemed to mind at all and we overheard the landlord saying that otterhunters drink a lot of beer. Dinner that evening was quite delightful, as Kate had cooked some of her native Austrian dishes. Newton was on top form and I could have listened to his stories all night. Kate's Sunday morning breakfast was no less special than her dinner and we sat listening to the church bells as we ate it, before walking up to see Newton's horses. On the way to the kennels, where I was to judge the puppy show, we lunched at the Last Drop Inn where I had met with the Holcombe Harriers the previous year. Various Committee members joined us and I was able to do my duty by the Committee of the MH&B Association by extracting a promise from Newton to bring his hounds to Peterborough Hound Show as the harrier classes had been rather thin the previous year. I was not overimpressed by the young entry but judged them to the satisfaction of the Master and did my best to give an amusing speech at the tea afterwards. We dined at The Tickled Trout on the way back to Mount Pleasant, and had some excellent quail pate. The Bacons did everything so well, and the happy memories of these times makes the adrenalin run even now.

Before going to the Lakes at the end of the 1972-73 season, I had furthered my determination to hunt with every harrier pack by making the necessary arrangements to hunt in the West Country on another jolly with my friend Stanley Tompkins. I had asked for help from the only contact I had in the area, namely John Budgett, Master of the Dartmoor Foxhounds. He made enquiries and, after a day or so, telephoned me to say that Major Farr could put up our horses at his stables in Ivybridge. When I contacted Major Farr he was pleased to accept our horses and agreed that Delia Andrews, my groom, could stay with his students which seemed ideal. When the arrangements for the horses and the groom were made, he asked where we would be staying, to which I replied that I was about to ask him to recommend a good little pub which offered bed-and-breakfast. He said that he would be happy to put us up on more reasonable terms than a pub and, furthermore, he would personally see that a new bottle of Teacher's would be on the table every afternoon for a "hunting tea". I had some misgivings but he went on to say that his hunting teas were the real ones, with boiled eggs and toast and large cups of tea which we could lace for ourselves from the Teacher's bottle. I had been wavering but this statement gave me confidence (misplaced as it turned out) and it was agreed that Stanley and I would stay with him in his house, so all of us – horses, groom, Stanley and I – would be staying at the same place.

We returned from the Lakes on Sunday 11 March (1973) and set off for south Devon on the following Tuesday at ten o'clock in the evening. The earliest day we could hunt was the Thursday so we decided that after a long journey the horses ought to have more or less a day's rest before hunting. With this in mind, we thought it better not to go to bed at all rather than for a couple of hours, and leave at, say, two o'clock in the morning. With Stanley and I taking turns to drive we did not stop until we reached Honiton where we had a cup of coffee. We eventually arrived at the Beacon Riding School, in Ivybridge, at ten o'clock on the Wednesday morning. They had not expected us so early so, not surprisingly, they were not ready for us. Delia took the horses out of the lorry and tied them around it, then took each one for a walk in turn. I had taken Paddy and Tina, and Stanley Duke and Jim. By the time each had had his walk the boxes were ready and the horses were put away, but student girls were still busy cleaning out our bedrooms. This included the removal of a mouse cage but, unfortunately, the smell of tame mice did not depart with the cage and Stanley, being the quickest to locate which room had held the mice, elected to have the other, leaving me to put up with the fragrance.

The bedrooms could at best be described as very basic and the bathroom extremely so, but were just acceptable for two men on a hunting holiday. We slept from four until six o'clock, then rallied enough to sit with the bottle of Teacher's and the Major's telephone to ring home and some of the local Hunt Secretaries to arrange the next few days' hunting. The full enormity of our lodgings did not hit us on the first night as, although the Teacher's had revived us considerably, we were still rather jaded through driving all night. The Major and his wife Rosalind dined with us on our round table in the corner of the kitchen on the first night, and were very generous with an excellent Hock. Both of them showed the effects of it and were waxing quite lyrical by the time we went to bed at ten o'clock.

We slept soundly until six and then, at breakfast, the reality of our situation hit us. We ate at our round table and the students, about ten or twelve of them, at a long table down the opposite wall. The whole room was far from clean and the state of the Aga cooker was indescribable. The students appeared to take it in turns to cook breakfast and when the rest of them came in, they had not cleaned their boots very well and there was a wet path (diagnosed as horse pee by the smell) diagonally from the door to the Aga where they filed along for their bacon and eggs before sitting down at the long table. On this table was a half-gallon plastic container of tomato sauce. The weight and the size of the mouth caused the students to slosh two or three times as much as they wanted onto their plates or, quite frequently, over the edge as well. The table showed all the signs of many months feeble attempts to wipe it and had built up quite a crust of past spills which reminded me of the way the tide sometimes leaves the sand in small waves on the beach. The plates had obviously been washed in cool water as they were rather smeared and most of the forks still had food jammed between the prongs. None of these shortcomings appeared to worry the Major or, indeed, his wife when she appeared in her dressing gown while everyone else was eating breakfast, and proceeded to comb her long hair in the middle of the kitchen floor. She leaned over backwards and then forwards with her hair hanging down to the floor only just missing the moist path to the Aga.

We had finished our breakfast by nine o'clock, loaded up our horses and set off for the meet of the **Dart Vale and Haldon Harriers** at Heatherstone Head near South Brent (Thurs 15 March 1973). When we arrived where we thought the meet ought to be, we went past it several times as we were looking for a pub. We later discovered that Heatherstone Head was a clearing on the side of the road. Six other men turned up so the field consisted entirely of men, and was the only time that either Stanley or myself had been hunting without a female in the field. Our horses were the only ones which were properly turned-out and we noticed that his young whip had no hunt buttons on his coat, but we immediately took to the Master and huntsman, Jim Broom, who gave us a genuine welcome. He hunted both fox and hare with this pack, but used the doghounds for fox and the bitch pack for hares. On this occasion he had the bitch pack. He soon moved off to draw and after three-quarters of an hour they found and almost immediately changed to a fresh hare. They had a nice hunt but lost her in a wooded combe in spite of Jim getting off his horse and casting hounds on foot. The next hunt was a quick spin during which Jim dropped his horn, but managed to retrace his steps and find it again later. I thought the lemon and white West Country harriers rather flashy and wild compared with Stud Book harriers and this tendency seemed to be aggravated by Jim lifting hounds and helping them too often. It was a bitterly cold day and we both blessed Stanley's wife, Kathleen, for packing his flask and a bottle of whisky to fill it. Jim blew for home at three-thirty.

Major and Mrs Farr did not join us for dinner that evening which we decided was a blessing as the Major was a great talker. Dinner was a leg of lamb taken straight out of the freezer into the oven and when it was served onto our plates it was burned on the outside and still frozen in the middle. This occurred quite frequently during the course of our stay and how we were not poisoned at this place I shall never know unless it was the alcohol that killed all the bacteria. Next morning there was another eventful breakfast. When we were well into our plateful of eggs and bacon we could see the student whose turn it was to cook come out of the pantry with slices of bacon in her hand. She was walking lackadaisically, her arms swinging down, and the basset hound was walking behind her. At every backward swing of her arm he ran his tongue the full length of the bacon.

Stanley made a small choking noise in his throat and pushed his plate away but I said, "Don't worry Stanley. The basset was outside when our breakfast was being cooked."

When there was no more bacon to lick the basset amused himself by attempting to rape the Siamese cat, holding her firmly by the neck. She objected to this loudly by emitting those awful screams that only Siamese cats are capable of.

**Dart Vale & South Pool Harriers** *Huntsman Gilmore Lewis*

Photo kindly loaned by Gilmore Lewis

We know the sayings that "Hope springs eternal ..." and "Nothing ventured, nothing gained" but nature's design of their respective body lengths left the little Betty in no danger of losing her honour.

The morning was just the opposite of the day before, being hot and sunny as we made our way to where we had agreed to meet the huntsman of the **Modbury Harriers**, George Baskerville, at Yealmpton, in order to follow him to the meet at Lowesbury Cross (Fri 16 Mar 1973). George introduced us to the Master, Mrs Pinsent, who not only gave us a warm welcome but went out of her way to be pleasant to us all day, beginning by explaining that the Modbury, although harriers, normally only hunt the fox. The hot weather was not the only contrast with the previous day as when we moved off the draw I remarked to Stanley that if we had not been there the field would have consisted only of seven ladies. They found a fox in the first half-hour but marked to ground almost at once. They then went away with another which was eventually put to ground in some laurel bushes outside of which we sat for an hour. This always seems so tedious to people accustomed to hare-hunting where hounds are normally running most of the time. It seemed an opportune time to eat our sandwiches but when we opened them we found that they were bacon sandwiches and we just looked at each other and threw them away as the thought of the basset's tongue overcame our hunger. We had another good hunt of a half-hour or so until Stan and I, who were doing a bit of "thrusting" at the time, managed to head the fox which was most embarassing for us both. Hounds quickly put themselves right where we had caused the check and then we sat and watched him go back up a hill looking rather tired. We hunted him back to where he was found, then he went to ground and was left. The huntsman's voice was very good but he had a peculiar habit of using the same holloa when he was drawing as when he viewed a fox. As a result, his hounds never hurried to his view-holloas. Also he hardly ever used his horn, so was a long time getting hounds out of cover. His daughter, aged twelve, was enthusiastically whipping-in to him.

**Modbury Harriers** *Hunstman George Baskerville*
Photograph kindly loaned by Mrs Moira Major M.H.

Leaving the meet at three o'clock, we arrived back at Ivybridge at four o'clock for our usual hunting tea – a new bottle of Teacher's, cup of tea, boiled eggs and toast, all very correct. We were relieved that Major Farr, by now renamed Major Twitter, had run out of things to say so we had our tea in peace. After dinner Rosalind (Mrs Farr), who was considerably younger than the Major, suggested we might like to go to the pub. The Major declined so the three of us went in her little car which Stanley offered to drive. She was obviously very popular and had many friends in the pub. The rounds came thick and fast until, at least ten or twelve drinks later, we went home. The car was parked to one side of a little market square in Ivybridge and Stanley, not being used to the car, put on what he thought were the lights and drove off. Before we had left the square, we were stopped by the police who pointed out that he was driving on fog-lights only. They told us to pull into another pub yard to be breathalised. Stanley elected to wait the twenty minutes allowed which I thought was the worst thing he could have done but somehow he was negative. Appropriately, the pub was called the Sportsman's Arms and at a celebration party after we got back I laughed and said to Stanley that I doubted whether there had ever been a better sportsman than him in its yard. It really was a good party: the Major was in bed and Rosalind got out the remains of the Teacher's from the two previous teas. It ended at about four o'clock for Rosalind and me, Stanley having gone to bed an hour or so earlier.

"A joyful night brings forth a sorrowful morn" and I was not quite at my best for the early start necessary for the long journey to the **Bolventor Harriers**' meet at Trevadlock (Sat 17 Mar 1973) which was seven miles south of Launceston. As we had not taken much out of our horses with the Modbury and the following day was a Sunday I asked Delia if she would like to come and she was delighted to accept the offer. We parked the lorry and hacked up to the meet and I made myself known to Mr Lobb, the Master and huntsman, and he in turn introduced us to his son and daughter who whipped in to him. I was completely taken aback by the sight. All three were immaculately turned out to a very high standard which was particularly marked as we were in the middle of Bodmin Moor and by comparison with what we had seen during the week. Some of the assembled field were turned out to the Master's standard but others were very scruffy.

The Bolventor, like most of the West Country harrier packs, hunted fox and it was pure joy to watch and hear Mr Lobb drawing as his voice and hound language were perfect. After drawing for an hour hounds found and we had a sharp run over the moor until this fox was lost. Hounds then drew a bog and it was quite an experience for us to watch them doing so as it was being grazed by sheep and ponies. When they found a fox, it ran through the middle of the sheep and ponies which scuttled out of the way for fifty yards or so and then quietly resumed their foraging in the rushes. During this run there was a check near a farm where sows were being allowed to destroy the banks so the Secretary suggested we might like to practise jumping the banks. We had been a source of great amusement to all the field as our horses were jumping right over the banks with the result that they often landed on their knees on the opposite side. He told us to trot at the banks and make our horses stop on the top, change legs and then jump down the other side, a practice known as "banking". After about twenty attempts, we perfected this, especially Paddy who took to it quickly once I knew how to approach it. Tina was the longest to learn as she so enjoyed jumping right over, being a big strong mare. Later we were sitting on top of a hill watching hounds below and, when they found, the Master was convinced that they would come round below us. Unfortunately, he had misjudged this fox and they took off into the distance. A most frightening gallop followed over very rough and rocky country. We lost hounds and had to hack back to the meet with a couple and a half of hounds. It was comforting to me to realise that I was not the only one who made the occasional mistake and that even the most experienced of Masters could sometimes get things wrong. Before going home, we arranged to meet him at his kennels the next afternoon.

**Bolventor Harriers.** *At Jamaica Inn, March 1973. Left to right, Jenny, Reg and Patrick Lobb.*

Photograph kindly lent by Mr and Mrs Lobb

That evening we should have gone to a party at the new home of John Graham who now lived at North Bovey but, as we were so late home, we rang to tell his wife, Elizabeth, that we would not go. We were just starting our dinner when John rang and made such a great fuss, saying that he had put on a splendid party especially for us, that in the end I managed to persuade Stanley to go by telling him what first class parties the Grahams always gave. We left at ten o'clock, arriving at John's house at about eleven, to find a circle of chairs round the room like a Sunday School treat, all filled with solemn boring, dull farmers and their wives, all staring at us and each other, with not a smile or a joke between them. We drank the most dreadful cheap red wine and were very pleased to escape by twelve-thirty. We drove back across the moor via Princetown and accidentally hit a sheep whilst driving at speed. The sheep just rolled over six times, and then jumped up and ran away, apparently unhurt. We arrived home at four o'clock, firmly convinced that this was the worst hunting party we had ever been to and wishing we had never gone. We were below par for two days with upset stomachs due, we thought, to the quality of the wine. However, this one lapse in no way lessened the memories of the many excellent parties that the Grahams have given before and since.

After breakfast we walked out the horses as it was a Sunday, and then all three of us, Stanley, Delia and I, set off at ten o'clock to visit various local kennels. The first was the Dart Vale and Haldon with which we were quite impressed. They stood in an idyllic situation with a stream running past and could have been designed by the great Peter Beckford himself. We met the Master's wife, Mrs Broome, and she gave us coffee and biscuits before we left to go to the South Pool Harriers' kennels. There was no-one there so we had a quick peep at the hounds and then went on to the kennels of the Modbury Harriers, which were also deserted. However, as we came away we met George Baskerville, the Huntsman, so we went back with him. These kennels were terrible as they were built into the side of a hill and as a consequence were very wet and cold but George explained to us that new ones were soon to be built. After lunch in Plymouth in a restaurant overlooking the harbour, we went to the Bolventor kennels which we rated quite highly. We were also quite impressed with the hounds which were all of a type and fairly level. We were made very welcome by Mrs Lobb, the

Master's wife, who gave us an excellent tea. On the way home we called to visit Arthur and Margaret Gillard whom Stanley had met through stag-hunting on Exmoor. We stayed for supper and enjoyed Cornish pasties, made and eaten in Cornwall! He offered the use of a mare to Delia for a day's hunting which was gratefully accepted. Returning to Ivybridge at ten-thirty, we set to and helped Delia do the horses.

**Spooners and West Dartmoor.** *Meet at the Prison Officers' Mess at Printetown, 2 October 1975. Master and Huntsman, Major Michael Howard.*
Photograph kindly loaned by Mrs S Joynson

Monday morning was the start of my first ever full week's mounted hunting and we left in good time for the **Spooners and West Dartmoor Foxhounds** who were meeting at Warren Cross near Horrabridge (19 Mar 1973). I introduced myself and Stanley to Major Howard, the Master and huntsman, and to Mrs Howard who turned hounds to him. Warren Cross was a crossroads in the middle of the moor and the field of nine looked rather lost in the huge expanse of rocky moorland. The Master decided to draw off the moor in enclosed pastures. This area proved blank, but he then drew the moor, found at once and had a sharp run, during which I received a terrible scare. Tina was pulling so hard I was out of control and she galloped downhill and slipped for over twenty feet, coming to rest only inches from a hundred-foot drop into the river below. Her nose was over the edge and it would almost certainly have been the end of us both if she had slipped another two feet. There were beads of cold sweat running down my back as we galloped on until this fox was marked to ground.

Another was quickly found on Staple Tor but after a sharp hunt, hounds again put the fox to ground. They found a third fox in Langstone Bog, which is a huge one of several acres, and we could see the fox as he came running through rushes because we were up on some high ground. After an exciting run hounds hunted him onto Doos Tor. They were close behind their fox and in our excitement Stanley and I rode right up the tor. The

**Spooners and West Dartmoor:** ***"Phew! That was a near one... only just enough brakes!"***

rocks were formed rather like steps with us half-scrambling, half-jumping up from step to step but hounds were screamingly near their fox and nothing would have stopped us. It was wonderfully exciting going up behind hounds and we were right with them when they killed. I was presented with the mask and Stanley with the brush but then we had to face the prospect of coming down again with the blood cooling fast, and realising what a different matter it was to come down. Stanley's horse started to lift its front feet as if preparing to jump down in one leap. I got off and led my horse down, Stanley following but still mounted, keeping close behind me so that his horse was not tempted to jump. At times the ledges were so close together and so steep that when I was on one ledge ahead of Tina her front feet were level with my waist.

**Spooners and West Dartmoor:** ***"Going up was great fun!"***

Major and Mrs Howard invited us back to the kennels where they gave us tea, very well laced with whisky, and we met Mr and Mrs Clarke who turned out to be old friends of Captain Bernard, my mentor and predecessor as Master of the Easton. During tea, the Howards explained to us that they had absolutely no staff and, basically speaking, the Major did the hounds and Mrs Howard the horses. This was my first instance of finding a hunt where the Master did not employ any staff, but quickly found out that it was quite normal in this part of the country, as it is in many small packs nationwide. I was asked to be the guest speaker at a Hunt Dinner, but declined as it was two days after we had planned to return home. We arrived back at eight o'clock in very high fettle thanks to the generosity of the Howards.

Tuesday was the day that Stanley's friend, Arthur Gillard, had offered a mount for Delia so we left Ivybridge early and made for Arthur's farm where we picked up his horse. This horse had a striking resemblance to Happy Jack, a hackney-cross-cob that I used to hunt and loved dearly. The **East Cornwall Foxhounds** were meeting at Lower Langdon (Tues 20 Mar 1973) in the Drains Valley. Arthur took me to meet Charlie Smith, the Master and huntsman, whom I thought to be a down-to-earth type, and some of the field of a dozen or so. A large area of moorland all around the meet was drawn blank until two-thirty when we found and enjoyed a short but very fast hunt. The line was lost in heavy cattle foil but during this hunt, I had got Paddy well and truly bogged down in a river bottom by trying to get to the Master on the other side. The river was deep and quite wide, with a narrow sheep track leading down into it, and another leading out on the other bank, really too narrow for a horse, but Paddy was nimble and catlike and I had confidence that he could go almost anywhere. I urged him down the little track much against Stanley's advice which I thought was because he knew his horse could not follow. Pride goes before a fall and on getting into the river itself I found the bottom was so boggy that I had to dismount into the water. It was no good trying to get him up the steep path on the other side because he could barely stand on the soft bottom and would not have been able to start, so I had to lead him along the river some way before finding a suitable place for getting out. The whole field, including Stanley, stood on the bank watching me plunging about in the river and walking along with water up to my thighs. It was lucky for me that it was a warm and sunny day. We had a good hunt to finish the day, very fast over some rough country well into the dark. After his refreshing dip, Paddy went extremely well over some big walls with nasty drops on the far side. I can still visualise Charlie

**The East Cornwall:** ***"What's the drop like?"***

Smith ahead of me in the dusk clearing these walls and dropping out of sight. The excitement and exhileration of this run prevented me having any thought of caution and the memory of it makes the adrenalin run as I picture it all in my mind again. Most of all I remember the sound of Charlie's horn and his lovely voice, coupled with outstanding hound control, in this wild, open country. Arthur Gillard, who had followed by car, insisted that we had tea as we dropped off his mare, and we eventually got back to Ivybridge at seven o'clock.

One of the most enjoyable things about hunting in this part of the world were the small mounted fields and there was one of only six on our day with the **Axe Vale Harriers**, from Bone Hayne Farm, near Colyton (Wed 21 Mar 1973). We arrived half an hour early but we had a very interesting conversation with the earth-stopper which filled in the time. Martin Salter, Master and huntsman, came to us and introduced himself, explaining that he only hunted fox like most of the harrier packs in this part of the country. We found at once and galloped with the field but were sadly well out of touch with the hounds as there were no hunt jumps or gates in the boundary fences which would have enabled us to have kept with them instead of always returning to the roads. The boundary fences running along the tops of hills prevented movement from one valley to the next so the field had to come down every time and go round by the road. Eventually we came up to hounds when they checked, and we had a long hack back to the draw. We had another good hunt but we were galloping on the roads all the while which jarred our backs, and after six or seven miles we were getting rather fed up. We decided to stand on a high spot and watched them draw for a long time and a few little hunts, then the Master blew for home and we hacked back to the meet with hounds. We were impressed with his lovely West Country Harriers who hunted with a great cry and tremendous drive. During the day we had talked to a lady in the field whose grandfather had started these hounds, and she gave us a booklet of the history of the Axe Vale. While on the way home, we

**Axe Vale Harriers** *Act. Master and Huntsman C R Williams M.H. Opening Meet at Wiscombe Park, South Leigh*

Photograph kindly loaned by C R Williams M.H.

were so hot and thirsty that we stopped at The Buttered Scone cafe at Newton Poppleford for a real Devon cream tea. The proprietor was very understanding and kept bringing us more hot water, realising how thirsty we were.

I wanted to give Delia another day's hunting but dare not risk one of my horses as we had so many more days to do, so on Thursday I hired one from Major Farr. I particularly wanted her to come on this day as the **South Devon Foxhounds** were meeting at Rugglestone near Widecombe-in-the-Moor which, apart from its well-known fair, was set in a particularly lovely part of Dartmoor (Thurs 22 Mar 1973). We unboxed and hacked down a winding road into Widecombe, then stood around at the meet and were amazed to find that, as we moved off, there was a pub round the corner which we had not known was there. This was the first meet at which we had seen a pub and were very upset that we had not been able to get into it. The kennel huntsman was hunting hounds as the Master was away. They drew blank until three-thirty and then had only a ten-minute hunt. It was very, very hot, far too hot for scent, but although the hunting was almost non-existent, the scenery and views were so beautiful that time did not seem to drag. I sat on a hillside watching them draw below me, the sun so hot that I was almost asleep, when suddenly a loud voice shouted, "Tony! What are you doing here?"

It gave me such a shock that I almost fell off and had to clutch my arms round Paddy's neck to keep on. It was Richard DuPont, the equine artist, who used to live at Dedham in Constable country, not far from the Easton country.

An hour or so after moving off, Stanley's saddle broke, the stirrup-leather bar snapping off, and he had to return to the meet. How lucky that this should have happened on such a quiet day, and not when he was performing over one of the horrendous walls, or scrambling up a tor. Later on, Delia and I joined him, and had another real Devon cream tea in a cafe in Widecombe, Stanley lacing his tea with whisky from his flask. That evening we went out to dinner at the Anchor Inn at Ugborough. It was a most delicious and enjoyable meal, Delia having a T-bone steak, and Stanley and I sixteen-ounce Dover soles.

**North Cornwall.** *Meet at Temple Four Turnings, 1986. Master and Huntsman Nigel Wakley, with whipper-in T Pilgrim.*

Photograph kindly donated by John Treffry

I was just getting into bed back at the Beacon Stables when I heard Stanley shout, "Hey, there's something in my bed."

I went through into his room and saw him gently lifting up the covers. Curled up between the sheets was a ginger cat. His comments were unprintable and the cat disappeared out of the window. This was not quite as callous as it sounds as outside the window there was another roof. It seemed that the two cats were used to sleeping in these rooms and they would often sit on this roof and rattle the casement windows in the forlorn hope that we would let them in.

The rest of the night was undisturbed which was fortunate because we had to make an early start the next morning, leaving at eight-thirty for the meet of the **North Cornwall Foxhounds** at Ruthern Bridge, near Bodmin (Fri 23 Mar 1973). On the way we picked up Arthur Gillard and arrived at the meet in good time. Hounds found quickly and we had a good hunt over very rough country with big banks and rough woodlands. What a ride that was! Three-quarters of an hour of really hard riding, and only Stanley and I were reckless (or imprudent) enough to keep with the Master and huntsman, Mike Weir, until the fox went to ground and was left. There was another hour or so of woodland hunting, during which I was most impressed by the sight of hounds hunting very slowly and thoroughly across some burnt common land, a sight I had never seen before and have never seen again since. I would have thought it impossible for hounds to be able to hunt over ash, so few days after the fire, but this only goes to emphasise the vagaries of scent.

I greatly admired the Master's hound control as he had no whipper-in and had an amazing knack of getting hounds quickly out of covert each time and always all on. This high standard of hound control amongst amateurs seems to be a relatively common feature among these small packs, and possibly something to do with the amount of time the Master/Huntsman spends with the hounds in and out of kennels. Arthur insisted that his wife was expecting us for tea and we thoroughly enjoyed some saffron buns and his Teacher's-and-tea. Eventually we arrived back at Ivybridge at seven-thirty, sitting down for another full hunting tea, followed by a quick bath and change before climbing back into the lorry to drive to the Dartmoor Hunt Supporters Club Cheese and Wine and film show at South Brent. There was a great atmosphere, and it was fascinating to be amongst so many real Devon characters and to hear the accent all around us. During this supper, I was pleased to renew my acquaintance with John Budgett, Master of the Dartmoor, who had helped to organise this jolly. I had previously met him at the Easton kennels, many years ago, as he was a friend of Nick Brook's, my huntsman at the time. We arrived back at eleven-thirty in very high spirits to find the basset hound asleep in Stanley's bedroom. Stanley did some efficient whipping-in, or rather whipping-out and the hound disappeared downstairs with amazing agility.

It was a shame that we could not have hunted with the Dartmoor the day after this supper as they were meeting in Ivybridge but, faithful to my intention of hunting with all the Harrier packs, Stanley, Delia and I went instead to the meet of the **South Pool Harriers** (Sat 24 Mar 1973). This was the sixth consecutive day and the last of this jolly so, once again, I invited Delia to come with us. The meet was a very unusual one, held at a Retirement Home at Combe Royal, near Kingsbridge. Combe Royal was a lovely setting for a meet as it was a mansion before being converted and the matron dispensed hospitality with home-made wine and sausage rolls. Although we had never met, I was hailed like a long-lost friend by the huntsman, Angus MacDonald, who assumed I was a fellow hunt-servant and explained to me that hunt servants do not have to pay caps (I was paying Delia's cap at the time). I was to meet him again in 1982 when he was whipper-in with the High Peak Harriers in Derbyshire. Mrs Peters, the Honorary Secretary, was very pleasant and made us most welcome but the Field Master was probably the most horrid I had ever had the misfortune to meet in the field. It was hardly surprising, it seemed to us, that the field consisted only of one lady and two children. The huntsman spent most of the day shouting instructions to the Field Master about where the field should be standing, as though he was the Master, and there was no mention of a Master that I can recall.

We drew for hours with very little or no sport, and hounds appeared to be very slack, not drawing well for their huntsman. We were not surprised to hear that they had only killed a leash of foxes that season. The only slight diversion from boredom came when the lady became bogged down and then went home with the two children. The huntsman kept yelling for us to go up with him while the Field Master kept growling at us to keep behind him. They drew up an old railway line as far as a tunnel and at that point we were so fed up that we decided to have a race to the end of the line, so we galloped away from hounds to warm up our horses. When we reached the end of the line we decided that the best thing to do was to go home, and have a cream tea in Modbury to cheer ourselves up. It seemed to us that this hunt was going downhill fast and was in great need of a good Master or it would soon disband. In fact, it was not until 1991 that they were amalgamated with the Dart Vale and Haldon as the Dart Vale and South Pool Harriers.

This seemed to be a low point on which to end our holiday but that evening the three of us gathered in Stanley's bedroom to review the whole trip with the remains of the final teatime Teacher's bottle to stop us flagging and we were soon revelling in the happy memories of all the good days. Firstly, we amused ourselves with thinking of personal bests for each of us, the main one being that we had hunted mounted with nine different packs in ten days. From these nine days came some amusing points. One hunt had only men in the field and another would have been only ladies if we had not been there. Another thought that caused much merriment was thinking of what our Easton friends would think of going to nine consecutive meets without ever going into a pub (the Easton have only one of these each season). Delia threatened to tell everyone how totally converted we were as, even when there had been a pub at a meet, we had not entered its portals. We then took another sip of Teacher's and looked around the room and started to recall all the horrors of our lodgings that we could relate to our friends and families – the joints of meat burned to a cinder on the outside but still frozen in the centre; the filthy Aga cooker and dirty kitchen with its regularly renewed damp path; and the encrusted students' table with its wavy top. The breakfasts were of course mentioned with both the Major and Mrs Farr in their dressing gowns, the hair-brushing and the frequent attempts at rape, and lastly a good laugh at ourselves for throwing away our sandwiches on the day that the basset had licked the bacon. We graduated from the horrors of our digs to the joys of hunting. We particularly liked the small mounted fields and the rugged, grim but majestic splendour of the moors with the melodious cry of the West Country harriers and the general atmosphere of goodwill towards hunting everywhere in this area. This made us realise that five packs out of the nine had no staff and the Master and his family did all the work. Most of the horses were cobby types with perhaps an average of only one quality hunter at each meet which we thought proved that the cobby types were more suited to the rough terrain of rocks and bogs. Another observation was how much easier it would have been to keep with hounds if there were a few hunt jumps or gates in the boundary fences which was perhaps the reason that all the Masters, with the exception of Mike Weir of the North Cornwall Foxhounds, preferred to be on the moor. Most hunts jumped very few banks owing to the damage caused, and most packs, with the exception of Charlie Smith's East Cornwall Foxhounds, were very unlevel. When we had finished discussing these thoughts, and many others, it was time to go downstairs for a parting drink with the Major and Rosalind before having a reasonably early night and a final laugh as, when Stanley went into the bathroom, the ginger cat was curled up asleep on his towel which had slipped into the bath.

The following Sunday morning we left Ivybridge at seven o'clock, stopping for lunch at Oxford, and arriving home at six-thirty. Stanley drove the whole way, with Delia sitting in the middle, and me on the outside, balancing a pad of paper on my knee, writing a song later to be called "The Ballad of Stanley Tompkins". I would occasionally read out a verse and I usually got a good laugh, especially the one about the cat in his bed. As for the reason behind the trip, we had hunted with another five harrier packs so, including the Minehead (which I had been with in 1971), I had now been with fourteen packs in all. By this time, however, the Rochdale and the Sparkford Vale Harriers had been disbanded, the Sparkford Vale finding a reincarnation in the Blackmore and Sparkford Vale Foxhounds, so I was more than halfway to my ambition, there being only another thirteen to go.

The spirits of our return trip would not have been so high had I known that I had had my last day's hunting on Paddy. When the hunters were got up for the next season in September he ran away with my next groom, Heather Hamm, onto a concrete track, and, putting his foot half onto an edge, he twisted his foot and broke a fetlock. After this he had to be put down. I was heartbroken as I knew I would never have the same affinity with another horse as I had ridden him for eleven seasons and he knew every inch of the Easton Harriers country. I have often sworn that I could have hunted hounds from him with no reins. He was a cobby little horse with a great turn of speed and had cost one hundred and twenty pounds in 1962.

# Chapter 4

## Local Harriers and the Triangle Jolly

In the latter half of the 1973-74 season I made further progress towards my ambition by hunting with another three harrier packs which I could reach from home. I might have had a problem in my quest as the **Sennowe Park Harriers** were a private pack belonging to Lady Cook of Sennowe Park in Norfolk. However, most years I met Lady Cook on two occasions, at Peterborough Hound Show or in London at the lunch that preceded the Masters of Harriers and Beagles Association AGM. It was at one of these lunches that I explained my ambition to her and asked if I might come out with her hounds at a time convenient to herself. She agreed that I could contact her by telephone and a date was decided upon in January 1974, the meet being at Bintry Mill (Tues 22 January 1974). I had also managed to extend the invitation to include Stanley Tompkins and I said I would pick him up from his farm at Forncett St Peter on the way.

The day started badly as at seven-thirty my girl groom came to the door to say that the lorry had disappeared in the middle of the night. A few minutes later the telephone rang and it was a friend, Michael Becher, who had used my lorry to take a sick Suffolk Punch to Newmarket for an emergency operation. He explained that he had not wanted to disturb me in the middle of the night as he knew I would say yes so there seemed to be little point in waking me up. "I hope you don't need it," he finished.

I explained that I did but not to worry and immediately telephoned another friend, Maurice Scott, to ask if I could borrow his lorry for the day, to which he readily agreed. By the time I had fetched Maurice's lorry I was well behind schedule but, after driving much faster than we ought to have done, we arrived at Bintry at five minutes to eleven, just as her ladyship was moving off. We unboxed in double quick time and hacked off up the road after her to where they were drawing a large stubble. Just before we reached the gateway we could see an old hound walking towards us. He stopped in the gateway and looked back towards the others, then lifted his old grey head and looked at us in that way only an old hound can do, and then continued to walk back slowly towards the meet.

I rode up to Lady Cook, apologised for being late, and told her about the old hound on the road.

"Oh," she replied, " that's nothing to worry about. It's old Pickwick. He's done that for years now. He's very old but still enjoys coming to the meet, but as soon as we start to draw he walks home."

Shortly after this memorable start another old hound decided that he had had enough exercise and turned his back on the other hounds to walk resolutely off towards the kennels which lay just beyond the meet.

Lady Cook, riding sidesaddle on a beautiful little hunter, was immaculately turned out, and had a groom with her who was equally smart. Stanley, her huntsman,

**Sennowe Park Harriers:** ***"Old Pickwick... full of memories of days gone by"***

was seventy-six years old and rode an old dun cob which resembled an Old English Sheepdog as it was unclipped and had a long, curly coat. His old hunt coat had Napoleon-like three-cornered flaps on the outside pockets and was so long that it would have reached his knees when he was standing. I was quite fascinated with this lovely old coat as I had never seen outside pockets on a hunt coat in England and would love to have known what age it was. He had long since ceased to hurry and just walked about on his old cob. The pack had originally consisted of five couple but was now reduced to four, two couple of old "towlers" who were in full accord with their huntsman and took life steadily, and two couple of drafts from the Cambridgeshire who, as there were rather too many hares, were kept busy coursing them back and forwards with their high, squeaky, terrier-like voices.

Lady Cook introduced me to Mr Woods who was a veterinary surgeon and to Mr Bidwell on whose land we were hunting. When she had moved out of earshot Mr Woods asked me how on earth I came to be there. I explained about meeting Lady Cook in London and my ambition to hunt with every harrier pack in England.

"Well, you're lucky," he replied. "I've lived in this parish for ten years but this is the first time I've ever been invited".

It then occurred to me that Lady Cook had made a special effort to put on a show for us by inviting some others.

By this time we were off Mr Bidwell's farm and on to his neighbour's who had a large herd of milking cows. In the distance we could see him striding towards us. The way he walked suggested that he had not come out to watch hounds and Lady Cook rode up to Mr Bidwell and suggested very sweetly that he might like to meet him as they were neighbours.

"Oh no," came the quick reply. "I think it's better if you go. He's far less likely to swear at you, my lady."

At twelve-thirty old Stanley and his Master had a little conference and decided to go home as hounds were unfit owing to this being only the second day out this season. Stanley and I had a few drinks with Messrs Bidwell and Woods at the Red Lion, before coming home from what we both felt was a very special experience and, for my part, I would not have missed it for anything. What a refreshing change in this modern world to find a really private pack belonging to its original family which goes out hunting not regularly but just when the owner feels like it. It reminded me of the advice given by Peter Beckford to a young man who had started a pack of harriers to send a manservant round the day before to never more than six of his friends.

Another harrier pack whose country was within reach of Tannington was the **Aldenham Harriers** and when I decided to have a day with them the week after the Sennowe Park, Stanley again came with me. It was not perhaps absolutely necessary that he and his horse should find themselves benighted at Tannington Hall but it did make for a good fun evening and was convenient for an early start at six-fifteen for the meet at the Lilley Arms at Lilley near Luton (Wed 30 Jan 1974). We arrived at nine-fifteen and after some initial reluctance we persuaded the landlady of the pub to cook us breakfast. We enjoyed the meet and the warm welcome from Sir Maurice and Lady Lyell. Lady Lyell was unable to hunt hounds owing to a fall so her Kennel Huntsman, George Garford, carried the horn, but was obviously very out of practice using it. The field were immaculately turned out and I have never before or since seen a whole field correctly turned out in such a variety of styles. As well as the black coats and boots on clipped-out hunters, there were also unclipped horses with ratcatcher coats, farmers on trace-clipped cobs with tweed coats and brown boots, and so forth, a copy-book example of almost every type of dress in the hunting field.

I was asked to ride up with the huntsman which always gave me extra fun, especially when Stanley had to stay back in the field. Hounds were of a strong type of Stud-Book Harrier, just the type I liked best and have always considered quite fast enough to hunt hare at a pace likely to give a long and interesting hunt. They hunted very well, sticking to the line in the difficult circumstances of high winds. They were a little independent but there was no-one to turn hounds to the huntsman as, of course, he was usually the whipper-in. Too many hares rather spoiled the day's sport and we always seemed to run back over Lilley Hill up to the edge of a golf course.

We arrived home at six-thirty and walked into the kitchen to find that Sheila was just home with a freshly-killed bullock, one of Stanley's calves which I had reared and fattened. She had just unloaded the meat onto the kitchen table when the power went off and when we arrived we found her calmly persevering with her task of packing the various joints into plastic bags by candlelight. Stanley and I selected a steak each and Sheila put them into the Aga. We had just finished eating these when Michael Becher arrived with a silver punch bowl as a thank you present for borrowing the lorry on the Sennowe Park day the week before. The power cut and the atmosphere of the candlelight in the old kitchen prompted me to fill it with champagne and after adding a little brandy we settled down to mull over the day. At last the power came on again and Stanley and Michael went home and I helped Sheila to put away the remainder of the bullock into the freezer.

The third and last harrier pack within reach of home was the **North Norfolk Harriers** and I left home at seven-thirty on Tuesday 19 February 1974 for their meet at Kelling Hall near Holt. As usual, I picked up Stanley on the way and we arrived in good time at ten-thirty. Being early, we decided to have a cup of soup from our flask and a bread roll for our breakfast and while we were enjoying this there was a tap on the window. It was a farmworker who had been put in charge of parking the lorries and as I wound down the window he said,

"Excuse me? Could you tell me if there will be any hounds coming today?"

I replied that I rather hoped so.

"Oh," he said. "Well, sometimes they come here just to chase hares."

**North Norfolk Harriers.** *Meet at Kelling Hall, 1972. The Master and Huntsman, Billy Seaman, leading hounds away from the meet, with Joint-Master Patricia Gurney, whippers-in Janet Giblett and Alison McAllister, and also Jennifer Clarke (Hon Sec), Miss Helen Barclay and Mrs Blount.*

Photograph kindly loaned by Mrs Jane Bell, MH

Our host, Mr Jim Deterding, was very generous and the meet most enjoyable but I could not help feeling that the lemon-and-white West Country harriers looked rather out of place in East Anglia. When we moved off a hare was found in the first few minutes and hounds were away with a grand cry and what appeared to be tremendous drive. This I later found was more akin to wildness and they were decidedly flashy. They overran by hundreds of yards and their casts were great circles taken at the gallop. It was during one of these flying casts that they sighted a low-flying partridge and took off for two or three fields after the bird. I am not sure how many people realised that we were "hunting" partridge but everyone set off in earnest after the hounds and squared up to a stiff set of high post-and-rails. I am not fond of jumping post-and-rails at the best of times and doing so after a partridge was quite ridiculous. However, I did not want to be seen to be left by my near neighbours and I need not have worried as Shamara cleared them easily, just as the partridge disappeared from sight. There was no more "serious" hunting and some skylarking over a Hunter Trial course concluded the day. We called at Poringland on the way home for a proper hunting tea with Stanley's daughter Linda.

During that evening I heard that Ernie Nunn, our famous old kennel huntsman to whom I had whipped-in when learning my trade some fifteen years earlier, had died. His niece gave me some of the old man's books and a pair of his spurs which I have kept ever since out of respect for his memory.

The next trip, made the following season, was unusual in two ways. Firstly, the main reason for going was not to hunt and, secondly, that when I did hunt the pack was the only one in the U.K. which can claim to be totally unique.

I had advertised for a new kennel huntsman for the Easton and had shortlisted the applications down to five that I wished to interview. Instead of the normal practice of paying their expenses to come to the Easton kennels for their interviews I decided to visit them at their respective kennels. This decision was based on the fact that all five were roughly in the same direction and that the furthest was at the New Forest Buckhounds kennels from where there had been two applications. This gave me both an excuse and an opportunity to hunt with the Buckhounds which are the only pack in this country to hunt fallow deer. I left home at seven o'clock in the morning with my daughter Bridget, aged thirteen, and Stanley Tompkins, calling first at the Oakley Foxhounds kennels at ten o'clock. We were most impressed with a brand-new kennel set-up, complete with new stables and new houses for hunt servants and grooms. I liked the young man but got the impression that he had his sights set higher than the Easton Harriers. Leaving the Oakley kennel, we went to the Sandhurst Foxhounds where we had some difficulty getting to the kennels as they were inside the military compound. Getting past the guards on the gate without a pass was something of a problem but once inside our troubles continued as we went at first to the wrong kennels. These were the combined kennel of the Sandhurst Draghounds and the Sandhurst Beagles. Eventually we found the Foxhounds and were appalled by the poor condition of hounds and the dreadful kennels which rather went against the interview with the candidate. This was perhaps unfair as he certainly deserved something better than this. It had been rather a chalk-and-cheese sort of morning as far as the kennels were concerned as we had seen the best and the worst kennels in my experience.

Leaving Sandhurst we went to see a man who was temporarily out of hunt service who lived at Overton, and then went on to the Compton Arms Hotel at Stoney Cross in the New Forest, where our rooms had been booked for us by Mrs Miller, Master of the Buckhounds, at seven o'clock. After dinner I telephoned the kennels of the New Forest Buckhounds to ask the two interviewees to come to the hotel. However, the huntsman, who sounded very pompous, said that his men could not turn out at that time of night and suggested that I came to the kennels instead. As I had come so far for the purpose of seeing them I decided that I would go. The implication that it was too late for hunt servants to turn out but quite all right for a Master had not put me in the best frame of mind to engage either of them but, after talking to each of them in turn in the huntsman's house, I mellowed and we all four of us sat and talked hunting until I suddenly realised that it was eleven-fifteen and promptly left.

Mrs Miller, the Master of the **New Forest Buckhounds**, had not only booked our hotel rooms but had also kindly offered to arrange hirelings for all three of us from Mr Partridge, whose stables were next to the hotel. He had horses to suit us all. Mine was called Sharman, and Bridget's Tombola had screen fame, having appeared in the television series of "Ivanhoe". What Stanley's was called I cannot remember. We had quite a long hack from the meet, which was near to our hotel at Stoney Cross, at Bushey Brackley, to the draw where there were nine bucks, including a white one (Mon 6 Jan 1975). The tufters seemed rather slack and worked with little or no cry. The bucks often just stopped and looked at them, but eventually they got one away. We had a very fast fifteen minutes or so to a small check, after which Bridget and I were parted. After another hour's continuous running I had no idea where she was and got quite worried. When the deer eventually took to water a lady approached us offering her flask and as we drank she said, "Cheers to Suffolk".

**Hursley.** *Boxing Day meet in Romsey Square, 1974. Joint-Masters Colonel D B Drysdale and Mr Monty Olden, and Huntsman Clifford Pellew.*

Photograph kindly donated by Mr Olden

I replied, "How typical of someone from Suffolk to offer their flask", to which she replied, "Only people from Suffolk are nice enough to make me want to do so."

We met some horse-boxes at High Corner and the hunt staff changed onto their second horses. I said to Stanley "Our horses are rather tired. What shall we do?" and he replied, "Change hands, and hit them on the other side, and they will think they are fresh horses."

Little more hunting was done so we decided to go and find Bridget. She had become quite lost and very sensibly decided to leave her pony alone hoping it would take her home. This it did, coming to a wire-netting fence immediately opposite the hotel with a main road in between. She was sitting wondering what to do when the pony turned and went along to an underpass with which it was obviously very familiar. They were soon back at the stables which was where we found her.

At dinner, over quite a few drinks, with Bridget telling us of her adventures, and us telling her of the last run, we suddenly thought it would be a good idea to have another day as the **Hursley Foxhounds**† were out on the morrow. It was after ten o'clock at night when I started to telephone to find horses. This proved rather difficult owing to me telling the truth about Stanley's weight but after several refusals I began to reduce his weight until he was only twelve stone. At last, on the tenth phone call, and just as I was getting very fed up of finding enough change to operate the telephone box, a man agreed to hire us horses and deliver them to the meet at Home Farm, Emberley, next day (Tues 7 Jan 1975).

He duly arrived and the first thing he did was to ask us to settle up the hire charges. I shall never forget the scene when he dropped his ramp and led out the first horse, Ned. This was a skinny, ewe-necked screw and, with never a thought that it might need tying up, he just left it standing alone while he went back into the lorry to fetch out the next one. This was called Midnight and was for me. We stood in amazement as they grazed quietly, their reins tucked into their throatlashes to prevent them standing on

† See Map 3

them, while he returned to the lorry to fetch out Bridget's pony called Fifty. Stanley's sixteen stone looked so pathetically funny on the ewe-necked screw, looking more suited to eight stone if it had had a three-month holiday. I offered a lady a pound to take a photograph of him but unfortunately he noticed and kept hiding up behind sheds and lorries so that she could not oblige. I would dearly have loved a photograph of him as it was the only perfect living example of Uncle Tom Cobbley's old grey mare I had ever seen.

There were six adults in the field and a few children, all rather scruffily turned out. The day's hunting was to be perfectly in keeping with the quality of our mounts, who could only manage a shambling trot for most of the time, and very occasionally, with a concentrated effort from their riders, a short lumbering canter. The country was all woodland and full of open earths. The huntsman was good, and doing his best, but was greatly hindered by his Master, a rude, blustering, noisy sort of fellow who was a nuisance to everyone as he kept barging past us on narrow rides and was so busy shouting and hollering that he always had hounds heads up. I felt desperately sorry for the huntsman who deserved a medal for his forbearance. During the day we often passed a large house which had been converted into a school. This had a curved drive going up to the front door, and away again out of a different exit. Each time we passed the school, perhaps five or six times in all, the Master cut across the lawn instead of going round the curved gravel drive. The lawn was quite churned up by the end of the day and Stanley and I remarked to each other, "Is it any wonder that there are some members of the public who think that hunting people are arrogant and uncaring?"

We endured all this charade of hunting with the greatest amusement until, while we were standing in a narrow ride, a hound behind us got its leg in a snare. Anyone who has ever had the least thing to do with hounds knows that a hound thus in pain makes a screeching sort of cry that is instantly recognisable. Not so our intrepid Master who thought that the cry was a hound on a line and came galloping back down the ride, yelling "Hike Forrard, hike forrard. Get on to 'im, get on to 'im." He galloped through the middle of the field which was crammed into this narrow ride, knocking children and their ponies into the bushes and bruising our knees. I just looked at Stanley and he said, "I think we have had enough of this," so we walked back to the meet and handed over our horses. At three o'clock we started our journey home in the car, arriving at Tannington at nine-forty-five, where Sheila had a steaming hot-pot waiting for us.

As for the new kennel huntsman, after interviewing a few others, I eventually settled on Jim Wickham who had been first whipper-in at the Essex and Suffolk. He came to Easton on 1 May 1975 and proved to be an excellent choice. He suited the Easton perfectly, fitting in with the character of the hunt. He held the position until 1987 when he decided to retire. He had broken his pelvis in a dreadful fall and never fully recovered.

The highlight of the 1974-75 season were the two "exchange visits" with the Holcombe Harriers which were arranged through my friendship with Newton Bacon. The Easton invited the members of the Holcombe Harriers to spend four days in the Easton country, with their horses, and fifteen members came down from Lancashire to Suffolk in November 1974. They stayed with the Easton members and it was all great fun. The return match was fixed for February 1975 and on Wednesday the 12th the Easton Harriers members made their way north to stay with members of the Holcombe, hunting with them on Thursday, attending the Waterloo Cup coursing meeting on Friday, and hunting again on the Saturday. When the Easton returned home on the Sunday, Stanley and I did not join the convoy as we had made arrangements to visit Colin and Tizza Plumbe who were then living at Triangle, just outside Halifax. I was feeling extremely rough with symptoms of 'flu so when we got there I could not help to unload the horses and went straight to bed. All the boxes at the Plumbes were already occupied so they had arranged for our horses to be stabled in some original and beautiful stables which went with a big house on the opposite side of the road from their home. This belonged to Mrs Stansfield, a wonderful old lady who lived there alone. This week turned out to be an hilariously funny one domestically, as far as Colin, Tizza and Stanley were concerned, as I had had to ask them to do my horse. Grooming horses gives me an asthma attack and I had not brought a groom. In return they thought up a multitude of domestic jobs for me to do, like making their porridge and cleaning their boots, culminating in winding up the cuckoo clock.

I was still not well enough to hunt on the Monday so Stanley and Tizza went alone to hunt with the Middleton Foxhounds, but I was feeling much better on the Tuesday (18 Feb 1975). This was particularly fortunate as I had been looking forward to this day with the **Rufford Forest Harriers** which were a private pack belonging to Lady Anne Cavendish-Bentinck. She had been Master of the Grove and Rufford Foxhounds for fourteen seasons but resigned in 1966, as so many good Masters have done before, when hunt politics proved to be more than she could bear. It must have been a serious disagreement as her estate covers a considerable proportion of their country. Following her resignation Lady Anne declared that she would have her own pack of hounds, but on second thoughts decided to have two packs, one of foxhounds and one of harriers. A whole new kennel was built in the most lavish style. After some seasons she gave up the foxhounds and concentrated on her harriers which she considered much more fun, to my considerable personal satisfaction as this corresponded with my own opinion. Following this decision she wrote an excellent article on this theme stating that many packs of foxhounds whose countries had become cramped by main roads and so forth would show more sport if they changed to harriers. Her harriers were firstly called the Welbeck but changed their name to the Rufford Forest in 1972.

Stanley, Colin and I left Triangle at eight-fifteen and arrived at the kennels at Shire Oaks Hill, Cuckney, near Mansfield, at ten-fifteen. Before we left to go to the meet Stanley, the huntsman, showed us round the kennels and we were amazed by the grandeur and quality of them. The horses' boxes all had tiled walls and the lovely wide oak doors had the most enormous brass hinges and bolts all sparkling clean. The kennels were equally palatial with the walls of the yards topped with iron railings and every fourth spike was tipped with her ladyship's coat of arms. The boiler room was also exceptional with polished copper waterpipes leading to a stainless steel boiler in which the hounds' food was prepared. When the hunstman wanted to feed the hounds, this automatically tipped over, slowly pouring the food into the feed trough which then ran along a small railway line into the feeding yard. I had heard how wonderful these kennels were, but was nevertheless quite bowled over by their magnificence.

We hacked on with hounds to the actual meet, following the hunt servants, who were both turned out to perfection. These lovely hounds, bred mostly from Cambridgeshire blood, looked fit and well as we jogged through tracks and lanes, across the estate. Lady Anne arrived by car, and then walked round to greet everyone. I had met Lady Anne several times at Peterborough Hound Show, but first of all when she had come to Suffolk to look at a draft of five couple that I was willing to give her to help her start her new pack of harriers in 1966. A little bitch called Tarnish was the only one left of that original draft, as all the others had grown too old. While Lady Anne was greeting us all, her chauffeur was busy getting the polished mahogany mounting block from the boot of the car, and her horse stood waiting, an absolute model of the perfect hunter. Her side-saddle was covered with a special fitted canvas cover as it was raining slightly.

We found a fox almost at once after moving off and Lady Anne said to me, "Would you like to ride up with Stanley?" Turning to the rest of the field, however, she said quite firmly, "And the rest of you can keep behind me." As always, I received double joy from this as not only was it great fun to be with hounds but to do it in front of my friend Stanley, who was being held back, was even more amusing and gave me an extra kick. There was some nice woodland hunting with this fox and hounds went with plenty of cry although it was rather squeaky and high-pitched. We drew again and went away on a hare and had a lovely hunt over this fabulous estate where every hedge and fence was kept at an even height (set, I believe, by Lady Anne), and no barbed wire. What a joy it was to be able to hunt on an estate one hundred per cent dedicated to hunting. This run ended in an area with too many hares and, as no more serious hunting could be done, we returned to the meet. As we were hacking back, Lady Anne told me how she had sent her huntsman to the High Peak Harriers to learn how to hunt hare.

"Did he learn how?" I enquired.

"No," was the reply. "Their only advice to him was to just keep buggering on."

At the meet Lady Anne got into her car and we hacked back to the kennels with hounds. When she arrived we went into the kennels to have a last look at Tarnish, and then retired for coffee in the huntsman's cottage. We thanked her for our day and were about to depart when something caught my eye. It was a lifesize statue of a hare sitting serenely on the grass in front of the kennels and I must confess to breaking the Tenth Commandment as I really did covet that dear little statue. On rejoining the motorway, Colin and I decided to have a bet as to who could sing the most hunting songs. We took it in turns to sing and we kept it going for over one and a half hours, and were still singing when we got back to Triangle. Stanley Tompkins declared it a draw. To round off this lovely day, we met some of Colin's friends at the Fleece Inn for a steak supper and spent a very amusing evening, hearing of each other's hunting experiences.

We had planned to hunt with the High Peak Harriers the following day but this had to be abandoned as the meet was cancelled. There would, of course, have been foxhounds out on a Wednesday but I was still determined to keep to harriers whenever possible so we decided to go with the **Wensleydale Harriers** who were meeting at Palmer Flat, at Aysgarth (Wed 19 Feb 1975). The Wensleydale was a pack of lemon-and-white West Country Harriers, which were hunted on foot in the Yorkshire Dales. We met the Master, Mr Dormer Treffry, and Mr King who was to take over the Mastership in the following season. Mr King told me that he was born in the Easton country and lived at Benhall, near Saxmundham, and was blooded by the legendary Ned Watts, an old kennel huntsman of the Easton.

We moved off down a little lane and were later joined by two other men who were the only field apart from us. The day was sunny after a hard frost and scent was not good which gave us a chance to see these beautiful harriers working splendidly on a difficult line. I just could not understand how these hounds could have such little support, because they have a paradise of a country, with good walking on old pastures and gently-sloping fells, and good sound walls. The whole area was breathtakingly beautiful. Hounds hunted superbly and as I write I can still picture Dormer Treffry casting hounds on the side of a hill a quarter of a mile away from himself, just by blowing a few notes on his horn and changing the direction he himself was walking in. I was fascinated to watch as he cast hounds back and forward until they fresh found their hunted hare. Only very few men have hound-control like that, and very few people are lucky enough to be able to see it. It was an education to see him hunt hounds with no whipper-in or any help at all.

**Wensleydale Harriers** – *Chanter '81, bred by Giles Thompson M.H.*
Photograph kindly loaned by Giles Thompson

We went back to the meet at two-thirty as we had a long drive back and Colin and Tizza were giving a dinner-party, inviting John Loy and Bob MacReady (the Masters of the Rockwood who we were to hunt with on Saturday), and their wives. What a lovely evening it was, what North Country people call "a right good do".

For our sporting entertainment the following day we divided into two camps as Stanley and Tizza wanted to go foxhunting and Colin and I preferred to go with harriers. Various arrangements were made and Stanley and Tizza went with the Sinnington Foxhounds and had a very good day. Colin and I went for a private day with the **Windermere Harriers**, with which pack Colin had been whipper-in for several seasons (Thurs 20 Feb 1975). The day had been especially arranged for us, or rather, as it turned out, we put on the day for ourselves. There was no-one to drive the hound van as the new Master, Albert Benson, aged seventy-seven, could not drive, so Colin offered to drive the hound van which meant that we had to go to the kennels and then double back to the meet at Low Fold, Kentmere.

As soon as we drew, hounds hit off a drag and after almost an hour dragged up to the fox. Albert had realised long before that they were on the line of a fox as there was always a couple of Windermere Harriers who refused to hunt fox and would return to him immediately. However, they were too far away to stop and they found the fox, going away over to Long Sleddale. Colin and I took the hound van round to find hounds, but could not see them and returned to find that they had hunted their fox all the way back to Albert. Then we spent a most enjoyable hour over tea in the farmhouse, listening to stories from Albert and his friends. I always feel privileged to be able to sit and listen to such people as Albert Benson, and hear of the days when huntsman had to go on foot to the meet, eight to ten miles away, hunt foxhounds all day, and end up in a pub with a Tatie-pot and a singsong, and perhaps not leave until ten-thirty, and then have twelve, sometimes fifteen, miles to walk back to kennels, and would, of course, be ready to do exactly the same thing next morning. What men they were. They must have had constitutions of iron. We returned hounds to kennels and when we finally arrived back at Triangle we found we had travelled three hundred and fifty miles in all.

There was dismay in the camp the next day as there were no hounds out anywhere, so we decided to visit the Rockwood Harriers kennels at Blacker Farm, Emley, near Huddersfield. These were converted farm buildings and we thought them to be a very neat compact setup, and obviously a lot of careful planning had gone into the conversion. While I was there I looked for another stallion hound but could not see one that I liked which was not too closely related to Rockwood Pickwick who was already in the Easton kennel. We called at a little pub on the way back for lunch, and then I rode Shamara out on exercise. Later in the afternoon we went to visit Mrs Stansfield who lived alone in the big house over the road and had kindly lent us her stables. Before having tea, we were shown round her home which was full of antiques. It had an atmosphere of timelessness and I would guess that it had looked exactly the same when Queen Victoria was a little girl. Earl Grey tea with little three-cornered sandwiches and iced cakes on a cake stand perfected this visit. Tizza later told us how much Mrs Stansfield had enjoyed having our horses and our visits as it brought a new excitement into her rather staid life. In the evening, Colin had arranged that we should meet some of the Rockwood members at the Fountain Inn, at Ingerbertsworth. When we got there they told me that Colin had told them all to come as I was going to sing. He had given me no warning at all! In spite of this, I enjoyed meeting the members and both Colin and I sang several songs before the end of the evening.

It is always pleasant to be able to end on a high note and this is exactly what happened on our last day when we hunted with the **Rockwood Harriers** at Hazelhead Hall, near Penistone (Sat 22 Feb 1975). We unboxed and hacked up to the meet where our host, Derek Booth Mallie, found people to hold our horses and took us inside the house for a lawn meet to remember. Tables were laden with a selection of home-made savouries and tumblers of drinks were pressed into our hands. The atmosphere was delightful and we felt that we were truly welcome. It was with obvious reluctance that the Joint-Master and huntsman, John Loy, said that we must move off. He went to draw a boggy piece of moor and we had two good circular hunts, going on to draw a better piece of country, with firm old grass and good sound walls. Shamara hit one of these first high walls quite early in the day and came down amongst a pile of stones. This turned out to be a blessing in disguise as she had the greatest respect for walls after that. Scent was not brilliant so hounds had to work hard and this provided me with the sort of day I most enjoy with plenty of good houndwork to watch. We had a wonderful time following these splendid hounds with their deep, powerful voices over this paradise of a country. My earlier apprehension of the height and reputation of the Rockwood walls had now completely gone and I was thoroughly enjoying them, even though Shamara touched quite a few of them as she was only fifteen-two and they seemed nearly as high as she was! During the mid-afternoon, we came back to near the meet and our hostess insisted (with us putting up only a token resistance) on our calling in "to help with all the food and drink left over". After a large whisky and some sausage rolls we soon caught up with hounds again and all the fun continued as the field dwindled down to about six. Dusk was upon us when the Master looked at his watch and said, "It's five-fifteen. We must go home."

**Rockwood Harriers.** *John Loy, Master and huntsman, 1970–91.*
Photograph kindly loaned by John Loy

Just as he was saying this, a hare jumped up in the middle of hounds and away we went. I shall never forget jumping those walls in the dark, with the cry seemingly magnified by the night air. It was gone six o'clock by the time we finished this run and hacked back to the meet with tired horses and very happy company.

We returned to Suffolk the next morning with Shamara rather lame. She had hit a few too many of those high walls. One of the best things about these hunting trips were the great friendships which were formed and which extended my circle of hunting friends. After hunting with the Holcombe I had become great friends with Newton and Kate Bacon, and now the situation was repeated as I had started another longstanding friendship with John and Marjorie Loy. As with the Holcombe, I returned to the Rockwood country on 21 June to judge their Puppy Show (again accepting the wonderful hospitality of Colin and Tizza), and "exchange visits" were arranged, with the Rockwood coming to Suffolk in November 1976 and the Easton going back to Lancashire a year later. This "Triangle jolly" had therefore started with one exchange visit (with the Holcombe) and caused another (with the Rockwood). It had also been successful with regard to the proper business of the trip as I had hunted with another three harrier packs, making a total of twenty in all.

# CHAPTER 5

## A WIDE VARIETY

Another judging duty I performed in the summer of 1975 was the harrier classes at the Rydal Hound Show in the Lake District on 9 August. After the judging was finished, Newton and Kate Bacon took Sheila and me to their boathouse on the edge of Lake Windermere for drinks, before taking us to dinner at the Aquarius restaurant in Bowness. Newton insisted that he should be allowed to order the main course which turned out to be Windermere Char, the famous prehistoric fish only found in Lake Windermere, living at great depths which vary by hundreds of feet according to the temperature. Fishing for char is only allowed by special licence and very few are taken out. Eating this fish was a culinary experience not to be easily forgotten. The flesh is light pink and seemed to taste like a cross between a wild salmon and a trout, in short, exquisite. Before the evening was finished, Newton and Kate offered us the use of the boathouse for a holiday.

An exceptionally dry summer and an early harvest allowed us to take up the Bacons's offer later in the month. Sheila and I took all three of our children – Bridget at fourteen, Judith eleven and Charlotte six – and also Tim Bird, a friend of Judith's. Before supper one evening Bridget and Tim decided to row round an island in the lake and back again. This took longer than they had expected and it was quite dusk by the time they reached the island. Sheila was in a terrible stew, walking back and forwards on the veranda, reminding me of a broody hen which had been sitting on ducks' eggs the first time the ducklings took to water.

After a few days of this "domestic bliss", however, I began to feel like Jorrocks when he said that all time not spent hunting is wasted, and proposed to have a day with the **Dumfriesshire Otterhounds** (30 Aug 1975). Sheila was not in favour and said "Surely we can have one short holiday without involving hounds or hunting?", but the youngsters were keen to go so she was outvoted and off we went up to Scotland, leaving Sheila in the boathouse to have a peaceful day. I was breaking the speed limit going up the M6 and instructed the children to keep their eyes peeled for police cars. I made a small deviation from the route to take the children through Gretna Green and later a lucky wrong turn brought us to the Dumfriesshire Foxhounds kennels where we were allowed to view the black-and-tan beauties. These are unique in the foxhunting world and could be seen from a specially built catwalk so visitors were able to look over the yard walls and down on the hounds.

We got to the otterhound meet at their kennels at Kettleholme just as they were moving off and we followed them upstream. We watched them draw the Castle Milk Lake which lay below the home of the Buchanan-Jardines, owners of the famous foxhounds (which had been bred by his family), as well as of the otterhounds. As we followed the otterhounds I met Mr Bell-Irving who invited me to go out with his beagles as they were meeting at one-thirty. The otterhounds had drawn blank all morning so we thought it would be a good idea to take up the invitation.

We had lunch in Lockerbie and then returned for the meet of the **Bell-Irving Beagles** at the same place. They found at once and ran with a good cry but lost the first hare in a thick plantation. After some more pleasant little hunts, Mr Bell-Irving invited us to his home, for tea and to see his hawks. He was very kind and painstakingly explained to us all (because I was as green as the children) about the different types of hawk, hoods and jesses, and many other hawking accessories. The journey back to the boathouse seemed quite short as we had so much to talk about with the children having had so many new sporting experiences. Firstly there was the lucky mistake that took us to the Dumfriesshire Foxhound kennels where we had our first sight of the great black-and-tan foxhounds, and heard

**Woodland Pytchley Hunt.** *Joint Master and huntsman, David Reynolds, on the bank of the River Nene at Aldwincle.*
Photograph kindly loaned by David Reynolds

**Woodland Pytchley.** *Meet at Sutton Basset, January 1994. Master Mr Eric Comerford (on chestnut horse with white blaze, with left hand raised), Huntsman Tom Teanby, and, in front of hounds, whipper-in Mervyn Holmwood.* Photograph kindly loaned by Mr Eric Comerford

their deep powerful voices as they bayed at us while we were looking down at them from the catwalk. Another thing which fascinated the children were the woolly coats of the pure otterhounds which, like the foxhounds, they had never seen before and were a great contrast to our harriers. The afternoon with the beagles was an extra bonus and, to cap the lot, came the perfect ending, being entertained by a real sportsman who had wetted our appetites for hawking.

This varied day set the tone for the rest of the season (1975-76) as I hunted with another four packs and they were all different hounds – foxhounds, bassets, beagles and otterhounds. The first of these was the foxhounds as, soon after our Opening Meet, I was told that the **Woodland Pytchley**† were due to hunt in Norfolk by invitation of the West Norfolk Foxhounds (Wed 19 Nov 1975). Stanley and I thought this too good an opportunity to miss and he said that he would make the arrangements as he knew one of the Masters of the West Norfolk. I picked him up on the way to the meet at the Bell Inn, Brisley Green, and when we arrived we were astonished to find a huge field of approximately one hundred and ten horses. We were made very welcome by Stanley's friend from staghunting days, Jim Haggis, now one of the Masters of the West Norfolk.

**De Burgh and North Essex Harehounds.** *Meet at Streetly Hall, West Wickham, c. 1978. Left to right, Jack Webb of Streetly Hall, J S Humphrey (Master), T G Baynes (whip), a supporter, Paul Imber (whip), Charlie Jewitt (whip), Matthew Higgs (whip), and Neil Curtis (whip).* Photograph kindly loaned by J S Humphrey

After leaving the meet hounds soon found and we went away at a fast canter down a long stubble field. I saw hounds swing right through a hedge and head back the way they had come so I turned to go in the same direction as hounds and learned a very hard lesson. Foxhunting fields appear to not watch hounds, or care in which direction hounds are hunting. When I turned I was confronted by a line of galloping horses. I assumed that they would try to avoid me but could not have been more wrong. They made no effort to do so at all and cannoned into me, crushing my leg which took until the end of the season to recover. More importantly, Connors, my best hunter, was injured in the shoulder from the crash and, although he finished the day, he never recovered and had to be put down. This was a great blow to me as he was a grand hunter named after the famous Dr Connors who had brought him over from Ireland. I had paid a high price for him from Leicester sales, especially for visiting other hunts in order that I should have a hunter who knew how to perform over fences.

I was most unimpressed with these hounds. They were slack and had no drive, little cry and, at a check, they just stood still, looking for their huntsman. This was a great eye-opener for me as I just could not have imagined that a pack of hounds could be so useless that they did not try to cast themselves at all. The only bright side to the day was to see the Master's son, aged eight, bombing about on a grey pony whipping in like a professional. There was little else to the day and while our journey to the meet had been full of happy expectation, the journey home was flat and dull.

It was just after the Easton season finished that I decided to do some more visiting and made arrangements to hunt with the **De Burgh Basset Hounds** who were meeting at Streetley Hall, near

† See Map 3

Haverhill (Suffolk) on Saturday 20 March (1976) taking with me my aged grandparents and my youngest daughter Charlotte, nearly seven. Our host, Mr Webb, was a real old-fashioned sporting farmer who gave a lawn meet for five different packs of hounds every season – the Cambridgeshire Foxhounds, the University Draghounds, the Cambridgeshire Harriers and the Trinity Foot Beagles, as well as the bassets. He introduced me to his housekeeper, Miss Jackson, whose family, the Lings, had farmed Braiseworth Hall, Tannington, which has been in my family since the Lings left. It was a lucky coincidence that I had brought my grandparents along for the ride as I introduced Miss Jackson to them and they had a great time reminiscing while we hunted.

There were too many hares for any serious hunting but Charlotte and I enjoyed strolling over the rolling grassland listening to that glorious cry. There was one Cambridgeshire Harrier in the pack which looked singularly out of place. After hunting we all went into Streetly Hall for a delicious tea and on the way home I felt it had been a great privilege to have met Mr Webb who epitomised everything that an old-fashioned sporting gentleman should be. I have often wondered since if there is another host anywhere who entertains five different packs at his home.

It was a typical East Anglian March day of sun and bitterly cold winds for my next visit four days later. I took with me on this occasion Rupert Montagu who for many years endured the unenviable task of being Master's Secretary to me. The **Colchester Garrison Beagles** were meeting at Landmere Hall near Thorpe-le-Soken (Wed 24 Mar 1976) and we were in good time which gave us a chance to observe how very small they seemed to be and how light of bone. They hunted most beautifully over an area near Kirby Backwater and the adjacent saltings and we were both struck by the amazing hound control that Peter, the kennel huntsman, showed as although he had no whipper-in he could stop and turn the twenty-one-and-a-half couple with ease. We left at four o'clock having had a very enjoyable afternoon.

**Eastern Counties Otterhounds.** *Charles Corner, Master and huntsman on the Little Ouse, 1976. L to R, Graham Downing, Charles Corner, Lady Cook, Jim Buchanan and Catherine Corner, whipper-in.*

Photograph kindly loaned by Charles Corner

My next "visit" was not really a visit, as such, because the **Eastern Counties Otterhounds** were meeting at Gleveringham Fishponds which were just up the road from the Easton Harriers' kennels (Sat 3 Apr 1976). As they were so close I thought it safe to take all three of my daughters, then aged fourteen, twelve and nearly seven. I walked out the harriers first and then went to the otterhounds' meet. The pack consisted of some pure otterhounds and some three-quarter bred, the result of careful breeding by Charles Corner, the Master. Hounds drew upstream towards the Easton kennels where the custom was to kennel the otterhounds while the field had lunch in the White Horse pub close by in the village of Easton. We did not find an otter but some coypu were hunted and one was killed. The children were much more interested in, and impressed by, watching a terrier digging another coypu out of a hole in a bank and killing it single-handed. We returned home just in time to watch the Grand National.

It was not until after Christmas the next season that I went a-visiting again. I had had a fall on Boxing Day and dislocated my neck so I was unable to ride or hunt the Easton and my kennel huntsman, Jim Wickham (then in his second season), was hunting hounds for me. After four weeks of no hunting I decided that this was a chance for me to see the **Wimbish Beagles**, a little private pack of beagles. I telephoned Mr Hall, the Master, and invited myself to the meet on Cock Robin Green, near Attleborough in Norfolk (Sat 29 Jan 1977). Mr Hall hunted the hounds himself with his wife whipping-in to him. It was a short day but I saw some very good hunting, or rather I saw as much as possible as I was unable to hurry very much. After hunting our host Dr Apthorp took us into his house for a tea of cottage pie and fruit salad during which I got into conversation with a Mr Graham who told me that they were not going to breed any more and as the hounds got older the pack would gradually be wound up. I thought this was very sad as there are so very few private packs in existence, but the pack was eventually disbanded in the mid-1980s.

The BFSS were indirectly responsible for my next experience with a different pack. They launched a Membership Drive and I asked the Easton Members to each recruit five or more new "banker's order" members for the BFSS. This they all did and when trying to think of a suitable treat for my splendid members I thought of my old friend, Reg Wright, and his **North Warwickshire Bloodhounds**. I explained the situation to him and he immediately agreed to bring his hounds to Suffolk to meet at Bedfield Crown on 16 March 1977. Another part of our contribution to the Membership Drive were some coursing meetings I held on my family farm stipulating that anyone wishing to run their dogs must first sign up as a member of the BFSS, if not already one. For some reason unknown to me, these informal meetings attracted competitors from all over the country and raised several hundred new members.

On one of these days Sheila and I had some house guests staying with us to watch the coursing. As breakfast was ending that morning, the doorbell and the telephone rang at the same time. Sheila went into the next room to answer the telephone and I went to the door to find a group of swarthy looking gentlemen who explained that they had come from Birmingham for the coursing and, as they were so early, could I tell them where they could get some breakfast. The only place I could think of was the hotel in Framlingham which did not seem quite appropriate so, knowing that our guests had risen from the table, I invited them in for breakfast. Sheila returned from her phonecall and, without turning a hair, set to and cooked for the eight men. After the meal they made a great fuss of my youngest daughter who was then nearly eight and running round the table, and she was delighted when nearly all of them insisted on giving her some money. This I have found to be typical of their method of repaying hospitality, not to be so crass as to offer money to Sheila, but to spoil the child and, moreover, to be extremely generous. I had thought no more about this incident, a very small one in a busy day, until some weeks later I was at a party and overheard my wife's conversation.

"Honestly, you have no idea what it's like to live with him," she was saying. "The other day we had some friends to stay. I left them at the breakfast table to answer the telephone, and when I came back they had gone and the table was full of gypsies."

**Hambledon Hounds.** *Meet at Newton Green (by invitation of the Essex & Suffolk). The Master, Colonel Frank Mitchell, talking to James Barclay. The whipper-in is actually John O'Shea, Huntsman of the East Essex who came for a "busman's holiday".*

Photograph kindly loaned by Mr George Paul, son-in-law of Col. Mitchell, and Joint-Master of the Essex & Suffolk

I arrived home from one of these coursing meetings to find that Reg had arrived and his hounds were kennelled in the stables causing much excitement among my hunters. We thought it would be a good idea to exercise the hounds after such a long journey so we persuaded Sheila to run round the lawns and meadows and laid hounds onto her line. After a short spin, she was caught and duly licked all over by happy hounds. Having made a special arrangement with the landlord at Bedfield Crown, the twenty-five people who had recruited ten or more new BFSS members sat down in the pub to a hunt breakfast of homemade bread and salt beef provided by Sheila. At ten o'clock the others who had got five or more new members arrived and we moved off at about eleven. We had carefully planned the lines and had three boys who volunteered to be the runners. Maurice Scott and I rode the lines the previous Sunday, with each boy taking his turn to memorise the route. Each line ended near a pub and, after hounds had identified their quarry, the field refreshed themselves while the next boy was running. This all went very well and everyone thought it great fun. The day ended with a Hunt Dinner at Cretingham Bell, and I was proud to be able to announce that the Easton Harriers were the top hunt in the country for recruiting new members. They had found over three hundred, and the next best hunt had found forty. Our final total was six hundred and forty.

At the beginning of the next season (1977-78) I heard from Jim Wickham, through the hunt servants' grapevine, that the **Hambledon Foxhounds** from Hampshire were coming into the Essex and Suffolk

† See Map 3

country. This long-distance invitation came about due to Mary Paul, who was the very popular and first-class Master of the Essex and Suffolk Foxhounds, inviting her father, Colonel Mitchell, to bring his hounds to Newton Green, near Sudbury (Wed 23 Nov 1977). Although I did not know it at the time, the Hambledon were to take the ill-famed Hursley under their wing in an amalgamation agreement. As this meet was on a Wednesday, a non-hunting day for the Easton, a number of us were able to go. Geoffrey Ingram-Smith, my amateur whipper-in, insisted that we left to him all the arrangements for this visit, and invited us to a Hunt Breakfast at his home. After this excellent start, we boxed to the meet and had a quick drink in the Saracen's Head on the edge of Newton Green, before joining the quite large field. Colonel Mitchell was hunting hounds but did not get much of a chance to show good sport as there were too many foxes and the coverts were large and very thick. I was impressed with his ability to get hounds away from covert quickly, but time after time the fox doubled back after only a field or so.

There was an African Prince hunting who was, I understood, a regular follower of the Essex and Suffolk. We were soon in conversation with him, during which Geoffrey invited him to join us afterwards for tea which he had arranged in the Saracen's Head. We had a sumptuous tea in front of a huge log fire, and I was persuaded to sing a hunting song. This prompted the prince to order a bottle of champagne which induced another song, so the prince ordered another bottle – a dangerous chain of events. The upshot of it was that we were still there at six-thirty. When we went to the bar to settle the bill, the prince's valet stepped up and offered to pay his share but we said that there was no need for him to contribute anything. What we did not realise was that the prince did not carry any money but always left these mundane matters to his man, and the end result was that we had to pay for all the champagne, as well as tea, which came to £17.00 for each of us – a very expensive tea and a memorable lesson about princes which I have never since been in a position to benefit from.

**Mendip Farmers'.** *Meet at the Kennels, Priddy, February 1978. Acting Master Tony Younghusband (right) and Huntsman Robin Squires (left). On this occasion only the hunt staff were mounted because, after a fortnight of snow and fog, everywhere was waterlogged.*
Photograph kindly loaned by Mrs Marjorie Stratton

It was some time since our last, short, jolly to Triangle in February 1975 when I started to plan the next one in March 1978. Looking at my Hunt Countries map, I realised that there were several packs still to be seen in the West Country. My longtime companion, Stanley Tompkins, did not come with me on this trip as he had taken on some extra land to farm, but instead Terence Saffell, Field Master of the Easton, agreed to share this holiday. The Easton Harriers had ended their season with a joint-meet with the Sproughton Foot Beagles on Thursday 16 March, followed by a joint-dinner in the Crown Hotel at Framlingham. The dinner was great fun as usual and it was after one-thirty when we left the table which was perhaps not ideal for me as I had planned a four o'clock start the following day. We had arranged that I would take the horses down in the lorry with my groom, Heather Hamm, and that Terence would drive down by car with Sheila the following day. Heather and I set off in the box with three of my horses and one for Terence and arrived just before four o'clock, driving almost nonstop for nearly twelve hours with only two breaks. These were for breakfast in a motel and lunch in the Sparkford Inn, which I could not pass as it was obviously named after the Sparkford Vale Harriers and harriers were depicted on the sign. One of the local Masters had suggested that I might find suitable accommodation for the horses with Mr Peter Over at Yawlings Farm, Holditch, near Chard, and this was duly arranged, with a caravan nearby provided for Heather. Terence, Sheila and I stayed at the little Yarcombe Inn on the opposite side of Chard which we knew and liked having often used it when visiting our daughter Charlotte at Millfield School.

For the first day of the holiday I had arranged to go with the **Mendip Farmers' Foxhounds** at Burrington Farm, in Burrington. I went on my own, of course, as Terence and Sheila had not yet arrived. I left the stables at eight-thirty and when I drew near to the meet I saw other people unboxing in a quarry so did the same. The Master and huntsman, Tony Younghusband, made me very welcome and invited me to ride up with him and hounds. The first fox went to ground quickly but was soon bolted and gave us a very fast hunt before going to ground in an embankment which was too deep to dig. We had several more exciting little hunts during which I was very struck by the Master's uncanny control of his hounds. At one time we were on top of a hill and I had a wonderful view of Wales, the Bristol Channel and two Mediterranean-blue lakes. Another very memorable part of the day was when hounds hunted into a deep gorge similar and parallel to the Cheddar Gorge and they kept leaving the line to cross over to the other side of the gorge in answer to the echo of their own cry. This situation was a nightmare for the Master and huntsman as when he blew or called for hounds the same thing happened and they would want to go to the echoes, the sounds being repeated three or four times. Having seen the huntsman grappling with this unusual problem, it made me realise yet again the educational value of these visits as it gave me a chance to see difficulties overcome which I could never have experienced at home. When the Master at last got all his hounds together again, he very sensibly blew for home and we hacked back to the meet.

**Taunton Vale Harriers** *Meet at Hopkins Farm, Halse (near Taunton), 11 February 1993. Master and Huntsman, the late John Roffe-Silvester, being offered a drink by the host, Charles Burrough, while whipper-in Tony Pipe approaches on the grey.*

Photograph kindly loaned by Mrs K Hill

When I got back to the Yarcombe Inn, Terence and Sheila were there having had a more trying journey than they had anticipated. Terence had decided to drive through the middle of London as it was a Saturday, unaware that there was an international rugby match at Twickenham. They had become completely held up in the traffic jams and had taken much longer to drive through London than they would have done going round it. After a day's rest on Sunday, the Monday morning could not have been more gloomy for our visit to the **Taunton Vale Harriers** (Mon 20 Mar). It was overcast and pouring with rain as we parked in the yard of the Catherine Wheel at Hemyock. Terence and I went into the pub where there were a few farmers and foot-followers. When no other mounted follower came in we thought we ought to venture out and found the Master, Mr Roffe-Sylvester, sitting on a piebald horse in the yard with his lovely West Country harriers all around him. The Master, who later became a great friend, was wearing a raincoat over his Hunt coat and although the welcome was genuine the pleasantries were kept to a minimum as the pouring rain was even heavier than before.

Almost as soon as we left the village, a fox was found and hounds went away at a great pace, soon disappearing from view with us galloping hell-for-leather along roads and forest tracks. There was little traffic which was just as well as the field never slowed up in the slightest when galloping over a crossroads. We came up to hounds as they were marking at an earth near a glider airfield, not far from Dunkeswell. This had been a hunt of six and a half miles, very fast and mostly on roads, but quite terrifying as we were going up and down the hills at the same speed – i.e. a full canter. I was pleased to have been there and felt very privileged to have seen Michael Roffe-Sylvester hunting his hounds as this was to be his last day doing so after twenty-three seasons. During the day I admired his horn-blowing abilities and later learned that his son had just won the Horse and Hound Ball hunting horn competition. After returning our horses to the stable and Heather's care we drove back to the Yarcombe Inn feeling very wet and tired but happy,

**Taunton Vale Harriers** *William Roffe-Silvester, Huntsman, with hounds in the Blackdown Hills, 1997/98 season.*

Photograph kindly loaned by Mr Peter Hurman

**West Somerset Vale.** *Meet at Clayland Corner. Master and Huntsman, Terry Chidgey, taking hounds to draw.*
Photograph kindly donated by Mrs G Dodgson

and found Sheila comfortably sitting by the fireside with her knitting, dry, warm and equally happy.

The weather had improved considerably by the next day when we joined the **West Somerset Vale Foxhounds** at the Old Mill House, Over Stowey, near Taunton (Tues 21 Mar). The Master and huntsman, Terry Chidgey, made us feel very welcome as did our hosts who were very generous with the whisky and introduced us to the lady Field Master. She was very interested to hear about the Easton and told us that she was brought up in the Banwell Harriers country. The field numbered about twenty-five and were very smartly turned out. The amateur whip was a fabulous character, a real old horse-coper type and was whipping-in single-handed as the kennel huntsman had broken his leg in three places. Hounds found and went down a very steep place which frightened me and terrified Shamara who twice lost her nerve and stopped still, shaking with fear. When we reached the bottom, both hounds and Master had disappeared and the whole field hacked about the roads for five miles until we came across the Master but he had also lost hounds. Eventually we were reunited with them and we drew the edge of the Quantocks which gave an added bonus of being able to enjoy wonderful views.

My little bay mare, Shamara, was a hard little sort and could do the most incredible amount of work but had one bad fault in that she would sometimes take hold and virtually run away quite out of control. When hounds found their second fox and went away at a great pace she was in one of her "going" moods and bore off down a steep and narrow track which crossed the hillside from top to bottom. She put down her head and just went and my greatest worry was that she would be unable at this pace to negotiate the bends and would pitch over the edge into the trees below. After just managing to negotiate the first two bends I saw to my horror that a sawn-off tree protruded a foot or so over the already very narrow track. Being unable to stop or steer the inevitable happened and the tree struck my leg, catapaulting me off the other side, down the steep drop into some trees below. These knocked off my hat and cut my head. With blood pouring from the wound I climbed back up to the track where Terence had retrieved Shamara. I managed to finish the day with blood matting in my hair and staining my green coat from which it never recovered. I wrote up this day in the bar of the Yarcombe Inn between listening to Sheila's hilarious stories of the chambermaid who did her room and who had three sons called Dirk,

**West Somerset Vale:** ***"Happy Landing …luckily"***

Dean and Darren. We had invited Peter and Yvonne Over to join us for dinner and the Yarcombe Inn provided an excellent dinner which rounded off the day in the best fashion.

On the following day we thought we would enjoy a change of quarry so we went with the **Tiverton Staghounds** who were meeting at Bampton, near Tiverton (Wed 22 Mar). I was particularly keen to go as I would then have hunted with all four surviving stag packs in the country, as well as with the Norfolk Staghounds which by that time had been wound up. We left the stables at eight-thirty and made such good time that we stopped for breakfast at a cafe near Tiverton, but arrived in Bampton to find that no-one could tell us where the meet was. After going into the Post Office and the shop, and stopping several likely-looking people on the pavement we were no further forward. Everyone was most helpful but just said that there were several places where they met around Bampton but they had no idea where it was on this particular day. Eventually a man hacking through the village told us where to unbox, and others arrived to unbox at the same place so we followed them to the meet which was a lawn meet at a house behind the Exeter Inn. I was told that our host liked to harbour deer in his wood, encouraging them to stay with such methods as putting salt licks in the wood. He was very keen that they should hunt a deer which was easily recognisable because it had only one horn, but it could not be found so they settled for a two-year-old. Six couple of tufters sorted out which deer to hunt and they were allowed to hunt the two-year-old away.

We galloped over this beautiful country, all grass and gently rolling in most places so that we could really kick on for a mile or so at a time. It seemed such a shame that the six couple of tufters had to be stopped as they were hunting so beautifully but when after ten minutes the main pack had not come up, the Master let them hunt on again for another quarter of an hour. Then they were stopped again and this time the main pack did come up but as soon as they settled they took the line into some woodland. The deer twisted in and out of this wood, often within view of either the field or the car-followers which caused much frenzied holloaing and shouting. This unnecessary noise got hounds' heads up and there was a serious check of approximately an hour, after which they settled to the line again and hunted it right back the way we had come until it came to bay in a pond quite near to where it was found.

After a quarter of an hour's rest the deer was just about to leave the pond when most of the pack started to hunt a fresh deer. These were eventually stopped and brought back and about twenty minutes after the deer had left the pond hounds were laid on the line and hunted it well until it finally came to bay again in the River Exe where it was shot. Terence and I asked some people to hold our horses and climbed down to the river edge to watch the kill and see them open up the deer. We were offered the highly-prized liver but we declined, not knowing how to get it back to our base without soaking the pockets of our hunt coats with blood. Declining this highly-prized delicacy caused an embarassing situation because the onlookers assumed that the strangers had refused to take the liver because we were squeamish of the spectacle. Of course, as is always the case, the more we protested our innocence, the more they were convinced of our squeamishness, encouraging us to take it by saying how delicious it was, and so on. This situation ended when the Master presented Terence and me with a slot each.

The Master and hunt servants were very smartly turned out and well mounted but most of the field looked rather scruffy. Amongst the field there was a lady who was very interested that we came from the Easton Harriers as they had had in the Tiverton pack two harriers, Easton Herod and Hero, in about 1959 or 1960 and she said they had gone very well with the staghounds.

In the evening Terence, Sheila and I went to dine with John and Elizabeth Graham at Lower Bagmore near Bradninch and, appropriately, we ate venison and drank the most beautiful red wine from John's friend, Jean Cruise, who not only owns a large vineyard but is a Master of deerhounds in France. During dinner, not surprisingly, the conversation was mostly of deer-hunting and in particular my amazement at how long hounds could be held up on the line, even for an hour or so, and hunt on again with no apparent loss of scent. This was such a contrast to hare-hunting in a plough country where scent lasts for only a matter of a few minutes. This first class dinner party was a fitting end to a most enjoyable day and three tired but very happy people arrived back at Yarcombe Inn at one o'clock.

There was a considerable delay in leaving the stables next morning as when Terence led his horse out of the stable to be loaded up he noticed that it had pulled a tendon, a fact that Heather had missed. Luckily for Terence (but unluckily for Heather) she was to have come with us on this day so a third horse was already plaited and ready and it was just a case of changing saddles. By the time Terence had given exact instructions of what treatment he wanted her to give the tendon it was much later than we had intended when we finally left. We were therefore quite late arriving at Mount Pleasant, near Hooke, where the **Cattistock Foxhounds** were meeting (Thurs 23 Mar), but a foot follower told us where to find hounds. They drew for an hour or so and then got into plenty of foxes and a brace were put to ground quite quickly. I was asked to go on point and was very interested to see roe and fallow deer leaving covert. I was also most impressed by how rock steady these hounds were to deer and I often saw them cross the deer lines with only the slightest pause, and then continue drawing for their fox. When they found and ran to the far end of the covert I made the classic mistake of the inexperienced foxhunter and left my point too soon. When I reached the far end of the wood they were leaving from the point I had recently abandoned – most embarassing for a Master who, of course, is supposed to know better unless he could be excused on the score of his green, harrier, coat. On the other hand, and especially in this area, it was frequently mistaken for a Heythrop coat which only compounded the error. After this hunt, Terence and I were soon the only ones left in the field due perhaps to the weather which had been high winds, sleet, hail and thunder mixed with sunny spells. Despite this, the Master, Charles Stirling, decided to draw again. I viewed a fox away from a stick heap which gave us a large circular hunt over lovely country and part of a Point-to-Point course until scent eventually failed. Hacking back to the meet, the Master told me that he kept an enormous number of hounds, putting on about twenty-two couples of young entry each season and keeping about sixty couples of hounds in kennel. He hunted the country three days a week with eight horses. The field was very noticeably superior to others we had recently seen and were nearly all mounted on quality hunters. We said our goodbyes at five-fifteen and arrived back at the stables at six-thirty.

**Cattistock.** *Meet at Wraxall Manor, 1978. The Master and Huntsman Mr Charles Stirling.*
Kindly supplied by George Pinney

Due to pressure of work Terence could not stay at Yarcombe until the end of the week and so he and Sheila left in his car for home on the following day (Fri 24 Mar) dropping me off at the stables on the way so that I could be reunited with the horsebox which from now on would be my only transport. I took two horses to the blacksmith and visited Bowyers of Chard where they made new carts and sold all sorts of horse and pony driving harness. I was back to the Overs in time for a bread-and-cheese lunch and then drove the lorry to Mr Roffe-Sylvester's Reaphay Farm at West Buckland, near Wellington, to take up an invitation given on the Taunton Vale day to see all the hounds kennelled there. He not only kennelled his own private pack of foxhounds, but also the Taunton Vale Harriers of which he was a Master, the Beacon Beagles of which he was a past Master, and the Culmstock Otterhounds – over a hundred couples in all. They were looked after by David Allibone, an incredible character who made light of such work that in most kennels would have needed at least three men. His casual approach to all this work gave the impression of one who dropped in for a couple of hours a day to look after a pair of terriers. I have never seen a man who did so much work look as though he was doing nothing. I watched open-mouthed as Michael drew by name not only his own hounds but ones from the other packs as well, while reeling off the pedigrees out of his own head. I was taken indoors to meet his wife Brigid whom I thought a most charming lady who told me that her father was a doctor from Doddington in the Fens so she felt she had a connection with East Anglia. Tea by a huge log fire was quickly followed by copious gins and time just flew by as I listened to fantastic stories of hunting in this area. It was quite late when I forced myself to leave this fascinating company and drive the lorry back to Yarcombe Inn.

Once again I was able to finish a holiday on a high note, this time with the **Cotley Harriers** at the Cotley Inn, near Chard (Sat 25 Mar), and was able to repay Peter Over's hospitality by lending him Shamara for the day. The Cotley are, I would think, the most famous pack of West Country Harriers and have been under the Mastership of the Eames family for successive generations since 1850. What more appropriate meet for us strangers than the Cotley Inn with the famous Cotley hound called Mover for its sign? I had been taken down to the Cotley Inn the night before by Peter to meet some of the Cotley members and met John Eames who whips in to his cousin, Vivian Eames, who hunts the hounds for his father, the well-known Master, Colonel Eames. The whole atmosphere of this pub was hunting and if the locals were not playing skittles in the alley at the back they were talking hunting. Another great character was pointed out to me as being famous for his ability to come every evening to the pub, and immediately win enough from the fruit machine to pay for his beer all evening.

**Cotley Harriers** *Master and Huntsman DVD Eames M.H. His father Lt. Col. RFP Eames M.H. on foot.*

Photograph kindly loaned by TVD Eames M.H.

We unboxed at Red Post and hacked down to the meet where Colonel Eames made us very welcome, introducing us to his son Vivian. The hounds were just as smart as I had anticipated, all level and all of the same type with lovely necks and shoulders, and, of course, all lemon-and-white, standing some two inches higher than Stud-Book Harriers at about twenty-two or twenty-three inches at the shoulder. There were about sixty mounted followers who were mostly turned out very well, and standing at the meet I had the impression that this was definitely a superior hunt. However, I was not impressed with the way they drew Bere Wood as they tended to follow one another in Indian file, instead of fanning out over the draw. Moreover, they were not above speaking to the odd deer line now and again and – dare I say it – even to the line of a ginger cat I had seen creeping through the covert. But when they found the first fox all the slight imperfections of drawing paled into insignificance as they went away over this delightful country, which was all grass with mostly jumpable hedges which are always known as fences to the old brigade. The cry was outstanding and different from any I had ever heard before or since. That glorious sound re-echoes in my ears as I write.

The first two foxes gave us ten-to-fifteen minute hunts and then went to ground. These were sharp hunts with a lovely line of country to cross which was often on high ground so we could see and hear hounds below us, and had to kick on to keep with them. Peter and I got ourselves into the Field Master's bad books by jumping a gate whilst hounds were drawing for the third fox (a sin I condemn thoroughly and heartily when Master in my own country) but worse was to follow. Our adrenalin was running and I think the horses felt the same because, as the next fox went away, Shamara heard that glorious cry and, as she had done a few days before with me, just took off with Peter. He was see-sawing on the reins but the old mare, with her nose just above her knees, went flying down a hill towards a gate. I sat and watched in horror as I saw the Master going to the same gate at a collected canter, while the old mare was bearing down behind him to the same spot. They both reached the gate at the same moment. The Master's chosen position over the centre of the

**Cotley Harriers:** ***"I shall strip him of his hunt buttons at the end of this run"***

gate was quickly changed to one over the gate post as Shamara collided with him in mid-air. Somehow both horses managed to keep on their feet but the rebound of the collision caused both horses to take different directions on landing which was, perhaps, fortunate. For the next hour or so, I was quite sure my "horse was tired" and kept well to the back of the field and well out of the way of all hunt officials. During this fun-packed day we had again experienced every kind of weather, very cold, sunny and warm, with hail and rain, and the day ended in the best possible way by us all getting together again in the Cotley Inn, where I was persuaded to play skittles and, of course, lost to the gentleman with a sore leg, which went a little way to compensate for the old mare's nasty habits.

On the following day, I returned home to Suffolk after having enjoyed yet another trip. It had been a particularly successful one with hunting on every possible day except the Friday when no packs had been going. In many ways, however, this could be seen as the best day of them all, as my visit to Michael Roffe-Sylvester's farm was the beginning of yet another long and intimate friendship with the whole family, to rank alongside my other hunting friends made on these trips, the Plumbes, the Bacons, the Loys and a host of others.

I had now hunted with another two packs of harriers, making a total of twenty-two, with only three to go as the Eryri had become foxhounds in 1976 and the Clifton Foot had become beagles in 1978. In the meantime, however, I had also managed to hunt with thirteen French packs and thirty-nine other English packs. These included twenty-four packs of foxhounds, five of beagles, three of otterhounds, and one each of bassets and bloodhounds, but, most signficantly perhaps, all the surviving four staghound packs, as well as the Norwich Staghounds which had by now been disbanded.

**Mr Sinclair's Harriers** *These West Country harriers were a private pack and are no longer in existence. The Wensleydale Harriers were bred from a foundation stock from this hunt. Donald Sinclair was the Thirsk vet who was Siegfried Farnon made famous in "All Creatures Great & Small". When the height of the walls or barbed wire stopped his horse, he would dismount and caontinue on foot - his horse would wait where he left it until his return.*

Photograph kindly loaned by Giles Thompson

# MAP 4

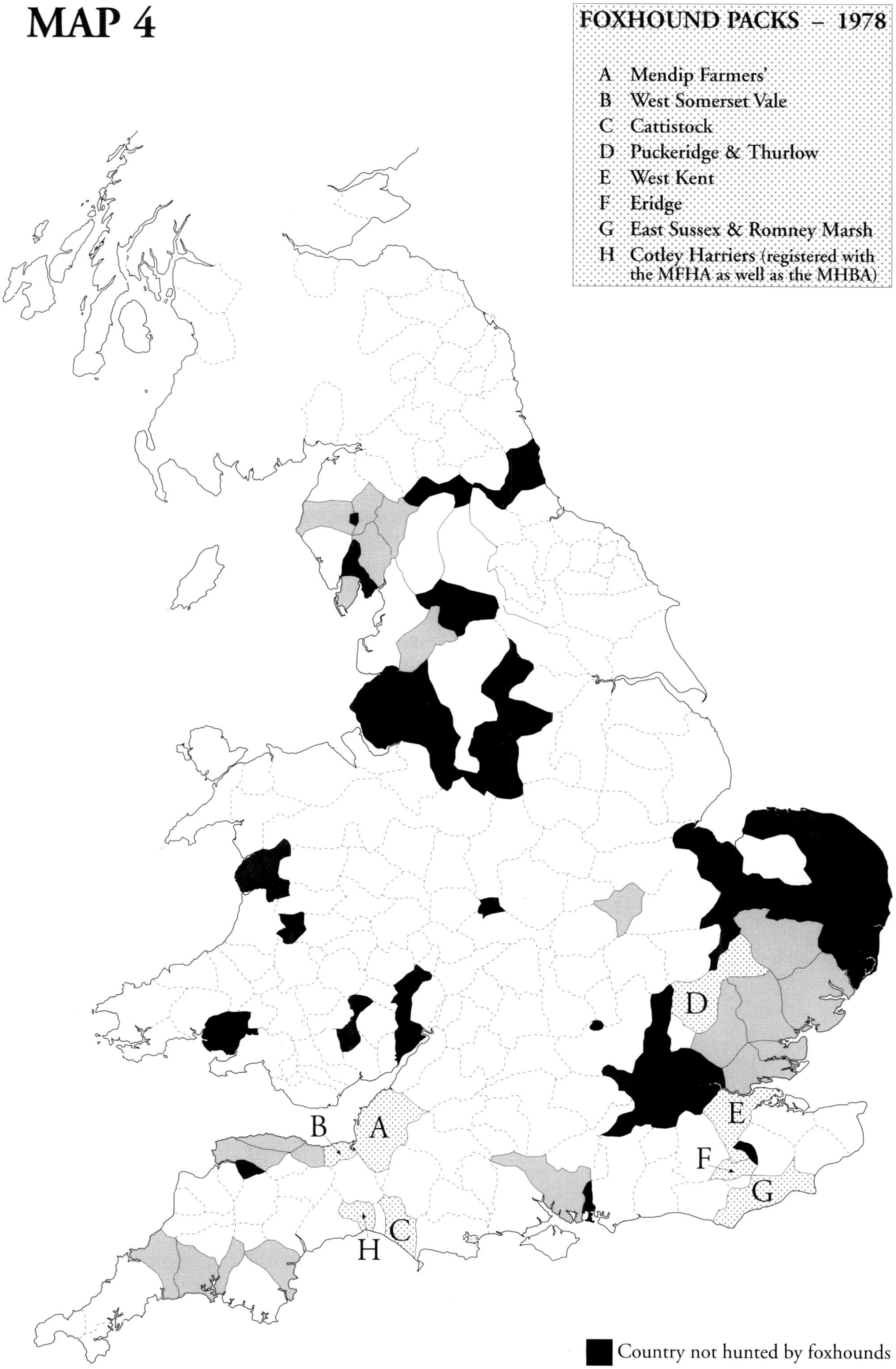
FOXHOUND PACKS – 1978
A Mendip Farmers'
B West Somerset Vale
C Cattistock
D Puckeridge & Thurlow
E West Kent
F Eridge
G East Sussex & Romney Marsh
H Cotley Harriers (registered with the MFHA as well as the MHBA)
A
B
C
D
E
F
G
H
Country not hunted by foxhounds

# Chapter 6

## Kent and North Devon

With the assurance that we would stop in her favourite hotel, I persuaded my wife to accompany me on a little mid-week jolly at the beginning of the next season. We had arranged with John Graham and Eric Furness, the Master of the Peak Bloodhounds, to meet them at the **Westerby Basset Hounds** meet at Wistow and to spend an evening afterwards in the Haycock Hotel at Wansford (Tues 7 Nov 1978). This turned out to be a non-starter as we naturally went to the village of Wistow in Leicestershire, but when we got there no-one had heard anything about a bassethound meet. Not to be outdone I quickly looked through Baily's Hunting Directory and telephoned the Trinity Foot kennels. I thought we could make their meet at Milton but was again unsuccessful. Wondering if we had come on completely the wrong day, we carried out the rest of the plan and went to the Haycock hoping to meet John and Eric. They duly arrived and I found out that the Wistow advertised referred to the name of a house twenty-five miles from the village of the same name.

We had a most enjoyable evening with John and Eric, both of whom were on top form, and the evening seemed far too short as we listened to tales from them both. One I recall was of Eric's early days with his bloodhounds who hunt "the clean boot" which means just a human being with no artificial scents such as are used in draghunting. The whole world is full of prospective quarry for bloodhounds, so it becomes a matter of the utmost importance that they are *de change*, which means that they will not change from one line to another. For example if the scent of the runner, Fred, becomes too faint they must not change to Sam with a stronger scent who had just happened to be walking that way! In his early days Eric's hounds were not always perfect in this respect and there is a story of them changing lines and taking a line across some marshes where the dykes were too wide for his horse to jump. By the time he had got himself round *via* the marsh tracks, hounds had long gone. When he eventually found them, they had a terrified, white-faced, marshman at bay with his back to a post, waving his spade at the baying hounds.

**Per Ardua Beagles.** *Meet at Car Colston, c. 1976. Left to right, Bill Pell, Myra Escombe (whippers-in), Leslie Levis, Tony Fillingham, Peter Gifkins (Joint Masters), Nick Thompson and Dick Giles.*
Photograph kindly loaned by Mr & Mrs W Pell

Another good story remembered from that night is of a certain gentleman, a pillar of society alive today, who was a Justice of the Peace. This gentleman also happened to be very fond of his gamecocks and the illegal sport of cockfighting. A main (a cockfight) was to be held in his area one evening, which he would certainly have attended if he had not been too ill. This turned out for the best as the police got wind of the arrangements and raided the barn. They arrested all who were there and the criminals were eventually brought before the Bench. As they filed into court, they all recognised the magistrate sitting with grave demeanour on the bench and one or two were remiss enough to wish him good morning. It must have been quite a test of his self-control to impassively listen to the evidence against all his friends and, when summing up, to deliver a sharp reprimand for their shameful behaviour.

The conversation of either of my dinner companions would have been sufficient for a whole evening's entertainment, and it was with aching ribs that I eventually went to bed feeling that, if the day had been wasted, the evening certainly had not been.

When I awoke the next morning in my four-poster bed it seemed a shame to go home having had no hunting at all, so I looked through Baily's and found that the **Per Ardua Beagles** hunted on Wednesdays and were within reasonable reach. Sheila was not desperately keen on the idea but agreed to it as she knew how disappointed I had been to miss the sport the day before. I had been friends with Air Commodore Leslie Levis, a past Master of the Per Ardua, for many years through meetings of the Masters of Harriers and Beagles Association. He was well-known to all hare-hunters as the first Keeper of the Map, appointed by the Masters of Harriers and Beagles Association to record all hunt country boundaries, produce a map of them, and then keep it up to date in order to settle all boundary disputes, a position he held for many years.

On the way we called to see the Fernie Foxhounds who were meeting at Carlton Curlieu. There were about eighty mounted but I was surprised to find that were not quite up to the standard I had expected. We drove on to the beagle meet at the Durham Ox, at Orston in Nottinghamshire, and arrived in time for a glass of beer and a cheese roll (Wed 8 Nov 1978). To quote from Baily's, "The pack was formed in 1951 under the auspices of the RAF Beagling Association to encourage beagling in the RAF, which relinquished them on April 30th 1977". Their unusual name comes from the RAF motto, "Per Ardua Ad Astra". The morning was as hot as early summer. As we arrived I was immediately greeted by Leslie and he introduced me to his wife and to the current Master, Tony Fillingham.

Hounds hunted as well as they possibly could in these dreadfully hot conditions, and persevered on very faint lines. The ground was rock hard and the sun so hot that they did well to hunt at all. The Master did the very best thing in just letting them alone to feather along on the poor scent. Hares were as scarce here as they were at that time in the Easton country. One of my principal memories is of the skill shown by Leslie in being in exactly the right place at the right time to hold up traffic on a main road while hounds hunted over it, not only once but twice, but sadly the day was chiefly memorable for the fact that this was the first time I had seen anti-hunt demonstrators in action. Fortunately they were not very effective as they had telephoned to say that they were coming. The police turned up and cruised around so the antis did not get out of their red van.

**Puckeridge.** *View of Huntsman, Ron Quarmby, cubhunting between Carlton and Brinkley, near Burrough Green.*

Photograph kindly donated by Mrs P D Thomas

Two weeks later the visiting bug was still biting so I decided to have a day with the **Puckeridge and Thurlow Foxhounds** who were meeting at Burrough Green, near Newmarket, which was within easy reach of my home (Mon 20 Nov 1978). This would be particularly interesting as it would be my first experience of a local pack amalgamation as in 1970 the Newmarket and Thurlow Foxhounds had amalgamated with the Puckeridge, an event which had caused much talk. One of the joint-Masters, Captain Charlie Barclay, greeted me warmly and immediately invited me to ride up with his huntsman, a gesture which I always appreciated to the full. Captain Barclay was well-known to all in the hunting world as his family had been Masters of the Puckeridge since 1896 and is generally acknowledged the most knowledgable plough-country huntsman in the country. His was not the only friendly face at the meet as I renewed my acquaintance with many old friends, including Liz Mitchell, Paul Rackham and Jerry Hudson.

Every day's hunting is a good one but some are better than others and this one was to be on the lower end of the scale as yet again there was a very poor, almost nonexistent, scent. From my privileged position I really felt for the huntsman as he tried his best with the foxes not pressed in any way, and consequently twisting and turning more like my beloved hares, and seeming often to be able to get to ground. The terriers bolted a brace from one earth, one of which appeared right under my horse's nose which caused much prancing and snorting. Conditions were so very unfavourable that there was little hunting and, although I stopped out until hounds went home in the hope of an afternoon hunt, it was not to be.

Three weeks later I was off to Kent for a short jolly which had been planned on the high seas the previous May during a cruise on the P&O liner *Uganda*. Sheila and I had gone with Stanley and Kathleen Tompkins and Maurice and Sue Scott and quite soon we met Georgie Fotherinham-Parker, who lived in Kent and who I quickly found out was a keen foxhunter. She and her husband Philip were the greatest fun and the upshot was that after a few drinks one evening I plucked up the courage to ask her if she would put up Stanley and I for a hunting jolly. She was enthusiastic and we made plans for the following winter. There were no stables at her home so she made arrangements for our horses to be stabled at the home of a friend of hers, Michael Gilby, at Hastings, while we stayed with her. This holiday was a new departure for me as it was the first on which I did not intend to hunt with any harrier pack at all. I now had a second ambition which was to hunt with every foxhound pack south of the Thames.

On Monday 11 December (1978) Stanley picked me up at ten o'clock and we called at the Easton kennels to pick up my horse. We travelled along peacefully until we got into Kent and saw a lady frantically waving a red flag on the roadside at Watlingford. It was Georgie, literally flagging us down, and she had been waiting to escort us to Michael's stables, and then back to her home at Kings Bank Farm, at Beckley. She had invited Michael to dinner to meet us and we all enjoyed an excellent meal which was faithfully recorded in my diary – fish pate, pheasant, and raspberry fool, all served with the finest wines. After dinner, amidst protests from Philip, Georgie insisted on taking us upstairs to show us a whole cabinet full of trophies, over three hundred in all, won by Philip in rally-driving all over the world. How typically modest it was of this lovely couple to keep these trophies upstairs and not on display in the sitting room as they would be in most houses.

We experienced an unaccustomed luxury on our first day as, after a superb breakfast, we were driven by car to the meet of the **West Kent Foxhounds**, at Harden Farm, Penshurst (Tues 12 Dec 1978) while Michael took our horses, with his own and Georgie's, to the meet in his pukka new horsebox. This was one of the long ones with a kitchen department at the front, which he used mostly in his other hobby which was competition driving with a team of horses. The heavy rain had just stopped when we arrived at the meet and Georgie introduced us to our hostess, Diana Clatterbourn, and to the Master, Tim Lyle. He made us most welcome and took us to meet Stan Luckhurst, his huntsman, whom we both agreed had an excellent voice and his horn-blowing was a pleasure to hear. It was just as well that we had the pleasure of listening to his horn and voice as it was not until three o'clock that hounds found. We then had a sharp run but were mostly galloping on roads until we came across a splendid old character, the sort one usually only sees in pictures or reads about in books. He was a rough old farmer out shepherding on his cob, riding in Wellington boots and a cloth cap, who decided to join the sport. He took charge of the field and piloted us expertly across his own and his neighbours' farms, galloping ahead on his grey cob. The country was really beautiful, lovely rolling pastures with plenty of reasonably low post-and-rail fences. I can see the sight again in my mind's eye of our unerring pilot who, although seeming at times to go away from hounds, always kept us in touch with them. He led us over a really lovely succession of rails and fences, never out of sound of hounds, only slowing up occasionally to go down steep places, which were very slippery after the heavy rain.

Unfortunately, our fox went to ground and, as it was in the Old Surrey and Burstow country, it was left there. We hacked back into the West Kent country where, due to the excessive wet, we were again restricted to galloping on roads. This did not appeal to us and so we hacked back to the meet with our hostess Diana, and discovered that we had a shared interest as she was also a keen driving lady and had a Welsh Cob stallion. As there had been a heavy storm of rain and hail on the way back, we were quite wet through, and were again very glad of that luxury of going home in Georgie's car, leaving our horses at the meet.

**The West Kent:** ***"The pilot"***

That evening we enjoyed a few pre-dinner drinks with Georgie and Philip before we all went to dine with Georgie's friends the Holmes' who lived at Saddlescombe. We enjoyed smoked salmon and prawn cornets, Chateaubriand steaks, and fudge cheese-cakes. Immediately after finishing our meal we went to the home of Derek Howard, the Master of the Romney Marsh and East Sussex Foxhounds who we were shortly to hunt with, where we had coffee and liqueurs. Stanley partook quite freely of the Glayva whisky, and kept referring to Gloria, instead of Georgie, much to the amusement of the rest of us, especially Georgie. The change of name was still being used when we bid her goodnight and I could hear her chuckling as I went upstairs.

**West Kent.** *Meet at Hever Castle, 1978. Huntsman Stan Luckhurst (right) and Richard Clemonson, amateur whip (left).*
Photograph kindly donated by Stan Luckhurst

For the second morning running we were chauffeur-driven as Michael had again agreed to bring our horses to the meet of the **Eridge Foxhounds** at The Cock Robin at Wadhurst (Wed 13 Dec 1978). Georgie did not want to hunt for a second day running so Philip drove us in his car. He was in the middle of a story about one of his rallying days over the infamous Wrynose and Hard Knott passes when he collided with another car at a crossroads. It was not a serious bump, just enough to cause a certain amount of amusement and leg-pulling for several days. Inside the pub we met the Master, Rodney Benstead, and his Joint-Master Mrs Schicht. The huntsman was John Cooke who I was to meet again in 1981 when he was huntsman with the South Wold in Lincolnshire. Michael's groom hacked our horses down to the meet and as soon as hounds started to draw we were away on an old fox. They hunted with a lovely cry but after half an hour changed to deer and the next hour was spent stopping them off deer which seemed to be everywhere. When all hounds were together again we drew Eridge Park during which we came to a very deep ditch with sticky clay in the bottom. I sat watching as the horses in front of me went down into the bottom of it and then struggled up the other side. I could imagine shoes being sucked off and, looking round, decided that, although the ditch was pretty wide, if I went along a hundred yards or so, I could jump from bank to bank. This I did and soon discovered the foolishness of not following the natives' example.

Mickey jumped splendidly and in midair I felt proud of him but, when he landed, it was one stride and then into an awful bog. He sank down completely up to the flaps of the saddle and I pitched forward onto his neck, then rolled off into the slime and was immediately blinded as my eyes were full of filth. I could only grope about with my hands and listen to Mickey struggling next to me. By the time my hands found a root I was in up to my waist and it was sheer fear that gave me the strength to pull myself out. Once I had my eyes cleared I could see the sickening sight of poor Mickey who had given up struggling and just lay there, looking sad and resigned. Luckily lots of people came to help the foolish stranger and, after joining many stirrup leathers together, I crawled across and put them round Mickey's neck. With about ten people pulling on the straps and me thrashing Mickey with my whip, he made a great effort and managed to get out. He stood there shaking every limb in his body with the black slime running off him.

I was also beginning to shake with cold but climbed aboard, manfully saying that I was going to carry on. However, I soon realised the impossibility of this, for not only was I getting very cold but I could not keep on Mickey because of the slime on my saddle

**Eridge.** *From the meet at the Rose & Crown, Mayfield, 1978. Left to right, Bill Swift (amateur whip), John Goodes (First Whip), John Cooke (Huntsman) and Rodney Benstead (served for 23 years).*
Kindly supplied by Rex Coleman

**The Eridge:** ***"Up to our ears in it... Always keep with the locals!"***

and clothes. I jumped a small gate, landed sitting behind the saddle and promptly fell off; and next jumped a tiger-trap, landed in front of the saddle clinging round his neck and again slid off. Stanley insisted that I went back to the box and it was necessary to jump the same two obstacles again to get to the road but I managed to stay on. Just to put a final touch to my miseries, a terrible hail storm blew up and within minutes the ground was white with hailstones. The wind tore small boughs from the trees which hit our horses and lightning struck a large tree only a few hundred yards from us and split it from top to bottom. After what we guessed to be about five miles, the box at last came into sight. As a Master, I had always been rather scathing about large, fancy boxes at meets as they took up so much room, but had to eat my words because I was so grateful for the kitchen department in Michael's. Stanley lit the gas, made me coffee and heated up soup. We waited quite a long while for Michael to return but when he did he invited two girls into the box for drinks. He did give me a large whisky which warmed me up a bit and telephoned Georgie and arranged to meet at a certain crossroads. When we got there, however, we had an hour's wait as Georgie was sitting on one side of the crossroads and Michael on the other and none of us realised it. It really had not been my day, and when we eventually got home I was very glad to get into a hot bath.

We had all been invited to an Eridge Social Evening, and I was disappointed when Stanley and Georgie decided that they did not feel like going and would have a quiet night at home. The system was so shocked by this "quiet night at home" that I awoke to find that I had a stomach upset. Georgie dosed me with Slippery Elm which is a type of milk drink similar to Ovaltine but made from the bark of elm trees. This worked and, although it was back to normal procedure in the morning, as we had to take our own horses, Philip drove ahead of us to show us the way to Michael's where we picked up our horses and then went on to Cripps Corner. Here we unboxed and hacked down to the Cross Inn, Staple Cross, where the **East Sussex and Romney Marsh Foxhounds** were meeting (Thurs 14 Dec 1978). Hounds were late arriving as their Land Rover had broken down so there was time for a few port-and-brandies to back up the benefits of the Slippery Elm.

Leaving the meet we drew Chitcombe and although scent was not good there was plenty of slow houndwork, most of which I missed because Mrs Jackson, one of the Joint-Masters, was not a very experienced Field Master. We lost hounds for over an hour but found them again as they were marking at an earth. This fox was despatched and I was given the brush by Derek Howard, Joint-Master and huntsman, whom we had met on the Tuesday evening. We then enjoyed a good run which took us into the dark, but just as hounds had their fox hard-pushed, sadly they changed to deer. The kennel huntsman managed to stop most of them and I then whipped-in to the Master as, leaving his kennel huntsman to bring on the few hounds still hunting deer, he hacked back along a main road. He went as short a distance as possible as by now it was really dark and quite dangerous with the traffic speeding past us. He stopped at the first place he knew he would be welcome to stay safely with the hounds while someone went to fetch the hound-lorry. Berdie, the Master's young wife, led Stanley's horse while a car follower drove him to fetch our lorry. When all horses and hounds were loaded we went into the house for tea and there was a marvellous atmosphere with the kitchen full of happy foxhunters, earth-stoppers, terrier-men and car-followers.

In the evening Stanley and I took Georgie, Philip and Michael to dinner at the Mermaid in Rye where we enjoyed a delicious dinner of soup, cod, Romney Marsh lamb which was outstanding, and finished with Stilton. Bottles of Pouilly-Fume and Chateau Latour were enjoyed with the appropriate courses and, after coffee and brandy, we all went home for a nightcap and then to bed feeling deliciously mellow. On Friday morning Georgie gave us a treat by bringing us tea in bed at seven o'clock, but we were packed and downstairs by eight o'clock. Sadly we could not stay longer as duty was calling and I had to be home to hunt the harriers on Saturday. Philip drove us to Michael's where our lorry was ready, the horses loaded, and we said our goodbyes to these charming people who had given us such a lovely holiday. What a lucky cruise it was that caused us to meet the Fotheringham-Parkers, and subsequently to have all this fun. As we drove home I realised how right Jorrocks was when he said, "Show me a foxhunter, and I know him instantly as a friend".

It had become a habit for Colin Plumbe to have an annual hunting holiday in Suffolk but when he arrived in February 1979 every mounted meet had been frozen off. We rang the Master of the **Mid-Essex Beagles**, Miss Phoebe Angus, and was delighted to find that she was hunting, although she had put the meet back to twelve o'clock (Wed 7 Feb 1979). We arrived at the Admiral Rodney pub at Little Barrow with an hour to spare which naturally was spent in the pub and the time sped by as there were several good friends there. The Master arrived and, before she had even opened the hound-van door, apologised to me for her hounds being old-fashioned. When she let them out, Colin and I were totally amazed as they were one of the best-looking packs we had ever seen. They were all level and had the same light tan and white colouring. They looked as if they had all been made from the same mould and I later found out that they were all descended from three bitches. To watch them draw for Miss Angus was sheer joy as she had only to change direction herself and the whole pack would do so too. We were spellbound as she drew a large field six times changing direction with military precision as hounds went backward and forward until she had covered the whole field. She did not once blow her horn or have any help from a whipper-in. These splendid hounds gave us two and a half hours of first-class venerie over lovely water-meadows and were shown off to perfection as scent was poor and every inch had to be thoroughly hunted.

On our return to the meet, hounds were "all on" (i.e. they were all present) so I was surprised to see Miss Angus insist on being shut up in the van with hounds. No-one else seemed to think this at all odd, but I could not contain my curiousity so went close to the van and looked in through the window to see her sitting in the middle of hounds with a list in her hand checking off each hound as she identified it. As I was saying goodnight to her, I saw a Fairy Liquid bottle on her seat so I asked what it was for.

"Oh," she replied, "it's full of water and if hounds start to wrangle in the van, I squirt them like a water-pistol. It works wonderfully well."

After another two weeks of disruption by frost, snow prevented any hunting with the Easton Harriers so Mary Garton and I decided to go to see the **Norfolk Beagles** who were meeting at Lodge Farm, Castle Acre (near Swaffham) (22 Feb 1979). This was an ideal opportunity to hunt with this private pack as they only went out on Thursdays (which was an Easton day) because the Master and huntsman, John Austen, and his wife Sarah, hunted with the West Norfolk Foxhounds on Saturdays.

I called at Dereham on the way, dropping off a wheel for repair at the workshop of John Gap, a wheelwright. The snow was piled eight feet high on the sides of the roads and we were unable to get all the way to the meet but as we could see hounds feet-marks in the snow we abandoned the pick-up and followed them, eventually catching up with John Austen with his hounds. John had perfect control of them and was hunting them totally alone as there would have been no field except for us. He could even stop them when a fresh hare jumped up and put them back on the line of the hunted hare using only his voice which I would not have thought possible. His hounds were the best drafts from the Bolbrooke Beagles and were very steady, persevering gallantly in these dreadful conditions. Sarah Austen was following in a van wherever possible, and had her young baby in a carrycot in the back. This early introduction to hunting obviously worked as the young lady has since become a very keen follower of hounds. It was a shame that conditions were not better as I had the feeling that here was hare-hunting at its best but I realised that if conditions had been any better I would have been hunting my own hounds.

To finish a very busy season of visiting, I went away again in the spring but this time the jolly was very different to all the others as, instead of having the

# MAP 5

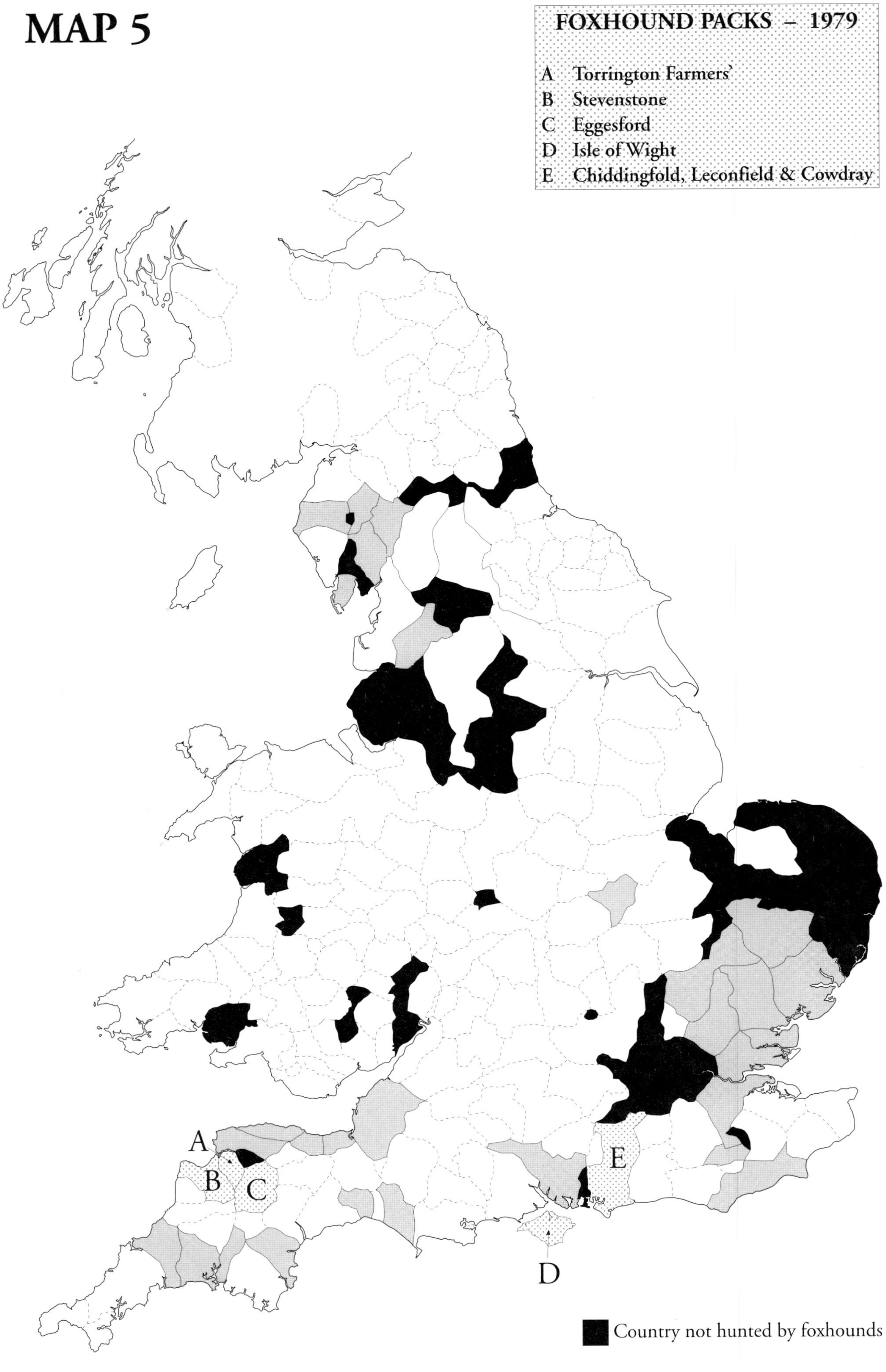
FOXHOUND PACKS – 1979
A Torrington Farmers'
B Stevenstone
C Eggesford
D Isle of Wight
E Chiddingfold, Leconfield & Cowdray
A
B
C
D
E
Country not hunted by foxhounds

company of another man, I went with my daughter Bridget, my friend Sue Gooderham and her three children, Mary-Jane, Lucy (who did not ride) and Jonathan. I was going to the West Country for the fourth time as, although my previous trips had enabled me to hunt with most of the packs in the south and mid part of the area, I still had several more to cover. Again this was to be an all-foxhound jolly but, although I was exceptionally lucky to catch two visiting packs, I also hunted with some packs I had already been with – the Exmoor, twice (which I had been with in 1971), and the West Somerset Vale by mistake (which I had been with the previous year). An opportunity to stay in North Devon came through Sue who mentioned to me that her mother had some friends who had self-catering holiday accommodation and also some stables. The idea was followed through and accommodation for ourselves and horses was booked with Mr and Mrs Ferguson at Middle Lea Farm at Berrynarbor, just outside Ilfracombe. The original plan was for Sheila to do the cooking for both families and for Sue to do my horse and supervise the equine side of the holiday but this was foiled by the illness and death of my grandmother. As my grandfather, aged ninety-two, could not be left on his own, Sheila volunteered to stay at home and look after him (the lesser of the two evils, perhaps!). The reviewed arrangements were for Bridget and I to go down with the lorry, while Sue and her children came by car, and we left home at four o'clock in the morning of Saturday 31 March. We were overtaken and flagged down for a cup of tea in a cafe by the Gooderhams at about three o'clock and arrived at Middle Lea Farm at four o'clock in the afternoon.

As I could not do my own horse and Sue would have to do all the cooking, I tried to do as much as I possibly could. As recorded in my diary, my daily routine was as follows. I woke Bridget up at seven o'clock and gave her breakfast so she could look after her pony, then cleaned all the boots and made up sandwiches (both cheese and bacon). After breakfast I looked to the dilapidated old lorry, filling it with oil and water (a daily requirement as it used a lot of oil and the radiator leaked) and starting it to warm up the engine. I then dropped the ramp and opened the partitions, ready for when the others brought their horses out. I did all the driving to the meets and back and, after hunting, I washed off all the girths, martingale straps, stirrup leathers and boots under the tap in the yard (a cold job on some evenings), and rubbed the boots dry with a cloth. I then went next door to use the Fergusons' telephone to make arrangements for the next day's hunting and to work out the route with either the Master's advice or the Fergusons'. In the meantime, Sue would supervise the cleaning and feeding of the horses, and cook our supper which we ate all together in their ground-floor flat. After supper, which was usually at eight-thirty, Sue and I usually went up to the Globe for a night-cap. Bridget and I had the first-floor of a pair of flats converted from old farm buildings. The "stables" turned out to be rather makeshift, and Mickey and Henry were in two converted bullock boxes, while the Gooderham's Robin and Jess were in the tennis pavilion.

On Sunday we drove onto Exmoor to show the children the moor and walked up to Dunkery Beacon before having lunch in the Black Venus at Challacombe. We then drove through Exford so that I could show them where I had stayed before at the Crown, and also where the stables were, and Rita's digs, but before leaving Exford they insisted that we bought them a Devon cream tea.

For our first day I decided to go with the **Chiddingfold and Leconfield Foxhounds** who had come west from Surrey to meet at the Fox and Hounds at Eggesford by invitation of the Eggesford Foxhounds (Mon 2 Apr 1979). Sue decided not to ride and kindly lent me her superb little hunter Robin and I set off with Bridget, Mary-Jane and Johnny. There was driving snow all the way to the meet and the visiting pack were late coming, a combination of events which left us sitting on our horses for a long time, very cold and fed up. When they did arrive the Master looked about as cheery as the weather, and glared at us all as if we had caused the snow to blow. Mr Barlow had been Master and huntsman of these hounds for many seasons and I had been looking forward to seeing them in the field but I was very disappointed with them as they went with little drive and seemed to get no encouragement from their huntsman. There was some woodland hunting and we went round and round the same tracks for an hour or so. Bridget caused the only excitement of the day when she persuaded us to take a different route. We jumped a couple of banks and then she fell off when Mickey got into some wire. We went home at three o'clock.

The next day there was another opportunity too good to miss as the Torrington Farmers' Foxhounds had invited the **Isle of Wight Foxhounds** to meet in their country at St Giles in the Wood (Tues 3 Apr 1979). This was particularly lucky as it would have been extremely difficult for me to have hunted with them in their own country as this would have entailed transporting a horse over to the island. Bridget, Mary-Jane and I arrived at the meet in good time and selected a downhill parking position where I could get a running start as the lorry battery was running down. I was surprised to see Colonel Mitchell from the Hambledon at the meet and during conversation he told me that he had made the arrangments for the Isle of Wight to be there. Mr Kingswell was Master and huntsman and his hounds looked very well. They drew thoroughly and hunted their fox along wooded combes with the field riding along above them. The sides of the combes were so steep that at times we could ride to the edge and look right down on top of their backs as they ran through the trees below us. Scent was not good and they had to work at it, but persevered, and if the riding was not very exciting, the lovely views and the cry of hounds rising up from below us made for a most enjoyable day. During the day I had met Mr Morrish, the Master of the Torrington Farmers' (the host pack), and we hit it off immediately. The children were rather cold so we went back to the box at three-thirty, and then went into Torrington for diesel and groceries. On the way home the lorry engine began cutting out at times which was very alarming on the steep hills but we managed to get home.

**Isle of Wight.** *Mr John Kingswell with hounds in 1979.*

Photograph kindly donated

On Wednesday Bridget and Mary-Jane volunteered to stay at the farm with Lucy, and Sue and Johnny came with me to the **Stevenstone Foxhounds** meet at Burford Cross, near Clovelly (Wed 4 Apr 1979). Sue took her Land Rover into Barnstaple for repairs and Johnny and I followed in the lorry to pick her up before going on to the meet. Colonel Elliot, the Honorary Secretary, took our caps and was amused that we should meet on the third concurrent day as he had been out with the Chiddingfold and Leconfield and with the Isle of Wight. The car followers were very generous and we were offered drinks and eats from the car boots at the meet. Frank Sumner, the Master and huntsman, had given me some old foxhounds for my drag hunt seventeen years earlier when he had been Joint-Master of the West Warwickshire Foxhounds, so we had plenty of catching up to do. I was pleased to be out with him as he was retiring at the end of the season. His hounds just sat around him and stared up adoringly at him, and when it was time to move off he said to them, "Are you ready, kids?".

Scent was poor but his hounds tried very hard and persevered and showed as much sport as was possible. Charlie, my horse, got stuck in a boggy place right in front of a bank so he could not jump it and I had to go a long way round, but I did manage to jump it later on in the day from the other side where there was a firm takeoff. There were only six other people out mounted, beside ourselves. Sue was very pleased with her son Johnny who was riding a young pony and had it performing well over the very varied obstacles. Hounds took a line into a large forestry plantation at three-fifteen so we decided that this would be a good moment to call it a day.

The following day I had great difficulty in finding the **Eggesford Foxhounds** who were meeting at Looseton Cross, near Wingfield (Thurs 5 Apr 1978) and arrived slightly late. There were only four others mounted other than Bridget, Johnny, Mary-Jane and myself, one of whom introduced himself as Desmond Isaac, and he kindly took it upon himself to look after us all day. The professional huntsman, Frank Heseltine, had a wonderful voice and was first-class on the horn. Both he and the amateur whipper-in were well-mounted and went across country with ease. For the last two hours there was only ourselves and Mr Isaac, and when our Welsh Cob, Henry, ridden by Johnny, refused to jump a hedge with a sheet of tin in the bottom he was obliging enough to jump off before I could do so myself and get behind him with his whip to make him go over. Mr Isaac persuaded the huntsman to draw a small cover and he found at once and we had a great hunt back into Staffords which was a large covert we had drawn earlier. This run was extremely enjoyable as there was only us in the field and we had our personal pilot to lead us across country. I tried hard to buy his mare which was rather plain but was a very good performer. Before going home I made a final top offer of £900 but he declined, saying that he would have a job to replace her. Three very tired and happy young people arrived back at Middle Lea Farm at six o'clock.

Although I had already hunted with the **Exmoor Foxhounds** in 1971, there were no other packs going on this Friday and it was a pleasure to be able to hunt more than once with this pack. They were meeting at Blue Gate, near Simonsbath (Fri 6 Apr 1978) and Mary-Jane and Johnny came with me. We left the farm at nine-thirty and arrived at the meet at ten-thirty, to be told that the meet was at twelve o'clock, not eleven as we had expected. Twenty minutes later the message came that Captain Wallace's train was delayed at Reading so the meet was to be put back to one o'clock. This delay gave us the opportunity, however, to notice a change in the habits of one of our horses, Mickey, who until this time had constantly pawed in impatience at the floor of the box, even while on the move, but did not do so on this day and stood quietly. I assumed that the four consecutive days' hunting had at least had this good effect on him. What was more important, perhaps, was that he never did it again either. I had the words of a new song in my pocket so I used the time to learn it while the children amused themselves planning various routes with the map.

Once the Master had arrived there was no delay in moving off and a fox was found at once which took us down a very steep place. The children were very nervous and had to be persuaded to come down. This caused a delay and we were rather left behind when I heard hounds turning back along the valley. Johnny and I tucked in just behind Captain Wallace and we had the Exmoor hounds virtually to ourselves for ten minutes when we were joined by Johnny O'Shea, huntsman to the East Essex Foxhounds, and his lady Master. I jumped down to move three very newly-born lambs which were in a gateway and too young to move of their own accord, so we were left behind again. Luckily, hounds checked for a little while which enabled us to get on terms once more and enjoy a fast run almost to Exford. This run was very alarming, as it was the first time we had crossed the moor at such a speed. Not only were we often going down steep and dangerous paths but we crossed the rough moor at such a gallop that our mounts were often almost down on their knees as they stumbled into holes and over rocks. Compared with ours, the local horses seemed to cross the moor with apparent ease as naturally they were accustomed to avoiding the obstacles. During this run, Johnny's pony shied violently and collided with an old gent who shouted at him, "Damn you child, why don't you learn to steer?"

Captain Wallace lived up to his reputation. When, only occasionally, he blew for his hounds, they flew to him, and his casts were always successful. He took the earliest opportunity to come across and thank me for moving the lambs which I thought was just the kind of attention to detail which had made him such an outstanding Master. The children had gone very well, once over their early apprehension, and the day could not have been better for us visitors. The sun sparkled on the remains of snowdrifts in some places and this enhanced the incredible beauty of the moor. Hounds often ran past herds of ponies which took little interest apart from just moving out of the way. Before boxing up we washed our horses' legs by riding them into the river opposite the hotel in Simonsbath and finally left at six o'clock with the children very tired and visibly fading before my eyes. We arrived back at the farm to be greeted by a very anxious Sue.

It was the Pony Club meet of the **Torrington Farmers' Foxhounds** on the Saturday and Bridget and Mary-Jane came with me to the meet at Weare Giffard (Sat 7 Apr 1979). We unboxed on top of a hill overlooking the village and there were several children out. When hounds arrived, ten minutes late, I went to watch them unload and it gave me quite a surprise to see that there were three horses in the back half of the lorry partitioned from hounds with only a low gate approximately three feet high. I would not dare to do such a thing as my harriers have been known to get over the partitions in my box which are five feet high.

We were unfortunately on the wrong side of a large covert as hounds went away, and had a long ride down a very slippery hill to catch up so we were well out of the first run. After a long gallop on roads, we were rewarded by seeing, ahead of us on the hillside, the hunted fox coming back towards us looking very tired. We were right in the guinea seats for a while until, just short of Bideford, the fox crossed a river and a main road together and hounds were stopped. Bridget had been left behind in this hunt but was quite jubilant when she caught up as she had enjoyed a private hunt with one hound speaking all along the line we had recently come along – probably an old hound which could not "run up". We had one more hunt, all of which was galloping on roads, as so much of the country was drilled with wheat, but decided to go home at two-thirty as we were fed up with the roadwork. In the evening we went to dinner with our hosts, George and

**Torrington Farmers'.** *Master Mr Henry Mannish with hounds at Harracott, November 1997.*

Photograph kindly loaned by Sue Barker

Jean Ferguson, and Sue's mother at the Black Venus at Challacombe and enjoyed a pleasant dinner with plenty of laughing as the children were on top form and were telling jokes which were most unsuitable for grandmothers.

We had a second day with the **Exmoor Foxhounds** on the Monday from their meet at Broad Mead Gate, near Challacombe (Mon 9 Apr 1979) and all of us (except Lucy, who did not ride) turned out. Unfortunately, we had rather a disappointing day, with thick mist to start with, coupled with foxes that went to ground quite quickly. During the day there was one particularly steep and dangerous place. I can picture it still – at first it was just steep, then got far worse. There was no turning back as the path was too narrow and it was so steep that it was difficult to remain in the saddle. In some places there was only one possible place for the horses to put their feet, and if they missed the mark there was a drop of a hundred feet or more. Matters got more dangerous as when the horses ahead of us reached the bottom they kicked on up the other side which caused our horses to lose concentration as they were inclined to watch the horses galloping up the other side. Sue was really scared and made me promise that I would not lead her or her children down anything like that ever again.

Ronnie Wallace called me up to speak to him and I was caused much embarassment as I was riding Mickey, my little cob, who just could not stand still. The wretched little horse kept backing and twisting round, several times cannoning into the Captain's horse. This made me feel such an idiot and an even more hopeless rider than I am. Bridget had her moment of glory when she followed the Captain over some bogs where the rest of us turned back, my horse having gone into it up to his knees, and I was out of touch with the hunt for over half-an-hour. During this time she was hunting with only the Captain, a whipper-in and another lady follower, and at one point the Captain sent her to stop some hounds from running heel-way. When she got home she got her full measure of fun by telling everyone that she had enjoyed a hunt almost alone with hounds having left her father in a bog. At three o'clock we were very wet and cold and the children were tired so we went back to the box.

I had been fortunate in that my last two holidays had ended with really excellent days but unhappily this good luck was not to continue. Our day with the **West Somerset Vale Foxhounds** from Aisholt Common near Bishop's Lydeard (in the Quantocks) was one of those days when nothing went right (Tues 10 Apr 1979). My first mistake was forgetting that I had already been with these hounds so I wasted an opportunity to chalk up another fresh pack. Secondly, the meet was an awfully long way in thick fog. We then drew for one and a half hours before hounds found, only to discover that there was no scent. There was heavy rain and we were wet through to the skin so we boxed up at two-thirty. The fog was even worse on our way back, and we had a horrendous journey. The only bright spot of the day was when we were asking for the meet and a

**The Exmoor:** ***"It's not like this in Suffolk!"***

man told us to turn up by the reservoir, saying, "You'll know that because it's full of water."

It was a disappointing last day but nevertheless it had been a good holiday and I had added another five foxhound packs to my list. The total was now thirty-two and, as I had hunted with another three beagle packs as well, my total was seventy-two English packs in total. The holiday was most memorable for the astonishing work put in by the little cob Mickey who hunted nine days out of the ten. This feat was remembered and commented on four years later when I was down that way again.

**North Dartmoor Beagles.** *Meet at Bowden Farm, Moretonhampstead, 1988. Left to right, Martin Whitley (whipper-in), Tim Whitley (Master and Huntsman), Harvey Paulger (whipper-in).*
Photograph kindly loaned by Mrs B A Fox-Ledger

# Chapter 7

## The Unplanned Jolly

The following summer Judith, my middle daughter, went to "au pair" in France and as I had to take her to the ferry at Southampton I decided to combine the journey with some minkhunting in the West Country. This sport had just been begun to take the place of otterhunting which had been stopped in January 1978. Charles Corner, ex-Master of the Eastern Counties Otterhounds, agreed to come with me and, although we had difficulty in getting petrol and breakfast in Southampton, we eventually saw her safely onto the ferry. Charles had telephoned the Master of the Culmstock Hunt, Norman Bartlett, who was a friend of his from the real otter-hunting days, and found out that they were hunting on the following morning (Wednesday 15 Aug). I then telephoned the Master of the neighbouring Ytene Minkhounds who, although he was not due to hunt on the Wednesday, offered to put on a special meet for us at seven o'clock in the evening. With this double treat in store, we still had all the rest of Tuesday to fill in so we decided to do a "recce" and find where the Culmstock meet was. We then drove to the Yarcombe Inn for a bar lunch and a few beers and all the wonderful memories of our previous visits there reminded me of Michael Roffe-Sylvester.

"How would you like to see four packs of hounds with over a hundred couples all kennelled on one farm?" I asked Charles.

The answer was inevitable and as we drove into the yard at Reaphay, Michael was just finishing a repair to the petrol tank on his flesh-waggon. I introduced Charles and Michael just looked at his watch and said, "Five o'clock. Time for drinks." It was just one tremendous party from then until one-thirty in the morning. Before it got dark he showed us all the hounds, and Charles was as impressed as I had been on my first visit. Michael and his charming wife Brigid insisted that we stayed the night with them and at nine o'clock took us into Taunton for a first class dinner in a French-style restaurant. On the way home, our road was blocked by a fire-engine attending a fire at a roadside house, and with never a thought of the breathaliser, Michael wound down his window to talk to the policeman on duty. We were told that we could not possibly go to bed without a nightcap, and we all enjoyed a very good brandy in front of the log fire.

Now, there are many types of log fire, but very few people, I suspect, have sat in front of one like this. Michael did not believe in wasting energy on cutting up logs and he considered that the length of the pieces of wood was of no importance. Michael always seemed to have his priorities right and filled our glasses with brandy, before he set about making up the fire which had burned low. As each piece was sticking out into the room by various lengths from six to twelve feet, this involved simply pushing each piece of wood further into the fire. To make the ends that were in the actual fire criss-cross each other in order to burn nicely, each long log protruded across the floor in different directions. The end result of this was that at least one log lay between each chair and this necessitated careful footwork which of course had become second nature to our hosts.

The huge fireplace was situated across one end of a long room which had a very homely feel about it. There was an abundance of furniture which, although I am no expert, was clearly of great age and value, all of which was treated in the same casual way as everything else. I should always count that evening amongst my most treasured memories of my hunting tours, as the Roffe-Sylvesters must be ranked as two of the greatest characters I have ever been privileged to meet. We sat and listened to his tales of when, considerably younger, he had hunted his own foxhounds and his harriers two days a week each, also hunting his beagles in the afternoon when home from foxhunting, all this fitted in between milking a herd of cows by hand, morning and night. He also gave us an insight into how early he and his brother had started to hunt hounds with a story that although his father was a rector he allowed the boys to hunt on Sundays, with a strict proviso that he could not hear hounds while he was in church. This condition sometimes was not met and he would complain bitterly to the boys that he had completely lost concentration during his sermon. What pure pleasure and joy it was to listen to real people, living characters, with absolutely no inhibitions, telling stories, often with a joke against themselves. Michael was in the middle of a tale when his wife Brigid came back into the room, saying, "Michael, Michael, darling," which fell on deaf ears until the tale was finished.

"Michael, Michael, darling. A most tiresome thing has happened. I've just been up to the bedroom to turn down dear Charles' bed and the ceiling has fallen down into the bed."

This was not allowed to mar the evening and two of the happiest men in the world went to bed at one-thirty and a mere "tiresome ceiling" did nothing to reduce our exhileration.

I awoke to hear one hundred couples of hounds singing in kennel and went to the window just in time to see them all passing under me on their way to the Grass Yard. It was without the slightest trace of a hangover, although we had consumed a great deal of alcohol, that I went down to sit in front of the house and write up my diary within sight of the kennels with the morning sun shining on me. Still feeling exhilerated from the pleasure of the evening's experiences, I wrote until Brigid called me in for an excellent breakfast.

**Culmstock Hunt.** *Meet at the Old Malt Scoop, Lapford, Devon, 5 August 1985. Left to right, Derek Hampson, Norman W Bartlett MH, Derek Myhill and Edmund Scott.*

Norman Bartlett, who had been Master of the **Culmstock Hunt** for over twenty years, was pleased to see us at his meet at Surridge Farm, Bathealton, near Wiveliscombe (Wed 15 Aug 1979). He introduced us to Bonjo Allen who, if my memory serves me right, was our host. Charles also renewed his acquaintance with another otter-hunting friend, Mrs Molly van de Kiste, who was President of the Courtenay Tracey Otter Hounds Club. Mr Bartlett and Mrs van de Kiste were well-known and greatly respected by all who follow hounds along the riverbank. The pack consisted of both woolly otterhounds and some Dumfriesshire Foxhounds. I had been told before that all otterhound masters like to have a few foxhounds hunting with them, as the otterhounds love to dwell on the scent and are lacking in drive. The combination of the drive of the foxhounds pushing on, and the water-hunting instincts of the otterhounds is the best choice. They drew the River Tone downstream for an hour before finding, then had a very exciting hunt of one hour and ten minutes during which the mink went to ground under a rock. He was soon moved and after about another half-hour went "to ground" again under a thick bramble bush where he would have been left but for an old foxhound who returned to the bush and marked very strongly. Once he was moved from the bush, we had a long hunt downstream with all hounds speaking beautifully as they swam, eventually killing the mink in midstream. This had been a most exciting hunt, with great cry from both the otterhounds and the foxhounds.

While drawing for the next mink, I saw two good, straight holly sticks in a hedge, ideal for making driving whips and as – shamefully – neither Charles nor I had a knife on us, we set about cutting these off with two slates found on the ground. This was much to the amusement of our host who, being impressed by our efforts, insisted that we went into the house for tea before leaving. The next hunt was most enjoyable, in spite of the heavy rain, and, having got thoroughly wet, we decided to accept our host's kind hospitality. After two stiff whiskies and a plateful of scones, we set off for the Ytene meet with the car-heater full on to dry ourselves off.

**Ytene.** *Meet at White House, Stourpaine, Dorset, 1979 or 1980. Huntsman Ian Arnott (right) and the late Jack Robins, whipper-in (left).*

Photograph kindly loaned by Bob Tucker MH

We arrived with just enough time for a quick glass of beer and a sandwich in the Martyrs, at Tolpuddle, before going to the meet at Moor Lane House, Briantspuddle, in Dorset. This was one of the placenames which had to be changed from -piddle to -puddle to avoid offending Queen Victoria when she passed through the area in a train. The **Ytene Minkhounds** had been formed the previous year in order to hunt mink in the country formerly hunted by the Courtenay Tracey Otter

Hounds. At the meet the members were very friendly but, as time was against us, we moved off quickly and drew the River Piddle downstream (also called the River Trent). Hounds found quickly and we saw a very difficult and twisty hunt. At one point, after swimming underwater, the mink popped out of the water for a breath right in front of the huntsman who was wading in midstream. This mink eventually went into some roots where it was given best as it was quite dusk.

Back at the meet, our host brought out large whiskies for everyone as we stood under the light over his porch. After our glasses were refilled, he persuaded the Masters to sing and I was drawn in to also give a song. The whole spectacle was quite amusing as for all the world we resembled carol-singers, standing in half-circle with the light shining on everyone's face. After saying our goodbyes to our host, who was highly amused and had recorded the whole thing, we adjourned to the Martyrs for sandwiches and a beer and were joined by Ian Arnott, the Master, and Molly van der Kiste. We eventually left at eleven o'clock to drive home to Suffolk. We took it in turns to drive until we came to London where I let Charles take over as I had no idea of the way through the city. We were having great difficulty keeping awake, so we stopped for coffee in London and arrived home at six o'clock in the morning.

I was getting very keen to hunt with as many different packs as possible and had started to shade in the hunts I had been with on my map of foxhunting countries. This highlighted the ones that it would be possible for me to do from home and, as a result, I had a day with the **Oakley Foxhounds** during the following season. I was especially looking forward to the day having seen the wonderful brand new kennels during our interviews for a new kennel huntsman in 1975, and I was hoping that hounds and the sport would be of the same high standard. I left home at six-twenty, picked up my horse from the kennels and was away smartly at seven o'clock, arriving at the meet at Harrold with a half-hour to spare (Tues 8 Jan 1980). While I was speaking to the Secretary about the meet I looked up "Harold" in my road atlas and the first place I looked at was right in the middle of London. I immediately asked him how they managed to hunt there and he said that I must be looking at the wrong Harold. The Master, Martin Lee, arrived with hounds and both he and his hunt servants were very smartly turned out, but I thought the field were rather scruffy and did him no credit. We drew Harrold Park blank, then found in some kale and I had the pleasure of viewing him away. I thought the hounds appeared to be very slack, and committed the greatest sin in my book which was to make no effort to cast themselves at all. However, they did run in some woods for a little while, but eventually I was so bored that I went back to the box at two-thirty.

However, the ambition to hunt with every harrier pack was still foremost in my mind, so I decided that, as I was taking Charlotte back to school at Glastonbury in January 1980, I would try to hunt with the Weston and Banwell Harriers. I telephoned one of the Joint-Masters, Mr Fear, and explained the situation, asking if he knew where I could hire a horse for the day but he very kindly offered me one of his own, a most generous gesture to a complete stranger. Sheila and I dropped Charlotte off at school at four-fifteen on the Sunday afternoon and arrived at the Yarcombe Inn at five-fifteen (Sun 13 Jan 1980). There were no hounds out on the Monday so went to visit the Roffe-Sylvesters and all four of us went out for a pub lunch. Just before we left, the local farrier telephoned to say that, while he had been shoeing a horse, it had reared up and killed itself by hitting its head on a beam in the roof. He wanted to know whether Michael would come to remove the corpse which was being a great inconvenience. During lunch I met one of Michael's old friends, Charles Hooley, a larger-than-life character who kept us in stitches of laughter. Lunch was such fun that I invited the three of them for dinner that evening at a restaurant to be recommended by them.

After lunch we went to the Weston and Banwell kennels to meet the Master who showed us round the lovely old buildings. His hounds, I thought, were rather rough but his stables and his horses were very good. We bathed and changed at the Yarcombe Inn then went to Reaphay (the Roffe-Sylvesters') for pre-dinner drinks and then on to the Castle Hotel in Taunton. Charles Hooley drove us all from Reaphay and we enjoyed a delicious dinner but I received quite a shock when the bill came. It was really my own fault as I had ordered very expensive wines and rather more than I needed to have done but this bill was nothing compared with the next expensive experience. It had rained and this had frozen on the roads to just a sheet of ice and, with sleet blowing, driving conditions were terrible. When we left Reaphay for the return journey we managed to get up the first few hills but when we came to a very steep one, the Volvo just stopped on the way up with the wheels spinning. There was nothing I could do except turn round but when I backed round the car slipped into the wall behind. Then I came forward and did the same to the front. When at last I was going downhill, even with the engine idling in first gear, the car started to glide sideways. I was completely helpless as touching the brakes would have made matters worse. There was a sickening crunch, and my side of the car nestled up to the stone wall.

As I could not get out, I asked Sheila to get out and push. She said that she could not so I said that we would have to sit there until morning and hope that there was enough petrol to keep the heater going. As is typical with most wives, the weather, the ice, the uselessness of the car, the amount of wine I had ordered, in fact everything, was all my fault and with a last cutting remark she braved the sleet. With the hidden strength the fair sex have when really angry, she pushed the car back onto the road and I found a route back to Yarcombe via Honiton without any steep hills. We arrived back at one-thirty.

**Weston and Banwell.** *Meet at the Red Cow, Brent Knoll, Nov. 1979. The Joint-Masters Gordon Jones and Jeff Fear to left and right, respectively, and Mrs Dianne Jones, whipper-in, in the middle.*
Photograph kindly loaned by Mrs M Dommett

In the light of dawn the car looked a very sorry mess, with front, back and side all well dented by the stone walls. With no hunting it was Sheila's turn to choose the entertainment which inevitably consisted of a shopping tour in Honiton. After the expensive day before I could have done without this, but she has always been a prudent shopper and she did not buy much.

A cheerful crowd greeted us next day at the **Weston and Banwell Harriers'** meet at the Knoll Inn, Brent Knoll, with most people inside the pub and that special atmosphere which seems to go with harrier packs (Wed 16 Jan 1980). There was still ice and snow on the ground and as it was very cold I had extra clothes on which made my hunt coat tighter than usual. To ease the situation, I handed my wallet to Sheila but a man said, "I shouldn't do that if I were you. You'll probably need it for tractor money to pull you out."

Sheila was terribly worried about this remark but I said, "Don't worry, the locals usually try to frighten strangers with these sort of remarks." I could not have been more wrong, as I later discovered. This flat Somerset country was all grass, divided by very wide dykes, some with hedges as well. The water table is high so that the dykes are full up to within about a foot of the top and as there is often a covering of green weed this could have confused the horses into trying to walk onto the water, a terrifying

**The Weston and Banwell Harriers:** ***"A little help is worth a lot of pity, when in you're in a rhyne"***

prospect for a stranger. Having been brought up in a ditch country I was firmly convinced that there was not a ditch I would ever be nervous of. I was also of the opinion that I would always much prefer my own horses. I was wrong on both counts as I was really scared of the wide dykes and was deeply grateful for the loan of the Master's sensible strong hunter who knew this country well.

There was little cover on these Somerset Levels so the Master was drawing the hedges and when it was necessary to jump the first dyke and hedge, his horse fell in and needed a tractor to pull it out. Not only were the dykes so very wide, but the banks were boggy so if a horse landed on the edge it broke and let him back into the water. In all five horses were pulled out of dykes by tractors during the day. The field, although not the smartest I have ever seen, were great goers, galloping at formidable places with such enthusiasm and often jumping awful places when they could easily have opened a gate. We were driving home to Suffolk that afternoon so I had to leave at three o'clock. They had not found by that time but, while I was loading up my horse, I was told that they had then found and were running well. I think very few hunting people could ever imagine a mounted field riding across such a formidable country in which, if you are brave enough and mounted on a very bold horse, there is nothing to stop you for miles as there is no wire to be seen. I have never jumped anything so wide or scary before or since, and shall always be grateful to Mr Fear for lending me his good old horse. Driving home I felt very lucky not to have taken a ducking. This was my twenty-third harrier pack and there were now only the Ross (in Herefordshire) and the High Peak (in Derbyshire) to go. However, it was the Easton which was mostly on my mind as I drove home. Their next meet was to be at Debenham and I was looking forward particularly to hunting my hounds that day as it would be a milestone day. It would be the seven hundredth time I had hunted them.

At the end of the season 1979-80 I decided not to go away for the by now traditional end-of-season jolly as my horses were very "jarred", a Suffolk expression. They had been worked hard as the season was an extremely good scenting one and furthermore we had hunted sixty-two days, losing only two for bad weather. However, Sheila and I were again going down to the West Country to visit Charlotte at her school and so I decided to have a day's beagling, ducking out of my immediate parental responsiblities by asking Sheila to drop me off at the meet of the **Chilmark Beagles** before going to the school. The meet was at the kennels at South Down which was very close to the school in Glastonbury (Sat 22 Mar 1980). As we had set off from Suffolk that morning, I was grateful that the meet was at twelve o'clock rather than the normal eleven o'clock, but nevertheless we arrived half an hour late, despite having left home at five-thirty.

Hounds had just moved off and as I caught up I was hailed by Mrs Buchanan from Norfolk. She told me hounds had been late moving off and she had overheard the Master, Alan Hughes, saying that he was waiting for someone called Tony Harvey from Suffolk. There were also some faces I recognised from the Sproughton Foot Beagles. I picked a moment during a long check when I thought it appropriate to apologise for being late, but was told quite sharply that this was *not* the moment, and I came away feeling like a little schoolboy who had been told off in front of the whole class. I climbed up to some high ground and saw some very pretty houndwork. From this vantage point, I could often see the hare as well as the hounds, and witnessed her fresh-found four times. It is extremely rare for this to happen and was possible because the scent was exactly as I like it for perfect hare-hunting, just enough scent for hounds to be able to stick to her line but not good enough to run quickly, thus giving her plenty of time to double and twist and enough confidence to clap down, thus enabling hounds to fresh-find. Ninety-five percent of this hunt was below us and in full view as she ran up the opposite hill, then turned back down and ran along the valley for a while before again turning up and then down the hillside. I wrote in my diary that this must be one of the most perfect places from which to watch beagles working, and would have been the most perfect day to teach someone about venerie. What a shame it could not have been filmed. There must be so very few times when a camera could have been in one place for ninety-five percent of a single hunt. There was a large field out, approximately a hundred and fifty people, as it was the morning after their Ball (after which it is a point of honour to be at the meet the next morning). Following this memorable hunt, the large field were scattered everywhere which spoiled the rest of the day and must have been very frustrating for the huntsman as the next hare was constantly headed by people spread all over the draw. I admired the style of the huntsman and he had his hounds in excellent control and let them persevere on this catchy scent.

I had arranged for Sheila to pick me up at two-thirty as she was far from well and was feeling pretty groggy, so I did not wish to be late. We drove to Yarcombe Inn with Charlotte who was staying out of school until the Sunday evening, and settled in for the rest of the weekend. Continuing the policy of trying to hunt wherever I went, I had put my hunting clothes and boots in the car so before dinner I tried to arrange for a few days. I sat on the stairs with a heap of tenpence pieces and Baily's Hunting Directory, using the payphone to try to find packs that were still hunting, combined with an Honorary Secretary who could tell where I could hire a horse. This proved very difficult for although packs were still hunting, no-one knew of horses to hire. I had twice been back to the bar, both for double gin-and-tonics to sustain my flagging hopes and for more coins when about the ninth or tenth Honorary Secretary said that his hounds (the Portman Foxhounds) were hunting and that it might be worth trying a Mr Ralph Coakes. He gave me his address and Directory Enquiries gave me his number and I was soon speaking to Mr Coakes. He readily agreed, not only to bring a horse for me to the meet, but also to hunt himself.

**Warwickshire.** *Meet at Upton House, c. 1978. Left to right, Sir Charles Smith Ryland (ex-MFH), K R Motion (Jt Master), Major R Dill (ex-MFH), S V Lambert (Jt Master), Lord Bearsted (ex-MFH and owner of Upton House), Major S Cayzer (ex-MFH) and Miss Boultec-Brooks (ex-MFH), and Clarence Webster (Huntsman).*

Photograph kindly donated by Mr K R Motion

I left Yarcombe Inn at nine-forty-five in pouring rain and sleet. All the rivers were over their banks as I drove the seventy-five miles to the meet of the **Portman Foxhounds** at Nineacres Lodge, Holtwood (Mon 24 Mar 1980). This was the home of Mr Mitchell and I arrived at eleven-thirty with fifteen minutes in hand. I found Mr Coakes, who was a very jolly sort of man and very easy to get on with, and soon realised that he was the owner of the world-famous Stroller and father of Marion who had ridden Stroller into showjumping history and the hearts of a nation. Mr Hugh Dalgety, the Master, welcomed me and said that he wished I had visited earlier in the season as it was now very "end-of-seasonish". He drew for two hours, then had a woodland hunt with the fox not wanting to leave a large wood. There was a Miss Large in the field who was riding an exact double of Shamara, one of my hunters, so much so that I am sure if she had been put in Shamara's stable my grooms would have got her ready for hunting and never have known that it was not Shamara. We boxed up at four o'clock and I got back to Yarcombe for a welcome hot bath as the day had been one of torrential rain. After getting out of the bath myself, I valetted my coat on the side of the bath by dipping the clothes brush into the water and not having to worry about how much I wetted the coat as it was already soaked. I then cleaned my boots by getting as much mud as possible off with loo paper and then washing the rest off in the bath. This resulted in a deep sludge in the bottom of the bath which disappeared with the help of a good flow from both taps.

Ralph Coakes had agreed to let me have the same horse the next day when yet again I was able to take advantage of the tradition of invitation meets as the **Warwickshire Foxhounds** were meeting at Stoney Cross by invitation of the New Forest Foxhounds (Tues 25 Mar 1980). By an extraordinary coincidence this was the very same meet as it had been for our day with the New Forest Buckhounds, back in January 1975. I left the Yarcombe Inn at eight-fifteen and arrived at the meet at ten-thirty-five to find Ralph there waiting with the horses. The hunt servants and their horses were very smartly turned out, and hounds looked extremely well for the end of the season. Sir Newton Rycroft, Master of the New Forest, recognised me at the meet and told me how well he could remember Ernie Nunn, the Easton's old kennel huntsman.

Hounds found a fox within ten minutes of moving off, and we had a fast woodland hunt with my horse stumbling about in the deep water-filled ruts in the forest rides. More than once she was down on her knees, with me clinging around her neck. It seems to me that there is really not much choice about how you ride to hounds in the New Forest during a wet time. The choice is either to go at a sensible pace and risk losing hounds, or to go much faster and charge through large puddles with no way of knowing how deep the ruts are below the water. I took the latter course, thus stumbling around as much as I did. Hounds marked this fox to ground after about three-quarters of an hour where it was left. The second fox also went to ground quite quickly and during the third draw the hunt staff seemed to be galloping around without drawing properly. Both Ralph and I were fed up so we decided to go back to the meet. On the way, Ralph saw three horses outside a little pub in the Forest so he decided to call in. He tied up our horses and we went in to find Chalk, the Buckhounds huntsman, and several others that Ralph knew, and in a few minutes there was quite a little party going on. As far as I can remember, they had also been with the foxhounds and were on their way home.

After a while the whole hunt came past and I quickly went out to hold our horses but they took no notice at all. Later the whole hunt came back again and this time I did not bother to go out as Ralph's horses had been so calm the first time. I can still picture the scene – the little bar was full of laughing, jolly hunting men and a ginger-haired girl sat in the porch with a plateful of sandwiches on her lap and a whisky and orange in her hand. The reins of three horses were looped through her arm, but they just stood quietly, seeming to be completely oblivious to the hunt trotting past. During this session I remembered just how many Honorary Secretaries had said they were still hunting. I asked Ralph what he could do about horses and he said he could manage to get "something" to whichever meet and as often as I wished. The upshot of it was that I decided that as I was likely to get several more days it would make more sense to move nearer to Ralph's farm which was just outside Milford-on-Sea in Hampshire as the eighty-odd miles each way to the meets was getting very tedious. Ralph agreed to book us in somewhere suitable for Sheila and I emphasised that it must be comfortable as Sheila was just sitting "at home" all day.

I arrived back at Yarcombe Inn at six-thirty and did some quick valetting, anxiously checking the green coat I had worn the day before which was in the airing cupboard. I found it almost dry so I left it until the morning. After the boot-washing and removal of all the sludge, I climbed into the bath myself before Sheila and I went to join Brigid and Michael Roffe-Sylvester and their youngest son John for an excellent dinner at Reaphay, arriving back at twelve-thirty. We were up early, packing and loading up the car, before sitting down to breakfast at eight-fifteen. We then paid our dues and set off to the meet of the **Wilton Foxhounds** at West Acre Lodge, Sixpenny Handley, near Blandford in Dorset (Wed 26 Mar 1980). At the meet I introduced myself to the Master, Angus Mann, and found out that he was related to the Manns of Thelverton Hall who own a lovely estate on the boundary of the Easton and Dunston Harriers' countries. This East Anglian branch of the family were also keen on hunting and hunted with the Dunston Harriers as well as foxhunting in the Shires.

This was not a very enjoyable day for me as my horse, a young cob, was green and very nappy. I would think that it had only just been backed. It was difficult to steer, as when I pulled on the rein, it would turn its nose round almost to my stirrup but continue going straight on. With my inability to steer I could not keep him away from some live electric fencing, and an alarming few minutes followed, with the best gallop of the day up a hill. This took us to where hounds were marking in a thick place and the cry was so lovely that I could not resist riding closer to see them. When they left the earth, hounds pushed past me on a narrow path and my mount went berserk when they brushed past his legs. By the time he had stopped leaping and snorting we were up to my knees in thick bushes. The Master was hunting hounds and it was my impression that he was one of the unlucky few to whom hounds do not instinctively respond. This sometimes just happens and whatever effort the person concerned puts into getting to know them, they just do not want to go willingly to him. Those who suffer this difficulty can draw comfort from the old hunting saw that hounds always go well for a rogue. This Master was very quiet and hardly ever used his voice or his horn, and was in my opinion too quiet for foxhunting.

This country, described so well by Thomas Hardy, was very inviting, being rolling grassland, and I could imagine how wonderful it would have been to ride across on a good horse. However, on this occasion with my green mount I was quite glad that we had had a woodland day. Ralph took me home to his farm in his lorry, where we unloaded the horses and then went into the house to meet Mrs Coakes and have a cup of tea. Ralph later drove me down to our new hotel, the White Horse Inn at Milford-on-Sea, where Sheila was already settled in as Ralph's daughter Mary had come to the meet with her father and had then shown Sheila the way. Ralph had booked us in simply as "Master of a Hunt", presumably because he could not remember my name, and everyone who came into Reception that morning had been asked if they were Master of a Hunt. The same question, of course, was asked of Sheila and, although she was very embarassed, things were finally sorted out. Having gone to the trouble of moving hotels, I could not hunt on either of the two following days. Whether this was due to bad weather, or simply to no packs going out on these days, I cannot remember. This was so impromptu a jolly that I had been simply spreading the hunting map open on the bed and, listing nearby packs, settling down with Baily's to see what their hunting days were and telephoning the Secretaries. On Thursday I took Sheila and Charlotte shopping in Bournemouth where they had a buying spree. I returned to the White Horse after lunch for a nap, then took my Border Terrier, Badger, for a walk in the Forest. Mr and Mrs Coakes, and their daughter Mary and her husband, joined us for dinner in the evening and we all had an amusing time as there is never a dull moment with Ralph. On the Friday we went up to Ralph's farm to see Stroller who was now a great age and was "strolling" around a meadow well-rugged up. I bought a saddle and an electric groomer from Ralph, then had lunch with them. Afterwards we drove to Glastonbury to watch the school play before leaving Charlotte and arriving back at Milford at eleven-forty-five, after a dreadful drive with gales and heavy rain all the way.

The Saturday was to be our last day and we had packed and loaded up the car before breakfast. We then left for Ralph's farm where we were to use our car and his trailer to get my mount to the meet of the **New Forest Foxhounds** at Vale Farm, North Gorley, near Ringwood (Sat 29 Mar 1980). The meet was easily found but I was very disappointed to find that Sir Newton Rycroft, the Master, was not hunting hounds. He told me that had given up due to ill health. It would have been a great milestone in my life to have seen Sir Newton hunting hounds as he must be ranked amongst the most famous of foxhunters in the world on account of his knowledge of foxhunting and hound breeding. The high winds, almost gale-force, were against us and there was little sport, the first two foxes going quickly to ground. This was not very exciting so I stopped at a pub for a drink with Stephen Sherwood who had been brought up in the Easton Harriers country, and was later to become Master of the New Forest. His father, Major Bugg, was a great character and well-known in the Suffolk hunting world. I asked Stephen why he had changed his name, and he explained that when he proposed to his wife she accepted only on condition that he changed his name as she did not wish to become a Bugg. We had much to talk about and, as sport was so poor and the wind getting worse, we decided to return to the meet where Sheila was waiting. Stephen suggested that he returned the mare and the trailer to Ralph's farm, and so we put my horse on his lorry. This was a very kind offer and very welcome as it saved a good two-and-a-half-hours of our journey home but meant that we could not say personal goodbyes to Ralph and his family, so I telephoned when we arrived home. However, we did not take full advantage of the head start because Stephen invited us into his lovely house for champagne and to watch the Grand National before leaving for home. Stephen's generosity made for a grand end to an enjoyable holiday. It was an unusual pleasure to have had Sheila with me, which livened up the evenings and she had enjoyed the peaceful days with her knitting and taking the terrier out for walks.

**Lauderdale**. *Meet at Brothershiels Farm, Berwickshire. Joint Master and Huntsman, Nigel Murray, with John Forbes, Kennel Huntsman and first whipper-in (Country Life, 9 April l987).*

Kindly supplied by Tony Hogarth

# MAP 6

**FOXHOUND PACKS – 1980**

A Irfon & Towey
B Sennybridge & District Farmers'
C Brecon
D Warwickshire
E Oakley
F Wilton
G Portman
H New Forest

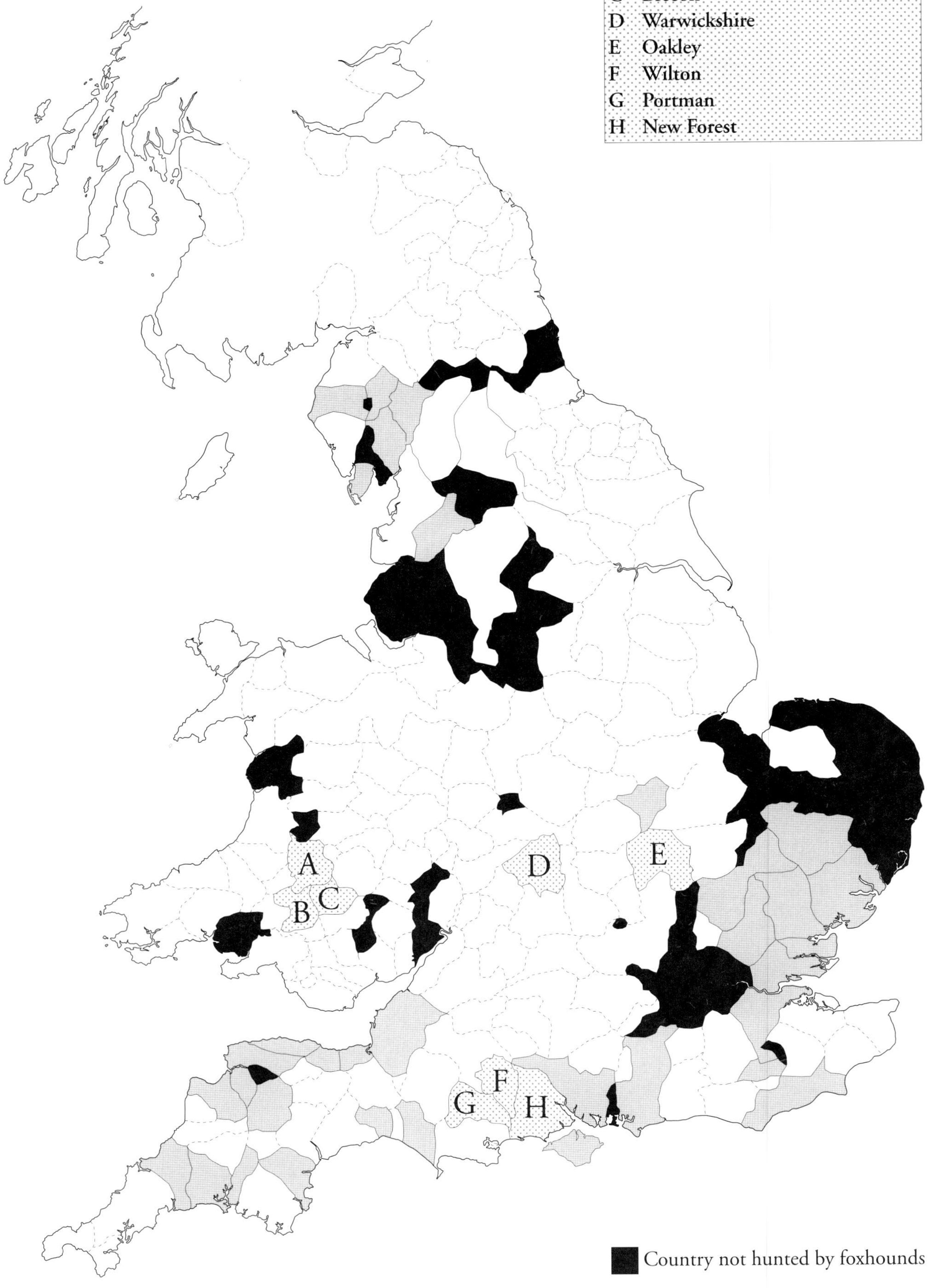

# Chapter 8

## Into Wales for the First Time

The wanderlust for hunting was now quite foremost in my mind as although I still had not achieved my original ambition for every harrier pack, I now had a new target. This was to have been out with a hundred different packs, of all breeds, and I had at that time been with eighty-one English ones and fourteen French packs. As I had finished harvest I decided to make the most of the remains of the summer by having a couple of days minkhunting on the Welsh border and was able to combine this with visiting my good friends, the Plumbes, who had moved to Orleton, near Tenbury Wells in Worcestershire. They were still away on holiday for the first evening I would be there but, telephoning ahead to discover where the meets were, I found that the Border Counties were to meet at the Cound Lodge Hotel and this seemed an obvious place, therefore, for me to spend the first night.

I set off to drive there on Friday 29 August 1980 and called at Braintree on the way to try to buy a baker's cart since one of my interests is that of collecting unusual horse-drawn vehicles, but the owner, a Romany, was not at home. The journey was dreadful. There was heavy rain all the way which no doubt was part of the reason why a car smashed into the back of mine at Milton Keynes. My bad luck continued when I arrived at the Cound Lodge Hotel as it was undergoing some improvements and there was no accommodation available. After much driving around and asking, I eventually found a bed in a hotel in Much Wenlock, the only one they had free. I soon found out why as it was an attic on the third floor up a narrow, twisting staircase and its only furniture was a bed and an old-fashioned washstand with a jug and bowl. I was feeling rather fed up so I set off to try to cheer myself up with a good dinner. Walking around Much Wenlock, I could not see anywhere that looked promising so I asked a gentleman who was filling up his Range Rover at the petrol station if he knew of a good restaurant in the town. His answer was brief and to the point.

"There isn't one."

He suggested that I drove out of town to somewhere else. I ought to have taken his advice but instead went into the Gaskell Arms where I was determined to enjoy a really good dinner. As I sipped a large gin-and-tonic and looked through the menu, the atmosphere in the bar reminded me more of the waiting-room at a crematorium than of a hotel bar. The barman asked if I was in town on business. When I explained to him that I had come to hunt, he went on in great detail about the Pony Club Dance that had been held there and how archaic he thought it was that there was a man there who insisted on being addressed as "Master". The more I tried to explain, the more I think I was put into the same bracket. I ordered soup and a schooner of dry sherry, fillet of plaice and a half-bottle of dry white wine, local beef and a bottle of red wine, and a pudding and glass of Sauternes.

The whole meal was a disaster. The soup was very poor, probably straight out of a packet; the sherry was cheap and nasty; the fish was soggy; the white wine was the best on the list but did nothing to help; the beef was tough and gristly, the vegetables hardly warm with water running out of them; the red wine was so sharp I could not finish it. The meal ended on a slightly better note, however, as the pudding and the Sauternes were just acceptable, or seemed so in comparison with what had gone before. All this was endured sitting alone in a large, cold dining-room. I returned to my garret even more miserable than when I had left it, wishing I had taken the gentleman's advice.

Next morning, as I was making my way back to the Cound Lodge Hotel for the meet of the **Border Counties Minkhounds**, I saw a group of men standing on a bridge who I thought might be minkhunters, so I stopped to ask if the meet had been changed (Sat 30 Aug 1980). After being told that it was still at the hotel, I was staggered when one of them asked, "Do you live in Worlingworth?"

"No," I replied, "but it's my telephone exchange."

It turned out that he had brought his lurchers to run at both of the coursing matches I had organised during the Membership Drive for the BFSS, and I said that he had gone a long way to have a day's coursing.

He replied, "It's no further than you've come to have a day's mink-hunting," a most reasonable reply although I was getting a little more than one day's hunting. We spent a jovial hour in the bar at the Cound Lodge Hotel, and then drove down to Cantlop Bridge to draw the Cound, a tributary of the Severn, and there was a good field of approximately sixty people. The Master, John Newton, hunted hounds and I liked the way he handled his hounds but, although they drew thoroughly, they had a blank day and had not found by the time I left them at five o'clock.

I set off to drive to the Plumbes' new home but, not dreaming that there would be two places called Orleton within fifteen miles of each other, I went to the wrong one and eventually arrived at seven o'clock.

Although the Plumbe family were only just back from holiday in Devon, Tizza produced an excellent dinner and they were amused to hear of my previous night's culinary experiences and the tale of the man called "Master". After dinner Colin took me up to a pub called The Fox where we got into conversation with a farmer who told me he bought his hop plants from John Wright who farms at Monewdon in the heart of the Easton Harriers country.

To amuse myself on the Sunday (31 Aug 1980), I took off into Wales to see some old friends. I left the Plumbes after a hearty breakfast with fresh orange juice – always a certain treat in their household – and drove to see John Lloyd, landlord of the Barley Mow in Builth Wells where I had stayed several times for the Welsh Cob horse sales. I arrived exactly at opening time (twelve o'clock) and, after a couple of half-pints, John and I put a crate of Double Diamonds in the car and went to see Roy Davies at his Tregare Farm Stud. He showed us round his Welsh Cob mares and their foals and I took such a fancy to one outstanding foal that I immediately wanted to buy it. With difficulty, I managed to persuade Roy to sell it to me before we left to drive *via* a very scenic route to the home of John Jones, Master of the Irfon and Towy Foxhounds, in the hope of seeing his Welsh hounds.

He took us to his kennel but there were only a few puppies there, and he then explained that his pack worked on a very rare and old-fashioned system. The hounds were trencher-fed during the summer, each hound returning to whichever farm it had been walked on as a puppy and was fed and looked after at the farmer's expense until the beginning of the next season. A century ago there were quite a number of packs that were trencher-fed all year round, i.e. only getting together as a pack on hunting days, but there are very few now. Casually I asked Mr Jones when he would begin cubhunting, as I imagined that in Wales, with no fields of standing corn, cubhunting would start early in September, and his reply was quite extraordinary and considerably advanced my hunting education. He told me that he did not know when he would begin hunting, as it all depended on when his hounds came back to kennel. At first, I thought he was joking but when I realised that he was not I asked him why he did not go to fetch them. It was at this point that he staggered me by telling me that the hounds return to the kennel one by one, entirely of their own accord, by leaving their summer homes and walking over the mountains straight back to kennels. He went on to explain that they themselves could sense when the season ought to start and that they all returned to the kennel within a week of each other. We were standing in his farmyard, just in front of his house, with mountains all around us, while he was explaining all this to me, when an amazing coincidence occurred. He looked up to a stretch of road in the distance and said,

"There's one coming back now."

Scarcely able to believe that I was really going to witness what he had just told me, I watched as a hound slowly walked down the road towards us.

"Now," he said, "I'm wondering if it will come home to me here at the farm, or if it will go to the kennels."

As we watched, we saw it turn off the road and disappear through the hedge.

"Oh," he said. "It is going directly to the kennels."

He seemed in no hurry, but eventually we went round to the kennel again and there the old bitch was waiting. He opened the door and she calmly jumped up onto the bench.

"Now," he said, "they will probably all be here before next Sunday."

As a hound man, I found this experience absolutely fascinating, to think that not only is a mental message of the urge to hunt received by all those hounds, almost simultaneously, but also the urge to reunite as a pack, coupled with a homing instinct of the way back to kennel. I think that the urge to reunite at the kennels is the significant point as the urge to hunt could have been easily satisfied as, wherever they had been staying for the summer, there would have been foxes just above them in the mountains within easy reach. I was thrilled to have learnt about, and to have seen at first hand, this phenomenal aspect of hound behaviour which could only have manifested itself in this circumstance of a summer trencher-fed pack. I was amazingly lucky in that, firstly, I was there at the right time and, secondly, that I asked the question which brought it up.

Mrs Jones then invited us in for an excellent tea, after which John Lloyd and I returned to the Barley Mow for a couple of whiskies before I drove back to Orleton. Tizza had a very flavoursome leg of local lamb all ready, to be followed by her homemade strawberry ice-cream. After coffee, Colin took me up to the Fox, rather late, as it was ten-thirty when we got there, but the landlord did not seem to mind and served us several rounds. There was a great character called Bert in the pub who Colin had wanted me to meet. Bert was a ruddy-faced, stalwart sort of fellow, a real yeoman of the old type, who amused us with a tale of his Point-to-Pointer. He had always been a great Point-to-Point enthusiast and often had a horse to run. There was one particular horse that he just kept on his farm, shepherding on it and hacking it around the place, but, in spite of the lack of special attention, it won almost every race in which it was entered. One day when the horse had won again as usual, it was loaded up in Bert's lorry and waited there while Bert celebrated in the beer tent and called at several pubs on the way home. Eventually he came to the Fox at ten o'clock where the landlord invited the victorious horse into the bar. Bert was in that particularly happy state of mind and readily agreed but, as he led the horse out of the lorry, he lost his footing and rolled down the ramp, followed by the horse which stood on his chest and then disappeared into the darkness. Bert told us that he found it the next morning standing in the yard, with its saddle and bridle still on, and only one rein broken, and in spite of this adventure it won the Open Race the following Saturday.

I went to bed feeling how lucky I was to meet so many characters and listen to their tales. On the Monday morning I set off to the meet of the **Three Counties Minkhounds** at Brinkwood Ford, near Ludlow (Mon 1 Sept 1980). I was disappointed to find that Ian Coghill was unable to be present as I had been looking forward to seeing him hunt hounds. John Newton, Master and Huntsman of the Border Counties, had agreed to hunt hounds and had brought three couple of his own hounds to mix in with the Three Counties. I have since wondered whether this was to encourage the Three Counties hounds to come with him or, perhaps, that they were very exceptional hounds and that they would help him to show sport. Show sport he certainly did. He drew the River Teme downstream and hunted a long drag through a lovely gorge and over some meadows to an old pump. Although they dug for half-an-hour, only a rabbit came out. This led to some ribald comments from the field, and much leg-pulling of the temporary huntsman, but I am fairly sure that the drag was not rabbit because I have always been led to believe that rabbits do not cross rivers with any degree of ease.

The second draw was around Downton Water, below a castle, and after quickly finding, we hunted up through some woodland and back across the meadowland to kill the mink just before it gained the river. I was presented with the tail of the mink which still hangs on my office wall. When sending it off to the taxidermist I was not sure whether to call it a tail or whether to elevate the mink to the status of an otter and call it a rudder. I enjoyed another good hunt of a half-hour in and around the remains of old tin mines, all overgrown and, I imagine, a paradise for mink, until they marked to ground under a bridge and I sadly had to leave them.

It is said that one should always finish on a high note and the dinner-party at the Plumbes that evening was exactly that. Diana Fraser, a friend of Tizza's, had arrived with her groom, Nicky, and was a fund of funny stories, mostly about their unfortunate experiences in the catering business. Colin and I disappeared to the Admiral Rodney for a drink, catching sight of a fox cub in the car headlights, and then returned to play tapes of hunting songs from the Lakes and an Easton hunt dinner, finally going to bed at twelve-thirty. With the usual heavy heart I left the wonderful company of the Plumbes on the following morning, calling at Luton Airport on the way home to pick up Sheila, Judith and Charlotte who had been on holiday.

While with John Lloyd on the Sunday I made provisional arrangements for a hunting holiday in the area as he had confirmed that I could stable my horses on the Royal Welsh Showground and stay myself with him at the Barley Mow. It was planned to fit in with my annual visit to Wales for the Welsh Cob Sales which are held on the Showground which is situated on the very edge of Builth Wells. To combine hunting with the Sales made good sense as it meant that the lorry would be there if I bought anything, killing two birds with one stone. We had been given permission to use the loose boxes at the back of the stable block which would not interfere with the cob sales. Nowadays there would be no chance at all of being allowed stables as the Sales are now so big that every box is used.

Consequently, a few weeks later I was back in Builth. I left home on Wednesday 15 October at six o'clock, picked up the two horses (Robin, who I had borrowed from Sue Gooderham, and Mickey) from the kennels and then my friend Maurice Scott from his farm at Kettleburgh. We were finally *en route* for Wales at seven o'clock and arrived at Builth Wells at three forty-five. Another friend, Bill James, had agreed to join us for this hunting/horse-sale holiday and it was arranged that he should bring my groom, Di Williams, with him in his car. Bill and Di arrived just as we had finished unloading the horses and when everything was settled we went to the Barley Mow which is in the centre of the town and where the car-park was barely large enough to reverse my lorry into. All four of us stayed in the Barley Mow and we used up all the accommodation they had. Di and I had a room each, and Bill and Maurice shared on the grounds that I ought to have a room to myself as I had all my hunting gear to spread around. The atmosphere in the bar that evening was so good that I had to use all my willpower to force myself to leave my friends in the bar to make the necessary arrangements by telephone for hunting on Thursday and Friday.

On the first day I went with the **Irfon and Towy Foxhounds** which were the pack that were trencher-fed during the summer and returned to the kennels on their own in the autumn (Thurs 16 Oct 1980). I collected Mickey from the showground then stopped in the street to pick up Marie Lloyd, the landlord's daughter, and her mare, and Marie guided me to the

**The Irfon and Towy:** ***"A large drop of the 'medicine' will make things feel better!"***

meet at Groswen, Llanafan-Fawr. The meet is pictured forever in my mind. The weather was foul, with high winds blowing sleet horizontally across the mountainside, cutting our faces and ears as we stood fully exposed. Mike Davies, one of my Barley Mow bar-friends, was giving the meet from a railway carriage on the mountainside which he used for keeping his sheep dips, spare stakes, and so forth. He disappeared into it and reappeared with assorted glasses of whisky, served on a tin lid held upside down, a wise precaution as the winds would have blown them off a flat surface. After a generous glass or two of Mike's whisky, things seemed a little more cheerful and I even began to realise how pretty the rowan trees looked with their red berries set off against the sleet. Maurice and Bill were following

**The Irfon and Towy:** ***"The first one home... Now the season can begin!"***

on foot and I was so cold by the time we moved off that I wished I was on foot with them.

Hounds drew a small forestry plantation and then the mountainside but both were blank, which was hardly surprising in the conditions. A fox was finally found in some dense bracken but hounds divided almost immediately on a second fox and both halves of the pack ran hard for half an hour before joining up again. The country was very difficult to cross on horseback as it was either very boggy or steep. The bogs were huge and I took my cue from the locals who got off and led their horses over them. The local horses did not panic in the wet places and took quick little steps thus keeping near the top. Mike Davies himself was hunting on a little fifteen-hand mare which seemed too small for him but she carried him beautifully all day. It was an education to watch her skip across the bogs, looking like a ballet dancer on stage. However, I was at a serious disadvantage with my little cob Mickey as he was not used to the bogs and would try to jump them with the consequence that he floundered deeper and deeper into the mire, trying continually to jump onto me. It is a natural instinct in horses in this situation for they reasonably assume that where others are standing must be safe ground. The experience of the bogs was really frightening as I was often pushed over and the reins got through his front legs, were covered in slime, and were eventually broken. I managed to make do with broken reins and, getting out of the bogs onto the hillside, I carried on with a lovely valley below. The hillside was so steep that as we rode across the side of it my inside foot was dragging through the bracken.

Hounds were going very well considering the terrible conditions but lost the line completely on a very exposed part of the mountain and Glyn, the huntsman, decided to return to the meet. We then moved off the mountainside to where Mike Davies and his wife lived in a caravan in a farmyard close by his mother's house and offered open house to all the frozen followers. Mike's hospitality in that caravan is amongst the most treasured memories of my hunting holidays. The caravan was packed full of hunting men and women and the three of us visitors sat and listened as Glyn compared notes with the huntsman from the David Davies and another hunting friend from the Lake District. Mike's wife was filling bowls with cawl which Mike handed round, his rugged and powerful appearance seeming singularly out of place as a waiter. Cawl is a traditional Welsh soup best described as a thick meat and vegetable soup, and was absolutely delicious and so warming. This left such a lasting impression on all our minds that if ever Bill, Maurice or myself start to reminisce about Wales, the cawl will always come into the conversation. It was followed by Welsh cakes and whisky, and my pen cannot begin to do justice to the unforgettable atmosphere in that caravan. It was only the greatest will-power that made me leave them to drive the box back to Builth Wells.

The next day was lucky on two counts, one that there was a pack hunting on a Friday and secondly that it was the **Ross Harriers**, one of the three harrier packs I had not yet hunted with (Fri 17 Oct 1980). They were meeting at Yatton Church near Ross-on-Wye and Bill rode with me in the lorry while John "the Barley" (as he was known locally) drove in front with Maurice to show us the way. We left the Barley Mow at eight-thirty and arrived at around ten-thirty but our guides, whom we had lost in Hereford, arrived at the meet a half-hour later. I was particularly interested in these Harriers as I had sent them drafts on several occasions and was looking forward to finding out what Robert Okell, the Master, thought of them. He was hunting hounds and, sitting in the middle of his unlevel pack looking exactly like Mr Jorrocks, he pointed out a couple of Easton doghounds, Hamish and Warrior. Maurice and Bill again followed on foot and found out that the kennel huntsman came from Cambridgeshire. The country was glorious with rolling grassland and very little arable, and I was very glad that I had borrowed Robin from Sue Gooderham as the fences were quite stiff and he was a bold little performer. The day consisted of several short hunts, all spoiled by the high winds and driving rain. Robert Okell helped his hounds rather too much, and they consequently made no attempt to cast themselves. I left at two o'clock when they had got into twenty-six acres of rye grass which was full of hares and hounds were going in all directions.

**Ross Harriers.** *From the meet at Wharton Farm, 29 October 1983. The Acting Master, Mr Robert Okell, hunting hounds.*

Photograph kindly loaned by F E Okell

The Welsh Cob Sales were held on the Saturday and the following Monday, the Saturday sale being held on a stud belonging to the famous old lady Miss Taylor, the doyenne of the Welsh Cob world. This stud sale was always very crowded so I said I would prefer to go hunting and Bill took up my offer of the little cob Mickey. One of the customers of the Barley Mow was terrier-man to the **Brecon Foxhounds** so we arranged to follow him to the meet at Bailey Bucham Common near Talgarth. We were ready and waiting outside the Barley Mow at eight o'clock. When we arrived at the meet, at a time when we ought to have been ready to move off, I was amazed to find that only the huntsman, John "Brecon", and his amateur whip were there. John explained to me that this often happened on a Saturday at this time of year as all the farmers were at sheep sales. I liked John's hounds which were level and smart, and stood gazing in adoration all around him. John moved off along a track, his hounds drawing the mountainside above him, and they soon found and ran along the mountainside. How thrilling it was to gallop along the track, looking up and seeing these wonderful hounds hunting over the rocks with a great cry just above us and in full view. Hounds next turned uphill and hunted right to the top of Mynydd Bychan. John turned his horse up a track and I followed him, like a lamb to the slaughter, not knowing what was ahead of me. We climbed and climbed, with John's horse leaving more and more space between us until he was out of sight almost all of the time. The track became narrower and narrower, and steeper and steeper, and Robin was slipping and scrambling on the loose stones. At times he seemed to be taking two or three strides without getting any further forward. The track became still narrower and steeper. The ground fell away to my left and, as we climbed further, the drop became greater. I was absolutely terrified. There was now a five-hundred foot drop to the left of the track, and sheer rock to the right. The path was so narrow that if I looked down my left side I could see no track at all, just the rocks five hundred feet below, and to my right my stirrup was brushing along the sheer rock face.

Worse was to come as the track was becoming icy. I was again thankful to have borrowed Robin as he was so nimble in correcting the frequent slips. I was by now so scared that when I tried to speak to Robin no words would come. The ice was getting worse, the drop even deeper. Great beads of cold sweat were running down my back and the hairs on my scalp were prickling like a dog with its hackles up. So realistic was this prickling that I constantly pressed down my hat as I was sure it was balanced on top of vertical hairs. At last the top came in view and the path widened out, until I could find a place to stop to let Robin catch his wind. I looked back and could see poor little Mickey labouring up slowly under his considerable load. There was so much steam coming off him that it was impossible to see Bill on his back until occasionally a gust of wind blew it momentarily away. I had always known that little Mickey had the heart of a lion but would have gone to any lengths to have prevented such a test as this. However, both of us were presented with Hobson's

**The Brecon:** ***"Past the point of no return"***

**The Brecon:** ***"The others will never believe us"***

Choice as it had been impossible to turn round and impossible to get off.

I decided not to wait for Bill as he would be at least another fifteen minutes coming up, so I set off after the huntsman. The mountain top was covered in snow about twelve to fifteen inches deep and although the huntsman was long gone out of sight I could follow his tracks in the snow. I was more than a little concerned about rocks or bogs under the snow or, worse still, holes that had drifted full so "in the huntsman's steps I trod". The snow crunched and crackled as I cantered on across the mountain top, listening for the cry of hounds and breathing in the beauty all around me. At last I heard hounds and then I could see them way over to my left so I had to abandon following the tracks and take my own line. After a few blunders I reached hounds without serious mishap. They were hunting brilliantly across the snow, back to the very edge of the mountain top and then marked to ground just below us. I held John's horse while he climbed down but he decided to leave the fox as it was in an impossible place. While I was holding his horse, Bill came into view, sensibly letting Mickey walk, and then we both dismounted to rest our horses while we discussed our ascent. John pointed out Builth Wells in the distance and said that we could see for over thirty miles. When the horses were sufficiently rested, John started to draw along the mountain top with his hounds below him. I was quietly wandering along, admiring the breathtaking beauty of the place, and thinking of all the millions of people working in their warm offices who would never experience this place, until jerked out of my daydream by Bill.

"Tony, Tony," he shouted. "Come over here. There's an aeroplane flying below us."

As I reached the edge there it was, way below us – a small aeroplane flying along so peacefully in the valley.

Bill and I sat watching hounds draw, enjoying the spectacular scenery, with the snow glistening in the bright sunshine and the lovely green lowlands below us with cattle looking like flies. Hounds found again and hunted down and down until we could see them in the meadows below looking like ants as they screamed through pastures before turning up the mountain again. John had seemed confident that the fox would return to the mountain but had nevertheless dropped down from the mountain top to a lower track which ran along the mountain side. Hounds ran past us on up to the mountain top again and we had another memorable ride to the top. There were no narrow tracks this time, but wide slippery rocks which in normal circumstances no-one would ever have tried to ride up. As we were going up, I could see a sheer face of rock about six feet high ahead of us and wondered why John kept determinedly riding towards it. When he got to it he climbed up onto his saddle and jumped to the top, leaving his horse to jump up behind him. We had no choice but to follow his example and I was so glad that we had these nimble little horses. This happened once more, and again I was thankful to Sue for lending me Robin as most of my other hunters could not have managed this day at all.

**The Brecon:** ***"Come hup," I say "come hup."***

Hounds turned down again and I was very glad that John took a different route as I would not have fancied jumping my horse down those two huge steps. About half-an-hour later hounds took the line into a plantation where there were four foxes and hounds split. We were quite grateful for the rest as it took some time to get hounds together again. While we waited we were entertained by tales from the terrier-man who John later told us had been known on several occasions to take off foxes' brushes with his teeth. The next draw was at the bottom of the mountain in a dingle called Bwll-y-Wrack. Hounds found and had a slow hunt but the sun in the valley bottom was by now too hot for scent and John decided to go home.

As we were boxing up at three o'clock we both agreed that we had never known six hours to go so quickly. Bill insisted that I stop on the way home so that he could buy an O.S. map and was delighted to inform me that we had climbed to 2,400 feet on the first hunt. We dropped off the horses and returned to the Barley Mow at four o'clock to find that Maurice was just back from the auction. We asked for a pot of tea and, while we waited for it to come, I savoured the old-fashioned atmosphere which was completed by characters to match. Sitting on either side of the fireplace were two wizened old men in Wellington boots, their collie dogs under their seats and their rams-horn sticks leaning against the fireplace. At various other tables sat more farmers, some with their wives with two or more shopping bags full of groceries. All the men had one thing in common – the sort of faces that can only come from many hours and years out in severe weather. Their ruddy craggy faces showed a great contentment that is seldom experienced by any but those who work on the land.

It was in the midst of this special rural atmosphere that I told my two friends that I wished them to have a whisky with their tea as I had something to celebrate. They accepted the whisky without enquiring what the celebration was, so I went on to explain that this had been the hundredth different pack of hounds I had hunted with, which included foot packs as well as mounted. The atmosphere, the whiskies and our reminiscences of the experiences of the day led to a rather long "tea-party", and it was after six o'clock when we went upstairs to wash and change.

When we came down I asked John "the Barley" if he had any good wine in his cellar as I was of the mind to spoil my friends.

"Well," he said, "I have some Hirondelle."

I explained that was not exactly what I wanted so we kept to our whisky. The dinner was superb with a choice of duck or pheasant which were both brought out for me to carve at the table. When we returned to the bar we found so many friends, all of whom wanted to do their part in helping me celebrate. In the corner behind the door there was a table of ladies who sang most beautifully and I can especially remember them singing "The Old Rugged Cross". The evening flew by, with singing, jokes and tales. I sang several songs and groups of men sang in competition with the ladies in the corner. Standing at the bar all evening were two real little old characters who were regulars at the Barley, both in their late seventies and one with odd Wellington boots on. They had thoroughly enjoyed the singing. At one-thirty they stood facing each other, gripping each other's arms and swaying backwards and forwards as they tried to think of a new song to sing.

One of them said, "How does this one start?" and the other said, "I cannot remember."

"Don't be so silly man. You must remember. You know you learnt it at school."

I caught Maurice's eye and the pair of us dissolved into laughter, and still do whenever it is mentioned.

After about two o'clock, people began to drift away but the party continued in full swing until six o'clock when the last of the customers left. John "the Barley" insisted that we have a nightcap with him, and we finally went up the stairs at six-thirty.

At breakfast next morning at ten o'clock, John "the Barley" brought a gallon bottle of whisky to the table, and made the three of us sign our names on it as he said we three were the only ones drinking whisky and he knew we had drunk it all. To this day he still has the bottle in his cellar but I have since discovered that there was a fourth, a local butcher who was called "Mohammed Ali" because he used to shadow-box in the bar, flitting about with footwork to equal the great World Champion, all while continuing his conversation. After breakfast, and not feeling hungover at all, we set off, armed with a case of Double Diamond, for a visit to Roy Davies' stud. This was a regular feature of our trips to the Sales and was as enjoyable as ever. We walked up the hillside to see his mares and foals and on our return went into Roy's house and pulled the top off a few of the bottles. On the way back we accepted an invitation to call on Roy's nephew Derek for tea and, after first looking at his foal, we went into tea with lovely sandwiches and Welsh cakes. Sadly this was when the effects of the night before began to materialise. The alcohol was fast disappearing, and with the lack of sleep and the comfortable chairs, we all felt very drowsy. It must have looked really bad as the three of us were falling asleep while eating our Welsh cakes. Derek understood the problem and was doing his best to engage us in conversation but was on a losing wicket because while he was talking to me the other two would be dozing off. I have often wondered what his wife said to him after we were gone. Needless to say, very soon after dinner that evening, three weary souls climbed the stairs in a far less jubilant mood than the night before.

On Monday we all attended the Welsh Cob sale on the showground, and I bought two foals from Roy Davies' stud, and one from Mike Davies (of caravan hospitality fame). Maurice and Bill also bought a foal each, Bill's eventually growing up to be a fine type for hunting in our plough country. For our last day's hunting before going home Bill and I decided to have a day with the **Sennybridge and District Farmers' Foxhounds** (Tues 21 Oct 1980). We took Marie with us and she was not sure of the way but luckily we again had the terrier-man with us and he showed us. We arrived and unboxed in a quarry in good time. Hospitality was dispensed from the back of a Land Rover before moving off to draw country which was rough and steep. Unfortunately the Master took us in the wrong direction and lost touch with hounds which meant we were galloping around on the mountain top for an hour before finding them. We had quite a difficult climb up to the top so imagine my surprise when we suddenly came across a tractor and baler which had been baling up bracken for bedding. Soon after finding hounds again, Robin, my mount, was badly cut on some barbed wire submerged in a river crossing and after disinfecting and bandaging it at a farm, Bill, Marie and I returned to the meet.

An amusing incident happened on the way back to Suffolk on the next day. I stopped to fill the lorry up with diesel and I had been looking at the pump attendant thinking that I knew him, when he looked at me and remarked that I was the exact double of a fellow named Harvey who was Master of the Easton Harriers in Suffolk. When I could get a word in edgeways I introduced myself and found out that he was George Steele whom I had met many years earlier in 1971 when he was huntsman of the Pendle Forest and Craven Harriers. I reminded him of the time Stanley and I had had tea with him at the kennels when he had been teasing his artist wife.

# Chapter 9

## The Ill-Fated Trip to Cornwall

Every opportunity was now to be taken up and, before going away on another major jolly at the end of the season, I managed to combine a day with the **Beacon Beagles** at Rodway, near Bridgwater, with a visit to my daughter's school in Somerset (Sat 28 Feb 1981). This was one of the packs kennelled at Reaphay, the home of Michael Roffe-Silvester who was an ex-Master. After a muddled sort of start, with no-one knowing where to draw, I enjoyed one good hunt with hounds often crossing big dykes, but later on I was rather left behind. When the huntsman returned he told me that, when he finally got to them, they were swimming in an old lock and speaking like otterhounds. I did not see much more of them as I had arranged for Sheila to pick me up again at three o'clock and we went on to spend a most enjoyable evening with the Roffe-Sylvesters at the Rock Inn at Water Row. The dinner was good, the company mostly hunting people and the evening, like all such evenings, went far too quickly.

During this dinner Michael suggested that a friend of his, Captain Mickleham, who lived near Falmouth, would be able to offer me stabling for a hunting holiday in that area. I followed up this tip and arranged with Stanley to go away again at the end of the season. These jollies were getting longer and longer, and this time we planned to be away for over two weeks. However, my wife says that I can never do one thing without trying to do another at the same time, or on the way, and the beginning of the holiday was combined with another trip to visit Charlotte at school and with a day with the Clifton Foot Beagles as I had been invited to speak at the retirement dinner for Tim Pearson, the Clifton's long-standing kennel huntsman. Mr Gardiner, the Clifton's Master, in inviting me to speak, had suggested that Sheila and I stayed with him. When I explained that we were taking Charlotte out for the weekend, he kindly offered to include her in the invitation. Stanley was to drive the horse-box down from Suffolk on the Sunday with our horses (two for each of us), and my groom Di Williams, and Sheila's sister Rita. We would meet at a service station and I would go on with them while Rita went back to Suffolk with Sheila. I also had to arrange to go home in the middle of the holiday as the Easton Point-to-Point was to be held on the 28th March.

Sheila and I left home on the Friday (20 Mar 1981) in our car and deviated from our route to pick up a spaniel puppy at Downham Market for James and Susan Osbourne who were friends of the Roffe-Sylvesters. The Osbournes lived at Remington near Wellington in Somerset and we stayed the night with them and enjoyed a fabulous dinner party. Next morning Sheila dropped me off at the meet of the **Clifton Foot** at the Strawberry Special Inn (which was named after a train) at Draycott and went shopping with Charlotte (Sat 21 Mar 1981). There was a good crowd because it was Tim Pearson's last meet and I was greeted by John and Clare Boyd who were ex-Masters and who I knew quite well as they had stayed with us in Suffolk when collecting drafts from the Easton Harriers. The Clifton Foot Beagles had, until three years previously, been foot harriers and I thought it a great shame that they should change to beagles as there were only two packs of foot harriers left in the country and the change lost some of the character of hunting. There was a practical reason for being harriers in that the rines or dykes are so large that harriers could negotiate them better than beagles, but they had been small harriers, preferably under eighteen inches. I had always sent my small harriers to either the Clifton Foot or the Windermere Harriers (the other foot pack) and had first started sending drafts to the Clifton Foot when Captain Wills, of cigarette fame, was Master. I remember an embarrassing incident when, as a nervous young Master, I was asked to judge their puppy show and was invited to lunch with Captain Wills. As we were driving up the long drive to his beautiful home, the rooks were at their noisiest in the trees beside the drive. Desperately trying to make conversation, I asked the Captain if he had ever eaten rook pie.

"No," he replied, with a visible shudder and such a look of horror on his face that I wished I had kept quiet about what was obviously only a rustic delicacy.

John Boyd introduced me to Mr Gardiner, his successor as Master, who explained to me that his reason for changing to beagles was the lack of success in attempting to breed small harriers as the bitches always seemed to throw bigger offspring than themselves. This, of course, was understandable as all my drafts to them were of small hounds which had bigger brothers and sisters and they would naturally be likely to breed normal harriers of up to twenty-one inches. I was shown Jailer, one of my drafts to the Clifton Foot and the only harrier they had left, and was delighted to hear that he had been kept for his outstanding working qualities.

The day's hunting is difficult to describe as there were rather too many hares and hounds changed quite often. This meant that hounds were running hard almost all the time with Jailer noticeably in the lead. Much of the time hounds were well away from me, running across the flat, open grassland, but I was able to see all of one hunt towards the end of the day as hounds settled on one hare and, after half an hour, killed at four-fifteen. Tim Pearson was presented with the mask and myself with a pad.

Sheila and Charlotte were waiting for me at the meet and we all went to an excellent beagling tea at the Boyds' before following the Master to his home. After bathing and changing, we were refreshed with a large gin and tonic then went off to the presentation dinner at Clevedon. The dinner was superb and the speeches good but, unfortunately for me, I was the last of five speakers. I listened in horror as, one by one, every point I was going to make was included in the earlier speeches. When it came to my turn to stand up there was not a single item in my notes that had not been fully covered. I arose and simply said how long I had known Tim since the days he had been at the Trinity Foot and as everything I had intended to say had already been said, the only thing I could think to do was to sing a song. This I did and followed it up with two more. I had hoped it would make a welcome change to the speeches and was pleased when, after dinner, several people remarked that they preferred it to yet another speech. I am often reminded of the day and the dinner as I bought a lovely print of the Clifton Foot and have it hanging at home.

Next morning (Sun 22 Mar 1981) we met Stanley at our pre-arranged rendezvous at the Dene service station and, after refreshments, Rita set off with Sheila back to Suffolk and I went on with Stanley and Di. I took over the driving and attempted to follow the directions to Captain Mickleham's riding school at Molehill, near Falmouth. While he had been speaking to me on the telephone he continually referred to the fact that his directions would be accurate as he had been in the Armoured Car Corps, but in spite of this assurance we could not follow them and it was seven o'clock before we arrived at Molehill. The stables were worth waiting for and, after getting the horses settled, we relaxed with an enormous whisky from Captain Mickleham. Di Williams brought her bags into the house and was shown to her room and we set off feeling in much better spirits to find the Green Bank Hotel in Falmouth where the Captain had booked rooms for us.

We had difficulty in parking the lorry as although there were plenty of spaces in the car park, they were not set out for lorries. After a while we gave up trying and, finding a piece of waste ground, we left the lorry there, and carried our baggage back to the hotel. It was rather plush and the reception area had deep carpets and velvet chairs, all of which made us feel and look out of place. The horrified receptionist, who had obviously witnessed the attempts to park the lorry, was now confronted with two rough-looking men who, with their plastic dustbin bags of kit, looked like ruining the reputation of the hotel for ever. In desperation she tried to tell us that we were not booked in but eventually admitted that she had rooms and asked for a deposit of £20. Stanley asked her what the rate was for the room to which she replied, "£20". This immediately struck our sense of humour and we both dissolved into helpless laughter but we could see her side of the whole episode. She was obviously thinking that, as she had let in these two undesirable roughs who had arrived in a lorry, baggage in plastic bags, the least she could do to justify her action to the manager was to assure him that she had taken all the money in advance. We were still in uncontrollable giggles as we started up the stairs and took a last look back at the poor girl standing behind her desk wringing her handkerchief in her hands and, I am sure, feeling convinced that she would be sacked.

Our room was very comfortable and we both wished our wives were with us to appreciate the luxury. Over an excellent dinner we tried our best to remedy our earlier impression but we came to a decision that we could not stay here for the whole holiday, thinking of mud-caked boots crossing the deep-pile carpet in the reception or, worse, the pink stair carpet, and trying to valet our clothes in the immaculate bedrooms was out of the question.

It was the following morning (Mon 23 Mar 1981) that we heard the news that was to spoil the holiday. I turned on the radio, which happened to be tuned in to a local station, to hear the disastrous news that Foot and Mouth disease had been confirmed in the south of England. Although I was considerably cheered up by the next announcement which was the results of the Cury Foxhounds Supporters Club horn-blowing competition, I had the greatest fear for our hunting plans. We were to have hunted with the Redhill Beagles but they had cancelled the meet so, after breakfast, we hired a car and set off to find a more suitable place to stay. We eventually came across the Seven Stars at Stithians, a few miles inland of Falmouth. Thinking that this looked a likely place we went in, ordered a beer and enquired if they did "B&B". The landlord explained that they did not but that he certainly could accommodate us if we could wait a little while. While we returned to the Green Bank Hotel for our belongings, a great upheaval went on in the Seven Stars. The landlord and landlady moved themselves out of their bedroom into the sittingroom and their daughter moved her things out of her room into a boxroom. Stanley had the landlord's room and I had the daughter's room and after getting our luggage in we felt we had made a good move as the bed-and-breakfast at seven pounds a night was much more to our liking than the twenty pounds a night at the Green Bank. We then went to check the horses and had lunch with Captain Mickleham, after which we drove to Lands End and stood on that famous point, discussing the banks we had just passed and wondering if our horses could manage them as they were so high. We dined at the Green Bank Hotel as the meal had been so good the night before and were back at the Seven Stars in time for a nightcap before they closed.

We were up early as this was to be our first day of mounted hunting. We picked up our horses from Captain Mickleham's and drove to the meet of the Western Foxhounds at Nancledra, only to find that it was cancelled for fog. Our spirits rose when a man at the meet told us that the Four Burrow Foxhounds were not far away and off we went hoping to find them even if we were rather late. We arrived at the Four Burrow meet to find that it was also cancelled for the same reason so we took the horses back to the stables and rode them out on exercise instead.

Next morning we started very early for the Lamerton Foxhounds meet at Brentor, near Tavistock, just over the Tamar into Devon and arrived in good time but suspected the worst when we saw a policewoman standing at the bottom of a farm drive. She would not let us park anywhere near so we drove on until we found another man unboxing and hacked on to the meet with him. As we rode up to the meet which was in a farmyard we could see that all was not well. There were none of the usual happy faces and jolly atmosphere of a meet. We were told that we must await the outcome of a test for suspected Foot and Mouth at the next farm. After an hour or so a man drove up to say that the disease had been confirmed so we all had to go home, in our case seventy-five miles each way for nothing. With the first two days cancelled and the prospect of all the hunts in the area being forced to stop early, our spirits were at a very low ebb.

We had returned our hired car as it was much too expensive so, after an excellent breakfast at the Seven Stars, we followed a tip given in the bar and set off in the lorry to a scrap yard. Here we managed to hire a car for £30 until the following Monday. This was a great bonus as the lorry was not easy and often extremely slow, sandwiched between the high banks on these narrow roads. We returned the lorry to the Seven Stars and set off in our rusty acquisition for a tour of local kennels and Masters. Our first stop was to have lunch with John Congdon, Master of the Tetcott Foxhounds. This would have been very enjoyable if it had not been spoiled by the company of an unpleasant man who had taken over the Mastership from him. Leaving John we went to the South Tetcott kennels and met the Master, Dick England, a wonderful old character and a real old-style English gentleman who took great delight in showing us his hounds and his kennels.

We next went to the Lamerton kennels where we met the huntsman Clifford Pellew who told us some horrific stories. It seemed to us that this hunt was in total chaos. I met him again years later out hunting when he was kennel huntsman with the Tredegar Farmers' Foxhounds, and he clearly remembered our visit to the Lamerton.

The day ended on a higher note as the Master of the **Redhill Beagles** put on a meet especially for us (as we had been disappointed on the Monday) at Lord's Park, St Neot, on Bodmin Moor at five-thirty (Thur 26 Mar 1981). Sadly, the evening was sunny and warm and, although hounds were occasionally speaking, it might been only a drag, and it was a blank evening. The pack was made up of Chilmark and Cattistock drafts and I was surprised to find that it included a beagle/basset cross. On the way out of Lord's Park I was thrilled to see a badger. This was the first time I had ever seen one as they are extremely uncommon in Suffolk. We had supper in the famous Jamaica Inn, an isolated place situated on a lonely stretch of road in the middle of the Moor, then drove our scrapyard car back to the Seven Stars.

We made our second attempt to go out with the **Western Foxhounds** the following day and, allowing plenty of time, we arrived at Sancreed, near Penzance, with an hour in hand (Fri 27 Mar 1981). On the way we had been observing the banks which divided the meadows and deciding which of them we would dare jump. The Master was the first to arrive. He was most unfriendly and was blessed with few manners, but I did manage to discover that his son whipped in to him. As the field began to arrive we were relieved to find that they were a marked contrast to the Master, being most friendly and welcoming and were intrigued to find out how far we had come for our hunting holiday.

We moved off to draw a rough, gorse-covered hillside where there were three foxes but they were reluctant to leave the gorse. After hounds had chivvied them around with a good cry for about forty minutes, one fox did break and we had a short, sharp hunt across this country which was a fox-hunter's dream. It had lovely solid banks, no wire to be seen, and the hunt was welcomed enthusiastically by all the farmers. This run will remain firmly in my memory until my dying day. I would have enjoyed it much more if Di Williams, my groom, had not forgotten Mickey's martingale. He was rushing the banks with his head in the air but somehow he could always manage, cat-like, to land on the top of the bank, change legs and off the other side. He was definitely over-corned due to our earlier missed days and, like Multum-in-Parvo, he was having "one of his going days". Then hounds turned back and we had to retrace our steps down a long farm track with a bend at the end. Mickey changed his tactics and, instead of putting his head in the air, he put his head down and just went.

I was completely out of control and getting very scared as I knew there was a cattle-grid around the bend. Despite desperate attempts to slow him up I found I could not and thoughts of this gallant little cob lying in the cattle-grid with broken legs filled my mind. As we rushed round the bend at top speed I kicked my feet out of the stirrups hoping that I would fly clear when we crashed down. Suddenly the grid was in view. An instant feeling of nausea came over me, and then we were upon it. The rattle of horse-shoes on iron bars echoes in my mind still. Somehow, miraculously, his feet at that speed had landed on the bars and not between them and suddenly the danger and fear all seemed worth suffering just in order to feel and enjoy the immense sense of relief when it was all over. When Stanley and I later compared notes, I found that he had had a similar experience, but his horse – Tiger Tim – had seen it at the last moment and had cleared the whole grid.

could sell them, and he had sold over twenty this season. He was riding a six-year-old and his son and daughter were both on four-year-olds. They were not pretty horses, but were real tough, hard-looking sorts. I was full of admiration for the sheer pluck of hunting hounds on young, green horses, over these high banks, and realised that the whole family must be good "nagsmen".

That evening I had to return to Suffolk for the Easton Point-to-Point the following day so after supper a young jockey, Alan Rowe, who was one of the customers of the Seven Stars, drove me to Redruth station to catch the sleeper train which arrived in London at six o'clock. From Paddington I took a taxi to Liverpool Street and telephoned Sheila to pick me up from Ipswich station. She took me home for a hearty breakfast then off we went to the Point-to-Point in a convoy headed by my eldest daughter in her boyfriend's sports car, with my middle daughter bringing up the rear, rather less stylishly, in a Transit van bearing the slogan "Zodiac Disco". We shared our Point-to-Point course with the Essex and Suffolk and, as it was their course, they did most of the organisation which was very convenient for me as it meant that I could just turn up on the day. I am totally uninterested in Point-

**The Western:** ***"Only a miracle can save us now!"***

It was a shame that the Master was so unfriendly as I felt we could have got on so well. I was sure that we must have a lot in common when I found out that he sold his farm to take on these hounds and was living off the hunt guarantee, and that his wife and daughter did the horses while his son and himself did the hounds. He supplemented his income by going over to Ireland and buying young horses which he hunted until he

to-Point racing and it was only a great sense of the duty required of the Master that made me leave my hunting holiday to attend. The only race I ever watched with interest was the Members' and this was won on this occasion by Moggy Hennessy riding one of Brian Bird's horses which was sired by my stallion Double Bleep. The only part of the races that I really did enjoy was the Easton tradition of a Master's tent where the Master can dispense hospitality to hunting farmers at the hunt's expense. As we had a wonderful lot of farmers it was always a pleasure to entertain them. Duty over, I caught the eight-fifty-five from Ipswich, and the eleven-fifty-five from Paddington, arriving at Redruth at eight o'clock in the morning, to find my jockey friend, Alan, waiting to drive me back to the Seven Stars Inn.

This pub proved to be the perfect place for us. The landlord, Lesley Williams, was an ex-sailor with a bushy beard, always telling jokes and laughing. His wife Sheila, a homely sort of lady, was always pleasant and nothing was ever too much trouble for her. All the pub regulars were keen foxhunters and supporters of the Four Burrow. Every evening was spent talking hounds and hunting. One evening Stanley persuaded me to sing and this was followed by a song from "Big Arty", the terrier man to the Four Burrow, and in no time there was a great singing session going on, with songs from the landlord and Alan Rowe. Every morning the atmosphere in the kitchen was like something from Surtees, with us eating our breakfast in our hunting clothes, and yesterday's coat and boots drying in front of the old Range, and the buxom landlady, with her wrapover apron, in the background. The evening meals were somewhat of a puzzle for us because she never seemed to mind if we were late coming through from the bar to eat, or even if we had given her no notice at all that we wanted dinner. Whatever the situation, there was always a lovely, piping hot roast dinner ready for us, whenever we felt like it. After a few days we had to ask her her secret, as our wives, both excellent cooks, could not manage miracles like this. The answer was our introduction to microwave ovens which fascinated us as neither of us had ever heard of them.

**Lamerton.** *Longstanding Huntsman Tony Booth with hounds 1980, now in his eighteenth season.* Photograph kindly loaned by Mrs M H Bury

On the Monday morning Di Williams and I left the stables shortly after eight for the meet of the **Lamerton Foxhounds** at Langworthy Gate, Bratton Clovelly in Devon (Mon 30 Mar 1981). My diary does not say why Stanley was not with us but the reason must have been important as he would not miss a day if he could possibly help it. We arrived in comfortable time and, after hearing Clifford Pellew's tales, we wondered what to expect but the meet was pleasant with plenty of sherry and cakes offered. However, the scene was not very impressive and the Acting Master, Alan Robins, and all his field looked rather scruffy and seemed to have made little effort with their turnout.

We found at once and had a short burst, then lost the line completely. We then drew for over an hour, and Di and I had a lovely view of the next fox which gave us a slow hunt of just over an hour. The Field Master persistently held us back so far that we were out of touch for the first part of the hunt but, luckily, I saw a farmer leaving the field. I went with him and he and I had hounds to ourselves for over twenty minutes. This was the only highlight of the day and after this rather slow hunt hounds again lost the line. The next hour was spent drawing blank so, as I was getting fed up, we left at three fifteen. Hounds had been very slack. This may have been because of the warm day but the field were really excited and declared it to be the best day of the season so I did not think so. I recorded in my diary that evening that I thought them easily pleased.

We again had an early start the next morning, leaving at eight-thirty for the meet of the **South Tetcott Foxhounds** at the Junction Inn, Halliwill (Tues 31 Mar 1981). As we had forgotten our

**South Tetcott Hunt.** *Meet at Burdon Grange, Highampton, Nr Beaworthy, January 1981. Dick England, Joint-Master and Huntsman, in front with hounds.*
Photograph kindly loaned by Mr Maurice Thomas, MFH

sandwiches, we stopped at a cafe and enjoyed a cooked breakfast, arriving just in time at eleven-thirty. The Master, Dick England, arrived just after us and came into the pub carrying his red coat. His woollen sweater was the same as he had been wearing when we visited his kennel the previous Thursday and was easily recognised as it was full of holes. In spite of the sweater, he had that quiet dignity and presence that would always command respect wherever he was.

Our first fox ran to some forestry where it proved difficult to get hounds out, but after about an hour hounds were "all on" again and the Master drew some marshes near an old railway line. They found and went away but on a poor scent. The Chairman, who was also Field Master, held us up at the bottom of a hill and we were so frustrated that in the end Stanley rode up to him and asked permission for us to go on. This was granted, but hounds were long gone and in spite of riding in every direction we could not find them. At four-fifteen we gave up the attempt and were on our way home when we met the Master hacking back to the meet alone with his hounds. We stopped the box and he told us he had had a wonderful run. This made us really fed up, especially as we had only missed out because of the Field Master. Although this was a lovely country we had been on the roads most of the day and it desperately needed a lot of work done on it – scores of hunt jumps and gates were required everywhere and like so many other hunts it could have done with a wealthy, keen, young man to become Joint-Master to combine with the great experience and wisdom of Dick England.

That evening we had the best party of our stay, the singing going on until two o'clock. A great deal of whisky was consumed and, as a result, I had a terrible hangover the next morning. I did not get up until nine-forty-five, an unheard-of thing for me as I am usually an early riser, and felt a proper April Fool (Wed 1 Apr). As Stanley was a cattle man he suggested that we went to see the huge Truro market which had many hundreds of calves and sheep. We then visited the town and bought some items from the largest tack shop we had ever seen. After lunch we drove back to the stables and led out our horses to graze on the roadside. After a wash and change at the Seven Stars, we took Captain Mickleham and his wife Anne to dinner at a restaurant of Anne's choice where we enjoyed an excellent meal with the Captain on top form, keeping us in stitches all evening.

There was still no hunting on the Thursday so, after breakfast, Stanley went to the stables to ride out while I cleaned coats, boots, etc. for both of us. Stanley had been reading the local paper and had seen harness and some horses advertised. With nothing better to do, we thought it would be fun to see them and, while Stanley was at the stables with the car, another regular of the Seven Stars called Steve drove me to see the harness. This turned out to be rubbish but, after being reunited with Stanley at the Seven Stars, we went off to lunch in Redruth and then we went to look at the horses which had been advertised by a dealer. I bid for two of them and eventually bought a five-year-old bay gelding.

Again we had an early start, up at six-thirty and leaving the stables at eight o'clock with Di to drive the seventy-five miles to the Dartmoor Foxhounds meet. We arrived ten minutes late but there was no sign of a meet. With the aid of Directory Enquiries, I found the Dartmoor kennels number and rang John Budgett, the Master. He explained that he had telephoned my home and left a message with Sheila (which she had forgotten to pass on to me) to tell me that he had a virus in his kennel and had finished for the season. Once again we had had a 150-mile round trip for nothing, and as we drove dispiritedly back we felt that this was definitely the most ill-fated trip we had ever had.

During the early evening we settled up with Captain Mickleham, thinking it would be preferable to doing so on the Sunday morning in all the rush of leaving for home. His charges had been £20 per week per horse, and £30 per week for Di's board and lodging.

Our last day was with the **Cury Foxhounds** who were meeting, very appropriately, at the Wheel Inn at Cury, not far from Lizard Point (Sat 4 Apr 1981). We arrived over an hour too soon so we had a snooze in the lorry before hacking to the meet and a warm welcome from the Chairman who introduced us to the Master and Huntsman, Mr Harris, and to the other Joint-Master, Major Grimshaw.

The first fox ran two large circles then, after

**Cury Foxhounds** *Bonallack Farm. L to R, Larry Truwern with his son, Andrew Richards, 1st whip, Jt. Masters Geoff Thomas and Bill Nicholls. Halford Passage in the background.*

going to ground, was quickly bolted and hounds went away with a great cry. They lost the field but killed their fox. Stanley had to return to the meet as Tiger Tim had lost a shoe. The next draw was Goonhilley Downs in full view of the huge satellite dishes. We found here but hounds could not hunt it at all and it was left. I was fascinated to watch the amateur whip who, during the day, often jumped such high banks that no-one could follow him. His lovely grey mare negotiated banks much higher than her withers, dropping down the other side so that only his hat was visible. I just could not take my eyes off her and asked the Chairman who the whip was and if he was likely to accept an offer for her. He said his name was Lawry Collins, that he had been amateur whipper-in for some time, and that was he was sure he would not be offended if I asked him to sell the mare. At the first convenient check I rode up to him but he explained that she was the best hunter he had ever had. His brother had bred her and let him have her as a yearling and he said he would never part with her. Nevertheless, I offered a large sum for her if he ever changed his mind. An hour or so later, I twice saw him leave the whole field again over enormous banks, so I rode up to him again and offered even more money for her. He still shook his head firmly but acknowledged that I had offered him a very high price.

The third draw produced too many foxes and the pack split three ways. Mr Harris asked me to go with one of the splinter groups to bring them back to him, and I thoroughly enjoyed myself riding across the moors with my little pack. I was rather disappointed when at a check they could just hear the horn but dutifully I pushed them back to their huntsman. He had, of course, gone with one group while Mr Collins, as amateur whip, had gone with the third and, after pushing my group back to the horn, I followed them back and could see Mr Collins doing likewise far to my right. The nearer we both came to the huntsman the less distance there was between us and as my hounds were already going willingly to the horn I left them and started to approach him again. Suddenly he caught sight of my green coat approaching him across the open moor and, at a distance of five hundred yards or so, began to wave his arm menacingly in the air, not exactly with a clenched fist but leaving me in no doubt that he did not want me near him, tempting him to part with his mare. I took no notice and rode up to him, offering even more money. The figure was now more than twice the most I had ever paid for a horse before. He still refused firmly in a determined manner but, as a parting shot, I said to him, "If you change your mind, I'm staying at the Seven Stars at Stithians". With that I rode away.

We had a five mile hack back to the meet, across the wild, open beautiful moor, but I found myself continually looking at this lovely dappled grey mare. Before we boxed up, a gentleman amused the assembled field with a tale of meeting me before, in March 1973 during a day with Charlie Smith's East Cornwall Foxhounds, when I had become stranded in a river bottom. He was a very good story-teller, with a few little embellishments he had the field in helpless laughter.

We returned to the stables and dropped off our hunters, then, in order to save time in the morning, we went to fetch the bay gelding I had bought the previous Wednesday. He was very difficult to load, and then threw himself down twice in the lorry on the way back to the Micklehams', so I rode in the back of the lorry suspecting that he was claustrophobic. In the end, however, I decided it was just temper and left him on the lorry all night to avoid the problem of loading him again in the morning. We returned to the Seven Stars and settled up our account at six pounds per day inclusive of evening meals. This was originally quoted at seven pounds but the landlord said that he would knock a pound off as we had been such good spenders in the bar and he had enjoyed the singing and our company. Before going to the Micklehams' for dinner that evening we were enjoying a drink in the bar with our friends when the telephone rang and the landlord said it was someone wanting to speak to me. It was Lawry Collins who said that he had been discussing my offer with his wife and they had decided to let me have the grey mare. My immediate thought was pure joy and I quickly found myself regretting that I had bought the troublesome bay gelding as there was no room on the lorry for my new purchase, Demelza. Nevertheless, I was in very high spirits, and more than ready for the excellent dinner at the Micklehams with the Captain regaling us with tales of the old days with the Four Burrow when there was no restriction on bank jumping and up to eighty banks a day could often be jumped.

On the Sunday morning we loaded up and were away in good time and mercifully were spared any more tantrums from the bay gelding. He was sold on in fairly short order, but my other purchase was soon my favourite horse. I returned a week later to collect her and, borrowing a single trailer and pulling it with the Volvo, I combined the trip as usual with a visit to Charlotte at her school. I took her best friend Jeanette but it was a terrible journey with the M4 reduced to a single carriageway by drifting snow and at one point I thought we were going to have to spend the night in the car. Eventually we managed to get through, picked up Charlotte, and spent an amusing evening with the two girls, then twelve, in a pub where I had booked

"B&B". Next morning the three of us drove on to Exeter where I had arranged to meet the amateur whip and change the grey mare over from his trailer to mine in a large carpark. My heart sunk when, after I had paid him, he said, "There are a few things I ought to tell you about Demelza."

Fearing the worst, I asked what it was, to be told that after each summer at grass it was necessary to almost re-break her as she was a terrible bucker. This proved to be true. She could break girths easily and we had to buy one with elastic in it to prevent her getting the saddle off. Once we knew her, it was only a few days of bucking like a bronco on the lunge-line before she would settle down and she never once bucked when out with hounds. She turned out to be one of the finest hunters I have ever had, carrying me for ten seasons and then producing a foal, sadly having to be put down when a second foal kicked a hole through the wall of her stomach.

**Suffolk Foxhounds** *L to R, Mrs James Aldous, James Aldous M.F.H., Geoffrey Sale on Paul Rackham's grey, 'Basil', and Mrs Gordon-Lennox.*

Photograph by Jim Meads

# MAP 7

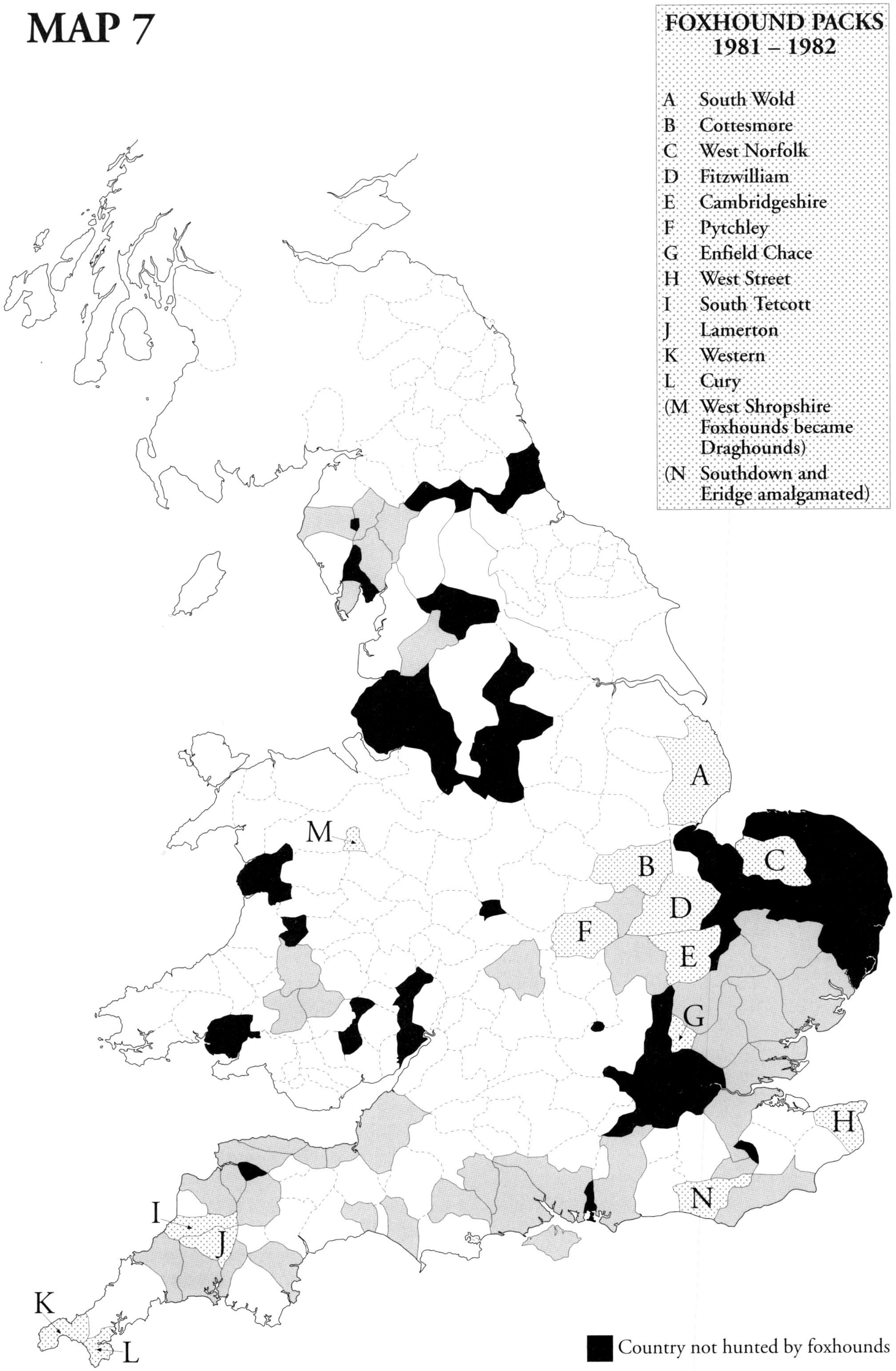
FOXHOUND PACKS
1981 – 1982
A South Wold
B Cottesmore
C West Norfolk
D Fitzwilliam
E Cambridgeshire
F Pytchley
G Enfield Chace
H West Street
I South Tetcott
J Lamerton
K Western
L Cury
(M West Shropshire Foxhounds became Draghounds)
(N Southdown and Eridge amalgamated)
A
B
C
D
E
F
G
H
I
J
K
L
M
N
Country not hunted by foxhounds

# Chapter 10

## Day Trips

I had no official jolly during the season 1981-82 but I made up for it by having several single days away and also several days from home which I started to call "day trips", much to the amusement of Hilda Wickham, wife of my kennel huntsman, who was in charge of the horses at the kennels.

The first of these followed from a party at which Charles Corner and I had been reminiscing about our day with the two minkhound packs. We decided to have another outing and managed to combine it with taking my daughter Charlotte and her friend Jenny, who had been staying with us in Suffolk, back to Jenny's parents at Templecombe in Somerset. Before we could leave, however, I had a job to do. I had recently bought some water-meadows and I urgently needed to make a gateway so that the dredger I had hired could get to the dykes. I would not let this difficulty stop me going hunting, so I started at five o'clock in the morning and, with the help of three others, had the gateway finished by twelve o'clock.

We then set off for Somerset and were on the road by two-thirty, arriving at Sheriden House, Jenny's parents' home, by seven-fifteen. Her father, Mr Fredmore, insisted that we went in for a drink and we were then easily persuaded to stop for an excellent dinner. Over more pre-dinner drinks, Mr Fredmore got out his AA book and booked us in to the Easton Court Hotel, which we thought very appropriate as it reminded us of our harriers. After a final brandy, we left the Fredmores' at ten o'clock, arriving at Easton Court at eleven-thirty.

During a quick nightcap we discovered that the South Devon Foxhounds were cubbing in the morning not far from the hotel, so we were up at five o'clock (Sat 22 Aug 1981). We became rather lost and arrived to find them returning from a run on an old fox which had taken them to the top of Hunters Tor. Some very good cub-hunting followed with circular hunts in the combe below us, their lovely voices amplified by the depth of the combe. We returned to the hotel for breakfast before setting off for the meet of the **Devon and Cornwall Minkhounds** at Fingle Bridge, near Drewsteignton.

We arrived to find a happy crowd at the Angler's Rest and moved off promptly to draw the River Teign downstream, finding after five minutes. This hunt took place in one of the most perfect settings for a minkhunt – the river wide and shallow, its water tumbling over rocks, with a good path for following which was high above the water in some places, and at the water's edge in others, but always in sight of hounds hunting below us. We enjoyed a forty-five minute hunt downstream and killed our mink in mid-stream. Then we drew on downstream for about two and a half miles to an old weir but, apart from a few hounds speaking occasionally, we did very little more so a decision was made to return for lunch. Our arrival back at the pub was amusing as it was one-thirty and the pub was surrounded by people enjoying picnics on the river bank. There were happy little family groups all over the place sitting on the ground with white cloths loaded with goodies. I took one look at these picnickers and felt very relieved that it was not me who had to take a pack of wet hounds through them. And through them it had to be as there was no room to go around. However, after some fairly nippy whipping-in, hounds were boxed up with the picnickers taking no notice of us whatsoever.

After a ploughman's lunch we drew upstream and had a pleasant little hunt of twenty minutes or so until the mink went to ground in some rocks. We then drew further upstream to Mill End Bridge. It was decided to blow for home at six o'clock and miraculously the hound van appeared on the bridge. Charles and I watched in astonishment as, after hounds were loaded into the hound van, there was a stampede of followers hurling themselves in with the hounds until there was no more room. Twelve of them managed to hitch a ride back to the meet in this way. Charles and I had a more dignified lift – at least by comparison – in the back of Mrs Miller's pick-up truck. She was an ex-Master of these hounds, and of the Tetcott Foxhounds. We waited at the meet for the pub to open at seven o'clock and were quite glad we did as we were joined by Mrs Miller. She had a fund of interesting stories, one of which was that she had been a professional whipper-in in her young days. Her father and grandfather had been Masters of longstanding and Charles and I could imagine the tut-tutting when the young offspring went professional.

We dined at the Angler's Rest with some fellows who told us of a lovely pub nearby so after dinner we set off to find the Drew Arms, at Drewsteignton, finding it delightfully old-fashioned and full of characters, three of whom were playing accordions. I sang three songs before we finally left at closing time. We arrived back at the Easton Court Hotel at eleven-thirty and went straight to bed, having spent a truly excellent day in most delightful company.

The following October, three friends and I set off from Suffolk to go to Wetherby in Yorkshire with seven Cleveland Bays and a foal for the special breed sale held there annually. Trade was rotten and the bidding on none of mine reached the reserve I had set. To see my beautiful four-year-olds in the ring, with the auctioneer struggling to get a bid of £350, was heartbreaking, especially as at a previous sale one of my horses had made the top price of a thousand guineas. After settling the bill for the bed-and-breakfast for all of us – an expense very much grudged as I had sold nothing – my friends Ernie Calver and Derek Read went back to Suffolk with the unsold horses in two lorries while Bill James and I set off in his car. We were heading eventually for theWelsh Cob Sales at Builth Wells but had planned to have a day's hunting "on the way" with the **West Oxfordshire Basset Hounds** who were meeting at the Mill Hotel, Kingham, near Chipping Norton in the Cotswolds (17 Oct 1981).

At the meet, Mr Humphries, the Honorary Secretary, made us very welcome and dispensed hospitality before we moved off in very high winds. Conditions were very much against scent, with most of the fields either just harrowed or being harrowed. Moreover, artificial manure had recently been spread on most of them and this, combined with the harrowing and high winds, did not make for good hunting. However, the bassets, in their usual indomitable style, persevered and we enjoyed their tremendous voices which were in marked contrast to that of the one beagle hunting with them. Leaving the bassets we went on to Builth Wells but the Barley Mow was fully booked so we stayed in the Swan Hotel during the Sales.

Less than a month later, I had the first of my "day trips", to the **Enfield Chace Foxhounds** (Tues 10 Nov 1981). They were meeting at Datchworth, near Stevenage in Hertfordshire and Peter Bailey, a member of the Easton, came with me. I had arranged for my horse to be ready at the Easton kennels at seven o'clock but when I arrived there, the staff had overslept and no-one was stirring. After a hasty corn feed and some rapid plaiting, we finally left at seven-thirty but, in spite of this delay, we arrived at the meet far too early with an hour to spare, so we sat in the cab eating the soup and rolls we had brought with us. Jack Batterbee, the huntsman, whose brother Tom Batterbee, was huntsman to the Suffolk Foxhounds, arrived with hounds and explained that there was so much anti-hunt feeling in the village that no-one could unbox anywhere near and there always had to be a special arrangement for unboxing in a farm yard. This was such an unhappy contrast to our jolly Easton Harrier meets where the pubs were crowded with local people. We were not impressed by the turnout of the field and noticed that even the hunt staff had no spurs on. The field were a friendly crowd but had no knowledge of hunting or hunting etiquette, and the only thing they understood was not to pass the Master. There was only one person who I could call a real hunting man and he was an ex-Master.

The first fox went away along the side of a stubble field but unfortunately the Field Master took the field for a gallop along the line before hounds arrived, so they could do nothing with this fox. They found again and had a slow hunt with the huntsman doing most of the work. I was not sure if the hounds were slack or the scent nil, but in either case there was little hunting. We were hunting within sight and sound of the A1 road at Stevenage and I would have been terrified to have hunted hounds so close. I wondered if that was the reason they preferred hounds not to be too independent. At one point we were sitting watching hounds work below us when the Field Master suddenly shot off at a fast canter, hotly pursued by the field, including us, as we assumed that he was leading us down into the valley. However, he only made a circuit of the field, returning to the spot he had left. This occurred several times more, but we were not fooled again and stayed where we were. When the happy field arrived back after one of these jaunts, one of them rode up to us and said, "I'm sorry you missed that run. You must keep your eyes on him," he went on kindly, indicating the Field Master, "as when he gathers up his reins you know you're in for a run."

At three o'clock we had had enough of this farce so we hacked back and made our way home.

The following Tuesday both Peter and Sue Gooderham came with me to the **Cambridgeshire Foxhounds** and we arranged to meet at the Easton kennels (Tues 17 Nov 1981). After loading up Demelza, who had become my pride and joy, we set off at seven-thirty for the meet at Stow Longa near Huntingdon, and arrived far too early. However, we were sportingly entertained as we were able to sit in the lorry cab and watch some whippets coursing in the field next door. As we hacked into the village I was hailed by a man who said, "You'd better have a whisky with me," and disappeared into his house, appropriately named The Fox Earth, and returned with three drinks on a tray. It was one of those embarassing moments when he was sure I knew him, but I could not remember his name or from where I knew him. I was later told that I had judged the Sproughton Foot Beagles Puppy Show with him, over fifteen years before.

The Senior Master was Mrs Crossman whose husband's family had provided a Master for the Easton in 1911. She introduced me to her Joint Masters, one of whom had been amateur whipper-in for over twenty seasons, and to the huntsman. The hunt staff were immaculately turned out and hounds looked very fit and well. The mounted field of thirty moved off to draw a large covert very near to where we had left our box. This was blank, which was not surprising after the coursing which had been going on next to it, and we then drew on until one o'clock before finding. This fox proved to be injured and was killed within a hundred yards. We drew again and at three o'clock found, but this fox was headed by a Water Board van and ran straight back into hounds and was killed. We continued to draw until stopped by failing light but did not find again. David, a young man who used to hunt with the Easton, drove me to fetch our box. So ended a disappointing day which could be blamed on nothing in particular but which just emphasises the glorious uncertainty of a day's hunting. We arrived back at Easton at eight o'clock having been away for over twelve hours.

Three days later Sheila and I were off again down to the West Country for a combined school visit to Charlotte and a day's hunting. We arrived at our favourite Yarcombe Inn on the Friday at six o'clock and that evening invited the Roffe-Sylvesters, who were on top form and as entertaining as ever, to a dinner which was as delicious as usual. Sheila persuaded me that as the meet was at twelve o'clock we would have time for shopping in Honiton. This mission accomplished, she dropped me off at the meet of the **Crealy Basset Hounds** at Combe Farm, Tipton St John (near Honiton), going on to collect Charlotte from school and do more shopping in Street (Sat 21 Nov 1981). Mr Takely, the Master, and I had a lazy day on the hilltop and watched while Mr Mills hunted the bassets below us but sadly it was a blank day, although he drew until four-thirty. Sheila was not at the meet when I returned so I walked to the end of the lane and sat in a bus shelter. When she did return she went straight past and I had to run after her the length of the lane which made up for my idleness.

We were back in Suffolk again on the Sunday and the following Wednesday I had a day with the **West Norfolk Foxhounds** from the meet at Hunts Farm, Saham Toney, near Watton (Wed 25 Nov 1981). Wednesday was a good day for these "day trips" because the Easton hunted on Thursdays and Saturdays. Peter Bailey was waiting for me at the kennels with his horse and we arrived at the meet in good time. Hounds looked well and the hunt staff were well turned out, but sadly it proved to be another blank day. We were told that the new young huntsman had been showing very good sport so this was particularly disappointing for us. He drew very thoroughly and carefully until four-thirty and most of the field of thirty kept out until he blew for home, like us obviously hoping for a late run. The main amusement of the day had been flirting with a pretty young lady called Celia, but re-named by us "Cuddles" (from Surtees), as her horse continually sidled up to ours most of the day.

The next foray was considerably further, to the meet of the **South Wold Foxhounds** at The Paddock, Edlington, in Lincolnshire, and I was particularly pleased that Peter Bailey was again able to join me as he knew this part of the country very well owing to his game-dealing business (Tues 1 Dec 1981). We enjoyed a most hospitable meet provided by Mr Robert Booth, our host, who handed round large port-and-brandies, and trays of delicious eats. Cook, the professional huntsman, I remembered meeting when he was hunting the Eridge in Kent three years earlier on the day Mickey got so badly bogged. Sadly, after starting on such a high note, we drew for over two hours before finding, and then only had a short run before scent failed, and we then drew for the rest of the day without finding again. Our flagging spirits were uplifted by our host inviting us in for tea, during which I suggested they might have an invitation day in the Easton country, with us bringing our hounds for a day in their country. This suggestion was enthusiastically taken up by everyone present but somehow never materialised.

Peter Bailey had by now firmly caught the visiting bug and again was my companion when I went for a day with the **Pytchley Foxhounds** (Mon 7 Dec 1981). We left the Easton kennels, surprisingly late, at eight o'clock and as the roads were very slippery we arrived only just in time to unbox at The Elms, Pytchley, the home of Joint-Master Mrs Reynolds. Although the field was small, the meet on the village green at Orlingbury was idyllic. The field were dotted around the green, looking very smart, and in the centre sat the huntsman with his hounds all around him, sitting on their haunches and staring up at him. Mr Saunders, the Joint Master, introduced himself, and then us to the Honorary Secretary who with practised ease extracted a cap from Peter. Hunting etiquette says that Masters of Hounds may hunt with other packs without paying a visiting cap, a system which works very well as most Masters do not have the time to do any visiting. I was soon hailed by two old friends from my days of hunting in the Lakes, Frank Taylor and Hugh Davis, and the remaining time before moving off were filled with reminiscences.

The huntsman moved off to draw some low meadows in a valley, and then tried a large covert where they found and went away with a most melodious cry over a lovely piece of country until they split, one half taking the line of a hare. This caused a delay but the huntsman soon had them all on the line again and although they were now fifteen minutes behind their fox, they hunted on and we were treated to some beautiful slow hound work. Sadly this example of hound perseverence was ended when some of the pack again rioted on a hare. I was quite taken aback by this as I had expected that a pack of this high calibre would have been rock steady to hare. The next draw was Badsaddle Wood which is famous for being where the last wild boar in England was killed. Finding in Badsaddle, the fox went away close by me and this was followed by an enjoyable little spin into a large covert outside which we sat and listened as they rattled him round and round. Although we were standing still, I thoroughly enjoyed this piece of woodland hunting – the glorious cry of twenty-one and a half couple, complimented by the exceptionally good voice and horn of the huntsman. It was while we were waiting outside this covert that I learned that Mr Saunders had won the Grand National. We were amongst the very few left out when, after watching the terrier-man (who was also the local grave-digger) unsuccessfully trying to dig a fox out of a very difficult place, we finished in the dark. Mrs Reynolds, mother of my old friend David Reynolds, kindly invited us in for a cup of tea and an early taste of Christmas cake, and we finally arrived back at Easton at eight-thirty.

**East Lincs Harehounds.** *Meet at Dalby House, Boxing Day 1984. Messrs C Cooper (Joint-Master), S Brocklehurst (Huntsman) and B Ramsden (whipper-in).*

Photograph kindly loaned by Mrs C Ramsden

As I drove home from the kennels, it started to snow and there was no more mounted hunting in the Easton country for another six weeks until 21 January. By the beginning of the New Year I was desperately bored with having no hunting at all so I started to telephone around and soon discovered that the **East Lincolnshire Hare Hounds** were still able to hunt (Sat 2 Jan 1982). Tony and Anne St Quinton, who are not only good friends and neighbours but also basset hound fanatics, needed no encouragement to accompany me on this trip. We left at nine-thirty and arrived at twelve with an hour to spare so we decided to have lunch at the Butter Cross restaurant in Spilsby. The otherwise jovial meet at the White Hart was marred by a rumour that the hunt might have to disband owing to a shortage of members. If the quality of hunting on this day was an example of the sport show, there certainly should not have been any lack of support. The first hare was hunted around us for three full circles. She was never hurried and had plenty of time to double and twist with the bassets carefully unravelling all her ruses until finally being distracted by fresh hares. This was one and a half hours of pure venerie, with that special cry that only bassets can produce, and well worth the trip to Lincolnshire. There was one more very pleasant hunt, before we adjourned for tea at a nearby bungalow and finally arrived home again at six-thirty. I was glad to see that they were still going in 1990.

Two weeks later Tony and I set off again to the **Albany Basset Hounds**'s meet at The Woodman, Nuthampstead, near Royston in Hertfordshire. This day's hunting was the most unusual of my whole experience and was conducted in a manner which I did not know existed. We left at ten o'clock and arrived with just enough time for breakfast in a transport cafe. When we arrived at The Woodman we found that the Hunt was holding a Committee meeting before hunting. This we thought very odd until matters were explained to us. The members of this very unusual Hunt come from such a wide area that it made good sense to hold a meeting when they were together for hunting. The Master, Mr Tucker, came from Derby, the lady whipper-in and her

**Albany Bassets.** *Meet at The Woodman, Nuthampstead, 1986. Huntsman Peter Baker.*

Photograph kindly loaned by Mrs S Money

husband from Bradford, the Field Master from Suffolk and the Honorary Secretary from London. The most unusual thing about this Hunt, and I would think that it is unique, is that the general public are allowed to bring their pet bassets and let them hunt with the pack. This sounds as though it would cause total chaos but in fact it worked quite well. The regular pack were kennelled and hunted as normal and there was a Field Master who told the Kennel Club basset owners when they could let their hounds off the lead and to catch them up again. The regular pack moved off to draw, followed by eight bassets on leads with their owners. Only one of the pet hounds was allowed off the lead to draw with the pack and this was obviously a singular honour which every owner strived to attain. When a hare was found and the pack had settled on the line, running with a strong cry, the Field Master allowed most of the others to be let off their leads. At the first check, he ordered any pet hounds that was in danger of distracting the pack from its cast to be caught up again. Then, after the pack had regained the line, these were released again. One or two of the owners were only allowed to let their hounds off for a few minutes and we assumed that these were new to the system, or what, in normal hunting, we would call "unentered". I was very surprised at how well the system worked but this was due to the strictness of the Field Master in insisting certain hounds were caught up quickly at checks.

The hunting was quite good considering the terrible hunting conditions with melting snow still in most places and, as there were not many hares, hounds could persevere on the faint scent without the distraction of fresh hares. The day ended with a tea-party, where our host offered whisky in the tea for all in hunt livery but later included me as I was a visiting Master. We eventually arrived home at six o'clock, feeling that we had learned something new and were privileged to have seen it.

The snow eventually went away and I was soon able to resume my daytrips. The next visit was to the **Fitzwilliam Foxhounds** and Peter Bailey again accompanied me (Wed 10 Feb 1982). We also arranged to meet Stanley Tompkins at the Crown at Stowupland (near Stowmarket) at nine o'clock, transferring his horse onto our box so we could all go together. We could not resist going to the back door of the Crown where we thought John the landlord would give us an early pint. This he did and, as always in drinking beer out of hours, it tasted especially good. John also got out his collection of antique shotguns and the combination of the beer and the guns caused us to be slightly late for the meet which was at Bythorn, near Thrapston (Northants). However, we arrived just in time to join the field of forty-five which included our old friends Hugh and Betty Gingell of the Cambridgeshire Harriers.

The first draw was along some rough hedges and a fox was soon away and gave us a long but very slow hunt until hounds changed onto a fresh fox which gave us a sharp hunt of over an hour. This run was over some unspoiled country with a few jumpable fences which Demelza managed in style. The pace and the sticky going had told on the horses and Stanley's was badly blown so he returned to the meet. Peter and I stayed out for another hour but most of this was spent drawing blank. We eventually left at four o'clock as I dared not stop later, as I had to be at a meeting at eight o'clock that evening. We made good time on the return

**The Albany Bassetts:** ***"Your turn will come!"***

trip and so had another beer before changing horses again at the Crown, and there was time enough for Stanley to sell this horse to Peter.

Another of the smart "Shires" packs within reach of home was the **Cottesmore Foxhounds** and Peter and I went with them two weeks later (Tues 23 Feb 1982). The day started badly for me as I overslept and was woken up by the kennels telephoning me at six o'clock. They were so used to me being punctual or early that they realised what must have happened. To save time I suggested that Peter should bring the lorry to the village of Earl Soham and I would meet him there at six-thirty. I had a very quick shave and dress, but no coffee. However, we made such good time that we allowed ourselves to stop at Wansford for breakfast and, because we decided on the Little Chef rather than the Haycock Hotel, we collected some funny looks in our hunting clothes. Arriving at the meet comfortably for eleven o'clock, Mr Samworth, one of the Masters, welcomed us warmly but Brian Fanshawe, joint Master and huntsman, seemed out of humour with everyone. I had hoped to see Jill Sillers, an ex-Easton member, but was told that she only hunted on Mondays and Thursdays.

We drew for two hours before finding but then the fox ran immediately into some large woodlands. This was just as well for me as I missed most of the run and would have been completely lost as I could not get Demelza over a hunt jump. There were two more little runs which were just enough to give us a taste of this glorious country which was over fifty per cent permanent grass. The field were all very friendly which made for an enjoyable day and we were sad to be obliged to leave at four-fifteen owing to me having another meeting to attend. On the way home we stopped at a caravan on a lay-by for a mug of tea and a bacon sandwich and had an interesting conversation with the proprietor. He was a keen foxhunter – keen on the principal of hunting, that is, because he had read about it but had never been.

My habit of visiting other packs had by this time become well-known and was the topic of conversation one day at an Easton meet while we waited for the fog to lift (Sat 27 Feb 1982). Bruce and Lela Turner were there and suggested that their friend Ron Hutchinson would put up us (them and myself) and our horses at his home, Ringwould Manor, in Kent. As there were several packs in that area that I had not yet hunted with I was very keen for them to make the necessary arrangements. This was very promptly done and they even agreed to bring my horse down with Lela's so I was able to travel by car and have a day with the **Surrey and North Sussex Beagles**, *en route*. I stopped at Otford (Kent) for an early lunch and arrived at the meet at The Half Moon at Balcombe (West Sussex) at twelve-thirty. Gordon Laing, the huntsman and a great friend of Jim Wickham, my kennel huntsman, boomed out a welcome in his broad Scottish accent and explained that we were to motor some way before drawing the other side of a lake. We drew blank all afternoon but hopes were raised at the end of the day when a farmworker siad he had seen a hare pass by him. Gordon put hounds on the line but only one old bitch could own the line, so after a time he blew for home.

Leaving the beagles, I reached Ringwould Manor at six o'clock, to find that Bruce and Lela were already there and had settled both horses into the stables, Demelza for me and Sansoin for Lela (Tues 2 Mar 1982). We had an early dinner then walked through the churchyard to the Five Bells for a game of skittles.

The next morning we all went to the meet of the **West Street Foxhounds** at the Fitzwilliam Arms at Goodneston (near Nonnington) but sadly, there are no details in my diary of this day, other than the meet (Wed 3 Mar 1982). I must have been distracted when starting to write it, and never came back to finish it. I do remember having a most enjoyable day in a country fairly easy to cross with plenty of little coverts and of coming away with a great desire to hunt with them again.

The Easton Harriers had their last meet of the season on Saturday 20 March and, after hunting, a few of us agreed to meet the next day at the Brome Grange Hotel for a hunt breakfast and then to follow the **Coakham Bloodhounds** who were meeting at Thornham Park nearby (Sun 21 Mar 1982). These hounds came up from Kent at the invitation of Lord Henniker over whose estate they were to run. The hunt officials were very smartly turned out and the hounds set off at a tremendous pace but I did not stay with them very long as my ribs were very painful following a bad fall the day before. I returned to the meet but my daughter Bridget stayed out and later told me that it was a great gallop but the field were rather inclined to barge and push at jumps.

At the beginning of the next season I decided to have another couple of days with basset hounds, planning it in conjunction with another trip to Builth Wells for the Welsh Cob Sales which was getting to be as useful an excuse for a jolly as going to see Charlotte. I telephoned Dr David Rees, Master of the **Hydfer Hare Hounds**,explained the situation and arranged to introduce myself at the meet which was at Carno Farm, Libanas, near Brecon (Sat 16 Oct 1982). This proved very easy as he was the only person at the meet but was later joined by his Joint-Master, David Evans. The hounds were an unbelievable mixture of almost everything in the hound world. There were Kerry Beagle crosses (famous Irish black-and-tans), bloodhound crosses, basset and harrier crosses, a couple of pure beagles and a Clifton Foot harrier bitch. When they were gathered around their Master and huntsman they presented an unforgettable picture but they tended to wander around a little. There was every colour one could think of and to say that they were unlevel would be a gross understatement. Dr Rees moved off with his mixed bag of hounds and found very quickly.

The hunt that followed came right out of the pages of hunting history. In conditions that were really terrible, with drizzling rain driven by near gale-force winds, they hunted slowly up the mountain into the clouds above us and back down to the valley bottom, time and time again. We had climbed up to the boundary fence (the highest one on the mountainside which is usually fairly horizontal with good walking behind it) and we could walk relatively easily, either watching them above us or in the valley below, and best of all when they came past us. When close enough to them I could see how wonderfully old-fashioned was their style of hunting – no rushing along the line but instead they hunted slowly with the Kerry Beagle crosses several times stopping, turning their heads over their shoulders to throw their tongues with that delightful double note which they hang onto seemingly for ever. This enchanting spectacle went on for two and a half hours with hounds hunting completely unaided, requiring no help in spite of the high winds. The Master considered they had changed hares during this long hunt after one and a half hours, and although I could not see why he thought it, I expect he was right as it is not the sort of thing one would suggest to a fellow huntsman if there was any doubt.

This had been a great day's hunting in some of the loveliest country imaginable, with spectacular views and these wonderfully old-fashioned hounds. Sir Roger de Coverley would have been quite at home and would easily have had time to carry out his alleged habit of picking up a tired hare in front of hounds and placing it in one of his voluminous pockets to give it an honourable retirement in his orchard. I bade Dr Rees and his Joint-Master goodnight and thanked them for what to me was hare-hunting at its best, but as I drove on to Builth Wells I could not help wishing I could have seen these remarkable hounds in fair conditions.

The Barley Mow was as delightful as ever, with the BFSS shield proudly displayed both in the window and over the bar, and was packed full of characters. I, of course, was "on a high" after the exhilerating day and when, during the evening, a singsong started I was more than ready to contribute. A group of gypsies came into the back bar and started to sing some good songs, but sometimes got stuck for the next line. Twice this happened with a song that I knew so I just said the next line and that was enough prompting to enable them to finish the song. After the second time this happened, they asked me where I came from and said that, as I had put them right twice, I must know some songs and asked me to sing one. When this was finished one of them put a whisky in front of me and said,

"There you are, Punch. Sing us another."

**Hydfer Hare Hounds:** ***"Handsome is, as handsome does"***

This process was repeated time and time again and the next day at the cob sales one of them told me that I had sung over twenty songs so presumably I had consumed over twenty whiskies, with no trace of a hangover. While this mammoth singsong was going on, every room in the Barley Mow was packed and one could hear music or songs coming from other rooms and the atmosphere was electric.

At two in the morning a policeman pushed his way through the crowd until he reached the bar and said to the landlord,

"You're very busy tonight, John Barley."

"Yes," said John, "but they are all residents."

"Oh," said the policeman. "Then I suggest that you lock the doors in case some of them get out."

The evening ended with a gesture I shall never forget. When the gypsies decided to leave, an old man, who rejoiced in the name of Grandfather Vandal, stopped as he passed me and shook me by the hand with tears running down his furrowed, weather-beaten old face. He said simply,

"Boy, how I wish my wife could have lived long enough to hear you sing those songs. They were her songs, you see. She came out of your country."

I have always felt that this was the greatest and most genuine compliment I have ever had after a singing session.

On the following morning (Sunday) I went to Aberystwyth University to visit Charles Corner's daughter Sarah who was studying there. She was not yet up so I had to wait while she dressed but then I took her out to lunch at her favourite country club. I then went to see Derek Davies (and this time I managed to keep awake during tea) before going back to the Barley for another party which ended at four o'clock. At Monday's sale I bought eight Welsh Cob foals and then the next morning left the Barley to drive to the meet of the **Westerby Bassets** at Theddingworth, near Lutterworth (Tues 19 Oct 1982).

This time, unlike my previous unsuccessful attempt to hunt with these hounds in 1978 when Sheila and I went to the wrong place, I managed to find the meet and arrived in good time. I met Mr Bragg, the Master, and also saw Dr Arthur of the Pipewell Beagles who enquired after Bridget. He remembered the fuss in the Lake District when she had disappeared while hunting with the Windermere ten years earlier and it had been thought that she was lost in the fells. I had read that some Dunston Harriers blood had been crossed into the Westerby Bassets and the effects of this could clearly be seen as their legs were straighter. Whilst hunting, the pack ran with more drive than bassets usually do, which again showed the harrier influence. There was one extremely good hunt of two and a half large circles and then they changed hares and ran into some country where there were too many hares for any serious hunting. As by now it was four o'clock and pouring heavily with rain I decided to leave.

**Westerby.** *Meet at Mowsley, 29 November 1986. Left to right, Chris Weston and Clive Hillcoat (whips), William Bevin (Master), and Mark Valentine (whip).*

# MAP 8

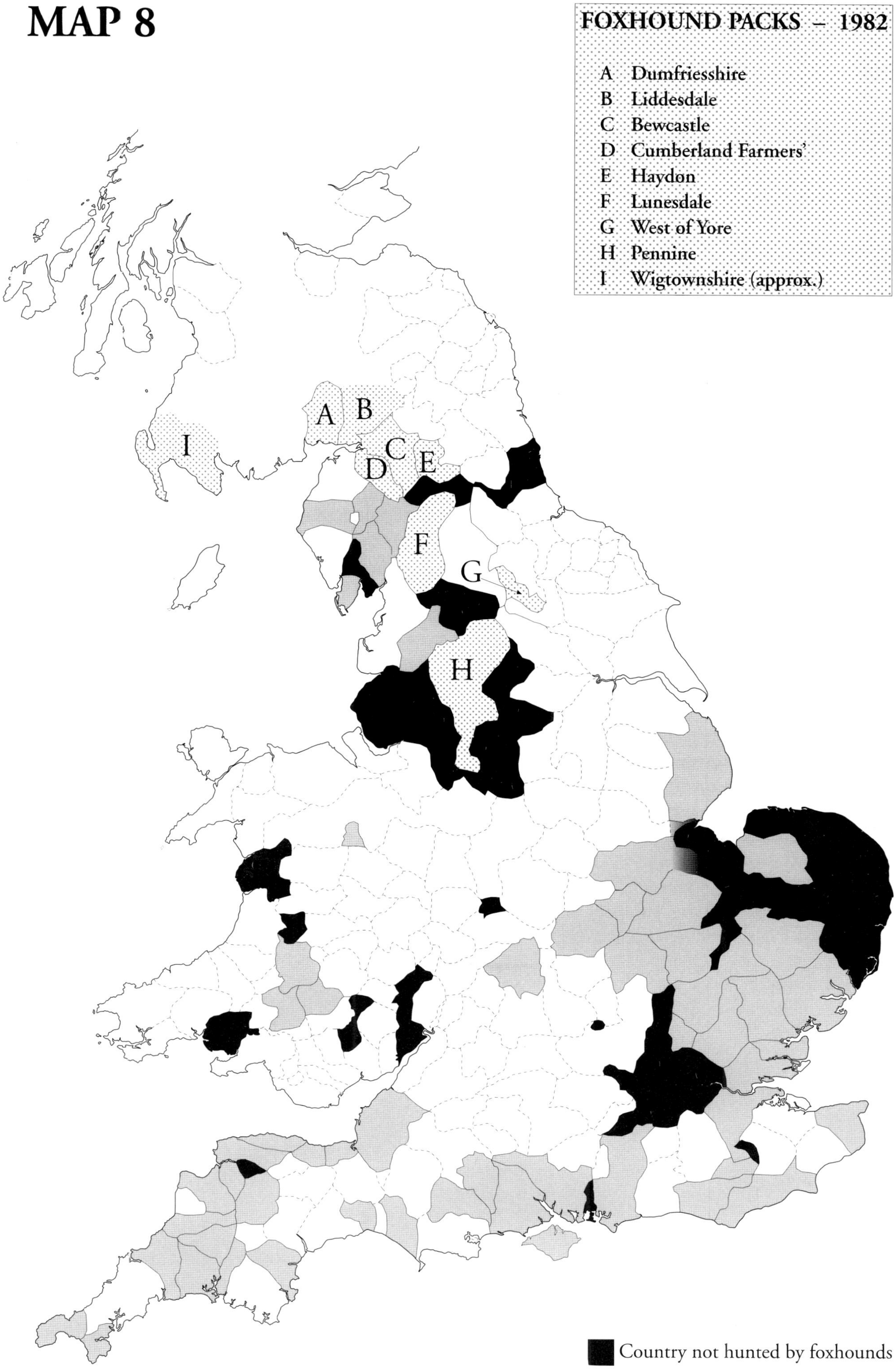
FOXHOUND PACKS – 1982
A Dumfriesshire
B Liddesdale
C Bewcastle
D Cumberland Farmers'
E Haydon
F Lunesdale
G West of Yore
H Pennine
I Wigtownshire (approx.)
A
B
C
D
E
F
G
H
I
Country not hunted by foxhounds

# CHAPTER 11

## SCOTLAND AND THE NORTH

Having had no jolly in the 1981-82 season I made up for it by having two in 1982-83. This first came about because I had arranged another exchange visit with the Holcombe Harriers. Twenty members of the Easton, together with their horses, went up to stay with members of the Holcombe and have two days hunting combined with a full social schedule and I arranged another hunting holiday in addition to the Holcombe festivities to take advantage of being so far north. Even though I did not know him very well at the time, I had arranged with Eric Elliot, Master of the newly-formed Staffordshire Moorland Harriers (to whom I had drafted some harriers to help start the pack), to stable my horses at his kennels for the first night and he kindly insisted that I stayed with him. To make these hunting holidays both easier and cheaper, I had bought a little caravan for my grooms to sleep in and put a draw-bar on the back of my lorry to tow it. This meant that the groom could always be near the horses, wherever they were, and also I would not have their accommodation charges.

I left home at just after seven o'clock, a day earlier than the other Easton members, with my groom, Theresa Pomroy, and we arrived at the Staffordshire Moorland kennels, at Sutton, near Macclesfield in Derbyshire at three-thirty. Paul Goddard, the huntsman, had everything ready for us, even a cup of tea. I had taken Charlie and Demelza and when they were settled in, Eric arrived to take me to his home a few miles away. He and his wife Marcia were perfect hosts. They had arranged a dinner party that evening and the other guests had obviously been invited especially because they had something in common with me. They were the Chairman of the National Farmers' Union and his wife, and the local National Parks Commissioner and his wife who had come from Helmingham (in Suffolk). The evening should have been very enjoyable but, once we had sat down at the table, things started to go horribly wrong. There are three things that I have a serious allergy to – nuts, spinach and blackcurrants. If I eat any of these my mouth and throat contract, I become terribly nauseous, and the end result is awful. The first course that Marcia served was Egg Florentine which, of course, is spinach based. To refuse this was highly embarassing but, when the next course arrived – trout in almonds – I just wanted to crawl under the table. To make it a hat-trick, the pudding featured blackcurrants. What embarrassment and seeming ingratitude to these kind people who, in spite of not knowing me very well, had put up my horses and myself, and arranged this lovely dinner party around my visit. We have since become good friends and the saga of the first night is a standing joke. When we meet Marcia often laughs and says, "Nuts, spinach and blackcurrants."

While enjoying Marcia's excellent breakfast I apologised once again for the fact that my schedule did not allow me to hunt with my host's hounds as his hunting days clashed with those of the Holcombe programme. He drove me back to his kennels where Paul Goddard had a good route worked out for me to find the meet of the **High Peak Harriers** at Sparklow (Wed 10 Nov 1982). This, apart from the new Staffordshire Moorland, was the last of the harrier packs but unbelievably it was to be eight years before I returned to hunt with the Staffordshire Moorland and complete my original ambition of hunting with every harrier pack. It was not without a little trepidation that I faced this day's hunting as the stone walls in the High Peak country are quite famous. Of the two horses, I had decided to take Charlie as I was afraid that Demelza might try to bank the walls as she would in her native Cornwall. At the meet I was hailed by the ex-Master, Jack Morton, whom I had known for years, and he introduced me to the new Master and huntsman, Martin Salmon, and his Joint-Master Val Turner.

**High Peak Harriers.** *Meet at Sparklow, 1989. Huntsman Tony Herring, with Mrs Helen Herring.*
Photograph kindly loaned by Mr Geoffrey Biggin

Another familiar face was Dick Deakin who had been a Kennel Huntsman in Essex.

There were perhaps rather too many hares, and hounds changed quite often, but the end result was that hounds were running almost non-stop across this glorious country. The old pasture and good sound going gave that lovely drumming sound when the field were galloping together that can only be heard on good, old permanent pastures. I was relieved to find that we were in an area where the walls were of jumpable height for me and, although I was scared stiff most of the time, I did not get left out of the running and thoroughly enjoyed my day. I was quite spell-bound by the beauty of it all, the countryside so neat and tidy, with the meadows looking like lawns, divided by the stone walls of the prettiest blue-grey stone. There were spectacular views all around, seemingly for tens of miles in every direction. When they returned to the meet for second horses, I thought I ought to stop as I had to go on up to the Holcombe to meet Sheila and the other Easton members. I returned to the kennels at Sutton to collect my other horse and the caravan, and went on to stay with Tom Bracewell, who had succeeded my old friend Newton Bacon as Master of the Holcombe on his retirement after fourteen seasons in 1979.

We hunted with the Holcombe on the following day (Thurs 11 Nov 1982) at Deerplay in very high winds and discovered a tradition with the Holcombe that all men remove their hats when "Home" is blown at the end of the day. I renewed my acquaintance with Alex Sneddon, the huntsman, and also with his whipper-in, Angus MacDonald, who had been huntsman to the South Pool Harriers when I had hunted with them in 1973. On the Friday Anthony Barker, Master of the Windermere Harriers, brought his hounds to the Plough Inn at Selside, especially for the Easton visit, but with sixty-five mph gale winds, sport was minimal and some hounds were lost for a considerable time. On Saturday we hunted again with the Holcombe at Mr Slinger's farm, at Hesketh Bank, finishing the day with a dinner. When I returned to Tom's house I was delighted to see that Newton and Kate Bacon had also been invited to the dinner.

During pre-dinner drinks Newton told me that I could hunt on the Sunday if I wished, as the Pennine Foxhounds, a foot pack, were out at Anglezark. I had not heard of this pack, but was keen to go so we got out some maps and found the spot. I desperately hoped to be offered a car and broadly hinted, asking how long it would take me to reach the meet in the lorry, and would the roads be alright for a lorry. Newton helped with comments like the roads are terribly narrow, but no offer of a car was forthcoming. I was silly not to ask outright for a car or Land Rover as there were plenty in the yard. Tom Bracewell was very generous with his gin-and-tonics and the pre-dinner party was over all too soon. We moved on to the dinner at a Leisure Centre where they had arranged a typical Lancashire hunt supper of Hot-Pot and apple-pie. Dinner was partly formal, but after a few toasts, and a vote of thanks from the Easton proposed by myself for the hospitality for the three days, the evening ended as usual with a singing session. The singing was kicked off by me having to reply to a toast to the Horse, so by way of a reply I sang the "The Battered Brigade" –

*"The mark of a stake on the shoulder,*
*The brand of a wall on the knee,*
*Are scars to the careless beholder,*
*And blemishes so it may be.*
*But every such blemish endorses*
*The pluck of a steed unafraid,*
*And the heart of a lover of horses*
*Goes out to the battered brigade."*

This song always seems to me to sum up all the courage of a good hunter and seemed especially appropriate as I had recently been over those High Peak walls and had been jumping some Holcombe walls that very day. We returned from the dinner at one-thirty and I must have expected to sleep soundly as I thought it necessary to set my alarm-clock for six-forty-five.

I set off to the nine o'clock meet of the **Pennine Foxhounds** driving my horse-box, but with no horse in it,

**Pennine Foxhounds.** *At Alport Castle, Glossop, 1982. Huntsman Chris Wood, first professional Huntsman to the pack.*
Photograph kindly loaned by Miss S E H Elders

and was glad of my good directions and a map, for Anglezark was a difficult place to find, made more difficult by the discovery of snow as I got into the Pennines (Sun 14 Nov 1982). The nearer I got to Anglezark the narrower the roads became, and the deeper the snow. The roads were so narrow that quite often I was reduced to creeping through narrow places watching in both mirrors to see if the box was clearing the high stone walls, often only missing by an inch or so. I began to wish I could turn round and go back but I was in quite a predicament as I had gone some miles and there was no room to turn round and I did not relish the thought of having to reverse three miles or so between such narrow walls. I crept on and on for another mile or so, desperately worried that the lorry would get stuck going up a hill as it often slipped on the snow, and was hoping either for a place to turn round so I could go back, or to arrive at the meet, when suddenly a large board announced "Anglezark" and in large letters, "Narrow and tortuous route – Not to be attempted by Heavy Goods Vehicles or Caravans". I wondered whatever could lie ahead to warrant that sign as I considered that the last five miles had been all of these things. However, I pressed on and then, rounding a corner, I saw a group of grim, tough-looking men standing in the road. I wound down the window and asked if this was the meet and the reply from one of them was, "I hope you haven't got a b...dy horse in there."

When I explained that this was my only form of transport he suggested that I left it on a wide verge near the Keeper's Cottage. I decided to turn it round before parking, which took several minutes and about twenty shunts, but I finally managed to leave it on the verge facing downhill. I walked down to the group of about nine men standing together, all looking grim and tough, and mostly glaring at me. I felt most uncomfortable and unwelcome in what must have been a semi-private hunt. I tried to get into a conversation with them and explained that I was on a hunting holiday but this seemed, if anything, to make matters worse as they obviously did not want anything to do with "them sorts what go on horses". Hounds, which were mostly fell-hounds, were very late arriving as they had to turn back because of roads blocked with snow but they soon moved off to draw a lovely valley. One man had melted enough to tell me as we walked along that the hunt had about two hundred and fifty members, each paying about three pounds. As they drew the fell-sides men appeared at the very top while the young huntsman, who had come from the Holderness Foxhounds, walked along about half-way up and the rest of us stayed on the valley floor. Hounds drew very well, but had not found by the time I had to leave which was sad as I would have loved to have seen them hunt. I had a deadline to leave as I was moving the horses and myself up to Clifton, near Penrith, and so ended my day with this relatively new pack which had been first recognised by the MFHA in 1964. My journey back was just as slow but not so worrying as I now knew it was possible to get through. When I arrived back at Tom Bracewell's Theresa had everything packed up and ready, and we were quickly on the road to John Robinson's yard at Clifton.

I had first met John at Lowther Country Fair. I had been having a drink in the Members' tent with Anthony Barker, Tom Wales and some others and Anthony had been telling them of my travels around the country. I had jokingly said that what I needed was a base in this area and Anthony had said, "I know just the man." He introduced me to John later in the day and his place was ideal. There was a large square cobbled yard, with his house on one side and loose boxes all around the other three, and room for Theresa's caravan near the gate. It had been built as a training yard for the Earl of Lonsdale's racehorses, and the boxes were large and very comfortable. When the horses were unloaded and settled in, John took me and my cases up to my "Bed-and-breakfast" with Mrs Carruthers, a delightful old lady who was everybody's dream of a perfect landlady. After supper I walked down to John's house and used his telephone to arrange the next day's hunting. As this was to be with the **Bewcastle Foxhounds**, which were a foot pack, John insisted that I took his car.

**Bewcastle.** *Meet at Lime Kiln Inn, Shopford, 1985. Master and Huntsman Mr Robert Proud. The Chairman, Mr C D Bland, is handing over a cheque from the hunt for cancer research.*
Photograph kindly donated by J H Cairns

In the morning there was a very sharp frost. I had some difficulty getting away from Clifton as the petrol cap was frozen on and it was lucky that the Bewcastle were a foot pack as it was much too hard for any mounted hunting (Mon 15 Nov 1982). The meet at Craigbarn Farm, Penton Bridge (near Longtown, in Cumbria), was over one mile from the road but I arrived to a great welcome and was taken into the huge kitchen where the tables were filled with sandwiches and cream cakes and sausage rolls. Whisky and coffee flowed equally freely and the old settles around the kitchen fire were full of wonderful old characters who were laughing and joking and telling tales in a Borders dialect that I could not fully understand. The Master, Mr Proud, let hounds out of the van and I thought that they looked very lean, hard and workmanlike, and were mostly fell-hounds. We drew until ten-thirty before finding below the farm and then they went away with a tremendous cry up into a large forestry plantation where they rattled him round and round for some time until I viewed him leaving the trees looking very tired. He only ran a little circle before returning to the forestry where fresh foxes saved his brush. I walked with the Master's brother, Eddie Proud, for the first half of the day and then with our host, Jack Lawson, for the latter half. When fresh foxes intervened hounds split into three groups and we went away with one group and had a really good hunt up to a fast-flowing salmon river. Hounds were racing along so fast that we were glad of a lift in a pick-up truck to keep up with them and finished up eight miles from the meet as the crow flies. It was by now very dark and the Master blew for home. In spite of picking up lost hounds on the way back to the meet he was still four couple light (ie. missing) when we reached the farm. Once again we were pressed to come into the kitchen for tea and whisky, followed by soup, black pudding and swedes and potatoes, ending with a lemon crumble. During tea I learned that although they had not caught a fox this day, they had killed eighteen and a half brace during the season so far, and forty-two brace the previous season, hunting three days a week. I was also impressed to hear that they had killed a brace and a half of foxes on each of the last two days they were out. As I left the remaining four couple were back in the farm yard, which was a satisfactory ending for such an enjoyable day amongst such genuine country people.

Next morning I had allowed far too much time to get to Paddock Hole Bridge where the **Dumfriesshire Foxhounds** were meeting and I had over an hour to wait, partly due to the meet being at eleven-thirty instead of eleven as I had assumed (Tues 16 Nov 1982). I unboxed Charlie on Bank Hill and hacked to the meet, and sat in a warm sunny spot in a farmyard out of the bitterly cold wind. About twenty members were out including an ex-Master of the Vale of Lune, whose face I could remember from when I hunted with them in 1971. There was considerable astonishment when a Frenchman, Christian Longville, loudly hailed me as "Tony!" He had had a draft of harriers from me to start his own pack in France. The Honorary Secretary told me that they had about one hundred and fifty members and the subscription was £300 and that 98% of them were farmers (very gentlemanly farmers, they appeared to me, and I could not help wondering if "landowners" would not have been a more accurate description). He also told me of the amazing flesh round, where collection was guaranteed within twenty-four hours. This involved two men with vans working full-time and each year they collected over a thousand cows, three thousand calves, and sheep beyond counting. All surplus flesh was sold and this, coupled with the "skin money", went to hunt funds. This was unusual as the skin money (i.e. the sale of hides from fallen stock to a tannery) is more normally a perk for the huntsman.

Sir Rupert Buchanan-Jardine, Master and Huntsman, arrived and hounds were let out of their smart hound trailer – which had obviously been custom-made for hounds as they could look out of the sides through a row of bars at head height. They were even more impressive than when I had seen them in kennel with the children in 1975. These big black-and-tan hounds were originally bred by crossing bloodhounds with French hounds and had no white markings at all. They were all exactly the same in conformation and were so alike that I wondered however a new hunt servant could ever possibly learn their names. The hounds obviously adored Sir Rupert and sat staring at him, watching his every move, and when he blew his horn to move off, there was a surge of black-and-tan as the twenty-two and a half couple went up the road.

A fox was soon found and we went away across what was obviously a beautifully-maintained country with hunt jumps in every direction. Whichever way hounds had run it would have been possible to keep with them. We ran through a valley and crossed a river with a hunt jump on the far bank. This had a pole poking up which could have caught a horse' chest or a rider's leg, but after I saw the Master go over it, I was not going to let anything stop me from following these wonderful hounds. I had wanted for so many years to see these world-famous hounds hunt, and there they were before me, running hard with a very wide head (i.e. running many abreast at the front) with those tremendous voices, so deep and loud, that even now as I write I can feel the shivers of excitement and the adrenalin pumping. They ran on across rough country but then entered a large forestry area and did not come out for two and a half hours. There was no let-up in their hunting and with only an occasional check they ran back and forth in this huge plantation with us able to keep with them on the rides, hearing them although we could not see them.

I, unlike most foxhunters, enjoy a woodland hunt but always prefer to get away from the chattering field so as to be able to savour the cry and especially the thrill of the first hound to open after a check. Their voices were amplified by the forest and the tremendous volume of their cry was quite deafening. Charlie and I were all on our own in a ride when an unforgettable incident occurred. Suddenly the hounds poured out of the trees further along the ride, and turned and hunted towards us. They filled the ride from side to side, a solid mass of black-and-tan, and those tremendous voices were more than Charlie could stand. He reared up, spun round, and took to his heels. There was nothing I could do to stop him. Away we went, right out of the trees, clearing a little forestry gate as we went, but once out in the open I could turn him and managed to stop. He was quivering all over and, with bulging eyes and continuous snorting, he stood staring back into the trees, absolutely terrified. Considering how often I have hunted hounds off him, and how often he has been right amongst hounds, his behaviour gives an indication of the incredible effect of these hounds. I managed to persuade him back into the forestry but was then told by the field that we would be unlikely to leave the place so as it was four o'clock I decided to go back to the box.

My lodgings with Mrs Carruthers at Midtown Farmhouse were charming and delightfully old-fashioned, with ornaments crammed onto every tiny space, even along the edge of the passages and the stairs. We soon developed a routine for the evenings. Theresa would walk up and join me and the other lodger (unbelievably called Roger), who was a building foreman, for an evening meal which was always first class. Then I would walk back to the stables with her and go into John's house to use his telephone to make future arrangements, and pore over maps to plan routes with John's help. All this concentration and forethought was aided by very generous helpings of John's whisky and always ended with an account of the day's hunting.

As there was to be no mounted hunting for the following two days, I asked Theresa if she would like to have a day on the Wednesday and we left at ten o'clock for the meet of the **Cumberland Farmers' Foxhounds** at the Travellers' Rest, Cowrigg (Wed 17 Nov 1982). As we were only just in time, we unboxed straight away instead of going into the pub and, as I sat on my horse, I was offered a sherry and then a cup of soup, the only time I have been offered soup as a stirrup cup. When Tom Wales, the Joint-Master, came out of the pub he quickly organised a large whisky for me. Tom and I had struck up an instant friendship when we had met at Lowther Country Fair, and later we had met again at Rydal Hound Show. He was an unforgettable character, with a white moustache which stuck out at least four inches each side of a very benevolent face. He had the knack of making a stranger feel at once like an old friend. It was snowing intermittently and we did not find until one-thirty but then had a nice circular hunt which took us through a farmyard where they were marking some sheep. Tom looked at me and said,

"Could be trouble. The wife. A bit sharp."

This turned out to be correct. The housewife came out of the house and gave Tom such a mouthful of abuse that the four silly giggling girls who had been the only other field were so upset they promptly went home. I had a spot of bother getting away from this farm, and neither my horse or Tom's would jump a collapsed gate, but we did eventually get over and caught up with hounds again where they had marked to ground in a quarry. The quarry was still in use and quite busy with large dumper trucks roaring around, and the huntsman, Tom's Joint-Master Mr Wybergh, could not believe that a fox would stop there so he cast hounds all around the quarry but had to come back to where they were marking. As the terrier men were digging, it started to snow even harder and the high winds were very unpleasant so I decided to go home. When I asked Tom the way back to the meet, he said, "If you've had enough, then so have I," and we went back together. He had little difficulty in persuading me that I needed a warming toddy before going home and I left as usual with the feeling that I would have liked to have talked longer with him.

Next day I went with the **Lunesdale Foxhounds** which are hunted on foot. Their country is on the edge of the Lake District and the meet on this occasion was at Aughton, near Gressingham in Lancashire, at nine-thirty (Thurs 18 Nov 1982). I was made very welcome and hospitality was offered from a broken pallet used as a table outside a farmhouse door. After cakes and coffee we moved off to draw a river valley. I climbed up as high as I could thinking that I would get a good view of them hunting for most of the time but I was wrong. After finding they ran so fast that John Nicholson, the huntsman, often needed to get a lift in a car and at one point I saw him stop, get out of a car where hounds had checked, cast them on over the road, watch them settle to the line, and then get another lift round to the other side of the hill and watch them coming down to him again. One of the best things about doing all this visiting was being able to observe different styles of hunting hounds, each suited to their own countries. During this hunt, some men with a North-East Gas van working on the side of the road stopped to watch hounds and said that they knew nothing about foxhunting and would like to come again and learn more. I have often wondered if they did come again and perhaps became members. I left them at twelve o'clock as I wanted to get to the Windermere Harriers' Shepherds' Meet at Troutbeck, and was lucky to get a lift back to the meet with a man who had four lovely Border terriers in his van.

I had often heard the Lake District hunting folk talk of Shepherds' Meets and had wanted to see one for myself. A Shepherds' Meet was an old tradition and every Lake District hunt had one or more during the season. It was originally, and still is to a certain extent, an opportunity for each shepherd to bring along any sheep that are not his own and, after a sort-out at the end of the day, each shepherd goes home with his own sheep. They put the strays into a walled paddock near the pub. This get-together has, of course, led to it being a great social occasion, with much eating, drinking and hunting. On this day the Coniston Foxhounds had met at nine o'clock and the harriers at eleven o'clock, but this was not a joint-meet since both packs hunted separately. This happens fairly often on special occasions in the Lake District, made possible by the country and the different quarries. The foxhounds met first and, as the fox would be likely to run away in a straight line, they would probably be over the fell and gone by the time the harriers started, and they (the harriers) would probably stay in the valley.

**Windermere Harriers.** *Anthony Barker, Master and huntsman, far right, Heather Barker, later to hunt hounds for her father.*
Photograph kindly loaned by Anthony Barker

By the time I arrived the harriers were well away from the meet which had been at the Queen's Head in Troutbeck. I could see them on the fell-side and although I was quite tired from my efforts with the Lunesdale I walked up to them and arrived just as they were at a serious check caused by sheep foil. They drew again but could not find as hares were in very short supply due to men coursing at night with lamps. A real good old-fashioned singsong in the Queen's Head followed, with "Tatie-pot" served. I enjoyed a fascinating conversation about venerie with Chris Ogilvie, the Coniston huntsman. I did not often have the chance to enjoy this sort of conversation, especially with someone as knowledgeable as Chris. About fourteen people sang, including Joan and Heather Barker, Anthony's daughters, who had respectively been hunting and whipping-in to the harriers. Everyone was highly amused when a young man said, "If it's the Shepherd's Meet, then we ought to have a sheep." He went outside and came back with a sheep which jumped up onto the settle and just stood looking around until a young lady went out and came back with some handfuls of grass which it calmly started to eat. As I drove Anthony Barker home over the Kirkstone Pass there was a dreadful hailstorm, and we were really glad to arrive safely at his home, Norran Bank, in Patterdale, where Sheila had tea ready for us.

After tea Anthony telephoned his old friend, George Laing, Master of the **Liddesdale Foxhounds**. Knowing how desperately I wanted to hunt on every day of the week, Anthony had asked George to take his hounds out on a Friday. This he readily agreed to do but said that we must telephone the night before to make sure the weather was suitable. The message came back that they would try to go on foot but on no account to take a horse as the snow was too bad. I eventually arrived back at Clifton at ten o'clock. Anthony and his wife Sheila, and the younger daughter Diana, picked me up again the next morning and we arrived at Twislehope, where the Liddesdale were kennelled on George Laing's farm, at eleven o'clock (Fri 19 Nov 1982).

The farm was at the end of this beautiful valley and, in fact, was so far up the valley that Mrs Laing was given official permission to educate her own children, I think seven of them, as it was too difficult to get them to school. She was the sister of Jo Paisley, Master of the Airedale Beagles, and she was also Secretary of the Fell Pony Society. George hunted his own hounds and his sons whipped-in to him, using either horses or motorbikes and both mounts were used for shepherding on non-hunting days. The last, but certainly not the least, member of the household was Jenny, who had originally gone as Nanny to the children. As they grew up and had less need for her services, she gradually took the hounds under her wing and I heard the most remarkable story about her. She was the only one who could control the hounds in summer and neither George nor his sons ever walked hounds out during the summer because they would not stay with them.

We first looked at the lambs in a large yard, then went indoors, where Jenny was busy baking, for coffee and cakes straight from the oven. Sheila settled down for a chat with Mrs Laing, while Anthony and George sat talking hounds and hunting, with me listening intently, anxious, as always, to learn from men more experienced than myself. Although the conversation was very interesting, after an hour or so I was getting anxious as there was no mention of going hunting. Then to my horror Jenny started to set the table for lunch. The meal was most enjoyable, with hunting stories going back and forth across the table, and with me dropping hints that perhaps there was going to be some hunting today. After lunch had been digested, they decided that they would get hounds out for me, and George and his son went into the stable to get their cobs. Jenny let out the hounds, which were mostly fell-hounds, and they went off up a track with us following in a car.

**The Liddesdale:** ***"Keeping an eye on the enemy"***

I had got out to watch them draw when suddenly a snowstorm blew up. It was difficult to see anything and I started to feel very guilty for persuading them to get hounds out in these unsuitable conditions. To make matters worse, the cold winds brought on an asthma attack and I had to sit in the car for a while. This looked really bad and I have often thought that George must have had a very poor opinion of me, having caused him to be out in that bad storm while sheltering in a car myself. However, the storm blew itself out and the inhaler cured my asthma, and I could continue following them. They drew the hillside back towards the farm, but could not find despite the fact that, as they told me, there were earths in the hills above the farm and in the summer they could see the cubs playing on the hillside. After putting hounds away we stood in the kennels for a while as Anthony and George discussed the merits of various hounds. Leaving the kennels we returned to the farmhouse for a tea of homemade bread and cakes, after which we were ordered out of the kitchen into the sitting room. George and Anthony continued to talk of hounds, past and present, and of their family traits, and once again I found it to be a great education. When we got up to leave, we were ordered to sit down again until told that we could go, and after our glasses had been refilled several times we sat down to more hospitality in the form of a delicious boiled ham which they kept telling me was Danish, just to tease me, as they knew I was a pig farmer. Eventually we left and arrived back at Clifton at eleven o'clock, having had a wonderful day in spite of not finding a fox. Although I had not seen them hunt, I had the feeling that when I did I would be impressed and when I eventually did go out with them again, in 1990, I was not to be disappointed.

As the horses had not done very much work I asked Theresa if she would like to come with me on the Saturday to the **Wigtownshire Foxhounds**. We were loaded and away by seven o'clock with a hundred and twenty miles to go and arrived only just in time (Sat 20 Nov 1982). The Wigtownshire were only in their second season as foxhounds, having previously been draghounds, and were obviously still quite inexperienced. The meet was at the Torwood Hotel, The Gass (near Glenluce) which had obviously been an old country house. Hounds were everywhere except with their huntsman, chivvying in and out of the laurel

**The Wigtownshire:** ***"Instant sport while we sip, they'll keep themselves amused"***

bushes which surrounded the wide lawns in front of the hotel. I watched in amazement as they suddenly found a fox which ran for about fifty yards before popping into an open earth. The huntsman totally ignored this little performance but the amateur whipper-in was making mild attempts to keep them together when suddenly another fox appeared and popped into the same earth. While this was going on, Theresa and I were capped to the obvious delight of the capper, who had probably never before had the chance of getting two caps at one meet. As they knew that I was a Master before they capped me, I assumed that they did not know the tradition of not capping Masters, and paid up rather than embarass them. The capping ceremony being over, I was taken to meet the Master, the Countess of Stair. While pleasantries were being exchanged, the hounds found a third fox in the laurel bushes just behind us and, this one declining to use the same earth as the others, went away and this signalled the end of the meet.

This run soon petered out but hounds soon had another fox away and we had a nice little run over lovely country but I was surprised at how few hounds were hunting. At the end of the run I could count only five and a half couple out of the original twelve and a half. Later I discovered that some had never left the laurel bushes, and others had gone off on a line of their own. The whippers-in seemed quite oblivious of the fact that one of their main duties was to get hounds away out of the coverts and on to the huntsman. One of them, who I believe was the huntsman's wife, had a frightful experience when riding through a gateway. Her stirrup became caught on the hinge and jammed her foot tight in the stirrup so that as her horse moved away she was forced to do the splits until she eventually fell off. It was awful to see it slowly happening, and miraculous that she did not break her pelvis. At two-thirty I said my goodnights to the Master and the field, which consisted of one man and four children, and as I drove the hundred and twenty miles back, I kept thinking how I would love to be Master of these hounds. Everything was there except knowledge. The country was first class as the farmers were welcoming, the roads quite quiet, and there was plenty of it as there were no other foxhound packs nearby. We got back to Clifton at six o'clock and, after a quick bath and change, I drove down the motorway to Newton and Kate Bacon's at Silverdale for dinner and to stay the night. Kate was an excellent cook and dinner was as enjoyable as ever. Newton rocked with laughter as I told him of the day's sport, and told me of a "pirate" pack called the Wensleydale Foxhounds which hunted on a Sunday. He asked if I would like to go and of course I said I would, so he telephoned the Master, Mr Bell, and arranged for us to go. As always happens, the evening was over far too quickly and I eventually tumbled into bed at twelve thirty.

Newton and I had our breakfast at eight o'clock because the meet was at nine-thirty and Newton then drove to Hawes where the Master of the **Wensleydale** lived (Sun 21 Nov 1982). I was very surprised when he drove into the town and moved slowly along a residential street looking for a particular number. He stopped outside the Master's house which was in the middle of a row of houses and suddenly Mr Bell appeared with ten couple of foxhounds from behind the houses. I thought that he must have some very tolerant neighbours. Newton and I followed the hound van to some forestry where about twenty men and boys were waiting. The conditions could not have been much worse with high winds and slashing rain. Hounds soon found and rattled around in the trees, and then most of them went away over the fell. By now the wind was so bad that it was almost impossible to stand up in the open so Newton and I kept in the trees and listened to the two couple which had not gone with the main pack. These two couple were making quite a good job of exercising the foxes remaining in the forestry of which there seemed to be several. By twelve-thirty we were very wet and cold so we decided to go back to Silverdale where Kate had some tea ready for us. I was pressed to stay for dinner but declined and drove back to Clifton so as to be ready for hunting the next day when I was to go with the **Haydon Foxhounds** (Mon 22 Nov 1982).

**Haydon.** *Meet at Greenshaw House, January 1981. Donald Edgar (Master and Huntsman), Tony Dale (Kennel Huntsman), and Roy Charlton (ex-Master and Huntsman).*

Photograph kindly donated by Roy Wallis

The meet was at Hadrian's Wall, in the National Trust visitors' car-park at Steel Rigg, and was one of the most memorable I have attended. The Wall was still very impressive, especially in the distance as it followed the undulations of the hillsides and stood six feet high in places. During the day I was told that in the past the top of the wall had been used as a road for soldiers marching and, where not too steep, for horses and carts. It was a wonderful feeling when, during the day, I was able to ride along the top of it, getting up and down at the places where it had collapsed. The weather was appalling, with slashing rain and freezing winds.

The Master, Derek Edgar, was the first to arrive and we introduced ourselves, then two ladies, one of which was the Supporters' Club Chairman, and these two and myself were to be the only field. Derek Edgar had hunted these hounds since 1967 and I was impressed to see how calmly he rode off with twenty-three and a half couple and no whipper-in. He drew the southern side of the Wall until we came to some crags where I felt privileged to watch these hounds drawing. It was a lovely sight to see them spread out over the crag face, going meticulously from ledge to ledge, not missing out any possible place where a fox could be lying. These crags were very steep so it looked as though hounds were working along a bookcase, each one above the next, as if each hound had a shelf of its own. In spite of their thorough efforts, the crag proved to be blank so the Master drew across country towards some forestry. While doing this we went through a deserted farm where a car follower was ready with an enormous whisky-mac for the two ladies and myself, the Master not being offered one as he never touched alcohol whilst hunting. This hospitable gentleman told me that he was a relation of the Greenwell family who have an estate at Butley in the Easton country and he persuaded me to have a second whisky-mac. As I was so cold I accepted with alacrity. This proved very unwise as I had had no breakfast and had left my sandwich box in my lodgings. The rest of the day was rather hazy but I remember cantering into a boggy place which made Demelza stop quickly, with the result that I went over her head into the bog. I was thoroughly wet before from the rain but was now soaked. The green dye was running out of my coat, and my white breeches were now mostly green. Luckily this was near the end of the day and after boxing up one of the ladies said to me, "Are you safe to drive home?", to which I replied, "No."

She kindly suggested that I followed her home where she cooked me eggs and bacon, after which my head cleared and I was able to drive home safely. It was a very stupid thing to have done which had spoiled the end of a most enjoyable day. I had been amazed at the Master's ability to hunt hounds so effortlessly and have them so completely steady on deer. I felt sick all evening, refused my usual whisky with John Robinson and went to bed early but was much better the next morning for my day with the **West of Yore Foxhounds** (Tues 23 Nov 1982).

When dressing I was unable to find the surgical collar which I had to wear while hunting after my Boxing Day fall in 1976, and then realised that I had probably left it at my kind benefactor's where I had had the eggs and bacon. I did the best I could to substitute it by winding my stock round my neck two extra times very tightly but the end result was that I was late getting to the meet which was at Redmire near Leyburn in the Yorkshire Dales. I unboxed as quickly as possible and managed to catch up with them while they were still drawing. I was greeted in such a friendly way by the members and they took me to meet the Masters, one of whom was hunting hounds. I was invited to ride with the huntsman but declined owing to still feeling rather rough. This proved to be a lucky decision as when hounds found he took a wrong direction and conseqently got left out of much of this hunt, while I chose a local farmer as a pilot and enjoyed the whole of it. Hounds ran continuously for over two hours and my pilot and I had them in sight all the time. As we galloped over some rough country I was worried about having no collar but the sport was far too good to think of stopping. Often we could see both the fox and the hounds at the same time and once it seemed that they must catch him in the open, but he dropped into a ghyll and gave hounds the slip. We galloped on across open moorland to a very steep drop into a narrow valley. The Master ordered everyone to dismount and lead their horses down and this we did. It was so steep that most of the men slipped down on their bottoms. Those with cutaway coats found that the tails dragged behind them and their horses were putting their feet on them and some were badly torn. When we reached the bottom I mounted again to cross the river and rode up the other side, but almost everyone else led their horses up so for a while I was well ahead and had hounds to myself. Then there was a serious check and when the huntsman came up he decided to blow for home as his, and most of the other, horses were absolutely cooked. This had been the best foxhunting that I had ever seen, and I could have missed it as, when I telephoned the Master, Mr Abraham, he said not to bother with this meet as it was usually very poor. This just proves again the glorious uncertainty of hunting. The sheer joy of being able to ride at that pace, keeping in touch with hounds all the while, made a great ending to a very good hunting holiday.

**West of Yore.** *Meet at Newfield, Mickley. Front three, left to right, George Cooke (Kennel Huntsman), Tom Ramsden (Joint Master and Huntsman), and Amanda Abrahams (Joint Master and amateur whipper-in). Also Peter Hill-Walker (behind Mr Ramsden), Captain Tony Warrington, Field Master (behind Mr Hill-Walker) and Nancy Staveley (to left of George Cooke).*

Photograph kindly loaned by Amanda Abrahams. Copyright Roy Parker.

That evening I took John Robinson and his wife and Theresa down to the pub for a last night's drinks. I was immediately recognised by two policemen who remembered me from the Royal Oak at Appleby in 1980 when I had driven my gypsy caravan to the famous gypsy horse-fair to raise money for Driving for the Disabled. When the Fair is over the policemen all get together for a big party in this pub, and they remembered my horseshoe-button suit and the songs that I sang. The landlord and landlady of the Clifton pub were a charming old couple and told me how "the Yellow Earl", Lord Lonsdale, had the gas main laid from Penrith to Clifton at his own expense. I had just read a biography of the "Yellow Earl" and the landlord was very interested in how much I knew about him. He later gave me a present of a book on the earl's collection of cars.

We were up very early the next morning, and were loaded and on the road by six-forty, arriving back at the Easton kennels at four o'clock. As usual I whiled away the miles by thinking back over the holiday. I had hunted every day for fourteen days, and had been out fifteen times with thirteen different packs, going twice with the Holcombe and twice with the Windermere. These included the Pennine Foxhounds and the Wensleydale Foxhounds which I had gone with on the two Sundays. The weather had been atrocious throughout and by the end of the two weeks all the rivers were full to overflowing. John Robinson, my host for most of the holiday, had been very helpful and was good company in the evenings. We found that we had a lot in common as he earned his living from horses, dealing in high quality show ponies, and running a livery and schooling yard.

# MAP 9

## FOXHOUND PACKS – 1983

- A Heythrop
- B Bicester & Warden Hill
- C Old Surrey & Burstow
- D Tetcott
- E Four Burrow
- F Dartmoor
- G Silverton
- H Tiverton
- I Seavington
- J Blackmore & Sparkford Vale
- K Whaddon Chase (amalgamated with the Bicester & Warden Hill)

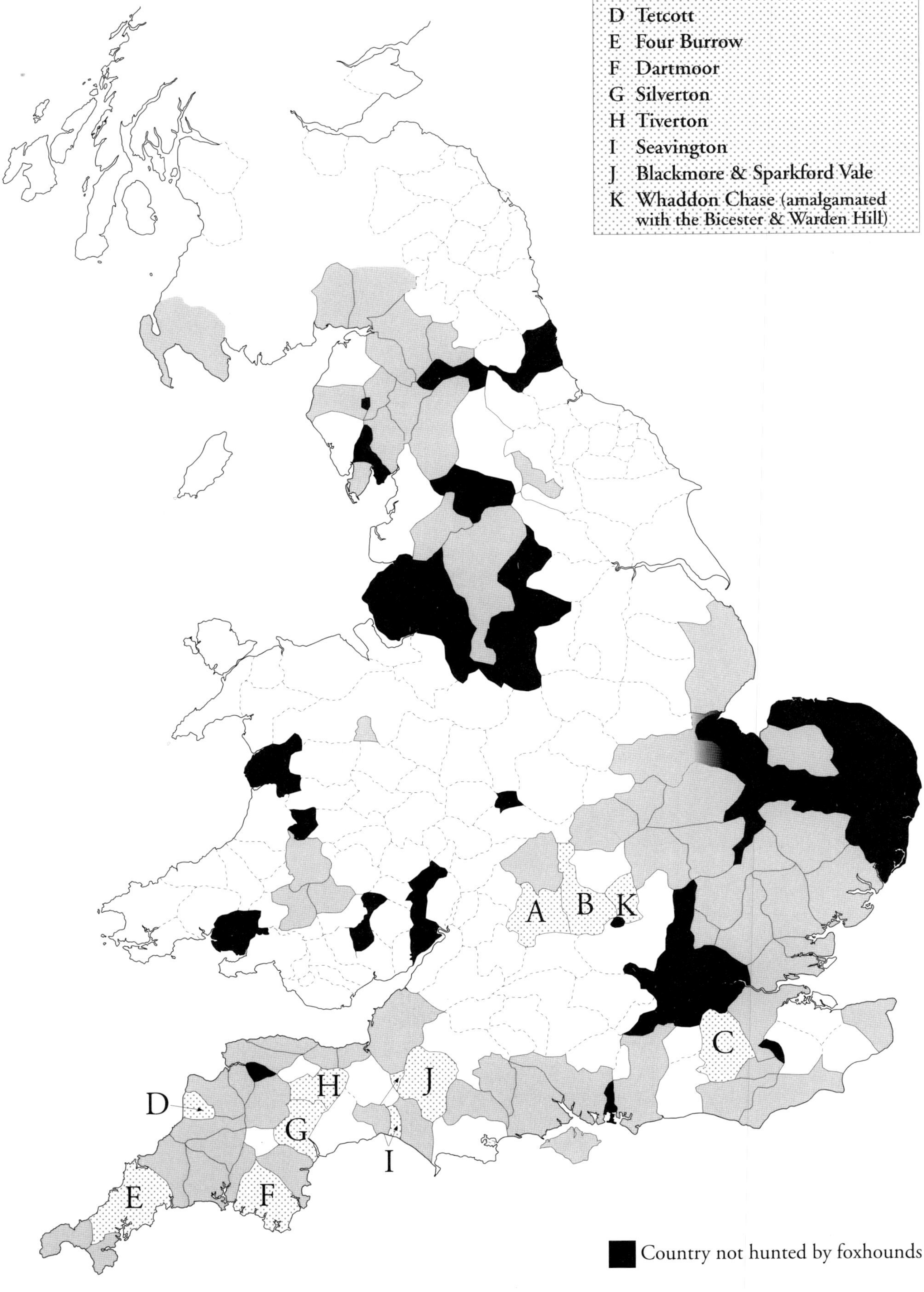


Country not hunted by foxhounds

# Chapter 12

## Dartmoor

Between the two big jollies of the 1982–83 season I managed to arrange a mini-jolly to Surrey, planning to have days with the Crawley and Horsham and the Old Surrey and Burstow on a Tuesday and Wednesday. I was able to do this because the Easton Harriers were meeting at the kennels on the Monday so I knew I could leave Jim Wickham to hunt hounds, returning home to hunt them myself on the Thursday. I easily found stabling and accomodation with Michael Gilbey who had put up our horses in 1978 when Stanley and I had stayed with Georgie Fotheringhay-Parker. The previous year he had stabled his horses at the Easton kennels while competing in a Horse Trials at Earl Soham Lodge and it had been a pleasure to renew my acquaintance with him. However, no good came of me shirking my Master's duties as this trip was singularly unsuccessful.

I left the kennels at nine-thirty with two horses (Charlie and Falcon) and with Theresa's caravan behind the lorry, and arrived at Michael's stables in Hastings at three-thirty (Mon 7 Feb 1983). We unloaded the horses but, as we were settling the caravan into position, it started to snow. During the evening it became apparent that there would be no mounted hunting the next day so, determined to have some hunting, I got busy on Michael's telephone. With the help of Baily's and after about fifteen calls, I found that the Radley College Beagles were hunting. Michael's daughter Susan was home from America and we all spent a highly amusing evening, with supper round the kitchen table, and finally went to bed at twelve-thirty.

By morning the snow was seven to nine inches deep and Michael kindly offered me his Land Rover to go to the meet which was at Common Farm, Kingston Lisle, in Oxfordshire (Tues 8 Feb 1983). After three and a half hours of furious driving I arrived just in time. There was some four inches or so of snow on the ground there, and the wind was very cold. The Secretary could not believe his eyes and greeted me with, "Not Mr Harvey, surely?" and said that although I had telephoned, he had not expected me to make it. The **Radley College Beagles** were a school pack and I was formally introduced to the four boys who were whipping-in and to their fellow-pupil who was huntsman. These teenagers were a joy to watch as they drew so quietly and thoroughly, with the whips always in the right place at the right time. The first hare ran a classical figure-of-eight, and I could often see her, and watched some of her doubles. The four or five boys who made up the field found out that I was a huntsman and, although they already knew quite a lot about hunting, they were continually asking questions as to what the hounds were doing and why. I had to keep my wits about me to give them satisfactory answers. After she had completed the figure of eight and hounds worked out her last ruse, she set off on a different circle and got amongst fresh hares. Twice the young huntsman had them stopped and put back onto the line of the hunted hare, but both times fresh hares again intervened which sadly spoiled this excellent hunt. During the day we were joined by Mr Colin Nash, Master of the Old Berkshire Foxhounds since 1963, and he offered to stable my horses if I ever wanted a holiday in his area. I said my goodnights at four o'clock, complimenting the boys on their very professional conduct in the field and saying that they were a credit to whoever had taught them.

As I made my way back through the driving snow, the visibility was so bad I somehow missed my turn and got into the London rush hour traffic. I was completely lost and had no idea how to get out of London on the right road, so I stopped a taxi and asked him to drive in front of me until I was on the right road.

"Would you like me to pay you before we go?" I asked.

"No, mate," he replied. "You look honest to me."

**Radley College Beagles.** *Meet at Cassington, February 1976. Left to right, M E Robson (Master 1976–77), J C Masters (Master 1975–6), A W H Tyndall (behind, Master 1976–8), and S H Cowan (Master 1977–8).*

Photograph kindly donated by Michael Linnell

I finally arrived back at Michael's at eight-thirty and although I had promised to take him out to dine, I found that he had cooked dinner and we enjoyed another fabulous evening in his home, with an excellent claret and several glasses of a most lovely brandy.

I got out of bed next morning at six-thirty and opened the curtains. With a sinking heart I saw that it was still snowing. I telephoned the Master of the Old Surrey and Burstow who said that he could not make a decision until nine o'clock which, although Theresa had the horse all ready, would have been too late for us to leave. As, in any case, it looked most unlikely that we would be able to hunt mounted, Michael suggested that I telephoned home to find out what the situation was there. This I did to be told that the Easton would not be able to hunt on the Thursday so Michael invited me to stay longer in order to hunt with the local pack of beagles, the **Pevensey Marsh** (Wed 9 Feb 1983). Michael came with me and it was still snowing hard when we arrived at the meet at the Bell Inn, Iden, near Rye in Sussex. Mrs Harrison, the Master, who I thought a great character, greeted us warmly and introduced us to Ian Cunningham, the amateur huntsman. Mrs Harrison, I was told, had been Master since 1965 and had revived the hunt from a debt-ridden state to a prosperous and happy concern. Although Ian Cunningham drew very thoroughly until four o'clock it proved to be a blank day. He tried in the open, and in the orchards, and finally in woodland which was perhaps where one could have expected to find a hare in these deplorable conditions. It had been snowing all day and was very cold, and by now there was over twelve inches of snow on the ground. After returning to the meet we went into a house nearby for tea and had muffins and lemon tea but, as there was no fire, we did not stop very long.

**Old Surrey & Burstow Hunt.** *Meet at Withyham, c. 1983. Huntsman Jack Champion, whipper-in Stephen Clipton, and amateur whip Rodney Fuller.*

Photograph kindly loaned by Mrs Sarah Lewis

As this was the last night I did manage to persuade Michael to let me take him out to dinner. He took me to an Italian restaurant on the sea front and we had an excellent meal but what was most memorable about it was that it ended with glasses of a liqueur which had beans in it, and were set alight before being served. Next morning, after breakfast, we pulled the lorry up to the top of a hill with Michael's Land Rover as the road conditions were so bad it could not have got up on its own. We then led the horses up the hill and loaded them into the lorry, then returned and used the Land Rover to pull the caravan up. When all was together again, we set off and arrived back at the Easton kennels at two-thirty where everyone was amazed to see the eighteen inches of snow on top of the lorry and caravan. This had been a three-hundred mile round trip, with two horses and a groom, for two days beagling in Sussex and Oxfordshire!

However, I was to get my day with the **Old Surrey and Burstow Foxhounds** rather sooner than I expected, as less than a month later Jim Wickham, my kennel huntsman, had heard through the hunt servants' grape-vine that they were coming up to East Anglia by invitation of the Puckeridge and Thurlow (Mon 7 Mar 1983). His enthusiasm to pass on this information was probably increased by the knowledge that, if I went, he would be left to hunt hounds himself from the Easton meet at Ashbocking Nelson.

I arrived deliberately early at the meet at Little Bradley Hall, thinking that there would be a huge field, but to my surprise it only numbered about forty mounted, which included the hunt servants from both packs. My early arrival was not wasted, however, as my old friend Charlie Barclay introduced me to his Joint-Master Mr Edmund Vestey who was destined later to become a leading figure in the foxhound world by being elected Chairman of the MFHA following the retirement of Captain Wallace. Cherry Barclay introduced me to our hostess, Mrs Clifton-Brown, who I was told was Mr Vestey's sister. The huntsman of the Old Surrey and Burstow was a legend in his own lifetime, and it was a joy to watch the famous Jack Champion hunt his hounds. He moved off from the meet with a cheery, "Come on, my ladies. Come on, my girls". His horn-blowing was the best I had ever heard and his hounds flew to him, seemingly almost before the horn touched his lips. The first fox proved to be a vixen and was left; the second was caught very quickly. When drawing for the third fox, I was asked to go "on point" at the far end of a large covert and when hounds went away I was rather left out of the game but later found that they did not go far. Scenting conditions were as poor as they usually are in East Anglia in March, with the drying winds, and tractors harrowing fields all around, and most of the fields having a good sprinkling of artificial manure. Due to this, there were no long runs, with foxes usually just running from one covert to the next. I got into conversation with one of the visiting Masters who continually referred to the "barking" of the hounds. I wondered whether he was using slang or whether he did not know any better, since it is more usual to refer to hounds "speaking". The day ended with a sumptuous hunting tea given by Mrs Clifton-Brown.

While making the preparations for my second major jolly of the season I heard of the death of my old friend Stanley Tompkins who had been my companion on so many of the previous ones. On 2 March 1983 Alec Burns, Field Master to the Dunston Harriers, telephoned to say that he had died whilst hunting on Exmoor. He was apparently in the middle of a great hunt and was galloping alongside the Master saying, "Now this is what I call a real hunt," and then dropped off his horse dead. Although obviously a tremendous shock to Kathleen, his wife, and his family, it was, I thought, a very fitting end for such a man and was as he would have wished to go. He loved every form of hunting but especially staghunting as he had been brought up in the old Norwich Staghound country. We had shared so many great hunting days together since the very first, when I had been up at the end of my first day with the Norwich Staghounds, to help Stanley "take" the deer. My diary entry simply states that Stanley had died, and that he was the bravest, boldest man I had ever seen in the hunting field, and all these years later it still holds true.

I had intended to go north again and had arranged to be based at the Staffordshire Moorland kennels but Judith Goddard telephoned to say that all the packs were stopping early so there would be no point my going up to Derbyshire. The visiting bug had now taken such a hold that I immediately got going on the telephone to arrange another holiday. I felt sure that they would still be hunting on Dartmoor so I asked John Budgett, Master of the Dartmoor Foxhounds, if he could suggest where I could stay in the Princetown area. He said that on Dartmoor it was not easy to find two stables near where I could stay myself, but he soon 'phoned back to say that he had found what I wanted at the Forest Inn at Hexworthy. I telephoned the owner of the pub, Mr Wise, to ask him if Theresa could stay outside the stables in her caravan and, although initially horrified at the idea, he reluctantly agreed.

I set off for Dartmoor, with Charlie and Demelza, on Monday 14 March and drove almost non-stop, except for a quick lunch, and arrived in the dark. The last few miles in the dark were an experience I shall never forget as the roads were narrow and the signs not very helpful. It was soon apparent why Hexworthy did not feature very prominently on the signposts, as there was only the pub and two cottages there. Theresa was horrified when she saw what we were told were the stables. They were old garages, their doors hanging on one hinge, and were right on the roadside. There were no lights and not even a water-tap; and it took some smooth talking to calm down her ruffled feathers. Luckily, we found a torch and managed to find enough string in the lorry to tie up the doors but we were none too sure that the horses would still be there in the morning.

Although the stables were a shock, I settled into the hotel and the first evening was a taste of what fun was to come. The food was first class and there were two smashing girls in the hotel – Prudence the waitress, and Susan the barmaid. Both girls were full of fun and caused a lovely atmosphere. Susan's father, John Coker, came into the bar every evening and told me that he had relations in Suffolk. What a small world it is. It turned out that I had been to school with his second cousin, Jack Coker from St Jacobs Hall, Laxfield. In our early days Jack and I used to take it in turns to be the bottom of the class. Also there is a Coker's Lane in Debach which was named after John's uncle who was well-known during the Depression years of the 1930s for bringing up ponies from Dartmoor to sell on for his brother.

I left the hotel at ten o'clock on the Tuesday morning and drove the lorry the sixty-odd miles to the meet of the **Taw Vale Beagles** at Woodburn Water, Roachhill, eventually finding it after some difficulty. We drew for two and a half hours before finding in this rolling, pasture country, but then had a lovely hunt through valleys and woods with very pretty houndwork, most of which I was able to see as I walked with the father of the Master and huntsman. As he knew every inch of the country we were always in a good position. I stayed out until five o'clock and was lucky in that a kind man not only gave me a lift back to the meet but drove ahead of me to show me a short cut back to the Tiverton road.

Next morning I was awake early and lay for a while listening to the dawn chorus in full swing, then went out to make sure that Theresa was awake. I need not have worried and I can still clearly picture the scene. The "stables" were slightly lower than the pub and as I walked down the road I could see her, dimly outlined in the half-light, standing on a stool in the middle of the road trying to plait Charlie's mane. Opposite her there were two Dartmoor ponies eating the straw that she had mucked out the day before, and then four more ponies trotted past, causing Charlie to try to make off with them. When I got to her I could see that she was nearly in tears.

"How can I manage to turn a horse out for you properly in this dreadful place?" she said.

When I stupidly asked why she was standing in the middle of the road, I was curtly told that this was the only place she could hope to see what she was doing. I thought discretion was the better part of valour and back-pedalled into the pub, returning with a cup of coffee for her.

I left at seven o'clock for the meet of the **Seavington Foxhounds** at Parham Park Farm, Netherbury (Wed 16 Mar 1983). When nearly at the meet I stopped to eat some of my sandwiches and soup, and then was lucky enough to come across a Land Rover and trailer to follow for the last few miles so I had no trouble in finding the meet which was in the courtyard of a very smart farm. An old lady was waving from a bedroom window and I was told that she had been very anti-hunting but that Mr Max Southwell, the Master, had done such a good job of charming her round that she had even offered a lawn meet. There was a special atmosphere as this was to be the last day of Jack Dark, the professional huntsman, who was retiring and everyone was very sad. It was rather foggy and raining, and we appeared to sit at the meet rather a long time, but as the eats were so good I did not mind.

Moving off, the huntsman drew some rough banks. Charlie was so full of himself I was afraid I would be bucked off and was relieved when the Master asked if I would like to go with his wife "on point" at the far end of the valley, as this offered me a chance to give him a canter. As we stood on point, Mrs Southwell told me of how the day before her husband had almost lost his life. He had climbed down a rock face to rescue a hound which had fallen and broken its leg. He slipped and fell a considerable way, but just managed to stop himself a foot or so short of a hundred-foot drop. The hound had been dislodged and fell over this drop and was killed. A mountain climber had to be fetched to rescue Mr Southwell. I also met a woman who had just bought a pony from the Gurdons who live in Easton country and hunt with us, and also a man who had been shepherding on his horse before hunting. This man reminded me of Stanley Tompkins, in his build and style of riding, and he told me that most weeks for the last twenty years he had sent around a hundred and fifty calves to Norwich market. By a curious coincidence, the next man I met told me that he had known Stanley Tompkins well from hunting on Exmoor and had just bought his dark cob that had been left in the Quantock country at his death.

**Taw Vale Beagles.** *Meet at Copplestone House, 2 April 1983. Left to right, George Hill, Alistair Hill, Harry Higgs, Norman Mills, Geoffrey Cox (Master and Huntsman), Stephen Mills, Donald Kine, David Mason, Donald Forbes.*

Photograph kindly donated by Lt Col J B Chanter

There was not much good hunting, only short bursts typical of the end of the season. At three o'clock the fog began to get thicker and I decided to go home. After a very anxious drive I arrived back at six-thirty. That night there was quite a session in the bar so, as there was no hunting, I did not get up until eight-thirty. I spent the first half of the morning using red string to do some essential repairs to the lorry and I then rode out across the moor where I once again marvelled at how these ponies and cattle manage to live through a winter, as the grass, although presumably of good quality, was shorter than any lawn. I then went to Ashburton to follow the advice of John Coker who, after listening to me moaning about getting wet so often and all the valetting of clothes after wet days, had said I ought to get myself an apron made. I asked Mr Wise if I could borrow his car and went to the Ashburton saddler, a Mr George, who proudly showed me a driving bridle he had just rebuilt, and agreed to make me an apron right away. As was becoming the norm, I had a wonderful evening in the hotel. John Coker had a herd of Gallowway cattle as well as a large herd of Dartmoor ponies on the moor and, as the pub was completely open to the moor, these cattle roamed around the pub as they willed. They always went to the muckheap, near to where the caravan had been parked, to sort out scraps of hay that had been thrown out with the mucking out. Susan, the jokiest of the two girls, built up an imaginary story about Theresa waking up in a haunted caravan which rocked with strange noises, meaning in fact that it would be her father's cattle rubbing on the caravan during the night. Mr Wise, the owner of the hotel, was a dear old gentleman but rather vague. He seemed fascinated about me doing these hunting holidays and enquired about Theresa's duties, asking whether she had to live in the tiny caravan all the while. When I replied that she had a larger one at the kennels, he became even more confused. I explained that her duties were to spend the winters at the kennels doing my hunters and in the summer the caravan was moved to my home because I like driving horses.

"Oh," he said, "now I begin to understand. You are a haulage contractor."

When I said that I was not a haulage contractor, but just liked driving horses for fun he shrugged his shoulders and said,

"How very odd. How extremely odd."

He looked so mystified that I explained how I had collected some old carriages and liked to use them on the roads. He suddenly brightened up and said, "Oh I see. You use the horses in the shafts, do you?"

When I said yes, he replied, "Oh, I was thinking that you put your horses in the lorry and then drove them around the roads for fun." It is difficult to believe that he really did think that, but nevertheless it is true.

Friday morning saw me on my way back to Ivybridge, but not, however, to Major Farr's riding school, but to the Hunting Lodge where the **Dartmoor Foxhounds** were meeting (Fri 18 Mar 1983). It was rather foggy as I followed another lorry onto a tourist car-park and was unboxing when the Master, John Budgett, hacked by with hounds. He paused to give the other man a severe telling off for using this car-park, but immediately added that I could stay there. In the bar the previous evening I had been told by a man that I would see some wonderful hound control from Mr Budgett. I was reminded of this as I saw his hounds absolutely motionless as they sat and stared at him. This was to be his last season as a Master of Foxhounds which he had been for thirty-five years, with one pack or another. His successor was to be Dr David Mills who was keeping on the kennel huntsman of six seasons (who had been kennelman at the Heythrop) to hunt hounds for him.

We moved off from the meet and hacked up onto the moor, but when we got there the fog was far too thick to hunt. John decided to take his hounds home because, quite apart from losing hounds, it is easy to get seriously lost oneself on the moor in fog. John Coker, who had lived on the moor all his life, told me that he could get lost even on his own farm in fog, and said how he had to rely on his shepherding pony to take him home on several occasions. The Master asked if I would like to see his kennels so I hacked back with him and tied Demelza up in his garage while we looked round, and then enjoyed a large whisky before hacking back to where I had left the lorry, determined to have another day with them before going home.

On the Saturday morning, as I was dressing, I realised that my hunting cap was in the kitchen where I had left it to dry but when I went to get it I found that the door was locked. In a panic I tried to find Mike, the barman, who was still in bed but only succeeded in disturbing a horrified old lady. I rushed outside and sent Theresa up to Mr Wise's house (which was situated a little way away on the top of a rise with a lovely view) for a key, but the general confusion had woken Mike up and he unlocked the door for me. I did not have to start until seven forty-five so I had time to have breakfast. I asked Ted the chef to fill my flask with soup, adding a request that it would be his own this time, as he had used packet soup for my day with the Seavington. He apologised and said it would always be his own in future. As he never knew what time I would start, Ted always prepared my sandwiches the night before and wrapped them in cling-film, and also introduced me to a system of taking hot water in a flask and making my own coffee cup by cup.

I had planned to have this day with the **Tetcott Foxhounds** and, as both the horses were very fresh, Theresa came with me. As we drew nearer to the meet at Stratton, near Bude, the fog became thicker (Sat 19 Mar 1983). It seemed rather pointless to carry on, but we did so as there was little else to do. Luckily the fog cleared during the last mile. A farmer told us where to unbox and Mrs Miller, an ex-Master of these hounds, who remembered me from mink-hunting with the Devon and Cornwall Minkhounds in 1981, said that she was both pleased and surprised to see me there. The meet was held in a meadow below a bungalow called Conways where the eats and drinks were excellent. I met the Master, Peter Hunkin, and Mr Honey who was a fabulous character. A splendid sight at the meet was of a large gentleman with a round rosy face, such a picture of contentment, reminding me of John Bull. He was sitting on his horse with a glass of whisky in one hand and a huge Cornish pasty in the other, happily munching while his cob grazed with the reins round his ears. The other members could see that I was highly amused, and told me that he was often to be seen sitting with a packet of sandwiches open on the pommel of his saddle.

I was not at all impressed with the hounds which were mangey and scruffy, continually scratching, and were very slack while hunting and terribly slow coming out of coverts. I kept with Mr Honey who proved to be a good pilot although there was little chance of getting lost as the Master was a very slow huntsman. Mr Honey took charge of me on the last hunt and took so many short cuts that, although I saw little of hounds, we were always in the right spot at the right time to watch them pass. This run took us through the yard of the farm where he was born so it was no wonder he knew the country so well. The day ended for me when hounds hunted up into an old quarry on real loose scree, and the Master climbed up on foot while we sat at the bottom for over three-quarters of an hour.

The kennel huntsman was riding a five-year-old iron grey, a real hard type, which I was told was for sale and he had it on trial. During the evening I telephoned the owner and said that I would be very interested if the kennel huntsman did not want it. He did not return my call so I presumed that it had been sold. Mr Hunkin, I was told, had taken on the Mastership of the Radnor and West Foxhounds, and that Mrs Miller was taking over the Mastership of the Tetcott for a second time the following season. Loveday Miller, the ex-Master's daughter, was whipping-in and looked very smart in her red coat. She also remembered me from mink-hunting so I asked her to say my goodnights to the Master, as he was high above us.

On the way home, it came on to torrential rain and I picked up a couple of young hitch-hikers who looked at my clothes and asked if I had been show-jumping. When I told them that I had been hunting, they shrank away from me, screwing themselves up against the passenger side door and looking at me in horror. If it had not been raining so hard, coupled with the fact that they by now knew that I was passing near the place they wanted to go, I am sure they would have wanted to get out. However, as we had a long way to go there was plenty of time to talk and they explained to me that they kept a Health Shop selling vegetarian food and were anti-hunting. I decided to talk about vegetarianism and asked if they would like to see a world where no-one ate meat. They agreed that that would be ideal because it was so cruel to kill defenceless animals. I asked about how they saw the countryside in this ideal world – would there be sheep and lambs in the meadows? Or would they cut the meadows with lawnmowers, or alternatively allow it to grow up with bushes and trees? They replied that they would like to see lambs skipping around as they looked so pretty. I then asked who would pay the shepherd, and for the fencing, and what would happen to this year's lambs when next year's lambs arrived. How would they cope with the overcrowding as successive generations arrived? I also pointed out that millions of animals would not experience life at all in their world. This and many other points were discussed in the hour or so that they were in the cab, and they relaxed and stopped pressing against the door. By the time I dropped them off they were becoming quite sensible and almost to the point when they would have agreed that there was no need for vegetarians. They had clearly not thought at all deeply about the matter, assuming that the countryside would always remain the same. It was a most fascinating conversation.

That night I had a superb dinner with fresh salmon followed by duckling and plum fool, and the company in the bar was such fun. Mike the barman appeared on Friday nights and worked in the bar on Friday, Saturday and Sunday evenings. He fascinated me as he drank glass after glass of gin, each a single measure in a small tumbler filled to the brim with water, getting through two bottles a day. He was always down at six o'clock in the morning and while I was drinking my coffee before going hunting he would be in the office doing the accounts. Even at six o'clock in the morning he would regularly go behind the bar for his gin. Even if I was not sitting so that I could see the bar (some mornings I preferred not to!) I could hear the glass hitting the optic. He never changed this system, even at two-thirty in the morning, it was always a single gin and the glass was always filled to the brim with water. I have often since thought that it was perhaps the amount of water that saved his liver. He was a big, well-built man, but not fat. What surprised me even more was how much he enjoyed his food. Most heavy drinkers do not eat much, but Mike would eat a large breakfast and as much dinner as I could (which was considerable). He made no secret about how much he drank, and did not attempt to conceal his early morning drinks. I laughed and said to him that I hoped he would donate his liver to medical research and he replied that I was not the first person to say that. He then went on to tell me seriously that he had drunk gin at this rate for over thirty years, except that he had recently cut down to two bottles instead of two and a half as he had had a minor car accident so had decided to reduce his consumption. Even at two-thirty in the morning he never showed the slightest sign that he had had a drink. Mike was an old friend of Mr Wise and worked all weekend for his gin and his food. The two happy, joking girls, Prudence and Susan, Mike and Mr Coker were the greatest characters in the little bar, closely followed by Mr Wise. There was always such an atmosphere that no-one ever wanted to leave and it was always well after midnight, and often one-thirty or two o'clock before I went to bed.

On the Sunday morning I borrowed Mr Wise's car again and drove over to lunch at Reaphay with the Roffe-Sylvesters. The day was spent in that especially delightful way which only happens at Reaphay. I met Michael's brother Peter who used to hunt the Tiverton Staghounds, and the brother of Dick Mickleham (with whom I had stayed at Falmouth) and was told that John was later to take on the Mastership of his father's hounds. With the greatest difficulty, I managed to leave this delightful place and drove back to the Forest Inn. After my large lunch, I tried to be sensible and insisted on a light dinner but the good resolutions soon evaporated and after a large dinner there was another long session in the bar.

Some days before I had realised that on the Monday there would be no packs hunting in this area that I had not already been with, so, as usual, with the aid of my map of foxhunting countries and Baily's, I telephoned round an ever-increasing radius until I found that the **Blackmore and Sparkford Vale Foxhounds** were having a meet in the New Forest by invitation of the New Forest Foxhounds. This was rather too far, I thought, to drive both ways, so I telephoned Ralph Coakes to ask if I could stay the night with my horse and he readily agreed. I breakfasted at seven forty-five and, like Dick Whittington, wrapped my necessary change of clothes and my spongebag in a bundle in my dressing-gown and, after reading Surtees for an hour, set off for the New Forest with Charlie (my horse) at ten o'clock. I was to do my own horse at Ralph's so before I left Theresa gave me the inevitable list of special things that I must do to him, and for him, and at what time. By the time I had read it through I felt as though I was hardly competent to feed the cat. I made much better time than I expected and arrived at two-thirty, thinking that I could just have managed to have driven both ways, but for the temptation of enjoying an evening with Ralph. I put Charlie away, managing to drop the ramp and shut the stable door without written instructions. Ralph was not at home when I arrived, but was there soon and, after a cup of tea took me to see the famous Stroller who was now thirty-three years old but looked quite fit. I also enjoyed an interesting chat with another veteran, Olive Coakes, Ralph's mother who had celebrated her hundredth birthday two months before. The evening was great fun, with me mostly listening to hilarious stories from Ralph.

I was up early and did Charlie (no plaits!) and, after breakfast, I left at nine-thirty with Ralph to show me the way to the meet at Campden car-park (Tues 22 Mar 1983). Marion followed with another lorry with horses that had been hired by Sir Newton Rycroft, Master of the New Forest, and his Honorary Secretary, and one for herself. As I rode up to the hounds at the meet, I was recognised immediately by the Master Mr Winslade who knew me because I had bought Charlie from him at Leicester Sales. He said that he had recognised Charlie before myself, and rather nervously asked how I was getting on with him. I replied, "Fine, fine. Such a good horse, I always take him visiting." In fact, he was a nappy swine, but I could usually manage to get him to go where I wanted. If he was in a bad mood, he would rear a little and spin round, and try to take off back the way he had come, but I was not going to let Mr Winslade know that I had had any trouble. I was not the only one to be recognised, as there was an extended whinnying greeting between Charlie and the whipper-in's horse who were obviously old friends. This was one of the longest exchanges of friendship between two horses that I have ever heard. At the meet I noticed that the whipper-in had a double row of buttons down the back of his coat like a Pytchley coat and wondered whether this was a traditon for whips in the Blackmore and Sparkford Vale or whether it had been borrowed since the Masters – Mr Winslade and Mr Cursham – did not have them on their coats. Mr Winslade told me his guarantee was £30,000 per annum, plus 90% of the skin money, the remainder going to the kennel huntsman and that 10% coming to £100 the previous week.

**Blackmore and Sparkford Vale Foxhounds.** *On the road with hounds are Chris Bowld and James Greenfill.*

As hounds went off to draw, I fell in alongside a lady who remembered me from when I hunted in the Romney Marsh country, and who kept with hounds brilliantly during the day. We viewed the first fox away – not easy in the New Forest, but this fox crossed an open paddock. The cry of hounds was, I thought, quite delightful, and the most musical I have ever heard. It was not a deep sound but very melodious: tenor rather than the usual bass of foxhounds. Hounds split and Sir Newton and I and the lady from the Romney Marsh had our splinter pack to ourselves. We had a most enjoyable run, but at the first serious check, Sir Newton took them back to the huntsman. These hounds had the reputation of going like the devil in their own country, but I felt that they were unused to running in forestry and did not feel at home there. The hunt horses had lost several shoes on the muddy rides so they decided to stop at three o'clock. I said my goodbyes to

Ralph and Marion and arrived back at Hexworthy at eight-thirty.

On Wednesday morning I left base at eight-thirty and arrived comfortably, unboxed and hacked up to the meet of the **Tiverton Foxhounds** at Ravenswood School, Stoodleigh (Wed 23 Mar 1983). Demelza was very difficult and spooky to get into the courtyard of the school which was a mixed preparatory boarding school, converted from an old country house. One of the matrons of the school, who was one of loveliest girls I have ever seen, approached me shyly to ask if she could take my photograph and I said it was a shame it could not be reciprocal at which she blushed and smiled. The huntsman recognised me from when he was with the East Sussex and Romney Marsh – two days running I had met someone from there. It is the custom at this meet for the boys and girls to follow hounds on foot and about eighty followed us from the meet, each clutching their packed lunch. The mounted field consisted only of myself and three ladies, each with a child, two of which came from the school. These two were treated to advice and comments from their pals at every stage of the day. I can remember at one obstacle a chorus of, "Go it, Nicky. Go on, girl."

The country was steep and, although there was good viewing from the higher points, there was also a lot of woodland. The first fox did not go far, and the second only for twenty minutes or so, as they were constantly being headed by the eighty children who had scattered all over the wooded hillside. It was a most unusual sight, the fox dodging in and out of the children who were each taking their own line. They were so thrilled to see the foxes, of which there were several, and the abundance of deer (both roe and red), that I thought it well worthwhile losing a little sport to see so many children out with hounds. The conditions were terrible with very heavy rain and very cold winds, and although my new apron kept my legs dry I was soaked to the skin after a couple of hours. The children and the mounted field disappeared and I was the only one left out with the hunt staff and the Master, Mr Pearcey, who had had these hounds for ten seasons. The third fox had no-one to head him and gave us a wonderful hunt of two hours, not a great point but venerie of the finest as he twisted and ran back and forth through these deep, steep valleys. There was constant opportunity of riot as deer were continually running in front of hounds but not a single one took the slightest notice of them. This would have been a day of exceptional pleasure if the weather had been more clement, and these were the best hounds I had seen on this trip. They received the highest accolade possible, with the single sentence that ended my diary entry for the day – "These hounds hunt a fox like the Easton hunt a hare" by which I meant unaided. I arrived back at five forty-five very wet, very happy and with a very tired Demelza who had been up and down the hills all day in the deepest going.

Next day I went with the **Cattistock** who were meeting at Widecombe-in-the-Moor (by invitation of the South Devon) although I had already had a day with them in their own country in 1978. I think the day is best described exactly as it is in my diary, without any added memories (Thurs 24 Mar 1983). I rode Charlie and it was very cold with strong winds and snow showers. Scent was good.

*"Lovely sight as I hacked down into Widecombe – herd of good-looking Dartmoor ponies coming up towards me while from left and right hunters were being hacked across the moor towards the meet from every direction. Large crowd at meet, approximately ninety horses. Betty and Hugh Gingell were there who told me that they had been down a week and were staying at Ashburton. Found at once. What a thrill to hear them going to a tremendous holloa, and the sound of eighty horses galloping on sound turf – grand hunt, often slow but real good houndwork, Mr Austen, Master and huntsman, casting them on foot at times. I was lucky and went with a farmer and got in a position to see all but missed out a lot of road work. Found a second fox and had a most exciting hunt round Hay Tor rocks – how wonderful to be so exhilerated. How do people live their lives without such excitement I wonder? I love hunting on the moor – such good views of hounds and such beautiful scenery – several hounds were mottled both blue and strawberry coloured and were very handy and very well hunted. Many people came up and said they remembered me from other places. Had quite a chat with David Miller. Near the box at three-fifteen so decided to finish on a high note after three of the loveliest hours I have spent for a long time. Heard that the Bicester are coming down. Grand feeling to be on a fit horse; grand to be alive and lucky to have health, and strength and the chance to live like this and long may it continue, God willing."*

Next morning I left at eight forty-five for a day with the **Heythrop Foxhounds** who were meeting by invitation of the Eggesford at The Fox and Hounds at Eggesford (Fri 25 Mar 1983). I had been to this meet before when staying in North Devon at Ilfracombe so I knew how to find it and was the first there. I found the concrete base of an old building which was perfect to park on and my example was copied by later arrivals. The meet is one of the most attractive of my experience, approached by a road higher than the pub, with a gravel drive sweeping up to it and along the front. I thought that perhaps this might be the reason why the Eggesford had invited the Heythrop to meet there, especially as they had also invited the Chiddingfold, Leconfield and

Cowdray to meet there when I had been with them in 1979. I went into the bar where a gentleman called Maurice remembered me from the otter-hounds and bought me a drink. As the others came into the bar and saw my green coat, they immediately assumed that I was a Heythrop official (since this pack wear green coats instead of the usual foxhound red), and I was treated with all due respect and reverence. Another peculiarity about the Heythrop livery, is that, like the Pytchley, the coats have a double row of buttons on the back. The day was very cold, and very wet with high winds – just about as unpleasant as it could be.

Hounds arrived so I went out to unbox Demelza. The Master of the Eggesford, Mr Gill, remembered my name and took me to meet the Heythrop Master, Mr Lambert, who was hunting hounds. At the meet hounds were allowed to wander a little and I thought that Mr Lambert and I had similar ideas about this because I did not have my hounds held up to me at meets of the Easton. The visit of these famous hounds had drawn together many neighbouring Masters and members and there were many faces I recognised. Mr Desmond Isaac, whom I had met when hunting with the Eggesford in 1979, asked if I had Mickey with me, and even remembered that the gallant little cob had done nine days out of ten when we were at Ilfracombe in 1979. He also drew my attention to the fact that he was riding a horse I had tried to buy the day I was hunting with his pack.

The first fox ran a small circle and the line was lost in thick undergrowth. I quickly saw that these hounds did not like the dense undergrowth and so did Mr Lambert, who got off and drew on foot. This again reminded me of my harriers and as he pushed his way through the dense undergrowth his hounds followed him in single file. This is very aggravating after you have pushed through and suffered the scratches and discomfort, and they still will not spread out to draw properly. Of course, it was of little help but somehow they did find a fox, and hounds went away. I got away with them and had a few glorious moments as I galloped across three pastures, alongside these world-famous Heythrop bitches. It was fortunate that I had had these few moments of ecstasy as the rest of the day was spent on roads and tracks, mostly out of sight and hearing of hounds. I was thoroughly fed up by three o'clock and went back to the meet. On the way I came alongside Mike Weir whom I had met in 1973 as Master of the North Cornwall Foxhounds but was now Master of the Silverton which I was to go with the next day, and who was of like mind. Mike and I had a couple of drinks together and talked of the day, and would, I am sure, have talked much longer but Mike had forgotten to bring any money and would not accept more than two drinks from me. I left thinking how I would love to see these hounds hunting in open country, as they were obviously very unhappy in the Eggesford country.

I arrived back at six-fifteen and, as I walked into the hotel, I asked Prudence if she would come up to my bedroom. She looked rather apprehensive but came, and was highly amused when I asked her to put her foot on the end of my boot-jack as I knew I would not be able to pull off my soaked boots by myself. Valetting hunt clothes was always difficult in a hotel. Sometimes I had the use of an airing cupboard or the kitchen to dry off coats and although I had two coats it was difficult to get one dry enough to wear next time. Theresa washed my gloves and stocks, but I would not let her do my Bedford cord breeches as they are so easy to shrink. To remedy this, when they were dry I would brush off the mud and the next time after I put them on, I would dab the stains with the Meltonian White that I used on my garter straps. "Be sure your sins will find you out", however, for at the meet that day, as I was sitting talking to Mr Lambert, the rain not only uncovered the stains but, to make matters worse, the Meltonian ran in white streaks down my boots. As much as I tried to distract his attention, I could see that his eyes were continually being drawn to my boot.

Dinner was as good as usual and I fell into conversation with a policeman and his wife who had been staying there for a few days, and always asked what sort of day I had. They were not sporting people, but just interested in a general way. His wife was always so pleased when I told her that we had not killed a fox. After dinner, the policeman bought me a drink and as we sat talking, he told me that he trained dogs for the Police Force then, in hushed tones from the corner of his mouth, whispered, "Tell me the truth, just between you and me. If a rider fell off in front of the hounds, wouldn't they have a go at him?" He obviously expected me to confess the awful truth, as one "dog-man" to another.

Next morning I left base at nine-ten for the **Silverton Foxhounds** meet at Cadbury Cross, near Crediton, and arrived in good time (Sat 26 Mar 1983). I immediately got into conversation with the Chairman of the Supporters' Club, who proudly told me that they had raised over £5,000 the previous year. I managed a quick conversation with Mike Weir, who was now Master and huntsman of these hounds, before he moved off to draw Cadbury Castle. He then drew up a hill which was so high that at the top we could see over twenty miles in every direction, and a member pointed out Exmoor in the far distance. Hounds found soon after drawing this hill but, after a short burst, he went to ground to a badger sett. The hounds had some Welsh blood in them and Mike hunted them very well, with that effortless ease that always goes with those who are good at what they are doing, coupled with melodious horn-blowing which ensured perfect control and made him a joy to watch. His son, aged about six or seven, was whipping-in to his father and was a sight that delighted my eyes. He rode his little pony in an old-fashioned style, now only seen in old men or on pictures, with his stirrup leathers long and his feet slightly forward of his knees. He carried an ash-plant whip (a hunting whip of normal size, but cut from ash naturally shaped like this, and correct to be used on informal occasions like bye-days and cub-hunting, or after 1 March). He carried it turned up against his arm, as professional hunt servants do. He did his duties like a true professional as well, never giving the rest of the field a glance, but always having his eye on his job, shooting ahead to open a gate, or flying off to be on point. To see this little lad doing such a wonderful job is one of the most cherished memories of this day.

**Silverton Hounds** *in 1993.*

Photograph kindly loaned by Mrs P H Bromell

Foxes proved difficult to find, scent was very poor and there was little to watch in the way of sport but the wonderful thing about hunting is that there are so many different things that go to make an enjoyable day. The lack of sport did not seem to matter because, as well as being able to watch Mike Weir hunting his hounds with that quiet extra-confidence and his little son whipping-in to him, the scenery and company were of the best. The views were so spectacular that I was moved to enter in my diary that it was one of the most beautiful countries I had ever seen, and the Field Master, with whom I spent quite a large part of the day, was most friendly and had a fund of interesting stories and comments. However, I suffer from an old back injury and was feeling particularly stiff. I attributed it to riding up and down these steep hills and, although the back pain had worn off a little, as sport was not all that good I decided to go home and arrived back at base at five o'clock. Brigid and Michael Roffe-Sylvester, and his brother Peter, were joining me for dinner and after an hour of hilarious pre-dinner drinks, we sat down to avocado with prawns, followed by fresh salmon and the cheese board, with plenty of good wine and port. During and after dinner, Michael and Peter told many good stories, three of which I recorded before going to sleep that night.

One was of a hunting farmer who had recently died and at his request hounds were to meet at his farm shortly after. They found a fox and after a long hunt it was killed on top of his grave. Another was of when Peter was hunting hounds and was hacking with hounds through Tiverton, and held his pack up at a busy main road. An old hound broke away and crossed the road, narrowly avoiding the cars, and when Peter managed to get over he found this hound jumping up and whining at the door of a council house. It was later discovered that the man who had been kennelman to these hounds all of his life was dying in the house at that very moment. The third was of a sporting parson who was called upon to bury a local bookmaker. As the coffin was lowered into the grave, the parson read from the Prayer Book "Earth to earth, ashes and ashes ... in sure and certain hope ..." but, as well as making the sign of the cross, he was also doing the tic-tac for four-to-one against.

On Sunday I borrowed Mr Wise's car again and I went on a local tour. I had lunch at the Ship in Plymouth in an upstairs room overlooking the harbour, enjoying a crab starter and a fresh sole to follow, then drove back to the Forest Inn and went for a long walk down by the river. I was just going upstairs to write up my diary, when about two hundred and fifty walkers appeared at the Inn, and as I was writing there was quite a din downstairs. In the midst of all this the telephone rang and it was Peter Roffe-Sylvester to thank me for dinner. The most lasting memory of this day was of Lord and Lady Harvey. This was a long-running story because they had booked into the hotel very early, and there had been a little confusion when some of the staff assumed that I was Lord Harvey when I arrived. However, what I remember best was the considerable disturbance when they went to pay their account at the hotel, as they argued that Mr Wise had agreed on the telephone that the £10 per night included their dinner and pre-dinner drinks. The entry in my diary describing my opinion of them was unprintable.

The day started with a bad hangover as I had attempted to keep up with John Coker's rate of drinking whisky and had stayed up into the early hours on one of those sessions when each of us was pouring out our hearts to the other. It was an unwise situation to get into, and I did not try to keep up with him again. Nevertheless, I set off for a day with the **Bicester and Warden Hill Foxhounds** who were meeting at the Fox and Hounds at Bridestowe by invitation (Mon 28 Mar 1983). Bridestowe lies on the boundary between the Lamerton and the Spooners countries and I did not put in my diary which hunt had actually invited them to meet there.

The hounds had some Welsh blood in them and drew well for their huntsman, Captain Farquhar, who was very quiet. Demelza was slightly lame so I stayed at the back of the field and came quietly along. We drew blank for hours, and what with Demelza being lame and having not found a fox, I was ready for home by two-thirty. As I walked Demelza back towards the meet, the hounds were drawing well above me, so in fact I was with hounds for another three-quarters of an hour. I arrived back at base at five o'clock. So ended a day when nothing had been right – headache, lame horse and no foxes.

On Tuesday I made my final attempt to hunt with the **Four Burrow Foxhounds** as earlier attempts had failed due to fog or frost (Tues 29 Mar 1983). The Four Burrow were the only West Country pack not shaded in on my hunting map and were meeting at Tehidy Hospital (or Point-to-Point course, since it seemed to be known by both names). It was a long drive but I knew I would never be nearer so I decided to go and left the Inn at seven o'clock. John Coker had strongly recommended breakfast at Smokey Joe's Cafe on the Camborne bypass and as I reckoned that I had thirty minutes in hand, I sat down and thoroughly enjoyed the full works of a lorry driver's breakfast. I must have looked very funny, sitting there in my polished boots and white breeches, amongst the grimy overalls of my fellow customers, eating three eggs, four rashers of bacon, fried bread, tinned tomatoes, baked beans and three sausages, with a door-step of bread-and-butter and a half-pint mug of tea which, from memory, cost a pound.

**Four Burrow Foxhounds** *at Tehidy Hospital on 19 March 1983, the day that Tony Harvey finally got to hunt with them. L to R, three Joint Masters Paul Hancock, Trevor Burley and Bruce Warren.*

Photograph kindly loaned by Mr Paul Hancock

At the meet I introduced myself to the Joint-Masters Mr Warren and to Mr Burley who hunted hounds. I found myself an excellent pilot who immediately took me to where the first fox would leave the covert and I had the pleasure of holloaing him away. He then took me to a high vantage point from where we saw the whole of this hunt. For over an hour, hounds ran round the bottom of the hill, until finally they killed in the open. I had deliberately taken Demelza because she knew about bank-jumping (having come out of this part of the country originally), but was told at the meet that there would be no bank-jumping. The farmers had said that they did not want it owing to so many having been broken down from this meet the previous year. The opportunity to watch from the top of the hill, rather than gallop around the valley with the field, was very welcome as it saved Demelza who was beginning to feel the effects of the deep going.

We moved on to draw some gorse and found a fox which immediately ran through a market garden. The sight was awful to see as the whole pack poured over the bank and ran through the garden which was full of glass cloches, while the angry owner loudly voiced his objections and waved his arms. It was the sort of sight that just makes you want to shut your eyes. This fox later went to ground in a badger sett and was left. We drew on for a long time before finding again, during which time I got into conversation with an old gentleman who told me that he lived in the oldest house in Cornwall and that his age and his horse's added up to 107 years. He also told me all about the Basset family who had owned the estate we were on, and that the hospital where we had met had been their home. He also pointed out a private road which ran for many miles and was built for their exclusive use, and must be one of the longest front drives ever made. We drew on into some woods and he again came alongside me and asked me if I would like to see the Basset family's foxhound kennels. We went into the wood and saw these lovely old kennels which were now full of cattle. To hear Mr Burley draw was not a very pretty sound, as his voice was deep and gruff, and not at all musical, and his "Try, try", sounded so forlorn, rather like an exhausted man's call for help.

The hounds, when running, had a very light cry and many of their voices were decidedly squeaky and high-pitched, so that even when they were close behind their fox there was no volume of music. The long journey back was not as tedious as it might have been as I picked up a student hitch-hiker who was with me for an hour or so and told me that his parents hunted in Essex. I eventually arrived back at base at seven-thirty.

In the evening I was lucky to find yet more good company at the dinner-table as there was a charming old couple who were car-followers of the Bicester and Warden Hill (visiting in the area), and were staying at the hotel. We had talked hunting on some earlier evenings and I found it particularly interesting to hear accounts of hunting from the point of view of an experienced car follower. It was quite an eye-opener for me to find out how much they knew and saw. My wooden boot trees caused some amusement as Prudence sent me to bed in a fit of giggles by telling me that another guest in the hotel had asked her if she minded telling them about the strange Man in Number Three (ie. myself) as they had seen little wooden feet and legs lying on the floor in his room.

The **Bicester and Warden Hill** were meeting again quite close to Hexworthy at the Two Bridges Hotel near Princetown, by invitation of the Dartmoor, and I left the hotel only at ten-fifteen (Wed 30 Mar 1983). The road from Hexworthy in that direction was very narrow and had an even narrower stone bridge on a double bend. John Coker had told me that this bridge could only be crossed in one direction by reversing over it as the bridge was so narrow and the bend so close to it. It had to be negotiated in this way every time I went in the Princetown direction which was for most of the hunts, and my lorry still carries the scars of it ten years later in the form of a very bent step. There was great merriment at the meet when someone put flippers on Captain Farquhar's boots as he sat with his hounds at the meet. This was because he had become seriously bogged down when hunting hounds the previous Monday after I had left. Hounds had not been drawing long when they marked at an earth. A terrier was put in and the fox bolted immediately. I was nicely placed and got away well with hounds, and there were several good walls to jump during this sharp run across the moor to some woodland. The hounds were hunting beautifully with a lovely cry and I wished that this woodland had been miles further away so I could have enjoyed a longer run in the open. However, they rattled him round the woodland and pushed him out for another sharp gallop across the moor before he went to ground in some rocks.

During this run, I became bogged when crossing a river but managed to struggle out all right, but when hounds checked at the rocks someone pointed out to me that Demelza had a cut. I dismounted and found quite a nasty cut just above her coronet which must I thought have been done while struggling in the river. I reluctantly had to return to the meet and get her back to the care of Theresa who put a poultice on it. After dinner, Sue and John Coker were going to the Two Bridges Hotel and John offered me a lift, and I thoroughly enjoyed my evening with the Bicester people. The large bar of the hotel was crowded with hunting people, both visiting and local foxhunters. I had a long and most interesting talk about venerie with Ian Farquahar and some other Bicester members. I had rather hoped that a sing-song would get going but this did not happen. I did not want to go when John Coker did, so I stopped with Sue until the bitter end in the early hours when she took me back to the Forest Inn.

Wishing I had not stayed quite so late at the Two Bridges, I left Hexworthy at nine-thirty for the meet of the **Dartmoor Foxhounds** at Moor Cross House, near Ivybridge, which was to be my last day (Thurs 31 Mar 1983). This was the second time I had tried to hunt with them as two weeks earlier fog had caused John Budgett to call it off. I unboxed at the kennels and quickly noticed that John seemed to be in a very bad mood, and hardly spoke to me at all. I hacked up to the meet with hounds, where there was a lovely hot punch waiting for us. Our hostess instantly noticed that the Master was not his usual cheery self and instead of giving him punch, brought him out a very stiff brandy. This soon did the trick and he invited me to ride up with him hunting hounds. His horses are never plaited for hunting, he explained, and asked how we would like to have our hair tweaking all day, but I secretly thought to myself that the fact that he did his own horse might have something to do with this theory.

There were about twenty mounted in the field and an equal number of car followers. We found a fox very quickly and had a lovely long run across good firm moor, with the horses' hooves making that lovely drumming sound until we ran into some woodland. He twisted around in the woodland for a while, then was pushed out and we had another sharp run across the moor. The hunting was superb and I was glad at last to be able to see John Budget hunting his hounds in this his last season before retirement. He had a lovely manner with his hounds, speaking to each one by name in a voice like an adoring grandfather does to his favourite grandchild. Every hound responded to this individual greeting with such obvious pleasure and enthusiasm that their whole bodies and sterns wriggled with pleasure. By three-thirty the length of the hunting holiday and the frequent days and the fact that I was riding up with the huntsman was telling on Charlie. Although he still wanted to go with hounds I could feel him weaving with tiredness underneath me, so I decided to go back. Some car followers described a route across the moor which was difficult to do and even more difficult to follow. However, I was very pleased with myself when I arrived at just the correct gate they had told me would lead me down to the kennels. It had been quite a long walk back across the moor with plenty of time to admire the beauty of the moor and to reflect on what a wonderful holiday I had had.

As I boxed up back at the kennels a terrible hailstorm blew up, and I was extremely thankful to have got off the moor as not only would it have been grim, but I would probably also have lost my way. Mrs Budgett called me into the house for soup and baps which were very welcome. The evening was a mixture of happiness and sadness as I had had such a good time. Sue and Prudence were genuinely sad that this was the last evening and Ted the chef had cooked a special dinner for Theresa and I that was not on the menu. The lobsters he cooked for the main course were out of this world and were complemented by the excellent Chablis he had chosen to go with them. It was difficult not to get involved in another heavy session but with the long journey in mind for the morrow I kept the celebrations to a sensible level.

Sue and Pru came down to the stables to see us off next morning, and helped push the caravan up the slope while I hooked it on to the back of the lorry. While this was going on, Mrs Wise was shouting for them to come back as I suppose that breakfast-serving had come to a complete halt while they saw us away. We left at eight-thirty and I drove non-stop, with Theresa passing me cups of soup and coffee, until we reached Baldock where we stopped for eggs and bacon at the little cafe that I always used when travelling to and from Barnet Horse Fair. I was getting very sleepy so I telephoned from Duxford and asked Bridget to collect Jim Wickham from the kennels and come to meet us along the route. When I saw them pass me on the other carriageway of the A45 I pulled into the next layby and they turned round and came back. We offloaded my cases into the car and Jim took the lorry back to Easton. Bridget and I arrived back at eight-thirty. It was Good Friday and on the way we had seen terrible queues up to thirty miles long on the M3 and M4 of cars going down to Devon for the holiday. We were very glad that they were going in the opposite direction to us.

When we got home Sheila told me the most extraordinary story. My little Border terrier, Badger, had been very miserable every day that I was away, spending most of the day in his basket, never sitting on his favourite window-sill from where he could see the drive, and only eating half his usual amount. When I got home Sheila told me that he had got out of his basket at eight-thirty that morning and jumped up to the window-sill and started waving his tail excitedly. Thinking he wanted to go out, she let him out but he came back in again almost immediately and resumed his position on the windowsill. He stayed there all day, staring down the drive with a happy expression and continually wagging his tail till I arrived home. After being miserable in his basket every day I was away, and then jumping up onto the windowsill at the exact time I left Devon for home, there can be no doubt that there must have been some form of telepathy which told him I was coming home.

I had enjoyed thirteen days' hunting, twelve mounted and one with the beagles and, although I had been twice with the Dartmoor and twice with the Bicester, and also went with the Cattistock for a second time, I had nevertheless managed to add another eleven new packs to my list. The total was now a round one hundred and fifty packs, the last fifty having been added in three years.

# MAP 10

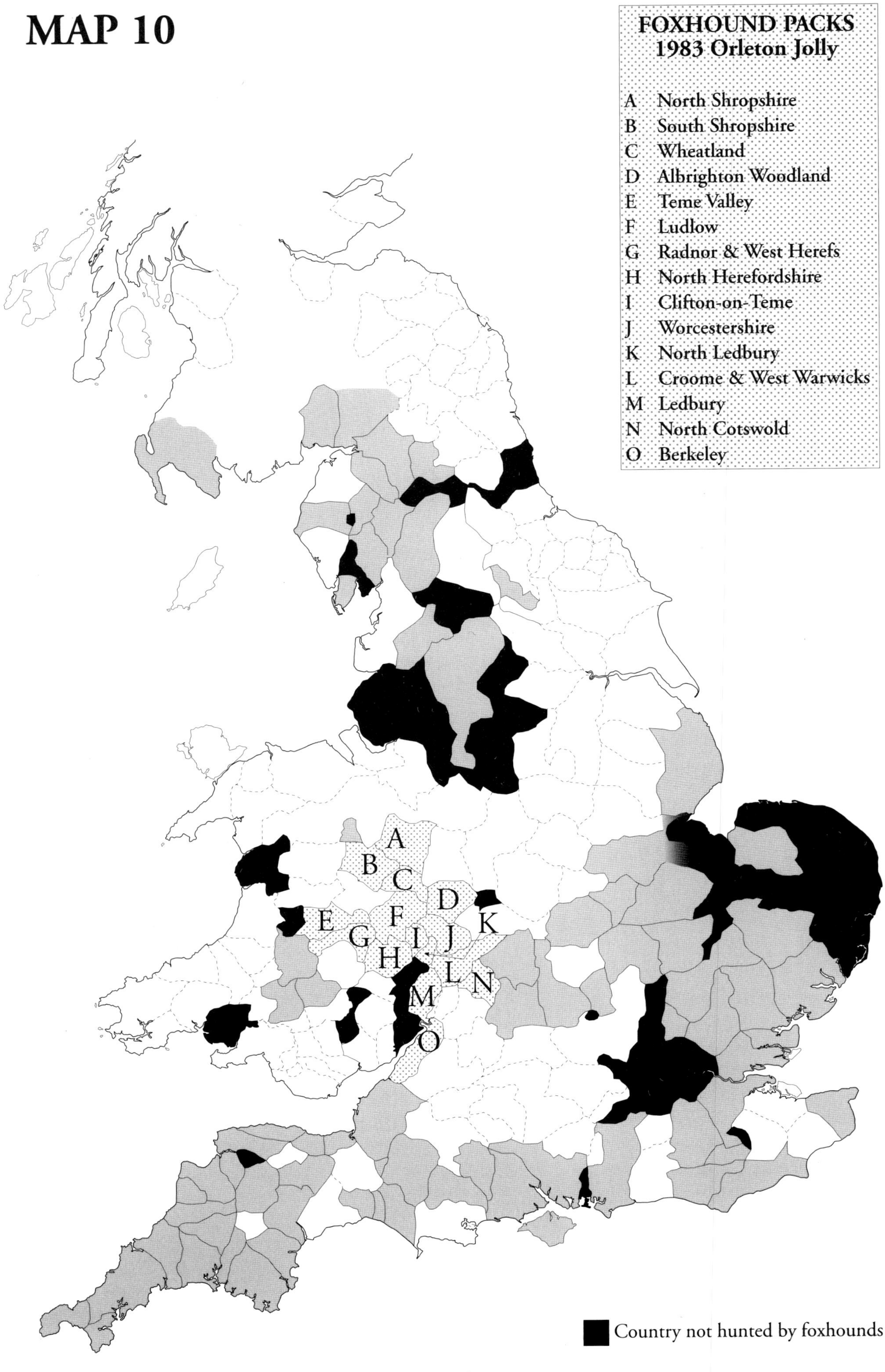
FOXHOUND PACKS
1983 Orleton Jolly
A North Shropshire
B South Shropshire
C Wheatland
D Albrighton Woodland
E Teme Valley
F Ludlow
G Radnor & West Herefs
H North Herefordshire
I Clifton-on-Teme
J Worcestershire
K North Ledbury
L Croome & West Warwicks
M Ledbury
N North Cotswold
O Berkeley
A
B
C
D
E
F
G
I
J
K
H
L
N
M
O
Country not hunted by foxhounds

# Chapter 13

## The Marches of Wales

At the beginning of the next season, in early September 1983, I drove to Scotland to arrange a hunting tour of the whole country, or to "do" Scotland as the Americans would probably say. I stayed the first night with Anthony Barker (Master of the Windermere Harriers) at Patterdale and, after looking at his hounds, we had a little unexpected sport when I went out with a terrier "pack". They had been asked to draw for a mink that had bitten a lady's bottom while she was sunbathing in her garden beside the river. Everyone was most surprised at this but in the true spirit of chivalry a number of gallant lads turned up with their terriers to find the offender and duly killed a mink. The terriermen assured the lady that this was the actual one which had bitten her but I thought this very unlikely.

I then moved up into Scotland and visited the Lanarkshire and Renfrewshire Foxhounds kennels. I was able to arrange stabling there with the huntsman and he even invited me to stay with him. He suggested that I next try the Duke of Buccleuch's kennels as there would definitely be boxes there. This I did and was dumbfounded by the magnificence of the old ducal kennels. The rows of loose-boxes were the finest I have ever seen – what a sight it must have been in its heyday. The next day I went up into Fife to see the huntsman of the Fife Foxhounds and he also agreed to give me a box and to arrange some accommodation. Thus I had arranged, subject to the approval of the various Masters, a U-shaped tour of Scotland with the idea of moving up the West coast and hunting with the Eglinton and the Lanarkshire and Renfrewshire from my first stop, then across to Fife, and back down to the Buccleuch kennels from which I was in easy reach of another four or five. However, like all the "best-laid plans of mice and men", this never came to fruition as I had some news from Colin and Tizza Plumbe that caused me to postpone my Scottish trip. They were shortly to be moving to Scotland to be closer to Galashiels where Colin now worked so, once they had moved, I would have a first-class and well-proven base in Scotland. More importantly, before they went there would be a first-class and well-proven base in Worcestershire as they were not going to get their hunters up and fit until after they had moved so their stables in Orleton would be empty. It was only sensible, therefore, to go to Orleton instead of Scotland, and wait until later to "do" the Scottish packs.

**Clifton-upon-Teme**. *A lawn meet at School House, Orleton.*
Photograph kindly loaned by Mrs Plumbe

Although I was to have a proper two-week jolly later in the season, I thought I would try to get in a couple of days from Orleton in conjunction with my annual trip to Builth Wells for the Welsh Cob Sales. Leaving Jim Wickham to hunt the Easton Harriers in my absence, I drove Falcon and Rose to School House at Orleton (near Stanford Bridge, Worcs). I did not take a groom as Tizza said she was willing to do the horses. Having left at ten-fifteen, I arrived at five-fifteen, unboxed the horses and let myself into the house (Thurs 13 Oct 1983). They had warned me that there would be no-one at home but they had told me where to find the key. Tizza soon returned but said that Colin, who was already working in Galashiels, would not be home until quite late. He eventually arrived home at ten-thirty and, after a quick chat, we all went to bed.

Next morning Colin and I went in a car to watch the Ledbury Foxhounds cub-hunting at Much Marcle, and that evening we went to the Harvest Festival where Alice, their eight-year-old daughter, and her friends were playing their recorders. The service was delightful and was followed by a real old-fashioned Harvest Supper, with the last surviving member of the Winnington family present. This family had built the church at their own expense some one hundred and thirty years before when they wanted to flood the valley for a trout lake where the original church had stood.

On Saturday morning we had decided to go to the local foxhounds, the **Clifton-upon-Teme**, who were meeting at Bromyard Hospital at nine o'clock (Sat 15

Oct 1983). I took Falcon and Colin had Rose. When we arrived at the meet it was actually on a common near the hospital and, as there was torrential rain, we stayed in the cab. Hounds arrived at the bottom of the common and Colin wanted to take the horses out but, as it was still pouring, I suggested that we waited until the actual time of the meet. At nine o'clock we unboxed and rode down to hounds but when Colin tried to introduce me to the Master, Mr David Parker, he just growled, "Right, now we can move off," and rode away. He was obviously furious that we had been sitting in the cab in the dry while he stood with his hounds in the open. Although I could, of course, sympathise, I could not see where we had committed any sin, as we were at the meet with hounds at exactly nine o'clock and were not the only members of the field.

Some of the views across the valley would have been fantastic but were of course spoiled by the driving rain. We killed the first fox after about thirty minutes and immediately found another and had a nice little hunt over to Burley where it went to ground and was left. The third fox gave us a short burst between coverts during which a young lady had a nasty fall over a hunt jump. When we retired to the lorry, my legs were dry under my Devon apron but the rest of me was soaked. When we got back to School House and I was able to change, I found that the green dye from the back of my coat had run and my breeches and even my underpants were bright green. Tizza had a lovely Lancashire Hot-Pot ready for lunch and then we slept all afternoon. In the evening Colin and I went out for a most unsuccessful evening of beer-drinking. Colin had arranged to meet a friend of his at the Bell Inn, and as he was not there, and it was full of yobs, we quickly left to go to another pub kept by friends of one of our local Suffolk landlords. This again was not a success as some big fellows started punching one another. A little friend of theirs walked in and, not knowing that they were quarrelling, he just walked up to them smiling and said, "Good evening." One of his "friends", without speaking, punched him so hard that he doubled up on the floor. When he got up, he dusted himself down, and then just turned and looked at the other chap in amazement before walking out again without speaking. We quickly followed him.

On Sunday morning we went to the Clifton-upon-Teme kennels, where David Parker showed me his hounds. They included some pure Welsh hounds and I asked him about the difference between pure Welsh and English. Not unexpectedly he said that it was in their voices, but chiefly, with their rough coats, that they were better at drawing thick places. All around the kennels supporters were polishing up the place as Ronnie Wallace was coming to speak at a cub-hunting dinner. I left that afternoon for Builth Wells and met several of my Suffolk friends in the Barley Mow, but there was not the usual good party owing to some half-drunken women screeching out a few songs, so we went to bed at eleven o'clock. I had enjoyed my usual supper of local lamb, and Monday's breakfast of twelve rashers of bacon with eggs and fried bread, but even with the new central heating in the bedrooms the bill was only seven pounds. The prices were high at the sale and in spite of bidding fifteen hundred pounds for a stallion and three hundred and eighty for a filly foal, I bought nothing and I drove back to School House after the sale. As Colin and Alice were away for the night, I said I would take Tizza out to dine and we had a very good fillet steak supper at the Fox and Badger at Bromyard, ending the evening with two Caribbean Coffees. Before going, I had telephoned home to tell Sheila that I had bought nothing as she always worried when I went to Builth Wells as I had been known to buy eight or ten cobs and bring them home loose in the lorry. Sheila had shocking news for me – there had been a murder in the next village and the victim was the wife of the man who had just painted our house.

I woke at four o'clock and could not get the thought of the murder out of my mind, so I came down at six and made a mug of tea for Tizza who was doing the horses, and then made porridge for both of us. An early start was necessary as the **Ludlow Foxhounds** were meeting at nine o'clock at Bromcrofts Farm Park (Tues 18 Oct 1983). Tizza and I left with both horses, Falcon for me and Rose for Tizza, and we got somewhat muddled in Ludlow. After a tour of the town, we eventually came out on the right road, and were pleased to see a Land Rover and trailer which Tizza identified as belonging to the District Commissioner of the Clifton Pony Club. We tried to follow her but a bus came between us and we lost her. Hounds had moved off before we arrived but we easily found them, still drawing. They did not find in this covert and moved on to the next where Tizza and I were asked to go on point at the far end. This was upwind and when they found we did not hear them go away, so we had a bad start but caught them up with both horses taking the hunt jumps in fine style. I was very surprised at how well Rose jumped one in particular which was uphill in a steep place. However, my pleasure was short-lived because, as we caught up with the field, we met this fine Ludlow fox on the way back. When hounds swung back again and she had to jump the same fence downhill she tried to stop at the last minute and demolished the whole thing.

The Honorary Secretary was a delightful-looking old character, with curly grey hair and a leather bag strapped around his waist. I laughed and said to Tizza that this was what Colin would look like in thirty years time. Tizza pointed out her ex-parson who was riding to hounds and went on to say that he had been defrocked for co-habiting with a farmer's daughter. Rose disgraced herself further by kicking a hound very hard and, as I felt very ashamed of what had happened, we left soon after as I was afraid that it would happen again. I knew she could not be trusted amongst hounds at home as a hunt horse, but had hoped that she would not do it in the field. When I had first had her and did not know how bad she was I saw her attack a hound. John Suckling, an amateur whipper-in, was riding her when I asked him to send a single hound back to me out of sugar-beet. Just short of the hound, Rose leapt into the air as if jumping a gate, and pounced like a lion on the hound, pawing at it with her front legs and pulling it underneath her before kicking it away with her back legs. This was definitely an aggressive act against the hound and something I had not seen before or ever imagined. It was a pity as she was such a good hunter in the field.

The Ludlow Master and huntsman, David Palmer (nicknamed "Charmer" Palmer because of his popularity with the ladies), hunted his hounds in a quiet manner but it appeared to me that they rather relied upon him and waited for him at checks, but of course it is impossible to get an accurate picture of a pack from a single day. The country was very "large" and had breathtakingly lovely views of river valleys. It was also very rideable, mostly grass and woods, with gently rolling hills. We again got lost in Ludlow on the way back and eventually arrived at three o'clock. While Tizza did the horses, I did the tack and washed off the boots, spurs, and so on, and then for good measure cut up a large box of kindling for her.

I needed to be home to hunt the Easton on the Thursday so I decided that, as the **Albrighton Woodland Foxhounds** were meeting at Wolverley, near Kidderminster, I could hunt with them on the way home (Wed 19 Oct 1983). Tizza followed the lorry in her car, dropping off her daughter Alice at her school. I was lucky as, after getting lost in Wolverley, I saw a trailer coming towards me and waved it down. The driver agreed to wait while I turned round and I followed him right to the meet which was held on a wide drive leading into the old Rover Works factory. It was surrounded by high chain-link netting and bushes, and could be said to be the boundary between town and countryside. Mr Pauli, the Master, made me very welcome and introduced me to his Joint-Master, Mrs Williams. The hounds looked extremely well and were a nice level pack. Stubbings, the huntsman, hunted hounds very quietly and well and his training under Captain Barclay was obvious.

We drew the thick bushes around the meet and found a very dark fox which hounds rattled around with a good cry, added to by a chorus of howls and barking from a greyhound kennel above the covert. They marked this fox to ground up above us and I saw the huntsman leave his horse and climb up to the earth. I asked permission to go with him and this was readily given. As I got up to where his horse was standing I thought what a lovely painting it would make. The horse standing there alone, in stirrup-high ferns, and

**The Albrighton Woodland:** ***"His trusted, faithful servant"***

**Albrighton Woodland Hunt.** *Hounds during season 1996/7.*
Photograph kindly loaned by Mrs Sue Jordan

Stubbings in his bright red coat was standing above him with hounds. The hounds and the huntsman showed as much sport as they possibly could in this rather cramped area, for there were towns and busy roads seemingly everywhere. It seemed very strange to me to hear the field coffee-housing at covert side in broad Birmingham accents, as that accent is more normally associated with heavy industry than rural pursuits. I left at twelve-thirty as I had to drive back to Suffolk and as I was driving home I thought how plucky these Masters were, to keep hunting alive with only these little pockets of country sandwiched between main roads and towns. They have fields of approximately one hundred on Saturdays when in jumping country, and a mere dozen or so when on the hills during the week. The members of the field were memorable because nearly all of them had every conceivable "extra" – most had skeepskin numnahs under their saddle, and sheepskin covers over them, and either sheepskin or brass browbands, with wire-cutters and sandwich boxes strapped to their saddles. To cap it all most of them had Range Rovers with matching trailers and those who wanted to upstage their compeers had had their tailboards stained and grained.

I felt rather like Mr Sponge as only five weeks later I was on my way back to my hospitable friends, the Plumbes, for the proper jolly. My conscience told me that I ought to be with my own hounds but I also felt that I had to take advantage of this opportunity because I did not know how much longer they would be at Orleton as they would be moving to Scotland as soon as they had sold School House. I left home with Charlie, Demelza and Falcon, and Theresa to look after them, and this was the first time I had ever taken three horses. As there were enough stables for them all, I wanted to be able to mount my host and hostess whenever possible. We arrived at School House at two-fifteen on Sunday 27 November (1983), only to find that Colin and Tizza had obviously not expected three horses as one stable was full of straw bales. After humping them all out, we got all the horses settled in. I telephoned to find out where the North Cotswold were hunting the following day but discovered that they had cancelled this meet owing to a member's death. I then rang around and found that the **South Shropshire Foxhounds** also hunted on Mondays and got directions to the meet at Steadment Farm, Ratlinghope, from the Secretary. Colin had to leave us for Scotland at four-thirty that afternoon so as to be ready for work at Galashiels on the following morning.

I left at eight-thirty and arrived far too soon but the host and hostess immediately invited me into the farmhouse kitchen for eats and drinks (Mon 28 Nov). There was a lovely atmosphere, and the old beamed kitchen was soon full of sportsmen, old and young, male and female, including three youngsters clearly playing truant and obviously enjoying that as much as the hunting. When we left the farmhouse to unbox the horses, a foot follower who had been standing outside recognised me and shouted to the assembly, "Oh, there's old Terry (meaning me). He's around again. He gets around all over the country". It was most embarassing and I never did find out where he had seen me before.

The meet was within the lovely moorland area of Shropshire called the Long Mynd, but as we moved off the wind had increased and was made worse by occasional sleet showers. We drew above the farm and I noticed at once that Michael, the huntsman, had remarkable control of his hounds. From a distance he could send them to draw gorse and coverts and blow them out again with unbelievable ease. We did not find until one-thirty as it had been a very wild night and most foxes would have been underground in the warm. We then found a brace of foxes near a rocky crag called the Devil's Seat, and three couple went away on one, while the rest of the pack went on the other. We had a nice little hunt over lovely country, hounds hunting with a deep and melodious cry and all on an even key, until our fox eventually went to ground. Michael immediately took hounds to join the other three couple but this involved a lot of furiously fast trotting on roads, technically known as "ramping", which always jars my back. I soon decided to go back to the meet as I did not want to overdo Charlie after his long journey the day before, or to upset my back.

As I was slowly returning along the road I saw them drop down into a covert way below me and I had the pleasure of holloaing a Shropshire fox away because he crossed the road in front of me. However, no-one heard my holloa as I was downwind and it was blowing very hard and sleeting but I could not resist following when four and a half couple came past me on the line and I had another little spin over this paradise of a country. There was grass as far as the eye could see and I was told that that would have included seven counties if the visibility had been better. My little pack lost the line after a few fields all of which had had jumpable fences so I had been able to keep up with them, and when "my hounds" went back to their huntsman, I slunk off. I felt very guilty about my private hunt which, although very naughty, had been great fun. When I got back to School House and put Charlie into his stable, I disturbed a gamecock which flew from a beam and landed on old Falcon's anti-cast roller. The picture would have made a wonderful painting entitled "Two Game Veterans".

For Tuesday's sport we decided to go with the **North Herefordshire Foxhounds,** who were at The Green Bank Stables, Marden (29 Nov). Tizza and I left at nine o'clock with Demelza for her and Falcon for me. The fact that I had lent my favourite horse to Tizza was, I must admit, not entirely an act of kindness to my hostess. Demelza tended to cat-jump her fences which I found to be very unseating but knowing that Tizza was a first-class rider I knew she would be able to cope with this small problem. We arrived in plenty of time and were highly amused when unboxing to watch a lady brushing her own hair and her horse with the same brush. We enjoyed the hospitality of hot punch and sausage rolls and I was relieved to think that there was actually no need for the warming drink as it was sunny and still, for a change. I was told that the huntsman, then in his fourth season, had come from the Blackmore and Sparkford Vale.

He first drew an old orchard which was blank, but then moved on to draw a derelict farm where a fox was found in an ivy-covered tree. I saw him peeping out from between the leaves and then he dropped down and I viewed him running along the top of an old garden wall. We had just got going nicely with this fox when it was hit by a car and went to ground soon afterwards in a pipe under the road. We then had another little hunt with an embarassing incident. The Field Master invited me to keep immediately behind him and we soon came to an overgrown gate leading onto a lane. He popped over it with ease and then moved to one side to leave me room. Falcon, however, did not rise to it at all. He halved the gate and shot me right up his neck, then made a hop over the remainder and I was hanging over the side as he turned into the lane. Tizza followed on Demelza who, always a suspicious sort of horse, made such a high leap that Tizza was jumped off. And all this happened in front of the whole field. We did not find another fox so at three o'clock we decided to go back to our box. They had fields of approximately fifteen on Tuesdays and thirty-five or so on Saturdays. The field on this day were not the usual hunting types and seemed more like riding school pupils who wore every conceivable type of coat, one even hunting in a Husky. To round off the day I took Tizza to dinner at The Waggon Wheel at Grimley.

Next day I arrived at the old station at Shrawardine, where I had been advised to unbox for the **North Shropshire Foxhounds** meet, and I was about to drop the ramp when Mr Avril, our host, invited me up to his house (Wed 30 Nov 1983). We were taken into the dining-room for drinks and eats where I was surprised to see Bridget Paul, whose parents were Masters of the Essex and Suffolk Foxhounds. She explained that she was staying with our hosts. I learned that Clive of India was to have built himself a castle there and the present house was to have been the servants' quarters but he changed his mind and returned to India. The rest of the stones which had been assembled for the castle were used to build the present range of impressive farm buildings. The forecast for the day had been terrible so I had taken my oldest coat, twice-worn breeches and my worst gloves. I felt quite ashamed of how I looked, especially in this elegant dining-room, and I hoped that Bridget Paul would not give a too-detailed description of meeting me to her parents.

I unboxed near the remains of the old railway station which was the official meet. We drew the first covert blank and set off across country over hunt jumps to the next draw. Charlie refused at the first set of rails as he was not yet warmed up, but I managed to get him over. There were hunt jumps in every direction and it was the policy of the Master to jump them in moving from covert to covert when drawing rather than the more usual practice of opening gates until hounds are running. This was unfortunate for me as Charlie was in one of his nappy moods and took great exception to jumping when hounds were not running. He stopped quite often, and once shot me out of the saddle. I landed on top of a gatepost where I hung, with the post in my midriff, head hanging down one side and legs the other, staring down at the ground before sliding gracefully down to my feet. We must have jumped over forty hunt jumps in all during the day, but only three of them while hounds were running. The policy of using them as often as possible seemed to suit the field, almost all of whom were only there for the ride. I was discussing this practice of jumping between draws with a member who replied in all seriousness that surely nobody went hunting just to watch hounds working, did they? That would be terribly boring! This hunt could easily have dispensed with all the expense of keeping hounds and just employed a bold Field Master to lead them around the country and they would have been just as happy. The field, although not interested in hounds, were turned out beautifully and were all riding well-bred hunters. There had only been one short hunt so I could not form an opinion of hounds.

After Charlie's behaviour it was a pleasure to take Falcon to the **Worcestershire Foxhounds** the next day (Thurs 1 Dec 1983). They were meeting in Shropshire by invitation of the Teme Valley and, as I rode up to the meet at Felindre, near Knighton, I was greeted by Ian Coghill whom I knew through the Masters of Harriers and Beagles as we were both Committee members. Hounds soon found and were to give me one of the best day's hunting of my life. The country was of firm moorland with big rolling hills which were not too steep, and could be ridden for many miles in any direction. The riding was particularly enjoyable as the hills were so firm underfoot, and the views spectacular. There were so many lovely colour contrasts with the brackens being all of different colours.

The first hunt was approximately ten minutes to ground. Finding again, they ran unaided for one and a quarter hours. The viewing was so good that I could kick on to the top of each successive hill and often see the fox going up the face of the next hill, twisting to left and right on different sheep's paths. I would watch the hounds follow his line and then gallop fast down and up the next hill and repeat the process. Hounds were a delight to watch as, each time they checked, they immediately cast themselves and hit it off again. At one point I saw the fox run into a small flock of sheep and follow them for a while, and I sat on the hilltop to see how these hounds would deal with this problem. They hunted up to the sheep foil and checked then, without hesitation, cast themselves in the classic manner of ever-increasing circles until they hit off the line beyond the sheep foil. This was done as well as if they had been aided by the best huntsman in the world. This one check gave me more pleasure than the whole of the previous day's gratuitous jumping. After one and a quarter hours they sadly lost the line which was a great shame as they richly deserved to catch their fox. This had been one of the most enjoyable fox-hunts I had ever participated in, largely because the country had enabled me to see the hounds working in this wonderful way. The combined field of the Teme Valley and the Worcestershire numbered about forty. One of the Teme Valley members told me that they often only had about four people out with them – what a terrible waste of a great country. My legs were so stiff from the previous day's jumping efforts that, when I needed to tighten my girths, I had to lift my leg in front of the saddle with my hand as my muscles were too stiff to do it on their own.

The next day I went with the **Ledbury Foxhounds** (Fri 2 Dec 1983). An added interest of this pack was that in the early part of this century they had been hunted by "Teasing Dick" Forster, second husband of the Duchess of Hamilton whose first husband had established the Easton Harriers. During that time he had also been Master of the Hamilton (as the Easton were then known) to keep them for his step-daughter, Lady Mary Hamilton. I found my way to the meet at the Drum and Monkey, Newbridge Green, quite easily and introduced myself to Mr Daley, the Master and huntsman. As there was no-one else I recognised, I got into conversation with the lady nearest to me. It turned out that she was godmother to the Blois children, the family farming a large estate on the boundary of the Easton and Waveney Harriers' countries. There were about sixty-five mounted, mostly turned out on very good horses, and hounds accounted for a leash of foxes in fine style.

They found as soon as we left the meet and the first fence was a long, evenly-trimmed hedge. It seemed that all sixty-five horses went at it abreast and I have never seen anything like it before or since. This was to be one of Charlie's "going days" and he flew over it effortlessly, as he did the other fences all day. Hounds lost the line of this fox after about ten fields, all of which had jumpable fences and it had been an exciting start, so different from the usual long draw. Mr Daley then drew some kale, and chopped one fox and a brace went away. Hounds settled beautifully onto the line of one of them, and we had an excellent hunt of one hour and twenty minutes. I was close behind the huntsman for nearly all of this run, including when he jumped into a meadow from which it was impossible to get out and we had to jump out again at the same place as we went in, which lost valuable time. Some hard riding was needed to catch up with hounds again. My blood was up and I was thoroughly enjoying this exhilerating ride across country, but when Mr Daley, without hesitation, took a formidable five-barred gate onto an extremely narrow road at such an angle as to land on the road and continue up it, I chickened out. Three or four of the field followed him, the rest us going through another gate which had been opened by a car-follower. I caught up again just before they killed in some stumps, and the Master asked me if I would like a trophy.

The kennel huntsman jumped off but it was already too late for the brush as hounds had already spoiled it. He grabbed the back legs of the fox and was struggling to get the carcase away from hounds, pulling with all his might, when suddenly they all let go at the

**The Ledbury:** ***"I hope the tip is worth a ducking!"***

same time, and the poor man fell backwards into a pond and was completely soaked. This sad state of affairs he completely ignored and climbed out of the pond clutching the dripping carcase in one hand and wiping weeds from his face with the other. I felt so sorry for him and guilty at the same time because if it had not been for me it would not have happened. I gave him a large tip which I hoped would help to ease the discomfort, and while we were in conversation he told me that he had applied for the huntsman's post with the Waveney Harriers.

The third fox ran a large circle into a drain from which it was bolted and ran another circle and again went into a drain quite close to where the boxes were parked. Charlie seemed a little stiff from a fall which had happened when a child on a twelve-two pony had cut in front of him just as he was about to take off, causing both horse and me to land in a crumpled heap in the next field, surrounded by smashed rails. As it was three o'clock and we were near the lorry, I decided that this was the best moment to go home. It had been a thrilling day, foxhunting at its best: good hounds, hunting on a moderate scent, which meant that the day was packed with good venerie, and with rideable country, which meant that I was able to be in touch with hounds for most of the day. It was all the more pleasant for being unexpected – the morning had been sunny after a white frost, which in my experience usually meant that scent would be very poor. As Mr Jorrocks said, "There's nowt so queer as scent, 'ceptin a woman."

On the Saturday I had hoped that Colin and Tizza would have been able to come with me to the **Wheatland Foxhounds** but sadly neither was free so I asked Theresa if she would like to come (Sat 3 Dec 1983). As usual she jumped at the chance to hunt. When we got near the meet at the Fox and Hounds in Stottesdon, a farmer's wife waved us into a farmyard to park. I had met Captain Foster, the Senior Master, before at Leicester Horse Sales, and had spoken to him on the telephone. He took me across to meet his son, who was hunting hounds. Just as he was about to introduce me, his son said, "It's all right Father, I can recognise Mr Harvey from a photograph in the Horse and Hound." As I sat at the meet, I was feeling rather nauseous and my stomach was gurgling and rumbling. I desperately needed a port-and-brandy to settle it but had forgotten my wallet and had no money to buy one, and did not know anyone well enough to cadge such an expensive drink. The field numbered about sixty, all beautifully turned-out on well-bred horses. The country was mostly wheat with very little pasture, and I believe that someone told me this was how the hunt got its name.

We found a fox in the first covert but he soon went to ground in a drain. The terriermen bolted him and he provided a good hunt, with several checks. This was just as well as I was trying to take my own line and making a very poor job of it. Demelza did another classic cat-jump over some rails which landed Theresa up her neck. The power of that mare's quarters was truly amazing. When she heaved herself over an obstacle in that manner, it was like sitting on an explosion. I would have been enjoying this tremendously as Mr Foster was hunting his father's hounds beautifully, except for the nausea which was getting worse and at one-thirty I went back to my box. The rest of the day was pretty miserable and even two large port-and-brandies at School House only helped a little.

I did not get up the next morning until nine-thirty. I was pleased to be feeling all right again but declined breakfast and decided not to go to church with my hosts. I knew that they had planned to move a large amount of logs from the paddock after lunch and, as I could not visualise this happening after one of Tizza's lovely meals, I found a wheelbarrow and stacked the logs in a very neat pile in the porch. This was a good two-hour job and I had just finished when they returned from church. Colin took me off to the Baiting House for pre-lunch drinks. We came back to a huge roast-chicken lunch which ended at four o'clock when poor Colin had to set off back to Scotland, while I fell asleep in a chair, waking up in time to chop a bunch of kindling for my hostess.

It was such a help on these hunting holidays if I could find packs which hunted on Mondays or Fridays as these were the most difficult days to fill for a full week's programme. On this particular Monday I was able to go with the **North Cotswold Foxhounds** who were meeting at Lynes Barn, Winchcombe, in Gloucestershire (Mon 5 Dec 1983). I arrived with Charlie only just in time to move off with them as I had taken a wrong turn close to the meet and had to ask at a farmhouse for directions. The Master and huntsman, Roy Tatlow, rode up and welcomed me, inviting me to ride up with him. We drew a big forestry plantation and had a fair woodland hunt, then went to draw some coverts in "combes" – steep ravines sliced out of the wolds. I did not keep with the Master as Charlie was not feeling as lively as usual and the close hunting days were obviously catching up on him. Coupled with this, the Master was so bold a rider that I probably would not have been able to keep with him in any case. Towards the end of the day, we jumped into the end of a long covert and when we came to the far end there was an enormous gate and I was thinking to myself with relief that at least they would have to open this one, but the lady Field Master, "Pinkie", just popped over it as if it was nothing. The next one to jump it luckily knocked it down which was a relief to me.

The members were obviously great "goers", and the Master's horse was one of the best I have ever seen. He would often turn and in a couple of strides clear a sizeable gate. I tried hard to buy it from him but he would not hear of parting with it. As we came through the last covert I was well left behind as Charlie was getting tired, and I saw in the dim light two enormous gates, over five feet high, across a steep downhill ride. The Master and the remaining two horses still out had cleared them both and as I opened and led through them, I could see the hoof-marks where they had landed on the downhill side. They were eight to ten yards away from the gate. The jumps must have felt like flying. I was invited to visit the kennels but as it was dark and getting quite foggy I declined in spite of being urged by a foot-follower who said it was well worth a visit as there were brass pipes polished so you could see your face in them.

**North Cotswold Hunt.** *Brian Fanshawe, Master and huntsman, at Lower Coscombe with his father Major Fanshawe and Mrs Charles Dickins in the foreground.*

Photograph kindly loaned by Christopher Houghton

I did not have quite so far to go the following day for the meet of the **Teme Valley Foxhounds** at Tin Rin Gate, near Felindre, but nevertheless arrived slightly late as I had not allowed enough time (Tues 6 Dec 1983). I was worried that this would inconvenience the Teme Valley Master, Mr Boundy, as the previous Thursday, when I had been hunting with the Worcestershire (in the Teme Valley country), he had kindly offered to meet me at Tin Rin Gate and show me the way across country to the actual meet. When I arrived he was still there, but hopping mad because his horse had not been delivered. The meet was across the rolling, fern-covered hills at a remote farm and, while we waited for his horse, he was telling me why he was so annoyed – the whisky always flowed particularly freely at this farm and he did not want to miss it. When his horse did arrive, he set off across the hills for a mile or two at a very fast canter. I followed him, Falcon slipping and sliding on the frosty ground. We arrived at the farm which stood in a hollow in the hills, and forded a stream which ran between the house and buildings. The farm was owned by a very old man who resembled Old Father Time with his long white beard. The Master told me that the two times that hounds met there each season were the only times that he saw anyone from the outside world as he never left the farm. There was a young man there who thrust a tumbler into my hand, then filled it three-quarters full of neat whisky. He was frowning all the time and did not speak to either the Master or me. There was another visitor out, an American, who said to me, "Gee, I'm kinda surprised that I'm the only one with a top hat." – obviously expecting every pack in England to resemble the smartest of Leicestershire turnouts.

We moved off and quickly went to a holloa. Hounds got settled onto the line and were running well across these lovely hills. I was riding with Mr Boundy, galloping knee-deep through the bracken, and I asked him if the horses ever stumbled over rocks or into holes hidden under the thick bracken. He said that surprisingly, they never seemed to, and in all the years he had hunted with these hounds he had never had a fall. This statement must have tempted fate, because a few minutes later he rode into a boggy patch and his horse went down, throwing him over its head. When he picked himself up he was bleeding profusely from his nose as his glasses had scraped a strip of skin from the top of his nose down to the bottom and it hung down from the end of the nose to his lips – a terrible sight to see. In spite of the pouring blood, he mounted and attempted to ride on, shrugging off the concerns of the field. It was with the greatest difficulty that he was persuaded to go home. He was escorted back to his car by a man with whom I had ridden the previous Thursday. I had not discovered his name but he was unforgettable as he had a black bushy beard. After these two had gone, the remainder of the field, six in all, seemed lost without the Master and just followed me so I became an unofficial Field Master.

Hounds had a lot of Welsh blood in them, and ran with rather a light cry, often no cry at all, especially when they were on sheep foil. The hunting was just as enjoyable as the previous Thursday, and I went home thinking that the Teme Valley country must be one of the finest hill countries I had ever seen. The scenery was breathtakingly beautiful, with relatively few bogs for this type of country, and to be amongst genuine hunting people who really wanted to watch hounds working made the day perfect.

Although the **Berkeley Foxhounds** were a long way off I decided to go with them even though I needed an early start (Wed 7 Dec 1983). I left School House at seven forty-five with Falcon, and drove down the M5 motorway in thick freezing fog which became worse the nearer I got to the meet at Arlingham, but nevertheless I still arrived one hour too soon. A girl drove up in a car with a message from Mr Shaw, the Hunt Secretary, that the meet had been put back an hour until twelve o'clock owing to the frost and fog, and I therefore had a two-hour wait. I unboxed and hacked up the two and a half miles to the meet which was outside the Crown Inn. There were about forty mounted which I thought an excellent number considering the conditions, and were, as I had expected, all well turned-out. Mr Shaw made himself known to me, and introduced me to several people and later on to Major Berkeley who had been Master of these hounds since 1960, and was late arriving owing to attending the funeral of an ex-huntsman's widow. We rode together for a while and I was pleased to be able to tell him that my daughter Bridget was doing her thesis on his ancestors, the Berkeley family, in the 14th century.

Hounds drew behind the village and found a fox which ran the gardens, hounds running in full cry between flower-beds, but no-one seemed to mind at all. This was just as well for, although the fox went out into the countryside several times, it would always double back into the village. It was explained to me that, because Arlingham lies within a great horse-shoe shaped loop of the River Severn, foxes born here do not know a very large area so they generally seem to stay around the village. The hound work was superb all day, with hounds quite delightful to watch, as they hunted very tightly as a pack and even when casting themselves they could be covered by a blanket. The cry was very melodious but not deep, and one lasting memory is of them pouring over a wall in full cry, ten or twelve abreast, into a garden and out the other side over another wall. Maiden, the huntsman, was very quiet and always allowed them to cast themselves. The frequent returning to the village and passing the pub proved too much of a temptation for five farmers who stopped and without much difficulty persuaded me to join them for half-time drinks in the pub. We left all six horses being held by one man who appeared out of the pub as soon as the horses stopped. Each time we bought a round one was taken out to him. While we were in there, the whole hunt passed once again and I went out quickly, afraid that the horses would play up and not willing to lose Falcon in the fog, but found the six horses quite content to stand quietly. On rejoining the field, I met a lady who knew Peter Bernard, an ex-Master of the Easton very well, and we had a few laughs recalling his exploits.

It was such a special occasion for me to be out with these famous hounds and to see the Master and hunt staff in their yellow coats with green collars, with a running fox on the collar. This unusual livery had its origins in the household livery of their earlier owners, the Earls of Berkeley. The hounds were a credit to whoever was in charge of the breeding and they all looked like peas in a pod. We finished in the dark, and had been lucky to have hunted. Indeed, we could not have hunted anywhere else but here because not only were they pretty sure that the foxes would always return to the village, thus minimising the risk of losing hounds in the fog, but also there was little traffic as the area was like a peninsular and the roads led nowhere. There was a sad note to the day that I was told that Major Berkeley was giving up the Mastership and this would mean that next season would be the first time that a Berkeley had not been Master since the Norman Conquest.

Next day it was Falcon's turn and we left at nine-thirty for the meet of the **Croome and West Warwickshire Foxhounds** at High House Farm, Abbots Morton (Worcs), arriving for once at exactly the right time (Thurs 8 Dec 1983). The Master and members were very friendly, and the hospitality, dispensed in the farmyard, was very good. There was another green coat at the meet worn, I learned, by a professional from the High Peak Harriers who may have been on holiday, but perhaps more likely to have been there on trial.

We found the first fox in an old farm yard, and I viewed him away over the village street and through some gardens. We had a short hunt but soon lost the line. They found again in some kale, and went away over lovely galloping and jumping country with Falcon clearing some sheep hurdles on top of a bank which stopped most of the rest of the field. My blood was up and I took a short cut across a wheat field where the drill had been blocked and a few rows unplanted. As ill-luck would have it, just as I was doing this the hounds checked which enabled the Field Master to look back and see me. When I came up he quite rightly gave me a terrible telling-off. I swept off my hat and apologised, explaining that I had ridden down an unplanted corridor. Luckily, this was immediately endorsed by another member of the field and my apology was accepted. I got away from the field as often as I could as they were not interested in the hounds and just sat coffee-housing at checks. The hounds were quite sharp but did not cast themselves as well as the Berkeley, but then, I thought, the Berkeley were a very difficult pack to follow. One lady asked me what pack I was from and went on to tell me that, when she had been a Master, she had employed one of my first hunt servants and was not very impressed with him. I commiserated with her and said that he had been the worst I had ever had. Another lady overheard this conversation and told me that she had relations in Orford. I went home, having had a most enjoyable day, with old Falcon on top form, loving the chance to gallop and jump – such a thrilling change for a plough-country horse.

I was pleased to find that the **Radnor and West Herefordshire Foxhounds** hunted on Fridays and were to meet at The White Swan in Eardisland (Fri 9 Dec 1983). Eardisland was a pretty little village, the houses being mostly built of brick and timber, the beams showing on the outside. I was pleased that Tizza was able to come, even though the weather was terrible, and I had Falcon again leaving Demelza for her. I met the Master, Peter Hunkin, whom I remembered from the previous season when he was Master of the Tetcott. There were about twenty-five mounted which was considered to be a large field. There were two girls at the meet, one of whom was the whipper-in. I did not know them but they obviously knew me and kept laughing about Suffolk hunting men, and how many jumps they demolished in a day's hunting, and saying that they supposed that I would break everything down today.

We found in the first covert and had a quick burst of four miles or so over a mixed country of grass and wheat. I was horrified to see how carelessly the field went round the wheat, leaving it looking a real mess. During this run, Falcon and Demelza went brilliantly, jumping the solid hunt jumps in fine style. When this fox went to ground in a drain, one of the girls asked, "Well, how many rails have you smashed?"

When I replied none, she asked if I had jumped any of the jumps. When I said that I had jumped them all she said, laughing, "Well, there was plenty of room for this marked improvement."

She then told me that she had been out with the North Herefordshire the day I had halved the gate.

My back was hurting and the pains were shooting down into my thighs, and seemed worse after this sharp run. While they were drawing for the next fox it started to blow even harder and with sleet hitting us at near gale force we decided we had had enough. At one-thirty we hacked back to the box, reaching it extremely cold and wet at two-fifteen. On the way home, I filled the lorry with diesel at a garage on the A44 at Kington. The girl cashier asked what sort of a day I had had and I offended her by asking if she hunted as she had been out for the first hour with the Radnor that day. She was not very pleased that I had not recognised her, especially as I had talked to her in the field. I told her how different girls look when they do not have their riding caps on and explained that the same thing has happened to me at Hunt Balls, when I have danced with girls I have known for years in the hunting field but not recognised them without their hats.

Colin arrived back from Scotland and we decided to go out to dinner. The gales were by now so severe that telephone lines were down so we set off without booking. Each of the first few places we called at were fully booked but we eventually got in at the Shrowley Arms, where there were about one hundred other people. It was a "carvery" where customers could serve themselves and most of them piled their plate up like a pyramid. Many of them were women on their own and these were the worst offenders. It was so disgusting to see that it quite spoiled our dinner.

Next day the Plumbe family came *en famille* to the meet of the **North Ledbury Foxhounds**, at Fromes Hill on the assumption that it would not be a very energetic day (Sat 10 Dec 1983). Depending on this assumption, Tizza rode her well-proven but unfit "Huff" (Muhuffas), and eight-year-old Alice came on her Shetland pony Smartie, Colin on Demelza and myself on Falcon. We left School House at ten o'clock and arrived comfortably, discovering to our great disappointment that the Master, Lady Waechter, was not hunting hounds. Lady Waechter had had these hounds since 1948 and I would particularly have liked to have seen her in the field. There was a slight connection with the Easton as the pack had been started by a loan of hounds and country from Mr Carnaby "Teasing Dick" Forster (Master of the Hamilton 1902-05) when Master of the Ledbury in 1905.

Lady Waechter came out of the pub and was very pleased to see us, saying how sorry she was not to have been able to hunt hounds for us. Her kennel huntsman had the hounds held up quite tightly and his brother whipped-in to him in a black coat so old that it had turned that delightful shade of green only seen in old black garments. The hunt staff were not what one normally expects of hunt servants, and sat with hounds looking wildly at us strangers with staring eyes. The rest of the field consisted of one man in a red coat, and one in black coat, and another Shetland pony on a leading-rein. Alice looked very colourful on Smartie as she had pulled her striped leg-warmers over her jodhpurs as it was so bitterly cold. The Master said that she had become worried about my visit as she had been unable to find any reference to me or my hounds in "the Bible" (i.e. Baily's Hunting Directory). She had telephoned the secretary of the MFHA who advised her to look under "Harriers". Her kennel huntsman enquired if he should move off. "Certainly not, " was the sharp reply. "Not until our visitors have finished their drinks."

The hounds were a slightly mixed bunch, with a couple of Dumfriesshire and some from the College Valley. These two distinctly different types of hounds added to the variety which included some harriers from the Pendle Forest and Craven. The Master obviously had a great love of her hounds, and told me with great pride of an occasion when the North Ledbury and the Clifton-upon-Teme had become mixed one hunting day. They had run to each other's cry and, when it came to separate them, she said, "Come on, my boys and girls," and took hers away from the Clifton hounds with no trouble at all. She followed by car during the day.

We moved off to draw the first cover and her two men disappeared into the wood without a sound. We remained outside and could hear absolutely nothing, not a cheer from the huntsman, or a touch of the horn, or a single whimper from the hounds. It was weird and felt most strange as one usually sits listening to the cheers of the huntsman urging his hounds to draw. One foot-follower offered his opinion that perhaps he was trying to creep up and surprise a fox.

Another foot-follower remarked, "I don't know why she was worred about you finishing your drinks. You would have had enough time for a four-course dinner."

Eventually they appeared out of the covert, having been unable to find a fox, and cantered off across country, the kennel huntsman in front and his brother just behind him, leaving most of the pack in the covert and those with them trailing along behind the two horses. Of course, a whipper-in is useless and no help at all when stuck to the huntsman's tail, and when the brother in the red coat suggested that the one in black went back to fetch the hounds a furious row broke out. They stopped in the middle of a meadow, yelling at each other, and brandishing their whips. The regular followers and the hounds took no notice at all of this, which suggested to us that it happened quite often.

Lady Waechter's Joint-Master appeared, an hour after we had moved off, and was easily recognised by his beard, but appeared to take little part in the running of the day. The other man in a red coat, who had apparently been a Master of the North Herefordshire, seemed even less knowledgable, and rode with a child's whip stuck into the top of his boot, and, despite his red coat, a checked stock with plain black boots (instead of mahogany-topped boots and a white stock) with no spurs or garter straps. I stopped to speak to Lady Waechter in her car, and she said that she hoped I would not mind if her kennel huntsman did not go on very well as he was riding a young Irish horse that she usually rode herself. Once out of earshot a foot-follower remarked that it would have made no difference what they were riding as they never jumped anything anyway. We went from covert to covert in the same style with the two brothers close together and the hounds coming along in their own good time, drawing each one blank.

**North Ledbury:** ***"Go back and get the hounds! Back, I say, back!"***

I had another conversation with Lady Waechter who said that the hunt was desperately short of money and she hoped that I did not mind her staff too much, and that she usually had the one in the black coat with her, his sole job being to get off and open gates as she never left the ground, and did not pretend to, but added proudly that she was always with her hounds. She also asked if her Joint-Master was making himself agreeable. I evaded the question as he had hardly spoken at all to any of us.

Towards the end of the day hounds found and the scene was unforgettable – hounds were rattling around a covert with a good cry, the Dumfriesshire couple's voices easily distinguishable. When the fox broke covert and went away across the middle of a large meadow the two hunt staff were very excited and set off after the fox, ahead of hounds, yelling at each other frantically, the one in black close on his brother's heels, cracking his whip for all he was worth.

"What are you doing?" his brother yelled.

"I'm pushing on hounds – which is what I'm supposed to do," came the answer (all hounds were still in the covert).

The one in the red coat yelled, "Go back and get the hounds." But his brother took no notice and kept up close behind him. So to encourage him to go back, the one in red started swinging his whip round and round his head in an attempt to beat his brother away from him. As though this cabaret was not enough to make anyone fall off their horse with laughing, Colin added more excitement to it. When he came out of the covert he dismounted to shut the gate, and when trying to get on again the saddle slipped round. This set Demelza off bucking and she broke away from him, and bucked stiff-legged all around the meadow like a bronco at a rodeo. Eventually Demelza was caught and I held her head firmly while Colin tried to clamber aboard, not an easy thing to do when you are weak-kneed with hapless laughter. The brothers came to a temporary truce and all was quiet. Hounds started to come out of covert and hunt very slowly across the first meadow where the fiasco had occurred but ran on very well once clear of the foil created by the two hunt staff galloping on the line. Colin and I took off after the brothers but always had to return to the road as without their Master the brothers could not remember the way across country. Each time we came back to the road on our panting steeds, we would come across Tizza and Alice wandering along in just the right place, looking very cool and decidedly superior, especially Alice who thought it great fun that her father was continually catching up with her.

So ended an unforgettable day, only marred by the fact that her ladyship was not hunting hounds as she had done for thirty-seven seasons. On the way home, I filled up the lorry at Bromyard. The attendant asked with whom I had been out and when he heard that it was the North Ledbury he said, rather sarcastically, that he supposed we had had a grand day. He was quite surprised when I told him we had had quite a good run. It seemed such a shame to me that this hunt is not taken seriously as Lady Waechter has dedicated her life (and I could guess an awful lot of money) to keeping it going and there is in my opinion a definite place in the hunting world for a hunt where it is known that there is never any jumping. There are many older people who could enjoy several more seasons with such a hunt and a lot more people than is generally known give up hunting because they have lost their nerve but would nevertheless thoroughly enjoy a season with the North Ledbury. If the pack had had these extra subscriptions, things would have been very different I am sure, because the Master definitely had the necessary knowledge and could have done with decent financial backing.

We had a relaxed Sunday. After coffee for breakfast, I chopped Tizza another box of kindling, then we all went to Stanford Bridge for a drinks party with some friends of the Plumbes. After bringing Tizza and Alice home, Colin and I went back again to Stanford Bridge to a pub, as we felt like a few beers before lunch. In the pub was an old man who Colin knew from hunting with the Clifton-on-Teme and Colin introduced me to him, telling me that whenever he was lost he would always look for the old man's car, as he was sure he would always be with hounds. Colin drifted off with other friends, leaving me to talk with the old character who presently asked if I knew what had happened to the man from Orleton (i.e. Colin). "He used to hunt with his wife, but I have missed him this season." He obviously had not recognised Colin out of his hunting gear.

We came back to a lovely roast lamb lunch but when we got up from the table it was snowing heavily. It continued to snow all afternoon and lay thick on the ground in the morning. I had planned to hunt with the Cotswold so I told Theresa to plait up and be ready in case there was less snow in that area, but when I telephoned Tim Unwin, the Master, he told me he had cancelled. Tizza had taken Alice to a dancing examination and when they returned I took them to lunch at The Hundred House and returned to sort out things for my return trip. Smartie the Shetland was grazing freely on the lawn, pushing the deep snow away with his nose. Alice asked if he could pull a sleigh, so I rigged up a harness with string and some blankets and the pony pulled her along. I don't know who had the most fun from this exercise, Alice or Tizza.

I went home, as planned, the following day, having been away just over two weeks and having hunted with twelve packs (not including the three I had been with on the visit in October). There had been a water problem with the lorry but we managed to get home safely, and received reports of good sport with the Easton while I had been away, so I did not feel too guilty. One person who definitely regretted my return to duty, was Jim Wickham, my kennel huntsman, who had been hunting hounds in my absence.

**North Dartmoor Beagles.** *Tony Harvey talking to Tim Whitley, Master and Huntsman at the Tor Valley Inn, Sticklepath (Wed 9 Nov 1988).*

# MAP 11

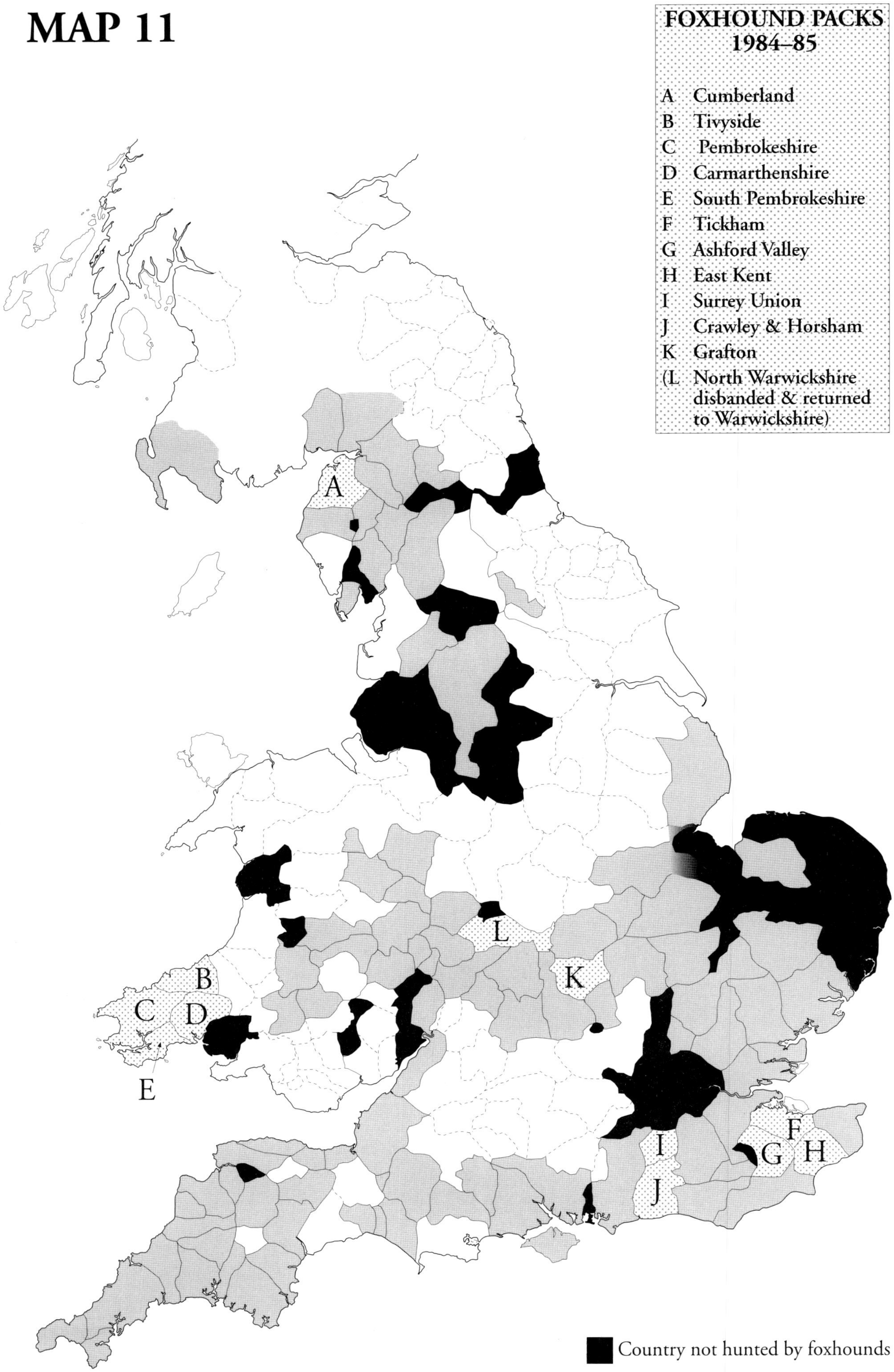
FOXHOUND PACKS
1984–85
A Cumberland
B Tivyside
C Pembrokeshire
D Carmarthenshire
E South Pembrokeshire
F Tickham
G Ashford Valley
H East Kent
I Surrey Union
J Crawley & Horsham
K Grafton
(L North Warwickshire disbanded & returned to Warwickshire)
A
B
C
D
E
F
G
H
I
J
K
L
Country not hunted by foxhounds

# Chapter 14

## More Day Trips and Wales Again

Having taken two weeks off in November I did not feel I could have another major jolly at the end of the season (1983-84), but I managed several more daytrips. I concentrated on the area south of London as, despite having organised two official hunting holidays in Kent, there were still packs in the area with which I had not hunted. The first of these was with the **East Kent Foxhounds**. Sue Gooderham had said she would like to come visiting with me and arrived at six-thirty with her horse, Robin, that I had had so many fabulous days on when she had kindly lent him to me. We moved Robin onto my lorry with my horse Charlie, and were away by six-forty-five, arriving just right at ten forty-five at the meet at Orlestone Woods (Wed 14 Mar 1984). There was a very small field out but Mr Alder, the Master, made us most welcome as did all the members. The huntsman had only been professional for two years and had been a farmer before that. He was very good at his job and his hounds clearly adored him. The professional whipper-in had broken his collar-bone, so he was not out, and his place had been taken by two lady amateurs who did a first class job. Hounds looked well and were hunted well, rallying to each other's cry in an exceptionally good way. We were lucky to find a pilot who had been a member for fifty-one years, and amateur whip for twenty-five years. He had us right almost all of the time and during two very good woodland hunts he was always in the right spot to see the fox cross the rides. It is difficult to describe a woodland day, but this was one when hounds were continually running with a grand cry. They eventually put a fox to ground about a mile from the meet and, as Sue said she did not want to tire old Robin out too much, we decided to return to the box although it was only two-forty-five, arriving home at seven o'clock.

Three days later I again travelled south through the Dartford Tunnel to hunt with the **Tickham Foxhounds** from the meet at the Harrow Inn, Warren Street (Sat 17 Mar 1984). With the Easton season over I could get away on a Saturday and I left home at six forty-five with Falcon, calling to pick up Ian McKay, one of the Easton members, from Kettleburgh. We only just arrived in time. Others were unboxing in a large park so we followed suit and then hacked up to the meet. The Master, Mr Hills, came and introduced himself to me, saying that he knew Bill James, a farmer and Committee member of the Easton (who had accompanied me on one of my holidays in Wales), because he bought pedigree Suffolk sheep from him.

The first two foxes went away in a direction where hounds were not welcome and they were stopped but the third fox obliged and gave us a lovely hunt. Unfortunately we were rather left out of the best of this as a young girl who was unable to hold her horse cut in front of an older lady at the first gate. She knocked the older lady off, breaking the gate and hurting the lady, which caused a considerable delay. Although stretched out on the ground looking rather bad, she proved to be only winded and she was soon on her feet again. This was most unfortunate as it was the only good hunt of the day. The rest of the day was spent scurrying from covert to covert, constantly changing foxes like a relay-race. I have never seen so many foxes in one place. The professional huntsman, who had come from the West Norfolk, was hunting them quietly and as well as he could in view of the quantity of foxes. We left thinking that we were unlucky in our chosen meet but with an overall picture of a fairly good country. Having left quite early and made good time, we were nearly home when Ian suggested that we stop for a drink. He went on to explain that if he got home from Kent earlier than when he hunted with the Easton it might take a bit of explaining to his wife who would probably take this as a precedent.

Alistair Jackson was due to retire from his position as Master and huntsman of the **Grafton Foxhounds** at the end of this

**Grafton.** *Meet at Wakefield Lodge, January 1984. Joint Master and Huntsman Alastair Jackson.*

Photograph supplied by Lt Col E G Walsh

season so I was determined to have a day with them before he went, and set off the following Tuesday for his last but one meet (Tues 20 Mar 1984). The meet was simply a clearing in Salcey Forest, near Newport Pagnell. Colonel and Mrs Hawkins made me very welcome and I was invited to ride up with Alistair hunting hounds. This being an end-of-season woodland sort of day, it was unfashionable and only a few people were out. This suited me very well and, from my privileged position beside the huntsman, I was able to appreciate these famous hounds having to work in the difficult conditions of dense ancient woodland, which made a refreshing change from forestry plantations. Alistair Jackson lived up to my expectations of him and hounds seemed steady to riot. We now and again had a foray out into the open, but the fox always returned to the woods. The cry was beautiful and I thoroughly enjoyed a good woodland day. The kennel huntsman told me that he had come straight from beagles to the Grafton, which is an unusually large step up the ladder as most have to work their way through several packs of foxhounds before reaching the heights of such as the Grafton. Leaving hounds at about four o'clock, I arrived home at seven forty-five, having to leave again immediately to go to an Easton Harriers Committee meeting.

**Crawley and Horsham.** *Meet at Wiston House, March 1983. Huntsman Dick Chapman, and Matthew Puffer, first whipper-in. Also Michael Cain (far right), an ardent foot follower, and Cicely Friar (to right of Huntsman on foot), who has hunted with the pack for over sixty years (fifty at the time of the photograph).*
Photograph kindly loaned by Mr Michael Cain

Having failed to hunt with the **Crawley and Horsham** as I had planned the previous season when snowed off, I made another attempt the following Saturday (24 Mar 1984). I left home at six o'clock and picked up Paul Yeldham, another Easton member, from Mickfield, on the way. We arrived at the meet at Wiston House, near Washington (Sussex) only just in time but were not allowed to unbox there and were sent round to a picnic area. There was a large crowd on foot and about thirty-five mounted. The Masters introduced themselves and then us to the huntsman, who told us that he was going to the Meynell Foxhounds the following season. We drew for ages before finding, then missed most of the first hunt as the Field Master was quite hopeless, continually stopping for conferences with other members of the field on which way to go. There were thirty couples of hounds out and the huntsman always seemed to draw away from us, so that when he did find he was in the next covert before the Field Master knew anything had happened. There was not a single real hunting person amongst the thirty-five mounted field, and the Masters seemed to be rather short of experience. It was a little difficult to judge the performance of hounds and huntsman because we were rarely within sight of them, and were usually out of hearing as well. Altogether, it had been a very disappointing day and we went home feeling rather flat.

I was delighted to be able to find a pack still going four days later and made arrangements to visit the **Surrey Union Foxhounds** at Effingham Hill Farm, Ranmore, for my last day in the 1983-84 season (Wed 28 Mar 1984). Compared with the Easton country, the meet appeared to be very much in the suburbs of London. The country was made up of little spinneys and commons, but there were houses tucked into every possible

**The Surrey Union.** *Meet at Effingham Hill Farm, 1984. Huntsman George Holder (right), and Joint Masters Michael Taylor (left) and Peter Parker (middle).*
Photograph kindly loaned by Michael Taylor. Copyright Stanley Hurwitz.

nook and cranny, and we came across them round every corner. I took Falcon and left home at six forty-five, just making the meet by the skin of my teeth. I unboxed in torrential rain which lasted all day, but received a wonderful welcome from the Master, Mr Parker, to whom I had spoken on the telephone. It was to be another woodland day, with the country "panelled" in every direction (i.e. liberally supplied with hunt jumps) so when we ran, as we did, from covert to covert, it was always possible to stay with hounds. The tremendous amount of work put into making these jumps made the best of a country restricted by urbanisation. We drew for an hour before finding, but then had a really good hunt, until the fox was headed by hundreds of children on a sponsored walk through the forest. After this check caused by "child foil", there was little more hunting, and as I was soaked to the skin I left for home at two-thirty. During the first part of the good run, Falcon had become very wound up and plunged in a rash and reckless manner down a very steep place, thoroughly terrifying me. This was a problem I frequently faced with my horses, used to being in front hunting hounds, and also used to our slow plough country, who tended to become over-enthusiastic when offered good, fast going and hunt jumps.

The next season (1984-85) began with a comparatively short jolly to south-west Wales, based at a pub which I had found while travelling with my youngest daughter Charlotte. I had picked her up from her school in Somerset and gone on to see a rare horse-drawn vehicle, a Staffordshire pottery cart (known as a "pot-cart") that I had heard was in a South Wales museum. During this trip we had stopped for lunch at a large pub in Tenby in Pembrokeshire where there were some old stables. I explained about my hunting holidays and the landlord was quite willing to clean them out for me to use. As a result, I left home a few weeks later on 16 October 1984 with three horses and Theresa at six o'clock and drove almost non-stop to Tenby. Being fairly ignorant of geography, as I crossed the Severn Bridge I felt as though I had nearly arrived, little realising that I was barely halfway there. How those last miles dragged.

**Pembrokeshire Hunt.** *Gary Barber, in his fourth season as Huntsman (1992/93), dismounted on the coastal path, the fox having run into cliffs.*

I was tired and the lorry was very sluggish at any sort of hill as we were towing the caravan. We finally arrived at five o'clock. We had brought some bales of straw which was just as well because, although the landlord had promised he could arrange for some, there were none there. There were only two boxes at the pub, so Theresa settled my old faithfuls Falcon and Demelza in them, and arranged the partitions so that Tiger could sleep on the lorry. Tiger was my hackney-Welsh Cob whom she had just broken in to ride and she was so keen to take him to Wales that in the end I had reluctantly agreed.

Next morning we set off at eight forty-five to go to the Vale of Clettwr meet near Pencader but three miles up the road the lorry broke down (Wed 17 Oct 1984) . I stood like an idiot, not knowing what to do, but a man stopped and inspected it and told me he thought it was the fuel pump that had packed up. We led Falcon and Tiger home (I cannot think why we did not ride them) and telephoned the garage to fetch the lorry which cost £283 to repair and a day's hunting missed. There was another embarassing problem in that the Master's wife had agreed to meet me in Pencader Square to show me the way to the meet. I telephoned her during the evening to apologise and explain what had happened, only to be told that I had missed a nine-mile point all on grass.

After this disappointing start, I was looking forward to my day with the **Pembrokeshire Foxhounds** on the Thursday but the winds were coming gale-force off the sea as we unboxed Demelza and Tiger at the meet at Haverfordwest Racecourse (Thurs 18 Oct 1984). The Master greeted me by saying that he would have cancelled the day if he had been able to contact me to tell me not to come and there were, beside ourselves, only the huntsman, his wife who whipped-in to him, another amateur whip, and three ladies out. The hounds surprised me in that they were all English and there were only nine-and-a-half couple. The huntsman told me he had thirty-three and a half couples in kennel, and I supposed that he had brought so few because of the terrible conditions. He had good control of his hounds and found fox after fox, but each one (having more sense than us) soon went to ground. We kept out until one o'clock when it was decided that the winds had made hunting impossible and we all went home.

That evening we had a very good dinner, which I had previously arranged with the landlord. I had ordered frogs' legs as a starter especially for Theresa's benefit and her face was the picture of surprise when she was confronted with them. This was followed by fillet of beef en croute. As frequently happened, I could find no pack that was hunting on the Friday so we took Falcon and Tiger to the Pendine Sands, a few miles round the coast from Tenby, to gallop on the seven-mile length of flat sands which at times had been used for racing cars. As we rode to the sea, there were red flags flying on the beach, so I asked Theresa what they meant. She said she did not know, and I replied that she ought to as she lived at Felixstowe on the coast of Suffolk.

"I expect it is to warn swimmers about dangerous tides," she said, and this seemed a good enough explanation to me.

We went for our gallop up the beach, five miles or so, but when we came back, we were met by a furious Ministry of Defence man, who said that any fool must know that no-one was allowed on the beach when the red flag was flying. They were about to fire some shells into the sea and we were lucky not to have been hurt.

Next day we went with the **Tivyside Foxhounds** and were lucky enough to catch their Opening Meet at Pant-y-deri House (Sat 20 Oct 1984). We left Tenby at nine-thirty and arrived in perfect time. The meet was in an idyllic setting, especially for an Opening Meet. The field of about fifty were standing in a paddock below a ha-ha wall at which the huntsman stood with hounds, and a lovely lawn stretched up to the house above us. The Master, Mr Moor, insisted that I have a drink and sent into the house for one especially for me, a lovely hot punch. Of the fifty or so field, about half were turned out well and the other half decidedly scruffy. The Master made a short speech which included a welcome to the Suffolk visitors, and we finally moved off and found a fox straight away which very soon went to ground. We found another which I viewed away, a very light-coloured fox which was killed in some kale after a hunt of about twenty minutes. A third fox was quickly away but the Master and all the field became lost, missing the first three-quarters of an hour of this hunt. Soon after we caught up he also went to ground in a wood. I walked into the wood with the Master and we both got into a very boggy area. I was nearly stuck, sinking down to the mahogany tops of my boots. This fox was left for the terrier-men to deal with and hounds drew for another, which was eventually caught and I was presented with the brush.

**Tivyside.** *Meet at Ngeadd Cross, 1986/87. Huntsman Norman Mathews.*

Photograph kindly donated by D H Ball

During the day, the Master told me how the hunt had almost disbanded three years previously, but he had stood up at the AGM and said that it was out of order to disband the hunt at an AGM. This was only a bluffing tactic and by the time there had been an Extraordinary General Meeting called, he had had time to get a committee together and with him as Master the hunt was saved. It would have been a crying shame to let this splendid little hunt go into extinction as it had such lovely country, with open grassland and the high ground interspersed with deep wooded valleys. According to Baily's however, the Tivyside had already come back from extinction twice having been disbanded between 1926 and 1937 and again between 1950 and 1954. The Master told me he would like to get some more Welsh hounds as he only had three and a half couple and these were proving so much better in the thick places.

That evening I was supposed to have had dinner with some friends of the landlord, Peter Parker, but they telephoned to say they could not make it. However, after dinner they called and picked me up, taking me into Saundersfoot to see their lovely new house which had every conceivable luxury, and was set high up on a hillside with lovely views over Carmarthen Bay. After leaving their home, they took me on a tour of the town to see the terrible damage caused by a recent gas explosion. A substantial part of the town centre was in ruins, looking like parts of London during the Blitz. We next went to their favourite pub where everyone seemed to know them and drinks came from all around. When we left the pub we went to a disco which was the last place I would have chosen, but what could I do when I was with a party of people? We went down a long flight of steps into a cellar where about three hundred people were dancing in a sunken area in the centre. The crush was terrible and the noise deafening but I had to admit that the lighting was cleverly done, creating several good effects. I decided to make the best of it and had a couple of dances with Peter's girlfriend then luckily they decided to go home.

On the Sunday morning I awoke with those dreadful loud noises still drumming in my head. After breakfast Peter lent me his old mini-bus to go again to the Museum of Romany Life where I had seen the pot-cart but it was closed. When I returned he asked me how I had got on with the mini-bus. I told him it was the worst vehicle I had ever driven and he laughed and said that it was being taken off the road for good the following week.

Once again I was lucky in finding a pack which hunted on Mondays. The **South Pembrokeshire Foxhounds** were meeting at The Folly Gate, at Cross Hands, but it was another very wet day, with high winds and there were very few people out (Mon 22 Oct 1984). I was disappointed that Mrs Evans was not there, as she had been Master of these hounds since 1942 and I would have loved to have met her. However, her daughter welcomed me and introduced me to the Field Master who told me that he had had a day with the Dunston Harriers (neighbours to the Easton) as he had relations in Norfolk. Hounds were bred on Beaufort and Heythrop lines but nevertheless did not seem to be very good at drawing thick places. Three times during the day they winded a fox in thick bushes but would not push in, just standing outside, baying, rather like marking at an earth.

The first fox gave us a very quick spin across country, so fast, in fact, that hounds left us behind, but we finally caught up with them in a small covert. The huntsman was of the old school, with the old-fashioned courtesy and charm. He had done twenty-seven seasons with this pack, and was very good on the horn and voice. I was soaked to the skin and the winds had reached such a pitch that it was nearly impossible to hunt, so I went back to my box at two o'clock.

On returning to base, I asked for somewhere to dry my coat and waistcoat and was shown the boiler room, which was ideal. The pub was fine for my purpose but, although far from the worst of my bases, was not the best of them either. My room was in a long corridor and, as a result, Theresa was able to tell me a strange thing she had noticed about her Alsatian dog which she had brought with her. Twice, when coming over from her caravan to see me about something, the dog had run ahead of her and stopped exactly opposite my door. There was a small swimming pool in the basement which I did not use but Theresa found very enjoyable on the days she was not hunting, and the food was very good throughout my stay. The stables were the original inn stables but had not been used as such for ages, probably since the War. They were barely adequate as the doors were nearly rotting off the hinges and we had to tie some strings across where the top door should have been, so they could not push against the bottom half which could easily have been broken. The landlord was a burly fellow, and a lot of fun. In contrast to my last holiday on Dartmoor, I did not get into conversation with the local clientele of the bar as they were mostly tourists. The hotel specialised in accommodating coach parties, which gave me rather a surprise as one night, walking past the bar, I could hear East Anglian voices which are especially noticeable when away from home. I walked in and discovered that there was a coach trip from Norfolk. This made a considerable difference to the holiday. I still cannot decide which was the best part of the holiday on Dartmoor – the hunting during the day, or the evenings in the Forest Inn.

There was a panic before I set out on the Tuesday for our last day as I had thought the meet of the **Carmarthenshire Foxhounds** was at eleven-thirty discovering nearly too late that it was ten-thirty (Tues 23 Oct 1984). When we arrived, just in time, at the Picton Country Club at St Clears, we found out that they were still cubhunting so there had been no need to plait the horses. It was also the Children's Meet and there were about twelve children of all ages out. The kennel huntsman was hunting hounds as Mr Thomas, the Acting Master, could not do so owing to having a boil on his bottom. It was an impossible place to hunt as we just went into some horrid forestry, where nearly all the rides were either blocked with fallen trees or overgrown. The kennel huntsman had his terriers running with him, and on one occasion they climbed up some rocks with him and bolted a fox which eventually went to ground again. It was such a lovely day, with sun and warm winds after the howling gales and rain, it seemed a shame that we were stuck in this dreadful forest. I thought it was enough to put the children off hunting for the rest of their lives.

I was forced to go home next day because I had promised to show a film of my Appleby Trip, as I did frequently to various W.I.s and so forth as it raised more money for Driving for the Disabled. I had asked David Steele and Tony St Quinton to meet me at Springfield White Hart just outside Chelmsford so that David could carry on home with the lorry while Tony and I went to Hanningfield Village Hall where I was to show the film to members of the British Field Sports Society.

We left Tenby at eight-forty, and made very poor time, as the lorry was not pulling at all well. To make matters even worse I was flagged down by a kindly passing motorist on the M25 to be told that Theresa's caravan had a puncture. I decided to try to get off the motorway, as to be rescued would have been very expensive and I felt that I was not far from the A12 turnoff. I crept along in first gear on the hard shoulder, hoping the rims of the caravan wheel would hold together. It was much further than I thought to the junction but we made it. I then discovered that the rims had not been damaged at all, a miracle which I put down to the fact that the caravan was so old it had been made in the days when really good materials were used. I left the caravan on some waste ground and telephoned home to say what had happened, only to find that I had made a mistake and that the film was not until the Thursday night, so I could have had another day's hunting in Wales. It was the last straw and I felt very fed up, but it was no-one's fault but my own. This holiday had not been a great success, with the lorry breaking down which caused me to miss the nine-mile point, and the gale-force winds and heavy rain, and finally the dreadful forestry. The only bright spot of the day was a roast beef lunch at Leigh Delamere Service station, carved off the largest joint of beef I have ever seen, and it melted in the mouth.

A month later, after our own season proper had begun, I had to cancel the meet at Clopton on Saturday 24 November. It had rained heavily all Thursday and Friday and it was far too wet. I decided on the spur of the moment to go to the Lake District with Kenny Warne, my stockman. Kenny had been through a very rough patch with both his father and his nephew, who were the only people who lived with him, in hospital. At the same time I knew he needed a holiday. Kenny had played a vital part in enabling me to go away on my hunting holidays and be able to enjoy them thoroughly without worrying, as I knew that my pigs were left in the best possible hands and that everything would carry on just as if I was there. Without that confidence, I could not have gone away so often, or for so long. We stayed with the Barkers at Norran Bank, Patterdale (where the Windermere Harriers were kennelled), and spent a lovely evening that Saturday night listening to fascinating tales from Anthony. The next day we spent driving around the Lake District so I could show Kenny the well-known beauty spots and this was especially enjoyable as there were so few tourists around.

Since I could not possibly be so far from home without trying to have a day's hunting, I found out that the **Cumberland Foxhounds** would be meeting at Tarn Cross, Aspatria (Mon 26 Nov 1984). These hounds were hunted both mounted and on foot, Mondays being the foot day. The Master and huntsman, Mr Bowes, was very fit and I did not think it would make much difference which day it was when it came to keeping up with hounds. The country, although not in the fells, would nevertheless have been too difficult to cross with a horse as there was a lot of barbed wire, and very wide dykes in places. We found a fox, and hounds settled very well to the line but soon crossed over a farm where they were banned. I was quite taken aback by this, as foxhunting is so popular in the region and the farmers usually welcome hounds, especially when hunted on foot. The farmer, known to everyone as "Smiler", was absolutely mad with rage, and my thoughts, as usual, were that I was glad to be a visitor and not have to deal with the problem. We drew for another two hours or so before finding and having another fairly good hunt, but hounds had to be stopped again as they were moving in "Smiler's" direction. It had not been the most successful of days, which was a shame as it was Kenny's first day's hunting and he had desperately wanted to see a fox. These were rarely seen in the Easton country but he had been unlucky. I left at three-thirty as I needed to go into Carlisle, before returning to spend another night with the Barkers. Anthony wanted to know all about the day, expounding his theories about certain problems with foxhunting. We drove home on the Tuesday *via* Burnsall in the Yorkshire Dales to collect an oil painting of myself and Demelza with the Easton Harriers, painted by Rosemary Lodge, which is reproduced on the dust-jacket of this book.

It was very nearly a year before I again hunted with another pack and then it was only another daytrip. This was arranged as I *still* had one pack in Kent to hunt with, the **Ashford Valley Foxhounds** (Wed 13 Nov 1985). I called for Paul Yeldham at seven-thirty, and used his telephone to check that the meet had not been cancelled as there had been a hard frost. Mr Bells, the Master, said it was too early to make a decision but he was hopeful and we could ring later on. Paul and I decided to risk it, and started off, telephoning again before we reached the Dartford Tunnel. This time there was good news. We unboxed in a riding school and hacked up to the village of Sutton Valence where the Master gave us both an enormous whisky. The field were all crowded around the front of the pub and no-one seemed to care that they were completely blocking the road. I was thoroughly shocked when the huntsman rode up with hounds and just pushed his way through the field, leaving his hounds to get through the rows of hooves and making no attempt to clear a path for them at all. Inevitably, one hound was badly kicked as it squeezed past the leg of a horse which was not accustomed to hounds. I have never seen anything so dreadfully negligent and callous on the part of a huntsman before or since, and could not believe my eyes, especially as the Masters said nothing to him. While we waited to move off, the hounds were all over the place, some having ventured their way through the horses, and some having not.

We moved off to the great relief, I am sure, of the many motorists who were waiting to get through, and went to draw orchards and hopfields. The first two hunts were quite short but they found a third fox and had a quick burst over lovely country, over a farm which I think from memory belonged to the Master. It was strange riding through the hopfields, the towering poles high above us and the stay wires poking out at each end. The day was memorable only for the fact that a lady of the field desperately tried to buy my horse, Fizz. We drove home discussing the day, the general opinion being that we were not very impressed and arrived home at eight-thirty.

**Ashford Valley Hunt.** *Huntsman Clive Knott leaving The Chequers, Smarden, 1986*

Photograph kindly loaned by Mrs R V Watson

That was my only visit of the 1985-86 season, but I made up for it the following one as I had two major jollies in 1986-87, one in Wales in October and one based in Dorset in March. However, I started with another two minkhunting days. I had been in the north for quite a while as Sheila and I, with Kenny Warne and Ronnie Kindred, had been at the Lowther Horse-Driving Trials and Country Fair. The other three had then gone home, leaving me to judge at Rydal Hound Show and then to travel to Whitby to sing for a week as guest of the Whitby Folk Festival. I left the Festival at three o'clock on Friday 22 August, and drove to the the Royal Oak at Gisburn, so as to be ready for the meet the next morning of the **West Yorkshire Minkhounds** at Whitewell, near Clitheroe.

I arrived at the meet at nine o'clock and we moved off at nine-thirty (Sat 23 Aug 1986). There were eight and a half couple of hounds, some Dumfriesshire and some Welsh. They drew along the bank of a tributary of the River Hodder (itself a tributary of the River Ribble), but there was little in the way of a definite hunt before stopping at Dunsop Bridge Country House Hotel for lunch, which I thought was very civilised sport. The idea of stopping for lunch was, I thought, very enjoyable and was a custom left over from the otterhounds. By coincidence, the Hodder Valley Foxhounds were to meet there when I hunted with them in 1992 on my last but one tour. After lunch and a few beers, sport improved dramatically, and we had a good hunt, marking to ground in some rocks. During this hunt, I noticed a boy of about eight years old who was whipping-in, and his voice and hound language were first rate. I was so impressed I could not resist giving him a £5 tip. The hounds were hunted very well by Mr O'Brien, the Joint-Master's son. I left at four o'clock having thoroughly enjoyed my day with the minkhounds. I usually do enjoy this sport, so different from most other hunting. It has all the qualities of a pleasant walk in the country, with the added magic of hounds speaking and hunting, without the speed of beagling. I then drove up to the Old Church Hotel at Watermillock beside Ullswater, preparatory for a day with the **North Lakes Minkhounds**. I would normally have stayed with my friends, the Barkers, at Patterdale but they were fully booked with bed-and-breakfast guests. My decision to stay at the Old Church Hotel was based on the fact that I knew the cuisine to be excellent, having been invited to dine there by Norman Robarts when he was judging the Private Driving at Lowther Country Fair that year. It was certainly an extravagance, but one that I found to be well worthwhile. Everything was of the best, my most vivid memory being of plates of home-made chocolates beside the armchairs in the drawing-room and on the dressing table in the bedroom. This did not help my weight problem which had been developing over the fortnight I had spent in the north and I came home over two stones more than my normal weight.

I left the hotel at nine-thirty and drove slowly through Mungrisdale, admiring the views, on my way to the meet at Caldbeck (Sun 24 Aug 1986). I met the Master, John Parker, who refused to take a cap from me. Hounds drew along the river and hit off some drag with a crash of music right behind the churchyard in which John Peel lies buried. For all his hunting

# MAP 12

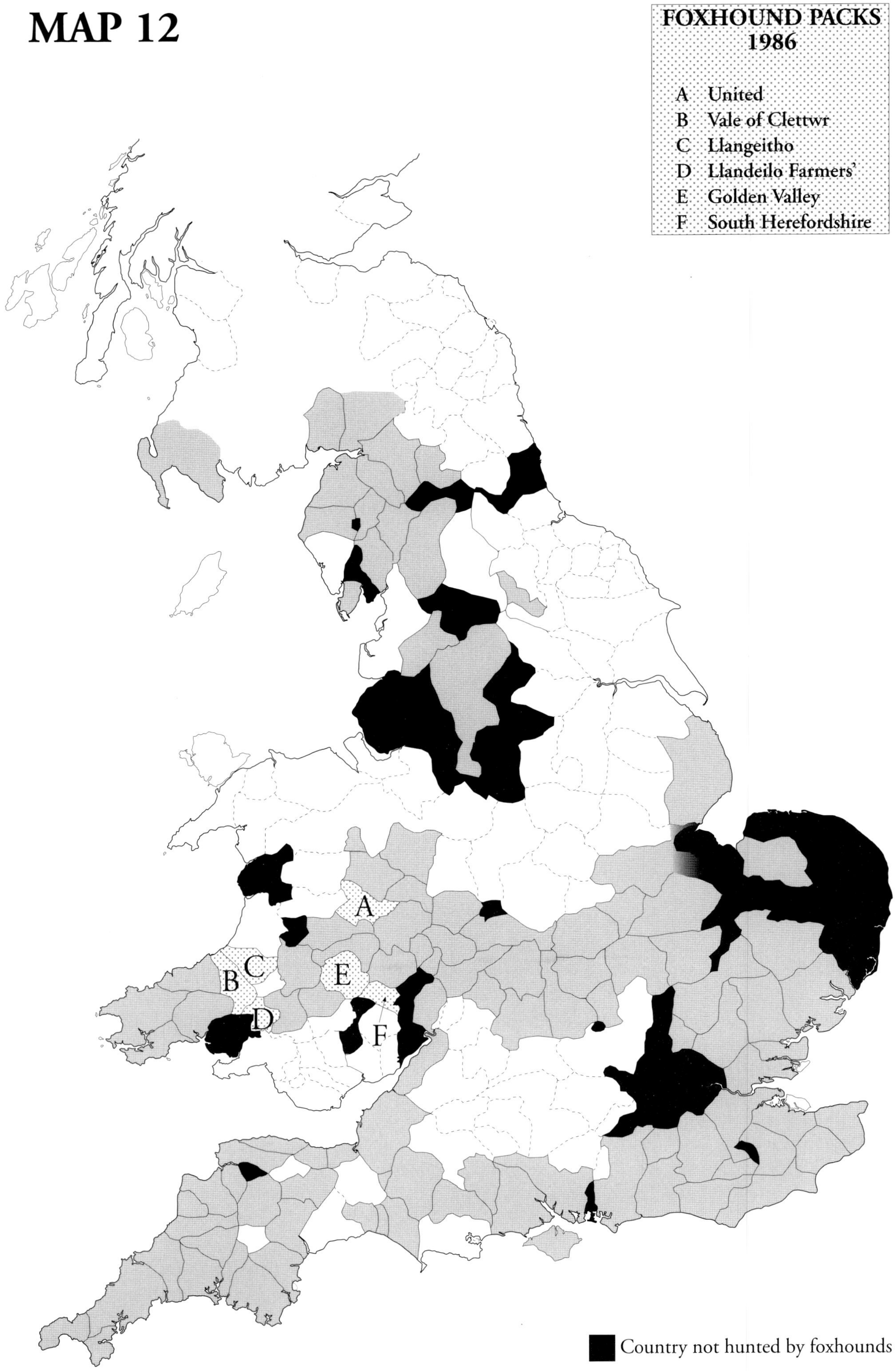
FOXHOUND PACKS
1986
A United
B Vale of Clettwr
C Llangeitho
D Llandeilo Farmers'
E Golden Valley
F South Herefordshire
A
B
C
D
E
F
Country not hunted by foxhounds

knowledge, John Peel would not have known what we were doing as there were no mink to hunt in his day. They hunted slowly on this drag for one and a half hours, then marked to ground in rocks. The mink was bolted and after giving it a good start the hounds were laid onto his line, and we had another good hunt upstream, finally killing it in the open as he was making his way to an old mine. Mr Parker drew on upstream to Hesket Newmarket where we stopped for lunch. I did not go on after lunch, but went to visit the Barkers at Patterdale to confirm the details of a Windermere Harriers' visit to the Easton country before, at last, driving back to Suffolk after having been away for over two weeks enjoying a variety of amusements.

The first jolly of 1986-87 was based again, as in 1980, at Builth Wells but this time we could not use the stables at the Royal Welsh Showground as they were all needed for the Welsh Cob Sales. Instead, John "the Barley" had arranged stabling for us with Mrs Biddy Williams, a keen sportswoman herself, at Dollywvy Farm just outside Builth Wells, and she had also agreed to provide bed-and-breakfast for my groom, Tracy Feavearyear, so she could be near the horses. The agreement was that she would provide good hay and straw, and we would take our own corn. Paul Yeldham was to come with me and he and I were to stay at the Barlow Mow. I left home in Paul's lorry with Demelza, Rose and Tracy and then called to pick up Paul and his two horses, and arrived at our stables by teatime.

The first day was my second attempt to hunt with the **Vale of Clettwr**. The first had been two years before when the lorry had broken down causing me to miss the nine-mile point. They were meeting at Ffynonhenri Square at ten-thirty and the morning was cold, with high winds and scattered snow showers (Mon 20 Oct 1986). When we rode into the square, the Master and huntsman recognised me immediately and explained that he had been out with the Carmarthenshire the day I had hunted with them in 1984. He made a little speech which was difficult to hear in the wind, thanking the farmers and welcoming us. Hounds found at once but the fox soon went to ground, and this was exactly what happened all day. There were plenty of foxes, but all went to ground quite quickly. If the hunts had not been short, I have no idea how he could have kept with hounds as there were so many deep valleys (of the type called combes in the West Country), which were difficult to cross, and there was wire everywhere. I saw the lightest-coloured fox I have ever seen, and watched him away. The Master then brought hounds and laid them on the line but the strong winds spoiled everything. Hounds were a mixture of Welsh and English, but rather slack in their efforts due, I was told, to the fact that the best had gone on with the previous Master to his next pack. The only field apart from Paul and me, were two adults and four children. My best memory of the day was of a little boy of about twelve years on a Welsh Cob, presenting a splendid picture as the two of them seemed to go as one. Demelza also came in for a lot of admiration which pleased me enormously. We left at three-thirty and arrived back at the stables two hours later.

**Golden Valley Foxhounds.** *Joint Master and Huntsman, Mr Vivian Bishop, with hounds.*

Photograph kindly loaned by W P Bishop

Next morning we were up early as the meet of the **Golden Valley Foxhounds** was at seven-thirty. We made our own coffee which was what we usually did at the Barley Mow when we needed to leave early, and went to pick up our two horses – Rose and Rosie. We left the stables with Biddy Williams (whose stables they were) and her horse, and arrived at the meet at a layby near Clyro in good time. Biddy introduced us to Mr Vivian Bishop, the Master, who had had these hounds since 1945, and was well-known for moving off strictly on time, but this morning he rode off five minutes early, with his hounds disappearing into the dark. As usual I had waited until getting to the meet before putting on my surgical collar and stock because they were so uncomfortable and this early departure put me in a fluster. In the rush I could not find my stock so I decided that, as it was only cubhunting, just my stiff collar would do and, in the general confusion, had ridden some way from the box before I realised that I still had my cloth cap on and we had to return to replace it.

In contrast to all this, Mr Bishop had a leisurely way of hunting hounds which, in my travels, I have noticed characterises the older huntsmen, in contrast to the more intense and earnest efforts of the younger

**Golden Valley Foxhounds:** ***"What a place to build a hunt gate!"***

generation. Hounds were quite often a fair way from him although some did often come back to him which, I suppose, were the young entry on one of their first mornings out. The rain was so heavy that at times it was difficult to see where I was going, and the hunting was limited to many short bursts. This was perfect to educate the young entry which of course was the main reason for cubhunting. There was one tricky place where there was a narrow gate set in the middle of a stream. Mr Bishop's horse would not go through it so I tried to give a lead with Rose, but she also refused to walk through. Paul then offered to give a lead on his Rosie, who took an enormous leap through the gateway, narrowly avoiding hitting Paul's knee on the post. The Master's horse again declined so I tried to give him a lead and Rose reared up and swung round, almost knocking the Master from his horse. We did manage to get through in the end, both of us with severely bashed knees. There was little sport and we were wet through so we went back to the box at ten o'clock.

Biddy told us it was the first time she had been cubhunting with Mr Bishop as he always meets at seven-thirty and it was far too early for her in normal circumstances, although today she had thoroughly enjoyed herself and was pleased she had come. On the way home, she told us that her godfather was Maurice Springfield, known to one and all as "Springy" who had been Master of the Easton before the war, and that she had often stayed at Easton and helped at the kennels when she was a child.

On Wednesday we went with the **Llandeilo Farmers' Foxhounds** who were meeting at Pen-y-groes (for Caer Bryn Bridge) and we left the farm with Demelza for me, Rose for Tracy and Buzzard for Paul (Wed 22 Oct 1986). It was the Children's Meet and Mr Roberts, the Master, made a good speech to the children, finishing up with a request that he hoped they would impress us (the visitors) with their good manners. This request they sadly did not comply with, the little darlings bombing around all over the place. There was a series of very short hunts to ground. I stayed with a foot follower just above a coalmine, who advised me that they would probably run in a certain direction. This proved correct and I had hounds to myself for quite a time, which included a furious gallop to get ahead to stop the traffic when they crossed a main road. I did not get much further with them as I was confronted by a very irate farmer who obviously did not want hounds on his land. He was brandishing a fencing stake, and left me in no doubt that he was going to use it if he could get near enough. Demelza and I made an about turn back to the road and when I was well along it I looked back over my shoulder and could see him still pursuing us up the road. This incident just stresses what can happen when you don't know the country and what trouble can be caused in all innocence. The hounds I thought were in rather poor condition and were mostly Welsh or Welsh crosses. We went home thinking what an enjoyable day we had had amongst such a friendly group of people – the farmer of course excepted.

The following day we went with the pack made famous by Dalesman, the **United Foxhounds**, who were meeting at Woolston, near Wistanstow (Salop) (Thurs 23 Oct 1986). We had fun and games getting to the meet as the road marked on the map was impossible to get through as it degenerated into a grass track and we had to find our way around. As we unboxed, there was just our box and the hunt lorry and I thought we were going to be the only ones mounted, but we were later joined by two girls and a man. The huntsman, Ron Ellis, recognised me from when he had been huntsman to the West Norfolk. The Master arrived in his pick-up truck and said he was going to follow on foot. Glasses of sherry appeared from a farmhouse before we moved off to draw just in front of the farm where we found at once. It never ceases to amaze me how a pack can sit at a meet and then move off and find a fox within five hundred yards. Hounds just flew and we had what the old hunting correspondents used to call "a quick thing". We were really going when Paul, unintentionally, jumped a cattle grid and I only just managed to avoid it.

The country was lovely and, with the excellent houndwork that persisted throughout the day, we were thoroughly enjoying ourselves in our almost private hunt, especially with a Land Rover following with an unending supply of port. Three times we viewed foxes and all of them were of the same very light colour as we had seen the day before. We were so interested in them being this colour that we asked if it was common in Wales, but were told that the majority were of a normal colour. Hounds were in very good condition and Ron Ellis told me that he preferred the pack to be part Welsh and part English, but they were now mostly part-bred Welsh. It had been a pleasure to listen to his voice and horn as he hunted them in his quiet style. While I was writing up this day's entry in my diary, Marie came rushing upstairs to see what Paul was up to as there was water running through the ceiling into the bar below. He had overflowed the bath while soaking after his day.

When planning this holiday, I had naturally telephoned Mr John Dix to ask if I could hunt with his private pack, the **Llangeitho Foxhounds**. When I started to explain who I was and what I was doing, he said, "I know all about you. I'm sitting here reading all about you at this moment. What day would you like me to hunt? Any day you choose!"

"Friday, then, sir," I said, promptly, "as no other packs go on a Friday." (Fri 24 Oct 1986). At the moment I rang he had been reading the write-up in Hounds magazine of "All Thanks To His Grace", the history of the Easton Harriers written by my daughter Bridget.

Marie Lloyd had been looking after us so well at the Barley Mow that Paul offered her a horse for the day and after leaving the stables at six forty-five, we picked her up at seven, and arrived at the meet at Strata Florida an hour too soon at nine o'clock. To while away the time, I looked around the ancient Abbey ruins. Mr Dix arrived and greeted me saying, "You know that your harriers should really have been my harriers, because my father was a cousin of the Duke of Hamilton." He went on to say that the duke had paid for his education as his father was rather impecunious. His two charming daughters, who then arrived, whipped in to him and we were the only others out apart from a foot follower who told me that he had been to an Easton Harriers meet at Rendham when we had made a presentation to an Easton foot-follower, Hilda Diplock, on her eightieth birthday.

We moved off and found at once, running two large circles over this desolate country – a wild moorland hill country, with not a house or farm in sight. There was not even a shepherd on these wild hills, and nothing to prevent a horse getting anywhere it wished, except for the bogs which had to be negotiated carefully. The girls were first-class whippers-in as one would expect from such training, and were always in the right place at the right time. After two and a half hours of pure, blissful hunting, it began to rain heavily and the Master asked us if we had had enough. Of course, we said yes, although we would have dearly liked to have gone on longer. When we got back to the meet we were two and a half couple light and while he was blowing his horn for them, he was telling us stories. He became so engrossed in telling us these that he forgot to blow and after a few gentle reminders from his daughters, which were soon forgotten, one of them surreptitiously slipped the horn from his coat and started to blow for them herself, and very well she did it too. One of the stories was of a very mean farmer who had always been known for being exceptionally careful with his money. When John visited him one day in making arrangements for hunting, he found the farmer carefully taking down the wallpaper from the walls.

"Are you going to re-decorate?" asked John, surprised.

"No," growled the farmer. "I'm moving and I'm going to take this to my new house."

John was a true gentleman of the old-fashioned sort – tall, lean and stately, a real old cavalry type, and I felt very privileged to have met him in the field. I shall never forget the sight of the grand old gentleman standing on a hillside, holding his cap round his ear to listen to his beloved hounds' cry from the valley below. When I complimented him on the deep cry of his hounds, he said, "I've never bred from a bitch unless she had a doghound's voice, but now, in my old age, I only breed one litter a year. I rely on drafts from my old friend, Vivian Bishop (of the Golden Valley). He is so slow, you know, that even his old hounds are not worn out."

John had been a Master of Hounds in Dartmoor, Cornwall, Worcestershire, Ireland and Italy, and possibly more that I cannot remember. From what I could make out, he had never been without a pack of hounds and had always managed without much cash. He went on to explain that his father had promised him money in his will but instead he bought a lifetime's stay in a grave, at Bealings in Suffolk. "No, no, Daddy," said his daughters in chorus, "It's the Grove, Daddy dear," going on to explain to me that this was a Retirement Home. I drove home thinking what a truly wonderful day it had been, and how lucky John was to be in such a wild part of the country with his hounds and daughters to hunt with him. When I asked him how often he hunted he replied, "As often as I can." He explained that he relied entirely on fallen stock brought in to feed his hounds as he could not afford to fetch it in himself or to buy meal, and that when supplies were low he was forced to stop taking his hounds out. He may not have had much money but he had always lived the life he wanted and would not have lived a different life if he had been a millionaire.

The Llangeitho were a hard act to follow but our last day, with the **South Herefordshire Foxhounds**, was not a disappointment (Sat 25 Oct 1986). They met at Callow, near Hereford, and although it was another day of high winds and heavy rain, this was to be a day of cubhunting at its classical best. Paul and I were asked to help hold up the cubs and I have never seen so many foxes together, often six or seven in sight at once. There was a brace accounted for, and I am sure it was an education from which the young entry would benefit greatly. The Master, Mr Jones, recognised me from when I hunted with the Weston and Banwell Harriers during his Mastership and his Joint-Master, Mr Fear, had lent me one of his horses. On the way back to Builth Wells, I became quite sick and shivery, so Paul drove the lorry. As a result of not feeling very well there was not the usual riotous last night's party in the Barley.

Driving back to Suffolk the following day, we had a puncture just over the notorious Spaghetti Junction, but luckily, as Paul was a haulage contractor, he had a number to ring to sort out the situation. It had been quite a short holiday, from Sunday to Sunday but, with the help of Mr John Dix who had offered to hunt on the Friday for us, we had been with six packs.

**Irfon and Towy.** *Welsh country on a bleak day*

Photograph taken by Tony Butler

# MAP 13

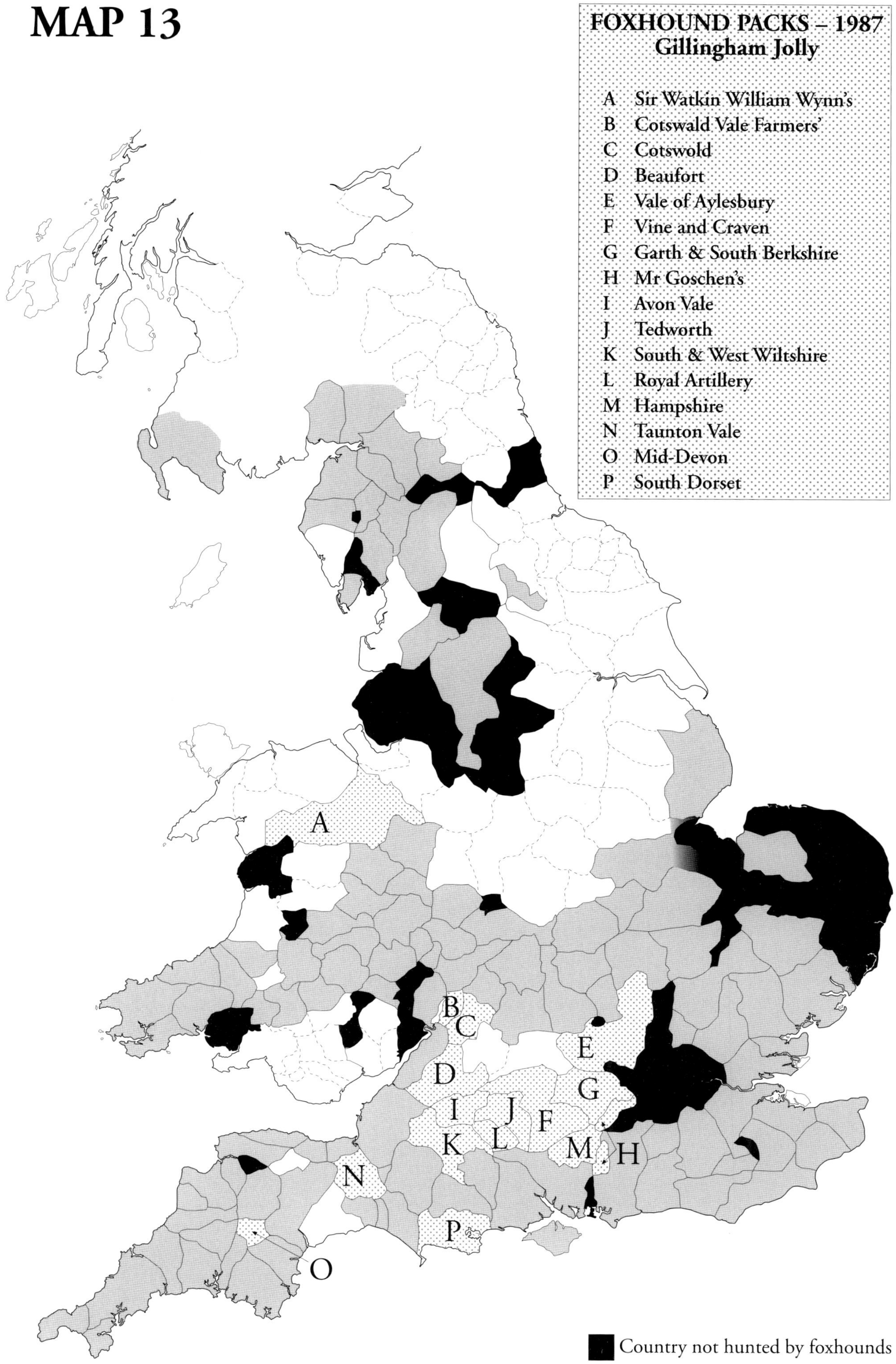
FOXHOUND PACKS – 1987
Gillingham Jolly
A Sir Watkin William Wynn's
B Cotswald Vale Farmers'
C Cotswold
D Beaufort
E Vale of Aylesbury
F Vine and Craven
G Garth & South Berkshire
H Mr Goschen's
I Avon Vale
J Tedworth
K South & West Wiltshire
L Royal Artillery
M Hampshire
N Taunton Vale
O Mid-Devon
P South Dorset
A
B
C
D
E
G
I
J
F
K
L
M
H
N
P
O
Country not hunted by foxhounds

# CHAPTER 15

## THE GILLINGHAM JOLLY

It had been a particularly difficult season and I was really looking forward to having a break away from home. All the arrangements for this holiday were made by Rupert Montagu, who was my Master's Secretary at the time, and he had not only telephoned all the Secretaries and worked out the schedule, with all the meets for each day, but also worked out the best routes and mileages to the meets. One of the Masters of the local packs told him of the Milton Lodge Hotel, at Gillingham in Dorset, where the old stables were still in use as a riding school. I planned to be away for four weeks from 8 March to 4 April, but would have to return to Suffolk twice during the course of it to attend the End of Season Ball and the Point-to-Point, so I had to have a car in Dorset for these lightning trips.

To add to the anticipated problems, one developed completely unexpectedly. I had planned to take with me my groom, Tracy Feavearyear, but her father came to me in the early evening on the day before I left to tell me that she was leaving my employ without notice. This was a terrible letdown as I had made all the arrangements and there was little time to find a replacement. I telephoned everyone I could think of who might be able to help, but no-one could come. That evening the Easton were holding their Mouse-Racing Evening, where I always acted as Judge. I spread the word through the village hall where it was held, and received an offer of help from Lindsay Baker who had been groom to me on the YTS scheme. Mr and Mrs Skepper, her present employers, agreed in the circumstances to let her go for a few days. Hilda Wickham, my kennel huntsman's wife, despite being rather apprehensive about pulling the caravan behind the lorry, had kindly agreed to drive the lorry down to Dorset and said she would help her settle in. A friend of Hilda's, Jill Bloss, followed the lorry in my pick-up truck to bring Hilda home and they had an uneventful journey and soon had the horses settled into the boxes and Lindsay into her caravan. They spent the Saturday night in the hotel using the bedroom I had booked for myself. This arrangement was ideal as it allowed Lindsay, who did not know the horses, to be more gently broken in to the situation. Hilda and Jill drove home the next day, as I was coming down the opposite direction in the car and I thought I might recognise the truck as we passed but I did not see them (Sun 8 Mar 1987).

I should have hunted with the Old Berkshire on the first day, and would have had the long journey for nothing had not Mrs Roberts, the proprietress of the hotel, insisted that I telephoned the Secretary to check, as customers had been coming in to the hotel saying that there had been snow in the Reading area (which was their country). I was told by another customer that the **South and West Wiltshire** were out at Loverton so I decided to go with them instead as my horse and myself were ready (Mon 9 Mar 1987). I therefore had my second day with this pack within a fortnight as two weeks earlier they had met at Great Bradley Hall, near Haverhill, in Suffolk by invitation of the Suffolk Foxhounds (Mon 16 Feb 1987). Colin Plumbe, who was staying for his annual visit to the Easton Harriers, joined me on my horse Falcon and we soon got into conversation with Simon Clarke, the Master and huntsman. When he knew that I intended to visit his area, he said he would be very pleased to see me in his country. He invited me to ride up with him, but I had to refuse as I was on a new horse, Manhattan, and I could not yet trust him with hounds, especially other people's. The day was one of very poor scent although it was snowing and I have often found that this brings good scent. The hounds appeared to me to be rather small but there were a lot of blue-mottled ones amongst them which pleased me as I love this colour because I feel that hounds of this colour usually have very good noses (ie. are very good scenting hounds). The day consisted of very short hunts from one covert to the next, and I was pleased with the performance of my new horse who jumped the hunt jumps without hesitation.

On my second day with them Mr Hugh Dalgety (whom I had met in 1980 when he was Master and huntsman of Portman Foxhounds) was hunting hounds as he hunted the dog pack and Simon Clarke the bitch pack. The first few coverts were drawn blank and then we found in a large wood near a park. Hounds seemed to run with a far greater cry than when they were in Suffolk, which I assumed was due to the fact that it was a better scenting day.

It was quite an art to pick a good pilot when hunting in a strange country, but this time I picked well, choosing a lady who I later discovered was an ex-Master. When she moved away from covertside, I followed her and as a consequence I got away well and we had hounds to ourselves for a while, and I was excited enough to jump a fair set of rails closely followed by a gate. This run over grass with lots of jumping was my undoing for the rest of the day as Fizz – Buck's Fizz –

lived up to his name and he became impossible. I do not normally have hot thoroughbreds but I had bought Fizz when I was assured that he was very calm in the field. His name, I was told, was purely coincidental and nothing to do with his temperament out hunting. I am always amazed at how such lies can tumble out of the mouths of such innocent-looking faces of the fair sex – this sounds chauvinistic but it is true that whenever I have been badly "had" in buying horses, the vendor has always been female.

There followed some woodland hunting which I did not enjoy at all as Fizz was throwing his head up and down in a desperate frenzy and pulling in such an alarming manner that I became quite frightened. I had many near misses on low boughs, and he stumbled onto his knees in wet spots. The end came when we moved out of the woodland and crossed the park, and it was necessary to jump some iron railings landing onto a tarmac road. I watched as some horses landed and slipped all over the place so I decided that discretion was the better part of valour. With Fizz being so hot I would never have been able to steady him enough to do the necessary neat little hop, so I hacked back to the box. This part of the country was new to everyone as it had been loaned to the Mendip Farmers for ten seasons. When Mr Dalgety joined the Mastership, he changed the South and West Wilts from a three-day to a four-day-a-week pack and needed the extra country. There was a lady in the field who told me that she had hunted with the Easton at Charsfield, seven years previously, and her friend said she knew the Gurdons, at Grundisburgh.

I decided to take Fizz again the next day on the grounds that more work might settle him down. I telephoned Dr Cameron, Master of the **Tedworth Foxhounds**, and he told me that he had changed the meet from Redenham to Upton Common. As he did not have my telephone number, he had arranged for a lady to wait for me at Redenham and bring me on to Upton Common (Tues 10 Mar 1987). He and Mr Guinness, the Field Master, gave me a great welcome, as did the dozen or so that made up the field, coming up and shaking hands, offering flasks, and so on. The professional huntsman, Ted Burton, was in his first season as huntsman, having previously been fourteen seasons with this pack as a kennel huntsman, whipping in to an amateur. He had an amateur whipping-in to him who looked rather scruffy but did his job very well, and I was surprised to hear that he was an ex-Master as his appearance did not suggest such a position. The day was mostly woodland hunting, but most of these hunts were spoiled by hounds not being steady to deer, or by changing foxes too often. I had tied Fizz's head down tightly with a standard martingale and felt a great deal more comfortable, but when the Field Master asked me to give him a lead over a quite small obstacle I wondered if he would be able to jump at all with his head tied so low. I need not have worried as he cleared it in fine style. The tracks in the woods were frozen solid and had a light covering of snow. Just before I went home at three o'clock, some foot followers introduced themselves and told me that they too were on a hunting holiday and regularly foot-followed in Essex. I arrived back at base at five-fifteen.

**Tedworth Hunt.** *Leaving the meet at Manningford Abbotts are Ted Burton, kennel huntsmanm and Bryan Read, amateur whip.*
Photograph taken 1987/88, kindly loaned by Mrs Gerry Beaton

The weather was still snowy and frosty next day when I had arranged to go with **Mr Goschen's** private pack of foxhounds from the meet at Woodmansgreen, near Midhurst in Sussex (Wed 11 Mar 1987). I telephoned to check if they were still hunting, and was told that the meet was put back to twelve o'clock. It was an eighty-mile drive each way, but well worth it to see these famous hounds who lived up to their reputation as they stood at the meet looking perfect. There were a few Old English hounds amongst them, which I believe were drafts from the Brocklesby. I was warmly greeted by Mr and Mrs Goschen who were on foot. They introduced me to Mr Parker whose wife was a descendant of Sir Thomas Boughey, whose harriers the Duke of Hamilton had bought to establish the pack in Suffolk which eventually became the Easton. I was surprised to see Jim Saunders mounted in the field as I did not know that he hunted. I had known him as stud groom at Hampton Court when he was in charge of my big coloured mare, Blossom, whom I had lent to Her Majesty for two years. They were trying to breed a large coloured horse as they had great difficulty in getting coloured horses big enough to be drum horses.

With the sun very warm after white frost, it was a classic case of no scent. Ken Hand, the huntsman, hunted them very well and tried woodland and open heathland, but they could do little with the brace of foxes that were found. Ken told me that he was moving to the Essex Farmers' and Union Foxhounds the following season. In spite of so little actual hunting, I thoroughly enjoyed myself among such pleasant people, and eventually arrived back in Gillingham at six-fifteen.

Next morning I left the hotel at seven o'clock and drove via Newbury and the A4 to Reading, then across country to Marlow, travelling at times on impossibly narrow roads, to get to the meet of the **Vale of Aylesbury Foxhounds** at Ibstone (Thurs 12 Mar 1987). I eventually arrived at eleven o'clock which was ideal as the meet was at eleven-thirty and I had time for a flask of soup and a sandwich. The field were a sullen bunch, hardly anyone speaking to anyone else. However, the ex-Chairman introduced himself to me and he then took me to meet Jim Bennett, the professional huntsman. Jim was sitting amongst his hounds which were the smartest pack I had ever seen, all exactly the same size and type. He told me that he had been whipper-in to our old Easton kennel huntsman Ernie Nunn at the Essex and Suffolk, and had in fact helped him to move to the Easton. He remembered the round house, and had all these years kept a pair of boots of the old man's out of respect for his memory. I was just about to say that I had his spurs for the same reason, when we were interrupted. It was Jim's last season, and I think possibly his last day, before retiring, and I count it a great privilege to have seen him in action, as to listen to his voice and horn was pure magic. To watch him draw those lovely open beech woods, with wonderful views into little valleys below, in the famous yellow livery, was a picture I shall always retain in my memory. The unusual livery was left over from the Old Berkeley, which had been amalgamated with the Hertfordshire and the South Oxfordshire in 1970 to form the Vale of Aylesbury. Scenting conditions were terrible, with hot sun following white frost yet again. There were deer everywhere and with very few foxes we did not see much sport. There was one short hunt, and I thought their voices were quite delightful, but unfortunately they were stopped as the whip thought they were hunting deer. In fact, I had seen that the deer had run the same line as the fox but I could not get the information to the huntsman quickly enough. I was riding in great pain having twisted my back during the previous day's hunting, and decided to go back to the box at three-thirty. I arrived back at the hotel at six-thirty, so the journey back was an hour quicker than the journey out.

**Vale of Aylesbury.** *Meet at Cholsey Farm, Ibstone, March 1988. Master Mr Alan Wynn, and Huntsman Nick Jones.*
Photograph kindly loaned by Mrs V Murray

I had another long way to go the next day to the meet of the **Taunton Vale Foxhounds** at Waterpit Farm, Kingston St Mary, near Taunton (Friday 13 March 1987). I unboxed along with some others at a picnic site and hacked up to the meet with a man who told me that he used to live in Stonham Aspel in the Easton country. His closest friend had been Andrew Turnbull, and both of them used to hunt with the Easton as boys. This was the last day of the Taunton Vale's season and the last time that Martin Lee would be hunting these hounds as he was giving up the Mastership at the end of the season. Consequently, there were official photographers and speeches at the meet, and Mr Honeyball's farmyard was packed with horses and foot followers.

The first part of the day was spent drawing hedgerows around the farm and jumping hunt jumps from one meadow into the next. This had the usual effect on Fizz and he became very fizzy indeed, and most uncomfortable to ride. At home, when I was hunting hounds and in front, he was a joy to ride, but visiting, and riding in the field, was absolute hell. The Master, seeing my plight, invited me to ride up with him as we went to draw some coverts and it was a great pleasure to watch his noticeably easy style of hunting hounds. When he sent them away from him uphill to draw some gorse they hit off a cold line but only a few couple could speak to it. Although we could not see hounds, Martin named all the hounds which were speaking, as he knew their individual voices. This is an expertise that I always rate very highly in a huntsman.

The last draw found us a fox and we had a lovely hunt over to and into the Quantock Hills. This was particularly enjoyable as only Martin and I were with hounds as the field had all become lost. This was a lovely ride across well-maintained country of steep grasslands, well-supplied with hunt jumps in the wire, and it was possible to go in any direction. When he got into the Quantocks I found that Fizz had lost a shoe and I suspected that it had been off for some time as he was quite sore, so I reluctantly had to make my way back to the meet. There I was pressed to go in to tea by a ruddy-faced horse-dealer who said he knew Ivor Constance, amateur whipper-in to the Waveney Harriers. He had also stayed with the Hawes family at Red House Farm, Stradbroke, which is in our Easton country. During tea I was invited to the Hunt Club Social, that night, for Martin's last day and although it was a long way I went to this and enjoyed a most pleasant party.

Next day I had another reasonable journey to the **Seavington Foxhounds'** meet at Eype, near Bridport on the Dorset coast (Sat 14 Mar 1987). I unboxed at Symondsbury and hacked on with hounds to the meet which was in a farmyard, with a field of about twenty-five mounted and perhaps as many as fifty on foot. The Master told me that all their meets are held at farms and that they were usually "a right good do". Each of the farmers come to each other's meets, thus creating a wonderful atmosphere, with all the farmers following by Land Rover. The hounds were small, rather like large harriers, and looked very fit and hard, having killed fifty-eight and a half brace of foxes so far that season, forty-six brace of them in the open. This very high tally I did not find difficult to believe as they looked like fliers. The setting was lovely – an old-fashioned farmyard, full of characters with such interesting faces of that special weatherbeaten colour only seen in fishermen, shepherds and the like, the whole being like a Wellington boot cocktail party. At the meet one of the foot followers said he remembered me hunting with them four years before when I had been staying on Dartmoor, as did several of the mounted members during the day. Although it was nice to be remembered, I was disappointed about this as, until they said this, I had not realised that I had been with them before. I must have slipped up in my system of recording my visits by shading in the map of hunt countries and had wasted an opportunity to add a fresh pack to my list. Nevertheless, it was a very enjoyable day amongst such lovely people, and plenty of foxes although all went quickly to ground so there were no good runs. I left thinking that I would like to have an exchange meet between them and the Easton Harriers but this never materialised. As a footnote to this day, even before I returned to Suffolk, my friend Maurice Scott amazed me by knowing all about my day with the Seavington – the name of the meet, and so forth. When pressed, he admitted that a friend of his daughter Kathleen (who was at university at Exeter) had been out, and the word was passed back.

From my bedroom in the hotel I could hear what sounded like hounds not far across the fields, but when I enquired in the hotel I was told that it came from the home of a lady who lived with a lot of shaggy-coated dogs. On the Sunday morning, with nothing else to do, I decided to walk over and find out if they were hounds, and to my great surprise found what was virtually a full pack of otterhounds. When otterhunting had been stopped in 1978, this lady had saved these hounds from being put down. She had fenced in her garden and the hounds had the run of the garden and most of the house. She saw me looking at them and I was asked in to the garden where she pointed out each hound, telling me which pack they had come from. I could hardly believe my eyes when she took me indoors, and I saw what havoc seven couple of huge hounds made of the house and furniture after paddling around in a muddy garden. It was a wonderful thing that she had done to preserve these valuable bloodlines because this ancient breed could easily have become extinct without such people as her. Who else would have kept otterhounds without being able to hunt them? Sheila was driving down to join me that day so I continued walking hoping to meet her, amusing myself trying to imagine her face if I had taken her into that house. When I did meet her and jumped into the car, I tried to describe it to her but it was an impossible task. The smell and the mud were simply indescribable.

Lindsay had had to go back to Suffolk as her employers were missing her help and needed her back but luckily Sandy Hewitt, an Easton member, suggested that I might like to take a young friend of hers, Karen Wainer. Karen had never groomed for anyone before but I knew that with Sandy she would have had a good training. Sandy therefore drove her down in my pick-up, following Sheila who was in my car.

Next day I left the hotel at eight-fifteen for a day with the **Duke of Beaufort's**, arriving at Inglestone Common only just in time (Mon 16 Mar 1987). I was unboxing just as Captain Ian Farquhar, Joint-Master and huntsman, hacked up with hounds as the kennels at Badminton were close by. Captain Farquhar was Joint-Master with the eleventh Duke, of course, and I had met him before when he had brought the Bicester and Whaddon Chase hounds down to Dartmoor. The Honorary Secretary approached me with a quizzical look in his eye, probably wondering why I had had the temerity to appear at the meet without approaching him first, so I quickly said, "It's all right. I've made my arrangements with the Master."

"Oh," he said. "That's odd. He has just asked me who you are."

I assured him that I had telephoned Captain Farquhar and he relayed the information. The Master then laughed and apologised for forgetting, and asked me to ride up with him hunting hounds, which is, especially with these hounds, a privilege that all huntsman would give their eye-teeth to be offered. It was to be a woodland day as we were getting very near the end of the season and it was too late to be out in the cream of the country. The hounds were most beautiful, as I had expected them to be, but, to split hairs, I think I was slightly more impressed with the Vale of Aylesbury as they were of the same high quality but slightly more level. It was a great thrill to have been able to follow the Captain into the wood to draw but I desperately wished that I was not riding Manhattan as he was still not completely trustworthy with hounds and I could not risk being amongst them, for to kick a Beaufort hound would be unthinkable.

As they found the first fox, a great shiver of excitement went down my spine – how beautiful those voices sounded as they hunted him round and round on the poor scent. When at last he left covert we had a little run in the open up to the top of some high ground, from the top of which we could see Wales and the Severn estuary. The rest of the day was spent entirely in the large woodlands, with scent getting worse all the time, and only a few hounds were able to speak to the line. There was one hound with a deep voice and it seemed at times to be the only one able to own the line and I think the Master said his name was Berkeley. The going in the woodland rides was very deep and sticky in places, and at four o'clock Manhattan over-reached, damaging his tendon quite badly, so I had to walk him back to the box. Scent had improved a little and hounds were running well as I left. It was heartbreaking to have to ride away from the lovely voices, and to miss precious moments being able to ride up with the Beaufort.

As I hacked back to the meet I had to pass the rest of the field and some of them told me that Captain Farquhar often stayed out until six-thirty at this time of the year. It was interesting to see that the field were mostly in ratcatcher coats, with their horses unplaited thus honouring the old tradition of reverting to ratcatcher after 1 March, a custom forgotten or unobserved in most hunts nowadays. At home with the Easton Harriers, it is only practised by one person, Lady Quilter, whose father was a long standing Master of the old school. Arriving back at the hotel at six-fifteen I found that Manhattan's leg was worse than I thought and was not an easy problem for young Karen to deal with, but she did her best and made a good job poulticing the injured tendon. However, it was obvious that I would not be able to hunt him again so I telephoned home and made arrangements for old Falcon to be prepared. I then telephoned Sandy to ask her if she would bring him down for me the following day, and this she was only too willing to do as she wanted to see how her young protegee was getting on.

I left at nine-thirty next morning for the meet of the **Vine and Craven Foxhounds** and arrived at the Master's house at Valley Farm, Stoke, at eleven-fifteen (Tues 17 Mar 1987). Mr Robin Mackenzie had been Joint-Master of these hounds since 1978 and he made me very welcome which was not surprising as he was the British Field Sports Society public relations man for the South of England. We had a quick drink and then hacked through bridle ways to the actual meet on a little common at Netherton Bottom. It was quite delightful to hack through the grassy lanes and come out upon a scene of hounds held up in the middle of the common and mounted followers dotted all around in little groups. It was like reliving one of Jorrocks' days. The hounds were hunted by his Joint-Master, Mr Crosbie Dawson, with an elderly kennel huntsman who had previously been at the Essex and Suffolk Foxhounds.

From what I saw on this day, there could not have been a better position for an elderly kennel huntsman as there was very little to do. Hounds looked very plain and their performance matched their looks. We trailed around from covert to covert, drawing each one blank which I did not find surprising as the hounds never left the huntsman's horse so they stood little chance of finding a fox. These were the slackest hounds I had ever seen and they made no effort to draw at all. In the whole day, until I left at four-thirty, there was only about five minutes of hunting, when they accidentally crossed the line of a fox, someone else had disturbed. During the day, I had a strange feeling that I had been in one of the coverts before but thought it was my imagination until I overheard someone mention "Bagdon" and "Windmills". I then realised it was a shared covert with the Tedworth and I had been in it the previous week from a different direction. To be fair, after these disparaging remarks, it was I would guess a very bad scenting day and sometimes hounds will not attempt to draw a covert when their instincts tell them there is no fox to be found in it, but I was not convinced that this was the case. As we hacked back to Valley Farm, I felt that the role of PR man was reversed, as I tried to think of something to say about his hounds that was not uncomplimentary. There was one easy compliment to them in that they were one hundred per cent steady to deer and, with deer going in all directions and hounds constantly crossing their lines, there was not one attempt to hunt them, or even feather on the line (ie. acknowledging the presence of a line by waving their tails, properly called sterns). Robin insisted that I came into the house for tea, and a chat, and I thankfully accepted after this long day. I finally arrived back at the hotel at seven-fifteen to find that Sandy had arrived at five-thirty with Falcon.

Next day I arrived at the meet of the **Garth and South Berkshire Foxhounds** one hour too early but eventually was able to meet Matt Maunder, the Senior Master (Wed 18 Mar 1987). The field of eight were very pleasant, and included a visitor from America. The meet was at Bucklebury near Newbury in Berkshire. Bucklebury itself was an open common area but everyone assembled round the pub which was called the Blade Bone – a most unusual name which I have never seen elsewhere. When we moved off, we went up a track and the Field Master insisted that all the field went into the first gate which hounds had gone straight past. Once inside, we were expected to jump little jumps from paddock to paddock until we could at last get to hounds. Falcon, straight from what he thought was the beginning of his summer holidays, was having none of this nonsense and stopped dead at the first two-foot jump, and I had to have a lead to get over it. At the next nothing would persuade or force him to go over it. It was acutely embarassing, especially for me, conspicuous in my green livery, on a beautiful quality hunter, unable to get over a jump suitable for a six year old on a Shetland pony. He did the same thing every time, going on at it and then stopping dead at the last minute, putting me up to his ears several times, until I finally lost my cap and had to get off to retrieve it. This was the last straw so, feeling most humiliated, I led him back to the lane, and then set off to try to find hounds. At the end of the day, while we were boxing up, Mr Maunder came up to me and apologised profusely for allowing me "to get involved in the gymkhana" and said that he wished he had asked me to ride with him.

**Garth & South Berks.** *Coming away from Bramley Green, November 1989. Ian Langrish (Huntsman) with his son Steven, Chris Syckelmoore (amateur whip) and Glyn Powell (whip).*

I found hounds in one of the stickiest, "bottomless" clay woods that could be imagined, and

**The Garth and South Berks:** ***"I'm a hunter, I don't play games!"***

in the bottom of a dip in one of the rides I saw two children dismount as their ponies were embedded in mud up to their stifles. There is nothing worse than a clay bog. I decided that I would not risk laming Falcon (even though I felt like burying his head in it) by jumping into it as the horses were trying to do. I found another way round and could see hounds again, across some meadows, but could not get to them by any route that I was able to take with Falcon, as he would not jump any of the hunt jumps. Whilst I had a certain sympathy for his refusals earlier, with hounds in front of us, this was quite a different matter. I was in a seething temper, which is unusual for me, just to think that I had this old hunt horse brought from Suffolk, with all the attendant costs, and could not get him over a single jump. Hounds luckily turned back into the Bucklebury woods, and I had a little while with them. A lady told me an amusing story of a wonderful old foxhunting character, now deceased, who always said that he imagined Purgatory was like having to hunt in Bucklebury Woods for ever. This just about summed up how awful Bucklebury Woods are, so sticky and deep that I felt guilty for making a horse go through it. My anger would not subside and I went back to my box at two o'clock. The Master was also fed up and decided to go home at that time, and while we were boxing up, he apologised for the day, but said that he had warned me not to come on this day. This was certainly true, but it was a warning that I frequently heard from Masters when trying to arrange these holidays, since they often told me not to come on the day I wished and suggested a better one. Most of the time I had to ignore this, understandable as it was for them to try to offer the best day possible to a visitor, as I would never have been able to hunt as often as I did. In addition, very often what the Masters considered to be a poor meet was for me pure bliss, in terms of country, if not of sport.

I arrived back at four o'clock and took Sheila to tea in Shaftesbury. This, however, did nothing to improve my temper and while writing up my diary that evening at nine-thirty I wrote "I still feel so wild that I could hurl my boot trees through the window", knowing that this was the first time that I have ever been completely thrown out of a hunt. I have never been so angry – with myself and most especially my horse, the brilliant old fellow, Falcon, whom I had previously had nothing to complain about in the six seasons he had been with me.

**Hampshire ("H.H").** *Meet at Andross Manor, Ropley, 7 March 1987. Master Mrs S J Maxse and Huntsman Steve Andrews.*

Photograph kindly donated by Mrs Maxse

Conditions were far from good as I set out next morning for the **"H.H."** or **Hampshire Hunt** (Thurs 19 Mar 1987). I left at nine-thirty and reached the meet at Old Alresford in time, in spite of often thinking that I ought to turn back owing to the amount of snow in Dorset, but luckily there was none at the meet. Mr Gray, the Master, seemed in a bad mood, barely grunted a reply to my greeting, and never spoke again to me or, as far as I could see, to anyone else. Hounds soon found and ran to a park within which stood a large Georgian house, and hounds hunted with a good cry along the top of a ha-ha wall until the fox was headed at the end of the park and turned back, taking a line behind the house. We drove on across open country at a good pace, making use of the plentiful hunt jumps, Fizz jumping everything very well but far too fast. When we jumped into and out of a lane he nearly landed on the second hedge but somehow managed to clear it. I really could not hold him for most of the time but, after Falcon's performance the day before, I forgave him for the pleasure of knowing that he would not stop at any type of jump. Hounds found a second fox in a pit in the middle of a meadow and I had a grand view of him going away. We had another fast run over to Ropley, passing through a large watercress farm, with seemingly acres and acres of watercress growing in shallow terraces dug into a gentle slope, filled with water, and made so each could be drained separately – something I had never seen before. We rode through these fields on wide tracks. At Ropley, there was a serious check and I accepted an offer of sloe gin from a gentleman's flask, followed by a pie from another kind benefactor, and after that I did not attempt to follow hounds again as it was four-fifteen and Fizz had really had enough. I finally arrived home at six-fifteen, driving most of the way through a heavy snow-storm.

On the Friday I had to go back to Suffolk for the End of Season Ball that evening and Sheila and I left the hotel at nine-thirty. We arrived home in Suffolk at one o'clock and I looked round all my horses and a lovely bunch of Hereford bullocks which my friend David Denny had bought for me while I had been away. I dealt with all urgent correspondence, before going to Brome Grange to change into my tails for the End of Season Ball. It was nice to see all my friends again and we had a most enjoyable dinner. Of my own choosing I had been strictly teetotal for the past ten weeks, and decided that this was the occasion on which I would give it up. Needless to say, I drank far too much, became hopelessly tight and cannot remember much of the last part of the evening. I had arranged for Tom Warne, who was most reliable in these matters, to drive me back to Dorset during the night, as I did not want to miss the Saturday's hunting. This he did, with me sleeping in a drunken stupor, all the way back, waking up outside the hotel feeling terrible.

**South Dorset Hunt.** *Meet at Middlemarsh, near Sherborne, 1987. Master Robin Gundry and Kennel Huntsman David Boulter.*
Photograph kindly donated by John Mennell

After forcing myself to eat some breakfast, I set off with Fizz to the meet of the **South Dorset Foxhounds** at Lulworth Park in Dorset, and arrived safely although I was feeling terrible (Sat 21 Mar 1987). I have never had such a bad hangover, and I can still visualise the stars, both red and white, which danced before my eyes as I rode across the park. Mr Gundry, the Master, and Major Dangerfield, the Field Master, welcomed me and introduced me to the kennel huntsman who asked if I knew that Sir Watkin Wynn's hounds were coming down on the Monday. This was good news as I did not have a pack to hunt with on that day and I had not been with them before.

**Sir Watkin Williams-Wynn's.** *The Wynnstay, 1990. Master and Huntsman N M L Ewart and Paul Connolly, terrier man (left).*
Photograph kindly donated by Jim Meads

In the circumstances, it is not surprising that I took little note of the hounds or my companions, and did not fill my diary very fully. Probably I should have decided to give this day a miss, and tried to go with them on another day. Every jolt made by Fizz sent pains shooting through my head, and later the stars decided to amalgamate and became a constant flashing. When I was cantering I could hardly see at all. This really worried me so at two o'clock I returned to the box and after a short nap drove carefully back and went to bed until it was time for dinner.

I took full advantage of the information received and made the necessary arrangements to go with **Sir Watkin Williams-Wynn's** hounds at World's End, Almer, by invitation of the South Dorset (Mon 23 Mar 1987). I left at nine o'clock and arrived at ten-thirty, but did not unbox until the last possible moment as it was raining in torrents. As a result there was no socialising at the meet. The hounds were not at all what I had expected and there were many with very heavy shoulders and some which were decidedly thickset. They were kennelled at Wynnstay, the home of the Williams-Wynn family near Wrexham, the family having been connected with the pack since 1788.

They drew very thoroughly, and were completely steady on deer of which there was an abundance, but could not find for ages. When they still had not found at two-thirty I decided, with most of the rest of the field, to go back to the box as I was soaked. Yet again the dye in my green coat had run. My yellow waistcoat had great green patches on it and my white breeches were green, even under my

Dartmoor apron. The country would have been lovely if we had been able to have a run, as it was of lovely rolling chalk hills, well-served by tracks and hunt jumps. I arrived back at the hotel at four-fifteen and valeted my coat, boots, and so on, as well as I could in the bath, then bathed myself and drove over to Titchfield, near Fareham, to enjoy a lovely dinner with Gordon and Fiona Corner, and Catherine, Gordon's sister. Both Catherine and Gordon were very keen on hunting as their father Charles had been a Master of the Eastern Counties Otterhounds, and had brought them up to understand and to love venerie. I had been offered a bed there to save the journey back to the hotel and this I gratefully accepted.

I awoke at five-thirty and left the Corners' house quietly, telephoning them from the hotel to thank them for their wonderful hospitality. I left again at nine-thirty for the meet of the **Avon Vale** at Costley Farm, Rode, in my second-best coat and boots as the ones I had used the day before were still far too wet (Tues 24 Mar 1987). I arrived in the village of Rode to find that no-one had ever heard of Costley Farm. I was getting desperate thinking that I must have made a tremendous mistake when I saw a Land Rover and trailer coming along, so I flagged it down and asked the driver if he were on his way to the meet. He said he was so I followed him to the farm which turned out to be in the next village and not Rode at all. I introduced myself to Sir John Fuller and he in turn introduced me to his Joint-Master, Mr Warden, who was hunting hounds.

Soon after moving off hounds found. They did not go far before losing the line but the second fox gave us a good hour of slow hunting in a large circle. This was full of interesting houndwork which I was able to see and was made all the more enjoyable as Fizz was going very quietly (for him) which enabled me to concentrate on the hounds. The third fox was found in an old walled garden and I saw him run across a roof, along the top of a wall, and then across a park. This produced another good circular hunt until we came again to the garden, this time to be stopped by an old man who had a sow farrowing in the garden (who had presumably been there when hounds found there) and naturally did not want a pack of foxhounds around her. The Joint-Master, Sir John Fuller, was great fun and this seemed to rub off on all the field who were a very happy bunch and reminded me of the Easton field at home. The girl I picked as a pilot was an artist. She was a great goer and a bundle of fun, and had that "keep with me if you can" look in her eye. Her sense of fun led to some friendly banter and one of her remarks I answered with, "You've left it too late, my girl".

She instantly replied, "It's never too late. It just takes a little longer," then touched her legs to her horse's side and flew away across country. She told me that she knew the Wales family from Norfolk and as they are notoriously bold Point-to-Point riders, it fitted in with her style across country. There were only about twenty out, but the damage done to the grassland was terrible. The frost and snow had all gone and the country rode very deep. This piece of country was to them their worst but, yet again, to a man from Suffolk it was really good and I thoroughly enjoyed my day amongst such fun people, and with a good pack of hounds, well hunted by Mr Warden.

Next day I made my second attempt to hunt with the **Cotswold**, the first time being when I was staying with the Plumbes in Worcestershire and the meet had been cancelled. I left the hotel at eight-twenty and arrived at Elkstone at ten forty-five (Wed 25 Mar 1987). There were about thirty-five out, most of whom were very friendly. The Master, Tim Unwin, was hunting hounds. The first fox went to ground after a quick burst, and the second fox was hunted for fifteen to twenty minutes until it entered a village and hounds were stopped. We then went to draw a big wood, called Tom Tits, I believe, and the amateur whipper-in signalled to me to go with him, and stand at a crossroads in the rides. This offered a good view to watch hounds run round and round us, or back and forth across a large valley, and would have been lovely as all was laid out before us and we only had to sit and watch as if sitting in a cinema. However, although this was expected to happen, it did not.

The fox went away from the other end of the covert and, what was worse, we did not hear them owing to the high wind. When the whip realised what had happened he went to find them and I had an enjoyable ride across country following him. They had killed their fox by the time we caught up, and they hacked back to draw the same big covert. The field were telling me that this was their worst meet, but again, to me, it was delightful, with ancient woodland and most attractive valleys. I told them what I have so often told others in the same situation, namely, that it ought to be compulsory for everyone to have one season in a plough country like Suffolk to make them appreciate their own country, on the same principle as a visit to a hospital makes you stop moaning and groaning about your own little aches and pains.

The last memory of this day was of Tim Unwin standing in a valley bottom, a huge covert stretching away up the steep hillside above him, blowing for the tail hounds to come out of the covert, as hounds filtered down through the trees making their way to him. Most of the seventeen and a half couples stood around him, as motionless as statues gazing at him, but not too close to him so they were showing themselves off to perfection. Each and every hound was perfect, all exactly the same height and conformation, and looked as if they had all been made from the same mould. They stood all around him, staring up into his eyes, their heads only moving to watch his hand as he pulled out his horn to blow. How I wish I could draw, or that someone had taken a photograph, as I would have said it was impossible to have such perfection but there it was before my eyes, and I just sat and stared at them. These hounds were and still are the smartest and most level pack I have ever seen, and it makes goose pimples rise on my skin just to write about them. I had had the best ride I had ever had on Fizz, jumping everything easily without rushing and as I left at four o'clock to drive home, I was feeling as if I could fly, as exhilarated as if I had taken some exotic drug.

There were no packs hunting on the Thursday or Friday that I had not already hunted with, and as Fizz certainly needed a rest, I went back to Suffolk, calling at Hampton Court to see how Blossom was getting on in her royal stables. She looked very well and was due to foal on 1 May. Friday was the Kelsale Harriers' Hunt Ball. These were a fictitious pack of hounds which enjoyed many good hunts under the Mastership of Captain Morgan, *alias* Dougie Ruth, with the members always holding a glass in one hand. The Ball is equally fictitious in that it is not a Ball at all but instead a great get-together in a pub for a proper "session". While we were at the "Ball" the wind was getting to a very serious pitch and we were all worried about the tentage for the Easton Point-to-Point the following day. On Saturday morning we thought we would probably have to cancel the meeting as the marquees were all smashed down, but the marquee people arrived with fresh poles to replace the ones which had broken in the gale. The men did a great job and all was ready and we were able to hold the meeting. Three members, Brian Sawyer, Kevin Lee and Harry Spencer, completed the Members' Race which is an unheard of feat for the Easton Harriers, setting a precedent which has yet to be followed.

On Monday I drove back to Milton Lodge again, this time with the company of Sheila and Bridget, as I had planned to go with the **Cotswold Vale Farmers'** the following day (Tues 31 Mar 1987). The meet was at Edge, near Stroud, and I left the hotel at nine-fifteen, arriving at eleven-forty, only just in time to enjoy the hospitality from the boot of Mr and Mrs Parrot's car. I would have been in good time, but unbeknown to me the meet had been changed and it was only by luck that I found out. A horse-box had broken down and when I stopped to ask if I could help they gave me the new directions. The meet was held on the edge of a quarry and I introduced myself to Mr Whitehouse and Mr Warner, the Joint Masters, and the amateur huntsman, Philip Whitehouse, brother of the Master. The field of about fifteen were all friendly and there was a particularly amusing foot-follower, a very tall man wearing a white cap as if he were a slaughterman, who kept everybody laughing.

All day hounds were running through the beech trees which clothed the steep sides of the valleys and we either rode along above them or below them. Both were equally enjoyable and we were always able to stay with hounds. The hunts tended to be mostly short runs to ground and although it was a busy day, with hounds always running, there were no long runs. Miss Stephens, a Joint-Master of the Cotswold with Tim Unwin, rode alongside me and said that she hoped I would go with them again next year, and Mr Warren reminded me that we had met before when out with the Cotswold.

Nick Valentine, the kennel huntsman, seemed to be enormously popular with the members, and was whipping-in on foot. I was greatly surprised to see that he was accompanied by his Boxer dog. He was on foot as they had run out of horses but, in fact, some members told me that he preferred to be on foot and they often came across his horse tied to a tree while he was running with hounds. When I got into conversation with him, he told me that he had a pack of French cross bassets which he hunted on Sundays. I naturally said that I wished that I had known this sooner as I would have liked to have gone out with them. All in all he was a most unusual hunt servant.

At one point during the day, we were on high ground and we could see the support towers of the Severn Bridge. Mr and Mrs Parrot insisted that I went to their home, Hill Farm, St Leonards, for tea before going home and as there was not much happening I said that the thought of tea seemed tempting. The Master, overhearing, said that if I was stopping then they would not carry on. We started our tea, surprised that no-one else came to join us, and we had enjoyed our meat pie, followed by an excellent trifle, when Nick Valentine came in with a brush for me. He said that as soon as we had gone they had had a good little hunt which the rest of the field had enjoyed. I accepted the brush with embarrassment as it is improper to receive a brush from a fox killed when you are not with hounds.

During the evening I met a couple who were on a riding holiday. The husband was one of the bodyguards of the Prime Minister, Mrs Thatcher, and he said that he was able to snatch a holiday as she was in Russia. There was another guest, Mr Smythe, who was the U.K. bacon buyer for Harris's and he thought he knew me, but he had mistaken me for my brother and we both commiserated with each other about the poor food at this hotel. He promised to buy me dinner at the Market Place Restaurant in Framlingham on his next visit to Suffolk but this he failed to do, and I have never seen him again.

**Cotswold Vale Farmers':** ***"Shanks' pony is best"***

As I had not taken Falcon any more after his disastrous day with the Garth and South Berks, I asked Karen if she would like to have a day on him when I went with the **Royal Artillery Foxhounds**, and she eagerly accepted (Wed 1 Apr 1987). It was pouring with rain as we left at nine-fifteen for Ivy Cottage, Netheravon, in Wiltshire. When we reached Netheravon I saw a Land Rover and trailer turn into a military compound so I followed, putting up my hand to the soldiers who were guarding the gate. I was expecting to be stopped but they let us through. The meet was in the small yard of a cottage on the edge of the compound and was given by Major and Mrs Thatcher, who were ex-Masters. The man who had turned in before us turned out to be the Field Master. He quickly excused himself and rode off to fetch hounds as Colonel Jago, the Master, who normally hunted hounds, could not be present. The kennel huntsman, young Greg Stokes, was a friend of my blacksmith, Graham Goldsmith, and they had been in the Army together.

We moved off through the village and the field stood on a hilltop to watch the kennel huntsman draw a low wood along the River Avon. He drew all along the valley blank, then crossed the main road and drew a little spinney on Salisbury Plain. Karen and I went on point which was just what we needed to do as we were getting cold and wet. Hounds found in the third spinney and we had a lovely gallop over sound turf, but with the constant danger of falling into the holes which had been caused by shells during many years of artillery practice. Hounds lost this line in a farmyard but soon found another which gave us another good gallop over the Plain until the fox crept under the wire netting perimeter fence of a Militarily Prohibited Zone. Greg Stokes was hunting hounds very well, always drawing upwind and thoroughly. Hounds swung themselves round at checks, casting eagerly, rather like harriers, and this was a wonderful area for keeping in close touch with hounds and being able to watch them closely. The shell holes were quite a problem and we had quite a few serious blunders as some of the older ones were grown over by gorse and what looked like good sound turf for galloping could be riddled with hidden holes. Karen only had a light jacket on and was soaked to the skin in the first half-hour but even when we were passing the horse-boxes she would not stop. The field were very keen but only two of them understood about hunting at all.

We went home at four-fifteen, thinking what an enjoyable day we had had, even in the terribly wet conditions. The Field Master had kept everyone busy by sending each in turn to be on point, thus keeping everyone happy and feeling that they had helped. There was one whipper-in who was a young officer and another who was an older man, and these two, and the kennel huntsman, wore green coats, while the other officials wore red coats. Looking up in Baily's to see if there was a reason for this, I noted that they used to be a harrier pack before 1946, and are now the only remaining recognised regimental pack of foxhounds. We arrived home surprisingly tired. I could not think why, but went to bed at nine-fifteen and did not get up until eight forty-five the next morning.

There was no hunting on the Thursday so I went for a long walk to Silton church to see if I could find any evidence of the Berkeley ownership which would be of interest to my daughter Bridget who was still doing her Ph.D. thesis on this family, but I was disappointed to find nothing of interest (Thurs 2 Apr 1987). In the afternoon, I wrote over twenty thank-you letters to Masters with whom I had been, and in the evening I met Mr John Robbings who was also having dinner in the hotel. He farmed in the South and West Wiltshire country and runs their Two Hundred Club. His groom was the sister of a man who had been in collision with one of the Easton members, Geoffrey Bowden, while in Suffolk. His car had hit Geoffrey's horse in such a way, that it scooped them up, horse and rider, up the bonnet, over the roof, and dropped him off the back. Mr Robbings told me that the man was very upset as Geoffrey was suing him for the loss of taste and smell which had resulted from the accident, and asked if I could intervene but I told him that I would prefer not to get involved in the dispute. It was an extraordinary coincidence that we happened to meet in this hotel's dining-room.

Later in the evening Nick Valentine telephoned to say he had managed to arrange a meet of his basset hounds on the farm of Mr Warren who was Master of the Cotswold Vale Farmers'. I was thrilled about this as not only was it another pack to add to my experience, but also it meant that I would be able to go out on the Friday. During the day I took Karen to Longleat House and, from memory, I think we also went to see the White Horse at Uffington in Berkshire. I arrived at the Cotswold Vale kennels at four o'clock which allowed me to have a good look at the foxhounds as well as at the **Bradley Vale Bassets** which were cross-bred English bassets and the rough coated French basset "venderei" (Fri 3 Apr 1987). The French coats were obviously dominant as most of these bassets were broken-coated. There were lurcher dogs tied up all over the place and some Old English game chicks hatching in an incubator. I had a cup of tea in Nick's caravan before we went to the meet at Southwick Farm, Tewkesbury, and was not a bit surprised to see that he had a box of game chicks in the caravan to keep warm. There was an enormous amount of flesh in the van which Nick unloaded, then washed it out, and placed rubber mats in it for the hounds to stand on. Nine and a half couple were loaded up with no trouble, the hounds jumping in willingly, including one and a half couple which were unentered, together with three lurchers. The Boxer dog rode in the front with us.

It was a joy to watch him draw as he could turn the bassets back and forth across the field with only his voice and the whole pack would do "about turns" like soldiers with only one shout from Nick. This was particularly impressive, as of all hounds, bassets are the most independent. The lurchers completely spoiled any chance of classic hare-hunting. On one occasion they coursed a hare into a spinney and put a fox out right at the feet of Mr Warren and myself as we stood at the covertside. We stayed out until dark and I was sure that if I could have seen these hounds without their long-legged friends, I would have rated them quite highly. Mr Warren showed me round his farm buildings before we went back to the kennels with the bassets and I finally got back to the hotel at eleven o'clock.

I had saved the **Mid Devon Foxhounds** for the last day as they hunted later than any other pack (Sat 4 Apr 1987) and I offered Karen another day on Falcon, while I stayed with Fizz. We left the hotel at seven-thirty after finding my sandwiches on a plate on top of the piano which amused me as I had never had my hunting sandwiches served on a plate before. These had been left like that because the owners had made them the previous evening before going to their daughter's eighteenth birthday party. Apart from getting in a muddle in the middle of Exeter, we arrived just in time. The meet at Throwleigh was a little over ten miles from Hexworthy which had been my base for a holiday in March 1983 but I had been unable to go with them then, for some reason which I have failed to note. The village lay at the edge of Dartmoor and we unboxed on the moor, and hacked in to the village. I noticed that the Masters and hunt servants

**Mid Devon.** *Huntsman Bernard Parker with hounds, meet and date unknown.*

Photograph loaned and taken by Miss Dianne Parr

were wearing red waterproof coats and white waterproof breeches over their normal ones. The coat and breeches were quite neatly made and at a distance they looked like normal hunting clothes. They must have been a godsend as the bogs on the moor and the frequent rain could make valetting a nightmare. They cost about £25 I was told which I thought reasonable. Mr Vickers, the Master, greeted me and invited me to ride up with him. Although he did not hunt hounds, this was a privilege because he went where he liked, and the field had to stay with the Field Master. As we moved off, he sent the field one way and he and I went another, and he turned to me, laughed and said, "That's got the rabble out of the way".

The first three foxes did not go far before going to ground, but the fourth gave us a very sharp hunt across the moor with us dodging in and out of rocks and bogs and jumping walls, but somehow I became separated from the Master and found myself behind the Field Master. He spoke in a broad Devonshire accent, and I could understand hardly a word of what he said. There were only four left with him, which did not include Karen, and the rest I could see in the distance, threading their way through a gate. I saw him go and look over a wall, then come back and gallop at it unusually fast. Fizz was bouncing on the spot and when I let him go at it, he went really fast. When I was in mid-air I saw to my horror a strand of wire on posts about three feet beyond the wall. This wire was the reason he had gone at it so fast, and was put there to stop cattle rubbing on the walls. Fizz cleared it alright, but it tipped up the other two which left only him and I with hounds. What a lovely ride we had across the open moor with hounds in full cry until they ran into a dense Forestry Commission area. It took some time to get hounds out of this forestry and then we went back to draw near the meet. As it was four o'clock, I decided that I had had enough. We boxed up and finally got back to the hotel at six-twenty.

On Sunday morning we left at nine o'clock with the caravan on the back, and I dropped off Karen in Ipswich at one forty-five after a non-stop drive. Both horses were sound but Fizz showed signs of all his hard work and there were plenty of work scars and minor cuts. This had been the longest and most productive of my hunting holidays as I had hunted with seventeen foxhound packs, of which fifteen were new ones as I had been with the South and West Wiltshire and the Seavington before, and one basset. My total was now two hundred and one different packs. This holiday was also the most expensive at £300 per week for the hotel for me, the board for Karen and, in addition, the extra journeys to and from Suffolk. The facilities were good, and the stables very good, but it was just a pity that the food was not more exciting.

**West Norfolk Foxhounds.** *The late Major Robert Hoare, Master and Huntsman of the West Norfolk, with the gamekeeper rowing him over to draw the island at Wood Rising, with hounds swimming in the background.*

Photograph kindly loaned by Paul Rackham

# MAP 14

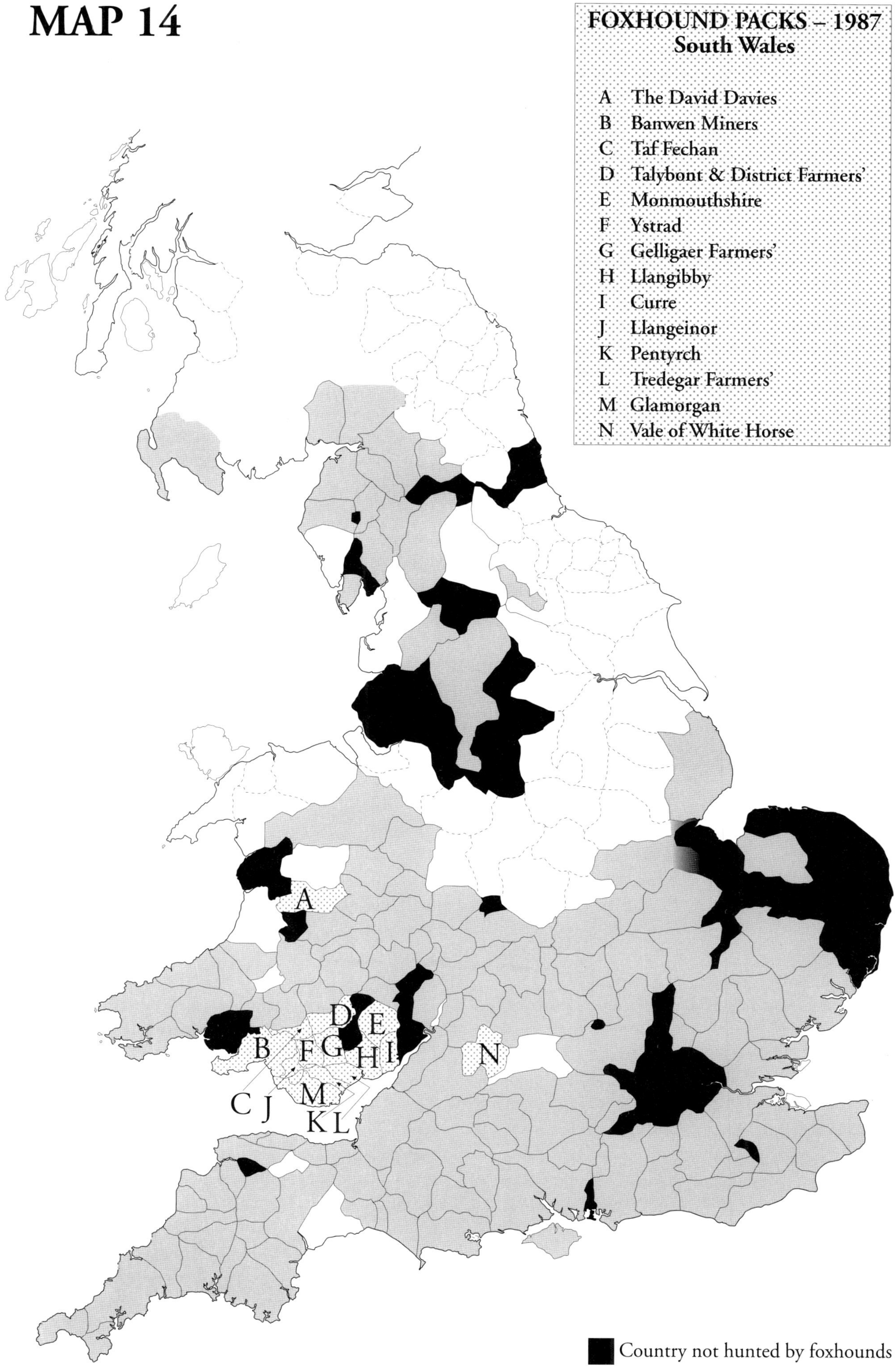
FOXHOUND PACKS – 1987
South Wales
A The David Davies
B Banwen Miners
C Taf Fechan
D Talybont & District Farmers'
E Monmouthshire
F Ystrad
G Gelligaer Farmers'
H Llangibby
I Curre
J Llangeinor
K Pentyrch
L Tredegar Farmers'
M Glamorgan
N Vale of White Horse
A
D
E
B
F
G
H
I
N
M
C
J
K
L
Country not hunted by foxhounds

# Chapter 16

## South Wales

At the beginning of the next season I made plans to go to Scotland, arranging to stay with the Plumbes for the first two weeks of September, before hunting started with the Easton. We got up the hunters earlier than usual and everything was ready, but then the weather spoiled our plans and for the second time I had to postpone "doing" Scotland. The harvest had been so wet in Scotland that hardly any corn was cut and consequently the packs that usually started early were unable to start hunting until late September.

I was so disappointed and gloomy that Sheila became fed up with me and said, "Surely you can find someone to hunt with."

I started to give it some serious thought and wondered about south Wales. I had a contact there in Mark Powell. He had applied for the position of kennel huntsman at the Easton and had been selected down to the final two but I had finally given the job to David Horsefield. I knew he was not too disappointed in losing this job as he went back to Wales to whip in to his father at the Monmouthshire Foxhounds, a country he really preferred. I telephoned him and was delighted to find that all the local packs were hunting but what was even better was that he said that I could put up my horses at the kennels and that Karen would be able to lodge with him and his wife. What a stroke of luck to find stabling and groom's lodgings all on one telephone call. Because of this I was able to make a lightning change of plans and go to Wales instead of Scotland. I asked Mark to book me in at the nearest comfortable pub and finally decided to go on 4 September. There was one small problem as I had for over twenty-five years taken Kenny Warne, my stockman, to Barnet Fair and I had forgotten the date. I resolved the problem by asking an old friend of his to take him.

Since she had come to my rescue in Dorset, Karen Wainer had become my regular groom and we left at five o'clock in the morning with a new horse Dolly, my old favourite Demelza and a hunter called Speedy for Karen which had been sent to us for improvement. Sheila had packed us up flasks of coffee and homemade soup and plenty of sandwiches which Karen fed to me as I drove non-stop. We arrived at the Monmouthshire kennels at Llanvihangel Gobion, near Abergavenny, by twelve-thirty having made much better time than I had expected. There was a little hiccup as I had forgotten to tell Mark that I was bringing the third horse. This was quickly sorted out and a box littered down with straw, before we accepted an invitation to share lunch with Mark and his wife who was appropriately called Diana. The kennels were most impressive, having been built in 1920, all in a glazed red brick, with lovely large boxes for fifteen horses. The kennels were approached by a very narrow lane, so narrow that the hedges knocked back both wing mirrors on the lorry. After going back and forth for several days one was eventually broken, which fortunately did not seem to bring any bad luck. Mark Powell's father, Glynn, had been a farmer, then a professional huntsman for several seasons with various packs, and then had returned as Master to the Monmouthshire, this being his first season. Mark got busy on the telephone arranging for me to hunt with the Talybont in the morning. I could have gone with the Monmouthshire but as they were to hunt on Monday, I thought it better to save them for a Monday when no other packs would be out. Mark got all the details of times, meet and directions to the Talybont kennels, and then I telephoned the Joint-Master, Mrs Pat Harley, to ask official permission. Mark then drove me round to show me some of the country, before I drove the lorry to the Clytha Arms where he had booked me a room. I unpacked and spent an hour or so relaxing before dinner. I was delighted with this small hotel as it was very comfortable and the owners were very pleasant people, full of fun and very obliging. In the course of the holiday Mark always arranged the directions and meets for me as I found the Welsh names and the Welsh dialect quite unintelligible over the telephone.

An early start was needed the next morning as the **Talybont Foxhounds'** meet was at seven o'clock (Sat 5 Sept 1987). I asked Karen to come with me and we left the kennels at six o'clock. As this would be cubhunting there was no need to plait which made the early start much easier for Karen. Stewart, the terrierman to the Monmouthshire, said he would meet us outside the Neville Hall Hospital on the A40, and show us the way to the meet at Pencelli, near Talybont-on-Usk. This kind offer almost proved a disaster as the hospital was in two parts, and I was waiting at one part while he was at the other. Luckily he realised what had happened and came to check. The heavy rain stopped as we unboxed and I met Mrs Harley who introduced me to the amateur huntsman, David Poulton. Both were wearing the green livery of the Talybont. There were very few out, just one man and two girls apart from us.

While hounds were drawing a dingle we were sitting outside an isolated cottage at the end of a track, when a tremendous holloa came out of the cottage. This really made us jump, nearly causing us to fall off our horses. The holloa came from a wonderful old character aged eighty-four who kept asking for the Secretary and insisted that he took ten pounds. This character had subscribed to hounds for over seventy years. The terrifying holloa had really upset Speedy and he gave Karen a really hard time, rearing up to such a pitch that he was almost coming over backwards. Luckily, after a few minutes, a fox was found and we had to go up the mountainside. It was very, very steep and a long way, with the horses slipping and scrabbling and really struggling at times in the steepest places. When we reached the top, Demelza's sides were heaving and Speedy showed no signs of wanting to rear. We had some good little hunts of twenty minutes or so which tended to be from one piece of forestry to the next. It was quite windy on the top of the mountain and this, with alternate heavy showers and sunshine, did not make scenting conditions any better.

I decided that I ought to stop at ten-thirty as this was the first time I had been on a horse since the end of the previous season, and I was afraid of being stiff, especially with the hills. I could just see the gate through which we had left the road, at the bottom of the mountain so decided to go back down the hill the way we had come up. This sounds easy and looked easy, but twice we got down to the wrong place and had to come up again. It was so steep it seemed almost vertical at times, and Karen was so frightened that she slid off and led her horse. After the second mistake, we saw hounds and rejoined them, and they drew towards the road. If only we had stopped with them they would have taken us to our boxes which would have been much more sensible than those two desperate scrambles. It had taken about twenty to twenty-five minutes to climb up the almost vertical hillside with us often climbing up beside the horses, hanging on to the breastplate.

We arrived back at the kennels at twelve-thirty and I returned to the Clytha Arms for a lunch of Gamekeeper's Pie and then went to sleep, not waking up until four-thirty. I started to read but fell asleep again, not waking up until seven o'clock. I telephoned Mark and Diana Powell to ask them to join me for dinner as they had been so exceptionally kind and helpful, telephoning an awful lot of hunts for me and stabling the horses. They had refused all offers of remuneration for either the horse boxes or the telephoning. I cannot remember what Mark ate but Diana and I had rack of lamb which was served in very generous portions with perfectly cooked vegetables, ending with a Pavlova topped with "wickedly thick cream" (as described in the menu). The food was superb and what with enjoying the dinner so much, and talking hunting (which we could do because Diana was as interested as her husband) we were very surprised when we looked at our watches to find that it was twelve-thirty and we were still sitting at the dinner table.

I had particularly looked forward to seeing the **Curre Foxhounds**, as much had been written about them and they were well-known for their lemon-and-white colour, so I was delighted to be able to join them at Itton at seven o'clock (Mon 7 Sept 1987). They had been bred by the famous hound-breeder Sir Edward Curre. The meet was at the bottom of Church Lane, just below the kennels where Bob Collins, in his first season as huntsman, stood with these famous hounds and two whippers-in, all three very smart and correct in every article. The Master, Mr Kathrens, said he was sorry that his Joint-Master, Mr David Broome the famous showjumper, was not out, but he made us very welcome. Apart from Karen and myself, there was only one other girl out in the field. She was the niece of Angela Miles, who is Honorary Secretary of the Suffolk Foxhounds.

Hounds found at once and rattled a fox round and out into the open and then ran to Chepstow Park which was a large piece of forestry. They ran with a great cry and pushed him round and round this large forestry until he went to ground. From a high point in Chepstow Park we could see the Severn Bridge and the Bristol Channel, with the Mendip Hills behind. The country was the neatest imaginable with everything in perfect order, beautifully smooth grass and large paddocks, enclosed by neat trimmed hedges, all exactly of the same height, but trimmed with a "bush-wacker" which meant that they were wide and stiff at the top and I would not fancy having to jump them, though I was told that they do during the season proper. This immaculate countryside stretched as far as the eye could see in every direction. Hounds were very smart, level and went with great drive, and good cry and very fast. It was about ten-thirty and scent had disappeared when the Master ordered "Home" to be blown. Bob Collins invited me to the kennels for coffee and a look around but, although I would have dearly liked to have seen the kennels, I declined as I was hunting again in the evening with the Monmouthshire at five o'clock.

I arrived back at the Clytha Arms at twelve-thirty, had a quick half of bitter, then upstairs for a bath before going downstairs to my host, David Hill, who said, "I know exactly what you need," and produced scrambled egg with smoked salmon for a late breakfast/lunch. After lunch I read the chapter from "All Thanks to His Grace" about Captain Bernard. David had a delightful little daughter called Alex aged seven or eight, and as she had said she would like to come hunting, I took her with me that evening. I tacked up her pony and loaded it, then went to the kennels for my own horse, then called back at the hotel for Alex on the way to the meet, thus allowing her enough time to get home from school. We left the Clytha Arms at four o'clock and followed Mark's father Glynn, the Master and huntsman, on to the meet at Pant Farm, Onen. One of Glynn's predecessors in the Mastership of the **Monmouthshire** during the 1950s was the legendary Colonel Harry Llewellyn of showjumping fame, and Glynn told me that in its heyday during his Mastership, his fellow showjumpers would come down to liven up their horses. The Monmouthshire country at that time was completely wire-free and every fence was jumpable and these visitors would ride fearlessly across country, jumping around fifty big natural fences (i.e.hedges) in a day.

**Monmouthshire.** *1987. Mark Powell takes hounds towards the Skirrid Mountain from Llanvapley.*
Photograph kindly loaned by Mrs Helen Manns

There were a good few foot-followers at the meet and the Master told them to get themselves around the covert. The first was blank but the second held a leash of cubs and an old fox which was soon gone. Scent was obviously very poor but somehow hounds kept chivvying around and managed to catch one cub above ground which was obviously very good for the young hounds out. They drew on into several more little coverts but could do little as scent was very poor. Mark was whipping in on a very gassy little thoroughbred-cross-Welsh Cob and was, I thought, a little over-enthusiastic in his job. At one point he gave a lift to his wife who had climbed up to a steep place. She was out of breath, so Mark put her up behind him and rode in Gretna Green style. This was quite a sight, and a feat of horsemanship on the hot little cob until he dropped her off near hounds.

Glynn had a very calm and relaxed manner with his hounds which were not a very level-looking pack, with a lot of bad curly sterns (ie. tails). However, "handsome is as handsome does" and although they may not have looked perfect, they persevered on this poor scent and I got the impression that they would have been very good if scent had been better. The first part of the

**The Monmouthshire:** ***"Gretna Green"***

evening was sunny and very warm and as Karen and I sat on point we could see the three cubs passing us in the covert below, at least fifteen times, and we got so that we could tell them apart from their colouring. Glynn and Mark were disappointed that I had seen their hounds on such a bad scent but I was well-pleased with the evening's sport and when he blew for home in the dark we hacked back to the boxes under a beautiful yellow moon, so yellow in fact that Karen and I both remarked simultaneously that neither of us had ever seen a moon that colour before. This had been my first ride on the new hunter, Dolly, and I was not too disappointed in her, but as a five-year-old she seemed rather green after my trusty veterans. Alex had also enjoyed her evening on her little pony.

Back at the kennels Mark helped me work out a route for the next morning when I went with the **Pentyrch Foxhounds** (Tues 8 Sept 1987). On the basis that the more work Speedy had the sooner he would calm down, I again suggested that Karen brought him. I left the hotel and drove my lorry to pick up Karen, Speedy and Demelza, and left the kennels at five-fifteen, arriving at the meet at the Black Cock, Tongwynlais, at six-fifteen. We had a cup of soup and then I fell asleep in the cab. Karen woke me to say that a lorry had arrived and I was leisurely putting on my collar and stock when suddenly hounds went away in full cry. We quickly got out our horses, who were naturally very excited having heard hounds screaming away, and soon managed to catch up with them. We were then told what had happened. The huntsman, Garth Morgan, had let hounds off the back of the lorry so that he could get his horse from the front compartment and, while he was in the lorry, they hit a line off at the edge of the car-park and were gone, across the valley and up the far mountainside. Mrs Basset, the Joint-Master, apologised for this rather unconventional start. The only other mounted follower was a man on a three-year-old cob which he had just broken and was still very green, but somehow he managed to be able to crack his whip on it, and he helped whip-in all day. The first half-hour provided most of the sport and the scent faded gradually thereafter. At one point, Garth Morgan drew a covert below us, right next to the M4 motorway which I found quite staggering as I would not have dared to take my hounds within two miles of a motorway. Mrs Morgan was whipping-in and as they left this covert she said to me, "Did you see the fox?"

"No," I answered.

"Oh," she said, "he crossed the motorway and I had to stop hounds."

I could not believe the calmness of it all – a pack of hounds close behind their fox which crossed a motorway, and stopping hounds on the edge, seemed just commonplace.

We were on the way back to the meet when a man shouted that there were three cubs in an old quarry. We hacked across and Garth put hounds into the quarry. We stayed on the top, and thoroughly enjoyed our excellent view of both hounds and the three cubs. They were having a rare game of hide-and-seek below us, with the cubs clearly in control of the situation. Scent was by now completely gone. The hounds were rather overweight and unfit, and rather shy, or horse-shy at least but, to be fair, it was one of their first mornings out. The hounds were small with very thick and tight coats which Mark later explained was the real old-fashioned Welsh type. When I returned to the kennels, and we had unloaded the horses, I walked down to the slaughterhouse which was well away from the actual kennels. Old-fashioned kennels were always made like this so that visitors to the hounds would not be offended by the gruesome sight of the carcases. Mark and Stewart (the terrierman) were very busy skinning a pile of carcases, and they told me that they had so much flesh that they threw away up to ninety barrels each week. I arrived back at the Clytha Arms at twelve o'clock and enjoyed a refreshing ham salad before having a soak in the bath.

In the afternoon Mark had arranged for me to go to the **Llangibby** meet at five o'clock. We unboxed Dolly and Speedy at the kennels at Llangybi (near Usk) and hacked up to the meet with hounds. I think the actual meet was at "Penny Park" but am not sure. The sun was still quite hot as we left the kennels but soon cooled down and it become quite cool and damp. I had told Karen to come out again on Speedy for the second time in the day as he still needed to calm down and to stop the dreadful rearing. I met the Senior Master, Mr Lewis, who was very old and had had a stroke. He was riding an old black horse that he had bought from David Broome over twenty years before. Naturally out of respect I kept behind him but quite soon hounds had disappeared from our view as he was going so slowly. He then told us to go on, and pointed out a hunt jump in the corner of a field telling us to go that way. We made a full circle trying to find hounds, with plenty of jumping before we actually came up with them. I had begun to get worried in case we would not find them again. In fact, there was little real chance of not finding hounds as all that was necessary was to stop and listen as the huntsman and both whippers-in were the noisiest trio I had ever heard. There was an elderly lady out who was very old-fashioned and immaculately dressed and I was told that she owned a large part of the Llangibby country and held all boxes and trailers in scorn, hacking to every meet throughout the season. The Master's son told me that he knew David Turner, a well-known Point-to-Point rider in Suffolk, and that he had ridden against him, both under

Rules and in Point-to-Points. At one time when the huntsman was blowing for hounds, a farmer asked if we had met at the kennels and hacked up. "No," I replied, and explained where we had unboxed. "Well, that is the kennels," he replied.

"It can't be because the hounds were in a lorry."

Various people heard this conversation and there was much laughter when the terrierman said, "Oh, he often brings hounds from the kennels to the stables in a lorry."

The explanation was that after drawing the selected hounds, the huntsman had popped them into the lorry to keep them from running around while he was tacking up his horse.

Mark Powell and Stewart had driven in front of us to the meet and were following on foot in this heavenly country of mile after mile of rolling grass, all well "panelled" with hunt jumps. Hounds were mostly English with one Dumfriesshire bitch. The huntsman and both whippers-in were very smart and the whole setup was of a very high standard. It had been a truly lovely evening. We hacked back to the kennels in the dusk for a second night running under the lovely moon still yellow, and boxed up at nine o'clock, arriving back at around ten-thirty. I had dinner with my boots still on and tackled the venison casserole with a vengeance. After dinner I got into conversation with John "the Pony" Hendy and heard some great tales about his time on the Beaufort estate. I pulled off my boots at eleven-forty-five and fell into bed very tired but deliriously happy.

I awoke early and as I was dressing I hoped that this day, with the **Gelligaer Farmers'**, would be as good as the previous one (Wed 9 Sept 1987). I picked up Karen and the two horses at four fifteen and drove to Merthyr Tydfil and turned off to the Tunnel Tavern, and thus up the mountain to the meet at a cattle grid near Pencuarra. In giving me the directions, Mark had remarked casually that the road crumbled away a little at the edges, which was the understatement of the century. The route (for one could not call it a road) was like driving a horse-box on the switch-back at a fair. The track was narrow, with sharp bends and sheer drops off the side, and the ruts were so deep that I was seriously worried about grounding the lorry. Karen became extremely scared and cringed away from the door, almost sitting on the gearstick, because she did not dare look down. On the way home I could understand why she was so frightened because looking down from the window there was no road, only the drop.

**Gelligaer Farmers Hunt.** *Huntsman Gary Barber with hounds at New Tredegar, 1988.*

Photograph kindly supplied by Mr David Burles MFH

The meet was at the top of a mountain and it was very bleak, with views for many miles in every direction. Before we could unbox, hounds came up with their huntsman and Miss Esher, the Joint-Master, made us welcome and advised me earnestly not to try to follow her huntsman, saying that no-one could go where he went. She went on to explain that she had brought some of the hounds with her from Kent where she had been a Master, as the previous Master, David Poulton, had taken most of the pure Welsh hounds with him when he had left to go to the Talybont. I later met Miss Esher twice more, in Scotland, with the Fife Foxhounds and the Grampian. Mr Davis, the Senior Joint-Master, arrived by car and explained that he could not have come mounted because of pressure of business. After moving off, we were joined by the remaining Master who had hacked across country from his home in the next valley, and he introduced himself to me as Mr "R" Jones.

The huntsman sat with his hounds on this mountain top, his hounds staring at him as if spellbound. His thoroughbred horse looked as hard as nails and had no underline at all, its belly going straight up from the girth to the back legs, just like a fit racing greyhound. At times, there would be as many as three hounds standing up on their back legs on each side of his horse, while he caressed their heads without speaking. This was most striking as a lot of horses would not let hounds rest their feet against their sides. It was a scene vividly held in my memory and it had a kind of eerie, almost ghostly, feel about it. Sure enough, he proved to be uncanny in his ability to ride a horse in steep places. It was terrifying to see the routes he took, jumping down places one would hardly tackle on one's own feet, and I was told that when shepherding he occasionally left his horse to go on foot, and his horse would stand for hours in the same spot, too terrified to move without him. He was quite

**Gelligaer Farmers':** ***"Mutual admiration"***

unbelievable and unforgettable in where he rode and what he did. He moved off by popping over a sheep-hurdle which was set in a very steep hillside and when he had drawn that part blank, he popped over it again coming uphill. This slope must have been at least one-in-five or six. This amazed us, but was nothing compared with what happened later when he rode up and down seemingly vertical slopes, with us on the top looking down. However a horse could keep its feet in such places I shall never know, and it must be one in several thousand horses to be able to do that.

Hounds hunted along the mountainside, usually out of sight below us, as it was so steep that visibility was made very difficult. As the cry was good we were able to keep in touch. We were seriously warned to watch out for subsidence cracks on the mountain top caused by the mines in the hillside below us. At one point we were looking down on the village of Aberfan, scene of the tragic landslip in 1966 which demolished a school. The cracks were quite wide in places and as they were often covered with bracken it made riding very dangerous. The situation was made much worse by the driving rain which on the mountain top was blown with such force that we could hardly see at all. The Master was a brilliant pilot all day and had us exactly in the right place at the right time. His cob was so sure-footed that on steep places he could just put his feet from one foothold to the next like a human being, while our horses were slipping and crashing around behind him. He told me that when he was shepherding on it, he could stoop down and pick up a sick sheep and put it across the pommel of his saddle and carry it home. This little cob stood at about thirteen-two and was very striking. We saw the fox cross the top of the mountain and hounds hunted the line over and down into a little den which was full of dense bracken. Hounds checked and were casting themselves around when the huntsman came up and cast them deep into the bracken and they fresh-found the fox again. Two hounds grabbed at him and pulled hair out of his coat, but he got away and eventually went to ground in some rocks.

We were very wet and at seven-thirty decided to go home as we were in sight of the horse-boxes. We had been the only field mounted, other than the Master and the amateur whip. The drive back down the mountain was even more terrifying than coming up, as, with fading light and the driving rain, the visibility was very poor. Another hazard was Welsh mountain ponies and sheep on the track which seemed to appear from nowhere. I was really thankful to get to the bottom as it had been quite frightening and had got the adrenalin running as much as any good hunt.

We had another evening meet the next day with the **Taf Fechan Foxhounds** at four-thirty (Thurs 10 Sept 1987). Martin Thomas, the amateur huntsman, offered to show us the way to the meet at Pontsarn Inn, Pontsarn, if we could meet him at the junction of the "heads-of-the-valleys road" and the Brecon road. I had Demelza and Karen had Speedy, who was by now beginning to settle down. Karen and I were the only ones mounted and we followed Martin up the path of an old railway line to draw. The first fox came up over the track and I holloaed it away as hounds ran up past us with a lovely cry, so very musical as they were all Welsh hounds. They hunted him beautifully until the fox went into a large pipe. A terrier was put in and bolted the fox, but he ran towards the pack. A young bitch grabbed him and they rolled over and over down the hillside but she did not let go and the rest of the pack closed in and killed it. Another fox had been seen by car followers and Martin laid hounds on the line twenty-five minutes behind him and a most delightful hunt followed, with hounds working slowly. They persevered and followed it as it twisted in and out of old hedgerows and meadows until they eventually worked right up to him. When he was fresh found, they ran with great drive, eventually catching him in the open. The third fox ran along a little tourist railway track. A train came along and blew its whistle, the driver waving to us and this turned the fox up the mountain and well over the top but he luckily turned back into our valley and went to ground in some rocks. It was by now seven-forty-five so Martin decided to go back to the meet.

We spent a very enjoyable hour in the pub, discussing the special problems of hunting in this part of the country. He told me the following story. The main problem with mounted hunting is that often it is too dangerous to try to turn round owing to the steepness, so it is necessary to keep going on. Once, at such a time as this, he was following a narrow track which became narrower and narrower, and the mountainside steeper. With no choice, he was forced to go on, unable to dismount on either side because of the steepness, until, to his horror, he found that the trail led along a narrow ledge in the rocks, with a river gushing below. Terrified out of his wits, he rode along this ledge, still unable to get off ,as the drop was far too steep to dismount. The ledge became even narrower and his knees were brushing along the rock face until the ledge at last dipped down into the river below. There was a waterfall above him and another one below him, so he could not ride either up or down the river. The far bank looked almost impossible but some foot followers found a rope and lowered it to help pull the horse up, and it just managed to make it with Martin climbing up behind. The nerve of this horse was amazing, but I suppose that they are used to the heights. Our Suffolk horses were not only unused to steep hills but were actually frightened of the heights, and before going down some of the very steep places, they would turn right and left, trying to turn back.

**Tredegar Farmers'.** *Meet at Five Lanes, Rhiwderin, 1987. Joint Master Mr Howard Jones, followed by amateur whipper-in, David Harvey.*
Photograph donated by Mr & Mrs Howard Jones

I got back to the Monmouthshire kennels at nine-thirty and enjoyed giving Mark a hard time about the quality of the Taf Fechan and what good hounds they were and that they had just caught a brace above ground. Back at the hotel I enjoyed a delicious supper of ripe melon and sea bass, which was so lovely as to be indescribable. I then made the mistake of getting into a session with George Peverley, a great character who had been huntsman to the Essex Farmers' for many years. George was on top form, and in the mood to recall all the faults he could about past Masters, especially one about me. He had been talking to Fred Hargreaves, my kennel huntsman, at the Peterborough Hound Show and had said to him, "Good God, Fred. I've just seen a man in a black bowler wearing brown shoes."

"Oh," said Fred, "that'll be my guv'nor."

He took great delight in telling this little story and to cut a long story short it was one-thirty before I pulled off my boots.

Next day as there was no hunting I went for a walk round a large park and picked some mushrooms that I noticed growing there. When I got back to the hotel, I handed them into the kitchen and was promised some mushroom soup.

This had not materialised by the following morning when Karen and I set off for the meet of the **Tredegar Farmers' Foxhounds** in a layby at Five Roads, near Rhiwderin (Sat 12 Sept 1987). We had to leave early as the meet was at seven o'clock but arrived without too many difficulties and unboxed in heavy drizzle. Clifford Pellow was the kennel huntsman and as we talked we were not sure if this was the third or the fourth time we had met with different packs when I was on my hunting holidays. We thought it was with the Hursley, Tivyside, Lamerton and here. The hounds were the most raggle taggle and bobtail pack I have ever seen. There were small ones, tiny ones, huge ones, thick ones, narrow ones, minkhounds, fellhounds, ordinary foxhounds and Welsh hounds, and every type of cross-bred, finishing off with one harrier from the Ross Harriers. Some of them could walk underneath others. The amateur whip, David Harvey, told me that they change hounds so often by drafting in and out that it was almost impossible to keep up with learning their names. The Joint-Master, Howard Jones (who was the local farrier), was hunting hounds, or rather trying to. When he went to draw they just followed him in single file, stopping when he stopped, and it looked as if his horse was pulling them along on a piece of string. The other Master, Mr Whitting, seemed a very friendly chap, but rather too soft and kind to be an effective Master.

I viewed an old fox over a ride and holloaed, and the Master brought hounds, in his own good time, and laid them on the line about ten minutes after the fox had crossed. There was action at last, and they left his horse and ran for about fifteen minutes, then the pack divided and lost both lines. Howard Jones kept getting off his horse at the least pretext, and it took a small army of helpers to get him on again as his horse had to be held firmly against a gate or stump. This little run was about the sum total of the day's sport. David Harvey told me that he worked in a factory five days a week and all week looked forward to coming out in his red coat on a Saturday. Mr Whitting told me that he preferred not to "get involved with the kennels and all that sort of thing". The field consisted of a bunch of silly children and a few incredibly ignorant adults who knew nothing about hunting and were very poorly mounted. The only one in the field who was any good, was an old ex-groom riding a very old horse. Clifford had previously hunted these hounds and I think that things would have been far better had he still done so. When we returned to the meet at eleven-thirty, the amateur whip asked Karen if she had enjoyed herself.

"Oh yes, very much, thank you," she replied.

"Bloody liar," he laughingly replied. "You have been looking just as bored as I have been."

That just about sums up the day. It was one of the most hopeless set-ups I have ever seen. No-one seemed to know what to do or when to do it and they were desperately in need of a few good old hounds to draw and to mark to ground.

On Sunday morning, after a leisurely breakfast, I stopped at the table and, with a fresh pot of coffee, wrote these comments in my diary.

*"Without doubt this is the best hotel I have ever stayed at, really good food – quite outstandingly good – comfortable room although small. When they saw the amount of kit that I had they offered me a double room but I declined because I was settled in. Sue and David Hill, the owners, are good hosts and nothing is too much trouble. Good company in the bar in the evenings, Tom and Reg always take an interest in the various packs I have been with. George Peverley comes in most evenings. He has had a pub, then a caravan site, and now a sewage pumping business since he has retired from hunt service, all in this area. He has a reputation for getting everyone on the booze but I have only been caught one night – last Friday – otherwise I have been rather modest in the booze line. One evening I treated myself to a bottle of Burgundy with an excellent sirloin steak. The hunts and the countries vary much more than one would expect. The lovely rolling grasslands of the Monmouthshire, the Curre and the Llangibby, the last two of which employ a professional huntsman and two whippers-in. The Monmouthshire has been badly let down and Glynn Powell has an uphill struggle. Lovely country but the farmers have been neglected because of an old, stuffy out-of-date Committee. Support gone to the Llangibby who are on top form. Do not envy him his job. He has one advantage in that he has been here before and knows many of the farmers and the country. The wild mountains of the Talybont and the Taf Fechan are splendid in their own right and were lovely – to be so far from anyone with hounds hunting by themselves over unfoiled ground. The poor built-up conditions of the Tredegar Farmers', with the main roads and towns all around them. Yesterday afternoon I went to the Usk Show, an old-fashioned country show with everything there. Terrible judging of the Private Driving. Stayed to the end to watch the "flapping" races – bookmakers and all ("flapping" races are unofficial ones; if anyone rides in one of these races, they are banned for ever from riding in the official ones run under Jockey Club Rules). I had Glynn Powell and his wife for dinner last night and Mark and Diane the Saturday before. Lovely meals on both occasions. Great excitement in this pub as there is to be a Llewellyn wedding – Dai and Roddy's sister. Dai Llewellyn is staying here and there is to be a special usher's lunch with champagne, lobster and the full works. Should be going fishing this afternoon !!!! with Stewart. Am not sure but have ordered an early lunch of leg of Welsh lamb to be ready. Telephone call – fishing cancelled – Stewart's boss back. Each day Mark provides me with a paper for each day with an exact route, huntsman and Masters' names, etc. – very good and ideal for me. There are an amazing number of rebel packs. Some seem to exist without friction with the registered ones, others are a serious trouble. I was told the name of one of the offending Masters who provides the rebels with hounds."*

I finished these notes and went for a long walk before lunch. I was amused when the Labour Mayor of Newport and his wife arrived for lunch, chauffeur-driven. The chauffeur lunched with them as well and he dealt with the bill while they went to the car. That night there was a party at the Clytha Arms. This kind thought of my hosts Sue and David should have been a surprise but Mark let the cat out of the bag. Sue and David provided a lovely buffet of chicken legs, quiche, Stilton and celery, French bread, etc. etc. – a really good spread which we ate in the Lounge, and then retired into the bar. Mark did all the arranging and contacted all the Masters and hunt servants of the local packs I had been with. Quite a lot turned up and it was a most enjoyable evening. Sue played the tape of horn-blowing which George Peverley had made while in hunt service. This was the first tape made of hunting calls and it brought him near to tears.

The Curre huntsman, Bob Collins, was the first to leave as he was cubbing in the morning but before he went he told me that he had brought his own horses from the Chiddingfold, and also his whipper-in, and both were mounted on his own horses on the day I went out. He said he was much worse off financially now as there was so much less flesh. In Kent he had only fed quality beef – cows, etc. – and never fed any young flesh, like calves. He had recently bought a horse for a pound as a lady had wanted to give it to him but, as he said he preferred to pay her, she said, "All right, a pound."

The rest stayed on and I left several in the bar when I went to bed at one o'clock. I was up again at four o'clock, picked up my horses at the kennels, and was away by five forty-five to go into England for the meet of the **Vale of the White Horse** (Mon 14 Sept 1987). I made good time to the Severn Bridge – three quarters of an hour – and arrived at the meet at Bledisloe Manor Gates, Coates (near Cirencester), at six-thirty. I had a ham sandwich and a cup of the mushroom soup which had been made with the mushrooms I had picked on Friday. Karen was rather hungover as she and Diana had a booze-up while the men were at my party. Karen and I were already mounted and waiting when the Field Master rode up and said how pleased he was to see us.

The huntsman, Sidney Bailey, laughed and said, "Oh, you've made it at last, then." He was referring to the awkwardness when Captain Barker, the Senior Master, had refused to allow me to go the previous spring, on the grounds that he was closed to visitors as he wished to minimise the damage to the spring grass. When I told him that I was a Master, he had grudgingly said that I could go but when I telephoned again to get the actual meet, he again refused quite curtly. His excuse was that he could not find me in his "green book" – meaning the MFHA list of all Foxhound Masters. When I explained that I was not in it as I was a Master of Harriers he replied that he was under no obligation to entertain Masters of Harehounds. I did go to the banned meet by car and there were only eight mounted and he looked very sheepish when I introduced myself. He had, I must point out, managed to say that I was welcome to come on this occasion.

Hounds were quite beautiful, all level and of the same type. They were full of quality, and were perfectly behaved. They were hunted with the utmost ease and quietness by Sidney Bailey. I could not help comparing it with all the noise and yelling of the Llangibby. I was spellbound to watch Sidney with his hounds and count it as one of the outstanding privileges of my tours to have seen this man in action. There was little scent and hounds could not do much with the first brace of cubs. They found a third cub in some sugar-beet and they rattled him around for some twenty minutes or so, then he slipped out, almost over the feet of a lady foot-follower who was standing next to me. He then ran a concrete farm road but their concentration on this poor scent was not helped by the Dummer Beagles who were baying frantically in their kennels nearby. Hounds lost the line somewhere along the concrete road, and although Sidney cast them back along the edge, they could make no more of it. They went back to draw the same sugar-beet again, and a tractor and trailer came along and Dolly shied so badly that she slipped, lost her feet and fell on the concrete road, cutting her hock and twisting my back. I stayed out a little longer but my back was too painful and I went back to my box at nine-forty-five. The drive home was, to say the least, most uncomfortable. After a long soak in a hot bath it became much easier. I enjoyed a huge plateful of blackberry and apple pie, with blackberries which had just been freshly picked by Sue and David's daughter Alex who had missed the school bus.

In the evening I went out again with the **Monmouthshire**, following on foot myself, owing to my back hurting, although Karen had Speedy out (Mon 14 Sept 1987). It was a blank evening which was as Glynn had expected, but he had gone for diplomatic reasons to please a local farmer. The greatest excitement of the evening was watching Speedy jumping a fair-sized fence. As there were no mounted packs going on the Tuesday that I had not already been with, I decided to take advantage of George Peverley's offer of the loan of a car and go beagling (Tues 15 Sept 1987). On the night of the big party George had suggested that I borrowed his car, provided his wife did not need it and when he tried to telephone her to ask her, he could not remember his own number, causing much merriment amongst the assembled throng.

I left the hotel in his car at six o'clock for the seven-thirty meet of the **Glyn Celyn Beagles** at the Cambrian Factory at Llanwrytyd Wells. I arrived in good time to see the Master, Johnny Andrews, who I already knew as both of us sat on the Committee of the Masters of Harriers and Beagles Association. Johnny was Master and amateur huntsman, and introduced me to the Senior Master, Colonel Jervis, a wonderful old gentleman who was still, in spite of his age, as fit as a fiddle. Later on in the day we were walking together going up a steep place and I found I could not keep up with him. The beagles were small and very smart and level, and when running went with a rather high-pitched cry. They soon found and they ran into the mist, and although the visibility was poor, it was not difficult to keep in touch with them as this hare was a particularly twisty one, and hounds were frequently at check, which allowed me to keep up. At each check they cast themselves beautifully, and hit off the line time and time again without any help from Johnny. I soon realised that I was watching an outstanding pack of hounds and wished that visibility was better so that I could have stood on a hilltop and watched them below. I dare not aggravate my back problem so I went back to the meet after two hours of pure joy.

**Glyn Celyn Beagles.** *Meet at Cwm Cynog, 1995/96. Master and Huntsman Johnnie Andrews.*

Photograph kindly donated by J M G Andrews

When I got back to the meet, I saw that the factory was open to visitors so I decided to take the opportunity to go in and look around. It was a woollens factory and I eventually bought a jumper for my wife before going on to the meet of the **Wentloog Beagles** at their kennels. Graham Best, the Master and huntsman, kennelled the pack at his home, "Beagledale" in Penylan, Bassaleg, near Newport and had kindly offered to meet me at the same layby at which the Tredegar Farmers had met the previous Saturday and which was only a mile or so from Bassaleg. In fact, he did not do so, but instead he sent two young men to meet me and show me the way to the kennels. The actual meet was to have been on Gelli-guer Common but was changed as the Clifton Foot Beagles were coming, so we followed the hound van from the kennels to a farm. This area, although known as The Moors, was not what one was expect of moors but a large flat low-lying area of first class grassland, divided by wide and deep dykes and high hawthorn hedges into small meadows. This was quite perfect for bringing hounds immediately to their noses (i.e. forcing them to start hunting rather than running in view because hares could quickly disappear from view). They drew for a long time before finding, through no fault of their own, as they drew most beautifully, fanning out and covering a large area of ground thoroughly. However, they were not completely steady to rabbits and there were several "little naughties after the bunnies". We were joined by Howard Jones, the Master and huntsman of the Tredegar Farmers', and he told me that he knew that these beagles also had "little naughties" with the Tredegar foxes.

They were very handy, and Graham could turn them wherever he wished, and although they had two whippers-in who went wide on each flank, they had nothing to do unless a rabbit came their way. The first hare found was quickly caught and the second one was found well into the dusk and when they ran away from us into the darkness with a great dyke before us, Howard and I walked back to the meet and I eventually arrived back at the hotel at eight-thirty. I would think that in fair conditions this would be a very good pack. Graham was very keen and I was told stayed out until all hours. The hounds were kennelled at the bottom of his garden, and are transported to the meet in a small trailer behind his car.

On Wednesday Mark had again arranged for me to go with two packs. The first was the **Llangeinor Foxhounds** who were meeting at Brynmenyn Park, Bryncethin, at seven-thirty (Wed 16 Sept 1987). I arrived at the Monmouthshire kennels to find it all in darkness so I quickly saddled Demelza even though she had a terrible stain on her side. Just as I was loading her, Karen appeared, full of apologies. I was away by five-thirty which was later than I had intended, and meant that I was on a very tight schedule to get there on time. I pushed the old lorry along the M4 as fast as I could get it, and turned off at Junction 36 and along to the Mason's Arms at Bryncethin where I unboxed on the common. I had just dropped the tailboard when Alex Ford, the professional huntsman, and his amateur whipper-in hacked up with hounds. Alex was mounted on a little blood pony and his whipper-in on a cob straight from the meadow, so I did not feel so bad about Demelza's stain. I followed hounds along to the meet where Alex introduced me to the Master Mr Board who apologised for not being out mounted himself as he had a cracked rib.

Hounds found at once and rattled round a large covert in grand style before marking to ground in a pipe. This fox was dispatched and as hounds were breaking it up, another came out of the same pipe and this one gave us a hunt of one hour and a quarter. During this hunt hounds hunted through a garden and when Alex tried to follow on foot the lady owner shut the gate in front of him saying that someone had jumped a horse into the garden the previous season and she was justifiably annoyed. I was the only one mounted apart from the huntsman and whip, and thoroughly enjoyed an excellent morning's cubhunting. I was impressed by the quiet way Alex had with hounds.

At eleven o'clock, Mr Board said to Alex, "You've had a brace of foxes and that will do very well." Reluctantly, we had to hack back to kennels. I then began to realise that I was going to be very short of time if I was to go back to the Monmouthshire kennels to fetch another horse for the next meet at four o'clock that afternoon. I thought that, if I gave Demelza a good feed, she could manage both hunts so I asked Alex if I could feed Demelza at his kennels and this is what I did. I gave her a bucketful of oats and nuts in the lorry, followed by a haynet, all of which she eagerly ate having had no breakfast. Alex showed me round the kennels which had benefitted from several recent improvements. Mrs Ford kindly provided bacon sandwiches and coffee and after tidying up Demelza a little I drove on to the meet of the **Ystrad Foxhounds** at Blaenllechau Mountain Grid, near Llanwonno.

I arrived with a half-hour in hand and was all ready when Graham Dunn, the Master and huntsman, hacked up with hounds. Graham was riding a little Welsh Cob cross Arab on which he had done eleven seasons, and had with him two rough-looking fellows whose horses were unshod and covered in white lather. I felt that I ought to apologise to Graham for coming out on a dirty horse but, as he was using a bridle made from plaited string and a cord running from a rusty bit for reins, it seemed as though my apology would be more like sarcasm in the circumstances so I did not give it. The three of them presented a very basic picture, but I was particularly struck that they seemed to suit these wild mountains and looked absolutely right in their setting. There were four other people out mounted, and all were memorable except for a girl on a pony. There was a fat gentleman on an enormous cob and I guessed he was only just learning to ride as he could not rise to the trot. Another gentleman was turned out properly in ratcatcher coat and brown boots but, although he was dressed correctly, he seemed to understand nothing about the hunting. The last one was a sight to remember. He was an Indian, which in itself is unusual out hunting, and he was carrying an umbrella in a case with a handle along the side so that it resembled a violin case with the umbrella handle sticking out of the end. I spent the day desperately hoping that it would come on to heavy rain as I would have dearly loved to have seen him riding along with his umbrella up. He was riding a wishy-washy palomino, of which he was obviously very proud, and kept asking anyone within earshot if they liked the lovely colour.

The hounds were rather over-fat and unfit but they had the truly lovely Welsh hound voices and when they ran it was with a cry that made my scalp prickle

**The Ystrad:** ***"Have umbrella, will hunt!"***

and it seemed that every hair on my head stood straight up. The evening consisted of many short hunts in this most wild and steep country and Demelza was coping with her second hunt of the day very well, although I did try to save her as much as I could. During a check Robert, a friend of Glynn Powell's (whose surname I never did learn), took me to a point from where we could see the farm which Glynn had had before he went into hunt service and the church where he was married. In the churchyard a famous local character was buried. He was a legend in his own lifetime for his ability to run and he could gather up sheep without a dog. I went back to the meet at seven o'clock and was shown a short-cut over a mountain road to Aberdare which saved me several miles and I finally arrived back at nine o'clock. A few weeks earlier I would never have imagined that I would ever hunt with two packs of foxhounds on one day, let alone on the same horse. A great party developed in the hotel that night. George Peverly was on top form, Mark had brought Diana and Karen down, and it was two-thirty before I climbed into bed.

I awoke not feeling quite at my best and as I had forgotten to set my alarm it was six-thirty before I left the hotel. I had arranged to borrow George's car again to hunt with the **David Davies** who hunted regularly on foot during the week and mounted on Saturdays (Thurs 17 Sept 1987). I was late getting to the meet at New Chapel, Montgomeryshire, but luckily a farmer saw me looking across the valley at hounds drawing and asked if I would like to ride with him in his Land Rover. I gratefully accepted and parked George's car in a gateway and he drove me up the mountain. It was raining quite heavily, visibility was very poor and we could see little of hounds. I decided it was a waste of time and when we were near the car again I left, thinking that I must definitely come again to see them hunt in this lovely wild country. This I did in 1992.

I called at the Barley Mow in Builth Wells on the way back, and Marie made me a huge ham sandwich. Old Tom, who was a great character in the pub, was very pleased to see me, and confessed how worried he was that his turnips would not be large enough by the time of the Welsh Cob sales as he always proudly gave us some turnips to take home. John "the Barley" told me that he had shown old Tom the picture of me on Demelza in "Hounds" magazine, and he said, "Oh, I know him. That's Norfolk." Old Tom had always called me "Norfolk". Tom also said how delighted he was to receive a five-pound-note for Christmas from Alfie Youngman, a Suffolk Welsh Cob enthusiast. It was addressed to, "The Turnip Man, c/o the Barley Mow, Builth Wells".

Back at the hotel before dinner, I tried to telephone the Master of the Banwen Miners'. I had been trying for several nights to get in touch with either Mr Stillman or Mr Thomas, the Joint-Masters, but this time I was lucky and got through to Mr Thomas who said that he was just off to a Hunt Committee meeting and that he would ring me back. After dinner he telephoned to say that his hounds would be out on Sunday morning. I was overjoyed about this as I had already planned to go with the Glamorgan on the Saturday and if I could get out with the Banwen Miners' on the Sunday I would have hunted with every pack in South Wales. I went to bed pleased with the results of the day, even though I had not seen much of the David Davies. This I was not too disappointed about, as it would be relatively easy to go with them again, as hunting on foot did not need horse boxes, stables and all the attendant arrangements.

As I had the week before, I spent the Friday relaxing and picking mushrooms in the park and was ready the next day to go with the **Glamorgan Foxhounds** (Sat 19 Sept 1987). I was up at four-fifteen and left the kennels, with Dolly for me and Speedy for Karen, only just making the meet in time after being mis-directed by a group of children waiting at a bus shelter. The majority had said one way and one boy had said another. He was the one we ought to have listened to. They were meeting at Fonmen Castle, the home of Lady Boothby who was a former Master (1951-62), and was quite near to Cardiff airport. She was directing boxes where to park which helped us considerably as we were rather later than we would have liked. The Senior Master, Mr Martyn, greeted me and apologised for being on foot, explaining that his daughter had been in a bad car accident during the night. He brushed aside my apologies for not having telephoned to confirm that I was coming out on this day and said that he would be pleased to see me at any time. There were about sixteen out mounted and eight keen foot followers who actually ran with hounds all day. The huntsman, Geoff Sales, drew for a long time, then chopped a cub but soon found another and chivvied him around on a very poor scent till he finally went to ground.

The hounds looked very lean and fit and had no Welsh blood in them at all. The huntsman told me he was in his second season, and that he had caught twelve and a half brace the previous season which had been a very poor scenting season, and his predecessor had only caught two and a half brace the season before. He had caught eight brace so far this season and I thought they looked set to catch many more as the whole set-up looked very businesslike with a professional whipper-in doing his job very well. This whipper-in told me he had been out of hunt service for a time but previously had been with Lady Lyell at the Aldenham Harriers. The country was lovely, a mixture of rolling hills and very steep ones, mostly grass with a little arable and was beautifully maintained with hunt gates and jumps everywhere. They hunted on Mondays and Thursdays during the season, with Saturdays as an extra day during cubhunting. The fields averaged about forty on Mondays and sixty on Thursdays. The Master said he had been under considerable pressure to hunt regularly on Saturdays during the season, and had, very wisely I thought, held a referendum amongst the farmers. They had voted overwhelmingly to keep to Mondays and Thursdays as they were afraid of the potential damage to their land from the huge fields that would probably come out on Saturdays out of Cardiff to hunt. "Home" was blown at ten-fifteen and I was pleased to be able to change into a dry coat as it had rained heavily all morning and we were quite soaked. The customary flask of soup was particularly welcome and this time it was mushroom soup, once again made from the mushrooms I had personally picked the day before. I got back and was pleased to be able to take off my green breeches and green pants and soak in a hot bath, before enjoying a late lunch of poached sole in a mushroom and cheese sauce, followed by nectarines and cream. As I was literally as hungry as a hunter, it was a lunch to remember.

I had wanted to give a dinner party this Saturday night and I had made a bargain with Sue and David for a set dinner of soup or melon, roast beef and plum duff as I planned to invite several people. I had invited Mark and Diane Powell, George and Mrs Peverly, and Glynn and Mrs Powell and their friend Robert who was visiting them and who I had met with the Ystrad. As expected it was an evening of great fun with stories galore and it was with difficulty that I eventually went to bed. This was at a later hour than was sensible as I needed to start at four-thirty next morning for the meet of the **Banwen Miners' Foxhounds** at Cwmgeidd Road Junction (on the A4067) (Sun 20 Sept 1987).

**Banwen Miners Hunt.** *At Llangenith, Gower, c. 1990/91 season. W Hancock (Master), G Burnell (Huntsman), and J Purnell and W Small (whippers-in).*

According to Baily's – "This pack was formed in 1963 on the demise of the West Glamorgan Hunt. Sir David Evans Bevan Bt, was President and gave the hunt the lamp-room of the local colliery when it was closed. This quickly became the Hunt kennels and "a legend was born". At first the Hunt was wholly run by the inhabitants of the little colliery village of Banwen, although it is now as cosmopolitan as any other hunt. ...The hunt went professional in 1975 by employing John Davies, late of the Sennybridge Farmers'."

I was at the stables by five-ten but Karen was once again not up so I quickly tacked up Dolly and was turning round the lorry when she appeared. It was the bumping down of the ramp that had woken her. I was away by five-twenty and arrived at the road junction where I had arranged to meet Mr Thomas, one of the Joint-Masters, and was dismayed to see that he was dressed to hunt on foot. When arrangements were being made, Mark had not thought to ask if they were going mounted as they usually do, and Mr Thomas had not thought to say that it was to be a foot day. I followed Mr Thomas for one and a half miles up a track into some forestry, and since I had the horse there anyway, I thought I might as well ride. I unboxed, and was of course the only one mounted.

They soon found and immediately divided on two foxes, one keeping in the forestry and one going out onto the mountainside. I decided that as I was mounted I would go with the latter and when I was out on my own I suddenly felt very vulnerable and lonely. It was a strange feeling and difficult to describe. The ground was very boggy and spongey and Dolly often went down in the wet areas. I pressed on as best I could and was relieved when after a mile or so hounds turned back and hunted back past me and into the forestry again. I was quite surprised at how nerve-racking it was to be on really wild open moor alone with no pilot as there was no track or obvious place where a horse could go. When I regained reasonably sound ground I found that Dolly had lost a shoe in the bog and was quite sore, so I boxed her up and changed out of my heavy green coat into a lighter ratcatcher jacket that I used for travelling in the lorry.

I set off after hounds in my riding boots but luckily was picked up by Gareth, the terrier man from the Sennybridge Foxhounds', who was an enormous man of approximately eighteen to twenty stone. He drove me round in his Land Rover with astonishing expertise since he had only a little over half of the steering wheel with which to steer, the rest being lost in his midriff. We lost touch with hounds and while driving around trying to find them we came across some hound puppies at walk. Gareth stopped to admire them and was told by the walker that they were by a David Davies stallion hound and after much discussion it was decided that one in particular was outstanding. It was appropriately called Topper. After leaving the puppies, Gareth stopped at the village shop and bought a bagful of bars of chocolate which he proceeded to eat one after the other, offering me my choice as well.

When we got near to the meet hounds were back and were loading up so at the Master's suggestion we all retired to the local pub. This was obviously a hunting pub as the Sunday morning crowd were all enquiring about hounds and what sport had been had, and where future meets would be. I heard lots of wonderful tales including one of an ex-Master who was very wild and smashed gates galore. When he asked a farmer how much a new gate would be and was told £50, he would get out his wallet and gave him £200. This was no isolated case and happened very frequently. He was a desperate rider across country and ruined many good horses and had even once jumped a Mini car which was parked across a lane. The chocolate could not have had much effect as I overheard Gareth ordering a roast pork lunch and emphasising that he would like a large portion. As I left he was settling down to a huge plateful. The lorry played up on the way back and there was diesel squirting out of the engine but luckily when I arrived back at the kennels, Karen was being chatted up by a young lad who turned out to be a mechanic and he put it right for me.

On Monday I had one last hunt with the **Monmouthshire Foxhounds** at Little Common, near Raglan (Mon 21 Sept 1987). They drew a thick fir plantation but there was absolutely no scent and hounds could do nothing. I felt so sorry for Glynn Powell as he had had a terrible start to the season; kennel cough for the first few weeks up to when I had arrived, and then such poor scent day after day, with his only support coming from foot followers and not one of the Hunt members ever showing their faces at any of the cubhunting meets, either on foot or mounted. I imagine they must be rather like the average Leicestershire hunt member, only wanting to gallop and jump. I asked Glynn again how much I owed him for the stabling but he would not hear of taking a penny, neither would Mark for his telephone expenses or for Karen's keep but I did send him a small cheque with my thank-you letter.

As this was to be my last night, David and Sue closed the restaurant and sat down with me for a private dinner party of sea food avocado, grouse and chocolate souffle, served with the most delightful wines, all most enjoyable. After dinner, all the people I had met came in one by one to say their goodbyes, some still in their working clothes on their way home from work but nobody went home and although it was a Monday night there developed the biggest and best party yet, with me finally getting into bed at five-thirty.

Next day I had an uneventful drive home, feeling tired and rather flat having had such an incredibly good time amongst such wonderful people. I had been away for eighteen days and felt that I had done fairly well to have hunted with thirteen foxhound packs (fourteen including the David Davies who I had hardly seen at all in the fog) and two packs of beagles. I had achieved what I had set out to do during this holiday, and that was to hunt with all the registered packs in South Wales.

# MAP 15

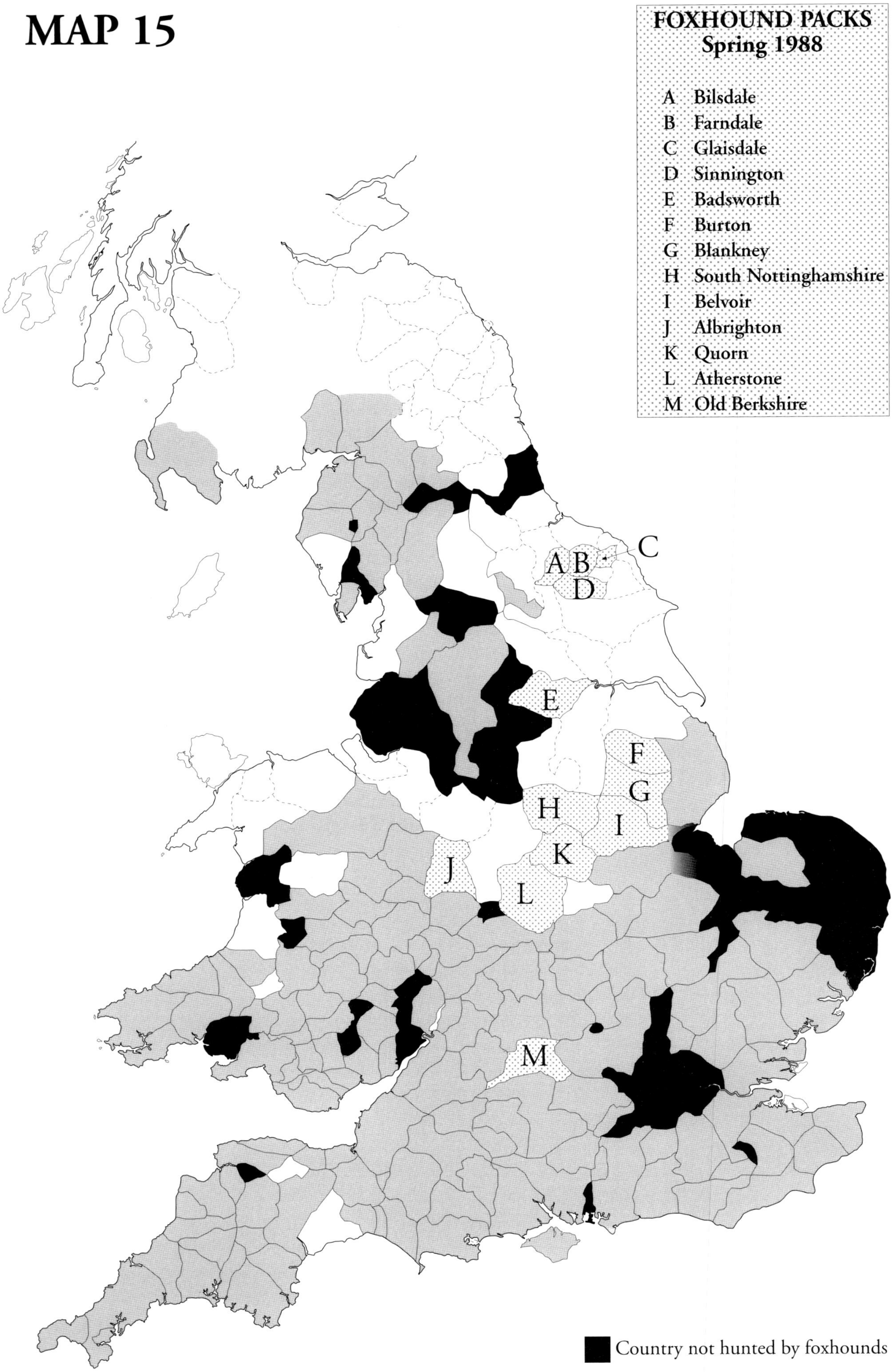
FOXHOUND PACKS
Spring 1988
A Bilsdale
B Farndale
C Glaisdale
D Sinnington
E Badsworth
F Burton
G Blankney
H South Nottinghamshire
I Belvoir
J Albrighton
K Quorn
L Atherstone
M Old Berkshire
A
B
C
D
E
F
G
H
I
J
K
L
M
Country not hunted by foxhounds

# Chapter 17

## The Shires Packs and Helmsley

Paul Yeldham had said how much he would like to go visiting again and this encouraged me to fit in another daytrip in December, before going away on my second major jolly of the season in February and March. The opportunity came when the **Old Berkshire Foxhounds** were meeting at Denchworth Manor in Oxfordshire (2 Dec 1987). I took Fizz over to Paul's at Mickfield the previous afternoon and spent the evening at home with John Howson who was professionally collecting folk songs and wanted to record some of mine. I arrived at Paul's next morning at five forty-five and he told me that his groom, Sally Dunlop, had not turned up as she was ill. Nevertheless everything was ready on time, but then Paul's lorry would not start. He soon used the jump leads from his Volvo and we were away. On the way to the meet we were unlucky enough to be pulled into a layby for a Ministry of Transport check, but still arrived in time. We were invited to unbox in a supporter's farmyard but unfortunately the top of the lorry caught and pulled down an electric wire and broke the post. They were lovely people and laughed it off, insisting that we went in for a drink. We were offered gin and ginger which we turned down very firmly as we had never heard of such a drink, but when we hacked down to a little meadow where the actual meet was, called Longcot Thorns, we discovered that gin-and-ginger was the traditional drink of this pack, and accepted the hospitality of the Beaverbrook family.

We moved off to draw hedgerows and rough places, drawing the first farm blank during which we had to jump about ten hunt jumps from pasture to pasture. Paul and I kept closely behind the Master, Mr Caudwell, who was also the Field Master. The field were quite badly behaved and did a lot of unnecessary damage to crops, and were always pressing onto hounds far too closely. Hounds found and hunted in a circle into a sewage works where John Smith, the huntsman, got off his horse and cast them on foot. He soon had hounds running again. I saw nothing of this second half of the hunt as the Field Master took us on a totally unnecessary jolly away from hounds. I was cross because I had followed him, thinking he was taking us on a short-cut and was not at all happy as I would have preferred to watch John hunt his hounds. I had known him for years when he was the kennel huntsman of the Rockwood Harriers. The next draw was so terrifying that I dare hardly look as they drew the overgrown railway embankment of the Great Western line, with the InterCity trains passing at 130 mph. The whipper-in and two volunteers stood on top of the embankment on foot and the field were held well back so as not to discourage a fox from leaving the railway in the right direction. One fox obliged and we had a fair spin across the lovely old turf, most of which was old-fashioned "ridge and furrow". This, combined with Fizz fighting me every yard of the way, caused my back to ache terribly and I was ready to stop at three o'clock, going back to the lorry. The lorry got stuck in mud coming out of the farmyard but with a pull from a tractor got out easily, and we eventually arrived back at Paul's house at eight o'clock. He kindly persuaded me to leave Fizz there, saying that he would bring him to the Easton meet the following day.

Later in the season I went away for almost the whole of March, returning for ten days in the middle to finish the Easton season and attend the End of Season Ball. The first session and half of the second were based in Leicestershire, the rest in Helmsley, Yorkshire. The visit to Leicestershire was made possible through Sally Hennessy whose family have been great supporters of the Easton for many years. She had introduced me to Charlotte Banks and when I found out that she had a yard in Leicestershire I asked her if by chance she would be able to put up my horses.

I left Tannington for Leicestershire on Sunday 28 February (1988) in very high spirits after having had the previous day the fastest run with the Easton that they had had in all the years I had hunted them. It had been like hunting a deer, both in distance and speed, and the day had ended appropriately with a "Swinging Twenties" party at the home of Michael and Jenny Lord at Mellis, near to where I had stopped hounds. My groom, Karen Wainer, came with me to look after Fizz and Max and we left home at one-thirty, arriving at the Grange, Rearsby (between Leicester and Melton Mowbray), at five-thirty. The boxes were all ready and presented a lovely Christmas Card picture, with the light pouring out of the doorways onto the old cobbled yard. The yard was quite delightful with boxes all round and a lovely tack-room with both walls and ceilings lined with matchboarding, the original fireplace and saddle-racks, and a staircase leading to the hayloft above.

My hostess, Charlotte, was not at home but she had left her sister Veronica in charge, with her Dutch boyfriend and his brother Peter. Charlotte hired hunters out to clients and these youngsters were preparing tack for the following day. They had got a double bridle in a terrible muddle but Karen was able to sort it out for them. After settling the horses, Veronica took me across to the house and led me into a large entrance hall where a log fire was burning. I was then taken up the wide stairs to an equally large landing from which I entered my "five-star" bedroom. It gave me an inexplicable feeling of excitement to know that I was in a real Leicestershire hunting "box". The entrance hall led, *via* a lovely old-fashioned brick passage, to an outhouse complex which included boot-rooms and valetting rooms, all with their original fittings. The remainder of the house was equally grand and included a butler's pantry and another sitting-room which protruded from the main building and was designed to catch the sun all day.

That evening I took them all out, with Karen, for a pub meal, but was home early, ready for my first day which was to be with the **Quorn**. I took enormous trouble valeting my clothes and left at nine forty-five for the eleven o'clock meet at Ab Kettleby, near Melton Mowbray (Mon 29 Feb 1988). I followed Charlotte's box containing four hirelings, and we had a half-hour to wait in a large farmyard. Although there were approximately eighty out, no-one offered to speak at all and when I tried to strike up a conversation I received only the briefest of answers. The Master, Mr Bealby, seemed not to speak at all, only acknowledging my "good morning" with a nod.

They drew various little coverts for three-quarters of an hour without finding. When a fox was found we ran for forty minutes or so with Fizz jumping the fences with ease and being so well-behaved that I even managed to stop when a man fell off in front of me, which I thought was quite a feat. There were two more good little runs over lovely country, which I could see had been terribly punished by previous runs. There was deep poaching not only near the jumps but also across some of the meadows. I rode with the Secretary for a while and got into conversation with him, and he told me that they had been over the same ground at least six times before that season. This amazed me, as did the number of broken rails and hedges, but what was most astonishing of all was the rapidity of the repairs. Twice we ran in a large circle and by the time we came back to the same place, we found that a fence smashed on the first time round had been repaired, only to be smashed again. This was carried out by two men who followed along behind the field making temporary repairs as the fences were broken, returning later to make a permanent job of it. The Secretary explained that the farmers did not mind about the damage done to their fences, as the replacement was always as good as or better than the original, and that the seemingly serious damage to the grass was superficial and disappeared in the spring. I asked him how the repair system was managed and he told me that Hunt employs two men full-time all the year round and that this cost about £35,000 per year. They spent the season doing the repairs of fences broken on hunting days, and the summer constructing hunt jumps. If a farmer wanted to re-fence a pasture, he rang the kennels and told them to put up a set of rails in a certain place and then he would strain the wire to the fence.

The field surprised me as I had expected to find everyone mounted on beautiful-looking brilliant hunters, skimming over the fences with ease. Nothing could have been further from the truth, and it was like looking at a well-known set of prints entitled "*Hunting Types*". There was the slim Cavalry Man with a handle-bar moustache and a cutaway coat, a Dealer's Man in a ratcatcher on a weedy chestnut, solid Farmers on even more solid and sensible cobs, and even The Runaway, with its head down, and mouth open, boring round the fields, often in the opposite direction to the rest of us. At one check, this unfortunate individual made several circuits round a large pasture until he finally managed to stop it. I could not resist riding up to him to make the needless enquiry if he was having any difficulty.

"It's his mouth, old chap. It seems a bit dead, old chap," was the reply given to me, with a very grave face. He appeared to be scared to death of what was obviously a hireling.

I met another interesting lady who was gate-shutting and was riding a green five-year-old belonging to Dr Connors, the famous horse-dealer. I thought she was the only really friendly one in the whole field and she told me that she was sister to Mr Shaw and to Mrs Gurney, well-known Norfolk hunting folk. Dr Connors saw me apparently taking an interest in his horse and appeared to ask if I needed a hunter. When I said I did need one for my kennel huntsman he said he had just the one to suit him at the low price of £3,000. He could not seem to understand that I did not think this sum to be cheap for a kennel huntsman's horse for a harrier pack. This led to a conversation with an American visitor from Pennsylvania. I asked if he knew Tony Garvin from the Springtown Harriers of Pennsylvania (to whom I used to draft harriers) and he said that he had heard of him but had not met him. When the hunt staff and some of the field changed to their second horses, I decided to go back to my box as I was getting a little concerned about Fizz who was getting quite old, and I did not want to overdo him on the first day of the holiday. While the hunt staff were changing horses I had an opportunity to look at these famous hounds. The bitch pack was out and they all looked exactly alike and were as full of quality as one would expect. They had been helped quite a lot during the day, but as the wind was very strong and bitterly cold I thought that perhaps scent was not at its best and wondered how I would have fared if this had been a "flying" day. Fizz was so excited that he was trembling all over as I tried to get him to walk back to the lorry, and after we were back at Rearsby he was continually walking round and round in his box in a terrible state of excitement and was still breaking out in hot and cold sweats in the late evening. I think he probably mentally relived his day with the Quorn all night.

On Tuesday morning I left Rearsby at nine forty-five for the **Atherstone Foxhounds** who were meeting at Brascote, near Desford (Tues 1 Mar 1988). I arrived in good time, unboxing with every one else in a meadow. Brascote consisted only of this farm, one cottage and the Windmill pub. I hacked up to the pub with the others who were friendly and quite the opposite of the previous day's crowd. An ex-Master introduced himself and bought me a drink. There were about forty mounted, and the hounds were mixed, with some Old English Foxhounds (Brocklesby, I think) and the rest Studbook Foxhounds. We moved off and stood in the same meadow as the boxes while hounds drew a covert two fields away. When Mrs Barber, Master and Field Master, decided to move on she just turned the head of her little bay horse and, in a couple of strides, jumped an enormous fence (i.e. hedge). To my great relief, only very few followed, and I joined the rest in going through a gate onto a track. I was riding Max whom I had originally bought for myself but found that he pulled too much for me, so my kennel huntsman, Jim Wickham, had had him for years. I had brought him on this Leicestershire trip as I knew that he could jump and on the grounds that it would be better to go across country out of control than be left stuck behind a big fence with hounds screaming away from me.

When hounds found a fox, one of the first obstacles that we came to was a moving conveyor belt standing about three feet high carrying gravel for several miles. I was told that they did sometimes jump it on Saturdays when it was still, but on this occasion a bridge was used. Hounds were running hard and were well away from us by the time we went round *via* the bridge. The next obstacle was a stile in the corner of a field with a very boggy take-off. I had tucked myself into fifth place and was glad of it as the take-off could only get worse. Max rose like a bird and cleared it in fine style but there were so many fallers soon after that the rest took another route. We ran on across this lovely country, mostly grass, with plenty of "lepping", both natural fences and hunt jumps, and Max jumped willingly all day. He refused only once after we had stood at a check for thirty minutes or so, and he had got cold and did not feel like jumping a quite stiff fence before he had warmed up again. To be slightly critical, I thought that perhaps the hounds were a little light of cry. At about three-thirty I asked for directions back to the meet, having thoroughly enjoyed my day amongst so many genuinely friendly people. Charlotte was home when I returned so I persuaded her to let me take her out to dinner. She said a pub snack would do but I insisted that she recommended a very good restaurant and we had a wonderful dinner at the Sixhills Restaurant, where the owner was a hunting man who hunted with the Quorn.

Next day I went with the **Belvoir** and, by a stroke of luck, they were actually meeting at Belvoir Castle (Wed 2 Mar 1988). What a thrill it was to ride up to the castle which must be the most imposing situation for a meet in the whole world. The scene was perfect for what most people would think a traditional foxhound meet should be. Deep straw had been laid over a stretch of lawn which the horses had to cross to reach the rougher area under a ha-ha wall where the huntsman stood with hounds, and behind him the lawns stretched back to the castle which towered above him. As well as taking Fizz in my lorry, I had agreed to take one of Charlotte's hirelings for a man called Robin who was a proper twit, and I spent a good part of the day trying to avoid him. As if the grandness of the meet was not enough, I really knew that I was moving in the upper echelons of Society when I realised that the lady unboxing next to me was the sister of the Princess of Wales. The Duke and Duchess were on foot amongst the crowd and there were servants galore handing out glasses of port and sherry – large glasses, too, not the thimbles more usual at lawn meets. Mr Blakeway, one of the Joint-Masters, came and introduced himself and took me to meet his Joint-

**Atherstone Hunt.** *Hounds in c. 1985–6, with whipper-in Jimmy Boyle.*

Photograph kindly loaned by Miss Felicity Vero

Masters, Mr Knight and Mrs Comerford, and then, to my great joy, said, "I know where you want to be," and took me right up to the huntsman, Robin Jackson, and told me to stop there. Robin and I sat in the middle of these lovely dark tan Old English hounds, and talked of stallion hounds and of the few remaining packs which were still pure Old English. There were photographers everywhere, and television cameras, and great interest was taken in my green coat. One of the things I enjoyed most on these tours was the contrast between the different styles and countries of the various hunts. No greater contrast could be imagined between the grandeur of the meet of these hounds, with the Ystrad in the depths of Wales, where the Master rode with a bridle made of plaited string and a rusty bit.

We moved off and soon found, and although it was called a "woodland day", and we were in woods most of the day, there was plenty of jumping and Fizz became very wound up. When he had to jump in and out of a lane, he jumped the first gate so high that he stuck my head into an overhanging bough and at the second gate I landed well behind the saddle. I must have jabbed his mouth terribly but could not help it. I shall never know how I managed to stay on and was very lucky not to have had a serious neck injury. We galloped on over old parkland down to the edge of a lake with the kennels beyond and, above and beyond them, the castle. It was a lovely view, and I could not help feeling what a lucky man I was to be there to see it and to be with these wonderful hounds. They were running with a glorious deep cry, every bit as good as I had imagined they would be. The field were very friendly and at every check there would be someone enquiring who I was and where I had come from, and wishing me a successful holiday. In conversation with the Field Master, he told me that he was originally from Stonham Aspal and had hunted with the Easton Harriers when Captain Bernard was Master. Towards the end of the day I hacked Fizz slowly back to the box, desperately hoping that he would calm down, and as I went I passed through part of the famous Belvoir Vale. This part was now mostly ploughed up, but it was easy to imagine what it must have been like in its heyday as permanent pasture with two hundred well-mounted sportsman riding across it, maybe twenty wide. This had been a really memorable day, one that really makes you glad to be alive and fit and well. Now as I write about it five years later, I can still hear those lovely voices ringing out from the huge woods below the castle, and the memory sends the blood rushing through my veins.

**South Notts Hunt.** *Huntsman Philip Watts with hounds and children at the local agricultural show.*
Photograph kindly loaned by Miss Anne Jepson

I left Rearsby at eight o'clock next morning for the meet of the **South Nottinghamshire Foxhounds** at Alderwasley, near Belper (Thurs 3 Mar 1988). When I could see by my map that I was almost there and had over an hour to spare, I called at a little shop-cum-cafe on a sudden impulse and ordered breakfast. When they asked me what I would like, I said "The full works," and the plate arrived well-loaded with everything, including a large helping of black pudding. This was a novelty since we do not have it in Suffolk, and I ate most of it, not daring to finish it as it was terribly rich. There was a huge car-park at the Bear, and as it was on high ground one could see for miles in almost every direction. Everyone left their horses in the boxes and piled into the pub, just like the Easton. This ought to have made me feel at home, but somehow it did not as I had become used to the foxhunting habit of sitting on the horses at the meet and drinking very little. Many of the field came up and made themselves known to me until eventually the Master said that we really ought to go hunting.

We moved off to draw the first hillside blank and then went across country to the next covert. This held a fox and we were away. Max was quite brilliant over the stone walls and went at them so willingly that he gave me great confidence. I am not ashamed to say that this was needed, as some of the walls were quite high. I was with the Secretary when the field turned to go up a long, narrow meadow.

"We want to be this way," he said. "There's no way out of here."

So we dropped down to a lower level and came out of a gate and hacked up the road. I was amazed to see the rest of the field jumping a low wall with a four foot drop onto a downhill tarmac road, with the horses slipping terribly. This proved yet again how important it is to find a good pilot who really knows the country as I do not think I would have jumped down onto that road. This was a sharp run and, when hounds checked, something happened that I had never seen before or since. The whole field (which included me as "when in Rome ...") paid no attention and just carried on across country as if hounds were still hunting, until they came to the next covert. They then stopped and waited there for the huntsman to bring hounds up behind them. It was quite extraordinary, and I shall never forget it – naughty it certainly was, but great fun. This was pure end-of-season devilment since they were not ignorant and clearly knew that they should have stopped when hounds did.

I was sitting in these steep Derbyshire hills, admiring the beautiful scenery, and thinking how lucky I was to be alive, when up rode an unpleasant memory from years ago in the Easton. How I wished he had kept himself to himself as it quite ruined my day, shattering my happy haze. He had been a member of the Easton but I had been forced to ask him not to renew his subscription on account of his behaviour, and he then moved on to the Quorn. He had actually been out with them the day I had had with them, and I had asked the Secretary how they got on with him. He replied that he had made somewhat of a nuisance of himself but when he had got out of hand the previous season, he (the Secretary) had suggested that he might like to pay for the Earthstoppers' Dinner.

The rest of the day was spent drawing blank with short jollies across country from covert to covert. The field were real "goers" and loved to ride across this lovely country and I would have liked to have seen both hounds and field go on a really good scenting day. It had been a day of intensely cold sleet showers with occasional warm sunshine, most extraordinary weather, with the temperature leaping up and down. I left them at three o'clock and arrived back at Rearsby at five o'clock. I said I would take three of the youngsters for a pub meal at the Wheel Inn, but when I came down after bathing, Karen was cooking something, so I took this as an unspoken refusal and took myself off in the lorry to the Sixhills restaurant again. It did seem funny to be parking this rough old lorry beside the Rolls-Royces and Bentleys in the carpark. I had so enjoyed my day with the South Notts that I thought the dinner ought to match it, so I ordered lobster to start with, followed by smoked salmon, then rack of lamb, and ended up with a steamed pudding. I ordered a half-bottle of Muscadet and another of Mouton Cadet, and ended the evening with the owner of the restaurant who joined me at my solitary table and insisted that I accepted two large glasses of the most delicious vintage port. I then drove the old lorry back, feeling like a prince, and very glad that the youngsters had not taken up my offer.

**Albrighton.** *Opening Meet at Whiston Hall, 1988. Left to right, Chris Wood (whipper-in), Philip Pearson (amateur whip), Nigel Cox (Huntsman), and Ted Watkins (amateur whip).*

Photograph kindly loaned by Mrs J Billington

I went home on the Friday to hunt hounds for the last few days of the season and catch the End-of-Season Ball, and then returned to Rearsby ten days later on Monday 14 March. I left Tannington to return to my "hunting box", feeling very grand, and this time took an extra horse, Rose, so that, when my friend Tony St Quinton came to join me in Yorkshire later on, he would have a horse to hunt that he knew. She would also, of course, be a standby for me if Max or Fizz crocked up during this eighteen-day jolly.

The following morning it was the last day of the season for the **Albrighton Foxhounds** and they were meeting at their kennels at Whiston Cross so I left early for the three-hour journey (Tues 15 Mar 1988). Nigel Cox, the professional huntsman (and a past huntsman of the Essex and Suffolk) asked me into his house for drinks and when Mr Webster, one of the Joint-Masters, arrived he could not possibly have given me a warmer welcome and offered me the honour of riding up with Nigel hunting hounds. At the meet there was an air of great excitement and amusement and I found out that, at the end of cubhunting, Mr Webster had said to Nigel, "Well done, you have caught twenty brace during cubhunting. If you can catch another twenty brace during the season I will throw a big party."

The tally was up to nineteen and a half brace and Nigel had only this last day to make the twentieth. The whipper-in, who recognised me from when he had been huntsman to the Pennine Foxhounds on the never-to-be-forgotten Anglezark day in 1982, was mounted on a heavy coloured cob, more than suitable to pull my heaviest gypsy caravan. It looked quite odd at the meet but was later to prove to be a brilliant performer in the field. The hounds out were all bitches and looked very smart

**The Albrighton:** ***"Knock, and it shall be opened unto you!"***

and level, like peas in a pod. Nigel and I went off to draw a covert which held three foxes, and hounds rattled them around with a very musical cry until at last we received the news that a foot-follower had seen one go away. Nigel laid hounds on the line twenty minutes behind him, and a most impressive hunt followed. Hounds persevered on this faint scent in terrible conditions of heavy rain and high winds, and hunted it into the garden of a farmer who was out with us. Without hesitation, Nigel galloped up to some high closed doors in a stable yard and rapped with his whip and shouted for them to be opened. This was done and he and I galloped through the coach-house and out at the back, rejoining hounds the other side, a most unusual line to take. I think we fresh found our fox soon after, but it might have been a fresh one, and we had a sharp hunt across country, I began to wonder if I had been wise in accepting to ride up with Nigel when he just turned his horse's head and in two strides cleared a fair set of rails. I followed him, knowing that Fizz would never refuse, but with all the usual worry about whether he would judge the take-off properly while at the same time fighting with me to go on faster. Wire, and fences with sheets of tin in the bottom, all took their turn, including jumping on and off a road, until hounds marked to ground and with Nigel and I well back with hounds, he was bolted amid much laughter from both mounted and foot followers. Hounds were laid on the line and another sharp run along some river meadows ensued, until he went to ground again and was dispatched.

This left poor Mr Webster to honour his bet, and he immediately invited me to the party which was very kind of him as I was a complete stranger. There was one snag in that the party was to be on Sunday 20 March which was the day I had planned to move from Rearsby to Yorkshire for the next part of my holiday. Four times during the day I was asked why I was not on Demelza, all recognising me and remembering the photograph so recently in "Hounds" magazine of the oil painting of me on her with my hounds. This had been a great day, spent in the best of company and ended with a lovely dinner cooked by Veronica while we all sat around in the kitchen with a glass in our hands, watching her prepare dinner. It was rather like the atmosphere that one always enjoys at a barbeque, that of hungry anticipation.

Before dinner, I valeted my coat on the draining-board in the kitchen, feeling guilty because I knew what Sheila would have said if I had tried the same trick at home, and then Peter drove me into Leicester to an off-licence where I bought a bottle of gin and tonics and a bottle of red and white wine. This I did a couple of evenings running and then thought that I was wasting time and next time bought several bottles of each. Next evening when I went to pour myself a gin-and-tonic to have before dinner I was shocked to find that it was all gone. I discovered that the youngsters had all sat up the previous evening after I had gone to bed, and stayed up until they had drunk the lot, three days' supply.

As I drove along next morning to the meet of the **Burton Foxhounds** at the Adam and Eve at Wragby, I was feeling deliriously happy, and a song suddenly presented itself to me (Wed 16 Mar 1988). I kept stopping in laybys to write down each verse as it came into my head but, in spite of this, I still arrived in good time. Everyone went into the pub and I soon realised that they were a really fun-loving field. We left the meet without unboxing, drove to a layby near some "pleasure woods", and then unboxed. Hounds found straight away but ran into fresh foxes soon after and divided. Luckily both lots ran into the same big wood so they were together again. Scent was very poor and hounds could only feather along, with an occasional short burst. The day was spent going from covert to covert, either through very deep and sticky rides or on roads, and would have been very boring if there had not been so many flasks offered and accepted, and so many interesting people to talk to in this most friendly field. I was treated as though I were a long-lost friend returned after a long absence. After hunting, I went with the huntsman to the kennels to see a horse which was for sale, but did not like it. The kennels were most impressive with large yards and lodges, all kept in apple-pie order by the Supporters' Club. Hounds were rather a mixed bunch but went with a lovely deep cry. I had a cup of tea and a sandwich in the huntsman's house before leaving and finally arrived back at six-thirty.

**Burton.** *Meet at Lissington, December 1997. Huntsman Jim Lang, with whipper-in Mark Melladay and, behind, Joint-Masters A W Lockwood and John Lockwood.*

Photograph kindly loaned by A W Lockwood

There was no pack hunting that I had not already been with on Thursday, so I took myself off to the Melton Mowbray horse sales where I was sorely tempted to buy two lovely young two-year-olds but I dared not because of the problems caused by finding accommodation and getting them home (Thurs 17 Mar 1988). After getting back to Rearsby I finished writing my song, "Thoughts of an Easton Master", and in the evening I went again to the Sixhills restaurant for a first-class dinner of crab and avocado, Dover sole, followed by Porterhouse steak and this time there was no room for pudding. The proprietor again kindly pressed glasses of a ten-year-old port on me.

Next day I left at nine-fifteen for the **Blankney Foxhounds** and arrived at Coddington in good time (Fri 18 Mar 1988). I was surprised to see two boxes already at the meet which was in a clearing on the edge of large woodlands. Two happy-looking men were carrying a table out of a lorry, and onto this was laid a white cloth which was soon firmly held down by bottles of whisky and sherry and large plates of sandwiches and cakes. All this was generously given by a very memorable character who rode a coloured cob. He was the local furniture dealer and had for many years before been a fairground proprietor. At the meet was a group of people I knew from Norfolk who were having a car-follower's hunting holiday, and also James Barclay, Master of the Fitzwilliam who had been Master of the Essex and Suffolk. Hounds were of a heavier type, similar to what I remembered the old Puckeridge to be like, and when they hunted they went with great drive and their cry was very deep, the deepest I had heard for some time.

The day was to be a woodland day, with me spending most of the time on point which pleased me because I was away from the coffee-housing field. The woods were a delight to hunt in, with good clear rides and not muddy as the land was very light. There was no classical hunting as there were so many foxes that hounds were constantly changing. Sometimes there were three or four hunts going on in different parts of the woods but there was nothing the huntsman could do about this as the woods were absolutely teeming with foxes. Our kind host was enjoying his hunting and jumped everything in sight. Any log or fallen tree would be made use of, and when Forestry Commission gates were opened, he always hung back until they were closed again so that he could jump them. I left at three o'clock which meant that I missed the Champagne Party which our friend had planned to complete his hospitality and to which I was invited. I got back at five o'clock and had hardly any valeting to do as there were only specks of sand on my coat and boots. I spent the early evening trying to learn my new song.

Another early start was necessary the next morning as the **Badsworth Foxhounds** were meeting at Cadeby, near Doncaster (Sat 19 Mar 1988). I left at eight o'clock, and as I was making good time I stopped for breakfast on a layby near Retford at a roadside caravan which I

**Badsworth Foxhounds.** *Meet at Stapleton Park, February 1988. Huntsman David Randall.*

Photograph kindly loaned by Dr E Wilken

had for many years used when travelling on the A1. This was run by a wonderful old man who had sponsored me on my trip with a horse-drawn gypsy caravan to Appleby in 1980. We had to give great credit to the Post Office as the request for payment had been sent to "The Caravan, the Layby on the A1 near Retford" but had nevertheless been received and the money sent back. This man worked seven days a week from six o'clock in the morning all his life, then retired and died a month later. The owner and customers alike were equally taken aback to see me in my white breeches and polished boots, tucking into my breakfast.

The Master, Mr Firth, had warned me that it was his worst meet, and very "end-of-the-season-ish", but I still said that I would like to go. I was astonished to see two vanloads of police at the meet, as well as two mounted policemen who followed hounds all day. What a lovely job! When I jokingly asked if there was much rivalry about who was picked for this duty, I was diplomatically told that it was just another part of their many duties, but the twinkle in their eyes said everything. There were very few "antis" out so there was no trouble. The policemen in the vans only followed for an hour or so but, strange to say, the mounted ones remained all day. Mr Firth invited me to ride up with his huntsman, David Randall, which of course I eagerly accepted, but unfortunately hounds could not find and although we drew from eleven to four-fifteen it was a blank day. Here again there was a connection with home and the Easton Harriers as the Secretary's brother lived in Wilby which is an adjacent parish to Tannington. During the day I met some girls who were riding horses which were for sale. I was interested in a four-year-old grey mare which might have suited David, my kennel huntsman, and I arranged to go to see them on the following Monday en route to Yorkshire. I had so many pressing invitations to hunt with them again at a special "breakfast" meet they were holding the following Tuesday that I promised to go, even though I would by then be in Yorkshire.

I arrived back at Rearsby at six-fifteen to find that my old friend William Gilbertson-Hart, known as "Wild William" by the Easton Harriers, had arrived to stay, with his girlfriend Susan and a friend of his, a Russian Count, called Andre. William was an old friend of Charlotte's. He was in his usual going mood and would not even give me enough time to wash off my boots before whisking me off to an old-fashioned pub in the middle of a housing estate where we enjoyed an excellent sirloin steak. Andre was very good company and accepted a considerable amount of ribbing from William with great tolerance. On my return to Rearsby after my evening with him I tried to write up my diary but after two lines realised that I would never be able to read it so gave up and finished it at eight-thirty the next morning.

Wild William had said that he would drive me to the Albrighton Eightieth Fox lunch party, and Mr Webster had agreed on the telephone that he would be welcome, but, at the last moment, William changed his mind (Sun 20 Mar 1988). Charlotte said I could borrow her Range Rover but warned me that it was not at its best. The battery was flat but I had jump-leads in the lorry and we got it started, and I took the leads with me assuming that there would be someone at the other end to help me start again. I had not gone far when something went wrong with the gears and I could only get it into third gear, and that only when stationary. By slipping the clutch I managed to draw away from each crossroads and cruised along at about thirty-five miles an hour. I arrived safely after an eventful journey during which I had concentrated on keeping to the correct route as I had no reverse gear with which to turn round. It was a very good party with everyone in high spirits and the atmosphere was really good. The whipper-in who was ex-huntsman of the Pennine Foxhounds sang a song and Nigel Cox asked me to sing "The Warson Hunt Song".

Next day I sadly had to say goodbye to "my hunting box" and thanked my young friends for their help and Charlotte for her generous hospitality. On the way up to Helmsley in Yorkshire, we called at the Timbertop Stables beside the A1 to look at the grey mare I had seen out hunting (Mon 21 Mar 1988). Karen rode her but thought her too green for David to whip-in on, so she next tried a six-year-old bay which I was told I would see out with the Badsworth the following day.

All the arrangements for the Yorkshire visit had been made on the telephone. I cannot remember now who it was who recommended that I tried to get stabling with Anthony Barker but whoever it was I shall be eternally grateful to them. I was given his telephone number and when I called him from Suffolk he was in the bath. I spoke to his wife and she relayed the message through the bathroom door.

"Tell him it will be £10 per day per horse", was the reply.

I sent a message back that I would bring my own groom and hard feeds and would not want full livery, and the word came back that it would be £6 per day. I sent back that it was still too much money, so another one came back at £5 per day. Finally I said that it was still too much just for stabling and straw and hay, and I would give him £3 per day per horse. His wife came back for the final time saying that he agreed and would I ring him again to make final arrangements when he was out of the bath.

*A home from home for my horses – Anthony Barker's stableyard in Helmsley, in continuous use in the Barker family for many generations.*
Photograph by Richard Wells-Furby

I arrived in the delightful little town of Helmsley and was directed up a very narrow street to Anthony's stables. This was most embarassing as the silencer had broken on the lorry and the narrow streets seemed to amplify the noise. The stables were the original coach-horse stables which had been in continual use without a break since the last coach-horses had been hired out by Anthony's grandfather who had been landlord of the Royal Oak. When I had spoken on the telephone directly with Anthony I had asked him to book me into a comfortable pub and Karen into a bed-and-breakfast as near the stables as possible. After settling the horses in, I took Karen to her lodgings at Park House which was very comfortable with a large bedroom and a long sitting-room with a log fire. Anthony Barker had booked me a room at the Crown Hotel but when I got there, my room was so poky and small that I could not possibly have coped with all my hunt gear. As this was the only room they had free, I booked out, losing my deposit, and decided to join my groom in her palatial bed-and-breakfast. Just as I came out of the door with my cases onto the street, Anthony was coming past with his pick-up loaded with horse muck as, of course, being in the middle of the town, he had to cart every bit of it away. I hailed him like a taxi and horrified him by throwing my cases, etc., on top of the muck, and asked him to drive me to Park House, where I booked in, and have since spent many happy visits.

*Park House, Helmsley home of my host and hostess Ian and Jackie Saggars.*
Photograph by Richard Wells-Furby

When I was settled in, I went for a walk round the town to find somewhere suitable to take Karen for dinner as she, and now also myself, were only in for bed and breakfast so needed to eat out. I walked into the Feathers at six o'clock and thought that that seemed quite nice, but I might as well look at some other places, so I then crossed the market square to the Royal Oak and went into the Public Bar. There was no-one else there as I ordered a beer. I asked the landlord if he did evening meals and then noticed over the bar a familiar face in the other room. Little did I know what I was letting myself in for when I decided to walk round into the other room and join him. We introduced ourselves and found that we knew each other's faces as we both belonged to the same club in Ipswich. Dr John Hughes was on holiday in Helmsley and was a regular there, and had many friends in the town. Each friend came in, one by one, and a terrible session was soon in full swing.

One of the first in was Anthony Barker, followed by various farmers, the local butcher, and a racing correspondent. All were interested in hunting, especially a burly farmer who at one time pinned me in a corner giving me a hard time about the sins of the local pack. Another farmer rescued me from this predicament. Before six-thirty the little room was crowded with what I felt were good, genuine people, and the rounds were coming in every minute. The landlord, Les Trowsdale, could hardly keep up, and as soon as one man had paid for his round, the next one told him to go round again. In the midst of this lovely party I remembered that poor Karen would be waiting for her supper, so I telephoned to ask her to come up to the Royal Oak. She caused quite a stir when she came into the room and the men were round her like bees round a honeypot. Poor girl, I am sure she wished she had never come. I had not eaten all day and I got quite tight drinking gin-and-tonics at this speed on an empty stomach. At eight forty-five when John Hughes suggested we go over to the Feathers for a steak I readily agreed. I would certainly not have won a prize for the most elegant eating and John laughs to this day about "the night when I could not keep the chips on my plate". My last memory of that night is of Karen guiding me like a blind man across the market square back to Park House.

I awoke not feeling at my best for the special Badsworth "Breakfast Meet" at Fishlake and wondered why I had agreed to go such a long way (Tues 22 Mar 1988). However, I had no other pack to go with that day and, amongst such lovely people, it turned out to be a most enjoyable meet with good food and good company. My diary entry is rather skimpy but I did see the six-year-old in which I was interested in the field, and as I liked it even more, I agreed to buy it. It turned out very well, still carrying the Easton hunt servants years after I gave up the Mastership. There were again vanloads of police, including the two mounted ones, and this time there were lots of antis blowing horns and making a nuisance of themselves. Sadly it was another blank day, or at least blank up to the time I left at three o'clock.

Anthony had kindly booked me in for the special last day of the **Sinnington Foxhounds** at Ravenswick, so I asked him if he would like to come with me on Rose, which he readily accepted (Wed 23 Mar 1988). I would never myself have ridden her from choice because of her nasty habit of kicking hounds, as this would prevent me from accepting any invitations to ride up with huntsmen. The day started with a sumptuous Hunt Breakfast in the lovely dining-room at Ravenswick, a most beautiful house with spectacular views down the valley. The dining-room was arranged so that the tables, which looked very inviting with their white cloths, led up to the large windows which overlooked the grand view. The full breakfast, with all the trimmings – orange juice, champagne, etc. – was very good and life seemed just as it should be. There were approximately eighty people sitting down to breakfast, mostly in their hunt clothes, and Anthony and I were enjoying every minute of it and already feeling as though we were old friends.

After breakfast, there was a cross-country ride over twenty-five or so made jumps, with hounds waiting at the other end. Anthony being an expert horseman and a very accomplished rider had not worried about riding a fresh horse at all, but as we were cantering towards the first jump he did ask whether Rose was used to jumping. I told him that I really could not help him as I did not know because we only ever jumped ditches at home. He took a firm hold of her and she went over the first and most of the others. We crossed a river four times which was quite hairy, especially one crossing when we had to jump down into the water. Glasses of whisky were waiting at the other end and, most important of all, the hounds. The Master and huntsman, Alistair Stewart, invited me to ride up with him and, as usual, I eagerly accepted. The hounds were mostly Welsh crosses and went with a very mixed cry, some high pitched and squeaky and others with very deep voices.

They drew the first covert and hit off a stale drag which they hunted slowly for a mile or so. They then found another and had a lovely hunt with the cry really ringing back across the steep valleys. During this hunt, Mr Stewart jumped a cattle-grid so I had to follow and this is the only time in my life that I have ever done this on purpose. As we went along this heavenly valley, with acoustics good enough for a concert, their voices were echoing back in our ears. Mr Stewart turned up a steep hill towards a gate and I expected him to open it but even on this steep slope he just flew over it, so I had to go as well, with my heart in my mouth. Fizz took it in great style and we climbed, or rather struggled, to the top of this steep hill where sadly hounds lost the line. As it was after four o'clock, Mr Stewart decided to blow for home. I had been impressed with his ability as a huntsman, particularly how he could "turn them on a sixpence", and all so quiet and easy. The end of the day matched the beginning (not an easy thing to do) as Anthony and his wife Jane had invited me to dinner. The evening started, as all evenings do in Helmsley, with drinks in that special room at the Royal Oak. Then we walked down the street and along a little path by the side of a stream to the Barkers' house. The dinner was superb, starting with a delicious home-made soup, and with a dish called "Elizabethan Beef" for the main course. I was so impressed with this dish that I telephoned my wife first thing the next morning to ask her to try to find the recipe. The whole evening was perfect as we had arrived back from the Sinnington still on a high, and Jane's lovely dinner kept us on the same plane, and I left at about eleven o'clock, after enjoying some of Anthony's fine brandy.

It was probably just as well that there was no hunting for the next couple of days as this gave me the opportunity to have a new silencer put on the lorry at the local garage. On the Thursday, after some wonderful beef sandwiches at the Royal Oak, I went for a long walk around Duncombe Park which belonged to the mansion of the Lords Feversham. The house was now standing empty but had been used in turn by the army and a girls' school and was shortly to be restored as a family home for the Fevershams.

On Friday morning I rode Fizz out on exercise across the moors, then took a bouquet of flowers to Jane Barker to thank her for the lovely dinner, before meeting my new friends at the Royal Oak at twelve o'clock. I had agreed to go to Doncaster Races with Anthony, John Hughes and Geoffrey Nicholson, the local butcher, whose daughter Susan was riding in the first race. I enjoyed myself at the races, largely because of the company I was in, even though I won nothing, as I refused to take the advice of my friends who all knew far more about it than I did. We were back in Helmsley by six o'clock and Tony St Quinton was waiting for me in the Royal Oak. We had a few gin and tonics together before going across to the Feathers for dinner, as this was by now the regular routine.

I could not possibly have guessed what sport awaited us from the joint meet of the **Glaisdale Foxhounds** and the **Farndale Foxhounds** at Mill House, in Farndale (Sat 26 Mar 1988). This day I would rate as one of the best, if not the very best, I have ever spent with foxhounds. It is, of course, impossible to say which was actually the best day, but this was certainly amongst the top five days of any pack of foxhounds I have ever been with. Tony St Quinton came on Rose, Karen on Max and myself on Fizz. The meet was unforgettable and and was obviously a very important event with the local farming community. It was held in the village hall and down each long side were tables laden with plates of sandwiches and cakes. Large ladies with large teapots were hurrying round, keeping everyone's cup full. There were, at a guess, over two hundred people in the hall, and I have never been amongst so many interesting-looking characters before. Some were small and some were tall, some were stout and some were thin, but all had that special tan, the weather-beaten face and honest, "son-of-the-soil" look that would enable anyone to pick them out of a thousand as a farmer. The whole hall hummed with local Yorkshire accents and Tony and I were pleased to be amongst such lovely people. The whole thing was like something relived from the past and I can still visualise the ladies up on the stage busily brewing tea for everyone. How busy they must all have been, baking cakes and making sandwiches, as the amount of food was easily sufficient for four hundred people.

When they decided to move off, both huntsmen got out their respective packs. The Glaisdale had twelve and a half couple and the Farndale eight and a half, and as both had brought every hound they had I feel justified in saying that although this was a joint meet I have hunted with them both. From memory, there were about twenty mounted. We moved off through a farmyard where we had to duck under a linen line and hounds hit off a drag. They were soon stopped as the two packs were hunting at different points of the same line and were not rallying to each other's cry. We drew on in the same direction as the drag had been going and found a fox in a fir plantation. I viewed him away

**The Farndale and Glaisdale:** ***"First hazard of the day!"***

and we went off at a grand gallop uphill and downhill over some very rough country. The level ground was very boggy, and full of holes and rocks. We galloped past many grouse butts and along the hillside, often going up and down very steep places. Fizz terrified me as he was so impetuous and would often plunge towards the edge of what looked like a vertical drop when we were about to go down a very steep place . The slope was so steep that it was extremely difficult to keep in the saddle, coupled with the fact that the ground was so rough the horses had a job to find enough sound ground for a foothold. The uphills were just as bad although this seemed less frightening than going down. One of the climbs was especially steep. Fizz was scrabbling up the side and, although his legs were going as fast as they could, he was actually losing height. It makes my stomach turn over now to remember what it felt like when he started slipping backwards. We were nearly at the top and if he had lost control or panicked we could both easily have been killed in the fall. Hounds were driving on, usually a quarter of a mile or so ahead of us as we rode along the top of the ridge, sometimes coming from the valley, over the top ahead of us, and down the other side, to hunt along the adjacent valley. Thus we carried on, either galloping along the top contending with the bogs, or struggling up and down the steep hillsides, for about twelve miles as hounds ran. We went over Harland moor, crossed the River Dove, over Sprowston Moor and Thorgill Bank, dropped down into the River Seven and finally killed our fox at Yates, fairly close to farm buildings in which he had tried to conceal himself. I was presented with the brush and Tony with a pad. Fizz, although a most unsuitable horse for such country as this, had nevertheless kept me close to the huntsman all the time, and I had seen all of this hunt which was a nine-mile point.

Sadly, Fizz had cut himself badly in two places and that was the end of my day. Blood was spurting out from his leg and running down the road. I was offered, and gratefully accepted, a lift from a car follower to go back to fetch the lorry and left Karen to deal with the cut and to take the horses on to Hutton-le-Hole so I would know where to find them. An extra pleasure was to see how much Tony had enjoyed it. This had been his first day with foxhounds and he was quite beside himself with joy and excitement. I followed my kind benefactor's car on the way back as I did not know my way to Hutton-le-Hole and we all eventually returned safely to Helmsley.

Tony and I bathed and changed and had a quick drink at the Royal Oak before leaving to go to a Mad March Hare Ball at Rearsby Grange which I had promised Charlotte Banks I would not miss. It was a long drive after a hard day's hunting but well worth it. Luckily, of course, we had the use of Tony's car and soon arrived to enjoy the Moet et Chandon and first-class eats. There were so many lovely girls that I did not drink much of the champagne as I was always dancing. I had not even finished my first glass before I was on the floor. Between dances I had a quick sip of the "rejuvenator" and then onto the floor again, dancing with ten girls in all, one of whom was my introduction to this place, Sally Hennessy, who looked as attractive as ever and was always surrounded by a crowd of admirers. Tony met a man he used to work with in Woodbridge and I renewed my acquaintance with Paul Quinn from the Holcome Harriers. "Wild William" was in full swing and wanted me to fly with him to Ireland for a few days. I kept telling him that I could not, but he would not hear of it, saying that life was too short to be as dull and dependable as I was. Tony and I would both have ended up in Ireland, without doubt, since he was not only persuasive but was beginning to talk about carrying us off bodily, but luckily, having stayed there twice before, I knew of an escape route. There were some servants' stairs at the back of the upstairs landing, so with the pretence of going to the loo, we went up the front stairs, back down the servants' stairs, and escaped at two-thirty. Tony took the chance on the breathaliser and drove his car as far as Newark where we stopped in a lorry park overlooking the castle. We left the engine running to keep the heater on and slept in the car. We breakfasted in a Little Chef at seven-fifteen and arrived back at Helmsley at eight-thirty.

Twelve o'clock drinks at the Royal Oak was followed by Sunday lunch at the Feathers and then we went to look round Castle Howard. A very pleasant evening was spent with the usual drinks at the Royal Oak and as it was John Hughes' and Anthony Barker's birthdays there was a special joviality about the proceedings which ended with a very good dinner at the Feathers and bed at eleven o'clock. There was no hunting on Monday so we went to visit the Army Museum at Beverley to see a horse-drawn ambulance for injured horses which is thought to be the only one, other than the one in my collection, in the country. I had hoped to see a perfect example but, like mine, this one had lost its original seat and pulley, and the First Aid box.

By Tuesday Fizz had recovered from his injury so I took him for a day with the **Bilsdale Foxhounds**, while Karen had Max and Tony, Rose (Tues 29 Mar 1988). The meet was at Boltby, near Sutton Bank, only a few miles from Helmsley, and was advertised for ten forty-five but hounds were half an hour late. This was a poor start and set the tone for the day. The hounds were a very mixed bag, very unlevel, mostly Fellhounds, with the worst sterns I have ever seen, some even curling round twice. They were very independent and would not go to the horn, so much of the day was spent trying to get them together. The most hounds I ever saw with the huntsman at one time with was five and a half couples, and he had out fifteen and a half.

**Bilsdale.** *Members high on the North York Moors.*
Photograph kindly loaned by R Barry

I met a man who had been manager of Colston Hall, Badingham, which was the next-door farm to where I lived when first married. We spent quite a long time on the Cleveland Way, and at one time were so high we could see for over thirty miles to the Pennines and right over the Bilsdale country to the Hurworth country. Tony was amusing himself chatting up the female whipper-in when they actually found in some forestry, and we did have a little hunt to end the day. At one time, Tony and I had the hounds to ourselves until they turned back into the forestry. We ended on high ground and had a steep descent to the horse-boxes below. I stupidly told Karen to go first, followed by Tony and then myself, but this upset Fizz because he was not in front and he started to plunge. Just in front of me, Tony decided to hang on to the back of his saddle. This struck me as very funny and I had a fit of uncontrollable giggles, so what with Fizz plunging and the loss of grip due to the giggles, I nearly fell off several times. However, we all arrived safely at the bottom.

Our last day was to have been with the Saltersgate Farmers' but, during the evening, the Master telephoned me to say that disaster had struck his hounds. Most of the pack had picked up poison when out hunting and he had lost most of them. As a result there was to be no more hunting that season. Instead Tony and I decided to drive, *via* a scenic route, to Whitby, where I renewed my acquaintace with my landlord from the Whitby Folk Festival, and then had lunch at the well-known fish restaurant, Trenchers (Wed 30 Nov 1988). The manageress, who was full of fun, remembered me from the Festival and asked me to take Mole away as he was chatting up the waitresses. When we arrived back at Helmsley, we went for a long walk in the Park where I showed Tony the follies and the lovely views from the Outer Walk.

Tony decided to go home the next day and took most of my kit which helped give some extra room on the lorry for the new horse I had to pick up. The Barkers kindly invited me to dinner again, and another first class evening ensued which was the perfect ending to a very good holiday. During dinner, Anthony's daughter, Emma, who was then about nine, told me how recently she had been hunting with the Sinnington and had stopped out so long that she had to hack home in the dark with the whipper-in. I was so pleased to see the obvious great pleasure she had to be with hounds and that the famous Barker tradition of hunting would continue. The story was particularly pleasing as I knew that the legendary Stanley Barker, who had been professional huntsman of the Pytchley from 1931 to 1960, was her great-uncle, and would like to have heard it himself.

I left Anthony's yard at seven forty-five and the long journey home was only broken by stopping to pick up my new horse, BJ, and for a sandwich at the Trinity Foot pub near Cambridge. Hordes of people were pouring out of London on this Good Friday and, as I was coming south, I passed a continuous traffic jam on the A1 going north from Thirsk to Peterborough where I turned off onto the A604, driving past the virtually stationary traffic for two and a half hours. As usual, I spent the long journey thinking of all that had happened and the time did not drag. I had hunted with eight more packs, or twelve if I included my first visit to Rearsby Grange. What a wonderful privilege to have experienced the contrasts in hunting that I so enjoy. I had stayed and stabled my horses at a real "hunting box" and had hunted with the elite in the famous "Shires". With my vivid imagination I could have imagined myself as a "Meltonian", and had then gone straight from this grandeur back to Surtees' days with the never-to-be-forgotten day with the Farndale and Glaisdale. I had been to a Hunt Breakfast, and ridden along the ancient Cleveland Way. I had met so many new friends and characters: Les Trowsdale, the landlord of the Royal Oak (a book could be written about his exploits); Jack Feathers, landlord of the Feathers Inn (which he named after himself), a real "mine host" character and if a film director had ever needed a Dickensian landlord he would have needed to look no further; Jack's son Lance who was such a fine chef, and a great character in his own right; Geoffrey Nicholson, the local butcher; Ian and Jackie Saggers who looked after us all so well in their lovely home; Peter "the Poof" the landlord of another pub three miles from Helmsley who was an ex-monk and now an alcoholic organist who played the organ in the private chapel at Castle Howard, and told funny stories of when he had had a few too many and played the hymns in the wrong order. Last, but not least, there was John Hughes, with his fund of amusing tales, several of which concerned his young son's pet python, which he could whistle for. The tales of this pet included several of occasions when it had wriggled out from under a chair unexpectedly when they had guests, one of a terrified vet who was called in to worm it, and, best of all, the one of when his son went into a pet shop to buy tame rats and mice to feed it and an old lady beat him about the head with her brolly. There were so many more lovely people, most of whom I have seen again on my subsequent visits to Helmsley. What else could one wish for on a hunting holiday? Good hunting, lovely food, non-stop laughter, and the first-class company of people who had welcomed me into their homes like a long-lost friend. All of this was the more enjoyable because of being able to share it with my old friend Tony and see his immense enjoyment of it.

**South Cornwall.** *Mr Parkin, Jt. Master and Huntsman watching hounds draw at Hellman Tor.*

# MAP 16

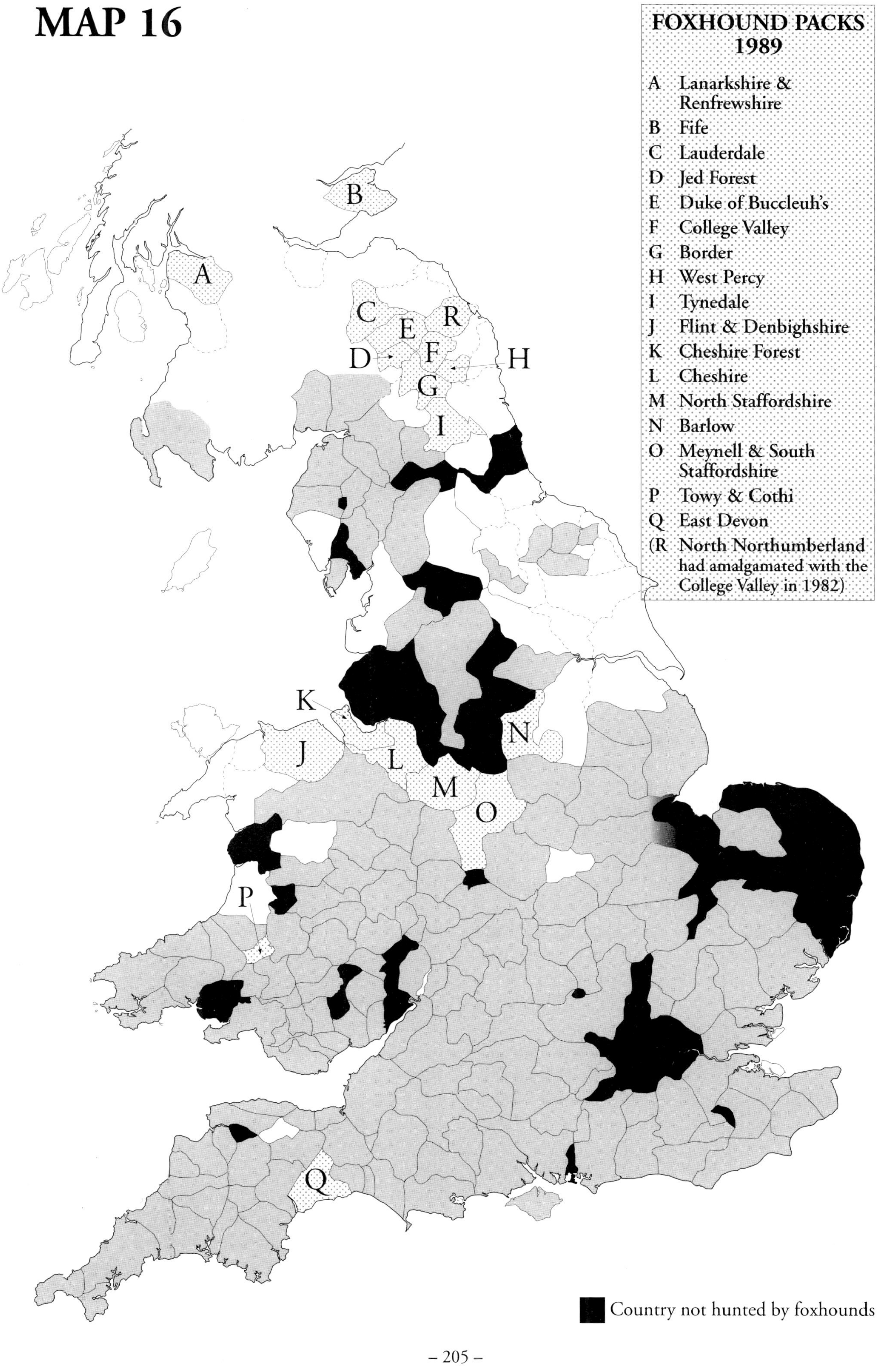
FOXHOUND PACKS
1989
A Lanarkshire & Renfrewshire
B Fife
C Lauderdale
D Jed Forest
E Duke of Buccleuh's
F College Valley
G Border
H West Percy
I Tynedale
J Flint & Denbighshire
K Cheshire Forest
L Cheshire
M North Staffordshire
N Barlow
O Meynell & South Staffordshire
P Towy & Cothi
Q East Devon
(R North Northumberland had amalgamated with the College Valley in 1982)
A
B
C
D
E
F
G
H
I
J
K
L
M
N
O
P
Q
R
Country not hunted by foxhounds

# Chapter 18

## The Painful Holiday – Scotland Again

During the summer of 1988 I made my annual visit to Appleby Fair in Cumbria with my friends Maurice Scott and Tim Last, and combined the trip with a day with the Lyth Valley Minkhounds. We went in the car towing a trailer filled with draft hounds, two and a half couple to go to the Holcombe as they were too big for the Easton, and three and a half couple to go to the Windermere as they were too small. We had arranged to meet Alex Sneddon, the huntsman of the Holcombe, at a motorway service station and, as he had parked on the opposite side of the road, he had to lead his two and a half couple over the walkway. We then continued up to the Windermere kennels where we were going to stay with Anthony and Sheila Barker at Patterdale. I had asked Anthony if he could find some minkhunting for us and he had suggested the **Lyth Valley Minkhounds** who were meeting at the Master's house near Beck Side (Fri 6 June 1988). Anthony, who needed little excuse for a day's sport, came with us to show us the way. The hounds consisted of six couple of Dumfriesshire Foxhounds.

When we got to the river the Master said, "Right now, lads. Are you ready for instant sport?"

He opened the door of the hound van and hounds went straight into the water and started to hunt. This was most impressive, but I assumed that he had seen a mink there while he was waiting for us to come so he knew he would be able to provide "instant sport". Hounds hunted very prettily with the deep Dumfriesshire voices, until the mink eventually went up a tree. Hounds were taken well back and the mink was persuaded to re-enter the water by a man who climbed up the tree. Hounds were then laid on and we had another ten to fifteen minute hunt, hounds finally catching it while swimming. This would have been an even more enjoyable hunt if it had not been for an idiot with eight terriers running loose. The Master quite rightly became very angry and said that if they were not kept on leads he would take his hounds home. The Master had also been the huntsman of the Kendal and District Otterhounds and we spent a couple of hours listening to his stories in the local pub before returning to Patterdale.

At the beginning of the next season the Easton were invited down to the West Country by the Mid-Devon Foxhounds with whom I had hunted in April the previous year (1987) from Gillingham. Many of the Easton members stayed at the Three Crowns at Chagford where everyone enjoyed the excellent dinners and splendid atmosphere which was frequently enlivened by the Irish postman who, at one time, had been kennel huntsman to the legendary Mr John Dix. I hunted the harriers on the moor but unfortunately had a blank day, and then the following day we all went with the **East Devon Foxhounds** (Tues 8 Nov 1988). Thirty-one Easton members had come down with their horses and over half of them came out again with these hounds who were meeting at Upton Farm, Payhembury. The Joint Master, Mr Bartlett, welcomed us all and said he would have liked to have given our hounds a day in his country, if only he had known we were coming down. The Easton members outnumbered the East Devon in the field but all the natives went out of their way to be pleasant to us visitors and that greatly enhanced the enjoyment of the day.

Hounds found in some fodder beet and ran over some lovely country which was teeming with deer. They were rock steady to the deer which were running in every direction, and completely ignored their lines. They stuck to their hunted fox and, although scent was poor, they caught him and I was presented with the brush. The second hunt gave us another good run across this lovely country of steep grasslands and twice we had a clear view of the hunted fox crossing the middle of a large pasture. During this run hounds had checked at the top of a hill and our horses were glad of a breather. As we sat there my brother-in-law, Michael Buckley, caught up on the horse he had hired locally. This horse must have been very quiet as he had forgotton to tighten his girth and the saddle had slipped back and was on top of his horse's quarters. He seemed not to have noticed his new position and the girth was swinging backwards and forwards hitting his horse on the sheath. I shouted "Michael, Michael, Get off quickly!". "Why!" "Why?" he replied. So I said, "Your saddle has slipped back", whereupon he took hold of it front & back and tried to hitch it forward. The rest of us just dissolved into hapless laughter and did so for the next three days whenever the subject was brought up. This second fox went to ground and was despatched by the terrier men. At four o'clock I said to Mr Bartlett that I had had enough so he said that if we were all going back he would not draw again. When we arrived back at Chagford most of us trooped into the tearoom next door to the Three Crowns for Devon Cream Teas and that evening there was a very good party at the Three Crowns which went on to the early hours.

**East Devon Foxhounds:** ***"Michael - Get off quickly". "Why!" "Why?"***

As the horses would need a rest, I had planned for the Easton members to have a day with the **North Dartmoor Beagles** at the Tor Valley Inn, Sticklepath (Wed 9 Nov 1988). On the way to the meet we passed very near to South Zeal and I could not resist calling in to see the landlord at the Kings Arms where I had spent so many happy hours during the Dartmoor Folk Singing Festival. Several of the Easton members followed suit and after half an hour or so with him we moved on to the beagle meet. There was an immediate atmosphere of fun and laughter as the two hunts mixed together and there was great laughter when my Joint Master, Mark Wayne, pushed a £50 note which I had placed on the counter for a round of drinks into the Poppy Day Collection Box. One of the Easton members was making a video film and was disappointed to have missed this incident, so it was decided to have a mock re-run. However Mark, in typical fashion, put the second £50 note into the box as well. This caused even more howls of laughter mixed with astonishment at such an extravagant joke, especially when the landlord commented, "It will go well with the £1.50 that was already in there." One of our young members, who was known to be quite thrifty, was all for cutting the top off the box with a knife. During the evening Mark refunded to me the second half of the joke.

Mr Tim Whitley, the Master and huntsman, moved off to draw some fodder beet above the meet and hit off a drag. Hounds followed the drag for a long way and I became convinced it was the drag of a fox, so lost interest in the proceedings. As the red mud was so sticky and the going very heavy I soon accepted a lift in a Range Rover, only to learn very quickly that car-following was not very successful between the high Devon banks. With the visibility nil, except when I climbed up on a bank, we soon lost hounds completely and so retired to the Drew Arms at Drewsteignton, a delightfully old-fashioned little pub. I felt I had not seen enough of these hounds and resolved to go with them again, hopefully on the moor and away from that sticky red mud.

The Easton visit lasted all week and we hunted with the South Devon at Hay Tor Rock on Thursday and had a joint-dinner with the Mid Devon at the Three Crowns at Chagford on Friday night, and ended the holiday hunting with the Mid Devon again on Saturday at Postbridge, near Princetown. This was made the more enjoyable because my great friends, the St Quintons, had come down by car for the dinner and Anne and Tony and myself followed on foot. It was all very enjoyable except when we received a rocket from a farmer who did not want us on his land and told us to stick to the footpath.

That season was my last as Master and huntsman of the Easton and, on my retirement on 30 April 1989, I resolved to make the most of my new freedom. During the next season (1989-90) I was away for all of November and for another five weeks in the New Year, hunting from bases in Derbyshire, Scotland, the Wirral, Wales and Yorkshire, and from some of these more than once. First of all came the Painful Holiday when I spent six days in Derbyshire and then moved up to Scotland for another two weeks, followed by short stays in the Wirral, Wales and Derbyshire again. I had received a kind invitation to stay with Eric and Marcia Elliott in Derbyshire in order to hunt with some packs in the area I had not yet been with. I left home on the last day of October at seven forty-five with my new groom, Hazel Chapman, and horses Fizz and Max, but I had never left home for one of these jollies in such doubt as to whether I would be able to ride or not. After my grand-daughter's Christening party the Sunday before I had slipped down and had struck my left buttock on the sharp corner of a small table. The bruise had turned inwards and I was in great pain. Had it been my right leg I would have been unable to drive as I could not have used the brake. As it was, I had to use my hand to lift my left leg onto the clutch every time I needed to change gear. I felt I was really mad to be driving up to Derbyshire in this state but "Hope springs eternal ..." and I assumed it would eventually wear off.

I had arranged to telephone to Eric when we reached the Post House near Junction 15 on the M6 and he was to come out to meet us. We arrived there at two o'clock and Eric then showed us the way to the livery stable where we left the lorry, horses and Hazel. She was going to share accommodation with one of the resident grooms. Eric took me in his car to his lovely home, Sutton House, at Endon, where I was greeted with a lovely kiss from Marcia.

Next morning I thought I ought to see if I could ride, as I had made arrangements to hunt with the Meynell and South Staffs on the following day, so Eric and I went to the stables to hack out. With great difficulty I got on with the help of a mounting block and managed to ride but it was extremely painful. The only way I could trot was to press my hand firmly on the pommel of the saddle to help raise myself up. I made the decision that, as I had come so far, I would try to hunt the next day. Hazel rode with us and, being Suffolk born and bred, was quite amazed by the Derbyshire hills. During the afternoon, Eric drove me to see a collar-maker that I had heard of in Woodville. I was most impressed with his traditional method of collar-making and, as I had recently lost all my harness in a fire, I ordered eight collars which I am still using today. In the evening Eric, Marcia and I walked down from Sutton House to the Plough Inn where they ran a first-class "carvery".

The walk back up the hill was good exercise but did not ease off my stiffness and I was not much better the next morning when I left Sutton House at eight-fifteen for the meet of the **Meynell and South Staffordshire Foxhounds** at Blithbury, near Lichfield (Thurs 2 Nov 1989). I arrived late and it took several attempts to persuade Fizz to stand still beside the ramp for me to get on. As I trotted to the meet with one hand pressed on the pommel I felt that indeed I was really mad to try to hunt, as riding was so painful that at times I was near to tears. I was unimpressed by the turnout of most of the field who looked more as if it was the last day of the season rather than the start of it. Hounds drew some sugarbeet and then some coverts near big cooling towers where they found and we had a little run across country which seemed a mixture of arable and old permanent pasture. With hunt jumps everywhere, it was easy to keep with hounds. The scent was not good and this run had many checks which I was very glad of because it helped me with my problem. When they decided to dig out this fox at one-fifteen I decided to go back as I was extremely uncomfortable and could stand it no longer. Back at the lorry I had to step off onto the ramp to get off. I arrived at the stables at three-thirty and then telephoned Marcia who kindly came to pick me up. We had arranged this as there was no room at their home for me to park the lorry, and this became the routine. Back at Sutton House, I had a good long soak in a hot bath but it did not help at all.

Eric was able to come with me next day to the **Barlow Foxhounds** and we set off at seven-thirty for the ten o'clock meet, with his horse Murphy and Max for me (Fri 3 Nov 1989). Just before the meet we made a bad mistake and arrived rather later than we would have wished. The meet was at Brackenfield, near Belper, and was held on what was once the village green but was now very "suburbanised" and cut with lawnmowers. Eric and I immediately felt a couple of idiots as we had turned out formally and they were still cub-hunting. This we both ought to have realised as the meet was at ten o'clock.

When they moved off to draw, I was asked to go on point near the edge of a reservoir and to stop the fox from going that way, but somehow he slipped by me in some brambles and we had a very nice hunt until he went to ground in a badger earth and was left. Hounds found again and had a hunt which consisted of many short bursts from covert to covert until he was eventually caught. They drew for their third fox near a large Hall and I was again put to stop hounds running to a fast railway line. This time I managed it. Hounds looked well and fit and were hunted beautifully by Chris Hill whose voice and horn were a joy to hear. Chris' father, Ted Hill, was a huntsman for many years until retiring in 1986 from this pack, and was a legend in his own lifetime. Ted's wife was out hunting helping to whip-in and she told me an incredible story. Ted's sight had gone while he was still hunting hounds but he did not give up on that account. Instead he had someone riding alongside him to tell him where the fences were so he knew when to take off, and to keep him away from low boughs and so forth. I was disappointed that Miss Wilson, the famous Master, known to all as Miss

Anne, was not out as she had to attend the funeral of the Master of the Grove and Rufford Foxhounds. Although I was thoroughly enjoying the hunting, I decided at two o'clock that I would have to give in as the pain was once again terrible and we eventually arrived back at the stables at four-fifteen.

In the evening we decided to go down to the Plough again and after another soak in a hot bath I still could not put my socks and shoes on and had to ask Eric to help me. The dinner at the Plough was hilariously funny as there were two fat women, with two fat children, sitting at the next table but one. They came back from the carvery with their plates piled up as high as possible, then proceeded to eat in a most revolting way. None of them used their knives to cut at all, but prodded the roast potatoes with the knife and ate them off the end of the knife as if they were apples. The meat was held likewise with a fork with mouthfuls bitten off as best they could. Funniest of all, however, were the large pieces of broccoli which were stabbed in the firm part of the stalk, then they tipped their heads back and stared at the ceiling while hanging the broccoli over their mouths and biting off from the bottom until they finally came to the stalk. To see the four of them eating in this manner gave us a fit of uncontrollable giggles and, as we did not wish to appear to be laughing at them, this made it all the more impossible to control. I can still visualise the scene of the four of them, their elbows on the table, knife in one hand with a potato on it and a whole slice of meat on the fork in the other hand, with the gravy dripping off it.

On Saturday Eric had arranged for me to go with the **North Staffordshire Foxhounds** (Sat 4 Nov 1989). I left the stables at nine o'clock and arrived just in time. The meet was held in the village of Norton-in-Hales near Market Drayton. This was on a busy road and, as no-one was allowed to stand their horses on the grass, there was considerable traffic disruption. We drew the first covert blank, then had a sharp burst across country to the next covert. While hounds were drawing this second covert, a friend of Eric's, John Burch, said: "Well, now you can say that you have jumped the only stone wall in the North Staffs country."

There were scores of antis out who blew horns and disrupted proceedings. I was surprised to see that the hounds were really keen to go to the anti's horn and would leave their huntsman's side to go to their blowing. At one time when the antis were well off the footpath and were in the middle of a large pasture, the Master called loudly for all the young members to come round him. He then told them to form a line and gallop towards the swarm of antis. This they did and the antis took to their heels and ran. Many of them ended up with torn trousers in trying to jump a barbed-wire fence. This was such a funny sight that I wished I had considered myself a "young member" and had joined in.

At two o'clock I could put up with the pain no longer so I walked back to the box standing up in my stirrups all the way. As Fizz was so excited and would not keep near the ramp, it took over five minutes to get off and at one moment I thought I would have to wait for someone to lift me off. I got back to the stables at three-thirty to find Eric waiting to take me off to his son's beagle tea at the Cheshire Cheese pub. The hounds – the North Staffordshire Moorland Beagles – had had a blank day but the tea was excellent and helped make up for it.

In the evening I had such difficulty in dressing that I seriously considered going home, instead of going on up to Scotland to stay with my old friends Colin and Tizza Plumbe in their new home at Roberton near Hawick, as planned. This was my third attempt to "do" Scotland, the previously planned trips in 1983 and 1987 having been abandoned, and in the end the stubborn side of me won and I decided to go on. In the morning I was stiffer than ever but nevertheless got into the lorry to drive to Roberton, still having to lift my leg onto the clutch every time I needed to change gear. This was not an ideal situation when driving a lorry in the Derbyshire hills. Just before I got to their home, Easter House, I met Colin on the road on his way to the Open Day at the kennels of the Duke of Buccleuch's hounds. He turned his car round and followed me back to his home, and then whisked me off to the Open Day as soon as I stepped out of the lorry. I thoroughly enjoyed the visit and was most impressed by the fabulous kennels and stables at St Boswell's Green. The day ended with a lovely dinner at Easter House with plenty of laughter.

The week started with a day with the **Border Foxhounds** (Mon 6 Nov 1989). Tizza came with me on her daughter, Alice's, pony and I took Max, but when we arrived at the meet at Hindhope there was hardly anyone there and we had to ask if this was the right place. Soon everyone arrived and there were Land Rovers and trailers everywhere. A little over half the trailers had horses in them but what really surprised me was to see the young men backing their motorbikes out of the other trailers. The mounted field was to be approximately fifteen motorbikes and twenty-five horses! It was quite a sight to see these lads riding their bikes over the hills. Some had three-wheeler bikes and some two-wheelers, and most had terriers with them – some under their arms, or tucked into their jackets with the head poking out, others were standing on the petrol tank between their owner's knees and one bike had a cage on the back with four terriers in it.

Some of the bikes also had radios and the Joint Master and huntsman, Michael Hedley, had one as well so he could stay in contact with them. This was the first time I had come across the whole concept of modern technology in foxhunting and it seemed very strange at first. I also thought it strange that the Master rode away with hounds without a word to anyone and as soon as Tizza and I were ready we hurried after him. However, the actual meet was at a farm a quarter of a mile up the road and once there the Master greeted us very civilly. He said that he knew I must think the radios very strange but explained how useful they were in these hills.

**Border Foxhounds.** *Meet at Upper Hindhope, 6 November 1989. The dramatic country enjoyed by the Border.*
Photograph kindly loaned by Lt Col R N R Cross

When we moved off to draw a small fir wood near the meet, the motorbikes roared off up the hills to watch from the tops or along the valleys in the far distance. Hounds found and ran uphill at a great pace reminding me a little of Fell hounds in their rather individual style. By the time we got up to the top with horses, hounds were well away across the next valley, but fortunately they swung round and brought the line back to the same wood where he was found. It was a morning of bright sunshine after a white frost and scent was not good. Hounds were frequently at check but they always cast themselves immediately and quickly regained the line. Their style of casting was very like Fell hounds: each hound would investigate his own theory with the result that the hounds spread all around the check and they hardly ever cast themselves as a pack like normal foxhounds. This fox was fresh found again in the wood and ran a similar circular route in these tremendous rolling hills and finally entered some farm buildings where there was a long check. I was leaving the farmyard via a little bridge when the fox overtook me, almost running under Max's legs as he squeezed past us on this narrow bridge, before going to ground in an earth in the next field. Terriers bolted him from here and hounds were laid on the line but, unfortunately, ran heel away back to the earth. They were soon put right by Mr Hedley and they ran on to catch their fox in the open. They richly

**The Border:** ***"When needs must, the devil drives!"***

deserved their fox as they had worked very hard in this very poor scent.

There were several more hunts, most of which were spoiled by too many foxes and too many changes as a consequence. The whole scene fascinated me, these huge, rolling hills with the motorbikes in every direction on the distant hilltops. Hounds would often be well away from the huntsman but he could speak through his radio to a bike in that direction who could perhaps tell him the hounds were turning back thus saving the horses considerably. It also meant that we could have the pleasure of first seeing the fox twisting and turning his way back below us, then watching as hounds unravelled his line. All or most of this we would have missed if we had been riding hard to catch up with hounds. Another very unusual thing was that there was not a single red coat in sight as the Border Foxhounds' livery is steel grey. The hounds seemed to be excitable to the extent that one could almost say they were wild but Mr Hedley was always so quiet and unruffled that he managed always to have them exactly where he wanted. It seemed strange at first to see all the motorbikes out hunting, but on reflection I thought how natural it was for all the young farmers to follow on the bikes which they use for shepherding, just as their fathers and grandfathers used their shepherd's cobs to follow hounds. The motorbikes had some distinct advantages over horses in that they could skim across boggy places where horses could not go and, of course, never got tired and could go from hilltop to hilltop all day. The only disadvantage was the noise but that was usually not a problem as most of the time they were in the far distance. The nature of the country, with very few fences, enabled them to go where they wished and they were very brave and skilful riders, often going in seemingly impossible places. I did, however, see one of them make a mistake in going up a very steep hill. When nearly at the top the bike tipped over backwards and both rider and bike tumbled to the bottom where, luckily, the rider was unhurt.

**Lauderdale Foxhounds.** *The Lawn meet at Nether Brotherton, 7 Nov 1989, Tony Harvey on Bucks Fizz, far right.*

I reluctantly had to give up at four o'clock, still very sore, and drove home with great difficulty. I had become quite worried as things seemed to be getting far worse and I presume that the bruised muscle was being aggravated by riding a horse. I wrote up this day in my diary while sitting in a charming little study at Easter House with a lovely fire burning in the grate and thinking how lucky I was to have such good friends and to be able to stay in such lovely places. I had my sock in my pocket and was waiting for Tizza to appear to put it on for me. I don't think that I can sum up my enjoyment of the day better than my actual first words in the diary:

> *"A lovely, heavenly, wonderful day, just my sort of hunting. Everyone who was there was there to hunt, Land Rovers, motorbikes, on foot or mounted. All were equally interested and played their own part in the hunt. There is nowhere else on earth I would rather have been today than where I have been."*

I left Easter House with Fizz at nine o'clock next morning for a day with the **Lauderdale Foxhounds** (Tues 7 Nov 1989). The meet was at Nether Brotherton, near Stow, and was held in a meadow below a bungalow from which delicious eats and drinks appeared. There were about twenty mounted and all seemed very friendly. The hounds were mixed fellhound and studbook foxhounds. They found at once and ran very hard across some "in bye" meadows of permanent pasture. "In bye" means enclosed land in the valley as opposed to the open hills. It was a very twisty fox which ran rather like a hare, frequently turning and doubling which made for a most interesting hunt to watch. The pace was good and when I found myself behind the whipper-in, I followed him over a wall and two fair-sized gates which Fizz took with his usual gusto. Hounds eventually lost this line and then proceeded to draw for over an hour without finding again. During this time I saw a blue hare for the first time and was surprised to see how much white she had on her.

I had read of the blue hares of Scotland which changed colour from browny-grey in summer to white in winter and was thrilled to see one. The changing of colour is triggered off by the length of daylight but this extraordinary feat of nature can be a great disadvantage to the hare when there is no snow on the ground as, of course, she is very conspicuous. On one farm in the Easton Harriers country there is a breed of white hares which stay white all year round. This fact alone, as far as I know, makes them unique among hares, and another interesting observation is that when they cross with the ordinary hares the resulting offspring are piebald. I have kept this fact a secret for many years at the farmer's request as he does not want them interfered with. He always asked me not to hunt them, which proved difficult for, as brown hares will not sit tight in snow, the white hares would get up three hundred yards ahead of hounds as they feel so conspicuous. One day when I was asking the farmer for permission to hunt on his farm he gave his usual request to avoid the white hares and ended with the remark that he was "breeding" them. When I asked him how he could "breed" wild hares, he said,

"Quite easily. I keep my rifle on the tractor when I'm working on the fields in spring, and I shoot the brown bucks."

This sighting of a white hare really made my day but, when it was announced that they were going into forestry, I decided to go back to the box as I was in agony having aggravated the situation by jumping the gates and so forth. The steepness of the hills made me even more uncomfortable as coming downhill put pressure on the sore part. The hills were exceptionally steep, so much so that I saw one man and his horse slip down the hillside for quite a long way before they could recover themselves. There was another fresh hazard in that there was mains electric fence running along the top of many of the walls. This had to be turned off when hounds were in the area. It was a terrible problem if the farmers forgot to switch it off or, more likely, if hounds ran to where they were not expected. One man came back to the meet with me and helped me get off, for which I was very grateful as Fizz would not stand still near the ramp.

Next day Colin took the day off work to come with me to the **Fife Foxhounds** (Wed 8 Nov 1989). We left at seven-thirty but we only just made it as Colin had to make a long telephone call to his work. As I was introducing myself to Mr Gilmour, one of the Joint Masters, a voice said, "Oh Mr Harvey, you have made it at last, then!". It was the huntsman, who remembered me from years before when I had visited his kennel in 1983 when I was originally trying to arrange a Scottish tour. The meet was held in a meadow in front of Cairnie Lodge, a most impressive house with a magnificent stable block, just outside Cupar.

**Fife Foxhounds.** *Meet at Cairnie Lodge, Cupar, 1989. Huntsman Ian Scholes, and Joint Masters Mr J Gilmour, Dr H Watson and Major W H O Hutchison.*

Photograph kindly donated

Hounds found at once and had a nice little spin over a farm where they were barred. They changed foxes three or four times, then settled to one which ran through a herd of Black Angus, then across another farm where they were barred. I was not surprised that they had been barred from so many farms when I saw how they behaved. When we came to a herd of Black Angus which were enclosed with a fairly new, tightly strained barbed-wire fence, this was promptly cut without hesitation even though it would have been quite simple to go round it. I was hailed by Miss Esher who had been Master of the Gelligaer Farmers' Foxhounds in South Wales when I had hunted with them and had since moved up to Scotland. The whole day was rather amateurish and I was not sorry to leave at two-fifteen, eventually arriving back at Easter House at six o'clock, where the order of the day was a quick change and off to the Buccleuch Supporters' Club Sausage-Tasting Supper at Denholm. I told everyone what a good singer Colin was and he sang a couple of songs as I later did. This was the first singing of hunting songs that the Buccleuch had heard and I left hoping it would build up.

Tizza was able to come with me again on Alice's pony, Quillie, for my day with the **College Valley Foxhounds** (Thurs 9 Nov 1989). We unboxed and rode up to the meet which was in an idyllic setting in a meadow under the ha-ha wall, with gardens stretching up to Melkington House above us, and the low ground stretching away below us. Martin Letts, the famous Joint Master and huntsman of these hounds, offered the briefest of civilities but the rest of the field (of ten mounted) were very friendly. One lady rode up to ask if I knew Cherry Barclay, Master of the Suffolk Foxhounds, as she and Cherry had been great "muckers" when they were girls. Sadly, the hunting was to be "in bye" which meant that we would be hunting over enclosed farmland and not on the open hills for which these hounds are justly famous. The first fox was found in some mangels and gave us a long and very difficult hunt. The scent was poor and hounds had to work hard but persevered mile after mile and were every bit as good as I had expected them to be. There were sheep everywhere and, as well as the poor scent, hounds had to contend with sheep foil. During the long, slow hunt, the Master had hunted them very quietly and unhurriedly, allowing them to concentrate, and no pack of hounds could have tried harder. When the line was eventually lost there was some more hunting in deep dingles, but very short bursts and it was impossible to see anything. The hounds were as lovely as their reputation led me to expect, all light-coloured, level and of exactly the same stamp. The light colour is highly desirable in a hill country as they are easy to see at a distance against the bracken. The whipper-in rode an Appaloosa cob, a most unusual sight. As there was no jumping and all the gates were opened, it was as gentle a day as Fizz would allow but I had had enough by two-thirty and we went back to the box.

On Friday there were no hounds hunting so I thought I ought to tackle the problem of washing four pairs of breeches. Bedford Cord breeches are very comfortable to wear but the devil to wash as they shrink very easily. I had never tried to wash any before, preferring always to wait to get home for Sheila to do them for me, not through laziness but from lack of expertise. I had been out with hounds seven times since leaving home and, as I planned to get out many more times, I felt obliged to pluck up the courage to make an effort myself. I telephoned to Sheila for instructions and was told to ask Tizza to set the machine as for wool and then to hang them out, and under no circumstances to spin dry them. I obeyed every instruction to the letter and all was well. I had often managed to get away with using breeches for a second time by brushing off the mud and touching up the spots with Meltonian White. This worked reasonably well, except for the one never-to-be-forgotten wet meet when the White started to run down over my boots.

While the breeches were drying I built a temporary stable for Tizza's grey pony as we were expecting a visitor to arrive with his horse for the meet next day. Ian McKay had been a member of the Easton for many seasons before his job took him to Scotland. As their local pack, the **Duke of Buccleuch's hounds**, were to have a lawn meet at Easter House, Colin and Tizza had invited him to come to stay, both to see me again and to have a day with the Buccleuch. Ian arrived at about ten o'clock that night and I am pleased to say that Tizza's horse did not escape from his temporary stable.

**Duke of Buccleuch's Foxhounds.** *Colin and Tizza Plumbe leaving their lawn meet at Easter House.*

Photograph kindly loaned by Mrs Plumbe

Next morning there was the inevitable frenzy of activity with glasses to get out, sausage rolls and other eats to make, as well as getting ourselves ready to hunt (Sat 11 Nov 1989). Ian and I were commandeered as waiters to dispense the drinks, and this was probably an expensive mistake on Colin's part. He gave me special instructions to see that the foot-followers and terrier men were well looked-after, as he had often noticed that they were left out at lawn meets, an attention to detail which was most typical of him. Approximately sixty-five mounted field arrived and, coupled with a large and happy band of foot-followers, we were kept busy with our trays of drinks and eats. Trevor Adams, the Joint Master and huntsman, arrived with his hounds and for the second hunting day in a row I was treated to the sight of a pack all of the same stamp, a sure sign of one Master's influence over several years. I was pleased to see that they included some of the original dark coloured ones amongst them.

Colin told the Master not to wait for us as we could easily catch up and, as they moved off, we took the last trays into the house. There was a crash of music before we had even reached the kitchen because as soon as hounds had left the meet a fox was winded over the road (i.e. hounds could smell the scent of a fox coming to them in the wind) and they were away at once. The cry was ringing through the valley as we desperately tried to mount with all speed (not easy in my condition) and hounds were well ahead of us as we started our ride across country to catch up with them. These lovely rolling hills, with their firm turf and either hunt gates or jumping places in every direction, were a joy to ride over and we caught up with hounds in a Forestry Commission plantation. Here hounds were thought to have changed to a cub which would not leave the trees, and hounds kept running round and round the plantation. They rattled him around in the trees for about an hour before losing him, and the Master blew them out and drew across country. Trevor Adams, had for a time been a professional huntsman and hunted hounds with the utter confidence which always denotes an expert at work. He was a joy to watch in the field.

We had not found again by the time Tizza and I decided to go home at three o'clock. Max was pulling like a lunatic and I was in great pain and not really in control of him. The field were very friendly and there were many connections with East Anglia, one having hunted with the Cambridgeshire Harriers, others with the Essex and one with the Essex Farmers'. I walked Max home, thinking what paradise this country was for a foxhunter. To me it had the best of everything – rolling hills, which often gave a clear view of hounds working, and good sound turf where one could mostly gallop with confidence. I was disappointed not to have seen more of the hunting. Colin and Ian returned later to say that I had missed a really great hunt.

**Duke of Buccleuch's Foxhounds.** *Colin Plumbe with his daughter Alice at Roberton.*

Photograph kindly loaned by Mrs Plumbe

The day ended with a first-class dinner party at Easter House. Ian was on top form and reminisced about some of the funny happenings in the old Easton days and the whole evening was packed full of laughter and merriment, frequently refuelled with the ever-generous Plumbe hospitality. There is no better way to end a good day's hunting than a dinner party amongst good friends and it was in the early hours when we finally went to bed.

Sunday was spent quietly filling log-boxes and valetting clothes (Sun 12 Nov 1989). I was grateful for this as my problem was, if anything, getting worse. To dress I had to sit on the edge of the bed and throw my pants, in hoop-la style, until the correct leg landed over my foot, and then work them up my leg with the other foot. In the bath, even after a long hot soak, I could not wash lower than my knees. To get in and out was an ordeal and to dry my left leg, I had to throw the towel and pull it back like a whiplash. I had to come downstairs to find Colin or Tizza to put on my socks, shoes, spurs, etc., and it took the top of the lorry ramp and a very patient horse for me to get on. Riding was quite a pinch but getting off was the worst. I was getting really quite worried as there was no improvement at all and if anything the pain seemed deeper-set and worse than when I left home. Everyone thought it terribly funny and I suppose it does sound such a stupid thing to have done. Why could it not have been caused by a hunting accident which would at least have been an honourable injury? It sounds so ludicrous, when someone asks, "How did you hurt yourself so badly?" to say that it had been done at my granddaughter's christening!

Despite the pain, I set off again on Monday morning, with Tizza and Quillie, for the meet of the **Tynedale Foxhounds** at West Newham, near Belsay (Mon 13 Nov 1989). We left Easter House at eight forty-five but, because of thick fog, we arrived rather later than we would have wished. There were only eight out apart from us and the Joint Master, Rosemary Stobart, with the briefest of introductions, rather ungraciously almost snatched the cap out of our hands. The field were very friendly and the hounds first-class, hunting with a very melodious cry. The scent was very poor but the first hunt was all the more delightful for it, and I enjoyed this long slow hunt with hounds casting themselves very prettily at each check – just the sort of venerie I enjoy to the full as I could always see the hounds, and they were doing everything they should. I was told that this was their worst piece of Monday country, but to me it was delightful, grass almost everywhere and it was always possible to keep with hounds. During this hunt we passed through and around Belsay Park, and could see Belsay Hall standing imposingly in the most beautiful setting. I was told that the gardens totalled twenty-seven acres. There was a bungalow in the middle of a large area of parklike pasture, seemingly with no connection with any road.

An old man, who could see me wondering about this, rode up to me, and said, "Do you know that you are looking at a boathouse?"

He went on to explain that we were standing where a lake had been planned but never actually created.

At three o'clock we decided to go home and when we were boxing up, one of the foot-followers pulled up in his car and said, "I think I know you from somewhere. Could it be the Welsh Cob Sales at Builth Wells?"

I told him that I did often go to the Sales but he said, "I don't think it was there that I saw you." Then, slightly embarassed, he added, "Where I think I saw you ... But it can't possibly be true... Can it?"

I began to get worried that he was going to bring up some murky details of past adventures best forgotten, when he said, "I know this sounds stupid but I think I saw you on the road to Appleby with horses and waggons."

When I told him that he was probably correct he said, "Well! I never thought I would see a man who travelled with a horse and waggon out hunting with the Tynedale."

It sounds particularly improbable since the Tynedale is usually considered rather a smart pack but it was true nevertheless as he was referring to the sponsored trip I had made in 1980.

**Tony and Sheila Harvey:** *Cooking time with the gypsy caravans.*
Photograph: Family album

This was not the last curious coincidence as, when I stopped on the way back to Roberton to fill the lorry with diesel, the woman said, "I remember you. You've been here before. I can remember that Norfolk accent and those mutton chops."

She was right. I could remember filling up the car there four months before when I was returning from Scotland, with my wife and mother, after seeing my daughter Bridget receive her doctorate at St Andrews University.

Next day Colin took another day off work to come with me to the **Lanarkshire and Renfrewshire Foxhounds** (Tues 14 Nov 1989). We left home at seven-thirty and after negotiating a cross-country route to the M8, bypassing Glasgow, we arrived in Houston where we were hoping to ask directions to the meet, since this is where these hounds were kennelled. To our delight we were waved down by a lady who told us that she was an ex-Master and introduced herself as Mrs Donaldson, saying, "I knew you strangers were coming and were bound to get lost, so I've been waiting here to show you the way to the meet."

**Lanarkshire and Renfrewshire.** *Meet at Wellees, 1988. Masters A R Campbell and M J Wilson (on the grey), Huntsman Peter McColgan.*
Photograph kindly donated by Mr Derek Parker

We followed her car to the meet which was near the new Master's home, at Strathkrype, near Bridge of Weir. We unboxed there and then hacked up to the meet where we were invited into the house, an invitation I would dearly have loved to have accepted but I dare not get off as I should have been unable to get on again. I held Colin's horse while he went in and the whole atmosphere was so friendly that, as usual, it reminded me of an Easton meet at home. The hunt servants were immaculately turned out and hounds were of predominantly Middleton blood, with some from the Beaufort. The field numbered fifteen, ten of whom were in red coats.

We found as soon as we left the meet and ran over very rough moorland, jumping rails and gateways blocked up with sheets of tin and walls with barbed wire on the top of them. The field were real goers and nothing stopped them. Max became so excited that I could not stop him. There were so many times that I could see what the locals call "a wet spot" and tried to steady him but could not with the result that he went into it at a full canter and stopped within a few yards. This happened so often that I was convinced he would have pulled tendons or, worse, a severe over-reach but luckily he did not. I have seldom ridden across country for so long completely out of control. One place remains firmly in my mind – a set of rails to be jumped going downhill with a "wet spot" a few yards the other side. The locals were popping over the rails and then turning off to one side but Max went at it full bore and in two strides was in the bog up to his knees, putting my face between his ears, but somehow I managed to wriggle back into the saddle.

There was an older gentleman who was very noticeable as he was immaculately turned out and was riding the most gorgeous hunter I have ever seen. He was always in the first flight across country. I asked his name and was told that he was Colonel Borwick who had at one time been Master of the neighbouring pack, the Eglinton. Later on in the day he asked me where I had come from and when I said the Easton Harriers he said, "I had a day with them in George Springfield's time." He explained that his best friend, John Henniker (now Lord Henniker), had invited him to stay and he had accepted, on the condition that his host fixed him up with a day's hunting.

He went on to say who else he knew in our area and then said, "There is a wonderful book about the Easton Harriers, you know."

When I said that it was my daughter who had written it, I thought he would never stop thumping my back in congratulation. He went on to say how much he appreciated it because he had written a history of the Eglinton and knew just how hard it was to put it all together in a readable form.

The scent deteriorated and hounds were not helped by the new Master who was supposed to be Field Master, but often galloped off to do some very amateurish whipping-in, the end result of which was that he just got hounds heads up and spoiled the hunt. We would undoubtedly have had much better sport if he had confined his activities to being Field Master. There was one lovely spin to end the day and it was for me the most frightening of the day. There was a set of rails to jump as we went down a steep hill, with a series of ledges on the downhill side. I could not steady Max and he went at it, cleared it easily but landed on the first ledge. One stride, and he jumped down to the next ledge. Another stride and down to the next. Eventually he landed at the bottom of the hill. I have been told that it is very good for your system to be thoroughly scared now and again, and I felt that this was my dose for at least a year. However he kept on his feet I shall never know.

Colin's grey mare, Countess, had lost a shoe and was quite sore so I went back to the box at two-thirty and fetched it back for him to save Countess' feet. We were told that we were in sight of the local farrier, but one or two members of the field advised against Colin using him, saying that his work was rather crude. The long journey home was spent in learning to sing a new song, "The Bold Buccleuch". By the time we got home, we could sing it without reading the words. What with the singing and the reminiscences about the day the time soon went and the long journey did not seem to drag at all. "The Bold Buccleuch" was written as verse by Whyte-Melville. As Colin was going to work one morning he had given me a Buccleuch Supporters' Club booklet with the words in it and said, "Find a tune to fit it. I'd like to be able to sing it." This was easier than I expected as the first tune I tried, from the staghunting song "Porlock Bay", fitted it perfectly and had just the right tempo. However, when Colin came home that night, Tizza and I had plotted to pretend that it had taken me all day. This joke went on for over a year until we finally told him how easy it had been.

**The Lanarkshire and Renfrewshire:** ***"Whoops! I did <u>not</u> mean to come this way"***

Tizza was able to come with me to the **Jedforest Foxhounds** the next day and we had only a short way to go as the meet was at Hawthornside, near Bonchester Bridge (Wed 15 Nov 1989). We left Easter House at nine-forty-five after trying our best to cheer up Hazel who was having a serious bout of homesickness. We found a place to unbox and hacked along to the meet which was a farm on the edge of moorland. We met Mr Walter Jeffery, Master and huntsman, hacking up. Gradually the field assembled from all directions until finally the kennel huntsman arrived with hounds. The field were a very mixed bunch, the mounts ranging from two Clydesdale carthorses to two Point-to-Point qualifiers, with just about every type in between.

**Jedforest Hunt.** *Wat Jeffrey with hounds at 4.45am, autumn hunting on foot in Burns Forestry.*

Photograph kindly loaned

We found just below the meet and we sat on the hillside watching hounds twisting and turning in the valley below us. A severely disabled young man was following close to hounds on a three-wheeler motorbike and it was heartening to see his obvious great enthusiasm for hunting. When he got off his seat to open a gate, he could hardly stand at all, but he could still keep with hounds and obviously knew this country like the back of his hand. A stranger like me could easily have been confused as to who the huntsman was, as there was an extraordinary character bellowing just as though he was the worst sort of huntsman. He was rather on the portly side and rode a delightful old-fashioned cob with a docked tail, the pair looking as though they had just stepped out of an old oil-painting. He galloped around, mostly ahead of the huntsman, holloaing and cheering hounds on in the most extraordinary way. Some of the rest of the field noticed my amazed expression as I watched this performance, and they explained that they managed to get rid of him once, but he had done the rounds of all the other local packs until he had turned up with them again.

Any actual hunt of that day is difficult to describe as it was a mixture of open moor and dense forestry, but the hounds were first-class. Some of the blocks of forestry were of over a thousand acres and held many foxes. Although the pack often divided, Mr Jeffery (known as "Wat" to one and all) could rally them together again with such ease, that one could easily imagine they were doing it themselves. It was an uncanny knack. At one moment there would be five or six little hunts going on and the next, just as soon as they had all checked, he would blow and they would all come to him.

We ran from forestry over moor to more forestry where, although there were so many fresh foxes, they marked a brace to ground. The cry was the best I had heard since I had left home and the whole day was packed full of pure venerie showing at its best, with all the problems of huge forestry and fresh foxes overcome. We left at four o'clock and I drove home with the distinct impression that if I lived in this area, these were the hounds with whom I would prefer to hunt. Wat Jeffery I rated very highly as a huntsman and his hounds obviously adored him. I sampled his ability to exert himself as Master when some of the field, including myself, set off across the moor after hounds before he had time to get out of the forestry – what a rocket he gave everyone when he finally overhauled us. The moor was very tricky to ride over as there were masses of little drains everywhere, mostly grown over, and Fizz stumbled almost to his knees many times. Days later, when I was out with another pack, I was in conversation with the huntsman and I mentioned my good day with the Jed Forest. He immediately remarked upon Wat Jeffery's uncanny skill with hounds and I was pleased to have my opinion verified. He went on to tell me a most amazing story.

After hunting one day Wat had been one hound light. He stopped and blew for her for a long time, but eventually went home without her. He and his kennel huntsman had hoped to find her waiting for them back at the kennels as the meet was only seven or eight miles from the kennels but she was not there so Wat left for home, telling his kennel huntsman that he would telephone during the evening to see if she was back. This he did every hour only to be told that she was still missing. His great love of hounds was obvious in how often he telephoned and on his last call he said, "I've got to go into Jedburgh for a dinner. I'll ring you from the hotel."

Before sitting down to dinner he telephoned the kennels again to be told that she was still not back, so he said he would ring again after dinner. He went back

**The Jedforest:** ***"The vibes were strong"***

into the dining-room and was just starting his meal when a man came into the dining room and said,

"Wat, there's one of your dogs lying beside your car."

He went out and found that the "dog" was the missing bitch. He made a great fuss of her and put her into his car. To reach him, this five-season bitch had moved up country in the opposite direction to the kennels and had entered a large town, found the right car park and recognised her Master's car. This was a splendid example of the extraordinary degree of telepathy which can exist between a huntsman and his hounds. She must have been able to sense his thoughts when worrying about having to attend this dinner without finding her.

As the **West Percy Foxhounds** hunted on foot on Thursday I decided to join them at the Blue Mill, near Thropton (Thurs 16 Nov 1989). To avoid taking the lorry when it was unnecessary, I borrowed Tizza's car and took Colin to work before going on to the meet which proved very difficult to find. I was getting desperate so I flagged down a motorist to ask. With my usual luck, I discovered that I could not have asked anyone better. He said, "Do you want the actual Blue Mill, or are you looking for hounds?"

When I introduced myself he said, "Oh I have heard and read all about you."

I soon discovered that I could have said the same to him as he turned out to be the notorious Willie Pool, Joint Master of this pack.

At the meet a supporter offered to take me in his Jeep and we kept hounds in sight most of the day. The huntsman was sometimes on foot, climbing up the steep hillsides, and sometimes mounted on a motorbike. It was an extraordinary sight to see him coming up a track on his motorbike, blowing his horn with his hounds all around him. The hounds were Fell hounds crossed with Welsh, a cross that I had never heard of before, but the proof of the pudding is in the eating and they hunted most beautifully all day. I hunted again with the West Percy later in the season when they were having a joint meet with the Border.

On the way home I picked up Colin from work again and took him to the Buccleuch kennels where, as Vice-Chairman, he had to attend an important Committee meeting to fix the level of the guarantee for the next season. I waited in the local pub, appropriately called the Buccleuch Arms, until the meeting was finished, and then we went to another appropriately-named pub, the Fox and Hounds at Denholm. Colin had arranged to meet a local singer here and we had a nice little singsong, with Colin and I doing a duet of "The Bold Buccleuch". We called for fish and chips on the way home.

Some days before, during dinner, we had been talking about the Easton Harriers' visit to central Wales

**The West Percy:** ***"The shape of things to come?"***

which the new Masters had arranged. Colin was quite keen to go, so we made the necessary plans, in the course of which I said that it was a shame they were going to central Wales as there were packs in north Wales and the Wirral that I had not hunted with.

Colin said, "Do you remember Chris and Mike Lloyd who used to hunt with us in the old Windermere Harrier days? They live in the Wirral."

I replied that I remembered them well and Colin just picked up the telephone and dialled their number. The most amazing conversation followed.

"Hello Mike, it's Colin Plumbe here. How are you? Can I visit you next Friday?"

"Yes."

"Tizza will come too?" asked Colin.

"Yes."

"We want to bring our horses. Is that alright?"

"Yes."

"Tony Harvey is staying with us. Can he come too?"

"Yes."

"He's got two horses. Can they both come?"

"Yes. Is that all?"

"No, sorry Mike, it's not. Tony has a girl groom with him. Can she come too?"

"Yes, and goodnight."

This extraordinary conversation struck Tizza and me as being very funny and each blunt, "yes" brought cackles of laughter and with the final question about the girl groom we were rolling around on our chairs. We were told later that he was about to settle down to a dinner party and would have agreed to anything provided Colin got off the telephone quickly.

The upshot of all this was that we moved down to spend one night at the Lloyds' en route to the Easton Harriers who were due to arrive in Wales on the Sunday. On the Friday I set off with my two horses and the Plumbes' two horses and Hazel and Tizza on the grounds that when Colin left work he could come down much quicker with no horses in the trailer. We arrived at the Lloyds' house in Gypsy Lane, Willaston, in the dark and settled my two horses into stables in a meadow belonging to a friend of theirs and the Plumbes' horses in the Lloyds' stables at their home. Colin arrived much later and we all enjoyed an excellent dinner which featured a most memorable sugar-baked ham as the main course.

The plan was for us all to hunt with the **Flint and Denbigh Foxhounds** (Sat 18 Nov 1989). We left the Lloyds' house after the most enormous breakfast and found our way almost as far as the meet. We were then met by the Secretary who showed us where to unbox. We hacked across Kinmell Park to the actual meet outside the Kinmell Arms. The meet was in such a lovely setting, so idyllic that it looked like one of those meet scenes from another century that are illustrated on biscuit tin lids or place mats. The Secretary introduced me to present and past Masters including Sir Watkin Williams-Wynn, joint Master and Huntsman of these hounds as well as Master of the pack which bears his family name. Ronnie Wallace was there and was very interested to find out about my most recent travels. As soon as he found out that I had come down from Scotland, he enquired how Trevor Adams was getting on at the Buccleuch.

I was sitting admiring the hounds, which were of Brocklesby, Belvoir and Middleton blood, when the Secretary said he would let us have a bulk discount on our caps, £30 instead of £35. This cap-paying was still coming as a shock to me as, of course, now that I was no longer Master I was liable to pay. Most Secretaries, however, said that as I had done such a long stint as Master they would still waive it. A young lady rode up to me to ask if I remembered her as she used to hunt with the Easton when she was a student at the Newton Hall Equitation Centre in the Easton country and was now married to the whipper-in. They had just moved down from the Percy in Northumberland. Another great character was Willie Tilly whom I met whilst contemplating a tiny cottage with just one room up and one down, and a lean-to cowhouse on either side. The country was delightful, mostly grass, with hunt jumps everywhere and, as the Lloyds were car-following with lots of sandwiches and flasks, we were well looked after. In fact, all we needed was a fox but, sadly, by the time we left, it was a blank day.

We all went out in the evening to the Champers Restaurant for a Beaujolais Nouveau evening and during dinner I plucked up courage to ask the Lloyds if I could stay again on my way back from Wales so I could hunt with the Cheshire and the Cheshire Forest. Whilst we were being entertained by the Lloyds Senior, Hazel was being entertained with a pizza by the Lloyds' sons, James, Richard and Duncan.

On Sunday morning we left the Lloyds' at ten-thirty to go on to central Wales. We knew that the Easton members had booked accommodation at Llanwrtyd Wells and had arranged stabling at the Central Wales Riding Centre. We arrived at the Central Wales Riding Centre at two-thirty, in spite of having made a stupid mistake at Builth Wells when I took the wrong road. This was probably due to lack of concentration when I was telling (probably boring) Hazel about some past exploit at Builth. We settled the horses in and then booked in to the Nevadd Arms at Llanwrtyd Wells, a very dreary sort of place which was not improved by the fact that my room was immediately over the front door which seemed to be banging endlessly.

A few days before, when I had telephoned the Master of the **Towy and Cothi Foxhounds**, Mr Powell, he explained that they used guns on Mondays and Thursdays, and hunted normally on Saturdays. I decided that I would like to go on a shooting day just to see what it was like (Mon 20 November 1989). I arranged to go to the kennels, as the meeting place was too difficult for a stranger to find and I arrived just in time to help the huntsman, Dewi Price, load up fourteen couple of mostly pure-bred Welsh hounds which included a couple of Fell hounds. I introduced myself to Mr Powell and he surprised me by saying that he remembered me going with them before. I had no record of this in my diaries but remembered meeting him so assumed that he was right. When we arrived at the agreed meeting place, there were about twenty or so farmers with twelve-bore guns standing near their pick-up trucks and Land Rovers. Quite a few asked me my opinion of shooting foxes, and asked if I disapproved of the practice. I replied that this was to be my first experience of such a day and I had come to see to make up my own mind. The farmers, whose number soon grew to over thirty, came together and discussed where they were going to position themselves around certain blocks of forestry and I asked if I could go with Dewi and the hounds. We went into the forestry on foot and hounds started to draw. After a few minutes they found and ran with the most delightful cry making the whole forestry ring with their voices and a huge fox passed close by us, the largest I have ever seen. It was not long before a shot was heard in the distance and Dewi explained that it was probably not the fox that we were hunting but another one that had been disturbed and decided to move away from hounds.

We drew numerous blocks of forestry until by the time I left at two-thirty there had been three brace of foxes shot. The hounds took very little notice of the shot foxes and did not attempt to rush up to them, or offer to break them up, as they would have done a properly hunted fox. Some of the farmers explained to me how the foxes come down from the mountains at lambing time and what havoc they cause. One farmer had lost over twenty lambs to foxes the previous lambing time. I came away with the opinion that, whilst it cannot ever be compared with proper hunting, it was nevertheless very necessary in this type of environment. Without the aid of a pack of foxhounds to drive them out, any serious attempt at a fox-shoot would be ineffectual in these huge areas of forestry. The damage done by the foxes justified these drastic steps. This necessary fox-shooting must never be compared with the abhorrent practice of shooting foxes in a normal hunt country where fox numbers are at an acceptable level.

We all had dinner with the Easton Harriers members that evening. After dinner the Easton members went through to the lounge for coffee but, as Colin and I went to follow, there was a little man called Donald playing an accordion in the bar and we went no further. We both started to sing, quite forgetting our coffee, and by the time the Easton members returned, there was quite a sing-song in progress. There was a story attached to this as the day was one on which

**The Towy and Cothi:** ***"Who cares about coffee!"***

an extinct Horse Fair had been held and the only surviving part of the fair was the accordion player, Donald, in the pub. He was delighted to have such an enthusiastic audience and played as long as he could stand and then some. As the accordion was so large in proportion to him, he spent the rest of the evening sitting cross-legged on the floor like an old-fashioned tailor with the accordion resting on his lap, still playing.

Next day I set off to hunt with the Tanatside Foxhounds but as I went the misty conditions became a thick fog and my speed was reduced to ten miles per hour. Ominously, it seemed just as thick on the high places as it was in the valleys. Although I was going so slowly, I almost hit a Land Rover which stopped dead in front of me. Two farmers got out to try to put a stray bullock back into a meadow. This was near Newtown and I decided that the fog was so bad I would turn back as there could not possibly be any hunting in these conditions.

When I got back to the hotel I rushed up to my room and grabbed the Baily's Hunting Directory to find out if there was a pack of beagles hunting in the area on Tuesdays. The only one I could find which hunted on a Tuesday was the Glen Celyn but there was no reply from the Master's house and only an answering machine at the kennels so I gave up and returned to take my horse back to the stables. When I made my way downstairs I saw a very disgruntled member of the Easton, looking as black as thunder, booking out at the reception. When I asked what was happening, I received a very curt reply.

"I've had enough."

Knowing that there had been shared transport on the way to Wales and that the angry soul was not very widely-travelled, I plucked up all my courage to ask, "How are you getting home?"

Turning to me with a withering stare, he squeezed out the word "Taxi!" from between clenched teeth, and then the angry soul was gone!

When the Easton members returned in the evening I told them what had happened with the angry soul and they just could not believe it, thinking that I was pulling their legs. I was not hunting with the same packs as the Easton members as they were going with packs that I had already been with and, of course, I was eager to clock up new ones on my list. This had been a very disappointing day for me, especially when I telephoned the Tanatside kennels in the evening and discovered that the fog had lifted and that they had had a very good day, with an eight-mile point.

After dinner we went to Builth Wells to see our old friends at the Barley Mow, and I was greeted as usual with, "Hello, it's Norfolk!" from old Tom Morgan. Marie told me how many people had said they would hope to see me on Thursday at the Irfon and Towy meet at the Barley Mow so, although I had planned to move back to the Lloyds' that day, I changed my mind and decided to move a day later.

Wednesday was the day that the Easton were going with the **Teme Valley Foxhounds** (Wed 22 Nov 1989). I had already hunted with them in 1983 when staying with the Plumbes at Orleton so, as my back was giving me hell, I decided to ride with Richard Lee, one of the Easton contingent, in comfort in the Range Rover. At the meet, which was at Knockston, near Knighton, I asked who it was best for us to follow and was told the terrier man. This we did and he kept us in touch with hounds all day. The Easton members had a wonderful day in this heavenly country and were as impressed with it as I had been before, which I was glad of because I had so often spoken of what a lovely country it was. When Richard and I got back to the boxes in the dark the Easton members were still not back so we went into Knighton to buy them a meat pie each as I knew they would be starving.

I was glad that I had changed my mind and decided to stay for the Easton's day with the **Irfon and Towy Foxhounds** as I had so many friends there, and particularly as they were meeting at the Barley Mow in Builth Wells where I had stayed so many times and had so many wonderful evenings. Again I followed with Richard Lee in his Range Rover and this time we had Mike Davies as our pilot. He had been a friend since his never-to-be-forgotten meet on my first visit to the Irfon & Towy in 1980. As he knew every inch of the country we were always near hounds. His directions across the mountainside gave Richard a few anxious moments but he always managed to get the Range Rover there and the day's exploits would have made a very good advertisement for the vehicle. However, the day was chiefly memorable for an incident when, after stopping for eats and drinks from Richard's vehicle, the Easton members were threatened with a twelve-bore gun as they tried to catch up with hounds again. All's well that end's well, and the angry farmer relented and let them pass, once he understood that they were visitors and did not know their way about. The Master, Ken Jones, came to our hotel at night and he and I spent most of the evening talking venerie and the qualities or otherwise of various huntsmen.

On Friday morning I settled the accounts at the stable and the hotel rather grudgingly as I had added only one new pack to my list but consoled myself that the visit had been great fun (Fri 24 November 1989). I said my goodbyes and drove back to the Lloyds' house in the Wirral, this time stabling my horse in the boxes at their home as the Plumbes had stayed on in Wales. This made things easier for Hazel. Chris Lloyd was the Pony Club District Commissioner for the Cheshire Forest Pony Club and she took me off in the evening to present the prizes at their Annual Prize-Giving. This was followed by a hot-pot supper and a disco which ended at eleven o'clock.

Next day, Saturday, I had arranged to go with the **Cheshire Foxhounds** but this was to be a day when everything went wrong (Sat 25 Nov 1989). I was stopped on the way to the meet and subjected to a Ministry of Transport spot-check which I only just managed to scrape through after some quick talking, saying that the lorry was booked in for a service when I got home. This delay caused me to be later than I would have liked getting to the meet which was at Bolkeley Grange, the home of the Master, but I was just in time to introduce myself to my host. Hounds looked very well and the hunt staff were turned out to perfection, as were most of the field.

After moving off, there were some hunt jumps to negotiate between draws and Fizz pecked badly at the second fence. I landed up his neck with my arms around his neck and in this undignified position I crossed the whole of the next field, only just managing to get upright again before the next fence. At this fence a lady who had befriended me at the meet had a very nasty fall, and I went to catch her horse and waited until a vehicle came to take her back to the road. I caught up with hounds again and then got involved in another accident, this time very gruesome. A lady just in front of me was about to take off over some rails when a girl crashed into her side, pushing her off course, so that her horse was opposite the post. The post was much higher than the rails and tore her horse's chest open, from just below the windpipe down between its front legs. The wound was terrible, gaping open one or two inches wide and very deep. The lady was, of course, distraught and I helped, with others, to get her to a farm where a vet was telephoned. I would guess that the wound would take at least forty stitches.

All this had, of course, taken some considerable time and hounds were well away by the time I left her. I listened and was sure I heard the horn in the distance behind the farm and rode off up the road in that direction. I stopped the horse to have another listen when a young couple stopped their car and asked if I was looking for hounds and gave me directions. I cantered off up the wide verge in the direction they had said, searched and listened for over an hour, but never found hounds. With hindsight, I realise that the couple must have been antis and had deliberately sent me off in the wrong direction. By the time I realised I had been fooled I was so demoralised and fed up that I went back to where I had left the box. Just before I reached it, a dog came out of a gateway barking and caused Fizz to shy violently sideways with the effect that I pulled a muscle in my left thigh. This was extremely embarassing as I was just getting over the other problem of my bruised bottom. I felt such a hypochondriac that I could hardly bring myself to tell the Lloyds and I felt a proper old screw, ready to be put down.

Mike and Chris Lloyd were there waiting at the box. They had been car following and were very worried as they had not seen me and wondered what had happened to me. Chris was ready with her flask of tea which helped soothe my disappointed feelings. This had been a disastrous day made all the worse by being capped £50 and then seeing so little of hounds. There were approximately 140 horses out and the standard was very high. The whole field were a great pleasure to see and I have never seen so many lovely horses all together in one place. Everywhere I looked I could see outstanding hunters and without a doubt this was the smartest hunt I have ever seen, both staff and field. My depressed feelings were uplifted by a lovely dinner party at the Lloyds with their friends who were just as much fun as I would have expected of friends of theirs. The dinner was excellent and Chris had made a lovely mushroom starter which was followed by hot salmon, with Summer Pudding and chocolate roulage to finish. This was all very enjoyable with lovely wines and was typical of the Lloyds' generous hospitality.

**Cheshire Forest.** *Meet at Yareangall Farm, Alvanley, 27 November 1990.*
Photograph kindly donated by Gordon Franks

On Monday, Chris and I followed the Watkin Williams-Wynn Foxhounds on foot as I did not want to ride with my torn muscle which was still very painful (27 Nov 1989). I had hunted with them before when I was staying at Gillingham in 1987 and they had come down to that part by invitation of the South Dorset. We kept in touch with hounds quite well and saw some good hound work. Since we also watched the field performing over some five-foot fences I felt quite relieved to be on my feet. Tuesday morning I spent in raking up leaves, then I took Chris out for lunch, after which we took the terriers for a walk in a lovely beech wood.

On Wednesday Chris came with me to the meet of the **Cheshire Forest Foxhounds** at Alvanley so I had no difficulty in finding it (Wed 29 Nov 1989). She knew nearly everybody, of course, as she was D.C. of the Pony Club. The whipper-in said how disappointed Stella Mitchell (who used to be a member of the Easton and had moved to this area) would be not to have seen me. We moved off to draw a steep covert and found at once. Hounds had to work hard to stick to the line so it was just the sort of hunting that I enjoy most. They were being shown to perfection as they continually checked and cast themselves, regaining the line time and time again without assistance. Max went very well and jumped all the fences willingly. These were mostly post-and-rails or hunt jumps and I was glad that he was in such an obliging mood as I had little grip with my torn muscle. I managed quite well by hanging on to the breast-plate and kept close enough to enjoy all the houndwork. I was, however, feeling very weak and useless and as the day wore on I felt so weak that at two o'clock I had to go back to the box. When I got home Mike and Chris' son, James, made me one of his medicinal toddies and I went to bed, by now realising that I had caught the virus from Chris who had brought it back from the visit to London. Three very stiff whiskies and some paracetamols revived me sufficiently to go out to dinner at an Italian restaurant with the Lloyds and James and his girlfriend.

Next day I moved the horses back to Derbyshire to stay with Eric Elliott again, but the stables we had used before at Rushton Spencer were full, so the owner had made arrangements for the horses to be stabled at her parents' establishment at Scholar Green which was some way away (Thurs 30 Nov 1989). This was far from ideal but when we got there there was some compensation in that the stables were first class. Eric collected me and took me to Sutton House where I was pleased to be able to rest as I was still feeling very weak and 'flu-like. Eric and Marcia had included me in an invitation to a dinner party in the evening and, after being bucked up by a couple of enormous gin-and-tonics, we went just up the road to Dunwood Hall, the home of Ruth Vincent-Kemp. She was a delightfully old-fashioned lady with a home to match, a real Victorian house full of Victorian furniture and curtains. It was a most delightful evening and I thoroughly enjoyed myself in these lovely surroundings and left feeling very privileged to have been able to see it all. I only wished that Sheila was with me as she would have been as fascinated as I was.

The 'flu bug was really at its worst next morning and I was feeling very weak-kneed and rough but nevertheless went to see four young Irish hunters at Mr Nigel Profit's farm at Acton (Fri 1 Dec 1989). I thought Mr Profit was a splendid name for a horse-dealer and could have come straight from the pages of Surtees. He had some good horses but not quite what I wanted, so I bought nothing, but was told that they would all be out hunting with the North Staffordshire in the morning, so I could see them in action if I wished. Eric drove me back to Sutton House where I sat near the fire and shivered and snivelled all afternoon, but rallied in the evening after two enormous whiskies from Eric and I took them out to dine at a Thai restaurant and enjoyed an excellent meal. I had now been away from home for a whole month which was something I had never done before.

Next day I had originally intended to go with the Grove and Rufford but, with the horses in their present stables, this made the already long journey even longer and in my present feeble state I could not face the prospect. I did not get up until nine-thirty and could not even get any enthusiasm to go to the North Staffs Foxhounds to see the horses and so I contented myself with the prospect of a day with the **North Staffordshire Moorland Beagles**. This pack had been formed by my host, Eric Elliott, in 1952 and he had remained Master until 1981, the season after he had formed the Staffordshire Moorland Harriers. At the time of my visit his son, James, was joint-Master of the Beagles and Marcia, James' mother, was the Secretary. They hunted a lovely part of Staffordshire which was once hunted by the Dove Valley Harriers (now defunct). These beagles were quite small and had considerable difficulty in getting over some of the stone walls. Discussing the problem over dinner on an earlier visit to Sutton House I had suggested that they ask the new Easton Master for a draft of small harriers, knowing that on my retirement I had left some at the kennels that were too small. This they had done and Easton Baffle, Bangle and Hostage were out and were going quite well for young unentered hounds.

I sat around until it was time to go to the meet at Basford, near Cheddleton at one o'clock, and sadly I can write little about the hunting as I was never close enough to hounds to make any serious assessment, but they did run well for most of the time that I could see. My weakness and those Staffordshire hills was not a good combination and I was relieved when it was time for the beagle tea.

Having spent these three days with the Lloyds to have one day with the beagles, next day I made the long journey home (Sun 3 Dec 1989). I had been away for thirty-four days, nearly five weeks, and had hunted with nineteen new packs (including the Towy and Cothi shooting day), as well as car-following with two I had been with before. My total was now two hundred and forty-eight packs, and there were thirty mounted ones to go. Many days had been spent in travelling, as I had moved base five times, having stayed with the Elliotts twice and with the Lloyds twice, as well as in Wales and Scotland. Poor Hazel was able to see her beloved Suffolk once again. It had been quite an experience for her, as she had hardly been away from home before, and had so recently been put in charge of horses. but had coped admirably.

**Cambridgeshire Harriers.** *Mrs Gingell with her harriers in the 1950s.*
Photograph kindly loaned by Michael Gingell

# MAP 17

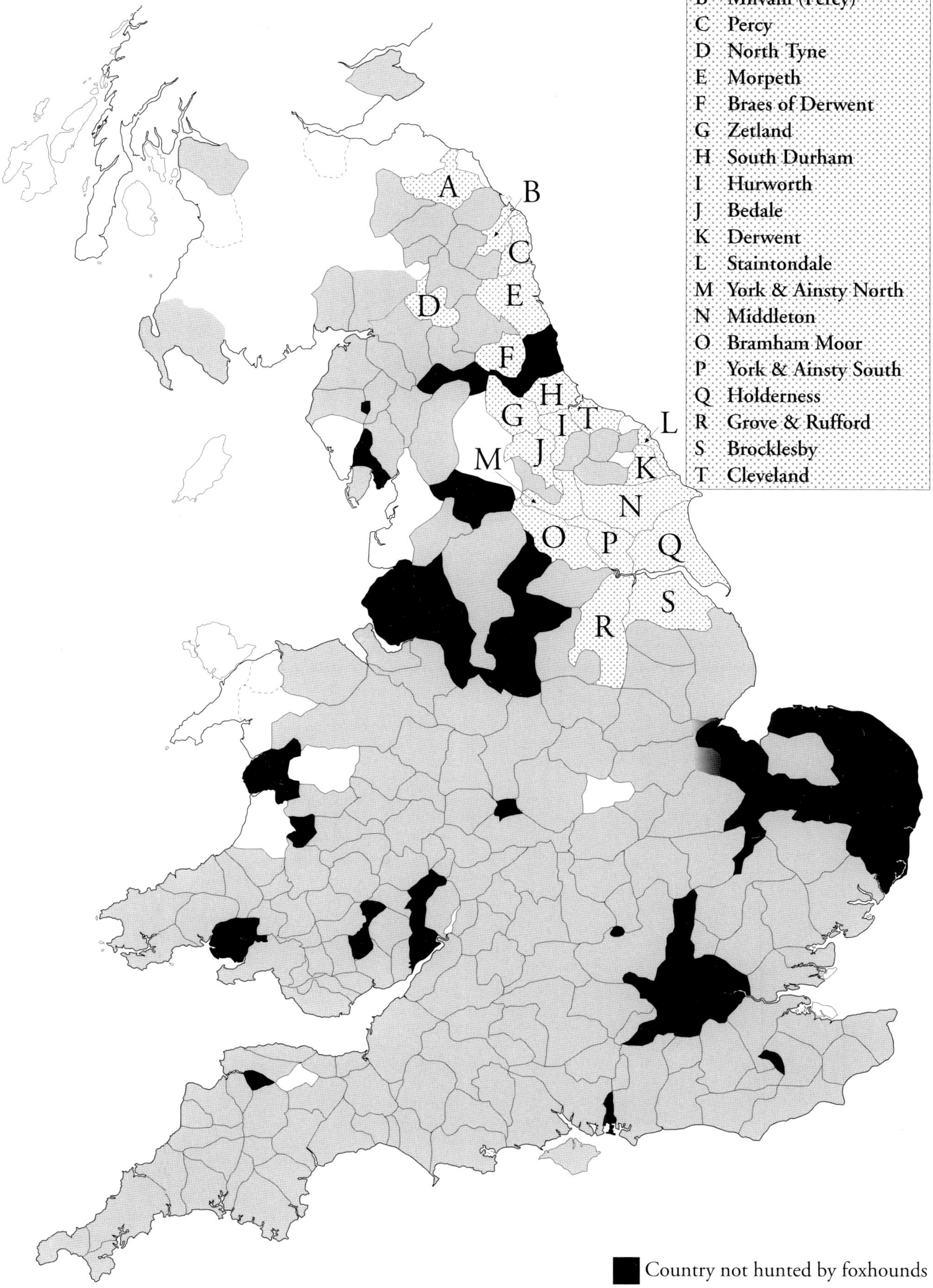


**FOXHOUND PACKS 1990**

A Berwickshire
B Milvain (Percy)
C Percy
D North Tyne
E Morpeth
F Braes of Derwent
G Zetland
H South Durham
I Hurworth
J Bedale
K Derwent
L Staintondale
M York & Ainsty North
N Middleton
O Bramham Moor
P York & Ainsty South
Q Holderness
R Grove & Rufford
S Brocklesby
T Cleveland

■ Country not hunted by foxhounds

# CHAPTER 19

## HELMSLEY AND THE NORTH

Before going away again, I had another daytrip from home, this time a "double day" of harehunting as the Newmarket Beagles and the West Lodge Harehounds were meeting within a couple of miles of each other, the beagles at nine-thirty and the bassets at one-thirty (Sat 16 Dec 1989). I picked up my friends Tony and Anne St Quinton, the basset fanatics, and when we were nearly at the beagle meet at Ufford, near Stamford, we called at the Little Chef at Wansford for coffee.

**Newmarket Beagles.** *Meet at Matching Green, c. 1992. Front three, left to right, Roy Alborough, Bobby Block and Sara Herbert, the three whippers-in.* Photograph kindly loaned by Nick Herbert

While we sat there a man came in wearing riding boots and we soon got into conversation with him, finding that he hunted regularly with the Cottesmore although he lived in the Puckeridge country. There were very few out with the **Newmarket Beagles**. I thought this was a pity as they went very well and ran with a good cry with the exception of a couple with very squeaky voices. There were too many hares for any serious hunting although they did try to stick to the line of the hunted hare. This was not made easy due to their rather wild and wide casts, which so often disturbed a fresh hare. This I assumed could partly be attributed to the fact that they were only hunting one day a week and partly that they were only beginning their third season since being formed in 1987.

Leaving the beagles, we drove the short distance to Helpston and enjoyed a well-earned lunch at the Blue Bell which was where the **West Lodge Harehounds** were meeting. The hounds were rather an uneven lot with some exceptionally bent legs, one so deformed that its foot pointed backwards. I was amazed to see that it could

**West Lodge Hare Hounds: *"A foot in both camps"***

*One hound so deformed that its foot pointed backwards*

run up all day. When hounds started to draw they were rather wild and rushed around in every direction, but a member told me that as they only hunt once a week the first half an hour was usually rather on the wild side. When they settled down they hunted most beautifully and the cry was quite delightful. We saw some lovely hunting and when we left at three-thirty they were running in some woodland and the cry was ringing in our ears all the way back to the village. It had been a day of very heavy going and by the time we reached the car we could hardly walk another step.

This made a round two hundred and fifty packs that I had hunted with, but there were still thirty mounted ones to go so, in determined pursuit of my ambition to hunt with all the foxhound packs in Great Britain, I settled down soon after the New Year to make the arrangements for going away again. Most of the gaps in my hunting map were in the north and I was pleased that most of them could be covered either from the Plumbes' at Roberton or from Helmsley, the two best bases of all my holidays for combining good stabling with good company. I planned to go away twice, the first time to Helmsley for nine days and the second time for twenty-three days, of which the first two weeks would also be spent at Helmsley and the rest with the Plumbes at Roberton.

**The Author's daughters with the Easton Harriers**
*L to R Bridget Harvey on Dora, Judith Harvey on Henry. Many years later Bridget compiled this book and Judith cooked the Celebration Dinner described in The Epilogue.*

Photograph from family album

I left home at six o'clock on the morning on Tuesday 16 January with Fizz and Max, the old faithfuls, and Hazel to do them for me, and arrived in Helmsley at one-thirty, having stopped only once for a bacon sandwich and a mug of tea. There was a very strong wind and as I unloaded the horses at Anthony Barker's yard in the town centre it whipped the straw out of the lorry and blew it all around the streets, which was especially embarassing as I now knew so many people who lived there. We were to stay, as before, with Mrs Saggers at Park House but found that, as we were so early, she was not at home. Luckily, an electrician arrived and he let us in. Later, after a rest, I walked up to the Royal Oak for the usual early evening drinks with my good friends, as this little get-together at six o'clock had become a ritual for me whenever I was in Helmsley. I returned to Park House and wrote up the diary of the day and then set off to find some supper. I decided to try something different from my usual custom of eating at the Feathers. Hazel had chosen to eat on her own, which was a change, as most of my girls have considered that eating as well as their boss on these holidays was one of the perks of the job. I found Monet's restaurant and had their Menu Surprise, a six-course dinner with a different wine with each course. Although I was dining alone, this was an exciting and most enjoyable evening, with both food and wine of the very best, and I thoroughly enjoyed myself, going to bed in a very, very elated and contented mood.

I had arranged to go with the **York and Ainsty North** for my first day, and they were meeting at South Stainley House, the home of Lord Mountgarret (Wed 17 Jan 1990). There were about thirty mounted in the field, which I thought was a lot considering the weather. It was an exceptionally wild morning as it was still blowing almost gale force and did not feel at all conducive to good hunting. The field were well turned out on good horses and described themselves as a friendly farmers' hunt who did not do much jumping. I got the immediate impression that these people really enjoyed the venerie and went hunting to watch hounds work. However, this was not to be the case on this day as the winds were so bad, I felt at times it would tear me from off Max's back. The hounds were very level with some Welsh blood. They were hunted by the kennel huntsman as the Master was away, and the Master's wife, Mrs Bailey, was whipping-in.

We went from covert to covert across this lovely estate for almost two hours and then found and had a short burst to ground, but then had to wait for ages while they tried unsuccessfully to bolt the fox. We drew on with little hope of finding a fox above ground after such a wild night. When we were in a sheltered spot I asked about our host and was told that Lord Mountgarret was not only justly famous for this large

**York and Ainsty North:** ***"What damned impertinence! The thing is ruining the drive."***

and beautiful estate, but also for the fact that he had shot down a hot air balloon which came over him while he was grouse shooting, as it was disturbing his birds.

I was most impressed by the careful way that the field went round the edge of wheat fields, such a pleasant change. If only all hunts would do the same, how improved would be most farmer-hunt relations. I drove back to Helmsley having thoroughly enjoyed myself, even though there had been virtually no hunting as the wind was so bad. The genuine welcome and interest from everyone out had more than compensated for the lack of sport. I was very touched when, during the evening, Major Bailey (the Master) telephoned me to apologise for the fact that his Honorary Secretary had capped me and said that he was sending it back. This he had no need to do as the Secretary had been quite correct to cap me, as I was no longer an active Master, but Major Bailey knew how long I had been a Master and decided to waive the cap. I think this story well describes the genuine friendliness of this hunt, and if I lived near there I am sure I would want to hunt with them regularly.

A nine o'clock start was sufficient to get to the ten forty-five meet of the **Bedale Foxhounds** at Atley Hill, and for once I arrived exactly on time (Fri 19 Jan 1990). The first person I saw at the meet was Major Smalley whom I knew well from his services at the Peterborough Hound Show and various committees.

**Bedale.** *From the meet at East Cowton, December 1989.*

Photograph kindly supplied by Sir Stephen Furness. Copyright Mr Roy Parker.

He was somewhat taken aback to see me and was very interested to know what I was doing. There were about thirty-two out and, while hounds were drawing the first hedgerows, the Field Master took the field for a "jolly" over a line of neat hedges. I walked sedately through a line of open gates in company with an ex-Master of these hounds, who also wanted no part in this skylarking – the pair of us feeling very grown-up and pompous while the children played.

**Grove and Rufford.** *Meet at Osberton. Huntsman Roderick Duncan, with Teddy Parks (on foot), the oldest surviving supporter who has hunted with the Grove since1912.*

Photograph kindly loaned by Ian Youdan MFH

Hounds soon found and went away at a great pace until they finally marked to ground in a very thick place and he had to be left. It was at this point that I noticed that Max was not himself as he was all white lather and had coughed several times. I still followed hounds for an hour or so longer, just walking along at the back, keeping well away from other horses. Max was quite content to do this, so I knew then for sure that he was not well, and took him back to the lorry and back to Hazel's tender care. I was sorry to have had my day cut short like this as I got the impression from my short time with these hounds that they would really be able to push a fox along in fair conditions.

Next day I took Fizz when I made my second attempt to hunt with the **Grove and Rufford Foxhounds**. I had intended to go with them the previous December when I was staying with Eric and Marcia Elliott in Derbyshire, but had been unable to go as I had the 'flu. On this day they were meeting at Saundby Park, near Retford (Notts), which was the home of two of the Joint-Masters, Mr and Mrs Youdan (Sat 20 Jan 1990). I was made very welcome, Mr Youdan telling me that he had recently been in Ireland hunting with various packs. When I asked what sort of country we would be in, he replied that he could either give me a jumping day or a hunting day, but not both. It seemed that it was going to be a jumping day as, when we reached the first covert and the huntsman had put hounds in to draw, he set off and took us on a "jolly" all around the covert over jumps, right back to where we had started from. It was just as well that the covert was blank as a fox would have been unable to have come out with a line of galloping horses going past. I resigned myself to the thought that this was how it was going to be all day, but events proved otherwise.

Hounds were put in to some old farm buildings and were away at once through a long covert and over a lovely sound turf, past a flock of sheep which had been put into some buildings for lambing, and swung round to re-enter the large covert. The Master took the field over a long line of Hunter Trial fences but I did not go with him and, when hounds hunted their fox out of the far end of the covert, I got away with another man whose father had farmed this land when he was a lad so he knew the country well. As a consequence we had a good hunt on our own, and were never out of touch with hounds. The next draw was a rough railway line near a power-station. Hounds found in some brambles on the edge of the line and then ran down the line for two miles or so. It seemed very strange to hear the horses' feet on the sleepers and I was quite relieved when we jumped over some rails to get off the line. The tracks were bright so the line was obviously still in use and I did not relish the thought of meeting a train head-on. At three-fifteen I decided that both Fizz and I had had enough, as hounds had been running almost non-stop all day and dear old Fizz was showing signs that he was getting tired. I got back to Helmsley at

**Tony Harvey** *on a low part of Hadrian's Wall near Steel Rig.*

Photograph by Richard Wells-Furby

five forty-five, just in time for the symposium in the Royal Oak.

On Sunday morning my daughter Judith telephoned to tell me that the straw-burner had set light to the barn at home and that it had burned down to the ground. All my driving harness had been burned in it, but the men from the farm had pulled my carriages to safety (Sun 21 Jan 1990). I decided that there was little point in going home as there was nothing I could do about it, so I stayed on for another three days' hunting as planned. The first of these was with the **Middleton Foxhounds** from Amotherby, near Malton (Mon 22 Jan 1990). One of my early-evening-drinking friends, Geoffrey Nicholson (the Helmsley butcher) had said that he would have a day's hunting with me and he met me at this meet having hacked on from his daughter's farm nearby. His daughter was married to Tim Easterby, a well-known and successful racehorse trainer. There had recently been a tragedy in the Middleton hunt as Mrs Crossley, wife of the Joint Master Colonel Crossley, had died while suffering an asthma attack. Colonel Crossley is the brother of Lord Somerleyton (who for many years was Master of the Waveney Harriers), and his wife had been buried at Somerleyton Hall in Suffolk. He was still in Suffolk so hounds were hunted by the kennel huntsman.

**Middleton.** *Meet at Amotherby, near Malton. Joint Masters Colonel the Honourable R N Crossley, Mr D Megginson, Mrs A Cooke and Lord Middleton.*
Photograph kindly donated by Mr and Mrs S Telfer

We moved off to draw a long length of river bank and a lot of "set-aside" land which was all grown up with weeds. In spite of this area seeming an ideal place for a fox to lie up in, it was over an hour before one was found. This fox gave us a run of just over an hour with only two small checks. After leaving the river, we crossed a main road and ran up to the Castle Howard estate. Max went well, and never offered to refuse, but I thought that discretion was the better part of valour when Geoffrey and his son-in-law squared up to a thick well-trimmed hedge of between five and six feet high, flying over it on their Point-to-Point horses. We were not with the rest of the field at this point so this faint-heartedness left me on my own. However, I soon found an alternative route and was up with hounds when they marked their fox to ground in a difficult place where it was left. At the meet I had sat thinking that these were not perhaps the best-looking hounds I have ever seen, which proves yet again the proverb "Handsome is as handsome does" as they had certainly hunted beautifully with a grand cry and great drive, leaving me at the end of the run with aching calf muscles for the first time in my life. There was a long hack back to the original draw and I watched them draw two more coverts blank. At three o'clock I decided to go back to the box, arriving back at Helmsley at four-fifteen. I spent a most enjoyable evening as Geoffrey and his wife joined me for dinner.

I took Max again next day to the **Hurworth Foxhounds** as Fizz had a slightly sore back (Tues 23 Jan 1990). I allowed too much time to get to the meet at Hutton Rudby, so I had to wait, sitting in the cab, for an hour or so. The meet was on the village green, a real picture-postcard type scene. I introduced myself to the Joint Master, Mr Smith, and the field arrived from all directions until there were about forty or so mounted, with apparently not a real hunting person amongst them. Nearly all had riding-sticks stuck into the top of rubber riding boots, and sat with their jackets undone. In marked contrast to this sorry sight was the professional huntsman, Robin Foster, who sat amongst his beautiful Old English hounds (which were mostly of Brocklesby blood) with no whipper-in to help him but every hound in perfect control.

When we moved off Mr Smith asked me to ride with him so I was at the front of the field when we came to the first covert. The sight of that huntsman sitting outside the covert is one I shall never forget, his hounds all around him quivering with excitement but not offering to leave him until he said, "Lieu in there," and then every hound flew into the covert. He had no whipper-in all day and neither did he need one. Hounds drew beautifully for three-quarters of an hour and then I saw a fox creeping along a rough bank. Hounds were laid on and we went away over a lovely line of country. I was not far from Mr Smith when I saw him turn away from hounds, but I kept going on with the field. When we were stopped by impossible wire I realised why he had turned away and wished I had kept with him. When we eventually caught up with hounds Max was getting quite tired (this being his second day running) so I decided to go home. It was fortunate that I did not stay out until the end of the day, as when I took his saddle off he also had a sore back. During the evening Hazel told me that my favourite saddle was finished, as the tree was broken in two places and this had obviously caused the sore backs on both horses.

However, on inspection the next morning, Fizz's back was thought to be up to another day so I set off with him at eight o'clock for the long drive to the meet of the **Brocklesby Foxhounds** at Little Limber Grange (Wed 24 Jan 1990). This was the other side of the Humber estuary and, after crossing the Humber bridge, I went the wrong way up the A18 so I arrived very late at the meet. Hounds had moved off by the time I was mounted but, after catching up with the field, I received a hearty welcome from Mr Burt, one of the Joint Masters. This genuine friendliness extended throughout the field. We were hunting in large and most beautiful beech woods which, after producing first-class pheasant shooting all season, still had plenty of foxes in them which caused hounds to change foxes at times. I had been in raptures for an hour or so, thrilled to the marrow of my bones by the glorious cry of these famous hounds when, at a check, a man rode up to me and asked if I had lost anything. I felt my pockets and realised that I had lost my wallet. He had noticed it in the mud of a woodland ride after all the field had ridden over it. I thanked him profusely and realised that in my haste at the meet I had not put it properly into my pocket when changing from my ratcatcher coat into my green one.

**Brocklesby Foxhounds.** *The 7th Earl of Yarborough, M.F.H. and Lady Yarborough with Huntsman Cooper Atkinson.*
Photograph kindly loaned by Mrs Colin Sanderson

These hounds were all very dark tan and all very similar, their appearance being that of large harriers in their size and build. I was struck particularly by this, having noticed it the previous day as well, since the Hurworth have so much Old English Brocklesby blood. They were fast and ran with great drive and exceptionally pretty voices. At one stage I noticed hounds slipping back and turned back with them, having the pack to myself for a few precious minutes. Then they left the covert and went away across wheat, dropping out of sight over the brow of a hill. I do not know how the huntsman and field had become separated from hounds and was sorely tempted to go on with them regardless, but resisted it. I could see someone in the distance and held up my hat, the message being relayed to the huntsman who came up to me and I explained where hounds had gone. We had a quick burst across country to find them marking at an earth in a disused quarry pit. The day was one of heavy snow showers alternating with sunshine which left the rides very slippery. Fizz, living up to his name, gave me many anxious moments as he slipped and skidded around.

At a long check Mr Burt told me how recently a well-known journalist had been out with the Brocklesby and had been invited to stay at Brocklesby Park with Lord Yarborough, the Senior Master, whose family have had these hounds since 1763. After hunting the visitor asked Lord Yarborough's son, Lord Worsley, to ask the butler to do his coat and boots. Not being inclined to ask the butler to do this chore, which was no part of his duties, but wishing to save embarassment, Lord and Lady Worsley did the chore themselves. Mr Burt was disgusted by the journalist's behaviour as was the small group of the field who had gathered round.

A very pleasant evening was spent with my Helmsley friends and after the usual six o'clock drink at the pub they all joined me for a Last Night dinner at the Feathers where I enjoyed one of the specialities of the house, Sirloin steak served with a Stilton sauce. As much as I would have liked to have found fault with the steak (just for fun) as I had the butcher, Geoffrey Nicholson, sitting next to me, I could not, as it was first class.

Next day I had to face the long journey home with the prospect of a burned-down barn and destroyed harness-room waiting for me at the end (Thurs 25 Jan 1990). It was a heartbreaking sight as not only was the old barn gone, that had stood there for hundreds of years, but also all the harness which had taken so many hours of careful craftmanship to make. However, all the vehicles had been saved so it was not as bad as it could have been, and it was only three weeks later that I was on the road again, on my way back to Helmsley. I had several business calls to make on the way, so I made a two-day journey of it, leaving on Thursday 15 February, and travelled in the car, *via* Burton, Walsall, Leeds and Worksop, while Henry Kemp, who worked for me on the farm, drove the lorry up to Helmsley with the two horses and Hazel. I arrived in Helmsley in the afternoon of the Friday and then Henry drove the car home again, leaving me with the lorry as usual.

The first day of this holiday was with the **South Durham Foxhounds** at Nunstainton East Farm which lay near the junction of the A689 with the A1 (Sat 17 Feb 1990). I decided to take Max and could not have made a better decision as he went beautifully all day. As I was already mounted, I declined the invitation to go into the house, but I could sense the camaraderie of this small hunt while listening to the sound of happy voices and peals of laughter coming out of the door. Although I kept outside on my horse I was well looked after by the hospitable host of this excellent lawn meet, and I had the company of a very interesting man who had been huntsman of the Sinnington Foxhounds for ten seasons. With the wisdom of hindsight I wished I had put my horse back in the lorry and joined them, as the party in the house went on for thirty-five to forty minutes, and, as always, reminded me of Easton meets at home.

**South Durham Foxhounds.** *Meet at Great Stainton, Boxing Day 1995. Huntsman Mr David Simms leading hounds away.*
Picture kindly supplied by Mrs A S Bowes

Just before we moved off I was invited to ride with the huntsman, and the first thing we did was to cross underneath the A1 motorway, canter across a meadow, pop over a flight of post-and-rails and then pass under the main railway line. What a place to hunt! I was immensely relieved when Max took the post-and-rails perfectly, as he can so often dig in his heels when asked to jump when hounds are not running. Hounds drew the railway embankment which terrified me to watch. I felt goose pimples all over me but all was well and a fox was found which ran away from the line and we had a lovely spin across country. During this run we had to negotiate a small river which necessitated entering at one spot, riding along the bottom, then up the other side. The huntsman stopped and explained to me exactly where to walk my horse, as there were very deep pools to avoid. The huntsman, whipper-in and I crossed safely, but a man out on a most beautiful heavyweight hunter which

**The South Durham:** ***"A wash before Wembley"***

had qualified for Wembley failed to navigate correctly and disappeared into a deep pool up to his neck. The horse had quite a job to get out but finally managed it. The rider, although thoroughly soaked, was determined to go on even though there was a very cold wind. From memory, I think his friends did persuade him to go home after an hour or so, which was probably very wise.

The hounds were rather a mixed lot but in perfect control, which was just as well as every fox they found ran to one of the two flocks of lambing sheep in the area. The huntsman drew in every different direction possible but wherever we found a fox, it always ran to one of the two flocks. Five foxes were found in total, and hounds hunted beautifully each time over delightful country, and it was such a shame that they had to be stopped every time. It seemed very odd to be hunting in this lovely country of grass with fences and hedges, but to be in sight the whole time of a major motorway and railway line. Late in the afternoon I hacked back to the meet (crossing over the A1 this time) having thoroughly enjoyed myself, largely due to the fact that I had been with hounds, but coupled with the fact that the field were so friendly and full of fun.

On Sunday I went to Sung Eucharist in the Helmsley church. It seemed very strange as I had not been to Sung Eucharist since I was at school (Sun 18 Feb 1990). I had a lovely walk in Duncombe Park in the afternoon, and I met Geoffrey Nicholson on his tractor. He had been working on the course for the Sinnington Point-to-Point the following Saturday and he invited me to have dinner with him that evening. It was a most excellent dinner, the joint of beef in particular being out of this world. It just melted in the mouth.

It was a most scenic drive on Monday morning along the coast from Whitby to the meet of the **Cleveland Foxhounds** at Saltburn Riding School, with spectacular views of the sea over the cliffs (Mon 19 Feb 1990). The meet, given by the proprietor of the riding school, Mr Hills, was first class with plenty of lovely food and glasses topped up continually. Most of the twenty-eight horses were rather weedy and there was only one other real hunter apart from Max. As we moved off, I could not help thinking that I had never seen a whole field of more unlikely looking hunters. However, pride comes before a fall, and later on, when it came to jumping a narrow stile set in the middle of a barbed wire fence on a steep downhill slope, Max and the other good-looking horse were the only ones which refused to jump it, and we were well and truly left.

**The Holderness.** *Tony Harvey standing in a12 foot deep Holderness drain.*
Photograph by Richard Wells-Furby

Conditions were terrible, with gale-force winds trying to tear us from our saddles and it was impossible to hear anything. Hounds had drawn for two hours but had been unable to find, which was not surprising as no self-respecting fox would have been above ground in these conditions. The draws were mostly hedgerows and small coverts on open moorland, and as they were drawing the farmer on the nice-looking horse and I got into conversation and were wandering along at the back, so when it came to the stile incident all the rest had jumped it leaving the take-off very slippery. Try as we would, neither of us could get our equally-experienced hunters to jump it. We turned back and, although my companion knew the country very well, we were unable to find hounds again as we could hear nothing in the winds. We had to hack back to the meet with our tails between our legs. During the day, however, I had seen the home of a lady who I was told was the richest woman in the country, and a little later on I had seen what I was told was the smallest church in the country.

Next day it was back into South Yorkshire for the meet of the **Holderness Foxhounds** at Apwich, and I decided to take Fizz again but this proved to be a great mistake (Tues 20 Feb 1990). As I rode up to the meet I was made very welcome by two of the Joint-Masters and was invited to ride up with the huntsman. There were about thirty out, which I was told was a very small field for this pack. The Holderness are famed for having very large ditches (or "drains" as they are known locally) but having come out of a country with large ditches I felt reasonably confident. The huntsman, William Deakin, was a very pleasant young man, obviously and justly proud of his beautiful hounds which were very level. I was really taken aback to find that this pack also were Old English. I had had no idea that there were so many packs with this blood, but was coming to realise that they shared the characteristics of drive and speed.

When we moved off, Fizz was acting like an idiot in spite of being in front with hounds. If it had been his first day's hunting ever, his behaviour would only just have been acceptable. I followed the huntsman over a few quite big ditches until we came to the first big "drain" which the huntsman carefully studied and then, after some consideration, jumped. I ought not to have tried to jump it with Fizz in this idiotic state of mind, but I did and he would not concentrate. He took off yards too soon and landed in a crumpled heap on the other bank, with the inevitable result that we finished up in the bottom of the drain which was twelve to fourteen feet deep. Somehow he more or less managed to land on his feet. In the confusion, we were parted and I let go of him. Some way further down the drain (and I shall never know how) he managed to climb out and careered off across country, leaving me standing "all forlorn", alternately looking at my disappearing horse and into the bottom of where he had just been. It is ironic that, having tackled all the horrors of stone walls and post-and-rails in galloping country, I should come to such grief in "ditch country". In my defence, of course, it could be said that this was not just a ditch. It took two kind men quite a while to catch him and return him to me, the Field Master wisely not having come this way, so no-one else was obliged to jump this drain. I had wrenched my back in the fall and stubbed my left wrist and had very little feeling in my fingers but soon forgot these troubles as I rode to catch up with the huntsman.

He put hounds into a covert which was owned by the Hunt. I later found out that they owned six coverts in the country and this was, I think, my first experience of hunts owning their own coverts. A fox was immediately found and we had a sharp run across country, mostly wheat fields with ditches, with a few hedges and one memorable leap over sheets of galvanised tin blocking a gap. Fizz thoroughly enjoyed the gallop and was tight, too tight, on the huntsman's heels. This was fine until we came onto a main road and galloped up it for a mile or so. He was completely out of control and, with my numb fingers, I just could not hold him. Ahead I could see a line of cars pulled up at a crossroad and I was sure that we would either jump or crash into them, but at the last moment he did try to stop. He skidded into a car with quite a bump, startling the occupants, but with extraordinary luck, it turned out that they were car-followers of the Hunt. I apologised profusely but was assured that I had done no harm and was firmly advised to get a severer bit. This fox was lost in some bungalow gardens, or perhaps "lost" was the wrong term as I expect the huntsman thought it politic to draw on, away from the houses.

My back was giving me hell and there was still no feeling in the fingers of my left hand so I was glad to take up an offer made by a member of the field, Mr David Osborne. I enquired how far it was back to the meet and he very kindly suggested that instead of hacking back to the meet, I put Fizz into a loose box at his home, Catfoss Hall, which was nearby, and he would have his groom take me back for the lorry by car. This I was very glad of, as it proved to be eight miles, which gave me an indication of how long the run had been and saved me from getting even wetter, as it had been a day of heavy rain and very stormy winds. My kind benefactor hacked with me back to Catfoss Hall, which was a very impressive place, with beautiful stables and a long drive paved with red bricks. I eventually arrived back at Helmsley at five-thirty.

My fingers were still numb next morning as I set off with Max for the meet of the **Bramham Moor Foxhounds** at Creskeld Hall, Arthington (Wed 21 Feb 1990). Conditions were nearly the same again, the winds being very strong indeed. There were three professional hunt servants out, but I thought the hounds rather ordinary and not as impressive as I had expected. They drew all around the meet and across Harewood Park, but it proved to be a blank day and I left at two-thirty, feeling that I had had enough of this dreadful wind. The whole day could have been very boring but for an auctioneer who was a great character and was very entertaining all day. Anthony Barker had invited me to dinner, which I was delighted to accept, as invitations to dine with the Barkers were most coveted, Jane being a first-class cook. The dinner party fully lived up to her reputation and a delightful evening was spent in excellent company. Brian Bourne, one of

**Bramham Moor.** *Meet at Kirkby Overblow, February 1990. Huntsman Stuart Coley (right), whipper-in Robert Howarth (left) and Joint Master L V Marshall, leading the field.*
Photograph kindly loaned by Michael Sharp

the six o'clock drinking crowd, was on top form and greatly added to the fun.

I eventually walked across the road to my bed at twelve-fifteen and left at six-thirty next morning for the ten o'clock meet of the **North Tyne Foxhounds** at Houxty House, between Wark and Bellingham (Thurs 22 Feb 1990). I was recognised as soon as I rode up to the house by the kennel huntsman, Kevin Parsons, who I remembered from days with the Windermere Harriers, and Mr Wybergh, the Joint-Master and huntsman, made me very welcome. He was, I believe, unique in that he was Master and huntsman of two packs simultaneously, for he was also the Joint-Master and huntsman of the Cumberland Farmers' Foxhounds, which meant that he was hunting hounds five days a week. The assembled field was like something I had never seen before. There were over thirty mounted and many more on foot. The Master was the only one who was wearing a clean coat, the others sitting there laughing and talking in coats bedaubed with varying degrees of mud, a few with such a heavy coating that it was most certainly the combination of more than one day's hunting. Most of the horses were the same, well mud-splattered and wearing dirty tack. Some of the bridles and saddles looked as though, at the most, they got an annual clean. All the field were either local farmers or their wives or children. There was no-one out who did not farm in the immediate area and, most delightful of all, was a three-generation trio of grandmother, daughter and granddaughter. I liked them all immediately, as even before we moved off I instinctively knew that I was amongst hunting people who went out to hunt and would only be interested in what the hounds were doing.

**North Tyne** *From the meet at Watergate Farm, Wark, 1990.*
Photograph kindly loaned by Mr Cyril Telford

**North Tyne** *The meet at Nunwich Hall, Simonburn (home of Mr & Mrs L Allgood), 1990. Peter Wyberg, Master and Huntsman.*
Photograph kindly loaned by Mr Cyril Telford

Hounds were mostly Fell types with some Welsh amongst them and they looked, I thought, like the hounds which Surtees describes as "fox-catchers". I loved the country as it was wild and open rugged moorland, free from all modern encumbrances and distractions, with small coverts and nothing to stop a good horse for miles on end. Unfortunately, this was to be another blank day although the Master drew thoroughly from ten o'clock until one-thirty. As the day progressed the Kielder Forest, which I was told was Europe's largest, came into view, a dark blanket which stretched for miles across the horizon. Gradually we drew closer to it, and each time we breasted a rise it was closer and filled more of the horizon. The day was sunny and warm (which made a pleasant change from the wind and rain) but I think it was probable that the three previous wild days had driven all the foxes into Kielder for shelter.

There was one incident in the day which I shall never forget. The Master was assured by a local that it was all right to go up a very steep bank out of a river bottom as he said he had been there with his spade and cut footholds for the horses. The bank was sixty feet high and very, very steep. It seemed almost vertical at the place where the steps had been cut. I almost chickened out and wished that I had had Max, as he was so much more sensible than Fizz, particularly as my fingers were still numb from our day with the Holderness. The climb was terrifying, and the one time I dared look back I could see only the river far below, so steep was it that the bank below me was all out of sight. To add to the hazards, there were trees growing out of the bank. When I was safely on top, I suddenly realised that the feeling had returned to my fingers, which I think must have been due to the increased blood pressure! At one-thirty the Master decided to draw the edge of Kielder Forest and so, as I was assured by everyone that a fox would never leave and that it would be the last we saw of hounds, I decided to hack the considerable distance back to the meet.

The meet of the **Staintondale Foxhounds** the next day was at the Windmill Inn at Stainsacre which was just outside Whitby so I telephoned Len Mison, an old friend who had moved from the Easton country years before, and who now lived at Whitby, and suggested that he met me at the Windmill (Fri 23 Feb 1990). He joined me at the meet and followed on foot and by car for a little while until his work forced him to leave hounds. The hounds, which had been a trencher-fed pack until as late as 1944, were being hunted by an amateur whip for the first time, as the huntsman was at his mother's funeral. This was a very homely, friendly little hunt which met on Mondays and Fridays. There were ten people out which was about average, and included a pair of identical elderly twin sisters riding identical horses. These two sporting ladies were, I was told, great supporters of these hounds. The amateur whip hunted them very well although conditions were against him, as it was very sunny with high winds. His first draw was some rough bushy ground where a fox was quickly found and we had a nice little run towards Raw, but lost the line on high country due to the high winds being worse on the exposed ground, the wind coming right off the sea. The rest of the day was spent in a series of short hunts which were always lost on high ground in the same way, leaving me feeling very sorry for the poor man hunting hounds for the first time. Nature could have been kinder to him on his first day. I left at two-thirty as my wife, mother and daughter Judith (with her husband and six-month-old daughter) were due to arrive at the Black Swan, Helmsley, for a "Secrets of Cuisine" weekend. I was delighted that they had agreed to join me in my second home and they thoroughly enjoyed their weekend, but for a small problem with a sauce which seemed to appear on our plates rather too often.

Saturday was the Sinnington Point-to-Point in Duncombe Park but I preferred to go hunting and, leaving my family to their own devices, I left early to drive to the meet of the **Zetland Foxhounds** at High Coniscliffe (Sat 24 Feb 1990). There were, as best as I could count, between ninety and a hundred mounted at the meet, which was quite a sight, with a high percentage of good horses, mostly well turned out. I was most impressed with the hounds and the immaculate turnout of the hunt servants. Unfortunately, it was just the sort of field whose behaviour I dislike most, with several people at once rushing at hunt jumps, cutting in and barging, Leicestershire style. This is unavoidable with these large fields and has to go on or you get left behind, but I hate it so I kept back and cut corners. As the first fox ran in a circular fashion, rather like a hare, I had a good view of houndwork, often seeing the fox cross first and then watching hounds hunt along the line. This mode of progress suited me particularly well this day as I was feeling the after-effects of an exceptionally good dinner, followed by a few too many brandies, the previous night. I carried on in this manner, cutting corners and finding myself "in the guinea seats". Gradually I built up a little field behind me, first one other person following me, then another until I soon felt like a junior Field Master. Eventually, however, I tried to be too clever and, along with eight others, became completely lost and out of the game.

**Zetland.** *Meet at High Coniscliffe in late 1980s.*
Photograph kindly donated by Mr and Mrs J Smith

At one o'clock we decided to go back to our boxes and I arrived back at Helmsley at three o'clock to rejoin my family. Sheila and Judith had enjoyed the cooking course during the day and we were looking forward to the dinner in the evening. This was good, although we thought that the sauce which was served with the lamb seemed to be the same as the one that had been served with the beef the night before. We also thought that it had gone better with the beef.

First thing in the morning the telephone rang in my room at seven o'clock (Sun 25 Feb 1990). It was Judith to ask if I would like to go for a walk because her daughter was keeping her awake, so she thought she might as well wake me up. I dressed and she and I, with six-month-old Daisy in the pram, walked through Duncombe Park, so I could show her the mansion. After soup and sandwiches for lunch, we drove to

Whitby for tea with Len Mison and his daughter. Sadly we missed Helen, his wife, as she was away in Canada. We drove back to Helmsley really looking forward to enjoying our dinner at the Black Swan but, although Sheila and Judith enjoyed their meal, Bill and I had chosen the monk fish and were shocked to find that it was served with a sauce which appeared to be the same as the one which had been served with the previous night's lamb and the night before's beef. My mother was disappointed too, as her chicken dish was also served with the same sauce. However, we did not allow these shortcomings to spoil our evening and thoroughly enjoyed our wines.

The family was due to go home on Monday but there was a terrible gale blowing (Mon 26 Feb 1990). I begged them to stop for another night but they insisted on going and later, when I saw the lunchtime news, I heard that the A1 was blocked in several places by overturned lorries, I was really worried and eventually relieved to hear that they were home safely. I had also planned to drive up to Scotland, but dared not venture as the gales were too bad. In a way I was glad to hear that conditions had been so bad as it justified what I was beginning to think of as my wimpishness.

I was forced to hurriedly arrange some more days from Helmsley but it is indeed an ill wind that blows no-one any good. My good friends Ian and Joan Cook were, unbeknown to me, in Yorkshire and had telephoned my landlady, Jackie Saggers, (who by now was more like a friend). She assured them that they would find me either in the Royal Oak or in the Feathers. It was a lovely surprise on this rather depressing day when they walked into the Royal Oak. After I had bought them a drink, I introduced them to Les Trousdale, the landlord, as friends and landlords of my favourite pub at home.

After a handshake he just turned, took a bottle of Jamieson's whisky off the shelf and filled two small tumblers, all without saying a word.

Ian turned to me and said, "I can see why you like this place so much."

We had a most enjoyable dinner at the Feathers and it was quite late when they left to go back to where they were staying with Joan's mother.

The gale winds were still raging next morning and I was quite surprised to find that the **Derwent Foxhounds** had not cancelled their meet at Woodlands Farm, Snainton (Tues 27 Feb 1990). The Joint-Master and huntsman, Mr Roberts, had come from Suffolk and his family, I think, farm in the Halesworth area. The hounds were of mixed types and included some very woolly Welsh ones. Ditches and small patches of bushes were drawn and several foxes found but hounds constantly turned to hunt upwind, which usually meant that they were running heel-way. The conditions were impossible. It was all we could do to remain on our horses. There was a good scent and in the odd place where a fox had run in the lee of a hedge, the hounds screamed along. At one o'clock I rode up to the Master to say my goodbyes and he replied, "If you're stopping, so am I. I was only keeping out because you were here." He then did exactly what I would have done at home in the circumstances, suggesting to the field of about fifteen that a light lunch (or was it a liquid lunch, it was difficult to be sure in the wind) at the Coachman Inn, opposite the kennel gates, should be the order of the day. After boxing and rugging up our horses, everyone went to the pub, and what a friendly, happy crowd they were. They reminded me of lines from a hunting song,

*"As evening comes, a merry crew*
*Are found in village inn.*
*In nature's haunts they've spent the day,*
*In men's they now begin.*
*With song and jest and laughter loud,*
*They pass the time away.*
*A happier lot you ne'er may find*
*Though search the world all o'er."*

The Master was the life and soul of the party and introduced me to his kennel huntsman with whom I had a very interesting conversation, as his grandfather had been huntsman to the Glaisdale at the time they changed from harriers to foxhounds.

I drove back with the winds no better and was sure that these hounds would show great sport in fair conditions if they could hunt as well as they had in these winds. I also reflected that this was one of the inestimable advantages of a small pack over a large one, that in these circumstances it was possible to make the best of a bad day by having this sort of party.

Next morning I had a long drive to the meet of the **Braes of Derwent Foxhounds** at Browney Bank, Five Lane Ends, but it was well worth the journey as I had a superb day (Wed 28 Feb 1990). Mrs Aldridge, one of the Joint Masters, made me very welcome and took me to meet her Joint Master, Mr Villiers, who also hunts hounds. Ed Bailey, the kennel huntsman, had been at the High Peak Harriers for several seasons so I knew him quite well from Peterborough Hound Show. Mr Villiers invited me to ride either with him hunting hounds or with his kennel huntsman, an invitation I was as usual delighted to accept. The field were the friendliest I have ever come across, even to the extent of pressing me to stay the night and offering to put up my horse. I had been surprised to see that snow was lying on the ground, although it was not a complete covering, as there had been none in Helmsley, but then realised that I was now on higher ground.

We found a fox in the first draw and went away at a great pace for some miles until the line was eventually lost. Max had gone very well over both stone walls and post-and-rails, often either taking off from a snow-drift or landing in one. The field were great "goers", even jumping a post-and-rails onto a road in these terrible conditions. At one o'clock it started to snow very heavily and was still doing so an hour later so I decided to go back to the lorry, as it was impossible to see anything. The snow storm continued all the way back and as I drew nearer to Helmsley I began to wonder how bad the notorious Sutton Bank would be. The road up the Bank was very steep and winding and was difficult enough in good weather. The first time I had driven the lorry to Helmsley my friend Tony "Mole" had been with me and he would not let me tackle it at all, insisting that I took the "caravan route" around it. I assumed that it would have been salted in the bad weather, but the lorry only just made it. It was really frightening to feel the lorry slipping back at times and I wished, knowing that it was as usual too late, that I had not attempted it. From the top of Sutton Bank to Helmsley was the deepest snow of the journey. It had been one of the most enjoyable day's foxhunting that I had experienced and I had thoroughly enjoyed every minute of it, even given the conditions. Scent had been very good as is so often the case when a snowstorm threatens.

After such a lovely day I was fortunate to have an evening to match, for after the usual early-evening drinks in the Royal Oak, I decided to dine in the Black Swan. Purely by chance, I met Colonel Leonard Gibson and his wife and a friend and was invited to join them for dinner. He was famous as Master of the Newcastle and District Beagles and the organiser of the Northumberland Hunting Festival. The impromptu "dinner party" was great fun, with the conversation mostly about hounds and hunting in general, all helped by glasses of the most delicious claret I have ever tasted. We ended the evening with a very smooth brandy, which must have been very impressive indeed, as I am not as a rule partial to brandy, preferring port. This is where this most enjoyable evening ought to have ended but, idiot that I am, as I was crossing the Square to go back to Park House, I decided to call in at the Royal Oak, where Les Trousdale was in one of his "you-drink-what-I-give-you" moods and set a large tumbler of Jamieson's whisky before me, which was not the best thing to follow wines.

I was grateful the next morning that the **York and Ainsty South Foxhounds** followed the old custom of putting meets back to twelve o'clock in March, although most hunts did not keep up this tradition any longer (Thurs 1 Mar 1990). The Joint Master, Mr Bloor, was on his feet again following a bad fall on Boxing Day and repeated the warning that he had first given me when we had spoken on the telephone, that Colton Lodge was the meet for their worst country. I had heard this so often, but usually took no notice of this as frequently their "worst meets" turned out to be bliss for me, but this time there was some justification for the warning. The Secretary asked Mr Bloor if she ought to cap me and to my surprise he said yes, so I had to pay £20 cap, the only time I was capped on this trip. There were only eight others out, but they were all very pleasant and friendly, especially the Field Master who was great fun. The kennel huntsman said that he recognised me from a picture in Hounds Magazine when "All Thanks To His Grace" was published, and I was again surprised to find that the hounds were Old English. They were all very smart and level and I was most impressed. The amateur whip was riding a wonderful little cob and I tried very hard to buy it, but he could not be tempted to sell. This was to be a blank day, or at least they had not found by the time I left at three o'clock. The country was mostly wheat and ditches, with little or no warm cover for foxes to lie in, and as it was very cold and wet, with snow on the ground, it was hardly surprising we did not find.

Eventually, four days late, we said our goodbyes to Helmsley next day, loaded up the horses and left at nine-thirty to drive up to the Plumbes (Fri 2 Mar 1990). When we arrived we found a note left by Tizza, saying that she was helping a neighbour whose flock was lambing, so we busied ourselves unboxing and settling the horses in until she returned at four-thirty. We had a cup of tea before taking one of her horses away to a friend so as to make room for our horses. This friend lived some twelve miles or so away, which shows how very hospitable and kind the Plumbes are to go to all this trouble to accommodate our horses. In spite of this journey, Tizza somehow managed to cook a delicious supper.

I was pleased that Tizza was able to come with me the first day to the **Berwickshire Foxhounds** (Sat 3 Mar 1990). We we left at eight forty-five, arriving at ten-thirty at the meet at Woodhead Farm which was off the Greenlaw-Duns road. Our host, Mr Peter Leggett, was busy dispensing drinks to everyone assembled in the farmyard. Mr Douglas Tweedie, the Joint Master, was also Field Master, and there was a professional huntsman who had been there for twenty seasons, seventeen as kennel huntsman and the last three as huntsman.

There were about thirty out and we set off to draw across a heavenly moor which was mostly firm going, except for one very bad bog. The huntsman drew small fir coverts which were dotted all over the moor, and his practice of travelling quite fast from covert to covert meant that we were kept busy and warm, as conditions were not good. There was a lot of snow on the ground and high winds. We eventually found in about the twentieth little covert and went away into the wind at a great pace. Max flew over a little gate and I was well away with hounds but sadly, later on, he faded rather. He was not used to these hills, especially coupled with the thick knee-deep heather. The line was eventually lost on an exposed hill-top where the wind had obliterated the scent.

Mr Tweedie pointed out to me two stone cairns in the middle of the moor and told me the story which lay behind them. In the days of the "Border rievers" one of the local laird's twin sons was stolen by the English during a raid, and he was taken to England to be reared as an Englishman. When he was grown up, he returned to claim half of the estate and fought a duel with his twin brother. They both died as a result of this duel and the two cairns were raised in memory of their deaths. Mr Tweedie went on to say how some Polish soldiers had used them as target practice and were made to rebuild them. I was about to ask why Polish soldiers were in Scotland when a fox was found, so I never discovered the answer, but I expect it was during the Second World War. At one time we dropped down into a deep ravine and rode along the bottom. Mr Tweedie called this pretty valley "Grand Canyon Corridor". Having had my first ever sighting of a white hare with the Lauderdale in the autumn, I was to be treated to the sight of twenty or more on the moor. They are properly called "blue" hares and they were very blue at the time. They were very pretty to see, and seemed to be much smaller than our brown ones. I was also taken to see the gravestone of an old gamekeeper who always insisted that the guns drink water from his favourite little well, way out on the moor. The guns, especially the visitors, would declare that it was the best water they had ever tasted. What he never did tell them was that he used to secretly pour a bottle of whisky into the water just before they drank it and this is the reason why he was buried near the well.

**Percy.** *Meet at the Shepherd's Rest, Alnwick, 30 January 1993. Huntsman Don Claxton, and first whipper-in, M Claxton.*
Photograph kindly donated by M Claxton

At two forty-five Tizza and I decided to go back and, although our host said it would be better to stay out, we decided to go. If only he had said how far we were from the meet, I would have asked one of the many young farmers who were following in their Land Rovers to take me back to the meet to fetch the lorry. We had hacked for an hour and a half along a very straight and exposed road and were very cold and wet when a car follower kindly offered me a lift and I fetched the lorry, thus saving the last six miles. It was far too late for Tizza to cook so I took her out to dinner at the Rendezvous Restaurant in Hawick, as our favourite, the Old Forge, was fully booked.

The **Percy Foxhounds** met on Mondays so at the beginning of the next week I was off to their meet in a car-park at Craster, a village on the coast near Alnwick (Mon 5 Mar 1990). It was some distance and the meet was at ten forty-five, so I had to leave at seven o'clock. I had some difficulty in Alnwick where I obviously missed the sign warning of a nine foot six arch over the road. I had to reverse the lorry a long way back down the street and every time I started someone would come right up behind me in a car. Eventually an old gentleman took pity on me and walked behind the lorry keeping the cars back.

**The Percy Foxhounds.** *The low arch in Alnwick – the cause of all the trouble.*
Photograph by Richard Wells-Furby

The Lady Master dispensed drinks at the meet to myself and the five ladies who made up the field. These ladies, I could instinctively feel, were real foxhunters and my instinct was proved to be correct as they were as keen on the venerie as I was. The hounds belong to the Duke of Northumberland, after whom the Hunt is named. The Master told me that she had asked to help with the field for a while after the Duke had had a stroke in the 1988-89 season and then found herself as Joint-Master, with the tenth Duke, after his death.

We found a fox at once and had one and a half hours of continual hunting, with hounds speaking all the time, as they hunted through thick gorse bushes on the sides of crags, which they were only able to do because the gorse sheltered the scent from the strong winds. I often had views of the hunted fox as he twisted and turned on the face of the crags above us before finally going away into the wind and hounds fairly flew after him, until the line was lost in an exposed place at a crossroads. Once again, this meet was supposed to be in their worst country but I thoroughly enjoyed it because of the spectacular views over the sea and of Dunstanburgh Castle. The huntsman reminded me of Surtees' description – *"too weak for a groom, too small for a coachman, too ugly for a postilion, too stunted for a footman, too light for a ploughman, too useless-looking for anything"* – and had a young whipper-in who had recently come from the Fife. The winds became worse and worse and at times it was quite difficult to keep in the saddle and when, at two o'clock, we got amongst several foxes and hounds split various ways I decided to go back to the box, having thoroughly enjoyed myself, as much, I think, as any day on this trip. There had been so much good, slow houndwork, all of which I had been able to see.

On Tuesday I was just about to leave for the meet of the Linlithgow and Stirlingshire when the Secretary telephoned to say that the meet had been cancelled because of the gale-force winds (Tues 6 Mar 1990). I was extremely grateful that she had thought to telephone early as I would have had that long journey for nothing. Following some hasty telephoning I found out that the **Morpeth Foxhounds** were going. I asked permission to join them and was given directions to the meet at Butternous Farm, Rothbury. The Joint Masters gave me a hearty welcome and Mr Cookson said he knew something of Suffolk and knew Lord Somerleyton.

We soon found but this fox went almost immediately to ground. He was bolted and gave us a sharp burst across country. Fizz was going like a bomb, far too fast for this wet and rocky country, and I was afraid that he would lose his feet but somehow he managed to keep upright. Inevitably the line was again lost on an exposed place, as the winds were terrible. Hounds were hunted by a professional and he had a professional whipper-in. They hunted with great drive and went with a very good cry. Quite astonishingly, this was considered to be their worst meet but, as usual, it seemed to me to be quite good, and wonderfully maintained as there were hunt jumps or wicket gates in every direction. It was always possible to take the same line as hounds. What a delightful day this would have been without the never-ending wind, but nevertheless I enjoyed myself amongst the field of about fifteen, most of whom were also interested in watching hounds.

Next day the same thing happened (Wed 7 Mar 1990). Tizza and I were ready to go with the Liddesdale Foxhounds but George Laing, the Master (whom I had met in 1982 with Anthony Barker of the Windermere), telephoned to say that he had cancelled because of the wind. As we were ready, we decided we would go to the Jedforest, as they were quite close, meeting at a farm on the Castleton road, even though I had already hunted with them when I had been at Roberton earlier in the season. Fizz gave me a terrible ride and I kept wishing that this would be the last time I ever had to ride him. I was so fed up with this terrible wind that I wished I had not gone out, as not surprisingly we had a blank day. The wind was so strong that after we had put the horses in the lorry it tore the ramp out of my hands and smacked it up with a loud bang, and it was even a struggle to close the little side door.

There were cards on the breakfast table next morning as Tizza had remembered that it was my birthday, and there were some more from the family when the postman came (Thurs 8 Mar 1990). My birthday treat was a joint meet of the **West Percy Foxhounds** and the **Border Foxhounds** (both of which I had been with before) at the Star Inn at Harbottle. With difficulty I found a place to unbox and hacked Max up to the meet. I thought for a time that I would be the only horse out, as both huntsman and whip were on motor-bikes and there were masses of people on foot and in cars. Before we moved off, some other horses arrived and there were about ten of us in all. One follower said to me, "Be sure not to overtake the Field Master", warning me that he was the one on the bright blue motor-bike. Amongst the mounted field were two ladies that I had met with the Braes of Derwent, and I confused one of them with a lady from another hunt and ended up in a most embarassing situation. There were plenty of radios so that all the Land Rover followers were able to be kept informed of the hunting. The woods would have been ideal for some good woodland hunting if there had not been so many foxes. The continual winds and rough conditions had brought them in for shelter and there seemed to be more foxes than hounds. The winds, if anything, were worse and I was fed up by two-thirty so went back to the box.

During the evening we had a lovely birthday dinner party at Easter House with Alistair Gibson and his wife, and Elizabeth and Wallace Donnan from "up the valley" who had recently moved into the area from the Eglinton country. Alistair was on top form and had us all in stitches all evening, no doubt helped by the lovely "Berry Bros and Rudd" claret that Colin was serving.

As so often, I did not hunt on the Friday and spent the day cutting up a large tree which had blown down in the gales (Fri 9 Mar 1990). I just managed to log it all, but could not burn up the sticks as everything was so wet. In the evening Colin, Tizza and I went to the Newcastle and District End of Season Dinner at Otterburn to which Colonel Gibson had invited me when we had met at the Black Swan. Unfortunately, Colonel Gibson was not there as that very evening there had been a false fire alarm in the Black Swan and he had had to go out into the snow. He had contracted bronchitis as a result and was still suffering. During the evening Colin sang "John Peel" and I sang "A Toast to the Harehunters".

Saturday was my last day and I went with the **Milvain Percy Foxhounds** who were meeting at Quarry House, Old Bewick (Sat 10 Mar 1990). I left home later than planned as the Master, Mr Barnett, had told me on the telephone that he would be late moving off. He had all the kennelwork to do as his kennel huntsman had had a heart attack. We drew for an hour and then found at one o'clock. We had a very fast run across good firm pasture with hunt jumps and post-and-rails. Every time we were on high ground we could see the traffic on the A1 and realised that hounds were running right to it, and this put extra zip into our ride across country. Max went very well and I was right with the Master (despite not being invited to do so!) so I could help him with hounds when they finally checked right beside the road. There were no hounds hurt, although we did have some anxious moments when they were getting very near to the traffic. They were marking at the bottom of a bank with the traffic roaring along above them. This hunt had been about six or seven miles as hounds ran, and was over lovely unspoiled country.

**Duke of Buccleuch's Foxhounds.** *Mounted followers at Easter House. Colin Plumbe on foot in the foreground with the Duke of Buccleuch in his car in the background.*

Photograph kindly loaned by Mrs Plumbe

Later, I asked Mr Barnett if the couple of Dumfriesshire foxhounds which I had noticed in the pack, were independent and he answered, "All the Milvain are independent. The hounds are independent, the President is independent, and the Master and all the members are too." Then, laughingly, he added, "We all get it from the President, you see."

The President was Miss Milvain, the owner of the pack and daughter of the founder. I was introduced to her and was so pleased to have been able to meet her as I had only read about her before.

The day with Milvain Percy was to be my last day's hunting that season, and as I sat in the study at Easter House filling in my diary, I ended with these words, *"I am feeling worn up, my clothes are worn out, my horse is old, and my lorry is very rough. I am wondering if all will hold together long enough so that I can fulfill my ambition."*

Jim Wickham, my ex-kennel huntsman, had previously telephoned to ask if there was a way that he could get a horse home from Scotland and I agreed to lend him the lorry, if he would bring my car up for me to go home with. He arrived with two friends, and spent the night in Hawick. Colin and I took them all to the Fox and Hounds at Denholm for a Last Night Party.

On Sunday morning Jim and friends set off in my lorry to go 250 miles into Scotland and back to Easter House to pick up my two horses and then bring all three home. Tizza kindly offered to feed my two horses for the two days before Jim would collect them, so that Hazel and I were able to go home in luxury in the car. However, all did not go quite according to plan as the 250 miles into Scotland proved to be the last straw for the lorry's poor old engine and it finally gave up. The extensive repairs took time and it was six o'clock on the Monday night before it was finished. Jim eventually arrived back at the Plumbes to collect Max and Fizz at one-thirty on Tuesday morning, and then carried on driving, arriving back at Tannington at three o'clock on the Tuesday afternoon, very tired.

# Chapter 20

## The Last Mounted Packs

At the beginning of the 1990-91 season there were ten mounted foxhound packs in the country that I had not hunted with. They were scattered all over the country, so I decided to make one last big effort to cover them all, and planned to be away for four weeks, staying at several different bases. I had decided to lend old Fizz to Mr John Dix who had asked if I knew of an old horse which he could use to quietly hunt his doghounds in the Forestry of Central Wales. This left me with just Max, who I desperately hoped would keep sound for the last few packs.

The first day was had en route to Derbyshire and I left Tannington at six o'clock with Max but without Hazel, this being almost the only time I have gone away without a groom, for the last of the "Shires" packs, the **Fernie Foxhounds** (Wed 14 Nov 1990). When I telephoned the Master, Mr Cowan, to ask if I could come, he had said quite firmly that I was no longer a serving Master he would expect a full cap. The meet was at Arnesby and I arrived only just in time, having driven through thick fog all the way. The field numbered around seventy and were as off-hand and unfriendly as these large, shire packs occasionally are. In contrast, when I eventually managed to find out who the Master in charge was and introduced myself to Mr Millington, he was very welcoming. I explained that I wanted to see as much of hounds as possible, but as I only had an old horse who would be hunting the next day as well, I wanted to do as little galloping as possible. He suggested that I went with his son who was qualifying a Point-to-Pointer and would not be doing very much. As the first draw was on their own farm he would know exactly where to go. "You will recognise him easily," he said. "He's the one with too much yellow hair showing beneath his cap."

**Fernie Hunt.** *Meet at Mowsley, 3 February 1990. Huntsman Bruce Durns and hounds on the road below Gumley Coves.*

Photograph kindly loaned by F B Hill

Then I found the Secretary and explained that I was going to be a "mounted road follower" and he said a voluntary cap would be in order so I gave him £30. I think the full cap was £70, and this was intended to discourage visitors, as their fields were often too large. When hounds moved off, the Master's son went in the opposite direction to hounds and turned down a long farm road. He went to a good vantage point and we could see both hounds and the field for quite a time, but there did not seem to be much hunting visible to us and the field seemed to be mostly cantering from one draw to another. When hounds found they ran for about two or three fields and turned into what in the distance looked like a pit or quarry. The Field Master, deliberately I expect, took no notice of them and kept the field going over another fifteen to twenty hunt jumps until he had completed a circuit nearly back to the pit. I judged that the field would have been very pleased with "the run", and I sat on my vantage point thinking how easily pleased some "foxhunters" are.

I left at two-thirty and drove on up to the Staffordshire Moorland kennels, arriving at five o'clock. This was perhaps my most significant move as it would complete my original ambition to hunt with every pack of harriers. This pack was not started until 1980, long after I had been "up north" hunting with the harrier packs and somehow, for one reason or another, it had taken years for me to be able to get out with them. The kennel huntsman, Paul Goddard, and his lovely wife Judith (who whipped into him) had agreed to put up Max and myself and that one of their three grooms would do Max for me. One of these girls was the granddaughter of the famous Molly van der Kiste of otterhunting fame. When the pack was formed in 1980 I was one of the Masters who contributed a draft to start them off, and subsequently sent them another two drafts, and I was pleased to see that they still had a couple of my Easton Harriers, Landsman and Laudable. I spent a very happy evening with Paul and Judith and when all was ready for hunting next day we went down to the pub where we had a good dinner. Perhaps the main character among many in the pub was the landlord who had been on jury service all week and had had a few on the way home. He kept us all thoroughly amused with his account of the various trials.

When I came downstairs in the morning, everyone was outside in either the stables or the kennels, so I made myself some breakfast, looking around until I found instant coffee and the bread bin (Thurs 15 Nov 1990). After an even more extensive search I found the marmalade. I found it was a constant battle when staying in other people's homes to be able to make myself breakfast. Other people never put things where you logically expect things to be, and everyone does it differently. We left for the meet at Wooton at nine-thirty and arrived slightly before eleven o'clock. It was a very good meet and our host, Mr Percy Clews, a retired farmer, was very generous with his drinks and the food was delicious.

**Staffordshire Moorland Harriers** *Master, Huntsman and founder Eric Elliott moving off from his own lawn meet at Sutton House with KH Paul Goddard.*
Photograph kindly loaned by Marcia Elliott

It was after twelve o'clock when we moved off to draw across country. The **Staffordshire Moorland**, although they were harriers, now hunted foxes. We eventually came to a high spot called the Weaver's and I stayed on this vantage point for an hour or so, being able to watch them all the time. Unfortunately, it was to be a blank day and by mid-afternoon we all went back to the meet. In true harrier style, we made the best of a bad job and sat down to a lovely meat-and-potato pie, with cups of tea, suitably laced with whisky. There was a lovely atmosphere in the bungalow and we had a job to tear ourselves away, eventually arriving back at kennels at five-thirty.

**Oakley Foot.** *Meet at Wartnaby, Boxing Day 1997. Master and Huntsman David Manning, and whipper-in Andrew Sallis.*
Photograph kindly loaned by Mrs Manning

I could not possibly go away without going to Helmsley, and I was delighted that two more packs could be covered from there, so on Friday morning I left the kennels, having given all three girls a tip for doing Max for two nights, and drove over the Pennines to my "second home". Just before I got there I was overtaken by my friend, Tony St Quinton, who had come up to join me for a few days and brought Hazel with him. We were both staying with the Saggers at Park House, as usual, and renewed our acquaintance with the Six O'clock Club at the Royal Oak before dining at the Black Swan. There we met Bob Handley, a great character, who used to be the landlord of the Malt Shovel at Hovingham, and who also happened to be dining there.

Our first day's sport from Helmsley was not, however, any of the eight mounted packs still to go. I had been invited to attend the party to mark Betty Gingell's Fiftieth Season as Master of the Cambridgeshire Harriers that evening so we arranged to have another "double day" of harehunting on the way (Sat 17 Nov 1990). The **Oakley Foot** were meeting at nine-thirty in their country which they share with the Quorn, and Tony and I had bacon sandwiches and coffee before leaving Park House at seven o'clock. We travelled in Tony's car and drove rather too fast through heavy rain but nevertheless arrived slightly late. We were lucky to find them at once as they were already hunting their first hare. We then saw some first-class harehunting and, as we watched, they had two more circles on a difficult scent before a fresh hare intervened. They were soon put back on the line of the hunted hare. I was pleased to see how they cast themselves as a pack and they were a joy to watch.

The rain continued unabated and we were

very wet by twelve o'clock so we decided to go on for lunch at the Plough at Long Clawson where the **Pipewell Beagles** were meeting at one-thirty. Outside in the street, I thought I recognised an elderly gentleman with white whiskers but could hardly believe it could be who I thought it was. I next saw him in the bar and asked if he ever sang a song about a prairie flower. He burst out laughing and I knew I had the right man. He was one of the Pipewell members who had often gone to the Windermere in March, as had the Easton. We spent a happy hour reminiscing about the old days hunting with the Windermere Harriers at Elterwater in the Lake District. I recognised a few other faces at the meet from those days, but I managed inadvertently to eat some nuts at lunch and was quite upset as I have an allergy to them. Hounds were rather unlevel and quite excitable, rushing around all over the place, but I thought that if they had been worked harder they would have hunted very well, as their cry was exceptionally good. We enjoyed a couple of hours with them, often seeing the hunted hare and watching them work out the line, but at three o'clock we had to leave them to make our way to the Landbeach Manor Hotel where we were booked in for the night.

**Pipewell Foot.** *David Reynolds, at his last Meet as Master and huntsman. Left, John Woodward, right, Stephen Reynolds, David's cousin and successor in the Mastership.*
Photograph kindly loaned by David Reynolds

The party was held in a marquee at Horningsea Manor, the home of the Gingells. Tony and I shared a table with Tim Whitley of the Dartmoor Beagles and his beautiful girlfriend, whom I had the luck to sit next to, much to the envy of my friend. The whole evening was delightful with good speeches from Michael Clayton (editor of Horse and Hound) and Hunter Rowe (Point-to-Point commentator) who was extremely funny. It was a thoroughly good evening and it was an honour to be there on this memorable occasion. What a tremendous achievement, to be fifty years the Master of one pack.

**Cambridgeshire Harriers** *Party to celebrate Betty Gingell's 50th season as Master and Huntsman of Cambridgeshire Harriers. L to R, Tony St. Quinton, Tony Harvey, Denis Raker, Pinkie Winton-Smith.*

Next morning Tony and I left the hotel to drive up to Whitby where I had to collect a gift for my wife (Sun 18 Nov 1990). On the strength of the visit I had arranged to meet our old Suffolk friends Leonard and Helen Mison for lunch. We lunched on lobster and Dover sole, and although the food was first-class, the meal was perhaps best described as a laughing lunch full of happy reminiscences. The evening was spent in the Royal Oak with Bob Handley who had just dropped in to bring his wife to meet us. They had intended to stay only for a couple of drinks, but when we discovered that we had a mutual interest in gypsy caravans it was closing time before they left. There was no hunting on Monday so Tony took charge of me and conducted me on a cultural tour, taking me to see the Railway Museum and the Yorvik Centre in York, both excellent and very interesting (Mon 19 Nov 1990). After a snack lunch we set off to find the Farming Museum but when, after a lot of difficulty, we did find it, it was closed for the winter. On the way back we called to see our new friends, Bob and Enid Handley, who lived on the top of Oswaldkirk Bank. Bob immediately produced two enormous gin and tonics, and insisted on taking us both out to dinner. We agreed to meet at the Royal Oak so, after bathing and changing, and a couple of drinks in the Oak, we set off, with Bob driving. After quite a pub crawl, as most places were not doing food on a Monday night, we finally enjoyed a delicious dinner at the Blacksmith's Arms at Hartoft.

Next day I had the first of my two mounted days from Helmsley, going with the **Goathland Foxhounds** who met at a railway bridge near Goathland (Tues 20 Nov 1990). The morning was frosty but bright and sunny, and the scent was to be as poor as these conditions usually denote. One of the Joint Masters, Mr James, welcomed me heartily and said how his Joint Master, Derek Gardiner, who was also the huntsman, was looking forward to having me out with him. This was because I had met Derek in August of the previous year when I was a guest singer at the Whitby Folk Festival. In a crowded pub he had noticed that I was wearing a BFSS tie and had introduced himself. Derek was now hunting hounds as an amateur but had previously been a professional with the same hounds.

**Goathland (with the Pennine, Farndale and Glaisdale)** *Joint Meet at Goathland, February 1990. Left to right, Paul Whitehead (Huntsman of Pennine Foxhounds), Derek Gardiner (Joint Master and Huntsman of the Goathland), Joe Tindall (Master and Huntsman of the Glaisdale), Danny Bowers (whipper-in, Glaisdale), Mick Featherstone (Master and Huntsman of tbe Farndale), and Mike Allen (whipper-in, Glaisdale).*

Photograph kindly donated by Mr J R Jefferson

We drew for two hours on the moor then hounds spoke to drag and took this line very painstakingly across to some forestry, where I thought they might get on better terms with him but an unfortunate incident occurred just in front of me. The field had been filing along a sheep track in the high bracken, one behind the other, and a tail hound was making his way up to the rest of the pack along the same track, squeezing past the horses. The horse just in front of me, ridden by a young woman, kicked the hound in the head and knocked it out cold. This brought all proceedings to a halt. I held Derek's horse while he examined the hound. I was sure it was dead but eventually it recovered. This has always amazed me about hounds. They must have skulls like iron. I have seen them receive a tremendous whallop, being hit by cars, and suchlike, but then getting up and carrying on as if nothing had happened. This one stood up and swayed a little, then staggered on up the track and a few minutes later was running with the others across the moor to the next draw. This serious distraction had spoiled what little chance they had of settling to the line so Derek drew again and soon had one rattling round the forestry. This eventually dropped down through a deep valley, over a railway line, and up onto the moors beyond. This railway line was the boundary between the Goathland and Saltersgate Foxhounds, and a very apt boundary it was too as it was impossible to cross, the bank being far too steep. The railway was still steam-powered, but carried only tourists now.

There were only four others mounted in the field which included a young man who was a professional horse-breaker. I sat with him on a high vantage point of the bank overlooking the railway line, and we watched the hunt on the opposite moor for as long as possible. He explained to me that most of their members were out with the Glaisdale Foxhounds as they were in their best country, while the Goathland were in their worst. I enjoyed my day on the moor but could see that it was very wet and boggy. Max was frequently plunging in very boggy places and a large block of Forestry Commission trees butted up to the impossible steep valley, presenting quite a problem. Derek hunted hounds very quietly and I noticed how readily they came to him when he needed them, and how rock steady they were to sheep. They were mostly light types, rather like Fell hounds, with evidence of some Welsh blood as some were "broken-coated" (ie. slightly rough after crossing with the curly Welsh hounds). They went with a particularly melodious cry which was quite enchanting to hear.

I arrived back at Helmsley at three-forty-five, not having taken much out of old Max, as we had stood still for such a long time at the railway line. I had an early drink at the Royal Oak and heard the result of the Conservative Party Leadership election, Mrs Thatcher winning (against Heseltine) 204 votes to 176 – "which must be good news for hunting" as I wrote in my diary, as she had stated that she would not interfere in field sports. I was the only one of the Six O'Clock Club to go across the square to the Feathers, where the young lad behind the bar immediately remembered my love for the Sirloin steak with Stilton sauce. On the strength of this I ordered one and was back in Park House by eight-fifteen for an early night.

I was therefore bright and fresh for the second pack which was the Goathland's neighbours, the **Saltersgate Farmers' Foxhounds** (Wed 21 Nov 1990). They were meeting at ten forty-five at Low Staindale, near Dalby, and mine was the only box at the meet. There was not even a hunt box as hounds were hacked from kennels to every meet except two each season, and I think this must now make them very unusual, if not unique. Their members followed their example and everyone usually "hacked on". It was still sunny and very cold, but there was a fair scent, especially when out of direct sunlight. The field numbered about twelve, and included some wonderful characters. All were pleased to see me and the Chairman, Mr Brian Funnel, and the Master and huntsman, Mr Brian Brown, gave me a most genuine and hearty welcome. I had previously arranged to have a day with this pack in March 1988, but had been unable to go because the pack had been poisoned while out hunting. Due to this disaster, hounds were of mixed type but looked very hard and fit. The first thing that impressed me was that, with the exception of a few young hounds, they were rock steady to deer of which there seemed an abundance. As Mr Brown moved off along a track on his way to draw the Dalby Forest, there were six deer running parallel to us on a track high above us.

**Saltersgate Farmers'.** *Meet at the Kennels, February 1990. Master and Huntsman F Bryan Brown.*

Photograph kindly donated by Mr Brown

**The Saltersgate Farmers'.** *The Bridestones in Saltersgate country.*

Photograph by Richard Wells-Furby

Hounds soon found and rattled around this large woodland with great drive, but at one point it was necessary to pass under low branches for a long time. With my neck in a stiff collar I had to dismount and lead back into more open rides. This put me out of the game for over half an hour, but they ran back in my direction and I viewed the fox and capped the Master onto the line. Hounds ran very fast down a deep valley, across a moor to the Bridestones. I left after this fox was lost and hacked back towards the meet with the Chairman, arriving back at three-fifteen. I could easily be very happy hunting with the Saltersgate, as everyone out was interested in the hunting. Even the children were asking intelligent questions. There were some very steep descents, scary enough to get the adrenalin running. The Master managed on a very small guarantee and fed his hounds with a free supply of trout innards from a nearby trout farm. The subscriptions were £7.50 for a car follower and £75 for mounted followers, and visitors' caps were £7.50. They were highly delighted when I refused any change from my ten pound note. The Chairman, who told me all these details, was very proud of the fact that he had shown a slight surplus on every year's accounts. Privately, I thought that the greatest credit was due to the Master for managing so well on such a modest sum.

I had been in some pain all day as, on the way to the meet, one of my teeth had split. The first thing I did on my return was to ask Jackie Saggers (my long-suffering landlady) if there was a dentist in Helmsley. There was and, because Jackie asked him, he fitted me in with an appointment at nine o'clock the following morning. Bob and Enid Handley met me at the Royal Oak and, after a few gin-and-tonics they took me to their son's pub, the Malt Shovel at Hovingham, where I had an excellent dinner of deepfried Lymeswold cheese, and duck breasts (very tender and ideal for my sore tooth), accompanied by a Mouton Cadet.

Next day there was no hunting – or rather, no pack going that I had not already been with (Thurs 22

Nov 1990). With only one horse, I dare not risk taking any extra days by duplicating hunts. The dentist in Mongate Street did a very good job in removing the splinter, making me feel much more comfortable and I returned to Park House and settled down to write twelve thank-you letters for the past days' hunting. Next morning I left Helmsley at eight o'clock to drive to my next base which was, as inevitably as Helmsley had been, the Plumbes' at Roberton (Fri 23 Nov 1990). From there I hoped to cover another four packs, the Linlithgow and Stirlingshire, the Eglinton, the Grampian and also the Liddesdale. The Liddesdale belonged to the unforgettable George Laing and I had had a day with them in 1982 but it had been a blank day so I wanted to go again. I had tried the previous season but the meet I had planned to go to was called off because of gale-force winds, as had the meet of the Linlithgow and Stirlingshire.

We made excellent time, arriving at Easter House at one o'clock and, as it was very warm, Hazel suggested that we put old Max into the orchard for an hour to enjoy a roll and a little relaxation. I busied myself unpacking and doing my usual Roberton chore of log-carting. As there were three open fires in Easter House, a good supply at each took quite a time. Colin's parents were due to arrive at four-thirty and would be using the bedroom that I mostly used, so that left me with a smaller one, and Hazel was billetted in one of the attic rooms (the old servant's quarters), much to her amusement and delight as they were very attractive.

It was therefore my second attempt to hunt with the **Linlithgow and Stirlingshire Foxhounds** when I set off at seven o'clock for their meet at the kennels, at Three Miletown, next morning (Sat 24 Nov 1990). I arrived at ten o'clock, to find the kennels surrounded by "antis". They lay between the M8 and M9 motorways and within easy reach of five of the Scottish universities. The Masters, Messrs Brines and Taylor, were pleased to see me, as were all the members. We moved off across stubble to draw endless coverts blank as the antis had been through them all. The country was very pleasant and was nearly all stubble and grass. We next drew a canal bank which also proved to be blank, then moved on to a deep pit where there was excitement for a few seconds when somone holloaed, but this proved to be an Alsatian dog so hounds were not laid on. The Master had a lovely touch with the children, getting them involved by asking a little boy on a fat pony to "help" the huntsman draw some turnips, and a little girl to lead the field across a stubble. I shall never forget the grin on her face as she bombed off on her pony ahead of everyone. I went home feeling very sorry for this hunt, as they had lost most of their members to either the Fife or the Lauderdale, as they had become short of country and suffered so badly from pressure from the antis. I felt that the MFHA ought to consider granting them a subsidy to keep them going on the "one down, one less to go" principle. The Masters were well aware of the seriousness of this problem and were determined not to be beaten by the antis.

I then had a few days off as it was not until the following Wednesday that I was to have my next day's hunting. The Sunday was very wet and I spent the day reading newspapers to keep up with all the news about the fight for the leadership of the Conservative Party, chatting with Colin's parents, and generally having a lazy day. Monday was spent putting up a long stretch of sheep netting for Tizza and in the afternoon I went into Hawick to buy a Coke tin which danced to music for my daughter Charlotte. She was then working in a hotel and I knew this would appeal to her sense of humour, and thought that she could put it on the shelf with the others, for a laugh in the bar.

I left Roberton at six-thirty on Wednesday for the long drive across to the **Eglinton** meet at Crosshands, near Kilmarnock, and arrived just as they were all unboxing (Wed 28 Nov 1990). All three Masters welcomed me most warmly and introduced me to Mr Tulloch, the Secretary, with instructions that I was to pay no cap. I insisted on paying something so we agreed on a half-cap of £15.

Hounds found at once and ran along a ridge but they could do little and scent seemed very poor. Max refused to jump a hunt jump which was overgrown and required bursting through, rather like a bullfinch. There was a farmer who had also been a Master at some time, whose horse also refused and was left with me. As he knew the country well, we were soon up with hounds again, finding that they had lost the line. They found another fox and went at a fair pace over delightful country, with old Max going like a dream, taking everything in his stride. I have heard people describe hunting country as "God's own country" when it was no better than this, and yet the field assured me that this was their worst meet. At one time, on high ground, I stood and could see nothing but grass for as far as the eye could see, four or five miles in every direction, with mostly jumpable fences. One of the Masters, the Honourable Robert Corbett, was a great character and after the introductions he made known to me some very forthright opinions about mutual acquaintances from Suffolk. Mr Corbett was obviously a much-loved Master of long-standing, and reference to Baily's showed me that he had been Master since 1975. The whole field were the greatest fun, constantly pulling each other's legs, and there was great camaraderie amongst them, just the opposite of what I had expected. I had an uninformed opinion that they would be stuffy and standoffish but nothing could have been further from the truth.

I thoroughly enjoyed a large circular hunt with scent just good enough for hounds to run, but not so good that they did not have to work for it, and we were able to be with them all the time. They ran this fox to ground in a difficult place where it was left. The next draw produced several foxes, and hounds split in several directions. As we were quite near the boxes and I had a long drive ahead of me, I said my goodnights and left them at two-thirty. I had gone to this hunt expecting to be outclassed in riding across country and quite expected to be left fairly often. Although I had enjoyed myself riding across country for its own sake, I felt sure that neither Max nor I would be able to keep with them in their best country, as they were obviously great goers. I left them, and the long journey home was neither tiring nor boring, as the adrenalin continued to pump in my veins until I reached Selkirk. I finally arrived back at six-thirty.

When I arrived at the **Liddesdale** meet next morning, the first words that George Laing, the Master, said to me were "Oh God, have you brought a horse?"

It was to be a foot day, with George, who must have been in his seventies, hunting hounds on foot while his son whipped in on a motorbike (Thurs 29 Nov 1990). There were only two other men in a car to make up the field. I followed on Max around the rides and was always fairly close to hounds as most of the rides were clear. They found almost at once and ran hard, checking only once on a well-used track, and killed their fox in under an hour, hunting through dense undergrowth where all the lower branches of the trees had been cut off and left on the ground. This had caused the sterns of every hound to bleed at the tip. After this most impressive hunt I put Max away, as I could ride with Jenny in her pick-up. She had been nanny in the Laing family and had transferred to looking after the hounds when the children, who had been educated at home by their mother, grew up.

*L to R Tony Harvey, Maurice Scott, Mike Davies dispensing hospitality from his railway carriage on a calmer day than that on page 90.*
Photograph taken by Tony Butler

The Master leant on the pick-up and quietly smoked his pipe for a half-hour or so until he was rested, and then drew again. Hounds were speaking again in a very few minutes but on a much poorer scent, and I think they were dragging up to him because after twenty minutes or so they began to run hard. Jenny stopped to pick up the Master so I got in the back of the pick-up which had a cage with some terriers and a couple of lost hounds in it. Hounds pushed their fox out of the forestry and Jenny drove frantically along the winding road, with me clinging on to the back of the cab, my fingers getting ever more numb hanging on to the thin edge. It was lovely to watch them flying along the skyline until they finally killed near Hermitage Castle. George had recently "gone modern" and had radios, but was getting very angry as his son was not answering his. He began to get very worked up, saying "What's the use of me buying radios if he won't answer the thing?"

It seemed so funny as he made no allowance for the fact that his son was riding fast across the rough moor at the time, bouncing high in the air as he hit every rut and hole, and needed both hands on the handlebars.

I rate this day as high as any I have seen for pure venerie. There is not a huntsman the length or breadth of the country who would not have been very impressed with these hounds. Firstly, they had killed two foxes in under two and a half hours with only nine and a half couple (which included some unentered). Secondly, they ran completely unaided, hunting through terrible undergrowth, with fresh foxes all over the place and deer everywhere. I have yet to find another pack of hounds which will hunt among deer and fresh foxes and be one hundred per cent sure not to change lines. Up here in the hills of the Border country was what must be perfection amongst hounds, yet it went unheralded, unnoticed and unreported by the sporting press. I thought some very famous huntsmen could learn from the Laing family who must have bred their hounds largely for this virtue of not changing foxes which the French call *"de change"*. This virtue definitely runs in blood lines. There was a famous hound called Tempest in the Windermere Harriers who would never hunt a fox as she had lived with a fox-cub. The Liddesdale did not always hunt in the forestry and more often hunted the huge rolling open hills around their farm. George told an amusing story about hunting in the hills. Hounds had run fast and straight for a while and the horses were really left behind. When George breasted a hill he

**The Liddesdale:** ***"Prompt action saves the day"***

could see hounds driving on towards a dual-carriageway main road, but unbeknown to him, one of his supporters was driving an articulated lorry down the road. The driver could see what was going to happen and, in a slight break in the traffic, swung his lorry across the road so it blocked both carriageways until hounds were safely over.

I was back at Easter House at three-thirty so had plenty of time to prepare for the last of my four Scottish packs. This was the **Grampian Foxhounds** who were kennelled at the Master's farm, Upper Craighill, Arbuthnott, near Aberdeen. When making arrangements on the telephone to hunt with this, Europe's most northerly pack, John and Wendy Agnew, who own the hounds, realised how far I had to travel from Hawick and said that they would have liked to put me up but had no spare stable. When I said that it would do Max no harm to stop on the lorry for one night, especially if the lorry could be in a sheltered place, they immediately said that there was a barn the lorry could be parked in and pressed me to stay the night before hunting. This I was very pleased to be able to do so, having done my valetting and packing the previous afternoon, and having dined at the Old Forge (which was as good as ever), I left Roberton at seven o'clock in the morning of St Andrew's Day (Fri 30 Nov 1990). It was nine hours non-stop driving, seven o'clock until four o'clock, except for a stop to fill up with diesel, so when the Agnews then offered to put me up for the Saturday night as well, I readily accepted. The original plan had been to drive home immediately after hunting on the Saturday evening.

The farm stood high up on a hill and was completely isolated, entirely given over to keeping hounds and horses. The hounds were kept in what was a cattle yard, so were completely under cover, while the lodges were at the back. There was the strong smell that always goes with completely covered-in kennels. The Agnews made me feel very much at home and just the three of us sat down to a lovely dinner of roast beef followed by cheese and biscuits. John and I had quite a few drams, and talked nothing but hounds and hunting all evening, finally going to bed at eleven-thirty. Wendy ran John's insurance office in Inverbervie and that left John at home to do telephone business in the farmhouse kitchen for, as he said, his clients did not know if he was stinking of hounds and flesh or in a pinstriped suit. The Agnews ran the Grampian Foxhounds single-handed.

I want to make it clear that I found experience of visiting the Grampian great fun. In the 1990s when there is a tendency for most people to be boring and predictable it was a breath of fresh air to find someone who is able to afford to be completely eccentric and just do as he likes, and hunt when he likes, as Masters did in the days Surtees.

As I wrote in my diary on the Sunday, "the last forty-eight hours have been a unique experience to me, in all my hunting travels", and there is no better way of describing the experience than to quote large chunks from my diary which was written while it was all fresh in my mind.

*"Next morning, John was so uptight about me being there, on account of my having hunted hounds for so long,*

*that he openly said he could not eat his breakfast and was almost wishing for a thick fog so that he did not have to turn out. He had spent two hours on valeting his clothes, even starching his stock a second time, and repolished his boots after I had gone to bed. We had more intense hound-talk over breakfast and details of exactly how he would draw and why. He loaded up the hounds with difficulty as some got past the ramp and while they were running around the hounds left back were squeezing under a gate and no-one had noticed. John was in a great flap but all was soon put right, and at the meet all was calm."*

During the journey to the meet Wendy Agnew had ridden in the back of the lorry with the hounds to prevent any fighting which may break out. The meet was at East Bogheadley Farm, Rickarton, and our hosts were Mr and Mrs Mitchell who provided a tray of port. This surprised me as, since we were in Scotland, I naturally thought we would be served whisky.

*"Although I did not find this out until the evening the farmer's wife had told her son, who had flaming red hair, that he was to behave himself as "the man from England was here", and also that she had broken the habit of a lifetime and had produced a tray of ports as this special occasion of my visit was so important. Then she had been too shy to bring one to me so Wendy (Mrs Agnew) had to bring the tray."*

The only field were the local laird in his Range Rover, twin girls and their sister on their ponies who were our host's daughters, and Sarah on an Exmoor pony. To complete the field, Mrs Margot Esher-Kennedy was out, easily recognised by her green cap from when she was Master of the Gelligaer Farmers'. I had met her in South Wales and she reminded me that I had seen her since then when I was out with the Fife. The hounds were ranging all over the place at the meet and the amateur whip, who had come up from the Ystrad country, was mounted on a very lame horse belonging to the Master. Margot asked how I came to be there and I replied that I had asked if I could come. "Oh, you're very honoured," she said, "because he only usually hunts on Opening Meet and Boxing Day." She has a good sense of humour so I took this with a pinch of salt but was later assured that this was more or less correct.

We moved off with one hound more than we thought we had, making thirteen couple in all.

*"Off we went to draw with the laird in front in his Range Rover, opening the gates, with our small field following. The scene was unbelievable. We drew along a hillside with mature trees along the river bank in the bottom. Beyond the river was a belt of young trees about four feet high and beyond that a stubble field then mature trees again. While we sat there on the hillside with about eight couple around John, a couple here, two couple there, and another couple somewhere else, were all fighting and snarling over dead rabbits. Below us in the little trees were the beaters for a shoot and four couple of hounds who were actually drawing. These went through the beaters, then drew the stubble between the beaters and the guns. The scene was like something even Surtees could not have dreamt up.*

*We drew along further or, to be more correct, we moved along further, then a most remarkable rabbit hunt started, with about four couple pursuing several different rabbits (some of which had mixy) in and out of the gorse. John just sat and watched, neither shouting at them nor taking any notice at all. A tan doghound caught a rabbit and held it in his paws while having his stomach on the ground and his quarters up in the air. He did not know how to kill it, so let it go, and caught it again in the same manner, and let it go again. Then several more joined in this particular hunt and despatched the rabbit.*

*Meanwhile, in the bottom, the four couple had found and were speaking through the middle of the beaters and the fox was shot. No comment or action at all came from the Master. It took a half-hour or so to get these hounds back, during which time the new whipper-in was riding about on a lame cob the Master had provided for him. He came up to the Master and said, "I think my horse is lame," only to be told, "Of course it's not lame. He's only testing you out. Just trying it on, that's all."*

*He was hopping lame, both front and behind. I only wish my pen could do more justice to the remarkable scene.*

*John decided to draw elsewhere and we hacked along a road to draw another covert blank, crossed the road and drew a covert which was full of pheasants and there was more rabbit hunting. This produced a great cry in the covert, and almost all hounds were in.*

*I saw two hounds run a rabbit into a stick heap, then all the hounds arrived, and finally the whipper-in on his lame horse. He asked me to hold it while he climbed over the wire and inspected the stick heap. John arrives and Margot holds his horse.*

*The whipper-in says, "It's to ground, sir."*

*John gets to the stick heap and yells, with the first enthusiasm of the day, "Yoi, wind him in there!" and so forth. In the midst of all this, the boy with the red hair came up on foot and said that hounds had been nearly up to a fox with three legs and would I tell John. Margot and I caught each other's eye and had the greatest difficulty in not roaring with laughter.*

*John arrives back at his horse and tells me how good they are at marking. My efforts to keep serious were not helped by Margot in the background. He goes to draw another covert and, surprise, surprise, all hounds bar one couple go in to draw. More great cry. I thought it must be*

**The Grampian:** ***"I've caught it... Now what do I do?"***

*deer and stood opposite a clearing, and saw them cross and recross twice. There was no deer and they were running too fast to be a rabbit.*

*Could it be a fox? Yes, they were away and we had a little ride of about a mile to get round the covert. As John and I galloped along he was breathlessly telling me how they can slip out of the back of this particular covert and be away over the hill and moor and be gone out of sight and sound.*

*When we arrived at the other side of the covert and stopped to listen, he said, "See what I mean? They have run from view and out of sound. I must put some hunt jumps in so we can get round here quicker." He was quite wound up and excited then, one by one, the hounds all trailed out of the covert behind us.*

*One of the Buccleuch hounds took the line on for a few fields into another small covert, speaking well in there, but John just sat with all the other hounds and made no effort to put them on to the hound which was speaking. He suddenly pointed across to a hill in the distance and said, "I think the fox will have gone over there." There was no reason at all that I could think of for this remark. The one hound brought the line out of the covert and was hunting towards another and yet he made no effort to put the others on. He was just deciding to cast his hounds over the hill in the distance when I suggested to him, "Why not try them where the hound is speaking?"*

*"What a good idea," he said, and slipped off his horse and took them back into the wood which the single hound had just vacated, but it came to nothing. He then decided to go home, having lost a couple of hounds and his whipper-in. As we were hacking back, another hound came up so we were only one hound light, as I had two good counts coming off the hill and was sure of the number. When John jumped off, he had a severe cramp and we had to load up hounds for him. Eventually I was able to put Max in the lorry.*

*As we drove away home, we picked up the last lost hound and John kept saying how pleased he was that she was doing the right thing by coming back to the meet. We arrived home and let out hounds, and I did Max and went indoors. Hours later John appeared and said he was a hound light in kennel. I said that I was sure of my count coming off the hill so it must be somewhere on the farm.*

*He telephoned the Marshalls in some embarassment to tell them that he had picked up the one he was short of but that he had miscounted and there was another one short. There was such excitement and flapping as I can't describe.*

*Would it have been one of the hounds that had got out of the kennel? I asked.*

*I had not thought of that, he said, and he went and checked his lists. No, all hounds that had not been hunting were there. Still even more concern.*

*We had supper and I heard a commotion in kennels and wondered if the hound was running around. As John made no remark I presumed it was usual for them to be noisy in kennel. Later when I went out to check Max's rugs, I saw the hound in my torchlight and it was one we had been out with.*

*During supper every detail of the day was gone over with – which hound had excelled himself where, and when, in such detail. Wendy also said that she had seen such-and-such a hound doing good work, and John, not agreeing, saying that so-and-so hit it off, and was a trustworthy hound. At nine o'clock I said I was tired and went to bed.*

*When you consider that Margot told me this was the first day out this year and that they only go out four or five times a year, it was truly amazing. It does seem extraordinary to feed and look after twenty and a half couple for 365 days a year to go out only a few times?"*

I woke up at two o'clock. As I was wide awake I decided to creep out of the house without disturbing the Agnews and drove off at two-thirty. On the way back I made a silly mistake and missed the Coupar Angus turn, landing up in Dundee, which probably put twenty miles or so onto my journey. When I got to Edinburgh I decided to be brave, as it was so early and a Sunday morning, and drove through the centre, through the famous Princes Street, arriving on the other side at the correct place, thus saving a few of the extra miles. At Galashiels I became very sleepy and was forced to stop twice in the last thirty miles before I got to Hawick. I went to bed for a while and then did my valetting and prepared to move the following day. I had a light lunch of soup and cheese as Colin and Tizza had gone to a luncheon party. I had been included in the invitation but dared not accept as I had not expected to be home on time. I telephoned the Agnews to explain how wide awake I had been and I hoped they were not offended by my early departure and thanked them for their hospitality. During the afternoon, in the tranquillity of Easter House, I ran through the events of the last forty-eight hours and put them down just as they came to me. It had been an extraordinary experience, but much of it could be explained by the fact that they had been formed only in 1976 and then as a drag pack, and had only just turned to hunting fox. However, as I said earlier it was a great experience to meet an M.F.H. who is truly his own Master, accepts no subscription, and never has to consider what his committee might think or do.

The Grampian was the last of the seven "northern" packs and there were only three to go, the Tanatside in Wales, and the Dulverton East and Mr Roffe-Sylvester's in Devon. I left Roberton and my generous and long-suffering friends at nine o'clock on Monday morning to drive to my next host, Mr & Mrs Humphrey Broad-Davies, who had invited me to stay at their lovely home, Netherwood House, at Rowton near Chester (Mon 3 Dec 1990). Humphrey and Anne's daughter, Louie, had been my daughter, Judith's, best friend since they had been through the Cordon Bleu course together. The Broad-Davies had been to stay with us at Tannington Hall where my treatment of them was not conducive to being asked to stay with them. I had taken them on a carriage-drive but had managed to turn over the carriage, the only time this has ever happened to me. I had made one extremely elementary mistake, one my father would have clipped my ear for when I was six years old. Both Humphrey and Anne were tipped out into the middle of the road, cutting both of them and ruining Humphrey's suit and Anne's dress. However, they were both very forgiving and, when they heard me say that I needed a base from which to hunt with the Tanatside, they kindly suggested that I stayed with them. This was particularly generous as they were not only non-hunting people, but non-horsey as well. By coincidence, however, they lived next door to the Duke of Westminster's old stables and they were able to arrange for Max to be stabled there. We had some memorable meals while I stayed there, as Humphrey is a noted wine merchant, and the excellent dinners were always accompanied by fine wines.

I had first tried to hunt with the **Tanatside** while staying in central Wales two years earlier (while the Easton had been there) but the meet had been fogged off. This time it seemed that I might not even reach the meet as I became lost but was put right just in time by a lady whose car I flagged down. It was an exceptionally pretty meet at Rhydygroesau, near Oswestry, in this Welsh border country (Tues 4 Dec 1990). The field consisted of six ladies and myself and the Master and Huntsman, Major Bonnor-Maurice, was very welcoming, and the hotel brought out a stirrup cup. Hounds moved off up into the hills to draw bracken, rushes and fir woods on the steep hillsides. They drew for two hours before finding and then there were too many foxes, at least five, or maybe six, in one covert. The members told me that it had not been cubhunted, so probably the whole family was still at home. Hounds settled to one fox and rattled him around the hills for forty minutes without a check. The cry was heavenly and most wonderful to hear. The hounds were all Welsh-cross which surprised me as I had thought that there would probably have been some pure Welsh considering their location. This was lovely country to ride over, with good firm turf on steep hills and at times the views were quite breathtaking and we could see for many miles. Most of the time we were jumping sheep-wire with a stick or an old stake tied along the top strand. Max did not like this at all and often stopped, but I always managed to get him over in the end. I said my goodnights to the Master at three o'clock as Max was feeling as though he had had enough, and arrived back at Rowton at five-thirty, having spent a most enjoyable day in good company.

Wednesday was another rest day so I went to the stables to see Max and had a coffee and a chat with the owner, Chris Lunt, who was wheelchair-bound and

**The Tanatside:** ***"Who needs expensive hunt jumps!"***

whose family had been master-saddlers for generations (Wed 5 Dec 1990). This was an extremely interesting conversation for me, as his father had been President of the Master Saddlers' Association and had been the owner of R Lunt & Son of Liverpool (est. 1830). This firm specialised in making driving harness, for all classes of horses, and their work was easily recognised by the shell design on the blinkers. The firm employed 87 harness-makers and a stove in the centre was kept going partly by the old scrap pieces of leather. To make a harness collar was a trade of its own and harness-makers would order the collar from another source. To put this firm in perspective, it employed fifteen collar-makers full time, and now there are only around five in the whole country.

John and Anne kindly extended their hospitality to include Tony ("Mole") St Quinton for the night, and he arrived just in time for an aperitif, before we settled down to yet another lovely dinner, with the lovely wines which were such an integral part of my stay here. It had been planned that Mole and I would go down to Somerset to stay with the Roffe-Silvesters at Reaphay, West Buckland, for the last two packs. They had agreed to stable Max but I thought it was unnecessary to take Hazel, and this meant that she had to be sent home. This was more difficult than I first thought because, to say the least, she was not an experienced traveller and she did not want to take a train to London and then another to Ipswich. The closest station from which she could get direct train to Ipswich was Loughborough so, when I left Netherwood House after breakfast with Max, Tony set off to Loughborough with Hazel (Thurs 6 Dec 1990).

He must have made very good time as he arrived at Reaphay only minutes after I had done with the lorry. In the yard was an old acquaintance, Norman Bartlett, who kennelled his otterhounds, the Culmstock (now called minkhounds, of course), at Reaphay. Norman was a great character and well-known to hundreds of people owing to having been Master of these hounds since 1957. Norman was talking to David Allibone, also an unbelievable character, who was kennel-huntsman to the Roffe-Silvesters. He had four packs of hounds to look after but never gave the impression of being hurried, as if he had less to do than the huntsman of one pack. After one bad spell of weather, there was an enormous number of carcases piled up down the drive, between six hundred and fifty and seven hundred of them, but he merely set to and skinned the lot of them as if it was a normal day's work. After settling in Max, Mole and I were shown round all four packs – the Culmstock Minkhounds, the Taunton Vale Harriers, the Beacon Beagles and their private pack, Mr Roffe-Silvester's Foxhounds. When Mole and I took our cases up to our rooms the happy memories of earlier visits came flooding back. What grand fun I had had in this house, with this incredible family. This was the first time Mole had met them and even he, a well-travelled man with a variety of friends and acquaintances from all spheres, could hardly believe them. John Roffe-Silvester now had Reaphay (a large farmhouse) to himself as his parents, Michael and

Brigid, had moved into a separate wing of the house which was now known as Reaphay Bottom. Mole and I had a room each in John's house but on this first evening we went next door to enjoy a fabulous dinner-party. In this hilariously funny company, a bread-and-cheese dinner would have been the greatest fun, but with a whole fillet cooked to perfection, and served with a wonderful sauce, preceded by enormous gin-and-tonics, it was one of the best dinner-parties I can remember. The talk, of course, was all of hunting and hounds and it was midnight before we went to bed.

Next morning Tony and I set off in the car to see the Taunton Vale Foxhounds meet at Clayhanger Cross, and followed them by car for an hour or so, then went to another old haunt of mine, the Yarcombe Inn, where I quickly sank three half-pints of bitter, as I was feeling rather hungover and dehydrated (Fri 7 Dec 1990). We then drove into Chard for lunch and bought some booze to take back to our hosts, including a bottle of Bailey's Irish Cream for Brigid as it was her birthday. After lunch we visited Henry Bowes' carriage workshop where I bought some modern driving whips. In the evening, John, Mole and I went to the Globe at Apperley, where we had a bar supper amongst real genuine country folk, and the whole pub with its local characters reminded me so much of the Hare and Hounds in Framlingham in the old days when Jimmy Finbow was landlord. Horror of horrors! On the way home it started to snow with the large flakes which made it look as though it really meant business. Was I so near to completing my ambition only to be "snowed-off"?

**Tanatside.** *Meet at Wynnstay Inn, Llansilin, c. 1990-91 (adjacent village to Rhydycroesau). Master Mr Charles Stirling and Huntsman Fred Hart.*

Photograph kindly donated by A R Vaughan-Evans

When I awoke in the morning I went straight to the window and was appalled to see that the ground was well-covered with snow (Sat 8 Dec 1990). My heart sank, and when I went out to feed Max the ground was hard with frost. When I met John busily doing his own horses, he said that he would have to cancel the meet, but over coffee, he and I decided to go up to Buckland Wood to see how bad it was. Without asking in so many words, John seemed to know that I was desperate to go out, and said that just he and I would go out with the hounds. We stopped up two main earths and returned to breakfast, then got out our horses and David Allibone let out the hounds, and just John and I rode off with the **Roffe-Silvester Foxhounds**. I was to be treated to the ultimate exclusivity in hunting, a private day with a private pack, although Mole was following in a Land Rover.

The roads were terribly slippery and it was really madness to be out at all. Neither of us cared and we eventually reached the draw safely. As soon as hounds were lieued in, a roe deer popped up right in front of them, and hounds could not resist the overwhelming temptation. All the hounds soon came back, however, except for one couple which kept on hunting the deer. John drew on and found a fox. They started to hunt it but scent was very poor and they had to work hard for it in these very poor conditions. They needed to be able to concentrate but were constantly distracted by the sound of the other couple chivvying the deer around which, amazingly, kept circling in our vicinity. Buckland Wood would not have been easy to hunt in even in good conditions, as the rides were overgrown, but the weight of the snow had brought the boughs much lower

**Mr Roffe-Silvester's Foxhounds.** *The late John Roffe-Silvester with his foxhounds at Reaphay. Tony Harvey on Max in the foreground. 6 Dec 1990.*

Photo kindly loaned by Tony St Quinton

than they normally would have been. The rides were very often steep and narrow and, of course, slippery with the snow but I think the worst of all the problems was the high wind which made hearing the hounds so difficult. To hunt woodland well, in my opinion, it is essential to be able to hear clearly so as to know which of your hounds is speaking and thus be able to cheer them on in confidence. In this wind we did not hear some of the hounds settle well to this fox and only found out later that they had hunted on their own as far as the Wellington memorial, where the fox turned back towards Buckland Wood. Just before they got back to us, these hounds ran across the road in full cry with no one with them, and collided with two cars causing both to crash as, of course, with the snow on the road, they were unable to brake effectively. One hound was killed outright and another injured slightly, and of the state of the cars we were not told. David Allibone, who was following in the car, brought us the news. So ended sadly, my private day with a private pack, and we hacked home in the bitter winds with our gloves soaked from the melting snow dripping off the trees and hands frozen stiff.

The evening was to be very jolly indeed as it was Brigid's birthday and this extremely gay and lighthearted lady was in an even jollier mood. Nine of us went to dinner at the Rock Inn at Waterrow, where I had been before in 1981. This was the first time I had met John's girlfriend, Kirstie, who was loveliness itself and everyone had a truly wonderful night. Brigid wanted to hear some hunting songs and Dove Granfield, who was Secretary to the Roffe-Silvester Foxhounds, sang the Porlock Bay staghunting song and I sang "Bachelor, King of the Kennel". As always in these circumstances, the whole evening ended far too quickly and we were on our way home on the snow-covered roads.

I woke up still feeling full of delight from the night before and went out to feed Max (Sun 9 Dec 1990). John had a horse already saddled and was about to go out on hound exercise with all his foxhounds. The sight was one I shall never forget, as I watched him ride up the drive in the first light, his lemon-and-white hounds all around him, the moon and the stars still shining above him, and the whole scene enhanced by the snow-covered fields all around. Later on, it was suggested that a move to the Merry Harrier would be in order, where we could have a light lunch, and John called to see a farmer, Mr Ward, on the way. Sheila would have said that this was a very Master-like habit, that every journey has to be combined with visiting a farmer, as I was prone to do it myself. Mr Ward insisted that with all this snow on the ground we would certainly have to have a large whisky each before going on to the Merry Harrier. When we returned to Reaphay I helped John to feed his cattle and did Max, then went round next door to Brigid and Michael and had a scrambled egg supper with them, and this remarkable lady even managed to make this simple supper something special.

It was still very cold with high winds, and the snow still deep on the ground as I set off on Monday for the milestone occasion, the meet of my last mounted pack, the **Dulverton East Foxhounds** (Mon 10 Dec 1990). I was convinced that I had hunted with this pack years before, during the 1970s, but I had not shaded in the hunt country on my map and, after thoroughly searching through my diaries, could find no entry. In these circumstances I decided that I would have to have another day with them. The meet was at the Exbridge Fisheries, but I had been advised to unbox at Perry Farm. Despite leaving Reaphay at nine-thirty I arrived only just in time and then hacked down to the meet with the owner of Perry Farm. He took a short cut which necessitated fording the Rivers Exe and Bar at the point where they met. This was successfully accomplished, although Max did look long and hard at this expanse of swirling currents before he would follow my guide's horse over. And to follow over is literally what had to be done, as it was necessary to avoid the deep pools, but with a good local pilot to lead me, this was done. The meet was chiefly memorable for the fact that it was held at a fish farm and also for the enormous whisky that I was handed. My diary is scant on this point but from memory I think it was Mr Billingsley, Joint-Master and also Joint Secretary, who welcomed me. Carol Rous came up and introduced herself and told me that she was a relation of Robert Rous, my neighbour and now Master of the Waveney Harriers.

Hounds found in the first draw, and a huge dog fox came out on our side of the covert, and I thought that we were "in the guinea seats", but there was a brace of foxes, and hounds went away with the other fox in the opposite direction. They hunted this fox for about an hour in these terrible conditions with the high winds and drifting snow, and riding on these steep hills was treacherous, with horses constantly slipping in the most alarming fashion. Quite a few slipped right over onto their sides, and Carol Rous had a particularly bad fall and had to retire. This fox was lost but we soon found another and had a good run on a better scent. After quite a long hunt, which necessitated crossing the river three times, this fox was killed in the open, just across the river from us. During my travels, I have seldom seen hounds run into their fox in the open and it was extraordinary that this should be so on my last day. Max was getting tired as at his age he felt the hills difficult to cope with, and on top of that I was really cold so I thought that this spectacular kill was perhaps the right moment to go home for the last time.

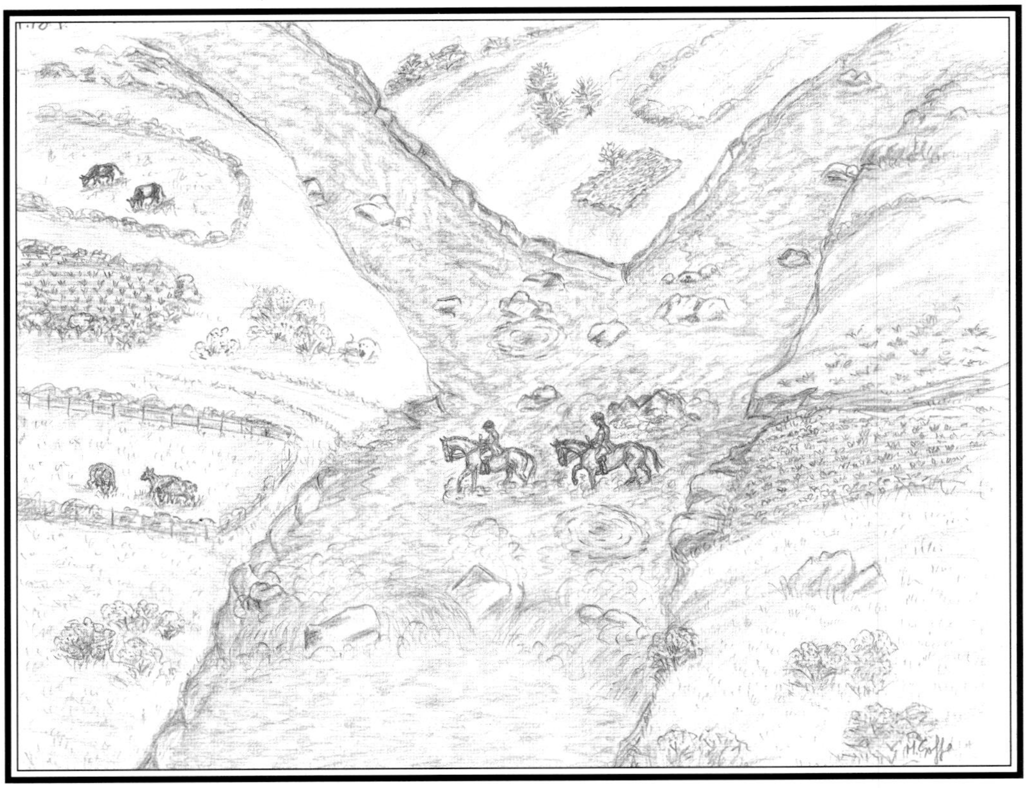

**The Dulverton East:** ***"In his master's steps he trod"***

In the evening, after the bathing and changing, I went across the yard to Reaphay Bottom and had some very stiff gin-and-tonics before taking Brigid and Michael, and John and Kirstie, out to dinner at the Castle Hotel at Taunton. The Roffe-Silvesters had protested very strongly at my suggestion of this venue as it was an expensive place, but I insisted as I had many happy memories of it from a previous occasion, and felt that it was the right setting for this milestone in my life. The Castle Hotel was very grand and the atmosphere in the dining room was hard to describe. At a suitable moment during this splendid dinner, I told them that I had fulfilled my ambition and had hunted with every mounted pack in Great Britain. I could not have been in better company and the general concensus of opinion was that we ought to go home where we could celebrate in safety. The malt whisky flowed until the early hours, and I only wish that I could relate all the wonderful stories that I heard that night. It was after two o'clock when I crossed the yard to go to bed. It was a very happy and contented man who drifted off to sleep on this momentous night.

I sadly left Reaphay at nine-thirty on Tuesday morning, with old Max in the lorry, feeling extremely flat (Tues 11 Dec 1990). I joined the motorway at Taunton, and drove to the Leigh Delamere service station where I stopped for breakfast and diesel. I then drove non-stop, finally arriving home at five o'clock and walked indoors after eight hours continual driving, excluding the breakfast break. The long journey was spent thinking that I had just completed what it had taken me twenty-two years to do since the spring of 1969, when I set myself the first modest challenge, to hunt with every foxhound pack in Essex. I had never really believed that it was possible to do, and it was still difficult to believe that I had now hunted with every mounted pack in Great Britain (excluding the drag packs).

# CHAPTER 21

## BASSETS AND FOOT PACKS

I had hunted with all the mounted foxhound, harrier and staghound packs and for a while this seemed to be sufficient. However, having caught up with the backlog of work caused by being away for nearly a month, and having rested on my laurels over Christmas, I started to think of other records which could be achieved without a horse. There were still quite a few packs of foxhounds which were hunted on foot and which would have to be seen before I could claim to have hunted with every single foxhound pack, and there were also not too many packs of bassets that I had not been with so another record, to have hunted with all of them, was to be had there.

It was with this in mind, knowing full well that they would jump at the chance, that I asked my friends Tony and Anne St Quinton, "the Moles", if they fancied a day with the **Huckworthy Bassets**. The Moles were great basset fans and I knew that they would come with me on this jolly. We set off at five o'clock on the Friday night and drove to Andover to stay with Paul and Avril Palmer. Paul was an Army friend of Major Mole. Several hours, and several drinks later, everyone had caught up with each other's news and it was time for bed. After a sumptuous breakfast all five of us set off on the Saturday morning for the meet, calling at the Milton Lodge, near Mere, to show the Moles where I had once stayed, and then driving on to the Trooper pub, at Stourton Caundle where the Master, Mrs Parlby, had agreed to meet us (Sat 2 Feb 1991). We followed her up a side lane to where the actual meet was, and we duly met her friendly field. I liked the hounds which proved to be very biddable. The hunting was not very good as there were deer everywhere and they were constantly crossing and re-crossing the draw, with the end result that the bassets could not concentrate on a single hare-hunt at all. The young man hunting hounds seemed to me to be very inexperienced, which did not help in the circumstances. However, all three of us, plus Paul and Avril, thoroughly enjoyed our day, and over tea at Henstridge we said that we would have to come down and see them hunt again in less trying circumstances.

**Huckworthy.** *Boxing Day Meet at Kings Colms, Charlton Horethorne, 1990. Huntsman Mark Hicks.*

Photograph kindly donated by Mr A R Parlby

It was not until the beginning of the next season, however, that I really set about this last target, but this one, the season of 1991-92, was to see the last of my hunting tours. As no horses were necessary it was a great deal easier to arrange to go and, rather than go away on one great long jolly, I had several short ones. The season was, in many ways, one of the best. During the summer I had discovered, to my surprise, that I had another mounted pack to go. I met the photographer Jim Meads, who had taken a keen interest in my travels all along, at Peterborough Hound Show, and he told me that the Gogerddan, which had been disbanded in 1989, had been reformed. As well as the Gogerddan, there were eight dismounted foxhound packs, ranging from the Lochaber and Sunart in Scotland, through the North Pennine in county Durham and the Eskdale and Ennerdale and the Hodder Valley in Lancashire, to the Eryri, Aber, Snowdon Valley and Nantcol Valley in Wales, as well as the David Davies with whom I wanted to have another day as I had not been satisfied with the day I had had with them in 1987. After the Huckworthy there were just three basset packs left, the Leadon Vale kennelled in Worcestershire, the South Wales kennelled near Cardiff and the Fourshires who hunted by invitation in Worcestershire, Warwickshire, Gloucestershire and Oxfordshire.

The 1991-92 season started in November when the Moles and I went up to Lancashire for the Opening Meet of the **Eskdale and Ennerdale**. We left at ten o'clock on the Friday and had a leisurely drive up to the Lakes. Tony wanted to show Anne and me a particularly favourite route of his over the moors to Sheffield and then I took over the navigating as I wanted to take them over

Wrynose and Hard Knott passes. We were booked into a farmhouse bed-and-breakfast at the village of Boot, which is perhaps best known for the fact that the legendary huntsman, Tommy Dobson, is buried in the churchyard.

Next morning we arrived at the nine o'clock meet at the George Hotel, Eskdale Green, in good time and stood in the cold wind to watch Edmund Porter, the Master and huntsman, walk up the valley with his hounds from the kennels, a rare and pleasing sight. There were not as many people as I had expected to see, considering it was the Opening Meet, but this was probably due to the pressure of work on the farms at this time of the year. After a glass of whisky we moved off up the fellside to draw blank for the first two hours. Although disappointing, this was not at all boring as the views were so enjoyable. At one stage we stood on a fell top and a local pointed out to us that we could see both the Isle of Man and Scotland from the spot. Edmund decided to change tactics and draw on the opposite side of the valley in some Forestry Commission trees. Hounds found in there at once, and rattled around very fast in the trees, soon accounting for a brace of foxes. We walked back and forth across a hillside listening to hounds hunting their third fox and I must have been pressing sideways on my thumbstick as it suddenly broke in half. I was very disappointed as I had had the stick for years and had used it on every hunt that I had ever done on foot, beagle, fox, basset, mink, otter and harrier, and felt as if I had lost an old friend.

**Eskdale & Ennerdale.** *Opening Meet at Eskdale, 1994. Master and Huntsman Mr Edmund Porter with hounds.*

Photograph kindly donated by Mrs Porter

At three o'clock, when we decided to go back to the meet, Major Mole took over the directions, stating confidently that he knew the best way home. His route may have been the shortest but it certainly was not the easiest as it was across a dried up bog. Very soon we were struggling through what appeared to be a moon-like landscape, falling into pits two feet deep and then having to climb up huge tussocks two feet high. It was around a mile across this bog and by the time we reached the other side Anne and I were ready with some serious leg-pulling concerning the soldier's ability to find his way across country. We should have remembered the old saying, "Never trust an officer with a map". When we got back to the meet, we enjoyed the traditional "Tatie Pot" and it tasted especially good.

Whilst walking on the fells, we had been told that the best singsong would be in the Brown Cow pub, a few miles away, where there was a sheep show and a Shepherds' Meet, so after our Tatie Pot we set off to find it. When we arrived, we soon realised that it was a wasted effort, as the real country people and the hunting people were well over the top. They were slurring their words and were too tight for any good singing. In addition, there were lots of youngsters who were playing the juke box so we made our way back to the George at Eskdale Green where the landlord had arranged for all the hunting people to be sitting together in one part of the pub. I sat down near Edmund Porter and enjoyed a very interesting chat about hounds and houndwork. These hounds have been in only two families since 1857, the legendary Tommy Dobson having them from 1857 to 1910, and then passing into the safe hands of the Porter family who have owned them ever since. The evening finished with an hour or so of good traditional singing with Stan Elwood as M.C., calling on Mr So-and-So to oblige with a song, and the best of possible order was kept for each singer. All three of us thoroughly enjoyed the evening and were still on a high at breakfast the next morning where the conversation was dominated by relating moments of the last lovely evening.

The long journey home was broken by calling at the home of Anne's brother, John, at Ilkley Moor where we had some refreshments. We then picked up an hilariously funny lady who was having a job interview with Anne's firm and had arranged for a lift to Suffolk, and the rest of the journey was enlivened by her.

Over a month later I set off to Wales to hunt with the Eryri Foxhounds and combine this with a "recce" for two of the other Welsh foot packs which it had been rather difficult to get hold of, the Aber and the Snowdon Valley. I left home with Major Mole at five o'clock in the morning, stopping for breakfast at a roadside bus just beyond Shrewsbury where we both agreed that we had seldom enjoyed a breakfast more

(Tues 10 Dec 1991). It was very foggy and we did not make the good time we had hoped for, arriving at Bangor at twelve o'clock. We were looking for the home of the Master of the Aber as there was not a telephone number in Baily's, and my letters had not been answered, and we found it, reasonably easily, in a quiet street. He was not at home so I knocked on the door of his neighbour. I was in luck as this proved to be the Master's brother-in-law and he told me that he was himself on the telephone and he would always give a message to the Master if I telephoned him. He also gave me the correct address – Penlon Gardens, and not Penlow, as given in Baily's – which explained why my letters had not been answered. I asked him if the Aber hunted as a normal pack or if they were a shooting pack, and he told me that they did not use guns, but looked a little sheepish as he said it, so I guessed that this was at least sometimes the case. We went away armed with the telephone number and the chance to correspond with the Master which was a considerable step forward over the last two years.

We next went to Beddgelert where we asked directions to the Eryri Foxhounds kennels and easily found them on Hafod-y-Llan, the farm of the Master Richard Williams, at Nantgwynant. He was just back from his honeymoon in Italy and was so young and keen that I could see myself as I was years ago. It really was most eerie to see oneself mirrored in this young man, so full of life, enjoyment and enthusiasm, and with his light stature and lean, dark looks he even looked uncannily as I used to. It was also really quite a jolt to realise how much I had slowed down and become less wildly enthusiastic, a process so slow that I had barely realised it. He explained to us that his grandfather had founded a pack of harriers in 1968 and had hunted fox with them for most of the next twenty years. Richard told us that he himself had first hunted them for his grandfather when he was seventeen years old, and that he was now twenty-five, and had a Joint Master, Mr Evans, but always hunted hounds himself.

He invited us into the farmhouse to see a video of his hounds hunting but as I could see he was busy with his farmwork I suggested that we would go away and come back after dark. He readily agreed to this suggestion, saying that his wife was going to her flower-club and he would be glad of our company. We set off again to find the Snowdon Valley Foxhounds, the second of the packs we had difficulty in contacting. When we enquired at a petrol station the way to their kennels we were told that they had disbanded, due to killing sheep. This seemed a little odd so we nevertheless went to the kennels which were near Caernarfon, and found them empty but obviously recently used, as there was still the unmistakable odour of hunt kennels. As we were going out of the drive a builder's van was turning in and had to stop. The driver looked rather angry so I quickly explained how we had been wishing to hunt with them, desperately hoping that he would believe I was not an anti. He told me that they hoped to start again soon if they could get drafts from other packs. For the time being, however, that was one of the remaining packs that I would have to cross off my list.

We returned to Beddgelert, bought a bottle of whisky, and went on to Richard's farm. When he answered the door we thought he was dressed very smartly for just showing us a video, but he very self-consciously said that, unbeknown to him, his wife had bought him a ticket to the flower club dinner and that he would have to go to this later on. We old-stagers sagely assured him that this, of course, was all part of married life. Mole and I both had the slightest of colds and used this as an excuse to ask him to put on the kettle and find some brown sugar. We sat down to watch the video with tumblers steaming with hot toddies from our bottle of whisky. We saw little bits of Puppy Shows, and meets, and then an unbelievable sequence of a single hound hunting a fox up a sheer rock face. This bitch was called Mayday as she had been born on 1 May, and she very slowly hunted up the rock face, from one narrow ledge to the next even narrower one, in impossibly steep places. The cameraman had also been able to film the fox going up the mountain face, so that when he turned back onto the bitch we could feel the excitement as she got ever closer to the fox, which had got as far as it could go. Imagine the excitement of the field watching below and the tremendous anxiety of the Master as he wondered whether she would fall and kill herself. What would happen when she got to the fox? Without doubt she would have a go at it and there was only one possible result of that, as the ledge was very, very narrow. However, when she got to the ledge next below the fox, it hurled itself off the rock and landed at the bottom where Mayday's sister was waiting and instantly killed it. Mayday herself came down the rockface at an incredible speed and joined her sister in the worry which was most well-deserved.

The kettle had been put on several times and the whisky bottle was empty when Richard went off to the flower club dinner in very high spirits. His wife told us the next day that he had spent the whole evening chatting up her colleagues in the club. We called at the Saracen's Head in Beddgelert for supper and had an excellent steak and a bottle of red wine, and then found the Bed-and-breakfast that Richard had booked us into. This farm Wernlas Deg belonged to Mr and Mrs Tom Roberts and lay only just outside the village. It was a new house built just in front of the ruins of the old farmhouse, and in the morning I went for a walk before breakfast to explore the ruins and a small waterwheel which Mr Roberts told me used to drive a chaff-cutter, a root-cutter and other small pieces of farm machinery.

The morning was sunny but cold, with white frost completely covering the ground and this boded badly for our day with the **Eryri Foxhounds** as this usually indicates bad scenting conditions (Wed 11 Dec 1991). After a good breakfast we set off at nine o'clock for Richard's farm so as to be able to follow the hound van, as he had suggested the evening before, to the meet which was at Cwm Pennant. This was a place situated as far as the road went up a valley and was a most beautiful spot. It was a real pleasure to be able to walk in such delightful surroundings, but scent was to be predictably bad. Hounds drew a small piece of forestry and came away speaking on a very cold line and could only feather up the hillside. After a mile or so they worked up to him and were away, but scent was almost nil. Hounds kept going on, but very slowly, which enabled me to keep with Richard as he quietly let them work by themselves. When they could make no more of it, he took them to draw again in an old slate quarry beyond the reservoir. The water was perfectly still and the mountain above was mirrored on its surface, a most impressive sight. They found in the quarry and went away over the top of this mountain from the top of which, I was told, we could have looked down onto the farm where we had stayed the night before. We were informed by walkie-talkie radio that they were marking to ground just out of sight over the ridge and that it would be a long time before they came back. This decided us that it was time to start home, as we had to drive all the way back to Suffolk. We left at three o'clock having thoroughly enjoyed ourselves in this fairytale setting.

**The Eryri: *"Hobson's choice"***

Two days later Tony and I left home again, this time with Tony's wife, Anne, as well, at five o'clock in the afternoon to drive down to stay with my daughter, Bridget, in Gloucester, ready to hunt with the **Leadon Vale Bassets** the following day (Fri 13 Dec 1991). The weather was dreadful, with fog and white frost, but the Master of the Leadon Vale had assured me on the telephone that he did not stop because of frost. Our first mistake was to drive past the turn-off for the A11 so we had to go on to Cambridge and join the M11. Mole took over at this point and drove round the M25 and up the M40. In the thick fog we overshot the A40 turn-off and carried on up to Junction 11. We were about thirty miles out of our way, which would be equal to a hundred miles in normal weather, since

**Eryri Foxhounds.** *Meet at Bryn y Wern, Cwm Pennant, December 1991. Hounds being held up waiting for a bolt from an earth near the river, with Mike Medcalf, Honorary Secretary.*

Photograph kindly loaned by Mike Medcalf

we were travelling at about fifteen miles an hour because of the fog. We studied the map and decided to go via Chipping Norton to Burford where we joined the A40, finally arriving in Gloucester at eleven-thirty. We telephoned Bridget from the Station telephone box and she came out and piloted us to her house. We had a large gin-and-tonic and then a plate of stew with bread-and-butter, plenty of red wine, and we all went to bed at approximately two o'clock, myself on the Mole's campbed on the sitting-room floor because there were only two bedrooms.

There was thick fog again in the morning but we set off to the meet which was to be at the Red Lion at Wainlode (Sat 14 Dec 1991). It was a delightful pub on the bank of the River Severn. The members of the basset pack arrived, all wonderful characters as they always are with bassets, and also my nephew Rupert McCowan who, hearing what my plans were for the weekend, had decided to drive from London to join us. The Master arrived with his hounds, but after waiting an hour or so there was no chance of hunting as the fog was so bad we could hardly see over the road. We set off home again and decided to go straight across country, via Bicester, Buckingham and St Neots but, after an hour or so, the car began to lose power. We crept along at fifteen miles an hour on a very bendy and narrow road where it would have been very dangerous to stop in this thick fog, as there was nowhere to pull out. We just made it to a garage and freewheeled in as the engine finally cut out altogether just as we turned into it. I rang Volvo Carcare but they said they would be two hours before they could get there as there were so many breakdowns, so Major Mole got to work. He diagnosed the trouble as the diesel freezing and managed to get the car going by putting petrol into the diesel tank which prevented the diesel from freezing. We stopped for fish and chips in St Neots and eventually arrived home by seven o'clock. Moral of the story – don't go out on Friday the Thirteenth!

**Fourshires Bassets.** *Hounds c. 1993–94.*
Photograph kindly loaned by Suzanne Huband

We were back in Gloucestershire two weeks later but this time to hunt with the **Fourshires Basset Hounds** who were meeting at Pastures Farm, Oddington (Sat 28 Dec 1991). Paul and Avril Palmer, who had come with us to the Huckworthy the previous season, were staying with the Moles, so I picked up the four of them from the Moles' home at seven o'clock in the morning. After a while we turned off the motorway in the hope of being able to find breakfast, but we had to go as far as Burford before we could find anything to eat. We located the meet easily enough and our host, Mr Lloyd, introduced himself and several others and told us that he was an ex-Master of these hounds and was going to follow on his horse. He also introduced us to the present Masters, Messrs Schuster and Meredith, who were justly proud of their Peterborough Hound Show successes. Although there were some very smart hounds among them, the hounds were unlevel and were of mixed types, and did not look like a pack as had the Leadon Vale. However, once again the proverb "Handsome is as handsome does" was proved to be correct, for when they found a hare, soon after we moved off, they hunted most beautifully as a pack and on a very poor scent. They were quite delightful to watch and especially to hear. Their voices were outstanding and this was the most stylish basset hunting that I had ever seen or thought possible. Whenever the amateur huntsman blew for them, they flew to him without a trace of the usual basset stubbornness and independence. In total they hunted four hares, two of which were lost in thick bramble bushes and it was a shame that the scent was so poor. One of the field said that they had seen me out with the local foxhounds and another one remembered me hunting with Pierre Bocquillon in France in 1962.

There was great laughter and fun all the way home which was only broken by a visit to the Bear at Beyton, near Bury St Edmunds, where the charming old landlady called Mrs Ostler was on great form and was as pleased as ever to see me. I had known her since I was seventeen years old, delivering day-old chicks for my father. She recalled how I once bought a coffin stool out of the bar from her husband for seven pounds. How cross she was when she found out that he had sold it for far too little. She told me that she had been in the pub for sixty-one years, so I gave her a big kiss across the bar and asked her if she remembered when the parson wanted to court her when she was a young girl. "Oh hush, boy, do!" she scolded.

Shortly after New Year I was off again, this time to Wales with Charlotte, my youngest daughter, to hunt with the David Davies on the Wednesday and the South

Wales Bassets on the Saturday. When we were twelve miles from home I suddenly realised that I had left my wallet behind, so we had to turn back. We stopped for an outstanding lunch in a bistro chosen by Charlotte in Kimbolton and eventually arrived in Builth Wells at six-thirty. Naturally, we went directly to the Barley Mow and we had a few drinks with my old friend Tom Morgan, a delightful old character. When I asked how he was keeping, he told me that he had fallen down on Christmas Eve. He added that he had fallen down in exactly the same place for the last three Christmas Eves. We took our cases into the Edam bed-and-breakfast and walked down to the Lion where we were assured we would get the best meal in town, with the exception, of course, of the Barley where they were not cooking.

I explained to the young waitress that we were both allergic to nuts, and that she must on no account let us order anything with nuts in it. I ordered mushrooms stuffed with Stilton cheese as a starter, but as soon as I had put the first half-mushroom in my mouth I thought I could taste nuts. I was not sure because of the strong taste of Stilton, so I called to the waitress and asked if she had carried my message to the chef. She assured me that there were no nuts in the dish so I stupidly believed her and ate the other half of the mushroom. Immediately I began to feel the effects of nuts – contraction of the mouth and throat and violent nausea. Charlotte called the manageress and she suggested that I drank some milk as it might have a neutralising effect. It did help a little but I was getting rapidly worse. Charlotte took charge and asked the manageress to telephone to the hospital. The manageress kindly took me in her own car, but along the way I could not open the door quick enough and, to avoid spoiling her car, was sick over myself. At the little hospital in Builth Wells they gave me an anti-histamene straight into my vein and this worked quickly. Soon I was back at the bed-and-breakfast and went immediately to bed. I was furious to find out next day that not only had I missed having an enjoyable dinner with my daughter, but also a great singsong in the Barley Mow. I went into the Lion and found out that there was a little crushed walnut in the Stilton cheese. Walnuts are the very worst for me but it is incredible that such a tiny amount can do so much mischief.

However, I was fit enough to hunt and, since Charlotte was quite happy to stay in Builth and potter around the shops, I set off alone for the **David Davies Foxhounds** and arrived at Oakley Park in good time for the ten-thirty meet (Wed 8 Jan 1992). Oakley Park was just a few houses and an old school standing on a T-junction and I watched as, one by one, the field of twenty-two arrived, most of whom were great characters, with faces that showed me that they had spent much of their lives outdoors. I fell into conversation with a lady who was the Secretary and was told that some of those present had been to the school. When she herself was at the school a boy had thrown a brick at her and the school mistress had tied him to the fence all day with the brick hung round his neck on a piece of string. On her way home she had hung it on his parents' front door. This caused a terrible fuss and a governors' meeting had to be called, which had the effect of consoling the injured parties and the incident was soon forgotten. There was a man going around taking one pound from everyone that he could see, and I was told that he was the Cap Marshal, a term I had never heard before, but I noticed how efficient he was. No matter how late in the day a new face appeared, he would get his pound.

There were about twenty-five couple of mostly Fellhounds, with some Welsh amongst them. When David, the huntsman, moved off to draw, a fox was found at once, and we had a lovely view of them hunting down into the valley and up the other side, right up to and over the top. When hounds went over the top, David went straight to a car so I followed in mine and made a complete circuit of the mountain. However, at one point we saw a very tired fox cross the road in front of us and slowly make his way across a meadow, stopping several times to look back. We were sure that this was the hunted fox and stayed at the spot for some time. Either we were wrong or, more likely, hounds had changed to another fox as they did not appear. We did not see hounds again until we were back where we started from. This showed how very difficult it was to hunt hounds in this sort of country. If David had not gone round to the other side, hounds could have been miles away without trace, but as it happened hounds had turned back and more or less retraced their steps. Those who stayed there had seen all the sport.

The cars were then left on a hillside and I walked with David, having the great pleasure of watching them hunting a difficult line very slowly but persevering for miles on end. Even on this catchy scent, their voices were superb and it was pure joy to follow them. The Master, Lord Davies, was not out, but his daughter was well up with the huntsman all day, and was obviously very interested in the houndwork. During this long slow hunt I saw how well they could hunt on their own, but also how David could rally them with his excellent horn and voice when required. The fox was eventually marked to ground in some shallow rocks, from which it was bolted by the terriermen, and I had a lovely view of it coming down the hillside past me, and through some farm buildings, across the meadow into a wood. As I watched him come to the edge of the wood, it was exactly as an odd hound was coming out

**David Davies:** ***"Should we be meeting like this?"***

and they stopped and looked at each other through the sheep-wire. The fox made a quick jink and was away into the trees but the hound, obviously a puppy, seemed at a loss.

While all this was going on, David was trying to lay the main pack onto the line, but with great difficulty for about fifty sheep had apparently followed the fox down the hillside. If the sheep had just crossed the line it would not have been a problem, but they were running away from the baying hounds (which were being held back) and took exactly the same route as the fox all the way down the hillside so they had spoiled the whole length of the line. Although hounds were cast into the wood where I had seen him enter, they could make little of it. This was probably because of the fright he had had on meeting the single hound, it being a frequently observed phenomenon that a hunted fox will leave no scent for a mile or so after a surprise encounter with, for example, a sheepdog. As it was by now four o'clock, I decided to say goodbye and drove back to Builth Wells. On my return Charlotte said that she had seen Marie Lloyd from the Barley and that I was invited to eat there that evening. This put us in an embarassing situation as I had said that I would eat again at the Lion as the manageress had been so upset. However, we ate at the Barley and enjoyed, as ever, a very good leg of lamb. Years earlier, Marie and her mother would always cook me a leg of local lamb as I so enjoyed it and can, or imagine that I can, taste the heather and the herbs of the mountains. The whole meal was first-class and Marie would not accept any payment for it, saying that it was a pleasure to see us in Wales again. After dinner, we walked down to the Lion to say "No hard feelings," and then back to the Barley, hoping there would be another singsong, but we were unlucky.

On the Thursday I had arranged a series of meetings all over the Midlands (Thurs 9 Jan 1992). We left Builth at nine-thirty in a blinding snowstorm, and had some anxious moments in climbing up the hill to Hundred House, as an articulated lorry spun to a halt and I had to overtake blindly in these slippery conditions. After a very slow journey, we eventually arrived at Cotterills in Walsall, a firm where I wanted to have some special harness buckles made for me. They eventually agreed, on the condition that I provided one of each buckle that I wished to be copied. We next went to Ashby-de-la-Zouch, to my collar-maker, Robert Denton, and ordered some more collars for the next season's carriage-driving.

I had also arranged to meet Michael Sagar, editor of Hounds magazine, for tea, and he was going to tell me what hotel he had booked us into, but I realised that I would not have enough time so I telephoned him from Robert Denton's. I apologised for having to miss tea, and he told me that he had booked us in to a hotel in Much Wenlock (Shropshire). When I heard this I was a little worried as Much Wenlock was where I had spent such a dreadful evening in 1983 when minkhunting. However, he then said that the hotel was the Talbot, so I was reassured. It seemed very appropriate that the editor of Hounds magazine and I should dine together at the Talbot with all its overtones of the ancient origins of hunting. When Michael arrived for dinner, I passed him my Baily's to look through. He quickly noted that there were dates beside each hunt's name and quickly flicked back to the Aber where there was no date. To save him the trouble of seeing how many hunts I had not been with, I gave him a list of the last seven. He seemed impressed but not over-excited and after dinner, when Charlotte had gone to bed, we discussed it again but I was very disappointed that he was not more enthusiastic. I had expected him to be very excited and keen about a hunting record being established in the 1990s, but with hindsight I have come to realise that no-one is able to realise just how difficult it is and all the determination required to fulfill it.

We left Much Wenlock next morning in bright sunshine and drove to Betws-y-Coed to call on some friends of Charlotte for coffee, going on to Portmeirion, the Italian village in Wales which Charlotte wanted to see (Fri 10 Jan 1992). We then moved on to Aberystwyth where she wanted to do some shopping and finally got to our destination, Abercoed Farm at Tregaron. I had seen this place advertised in Hounds magazine offering hunting holidays and hire of horses as well as bed-and-breakfast, and it was the perfect place to stay while I planned my last day's mounted hunting, with the Gogerddan.

Mr and Mrs Jones welcomed us and showed us their horses in the stables. Neither Charlotte nor I could properly pronounce Mr Jones' Christian name, which was Ednyfed, so Charlotte decided we would call him Ed as the closest English abbreviation. Ed sat down with me to talk hunting and thrust an enormous tumbler of whisky into my hand. After much discussion of various aspects of houndwork, he told me that he whipped in to his brother who was Master and Huntsman of the Gogerddan. To celebrate this extraordinary coincidence, I accepted a second tumbler of whisky. Janet Jones called us through to the dining room for a lovely dinner of homemade soup and leg of local lamb, which was very flavoursome, and finished up with a pudding and an elaborate cheeseboard. After dinner, Ed suggested that we went down to his local in Tregaron for a nightcap and this seemed a good idea. Charlotte came with us and at the time when we all ought to have gone home she said it was time to go. Ed, however, had other ideas and took her home, then returning to settle down with me for a serious session.

Next morning I was feeling extremely rough and hungover and did not enjoy my breakfast (through no fault of Janet's), but left with Charlotte to drive to Bonvilston where the **South Wales Bassets** were meeting at the Red Lion (Sat 11 Jan 1992). We arrived at the place at twelve forty-five and met Mrs Harrison, the Master, who took us into the pub. I was parched with thirst and readily swallowed two half-pints of bitter. As the three of us were the only members of the field to come into the pub, we went out to the car-park where Mrs Harrison told the Secretary we were to pay no cap, a gesture which always makes one feel so welcome. The landlord brought out a tray of sherries and, as we were sipping these, hounds were let out of the van. Taking into account the previous night's excesses and how I was feeling I could still hardly believe my eyes. The hounds were the most unlevel lot (I could not describe them as a "pack") I had ever seen. There were light, leggy harrier types (but with a basset's head and long ears), standing about seventeen inches high, down to the smallest at about eleven inches high, and every type and size between these two. It really was the most astonishing sight. The incredible harrier types were, I was told, a throwback to when the Westerby Bassets used a Dunston Harriers stallion hound. It is wonderful how long after an outcross the genes can produce the full harrier height.

**South Wales Bassets.** *Meet at the Red Lion, Bonvilston (Vale of Glamorgan), 11 January 1992. Tony Harvey with Dilwyn Bridgeman (Kennel Huntsman) and Ralph Langdon (Huntsman).*

Photograph kindly loaned by Mr Tony Blake

They proved to be yet another case of "Handsome is as handsome does." They were hunted very well by Mr Ralph Langdon and the kennel huntsman, Dilwyn Bridgeman, seemed a very keen sportsman and whipped in very enthusiastically. I felt sorry for them as there were cobwebs all over the fields and I knew this to be a sign of very bad scent. We drew for one and a half hours before finding. This Mrs Harrison had warned me about as there was too much "lamping" in the area (illegal coursing of hares at night using a powerful spotlight). When they did find, they went away with a lovely cry, but scent proved to be as bad as I had expected, and this quite soon reduced them to a slow walking pace. They tried very hard, just touching the line here and there, and managed on this difficult scent to take the line over several fields. I was desperately hoping that they would work up to her and fresh-find her as they deserved to because of their outstanding perseverance. However, this did not happen due, I expect, to the lamping, as coursed hares tend to keep running and will not clap down. Hares which are only used to hunting will clap down with confidence as they are never pushed as hard as when coursed. At four o'clock I said my goodbyes to Mrs Harrison and, after coffee and paracetamols in the pub, we drove to Bridget's home in Gloucester. We had a most enjoyable evening with Bridget and her husband Richard who had cooked a delicious pizza while Bridget had made an orange jelly (an accurate reflection of their respective culinary abilities). After dinner I was rather too sleepy to be other than boring company so went to bed at ten o'clock and we drove home to Suffolk the next day through thick fog all the way.

Within a week I was back in the area again, this time travelling with Tony and Anne "Mole" for our second attempt to hunt with the Leadon Vale Bassets, and also to go with the Nantcol Valley Foxhounds, a private pack. Leaving home on Friday at two o'clock, we drove to Bromyard in Worcestershire, where we were invited to stay with Tony and Janet James who were long-standing friends of the Moles. When we arrived at seven o'clock Tony James was at choir practice, but the rest of us went to the local pub for a delicious supper of beef stew and dumplings which were as light as a feather. To complement this old-fashioned dish the landlady was wearing a mob cap. After a very amusing breakfast four of us set off for the **Leadon Vale Bassets'** meet at the Bridge Inn, Hawbridge (Glos), for what was the last of the basset packs (Sat 18 Jan 1992). When nearly there we realised that we were far too early so we went into Tewkesbury for coffee, during which the proprietor told us horrific tales of robbers coming off the nearby motorway to steal anything from wheels of cars to the cars themselves. The previous week thieves had stolen all the golf clubs, from every Porsche car at the golf club – £11,000 worth. The Bridge Inn lay right on the bank of the River Severn and had a longboat (i.e. an original horse-drawn barge) tied up alongside with a fire burning in the stove and a pile of logs on the roof. I always get special pleasure from seeing these boats as I feel they are so close to my own hobby of horse-drawn gypsy caravans.

The pub was as delightful as the previous meet of these hounds when they had been fogged off. We renewed our acquaintance with members of the field whom we had met before, and some new ones, including one man who was six foot seven inches high and another whom we called Rupert Bear on account of his bright yellow scarf with a large check. He had with him a very glamorous girl who was a film star and on this dull day was hunting in sunglasses. There was a tremendous atmosphere in the pub and we were drawn into other peoples' conversations. It was during one of these chats that the Master told me that so far that season they had not killed a hare.

We moved off to draw lovely flat grassland which was part of the Ledbury Foxhounds country. The hounds were in perfect control and soon found and hunted most beautifully. This was the first time that Janet James had been out hunting with any sort of hounds and she was keen to learn what it was all about. The four of us were on our own when a hare crossed not far from us and I could hear some hounds hunting it. I explained to Janet how they would follow the line and pointed out the wind direction and how it would move the scent downwind, so she was not to expect the hounds to hunt exactly where the hare had actually run. I soon realised that these two couple were hunting away from the main pack, but we kept with them and this proved perfect for Janet as the hare stayed in a small area. The country had some wide dykes and as the hare was not pressed in any way she would not cross the dykes and kept circling around us, often passing in view, and we could stop and watch as the hounds drove on upwind or hunted slowly downwind. It was an ideal exercise to show Janet what hunting was all about and she thoroughly enjoyed her new experience.

This private hunt lasted about an hour and a half and when we rejoined the pack we found that they had caught a hare, the first one of the season, and we had not been there to witness the event. At three o'clock we were quite near the Boat Inn and thought we would enjoy a quick beer. We met the grand old landlady, who had been born there, and whose family had kept this pub for over two hundred years. Leaving the Boat Inn, we walked back to the meet along the river bank and arrived back at the Bridge Inn at four o'clock. During the day we had seen a four-year-old boy going very well, either with his father or without him. Back at the meet I remarked on it, and somebody told me that his father was the leading light in the new National Hunt Supporters' Club.

We arrived back at the James' home at five-thirty and, after a quick cup of tea, set off again armed with pork pies and cakes to eat along the way as we drove across Wales to Dolgellau. We arrived there at eight o'clock in a state of confusion, as I had forgotten to bring the address of the place where we had booked bed-and-breakfast. All I could remember was that it was the Ivy House and as Dolgellau was larger than we had expected this was not much help. Then Major Mole thought he remembered me mentioning Finsbury Square. That completed the puzzle and we were soon being shown to our rooms. The landlady was very pleasant and cooked us a lovely dinner which was served by her husband. He had an enormous beard and looked as if he had stepped off a pack of John Player cigarettes. We asked to pay our bill and have sandwiches packed up instead of breakfast as we wished to leave at seven-thirty in the morning. The landlady was convinced we were all mad but agreed to our request.

After coffee in our rooms we left promptly at seven-thirty to drive to the kennels of the **Nantcol Valley Foxhounds** at Pentre Gwynfryn, near Llanbedr, where I had agreed to meet the Master, Alan Owen, at nine o'clock and to follow him in his hound van to the meet (Sun 19 Jan 1992). He was owner, huntsman and joint-Master of the pack, which had been started by him in 1975. We got directions to the kennels from a paper shop and arrived forty minutes early so we sat in the car above the kennels and listened to the hounds singing. The kennels were set in a clearing in the wood and above them was a little car-park, presumably for walkers and the like. At nine-thirty Alan Owen arrived but drove straight across to the kennels, and through the grassyard, taking no notice of us or our car. I expect he thought we were tourists as we were parked in the little car-park. I walked down and introduced myself and he apologised for being late, explaining that he had been up until three-thirty in the morning picking up hounds which had been lost on the previous day. At the end of the day, hounds had got amongst masses of foxes and had gone off in all directions. There was still one couple missing and he said that, in these circumstances, his normal policy was not to hunt again until all the lost hounds had been picked up. My heart sank as I thought this was leading up to him saying that he would not be hunting today, but this was not so.

**Nantcol Valley.** *From the meet at Gors y Gedol, Dy-ryn Ardudwy, September 1992. Joint-Master and Huntsman Alan Owen with hounds and terrier.*

While I stood talking to him, he let hounds out into the grassyard, all amongst the chickens and geese which seemed to share the yard with the hounds, neither of which took any notice of the other. Several of the hounds were stiff and sore after the previous day's efforts but, after he had selected the fifteen couple for that day's hunt, we set off, following his Ford Transit, to the meet which was at Llanyrch in the mountains above Llanfair. What a job we had to keep with him, often touching seventy miles per hour, and the last five miles were up steep hills with very narrow roads and I felt as if I was driving in the Monte Carlo rally. The meet was on a hillside in a quiet and seemingly deserted valley. I stood and looked around at the majestic scenery with nothing but a few abandoned houses to show that Man had ever been there. The only field were the whipper-in (who had not been to bed at all on account of looking for hounds all night) and ten farmers with guns because, as it was explained to me, as it was near to lambing time it was necessary to kill as many foxes as possible.

Hounds soon found a fox amongst the rocks and hunted on up the hillside. We followed as best we could but were soon outstripped by the locals. I had long since learned not to try to keep up with the local people and to set my own pace. We could not see either the field or the hounds for three-quarters of an hour, but could hear their voices ringing above us, which kept us climbing upwards until we finally came up to the Master who stood, with some of the field, watching hounds hunt in the next valley below us. The Master strode off towards hounds with the effortless ease which typifies a hill-country huntsman, but the whipper-in said he was going to stop where he was for a while. We said that we would wait with him as we were only too glad of an excuse to rest, and I got into conversation with him. He told me how the previous year he had been made redundant and was so bored that he decided to see what foxhunting was all about. He had become totally hooked on the sport and had only missed one day since then, and that was the second day, as he was too stiff from the first to walk. He went on to tell us how he now worked for the Master for nothing, doing up the drive to the kennels and so forth. What a character he was, with a chain around his waist and a hunting horn stuck into it.

Suddenly the conversation was over, as he said he could hear hounds marking, and set off at a great pace with us following as best we could across the valley and up another small hill. When we looked down the other side there was a splendid sight, with the Master standing on top of a rock pile leaning on his stick, with his hounds marking below him. He wore a leather jerkin with a woollen sweater poking out below, and real Fell boots on top of which he wore the tops of Wellington boots. There were terriers yapping on leads and hounds baying at a number of holes, all of which was vividly set off by quartz showing brilliant white through the rocks. I climbed down, much to the consternation of the Moles who thought I might fall, but after twenty minutes or so they could not bear to be away from the atmosphere and gingerly climbed down as well. This was a very difficult place with deep cracks in the rocks all around, which were probably joined deep down inside the rock, so it was decided to leave this fox and draw again.

We kept with them for a time, but when they turned away from the meet we stopped, watching them for as long as possible before making our way back to the car, as we had to face the long journey home. We took turns to drive which gave me time to think over the main points of the day. The most memorable member of the pack was a noble old hound called Rockwood who had suffered an accident years previously and went on three legs. The fourth was held up and the muscle had all wasted away. He was such a knowledgable, sagacious-looking old hound and went as well as the others, jumping wire and walls all day. I only saw him lifted over an obstacle once, and this was a high fence of wire and rails. With only one back leg he lacked the power to clear it. The hounds were fell types and hunted well together, unaided for most of the time, and were rock steady to all forms of riot. I would certainly never forget the young man who had changed his life and become dedicated to hounds. Lastly, I thought how lucky we were to be in such majestic scenery. Only hunting would take me to such lovely remote places, but I had also to reflect on the abandoned houses in the valley. The inhabitants must have had to walk four or five miles to the nearest tiny village and I wondered how they had managed in a bad winter. The hunt was financed by a farmers' Fox Society which paid two pounds fifty per brush, or forty pounds per plantation to draw it, and this far into the season they had killed twenty-two foxes.

By the time we were nearing Bury St Edmunds in Suffolk, Tony and I were gasping for a beer, but Mrs Mole was reluctant to enter a pub in the town, as she felt so untidy. I assured her that I knew just the place, and drove straight to the Angel Hotel which was the smartest hotel in the town. She took it all in her stride and, after a mild protest, came in with us. We had a very pleasant half-hour chatting with the barman who had served there for fourteen years and then drove on, arriving back at ten-thirty.

**Gogerddan Foxhounds** *Jt. Master and Huntsman JC Jones standing with Tony Harvey.*

Photograph taken by Jim Meads

# MAP 18

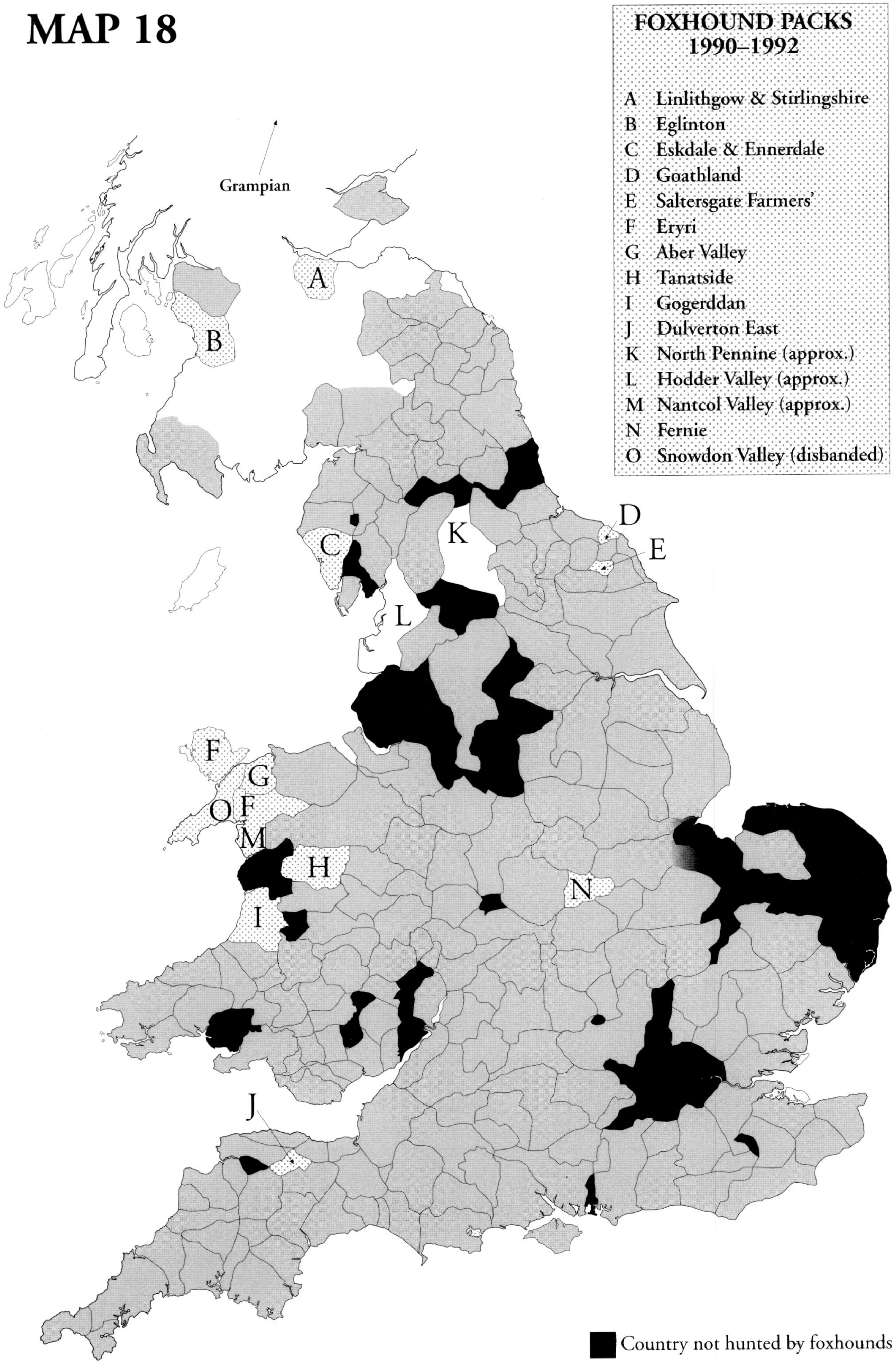
FOXHOUND PACKS
1990–1992
A Linlithgow & Stirlingshire
B Eglinton
C Eskdale & Ennerdale
D Goathland
E Saltersgate Farmers'
F Eryri
G Aber Valley
H Tanatside
I Gogerddan
J Dulverton East
K North Pennine (approx.)
L Hodder Valley (approx.)
M Nantcol Valley (approx.)
N Fernie
O Snowdon Valley (disbanded)
Grampian
A
B
C
D
E
K
L
F
G
O
F
M
H
N
I
J
Country not hunted by foxhounds

# CHAPTER 22

## THE EDINBURGH WOOLLEN MILL TOUR AND THE LAST TRIP

After the Nantcol, there were sevn foxhound packs to go, four in Wales and three in the north. I decided to tackle these in two jollies and set off on Monday 27 January (1992) for the north. As I had the added pleasure of Sheila's company, and as her priorities were not quite the same as mine, I soon christened this jolly the "Edinburgh Woollen Mill Tour". I was intending to hunt with the North Pennine, the Lochaber and Sunart, and the Hodder Valley but it was to be a real "tour", stopping at various different places to meet many different people on the way. I left with a trailer on the back of the Volvo, containing the front wheels of one of my Landau carriages, which were lying on top of two large bales of straw, weighing around three-quarters of a ton. The wheels were for Don Royston, my wheelwright, who lived near Leeds, and the straw was for Donald Hardy who had a coaching team and who shared premises with Don. The straw was a present for Donald as he kept some pigs as well and found it very difficult to get hold of straw for them.

We left at nine-thirty and a tyre burst on the trailer at Woolpit twenty-five miles on. Needham Tyres came quickly to our rescue and we pressed on to have the same wheel, with its new tyre, burst again at South Wickham, twelve miles short of Grantham. We waited for over three hours for Associated Tyre Services to come out, and then discovered that the bearings had gone in the wheel. We left the trailer at a service station and, fearing that they would be stolen, put the Landau wheels in the Volvo. As we were by now so late, we went directly to Park House, Helmsley, arriving at seven o'clock and were revived by a large gin-and-tonic from Jackie Saggers. This was the best part of the day so far. When fully revived I asked to use her telephone and rang Tony "Mole" St Quinton to ask him to sort out the mess. I asked him to come out the following day with another low-loader, and pick up our abandoned trailer and get everything to the wheelwrights. I suggested that he asked Kenny Warne, my stockman, to come with him, both to help and to give him a well-deserved break, and then that they came on to Whitby where Sheila and I had arranged to meet Helen and Len Mison again.

When all this was arranged, I took Sheila to meet Anthony Barker at whose yard I had stabled my horses all the times I had stayed in Helmsley. He gave us yet another large gin-and-tonic, and then we went on to the Feathers for supper, a steak and Stilton sauce for me, and fish and chips for Sheila. Afterwards I took Sheila to the Royal Oak to meet the rest of the gang but, being on my best behaviour, we had a relatively early night at ten-thirty.

The next morning was spent shopping in Helmsley but, instead of buying an expensive present for my wife, I was extravagant on my own behalf. I wanted to go with the Ampleforth Beagles but had forgotten to put my wellington boots into the car. I thought it would be simple enough to buy another pair, but the problem was that I could not find a pair in my size, which is unusually small. The only pair I could find in Helmsley was one lined in leather, at £90 in the Sale (with £50 off). After a thoroughly enjoyable time there, welcomed with enthusiasm by all my friends, we had a lovely drive across the moors to Whitby, arriving at twelve o'clock. We walked around the shops and then had a fish and chip lunch. We settled ourselves into the Kimberley Hotel and then did some more shopping in the afternoon. Mole and Kenny arrived at six o'clock and after a delicious Italian meal in the Kimberley, Len and Helen joined us for drinks. Mole was very tired and soon went to bed.

There was yet more shopping next morning and then I left Sheila relaxing in the hotel while I drove across to Beadlam Rigg, to the meet of the Ampleforth Beagles. Unfortunately the meet was cancelled as it was too foggy so I had gone to all that expense of the wellingtons for nothing. Len and Helen joined us for dinner at the Kimberley, and we spent a happy evening reminiscing about the good times we had together in Suffolk before they moved north. Next day we were on the move again and drove across country to the Barbon Inn near Kirkby Lonsdale, where we had arranged to meet some more old friends, Newton and Kate Bacon. We arrived at about two o'clock but the pub was cold and unfriendly and there was no-one around. Sheila was shivering in the corner and I was so cold I got into bed, but eventually the heating came on at five o'clock. Newton and Kate arrived at six-thirty and fulfilled the main purpose of the visit by giving me some good notes for this book. The quality of the dinner and the pleasure of seeing the Bacons again, more than made up for the shortcomings of the pub but, even though we were supposed to stay a second night there, we decided to move on again as it was so soulless and dismal. I rang Sheila Barker to see if she could put us up at Patterdale but she was fully booked and found us a room in another bed-and-breakfast place at Home Farm, Patterdale.

Next day I had planned to go to the meet of the Cumberland Farmers' at Hutton Roof to see my old friend Tom Wales, the Master, but on the way we saw the Blencathra hunting in Mungrisdale, so we watched them for a while before going on to the Cumberland Farmers' meet, which had been put back to twelve o'clock owing to the frost. We saw them away and then Sheila drove into Carlisle because I had had a few drinks with Tom, and we went on yet another shopping expedition. There were two Edinburgh Woollen Mill shops there, and we went into each twice, then I took over the driving and we went on to the Plumbes' at Roberton, arriving at four-thirty.

There was no Sunday morning lie-in as I had to leave Roberton at seven o'clock in order to reach the nine-thirty meet of the **North Pennine Foxhounds** at Bay Bridge, near Blanchland (Sun 2 Feb 1992). In fact, I arrived at the meet at eight forty-five but there were already many people there. I got into conversation with Mr Dodds who remembered me from hunting with the Haydon Foxhounds years ago. He told me that he was taking on the Mastership of the Haydon the following season. There were about thirty-five people out, which I thought was a jolly good field for nine-thirty on a Sunday morning. Mr Tones, the Master, made me very welcome and showed me the hounds, which were mostly Fellhounds with a few Sinnington and one or two with some Welsh blood. I later heard that he had had an uphill struggle for the first few seasons to get things going and to generate some enthusiasm for hunting, as there had been no hunting in the area within living memory.

We moved off down a broad, flat valley and drew wooded banks on either side of the valley but hounds were prevented from drawing properly by hundred and hundreds of rabbits everywhere, all either dead or dying from myxomatosis. It was a sight difficult to describe, as I have never seen so many rabbits together in one place before. I would guess they would have eaten more grass than several hundred sheep. While walking up the valley I saw a huge frozen waterfall which looked like a lovely crystal chandelier, but then we were obliged to climb out of the valley owing to so many fallen trees in one part. The field divided with some of us going up each side. They drew on for an hour and a half before finding, and then I was unlucky as they went away on the opposite side of the valley. We never really got on terms with them in this hunt, as by the time we had climbed down and then up the other side, they were well away. We could keep them in sight but could not hear their voices as the wind was very strong.

**North Pennine.** *From the meet at Bay Bridge, March 1991. Joint-Master and Huntsman, Mr M Tones, seeing hounds over a wall, with a young supporter.*

Photograph kindly loaned by Mr Robin Turnbull

The Master's mother picked me up and I followed in her car for a while. She told me that the Master was a school instructor and a specialist in Rural Science. She also told me that he now had a kennel huntsman, so life was a little easier than when he had to do hounds on his own, before and after work. Her car was full of masks, brushes and pictures which had recently been left to the Master by an old lady who had died in the Lake District, and I was sitting in the car with boxes full of hunting trophies in my lap. She was hunting this day without her husband as he was reading a lesson in church, but she normally picked him up from the church and brought him straight out to hounds. After an hour or so she took me back to my car as she was going out to lunch, and I followed another run up to a quarry. Hounds then came back to near the meet and at that point I decided to go back to the Plumbes'.

When I arrived there I asked Colin how Sheila had been getting on during the day and he replied,

"Oh she's fine. She's had two bottles of vodka and is now on the third."

He then explained that she had been drinking the miniature bottles provided by airlines as that was the only vodka he had in the house.

Next morning we left Easter House to drive to Fort William, which was to be our base for the Lochaber and Sunart. After the horrors of driving through Glasgow and its suburbs, we settled down on the scenic A82 which took us along the shores of Loch Lomond and over some high ground through lovely scenery, until finally we followed it up the edge of Loch Linnhe to our destination, the Mercury Hotel at Fort William. After putting our cases into our rooms we went for a walk around the town, window-shopping, and gave two more Edinburgh Woollen Mill shops a thorough inspection before having a cup of tea in a cafe which overlooked the water, and then strolling back to the hotel.

I enjoyed a fried breakfast, which included slices of black pudding and haggis, at seven-thirty with Sheila, and then left at eight o'clock for the nine-thirty meet of the **Lochaber and Sunart Foxhounds** at Dalilea (Tues 4 Feb 1992). I went west along Loch Eil and then took a wrong turning, but corrected myself and got to the meet just in time. Roy Newton, the huntsman, arrived with ten and a half couple of Fellhounds, and a local farmer was the only other field. Dalilea was a very steep place with fifteen to twenty miles without a road. The mist was very bad and Roy said that, as I was there, he would move the meet to the next Friday's draw in Glen Moidart, as the mist would be better and the seeing easier as there was a road all along the bottom. Even without the mist the only real way to watch hounds from this meet was from a boat on the loch, and Roy made plans with the farmer to have a boat ready for Friday. This was so he (the farmer) could row up and down the lake and watch hounds working on the steep hillside, using his radio to report to Roy.

Hounds were unboxed in Glen Moidart and, once Roy had given the farmer a radio, he took hounds to draw. The farmer and I stayed on the road as Roy had suggested, with some emphasis, that I did not follow him. He said I should walk along the road as I would be able to see far more than if I was up in the trees on the steep hillside. They drew for two hours before finding, and then the scent was poor. When they did find,the farmer picked me up in his Land Rover and, with the aid of the radio, we were able to keep in touch with Roy. They ran quite fast along the face of a hill and although we could not see them we could hear them easily. The farmer drove quickly from one vantage point to the next for some miles, then he suddenly turned off up a drive to a large mansion, opened a gate and went into a meadow with a lot of clumps of rushes in it.

We could hear hounds speaking nearer and nearer and then we saw the hunted fox coming through the rushes. The farmer had his twelve-bore gun in his Land Rover but was very upset because the fox would have been out of range by the time he got it out. I said it would make my day to watch them hunt it and luckily two and a half couple came down the mountain and took the line through the rushes. The fox headed back the way he had come and we then followed a great hunt up and down the mountainside and back along the valley. Then the farmer turned his Land Rover up to a farm and left it to climb up to try to get a shot. Hounds were really on good terms with their fox and the cry was making the adrenalin pump in my veins, so I was pleased when they hunted him down to the valley again and out of the range of the gun.

The farmer ran back to his Land Rover saying that he wanted to get ahead to shoot it, and would return to the rushy meadow, so I stopped riding with him. I was enjoying the hunt too much to miss any music by being in his vehicle. All the other hounds had joined in and the cry was very exciting. It prompted me to run as fast as I could along the road, but the farmer had rightly guessed that the fox would cross the meadow again, and when he did, he was ready. I heard two shots and when I got back to the meadow hounds were breaking up the fox, unlike the Towy and Cothi hounds who had not broken up a shot fox. When Roy eventually arrived I told him how wonderfully well his hounds had hunted. He asked me if they had killed it and seem rather disappointed when I told him it had been shot.

The mansion near which the meadow lay had been restored recently at great expense, even down to gold-leafing the weather-vane which, my Scottish farmer friend assured me in horrified tones, must alone have cost thousands. Roy examined the fox and found that it had not a tooth in its head. The lady from the mansion walked across to us and Roy told her that this fox would have been the one which had been eating her chickens' eggs as he was so old and toothless. She requested that the remains of the carcase be taken away, as the three King Charles spaniels that were with her would be sure to roll in the carcase and bring an unpleasant smell into her house. It was a lovely sight to see the three spaniels all amongst the hounds.

Roy told me that he had killed twenty-two foxes on top, plus eight dug out with terriers, and six killed with shotguns. During the day it had been lovely to see the hounds hunting up into the mist and back down into sight again, time after time. There was a bad place near this mansion where he had lost six hounds the previous year. He had spent three days getting them out, which included having to blast some rocks, but only managed to get one out alive. The others had jammed themselves tight into narrow slits in the rocks. He also told me of another two packs in the area that I did not know about. He gave me the telephone number of Lawton Evans, huntsman of one of them, and during the evening I rang him, but he would not let me go, saying that they were fox-catchers and not in the entertainment business. However, I was more successful with the other pack which Roy mentioned to me, the Three Straiths. He said that he would find out if they were hunting before Saturday and if I could go, and I said I would telephone him from the hotel to get the answers. When I did he told me they were meeting in the morning so I took directions and then went back to break the news to Sheila that her proposed shopping

**The Lochaber and Sunart:** ***"The toothless egg-eater"***

day was postponed. She accepted the fact with her normal resignation about hunting matters. I returned to the dining-room to ask the waiter to arrange for a packed lunch to be ready for seven o'clock and he agreed, provided they could prepare it at once and wrap it in cling-film.

I left the hotel at seven o'clock and drove to East Croachy where I had agreed to meet Paul Crofts, the huntsman of the **Three Straiths**, at the Grouse and Trout (Wed 5 Feb 1992). In spite of making another mistake, I finally arrived at the pub at nine-fifteen and then followed Paul to the meet which was at the Mains of Aberarder Farm. There were about ten men, most of whom were gamekeepers in plus-fours, at the meet, and all carried guns. Paul, whom I had known when he was with the Essex and Suffolk Foxhounds, arranged for a retired keeper called David to be my guide and pointed out on the hillside above us where he intended to draw. He then disappeared down a long track in the hound van. All the keepers went with him and he waited for twenty minutes or so for them to get up the hillside above him before he drew. From the road I saw hounds hit off a stale drag and work it very slowly round the face of the hill to a cairn on the other side.

My guide, David, had never seen a hound until six years earlier as there had been no pack in the area, but now hunted four days a week and amazed me by his enthusiasm and knowledge. He knew every hound by name and could identify most of them by their cry, and he used all the proper expressions and understood things like the drag. He advised me to drive round to the other side of the hill where we sat in my car and, using his field glasses, I could watch hounds drag up to the cairn. I expected to see a pile of stones but it was explained to me that in this part of the world a cairn is an earth in the rocks. We sat and watched for over an hour as Paul tried to bolt the fox with his terriers, one of which had come from Sir Robert Adene's gamekeeper at Ramsholt in Suffolk. When the fox bolted we had a wonderful view of hounds streaming down the hillside, and we moved to a spot where we were just right to see them cross the road into some young forestry trees standing about four feet high.

There was a considerable check here. A white hound found the line first, but ran ahead mute, which made it harder for the others to work it out, but eventually they did, and hunted very slowly along a rock face over loose scree. The fox then went to ground again above a large house which was now an electronic works. We could see them clearly above us with David's excellent glasses and after some time Paul arrived at the hounds. He had walked the six miles of this hunt in very good time considering the height of the hills. After another hour he managed to bolt the fox again and a keeper had a couple of shots at him but missed. We had another short hunt of two miles or so to ground again from which he was killed. It had been a most enjoyable hunt with hounds always in view working in difficult places on a very moderate scent, and I could not help thinking that they would have been better without the mute white hound which always seemed to be in front, as mute hounds so often are.

I left at three o'clock as, after the fox was shot, the other keepers all returned to their beats to feed the deer, and so forth, and David and I were the only ones left out. It had been a lovely day's venerie in charming company and with an excellent pack of hounds hunting by themselves, which always gives me special pleasure. The young hounds were "entered" by being taken on leads and being let off the leads only when a good hunt was in progress, the method of Beckford and as far back as Xenophon. Hounds were rock steady to deer of all species, red and roe, and the day could have been classed as a classic foxhunting day had it not been for the guns. The whole day had been spent in a huge, quiet and almost forgotten valley. During the day I asked David if there had been any opposition to the hounds starting up in this area as the pack was only seven years old and had only done one season when Paul Crofts came. He said there had been very little opposition as the pack had been formed deliberately to keep the fox numbers down, in conjunction with guns. Most of the farmers had joined the Hunt Club which was a Fox Destruction Society and the hunt was supported by farmers' paying so much per hundred ewes.

He did mention one particular anti, an architect who had bought a large wreck of a house and restored it. One day hounds were hunting through the valley and the architect saw some hounds which were making their way back to their huntsman along a road. He got out his car and drove through them at top speed. He had one hound wrapped round the prop shaft and dragged it for three hundred yards, still alive. When Paul finally managed to get it off the prop shaft, it was so badly injured he had to shoot it, in front of the architect. Strange behaviour for a so-called animal lover.

When he heard that I wanted to have a day with Lawton Evans, Paul volunteered to telephone him to see if he could persuade him to let me go, but after dinner when I rang Paul, he had been unable to succeed. With no hunting, we spent Thursday driving along beside Loch Ness to Inverness, where there was another Edinburgh Woollen Mill, and then returned for more shopping in Fort William. Next day we moved south to the Crown and Sceptre in Carlisle. We had great difficulty in finding its car park as it was necessary to drive through the Marks and Spencer's shopping alley to get to it, but the hotel was extremely pleasant and a great improvement on the Mercury at Fort William, although they both belonged to the same group.

On Saturday we made a grand tour of the north of England. After some more shopping in Carlisle, we drove to the Royal Oak at Appleby where we had a right "royal" welcome, and then went on to Don Royston's near Leeds to pick up the Landau wheels. We were given a conducted tour of Don's latest fad, growing rhubarb in black bin liners, and then drove across west again, *via* the M62, to the Scaitcliffe Hotel in Todmorden. This was a lovely hotel and very comfortable. We had a large old bedroom, and the original bathroom was entered by four steps down into it. The bath stood on legs and had enormous brass taps in the centre of the long side and an extremely primitive form of plug which comprised an eighteen-inch long brass pipe with a seal at the bottom. If the water became too high, the air pressure lifted it out – very clever really. We were told that Winston Churchill had stayed in that very room during the election campaign of 1946. I went for a long walk up Lovers' Lane, up to the high ground above the town, for about one and a half hours, then back to bath and change ready to meet some more old friends, Brian and Flynn Bird. They had recommended this hotel and we enjoyed a delicious dinner together. It was over ten years since they had left Suffolk, and we caught up on each other's news and recalled many happy memories until they eventually left at eleven-thirty.

I ordered a packed lunch for the last of my day's hunting, and a Continental breakfast in the bedroom at seven o'clock. We thoroughly enjoyed our breakfast at a round table in front of the window, and could not help thinking of Sir Winston sitting in his bed reading all the newspapers and having his breakfast as he read them. The meet of the **Hodder Valley Foxhounds** was at Dunsop Bridge at ten, and by an extraordinary coincidence I had been there once before, in 1986, when hunting with the West Yorkshire Minkhounds. They had met at Whitwell to draw a tributary of the Hodder and had stopped at the Dunsop Bridge Country House Hotel for lunch. I left the Scaitcliffe Hotel at seven forty-five and drove along very slowly admiring the views, arriving without a hitch an hour too soon (Sun 9 Feb 1992). The meet was up a No Through road from the War Memorial at Dunsop Bridge. I drove up this but it seemed so far that I was sure I was wrong and stopped. It was not long before a vehicle passed me so I followed it and found that it was gamekeepers coming early to close their fox snares. This district had traditionally not had a foxhound pack so the local keepers were accustomed to deal with the fox problem with snares. The long valley had a well-kept tarmac road for several miles and was owned by the Water Board, or now, presumably, by its modern successor. There was a trout or salmon hatchery half-way along the road, otherwise nothing but the occasional farm vehicle would travel on it. It was difficult to see how the expense of this long road could be justified.

Hounds arrived in good time and Mr Hatton, the Secretary, greeted me and explained that they had no Masters. He explained the draw and introduced me to the huntsman, Brian Robinson, who asked me what part of Suffolk I was from. When I told him, he said that he knew the nearby village of Bruisyard well, as he used to sell draining machines to Jacksons of Bruisyard. About sixteen to eighteen gamekeepers and farmers assembled with their guns and took their positions up a wide ride through the centre of a block of forestry. The Secretary, huntsman and myself walked up a very steep track to draw and I was soon well left behind. A fox was soon found and they rattled him around for three-quarters of an hour or so before he was shot. We drew for another fox for an hour but could not find, and went down to the cars for a very short break until Brian said,

"Come on you fellows. Swallows are beginning to settle on the wires."

The next draw was on the opposite side of the valley, which was even steeper, so the Secretary and I stayed on the bottom road and watched them drawing above us. That side of the valley proved to be blank and at three o'clock it was decided to call it a day. There were four couple of hounds in kennel and the rest of the hounds were trencher-fed. There were eight and a half couple in all which included one and a half now twelve months old, and which were out on leads being "entered" in the same way as the Three Straiths. This hunt had also been started as a Fox Club and had accounted for twenty-four foxes so far that season. The hunt was self-financing and raised its money by social occasions, and so forth, and a draw was held at every meet. During the day there had been references to cairns and I was interested to note that, in this part, cairns were stone marker posts.

That was the last day of the tour but I now had only the last two foot packs and the Gogerddan to go.

Eighteen days later I set off again, this time with Tony Mole, for Wales. We left home in a fluster and late at eleven forty-five, calling to see the collar-marker in Ashby-de-la-Zouch on the way. Mole had booked us accommodation at Betws-y-Coed in a very comfortable hotel called High Bank, and we got there at seven o'clock, having a large gin-and-tonic before enjoying a delicious dinner, washed down with a bottle of excellent New Zealand red, and ending the dinner with a glass of pudding wine. After coffee we went to bed early but unfortunately neither of us was sleepy. Mole started to talk about *Mr Sponge's Sporting Tour* which he was reading, so I persuaded him to go down to the car to fetch it. We had taken the precaution of bringing a bottle of whisky with us in case our "B&B" did not have a licence, so I poured a good measure into each of our toothmugs and climbed into bed. They we lay in our beds and Mole read from *Mr Sponge* while we sipped our drinks. Every time he said he was tired I quickly poured him some more whisky and so we went on until finally we both went to sleep.

Before breakfast we walked down to see a suspension foot bridge over a deep gorge which Mole, being an engineer, was particularly interested in. This gave us an appetite for a large breakfast, and we then settled up, agreeing that this was an excellent hotel and very good value for money, being of a much higher standard than our usual digs. The first of the hunts on our list was the **Aber Foxhounds**, so we drove into Bangor and went to the home of the Master, Mr Trefor Jones (Sat 29 Feb 1992). After getting his proper address from his neighbour when Mole and I had visited on our "recce" in December, I had contacted him by letter but he said that he had finished for the season. I was very disappointed as it meant that I would not be able to complete my ambition that season, but Mole remembered that the Master's neighbour (and brother-in-law) was called Edwards and had kept his telephone number. Unbeknown to me, Mole rang Mr Edwards to ask if he could arrange for Trefor Jones to be in his house if he rang back. This Mr Edwards very kindly did and Mole then explained to Mr Jones that I could fulfill my ambition if he would put on an extra day. This he agreed to do and so my first job was to thank him for his kindness in altering his end-of-season for me and to give him a suitable present. He asked us in to his house, but I said I wanted to get something from the car and went back to fetch a box with two bottles of whisky and two bottles of sherry. This he was very pleased with, and I had a charming letter from him afterwards. We joked about the date saying that, as girls could propose to men on 29 February, we felt we could propose to have this special day. We had coffee and biscuits in his sitting room and then, after I had taken another bottle of whisky next door to Mr Edwards to thank him for his kindness, we went off to the kennels.

The kennels were called Abergwyngregyn which meant "the mouth of the river of white shells". Mr Jones told us it would have been named after oyster shells in the river. The buildings had been converted from an old water-mill and were situated beside a rushing stream in a delightful setting. The quiet little mountain road was way up above them, and we left the cars there and walked down the grass track which followed the stream to the sound of ten couple of lovely Welsh voices. There were two men there, the new huntsman and the ex-huntsman, who had been hunting hounds up to Christmas when an unlucky step on a rock shattered his foot and had left him very lame. Mole and I followed the huntsman over a little bridge and climbed up a steep bank behind the kennels until we were well up above them. Then eight couple of hounds were let out and most of them came up to us and started to draw at once. Some of the hounds, however, stayed at the bottom and would not leave their old huntsman. This was very natural and perhaps it would have been better if he had hidden when they were let out, as he still fed and looked after them. Hounds disappeared into dense forestry and were a long time finding. Then there seemed to be three different hunts going on at once. We were sitting on a bench and listening to them hunting around us, when three men with guns came up and went to their various positions. We climbed higher and higher along forestry tracks until at last we came out onto the open mountainside.

Above us in the distance we could see hounds milling around out in the open and near them was a man waving a fox's brush. This man then calmly walked down a very steep place with his flask top in his hand full of tea. We would have found it difficult to scramble down there with two hands free, let alone hold a cup of tea. We went back down again to where the men were with guns and then walked with the Master for an hour, hearing his stories of past hunts and his early days working on a farm in that area. Hounds did not find again so the Master, Mole and myself walked slowly back to his kennels listening to his wonderful tales as we went. It was a most enjoyable walk along the high ground looking down to the kennels and listening to the two couple of hounds who had refused to leave the huntsman baying below us. The Master very proudly showed us the inside of his kennels which were spotlessly clean, all white-washed inside and much smarter than I had expected to find. There were ten couple of hounds in kennel, including one West Country Harrier, and two couple of part-Welsh.

We had a late lunch in the Aber pub and then drove to Beddgelert to the farm of Richard Williams, the newly-married Master of the Eryri, whom we had met when in Wales in December. Unbeknown to us, however, he had moved and it was his grandmother who came to the door of the farm. She was rather stern and frosty but told Mole that Richard did not live there anymore and gave us directions to his new house.

"Go back to the Post Office," she said, "and turn left. Then go over four grids and two gates."

We found Richard in a really old farmhouse which had not been lived in for seven years. He was just back in from hunting and greeted us with enthusiasm, lighting the fire in the old-fashioned grate. The whole setting was marvellous and time seemed to have stood still in the charming old room, with his red coat hanging on a post. It seemed really incongruous that he lit the fire with a gas torch. For a while we just sat and listened to his stories, and it was like listening to a man of seventy-six, not twenty-six, with his lovely style of story-telling.

He telephoned to the Tanronen Hotel in Beddgelert and booked us in for the night, agreeing to join us for dinner that evening. I sat in the bar with a gin-and-tonic writing up these notes while Mole had a doze in his room. Richard was rather late arriving, as he had had to fetch some sheep which had strayed, but we were soon in the dining-room enjoying our delicious dinner. Mole and I had the lamb which I think was over-yeared, i.e. mutton. It was so good that I sent a message to the chef that it was the best I had ever tasted. We told Richard not to feel that he need stay any longer than he wished, as we could see he was dead-beat. He had hunted five days running, one of which had necessitated climbing to the top of Snowdon, as his hounds were marking near the summit.

While we were in Richard's new home he had told us of another pack of foxhounds, the **Cambrian**, belonging to Dr Maurice Hughes and had telephoned to ask if we could go with them the next morning. Permission was readily given and so, having as usual asked for sandwiches instead of breakfast, we left the hotel at seven-thirty next morning for the meet at Nant-ddu at nine-thirty (Sun 1 Mar 1992). We were greeted with some suspicion, but as soon as I mentioned that we had spent the evening with Richard Williams, we were immediately welcomed. Dr Hughes had been a whipper-in to Richard Williams' grandfather and had expected to take on the hounds after his death, and was so upset when they were given to Richard that he had started his own pack. Later Richard had telephoned to arrange a meeting to end the animosity, a good move as they were now good friends. The meet, in fact, turned out to be a joint meet with another pack which belonged to a man who had been kennel huntsman to Richard's grandfather. Unfortunately I never learnt his name beyond Arthur. While we were waiting for Dr Hughes to arrive, he had drawn up with five couple of hounds in a trailer behind his car and it seemed that most Sundays they had a joint meet.

Dr Hughes suggested that we would see nothing if we went with him into the forestry, and told us to go in our car to a high spot on the road. The two huntsmen walked off with their respective hounds down an old railway track to the forestry and from our vantage point we watched them drawing. They found and rattled their fox round and round the covert with a grand cry. Then we heard a shot and all was quiet. Soon another fox was afoot and they rattled him round before he went away, and we enjoyed a lovely hunt of some three to four miles with us following by car. Mole spotted the fox way up on the hilltop and then hounds went over the top. They were out of sight and were gone so long that we decided to go home. As we could not hope to find them again we had to go without saying goodbye.

We had been given a key to the hotel so we returned there, but the bar was not open as it lay in the part of Wales which does not sell alcohol on Sundays.

We decided to go for a drive towards Ffestiniog, where we came across a car-park overlooking a wonderful view. We spent an hour there eating the rest of our mutton sandwiches and finished off the coffee, then I got out a bottle of champagne from the boot and we drank it in our coffee-cups. While we consumed this delicious repast and feasted our eyes on the magnificent scenery, we started to plan a special white tie dinner, which I thought I would give to celebrate the fulfillment of my ambition, talking over the different courses and wines, toasts, seating plans and so forth. After sleeping for an hour we drove back to Beddgelert by a different route, and let ourselves into the hotel with our key as there was still no-one there. We had a bath and another sleep, then went to a pub three miles up the Caernarvon road because it was open, and had a lovely steak, preceded by leek and potato soup. On our return, the landlord served us some drinks as we were residents and, with Obadiah the basset hound baying at times in the background, the three of us had a long talk about venerie and the different characteristics of hounds' working abilities.

Richard had promised to put on a special day for us with his **Eryri Foxhounds** so next morning we went to meet him at his kennels at Nantgwynant at ten o'clock (Mon 2 Mar 1992). As we were early we drove on past the kennels up the valley which was unbelievably beautiful, and we saw a young man making a first class job of a stake-and-bound hedge. We followed Richard to a place just the other side of Beddgelert, and when Richard went to draw we went to a spot with the other car followers beyond the river where we could get a good view of everything. The draw was very dense trees and there were too many foxes, but Richard's hounds fairly rattled them round. We spent a long time with a man who had hunted hounds for years until he had decided to have them all put down. There had been a great fuss in the newspapers about it. He told us an amusing story of walking back after hunting along the railway line and taking a short cut through a tunnel with his hounds. He could see some people walking towards him from the other end, silhouetted against the light of the far end of the tunnel, and then, when they were about seventy-five yards apart, they obviously heard something and shone a torch down the tunnel. All the hounds' eyes lit up and glowed in the torchlight and the people turned and fled. There was no sign of them when he eventully came out of the end of the tunnel. Another man told us of a beagling festival and how wonderfully well the beagles had hunted and kept together. He said in his lilting Welsh voice that they reminded him of "little white maggots".

We left at two-thirty to drive to our next stop, the Barley Mow at Builth Wells. It was market day and Roy Davies, the cob breeder, and a few of the farmers were still in the bar. I invited Roy and his wife to dine with us and he accepted, provided he could first go home and shut up his ducks and feed his cattle. He joined us at eight o'clock. Mole asked for soup as a starter but I advised him not to have a starter at all, and just as he was finishing his excellent steak he thanked me for the advice. After breakfast we left the Barley to go to the **Irfon and Towy** meet and were greeted on the roadside with whisky and cakes (Tues 3 Mar 1992). The first person I got into conversation with said he regularly sent sheep every year to Iken on the Suffolk coast. Ken Jones, the Master, drove us round, but we could see little in the very low cloud and fog and we eventually left. We went to have a beer in the Nevadd Arms in Llanwrtyd Wells which was the pub I had stayed in with the Easton Harriers in 1989. I was pleased to find that they had our local Suffolk beer, Adnams bitter, on as a guest beer. Leaving there, Mole took over the driving for the last leg to Tregaron, where we were going to stay at Abercoed Farm, where Charlotte and I had stayed in January with "Ed" and his wife. It was a nightmare of a drive over mountain roads in thick fog, and he was often unable to see where the road went as he topped a hill. Arriving at Tregaron, we enjoyed a delicious dinner and then were joined by Ed's brother John Jones, who was Master of the Gogerddan, and we talked hounds and hunting until after midnight.

At last, after more than a quarter of a century, it was the Last Day and the Last Pack (Wed 4 Mar 1992). The **Gogerddan** had been disbanded in 1989 "on the retirement of Marjorie, Lady Pryse, at over eighty years of age. Lady Pryse cites Fox Destruction Societies, wire, forestry plantations, the registration fee, private packs and rheumatism as reasons for her retirement." After a walk around the meadows above the farm, we came in to enjoy an excellent breakfast of bacon cured by the local village butcher, which was first class and more like eating small gammons. I had arranged to borrow a Welsh Cob belonging to Ed's wife, and was to ride in a ratcatcher coat as the green coat had become a little tight and would have looked out of place on a cob. I felt very strange dressing for mounted hunting for the first time that season. It seemed like years since I had done so and it was the first time I would be without my green coat for thirty-five years.

Ed took his wife's cob to the meet at Tynddol in a trailer behind his Land Rover and we followed him as he drove through the most amazing country. There was one valley which reminded me of parts of South Africa, which I had recently visited, and I almost expected to see a lion or an elephant appearing from behind a bush at any moment. It was five miles to the meet after we passed a No Through Road sign. The remaining country was lovely rolling hills, all rideable, but with care as there were plenty of "wet places" (as they were called here. Most of us would have called them "bogs"). There were only five horses at the meet or, more accurately, ponies, as there was nothing over fifteen hands. The Master had a very smart black cob and the other outstanding mount was a small thoroughbred ridden by a farmer, Dai Owens, who owned the whole area for miles around. I do not think I have ever seen a man who rode more naturally than he did, seeming to be at one with his horse as it plunged and sidled about. To see him crossing the hills, swinging off without stopping to lead over a "wet place" with his horse following exactly in his footsteps with utter confidence was incredible. Of course, this perfection is obtained by day after day of shepherding on the hills with the horse. To see it still messing around, plunging and so forth, after six hours in that steep country, one could hardly believe that it was seventeen years old.

**Gogerddan Foxhounds** *Hounds settling to the line of the first fox found. Jt. Master and Huntsman JC Jones in the lead. Tony Harvey on right.*

Photograph taken by Jim Meads

Jim Meads, who is world famous (as was his father) for photographing hounds and hunting, was also at the meet. I had known Jim for many years and, as he too had been with many different hunts, we had always compared notes in a spirit of friendly rivalry, whenever we met, on how many we had each been with. When I thought I had hunted with every mounted pack it was Jim who had told me that the Gogerddan had re-formed. He had also helped me to contact the new Master, and finally did me the great honour of offering to take photographs of my last mounted day.

**Gogerddan Foxhounds** *Jt. Master and first whip ED Jones with Tony Harvey at the end of the day.*

Photograph taken by Jim Meads

The first run was very fast and followed an instant find in the first draw, and we ran miles to a huge forestry area called Bwlchwallter. No-one was in touch during this hunt but Dai Owens showed us the way over his hills in great style. I felt my lack of riding this season and nearly came off several times when we hit a "wet place" and stopped quickly. When, as I often did, I got off to lead over a "wet place", I was glad my cob was only fourteen hands when I had to get on again, and even found that difficult at times. John, the Master, had to blow for a long time to get hounds out of this huge forestry and then drew for an hour or so before hitting off a very cold line. This was very enjoyable as it gave me the chance to see the good Welsh noses at work. An hour or so later we were within a few miles of the meet, so I decided I had had enough and would hack back. During this hack I managed a spectacular fall into a bog, where I finished up on my bottom in the wettest place, but somehow the little mare managed to get herself out and I decided to lead her for a long way. She was an excellent mare to have in a bog as she did not panic at all. I came across Jim, Mole and Ed so Ed came back to the meet to put the mare away. We carried on following in his pick-up until we stopped to walk up to the top of long hill which was not easy in hunting boots. We waited ages before hounds came into view, but then saw them hunt the fox down a hillside and kill in marshes below us. We found out that they had killed another fox during the time I was hacking back to the meet.

When we returned to the meet Jim took a photograph of John and I holding a brush each, and then we were all invited in to Dai Owens' farmhouse for some of the lovely Welsh soup called cawl that I always so enjoyed. Mole was fascinated to find that the electricity for this farm was made by a water-powered generator. This had been an unforgettable day in Red Kite country, miles and miles from anywhere and ending up in the wonderful atmosphere of Dai's kitchen, with his wife and family and members of the hunt. I did not do justice to Janet's lovely cooking in the evening as the effect of the cawl was still very evident. Jim autographed his new book for me – *They Will Always Meet At Eleven* – and he wrote,

*Congratulations on your Grand Slam. I am delighted to have been out on your day with the Gogerddan Hunt, the last on your list. Good hunting. Jim Meads.*

**Gogerddan Foxhounds** *Jt. Master and Huntsman JC Jones on a track with hounds, Tony Harvey in the background.*

Photograph by Jim Meads

**Gogerddan Foxhounds** *Dai Owens, centre, who generates electricity by water power.*

Photograph by Jim Meads

# Chapter 23

## The Celebrations and Latecomers

Having achieved my ambition at last, naturally my thoughts turned to celebrating the event. After a great deal of thought we decided on two parties, a White Tie Dinner for a select band of gentlemen, and a larger lunch party for all my other friends. The parties were planned as a pair, as I would not have wished to have the one without the other, but it was difficult to decide which order they should be in. Being as ever a male chauvinist pig, I thought the gentlemen should take priority.

response to this expensive request and I have ever since used every opportunity to give them all a chance to wear them. I therefore decided to give a White Tie Dinner. I also decided that it would be a stag dinner as the dining-room was really too small for all my men friends, let alone their wives. We tried to give the dinner the grandest name we could think of and finally came up with The CCCVIII[1] Venati White Tie Dinner (Saturday 14 March 1992).

**The Celebration Dinner.** *L to R, Back row: Michael Buckley, Tim Last, Richard Baker, John De Vaux, Colin Plumbe (red foxhound coat), Charles Corner (blue otterhound coat), Will Edmundson, Ernie Baker, John Finch, Bill James. Centre row: Mike Bryan, David Steel, Robert Bothway, Tony St Quinton, Maurice Scott, Jim Hardwicke, Gordon Grover, Rod Thorpe, Brian Sawyer. Front row: Ian Cook, Ernie Calver, Robert Haag, Paul Yeldham, Tony Harvey, Terence Saffell, Geoffrey Bowden, Chris Durrell, the late Rupert Montague.*

I have always loved giving dinner parties but to explain the nature of this dinner it is necessary to hark back a little. During my Mastership of the Easton Harriers I had let it be known that I would like to see more gentlemen to whom I had awarded a Hunt Button wearing a white tie at the Hunt Ball and to be sporting an Easton Harriers' tailcoat. There was a very good

Sheila was very enthusiastic and while I was in Wales she and Judith had given it much thought. They had planned a superb menu of nine courses which was more adventurous than I would have dared be, considering the number of people. I had invited thirty-one guests, three of whom were unable to come, sadly including Michael Sagar, editor of "Hounds" Magazine

[1] Owing to a miscalculation, we thought I had hunted with 308 packs of hounds by this date. In fact, the Gogerddan was the 286th British pack and, counting the fourteen French packs, I had hunted with a grand total of 300, a much neater figure!

who I had hoped would be a Guest of Honour, and also Patrick Edmundson and Nick Saffell. We had to divide them among three tables and Sheila and I spent hours over the seating plan, particularly the problem of how I could sit at all three tables. The solution was that I would sit at the table of six for the first two courses, and at the table of eight for the next two, and at the head of the large table for the rest of the dinner. Terence Saffell and Paul Yeldham, Acting Masters of the Easton, were to change places with me each time.

At last the great day arrived that I had been looking forward to for many months. The guests began to arrive punctually at seven o'clock and I greeted them in the front hall, giving them a glass of champagne before they moved on into the drawing-room. Rod Thorpe was wearing his tailcoat for the first time which added a special pleasure to the evening. We served canapés of smoked salmon and caviare that I had brought home from a hunting trip to Russia. Over the many hours of planning Mole had insisted throughout that there should be a group photograph, so one end of a bedroom had been cleared and a row of beer crates placed along the wall with a row of chairs in front of them. At a suitable time I asked everyone to come upstairs and posed them all, with one row standing on the crates, one row standing on the floor and a third sitting on the chairs, with myself in the centre and the two Acting Masters on either side. The photographer, Jim Overbury, had his patience tested to the full as there was much laughter and quips such as, "Who would own up to having been in a strange bedroom in their tailcoat?" It was difficult to get everyone into order but at last the photograph was taken and we could all go into dinner.

**The CelebrationDinner.** *In the dining room at Tannington Hall. Host, Tony Harvey, far right.*

Each guest had his name written on the menu and when all had found their places I said a Grace, followed by a few words of greeting especially for Colin Plumbe's effort in coming from Scotland. Then we settled down to our first course, Avocado and Smoked Chicken. The staff cleared the empty plates, served the sherry and then, when they had withdrawn, Michael Buckley proposed the first toast, "Absent Friends", with Louis Borrett very much in mind. Then the second course, Celery, Apple and Tomato Soup, was served, and this was to be the routine for the evening. After the soup plates were cleared, the hot saki was served, and Robert Bothway proposed the next toast, "The Staghound" with an excellent poem. This was followed by Chinese-style Prawns, the water glasses were filled, and Tony St Quinton proposed "The Basset Hound". A refreshing sorbet cleared our palates, and these plates were cleared but then a small mistake occurred. I had not explained the system carefully enough to Paul Yeldham who was to propose "The Harrier" and he jumped up to make his toast before the next wine had been served. Most uncharacteristically, then, this toast was drunk in water, but then the claret was served, followed by a space for talking where the toast ought to have been. The fifth course was Pheasant Chasseur, which seemed most appropriate, and when this was finished, the claret glasses were topped up, the staff withdrew, and Colin Plumbe proposed "The Foxhound". A green salad was served and water and claret glasses were topped up again for Bill James to propose The Loyal Toast. The cheese was served with a Sauternes, and "The Hare" was proposed by Rupert Montagu. Tartlettes aux Fruits followed and, after topping up the glasses with either the Sauternes or the claret, Charles Corner proposed "Venerie", bringing in every form of venerie that I had experienced, otter, mink, jackal and boar, as well as hare, red deer, roe deer and fox. Finally, the savoury, smoked salmon and scrambled egg, was put away and the port decanters started their rounds. My old Master, Captain Bernard, had persuaded me to buy this port, a Cockburn's '67, at Berry Bros and Rudd in St James Street, the year I had moved into Tannington Hall, and I felt that this was a rather pleasing end to the dinner as it spanned almost all the years I had been hunting with other packs. When we all had a glass Terence Saffell proposed "The Host" and thanked me most graciously for the dinner. Homemade chocolate truffles were served with the coffee.

At about twelve-thirty there was a general move to go home and about half the company went away. The rest of us sat round the big table and port decanters continued their journeys. At this point my memory fails me but I am told that we all adjourned to the drawing room but can only assume this to be correct as I woke at ten o'clock on the following morning in the recliner in the drawing room.

J. A. HARVEY
CCCVIII VENATI

***White Tie Celebration Dinner***

TANNINGTON HALL
SATURDAY, MARCH 14th, 1992

## MENU & TOASTS

*GRACE*
∞
AVOCAT AVEC POULET FUMÉ
∞
ABSENT FRIENDS
*proposed by Mr M. Buckley*
∞
POTAGE de CÉLERI, POMME et TOMATE
∞
THE STAG HOUND
*proposed by Mr R. Bothway*
∞
CREVETTE ROUGE – À LA MODE DE CHINOIS
∞
THE BASSET HOUND
*proposed by Maj. E.A. St. Quinton T.D.*
∞
SORBET
∞
THE HARRIER
*proposed by Mr P. Yeldham M.H.*
∞
FAISAN de CHASSEUR
∞
THE FOXHOUND
*proposed by Mr C. Plumbe*
∞
SALADE VERTE
∞
THE QUEEN
*proposed by Mr W. James*
∞
FROMAGES

THE HARE
*proposed by Mr R. Montagu*
∞
TARTLETTES AUX FRUITS
∞
VENERIE
*proposed by Mr C. Corner*
∞
OEUFS BROUILLÉS AUX SAUMON FUMÉ
∞
THE HOST
*proposed by Mr T. Saffel M.H.*
∞
CAFÉ avec TRUFFE en CHOCOLAT

## WINES

*APERITIF*
PERRIER – JOUËT
∞
*SHERRY*
LUSTAU ALMACENISTA
∞
*ORIENTAL WINE*
SAKI
∞
*CLARET*
CHATEAU SIGOGNAC '86
∞
*SAUTERNES*
BARON PHILIPPE '88
∞
*VINTAGE PORT*
COCKBURN '67

Those present, apart from myself, were Brian Sawyer, Rod Thorpe, Robert Haag, Gordon Grover, Bill James (who had been with me on some of my Welsh days), Maurice Scott, Rupert Montagu, Tony St Quinton (who had been on several of my days), Nigel Chapman, Colin Plumbe (whose various homes had been bases very frequently), Terence Saffell (who had contributed to the effort by taking care of the Easton during my absences), Ernie Baker, Richard Baker, Chris Durrell, Paul Yeldham, Charles Corner, Robert Bothway, Michael Buckley, Ernie Calver, John Finch, Will Edmundson, Tim Last, Mike Bryan, Jim Hardwick, Ian Cook, David Steel and Geoffrey Bowden.

Needless to say, the success of the evening was owing solely to the great efforts of the womenfolk in the kitchen and their staff. Judith had persuaded her great friend, Louie Eze, whom she had met during the Cordon Bleu diploma course, to come down to Suffolk to help. The combined efforts and expertise of Sheila, Judith and Louie ensured that every course arrived exactly on time, piping hot and served with style and elegance.

A week later we had the lunch party (Sunday 22 March 1992). Judith had just joined me as a fellow churchwarden but made a poor start by telling the Rector that we would have to skip out of church before the sermon as we had a lunch party. Eighty-four people out of the ninety-four invited turned up and again I greeted them all in the hall. Most of them had by now heard what the party was all about so many congratulations were in order. Outside my circle of hunting friends I had invited my immediate farming neighbours which included the Nesling, Western and Rous families who had cheerfully endured hounds over their land some times as often as four times a week and certainly over twenty-five times per season, and had thus contributed so much to the success of the Easton. I had also invited all my past hunt servants, who had also contributed a great deal. Fred Hargreaves, who had been my Kennel Huntsman 1964-68, Bernard Needham 1971-75 and Jim Wickham 1975-87.

With Sheila in charge everything was ready when we got back from church at eleven forty-five. I had been up since early morning doing what I could which included making the main dining-room table tiered by putting specially made boxes down the centre, carefully wrapped in a table-cloth. This provided the perfect setting for Sheila's masterpiece, which was six raised pork-pies in three sizes, the two largest in the centre, with a medium-sized one on either side and the small ones on the outside. These provided the centre-piece for the rest of the cold buffet which included Coronation Chicken. Wine was served throughout and the whole party went off splendidly and well into the afternoon.

Almost as soon as the celebrations were over I started writing an account of all my travels, using my hunting diaries as the raw material. However, publication seemed to be unlikely as the resulting book was so long, and would be so expensive to produce, that the project lagged. Then my good friend Paul Rackham took a hand and things started to move rapidly. In the intervening five years, however, there had been changes in the British hunting world, and several packs had been re-established or newly-formed. I could not let the book be published while there were packs in the country that I had not been with, so I started to check up on a few things I had heard, and as a result went with another five packs during the 1997–98 season. One hunt I particularly admired was the Granta, a new pack of harriers started in East Anglia this season: being so close, they would be reasonably easy to see. The Snowdon Valley, which had recently disbanded when I was in North Wales in 1992, had reformed and were now hunting regularly; and the South Cornwall Foxhounds had become fully established since I was last hunting in Cornwall in 1983.

My first important decision was that, although the Granta and the South Cornwall were mounted packs, I could be excused from my previous rules and follow them on foot. I had not been on a horse for five years and I no longer keep a hunter and, although I could have hired a horse and put up with the stiffness, I had also grown out of all my clothes. The final point was that the necessary arrangements would be much easier if I did not have to find transport and stabling for a horse as well as accommodation for myself.

It was fun to start to plan another hunting jolly but it soon fell into difficulties as, when I looked up the Snowdon Valley and the South Cornwall in my "Hunting Year" book, I found that both packs only hunt on Saturdays. Prospects looked brighter when I telephoned Mr Parkin, Master of the South Cornwall, as he told me that he was also hunting on Wednesdays in the North Cornwall country as they had kennel cough and could not hunt for the time being. Finally I planned to visit my accountant in London on the Monday, then drive on to Cornwall to hunt there on Wednesday, moving on to Wales to hunt with the Snowdon Valley on Saturday, making a nice round trip.

When I left the accountants on the Monday afternoon I did not get very far as driving conditions were terrible, and I spent the night in a soulless hotel in Salisbury. Tuesday morning, as I was so close, I decided to look at the Cathedral but was strangely disappointed at its interior and thought it very plain. Arriving in Cornwall, I decided to try Fowey as a base as it was not far from the South Cornwall kennels and would be likely to satisfy my passion for fresh fish. I had not driven very far into the village when I saw a sign offering half-price accommodation for out-of-season bookings. I decided to enquire, although this meant leaving the car blocking the narrow street as there was no parking place. There are always drawbacks to special offers and this one was the carpark half a mile away, but with plenty of time on my hands this was not a real problem. It was easily overcome by the quality of the dinner with an exciting choice of fish. With a gin and tonic in my hand I telephoned Mr Parkin to find out the meet for the morrow, but was disappointed to hear that the North Cornwall kennel cough was over, so the South Cornwall would not be hunting until Saturday. This was very bad news as it spoiled the plan but I decided to make the best of it and stay until Saturday. When I had overcome my disappointment, I thought I would like to go out with the Cury and see Laurie Collins again from whom I had bought my good hunter mare Demelza in April 1981. I telephoned Mr Thomas, the Master, to ask if Mr Collins would be out, only to be told that he had died a year or so earlier. When I explained how I had bought Demelza from him, more or less against his wishes, he laughed and said that he had sold another horse in an equally strange way. Mr Collins had some meadows that ran down to a bay in which was moored a schooner. The owner of the schooner came ashore and was admiring one of Mr Collins' hunters out to grass for the summer. The story was just like me buying Demelza, as he asked if it was for sale and was told definitely not. He nevertheless offered a very high price for it and said that he would give his name and address to Mr Collins if he should change his mind. The last thing he said was, "Do you have a shotgun?"

"Yes," was the reply.

"Well, I am sailing on the next high tide. If you decide to sell, fire your gun twice and I'll know that I've bought it."

The gun was fired and the deal concluded.

Before ringing off Mr Thomas gave me the meet and directions for the next morning.

The meet of the **Cury Foxhounds** (Wed 3 Dec 1997) was at the Penrose estate in front of the house which is still lived in by the original owner, although the estate now belongs to the National Trust. Michael and Shelagh Dickinson introduced themselves and as they were foot following, I walked with them. The estate was luxury for foot followers with paths and drives in all the right directions. As we walked, Michael said that he remembered me hunting in the seventies as he was also on holiday and hunting on most days, so we were often out together and he remembered my green coat. The scent was predictably very poor, with warm sun after frost. Hounds could only run in the shade and could not get on terms with their fox. There was talk at the meet of mange amongst the foxes, but the only one that passed near us was in prime health and its coat shone in the sunlight. Mr Thomas, the Master and Huntsman, blew hounds away from the woods surrounding the house and lake and went across country to draw elsewhere. We went round in our cars and parked on a beach carpark and climbed up the cliffs. Hounds arrived and the site was a joy to behold as Mr Thomas carefully drew the gorse on the clifftops, with the calm, deep blue sea behind him, complete with boats in the distance. At two-thirty I left, as hounds had gone well away up the coastline.

I had looked up the nearest pack of beagles in the MHBA handbook, thinking I could have a day with them, and discovered it was the Constantine Beagles, the most southerly pack in England. I asked the Dickinsons and other foot followers about the pack, but could not get any information so I drove across country to St Day where they were supposed to be kennelled. I enquired at a riding stable and was told that there were hounds just down the road but these turned out to be the Four Burrow Foxhounds. Mr Hancock, the Master and Huntsman, told me that the beagles had disbanded. However, he showed me his hounds and said that they were hunting the next day. He also remembered that I had written asking for a photograph and promised to bring one to the meet.

After another night at Fowey, I drove the next morning to the meet of the Four Burrow at the cross roads near Penrose in the Padstow area (Thurs 4 Dec 1997). Mr Hancock arrived with his hounds and horses and, with a broad grin, produced a photograph taken at the actual meet of the Four Burrow when I was there in March 1983. Before moving off to draw Mr Hancock beckoned me across to tell me that Mr Lobb, ex-Master of the Bolventor Harriers, was there. I went across to re-introduce myself, and he instantly remembered both me and Stanley Tompkins and the fact that one of us had lost a shoe. Reg suggested that I follow with him in his Land Rover and I readily agreed. He had hunted this country in the past so he knew where to be, and we were in touch with hounds all the time. The first fox kept doubling back through a large gorse area behind a chicken farm and was eventually killed. Hounds drew for some time before another fox was found. Scent was very poor and Mr Hancock let them concentrate and slowly hunt the line into more cover where they could run a little but it was not going to be one of the best days. Reg shared his lunch with me as we sat on a hillside watching hounds in the valley below and he told me of hunts in the past in this well-banked country. At three o'clock we decided to go back to the meet where I could retrieve my car and then follow

Reg home for a cup of tea. I asked permission to look at the wealth of paintings and photographs around the walls and found a meet scene of Reg with his son and daughter and the Bolventor Harriers at the Jamaica Inn. I said that it was just what I needed for this book and Mrs Lobb immediately took it out of its frame and packed it up for me to bring home. I returned to Fowey in the dark and heavy traffic.

Friday was a non-hunting day and I had not really made any plans of what to do so I was open to suggestion. I heard "the Lost Gardens" mentioned at breakfast and remembered reading about them in a magazine in a barber's shop, so I made enquiries and was given a leaflet about the Lost Gardens of Heligan, which were not far away. These proved very interesting as they had been abandoned and left to grow up like a jungle. At every stage there are photographs of "Before" and "After" and most of the glasshouses are restored. Rare plants and shrubs have been found and all the original paths have been uncovered from under feet of silt, but plant roots had not undermined and broken up the paths as the gardeners had made them up with silver sand from the beach and the salt content of the sand had repelled the roots. I ended my visit by taking the "Jungle Walk", which is all on raised, wooden paths down a long valley. I then thought it would be fun to go to see the Seven Stars at Stithians where I had stayed in 1981 with Stanley Tompkins. I was pleased to see that it was still open and the place where we parked our old lorry was still there. The inside had changed a little and some of the small rooms had been made into one. There were a few men in the bar and I amused them by telling them about when I stayed there and the landlord reduced our bill for "B&B" and evening meal from £7.00 to £6.00 per night as we had spent so much in the bar.

Breakfast overlooking the bay was made the more enjoyable by the fact that today I would at last be able to follow the **South Cornwall Foxhounds** which I had come all the way to Cornwall to see (Sat 6 Dec 1997). The meet was at Sweetshouse, near Lostwithiel, which was only a few miles from where I was staying. I arrived too soon and watched as people began to arrive. I was delighted to see a little girl on a leading rein with her mother. Upon enquiry, I discovered she was Amy, daughter of the Master and Huntsman, Mr Parkin. Mrs Parkin told me proudly that Amy had not missed an Opening Meet since she was born, attending her first one at nine months old in a basket saddle and now, at four years old, following every Saturday. I introduced myself to the joint Masters, Mr Parkin and Mr Stevens, and asked for a good local man to follow. This proved worthwhile as I was always in the right place at the right time. Car following in between high Cornish banks is not easy unless you know the country very well. During the first draw I met Mr Geoff White who was the first Master of the South Cornwall after they stopped being a gun pack and became recognised by the MFHA. I also learned that, after the kennel huntsman had left last season, Mr Parkin had been doing the hounds himself and I thought they were a credit to him, as did my fellow foot followers.

Hounds drew a wet lowland area and soon had a brace of foxes on the move. Scent was very poor but hounds persevered and the music was almost non-stop for two hours or so. This wet area was called "moor" which seemed strange to me as I think of moors as big, wild, open spaces, but this was moor in the sense that it was wild and wet. The moor ran in a horse-shoe shape and had a fair sized farm in its centre called an island farm. The third vantage point to which I was taken, Hellman Tor, was by far the best as it was a perfect place to watch hounds. We parked the cars at the bottom and walked up to the impressive grand boulders above us. On the way we were confronted by a herd of Exmoor ponies, all strikingly similar. From the top I could see for miles in every direction. Mr Parkin drew all around the tor but sadly blank. From this vantage point I enjoyed the quiet efficient way that Mrs Spurgeon whipped in, always seeming to be in the right place without hurrying. I then saw them going off in the distance but by the time I had come down off the tor, my guides had gone and I could not find hounds again. I telephoned Mr Parkin to thank him for the day and he said that hounds had found again and had a little hunt, and that there had been about twenty or so mounted followers. I came away feeling that I would like to see them again on a good scenting day and, by the casual way that they popped over

**South Cornwall.** *Mr Parkin, Joint Master and Huntsman at Sweetshouse, Sat 6 Dec 1997. Tony Harvey in foreground.*

barbed wire fences, judged that they would be fair goers as well. Mr Parkin's father had hunted these hounds and I thought how lovely it would be if four-year-old Amy could make it three generations.

The following Friday saw me wending my way up north for what was to be the most extraordinary hunting trip of all time. As I was once again adding to my list of hunts I thought I would make another attempt to hunt with Laughton Evans' Atholl and Breadalbane pack in Scotland. In 1992, when I was in Scotland to hunt with the Sunart and Lochaber and the Three Straiths, I had tried to hunt with him but was told I could not go because he was not in the entertainment business. Since then, whenever I have been in the company of anyone who would know Laughton Evans and his hounds, I have asked if there was a way that I could hunt with him. None of the answers were encouraging.

"Oh, you never know with him, a rum fellow, that one."

or

"He's a queer fish",

were the sort of answers I had.

Encouraged by having started touring again I decided to try once more and telephoned my old friend Anthony Barker in the Lake District who said that he knew Laughton and would try to fix a day with him. The date was to be Monday 15 December and the plan was to stay in Scotland on the Saturday and Sunday nights in a small hotel very near Laughton's hounds and have a good "crack" with him on Saturday and Sunday.

I left home with an infection in my left knee, hobbling along with a stick. I really should not have been driving but as it was the left knee I decided to risk it as all the arrangements had been made. Friday night at Norran Bank, was as lovely as always and ended with me sitting in a chair all night with my leg high up on a stool. On Saturday morning we all moved on in my car to the Logierait Hotel, near Pitlochry in Perthshire, Anthony and I, with Anthony's wife Sheila, and their daughter Diane doing the driving. The journey was enlivened by Diana recalling her memories of walking from the Lake District to Hyde Park to the big rally in the summer, and what wonderful hospitality they had received along the route, and the singing of hunting songs in the London pubs and in the train on the way home. Laughton Evans came down to the hotel and joined us in the bar for two hours or so. The "crack" was really good, and I thought him delightful company. Anthony asked him if he could come up to the kennels in the morning but Laughton said no, as he was delivering a Pointer that he had trained back to its owner. Before he went home, however, Laughton made arrangements with the landlady to give the four of us dinner on the following night and he and Mrs Evans would join us.

Next day we thought it would be fun to visit Paul Crofts at the Three Straiths Foxhounds, but we missed him and his wife said he would be back at about three o'clock. We went back at that time, Mrs Crofts made us tea and we waited until four o'clock but then had to leave without seeing Paul although we first looked around the smart kennels. In the evening we had an enjoyable dinner with Laughton and Mrs Evans, and returned to the bar for more hunting "crack". At about ten fifteen, Laughton seemed to be about to go home and not a word had been said about hunting.

I kept quiet as I had arranged to let Anthony do the talking. As he started to rise from the table Anthony said, "Are you hunting in the morning, Laughton?"

"Yes," came the reply, as he stood up to go.

"Well, we would like to come," said Anthony.

"Track is very rough," said Laughton in a voice that made it obvious that he did not want us to go.

Anthony had one last try and said, "We would love to see your hounds."

But Laughton just said in an offhand way, "You have seen Paul Crofts' hounds today. Mine are just the same as his."

With that, he was out of the door and gone.

It was such a disappointment to have come all this way and be treated to dinner and then curtly refused permission to watch his hounds, as car following was all that we had planned to do.

Sheila Barker said that all was not lost as Mrs Evans had mentioned the village where they were meeting and surely we could find the meet if we had the right village. I said that I did not think we ought to go as he obviously would not welcome us but Sheila said, "Oh blow him. It's a free country. We can go and watch."

With that, we went to bed. When we met at the breakfast table, I said, "Well that was a rum evening, wasn't it?" and Anthony turned to me and said, "Aye, the stinking booger," and then, as an afterthought, "You can put that in your book, an' all."

Sheila, Diane and I were laughing at this, in spite of our bitter disappointment, but Anthony was still seething with rage and turned to me and said, "If he ever speaks to me again about his hounds, I shall tell him to stick them where the monkey puts his nuts."

He was so angry that he could barely eat his breakfast. I again suggested that perhaps we ought not to go and that it would be best if we got off quickly and had a few hours with the Ullswater hounds, back in the Lakes, as at least we would be welcome there. Sheila said firmly no, since we had come all this way. We would try to find them as the meet was at Aberfeldy and it was on the way home anyway.

Off we went to hunt the hunt, as it were, with much laughing at the absurdity of it all. We came to the area we wanted and stopped on a lay-by to discuss where to "cast" next. There was a shout from the back of the car that served for a "view holloa" as Anthony had spotted the hound van passing us on the road, and we tore off, "running our quarry in view", around bends at breakneck speed until losing sight of him. Then, casting on forward, we saw that the hound van had come to bay at a keeper's cottage. Thinking it better not to approach Laughton directly, we kept our distance and then decided to try higher ground and came to a delightful spot where it was possible to see for a mile or so along the valley. We could hear Laughton's voice echoing across the valley as he drew some Forestry on the hillside. There we saw several instances of sheep moving quickly in the distance which suggested that foxes were stealing away, or perhaps an odd hound. There were two clearings in the forest and we saw a couple or so casting around in these and that was all we saw of the hounds apart from in the back of the van. We stopped for an hour or so and there were moments of excitement when we thought that they might run out of the Forestry and across the valley but it did not happen.

On the way back to the Lakes we laughed about what an extraordinary experience it had been. I would have been three nights away from home and had driven 1260 miles to see two couple of hounds in the far distance for a few minutes. I wondered how much per second it had cost to see Mr Laughton Evans' hounds. It was certainly the most expensive I have ever been to, without even having to pay a cap. I dozed for most of the journey, and was therefore fresh when we arrived back at Patterdale so I decided to go on and not stay the night as previously planned. As I drove home I had plenty of time to reflect on the disastrous nature of the trip. However, all hunting is fun, or causes fun, and I had thoroughly enjoyed, as always, the hospitality and company of the Barker family, and the crack in the evenings. It was a delight to listen to Anthony and Laughton go back through bloodlines of Fellhounds as Laughton sought an outcross for his hounds. All good fun, except for the last moments of Sunday night. I have since wondered if perhaps he was embarrassed about it being a gun pack. If so, he should not have been as I had a lovely day with Paul Crofts and his Three Straiths, and there are places where a gun pack is the only answer. The whole trip was one of those things that make up life's rich pattern and just emphasises the lovely North country saying, that "there's nowt so queer as folk."

It is very strange that it took my nephew Rupert McCowan, just back from Hong Kong, to tell me of a new pack of hounds kennelled only fifteen miles from my home, which he intended to hunt with on his way down from London to visit me. This was a private pack of French bassets, Bleu de Gascoigne, called the **Rally Beauvautrait** who were meeting at Home Farm, Starston, next to the church on Saturday 10 January (1998) at eleven o'clock. We had quite a carload as Mark Wayne, my ex-joint Master, and Penel Reinartz, my eight-year-old granddaughter Daisy Vaudrey, and a twelve-year-old nephew Ben Buckley and his friend Tim, all came with me. There were three and a half couple of blue bassets which made an impressive sight in the Norfolk countryside (we were just over the border). The Master, Mr Andrew Spillane, made us very welcome and introduced us to the huntsman and Mrs Spillane. Hounds quickly found and went away with a great cry for so few hounds, but were to be denied any serious hunting as there were rather too many hares. The huntsman was rather overkeen for my taste which had the effect of getting this rather young pack more excited than was necessary. However, I do not mean to be over-critical as it was pure joy to listen to their glorious voices, and to see them running over this lovely country of permanent grass, woodland and some arable. We left at three o'clock as the youngsters, who had been going well, began to tire and lost interest. I had welcomed the opportunity to show some points of venerie to my granddaughter who proved to be as enthusiastic as I could have wished. As we drove home we all agreed that we would love to be able to go again and to see this real private pack which are kennelled at Albugh, only seventeen miles from home.

**Rally Beauvautrait.** *Tony Harvey with Huntsman Mr N Green at Starston 10 Jan 1998.*

The **Snowdon Valley Foxhounds** had just disbanded when I tried to hunt with them in 1991 but they had assured me that they would start again as soon as possible. It was just over six years later that I finally saw them hunt on Saturday 24 January 1998 when they met at the Foelas Arms Hotel, at Pentrefoelas on the A5. I drove down on the Friday having tried to book into the Hotel but they were full so they reserved me a bed-and-breakfast at the Post Office next door which proved to be very comfortable. I had a moderate dinner at the Foelas Arms and as the music was so loud, went back to my B-and-B at nine o'clock. When I was making the arrangements for this trip, I had telephoned the Master, John Roberts, but he did not appear very interested in the proceedings of his pack and told me to make all arrangements with the huntsman, Ivor Davies. I had agreed to meet Ivor in front of the Foelas Arms and to go from there to the draw, so next morning I fetched the pick-up truck from behind the post office and parked up in front of the hotel.

There were three men standing near their vehicles, eating sandwiches, who looked very much like outdoor types, so I approached them and asked if they were with the Snowdon Valley.

"No," came the grim reply. "It's Richard Williams you want."

"No I don't," I said. "Richard Williams is the Eryri, and I want the Snowdon Valley."

There was nothing more forthcoming so I simply said, "Well, you look like foxhunters to me and I'm sticking here."

This remark brought a broad grin on the face of one of them and the whole atmosphere changed. We were soon in full conversation and they were like old friends by the time Ivor arrived with hounds. It was quite a long drive to the draw and on the way we overtook a postman, delivering at a remote cottage, who waved and wished us good sport. The morning was still, with bright sun after a frost, and as Ivor drew the first covert it became obvious that scent was predictably poor. There were about eight farmers out, all carrying a gun, and they stood at various vantage points. However, the fox would not leave the covert and finally went to ground in a badger sett where it was left. Scent was better in the second covert and hounds soon found another and rattled him around in short bursts for a while until he went away. As hounds crossed a busy road one was hit by a car: it was not too badly hurt although by the time we got to them the line was lost. The third draw was gorse thickets and a big deep red fox was killed by one of the guns. I left at three o'clock and drove straight back to Suffolk.

**Caerphilly.** *Huntsman Martin Arnold at The Village Inn, Rudry, with Tony Harvey and his granddaughter, Daisy Vaudrey. 21 Feb 1998*

My next outing was to be very special for me in various ways. Firstly, I had bought a Centenary Edition of Baily's Hunting Directory and noticed the **Caerphilly and District Foxhounds** recorded there. Seeing an unregistered pack, fully recorded in the hunting man's Bible, intrigued me and made me determined to visit them. Secondly, this would be the first occasion of mounted hunting for me since going with the Gogerddan in March 1992. Lastly, but certainly not least, was that I would be for the first time hunting mounted alongside my elder granddaughter and arrangements were made to fit in with her half-term. When I telephoned the Caerphilly Chairman, Mr Richards, he was most enthusiastic, but rather cautious with his replies which is quite normal now, with the constant threat of antis. He later told me that he realised that I was genuine when I telephoned him a second time and he could hear an anxious Mum in the background saying, "Ask him how steep it is, and is it suitable for an eight-year-old."

Mr Richards suggested that I rang his Field Master, Richard Morris, who could probably provide me with stables. Richard and Cathy were very helpful and encouraging and assured me that although their stables were full they would somehow fit us in which they did most handsomely as our boxes were first class. They also arranged the hotel for us and even faxed all details of the route, and so forth. We were a large party as, as well as Daisy and myself, my friends John and Rhian Ilott also came with us. Following their wedding in August 1997, they had hired one of the stable cottages from me and Rhian keeps her cob, Kizzi, in my stables. This was instrumental in me riding mounted with the Caerphilly as I had started to ride out a little with Daisy, borrowing Kizzi from Rhian.

Daisy had persuaded me to come out with her by making remarks such as, "Oh come on, Grandad. I really cannot have a grandfather who is a wimp."

Having ridden a little again, Rhian then tempted me to hunt Kizzi by making repeated offers and eventually I succumbed, even though my few little trips had not made me anything like fit. On Friday 20th February, John and Rhian left Tannington early in the morning with Kizzi and Daisy's Misty in the lorry, and Daisy and I followed in the pick-up truck an hour and a half later. I had expected to catch them up but we did not and eventually arrived at the stables a few minutes after them. Richard and Cathy were reluctant to charge for the stables so I suggested that they dined with us at the Griffin Hotel where we were to stay. They had arranged to dine out with their friends Peter and Liz Puresevic so they, of course, joined us and the seven of us sat down at eight-thirty for a delicious dinner. For me, home-made leek soup was followed by a first class sirloin steak and it would have felt like heresy if the meal had not ended with Caerphilly cheese. Daisy thought that "room service" sounded fun so had her supper in her room which suited us all and I stupidly thought that she was having an early night until she appeared at ten-thirty in the dining room with her Barbour coat over her pyjamas.

Saturday morning (21 Feb 1998) dawned very overcast with occasional heavy showers but by the time we had collected our horses the showers had stopped. We followed Richard and Cathy to the meet, unboxed on the village hall car park and were joined by the hound van holding thirteen and a half couple of mostly purebred Welsh hounds. We hacked up to the meet at the Village Inn at Rudry where there were twenty-five or so mounted waiting for us and a good crowd of foot followers. The huntsman, Martin Arnold, very proudly pointed out his prize- winning doghound, Bristol, who had been Champion at the Welsh Hound Show and thereby solved the Baily's mystery. It was because of his numerous successes in the showring that Baily's had wanted the full details of the Caerphilly.

The field were very friendly and came up and introduced themselves and the landlord was generous with hot punch and sandwiches, sausage rolls, etc., some of which disappeared into Daisy's pocket at the suggestion of the lady handing them round. There was that special happy atmosphere so often associated with the smaller packs and it was eleven-twenty before hounds moved off to draw the surrounding hills and coverts. There were foxes in most of the coverts and it was a joy to listen to those Welsh voices ringing in the hills. Scent, however, was very poor and hounds could do little outside the covert. One fox went to ground in a very deep cave at Parc-y-fan and the terrier man had to climb down twenty feet to rescue a small terrier which could not climb out. There was one short and sharp run from Y-gopi to Coesha-whips. I especially enjoyed watching the young huntsman with his hounds and listening to his horn, and the amateur whip, John "Cocoa" Hughes, had particularly good hound language. It was like watching two good professionals to see them in action together.

It was a special joy to be out hunting mounted with my granddaughter for the first time and to see her immense enjoyment of riding in the Welsh hills. Her pony, Misty, is very well known in the Easton Harriers and had been kindly lent to Daisy by Diana Greenfield. He had given her confidence to ride across Suffolk and now in the completely new experience of steep hills. A Pakistani gentleman called Mohammed Shad, who was a regular follower and great supporter of the Caerphilly, was riding a mare called Daisy and was jokingly saying that he would look after his two Daisies. Peter Puresevic was out and offered Daisy his hunting whip which she somehow managed to carry for the rest of the day. He was very jetlagged and was often accused of being asleep on his horse. The field proved to be even more fun than at the meet and wherever possible flasks were handed around and even slices of a black pudding.

I had arranged to have only half a day as I had ridden so little and Rhian took over at two-thirty. It was not a moment too soon as I was getting very stiff and sore, but she and Daisy stayed out until "Home" was blown some time after five o'clock in failing light. I followed with John in the pick-up which was the reason I had brought it down so as to have a four-wheel-drive vehicle to use across country. John and I were lucky in being able to enlist the help of four young people who climbed into the back of the pick-up and directed us to all the best spots. Ryann Bowden, Robert and Sara Morris (whose father had stabled our horses) and a tall dark-haired lad called Dai. Seven-year-old Robert asked me if the Caerphilly were going to be in my book and when I said, "Yes", he solemnly said that he would save up and get it. Later the poor lad somehow managed to annoy his sister and was forcibly held down while his head was ducked in a large puddle.

Back at the Griffin Hotel, Rhiann volunteered to stay with Daisy so John and I returned to the Village Inn, where we had met, and found the pub filled to overflowing. Some members had been home to change but quite a few were still in their hunting clothes. The atmosphere was terrific with dozens of people wanting to buy us drinks all at the same time. I had a very interesting conversation with Mrs Morris, Richard's mother, and at some time during the evening the Chairman, Mr Richards, called order and said how pleased he was to see us visitors from Suffolk. He suggested that the song specially written for the

Caerphilly & District was sung for us and this was most enjoyable. I replied with "Drink, puppy, drink" and forgot the last verse which is the best. Later on I sang "The Place Where the Old Horse Died", and a fellow came up to me and said that he remembered me singing it at the Welsh Hound Show at Builth Wells. I said that I had never been to the Hound Show but he insisted that he had heard me singing it as he remembered clearly the style and tune. It transpired that I had indeed sung it in Builth Wells but at the hunting festival, not at the hound show. The landlord served a very good curry and chips to all the hunting people and altogether the evening passed far too quickly. It was soon time for John and I to go back to the Griffin amid cries from all around to come back again.

## The March

Sunday 1 March 1998 is, in my opinion, the most important and significant day for hunting since the Normans brought scenting hounds to England after the battle of Hastings in 1066. I am sure that everyone there will share with me everlasting memories of the incredible spirit that prevailed throughout the March, especially the wave upon wave of cheering and holloaing that rolled along the length of the Embankment. I so wished that I had taken a hunting horn as those that were there prompted instant whooping and holloaing as the whole happy throng wended its way to Hyde Park. The whole thing was beautifully organised and went off very smoothly and I am sure that for about 300,000 protesters to walk so calmly through the London streets with absolutely no trouble must have impressed even the most "anti" M.P. The greatest success of the March must have been its numbers and I feel that all of us in the hunting world must remember those who put in the most effort to attend. They were the disabled and the elderly and those who came from Scotland, Cornwall and especially those who came from overseas. Besides the many coaches going from the Easton Harriers and the local shoots and farmers, I organised three coaches to go from my stable yard, leaving at seven-thirty. The return journey was one long party. I started off the singing and others came on to the microphone for jokes, stories and more songs, the last joke being told as we turned down the drive to the stables. Everyone who hunts or shoots or will do so in the future must always remember the depth of gratitude we owe to those who put so much effort and skill into organising this unique day.

So often the day after something as momentous as the March seems very flat but I was very lucky to be invited to a Hunt Breakfast. Philip and Janet Covell were hosting a lawn meet for the Essex and Suffolk Foxhounds and invited Maurice Scott, Peter Bailey and myself to a sumptuous breakfast of which Surtees would have approved . The atmosphere at the round table was reminiscent of Jorrocks, especially when a dish of kidneys appeared amongst all the other goodies. After coffee and toast the breakfast finished in style with a couple of glasses of champagne. There were so many old friends at the meet that I hardly had time to speak to them all before it was time to move off. The three of us, with our host and his friend Roger Partridge, followed together in my car and watched them draw for an hour or so without finding. Philip and Maurice are partners with me in a famous little pub called the King's Head at Laxfield, five miles from my home, and with this common interest in public houses Philip suggested that to show me one of his locals would be more fun than watching them draw blank. After seeing a couple of his locals we decided it was time for lunch, and so the day went on. When I eventually arrived home I was asked if the breakfast had been a good one, as it had taken such a long time to eat it! I assured them that it had been first class, as had the apres breakfast amusements, and after some more ribbing the matter was allowed to drop (or be stowed away for another occasion).

**Granta Harriers.** *William Burton, Master and Huntsman, with hounds at The Butcher's Arms, Knodishall, by invitation, 3 Mar 1998. R to L, Chris Durrell, M.H., Easton Harriers, Tony Harvey, Daisy Vaudrey.*

The following day the excitement was not allowed to flag as, for the second time, I set out to have a day with positively the last pack. This was the **Granta Harriers** and I was again mounted on Kizzi. Rhian followed in the car so as to be able to take over at half-time again, and prevent me from seizing up completely from stiffness. Although this was term-time, my granddaughter was out with me again as I had particularly wanted her to be with me on this momentous day. It was with a feeling of being a naughty boy called into the Headmaster's study that I telephoned Daisy's Headmaster, Nigel Johnson, to explain about my having been with every pack and how I would particularly like Daisy to be with me on my last day. He readily agreed, much to the delight of Daisy and myself, on the condition that we wrote a short account of the day to be put into the school magazine.

Baily's Hunting Directory says that the Granta Harriers were started this season by a group of farmers who were keen on harehunting. I have felt that a new pack of hounds, starting up in these difficult times, has given hunting a much needed tonic, and I am sure that many people would agree with me. The Granta rely heavily on being invited into other countries and it was by invitation of the Easton that they were at the Butcher's Arms at Knodishall on 3 March 1998. The three Joint Masters – Graham Wedd, Mrs Martin and William Burton (who also hunts hounds) – had suggested that permission to hunt in the Easton country was all that was desired and that a full invitation meet with all the Easton members out would come later, when they were better established. Two of the Easton Masters were at the meet to greet the visitors, Chris Durrell mounted and Brian Sawyer (who had made all the arrangements) on foot owing to pressure of work. All the visitors came into the pub to meet the six Easton members and also Cherry Clarke, Master of the Essex and Suffolk Foxhounds, with whom I had been the day before. Graham and Mrs Wedd reminded me that we knew each other years before when our respective daughters were at St Felix School together. This brought a cry from my daughter Judith who said that in all the time together at school she had never known that Louise Wedd was a hunting girl.

During the introductions, Graham took me to his whipper-in and said, "You two need no introduction, I know." I felt increasingly embarrassed as I looked at this pretty girl and had to admit that I did not know her, only to be told that she was Clare Williams who had groomed for me on the old Y.T.S. scheme.

The ten and a half couple were let out of the lorry and were better looking than I would have expected from a pack of draft hounds. The lemon-and-white West Country Harriers which had come from the North Norfolk Harriers, stood out because of their colour and I asked how the two breeds of harrier hunted together. Mr Burton said that they went well together, although I had expected him to say that the West Country were faster than the Stud Book. There were four mounted visitors, William Burton and Sarah his wife, Graham Wedd and Clare Williams, the whipper-in. Mr Robert Barr was out with us on one of his Point-to-Pointers and it was to his Manor Farm that we first went to draw. Conditions were all against hunting, with very high winds and strong gusts. Hares all seemed to be together in some rape but as soon as a line came to an exposed place the scent was completely blown away. William Burton hunted them quietly and if nature had been kinder to us, I am sure we would have had a brilliant day as after a heavy shower I felt there could have been a scent. I changed with Rhian at one-thirty thinking that I ought to not have Kizzi as long as I did in Wales and to let her have a longer ride but unfortunately Kizzi injured herself and had to go back to the meet an hour or so later. Lydia Fetto volunteered to look after Daisy so she was able to stay out and I followed with my daughter Judith. With this light sandy land and many tracks I was able to keep near hounds, feeling ever sorrier for the huntsman as everything seemed to be against him but I was very pleased to see that this did not faze him and he remained calm and quiet throughout the day giving hounds every possible chance. When hounds arrived back at the meet there was no sign of Daisy or Lydia. Daisy had persuaded Robert Barr to let her ride round his gallops with Robert leading her on his Point-to-Pointer. The landlord had a wonderful homemade soup waiting for us and there was that special atmosphere of a hunting tea and the day ended in a most perfect way.

In the evening I had a chance to sit quietly over coffee and a glass of port and reflect on what 1 had just achieved. I had actually hunted with every single pack of foxhounds, every pack of harriers, every pack of staghounds and every pack of bassets in Great Britain. These were spread from Lands End in Cornwall to the Grampians in Scotland and from Margate on the east coast to Pembroke on the west coast. 1 have always liked meeting and mixing with real characters and I had met an abundance of them and made lifelong friendships; the wonderful times in Helmsley where 1 now have so many friends; the fun-packed times in Builth Wells, particularly in the Barley Mow, where John "the Barley" proudly displays the BFSS shield; the great fun on Dartmoor and the never-to-be-forgotten evenings in the Forest Inn at Hexworthy; the long friendship and hospitality of the Plumbe family and the countless dinner parties which went on into the early hours. I have always felt that a good day's hunting with the adrenalin running high should end with a dinner party or some social event where you can continue to keep "on the high" amongst like-minded friends, and on my travels 1 have been very lucky and almost always found good company too numerous to mention with which to enjoy my evenings.

I also enjoyed the great contrasts of hunting - in one holiday I had the pleasure of being with the Curre Foxhounds where the immaculate hunt servants were mounted on first class hunters and a few days later to be with the Ystrad where the huntsman sat on his horse with a rusty bit and the bridle made from plaited baler twine. The styles were very different but the hunting spirit was identical. I also looked back to the contrasts of countryside that hunting had taken me into - the mountain countries and the pleasure of being able to sit and look over valleys that had remained unchanged for centuries and then sometimes to make the nerve-wracking descent into them with my horse's back hooves almost touching the front ones; the grimness of the Linlithgow and Stirlingshire country near Glasgow where hounds hunted between the M8 and the M9, the hop fields of Kent, the granite tors of Dartmoor, the ploughland of East Anglia, the fells of the Lake District, the moors of Northumberland, the rolling hills of Scotland

I refilled my glass and mused before going to bed of what it had taken to be able to be able to enjoy all this. It was a time to be thankful to my many friends who have helped me, to thank God for the health and strength to do it., for the loyalty of staff who enabled me to be away from home so much, for my family and the great luck to be born into farming as I cannot think of a better business to combine with hunting, and lastly to think how grateful all of us ought to be to the Masters and hunt servants who keep the noble sport of hunting going. Good luck, good health and good hunting to all who read this book.

P.S.

Just as this book was going to print a friend telephoned me and jokingly said "Ha, ha! Your book is out of date before it is published! There is a new pack of foxhounds that you have not been with". He went on to tell me the good news that there was a new pack of foxhounds established in Staffordshire. They are known as **The Staffordshire Moorland Foxhounds** and share kennels with The Forest and District Beagles at Hollinset Farm, Higher Sutton, Nr Macclesfield and are under the care of kennel huntsman Paul Goddard. The Staffordshire Moorland are a foot pack and will be hunted by Jt. Master Nicholas Stones. His Jt. Master is Richard May who is also Master and Huntsman of The Forest and District Beagles. I was determined to go and have a day with them and include them in this book, and with printing only days away I made arrangements to hunt with them on Wednesday 23rd September 1998. Unfortunately they telephoned me to say that they had kennel cough so I was unable to go. I shall hunt with them at the earliest possible opportunity and I wish them every success.

# Songs

## The Battered Brigade

The mark of a stake on the shoulder,
the brand of a wall on the knee,
are scars to the careless beholder,
and blemishes so it may be.
But every such blemish endorses
the pluck of a steed unafraid,
and the heart of a lover of horses,
goes out to the battered brigade.

Their knocks have been gathered in duty,
their scars in the front of the fray.
It isn't your cleanest legged beauty
that's there at the end of the day.
When 5ft of timber before us
has half of the pretty ones stayed,
if you mean to catch up with the chorus
come on with the battered brigade,

Turned out in the finest of fettle,
'tis sometimes the soundest that fail,
and would rather hear hooves on the metal
than follow the rattle of rail.
But out on the grass with hounds racing,
and fences as big as they're made,
the cream of the gay steeplechasing,
is left to the battered brigade

Their line is the line of the foxes,
their pace is the pace of the pack.
Though tomorrow they stand in their boxes
as stiff as the props of a stack.
But I'll lay you my cheque at the bankers
they're forward next week undismayed.
Here's good luck to the blemished front rankers,
Hats off to the battered brigade.

## The Six Fell Packs

Now I'll give you a toast, lads, to all the fell packs,
To Masters and Huntsmen and Whips of aw maks,
You can have your athletics and games of all sorts,
But this hunting is surely the greatest of sports,
Tally-ho, tally-ho, tally-ho,
Hark forrad, good hounds, tally-ho.

John Peel was t'first hunter to gain lasting fame,
At Caldbeck not long since they honoured his name.
Bill Porter, Jim Dalton are others we know,
Then rivalling Peel there came Bowman - Old Joe.
Tally-ho, tally-ho, tally-ho,
Hark forrad, good hounds, tally-ho.

On t'North side there's t'Eskdale, wi' Porter's son, Jack,
Harry Hardisty's proud of his laal Melbreak pack,
Geordie Bell hunted t'Cathra for many a year,
Johnnie Richardson now keeps those foxes in fear,
Tally-ho, tally-ho, tally-ho,
Hark forrad, good hounds, tally-ho.

And when Bowman retired, they engaged a new lad
As Ullswater Whip – and he hasn't done bad.
He's stayed 40 years and he's still going the rounds,
So here's to Joe Wear and his Ullswater hounds
Tally-ho, tally-ho, tally-ho,
Hark forrad, good hounds, tally-ho.

We next come to one who to hunting was born.,
He's the fourth generation to carry the horn.
Anthony Chapman's the name, as I hardly need say.,
And how those Coniston hounds love his "Hoo git away",
Tally-ho, tally-ho, tally-ho,
Hark forrad, good hounds, tally-ho.

So there's yan laal pack left, hunting plain open fell,
And whose foxes are apt to go straight-necked to hell,
But Walt Parkin's young pack has caught up with the rest.
And the Lunesdale can now hold its own with the best.
Tally-ho, tally-ho, tally-ho,
Hark forrad, good hounds, tally-ho.

So back to my toast to this greatest of sports,
Here's to hunters and hounds – and spare Reynard a thought.
May we follow the horn till it's our turn to die,
And if St. Peter has hounds he will hear us all cry
Tally-ho, tally-ho, tally-ho,
Hark forrad, good hounds, tally-ho.

*D. P. Todd, Kendal. 1950's.*

## A Fine Hunting Day

'Twas a fine hunting day and as balmy as May.
And the hounds to the village will come,
Every friend will be there, and all trouble and care,
Will be left far behind us at home,
See servants and steed on their way,
And sportsmen their scarlet display;
Let's join the glad throng, and go laughing along,
And we'll all go out hunting to-day.

*Chorus:*
*So we'll all go out hunting to-day,*
*All nature balmy and gay;*
*Let's join the glad throng, that goes laughing along.*
*And we'll all go out hunting to-day.*

Farmer Hodge to his dame says "I'm sixty and lame,
Times are hard and my rent I can't pay,
But I don't care a jot, if I raise it or not,
For I must go out hunting to-day,
There's a hare in yon planting they say,
Let's find her and get her away;
I'll be first up yon hill, and be in at the kill,
For I must go out hunting to-day.
*Chorus*:

See the doctor in boots, with a breakfast that suits,
Of strong home made ale and good beef,
His patient in pain says I've called once again.
To consult you in hope of relief,
To the poor he advice gives away;
To the rich he prescribes and takes pay,
But to all of them he said, you will shortly be dead.
If you don't go out hunting to-day.
*Chorus*:

Then the judge sits in court and gets wind of the sport,
For the lawyers apply to adjourn,
And no witnesses come there is none left at home.
They have followed the hounds and the horn,
Says his worship, great fines they shall pay,
If they will not our summonses obey,
But 'tis very fine sport, so we'll break up the court.
And we'll all go out hunting to-day.
*Chorus*:

Then the village bells chime there's a wedding at nine.
And the parson unites the fond pair;
But when he heard the sweet sound of the horn and
the hound,
And he knew 'twas his time to be there,
Says he, "For your welfare I'll pray,
And regret I no longer can stay,
You are safely made one so quickly be gone,
For I must go out hunting to-day.
*Chorus:*

None are left in the lurch, for all friends of the church,
The beadles and clerks, are all there,
They're determined to go, and shout "Tally HO"
And the bell ringers joined in the rear,
With bridegroom and bride in array,
Each one to the other did say,
Let's join the glad throng that goes laughing along,
And we'll all go out hunting to-day.
*Chorus:*

Theres' only one cure for all maladies sure,
That reaches the heart to its core,
'Tis the sound of the horn on a fine hunting morn,
Whatever the heart wished for more,
It turneth the grim into gay,
Makes pain unto pleasure give way,
Turns the old into young and the weak into strong,
If they all go out hunting to-day.
*Chorus:*

## The Chase

*Dedicated to Mr. Harold Floyd, Past Master of the Holme Valley Beagles.*

Come out, come out, my merry, merry men,
Aye, Girls also who care,
From farm and shop, from mill and forge
Come chase the sportive hare.

The hay and corn is gathered in
The russet tints the trees
And blood runs thin, so health come win,
In autumn's cooling breeze.

September is a merry, merry month,
The month we all love well
For then we start the chase we love,
As records past will tell.

Our hills and dales with sportsmen fill,
And echoes ring all round.
Then hark away, we all feel gay,
And quickly clear the ground.

Our hares are a merry, merry lot,
We chase both brown and grey,
For hours they double, twist and turn,
At sundown, love to play

They're hardy, fleet and tricky, too,
We love their merry ways;
If one we lose, we quest around
Another one to raise.

Our hounds they are a merry, merry pack,
They fill us with delight,
For when they find a romping scent
They'll hunt from morn 'till night.

Though puss may leave them in the chase
They still stick upon the trail,
Til sportsmanship demands recall
Before her heart doth fail.

We love to rise on merry, merry morns
When breezes softly blow
When cares are light , and hearts are bright
And sun doth gently glow.

And as we roam o'er fields and woods,
And huntsman's horn doth sound
A happier lot you ne'er will find
Go search the world around.

When evening falls, a merry, merry crew,
Are found in village inn
In natures haunts we've spent the day
In man's we now begin.

With song and jest and laughter loud,
We'll pass the night away.
A happier lot you ne'er may find
Though search the world all o'er.

## Main Index

**Hunt names** are in bold, bold page numbers denote hunting days

*Italics denote titles of book or songs*

## Main Index

## Main Index

## Main Index

## Main Index

## MAIN INDEX

## Main Index

## Main Index

## Main Index

## Main Index

## Main Index

## Main Index

## Index to Illustrations

## Index to Illustrations

## Index to Illustrations

## Index to Illustrations